CCENT® Cisco® Certified Entry Networking Technician ICND1 Study Guide with Boson® NetSim® Limited Edition

(Exam 100-101)

CCENT® Cisco® Certified Entry Networking Technician ICND1 Study Guide with Boson® NetSim® Limited Edition

(Exam 100-101)

Bob Larson
Matthew Walker

Mc
Graw
Hill
Education

New York   Chicago   San Francisco   Athens
London   Madrid   Mexico City   Milan
New Delhi   Singapore   Sydney   Toronto

Cataloging-in-Publication Data is on file with the Library of Congress

McGraw-Hill Education books are available at special quantity discounts to use as premiums and sales promotions, or for use in corporate training programs. To contact a representative, please visit the Contact Us pages at www.mhprofessional.com.

CCENT® Cisco® Certified Entry Networking Technician ICND1 Study Guide (Exam 100-101) with Boson® NetSim® Limited Edition

Figure 10-7 used with permission from SubnetOnline.com.
Photo in Figure 4-4 courtesy of Tripp Lite.

1234567890   DOC DOC   10987654

ISBN: Book p/n 978-0-07-183836-8 and CD p/n 978-0-07-183837-5
of set 978-0-07-183839-9

MHID: Book p/n 0-07-183836-8 and CD p/n 0-07-183837-6
of set 0-07-183839-2

Sponsoring Editor Stephanie Evans	**Technical Editor** Brad K. Hernandez	**Production Supervisor** Jim Kussow
Editorial Supervisor Jody McKenzie	**Copy Editors** Lunaea Weatherstone Kim Wimpsett	**Composition** Cenveo Publisher Services
Project Manager Harleen Chopra, Cenveo® Publisher Services	**Proofreader** Lisa McCoy	**Illustration** Cenveo Publisher Services
Acquisitions Coordinator Mary Demery	**Indexer** Rebecca Plunkett	**Art Director, Cover** Jeff Weeks

3 1327 00595 6115

This book is dedicated to Anita Rose Warner, my best friend's wife, whose miraculous recovery from traumatic brain injury has inspired me; and to my three graduate assistants, Korissa Fitterer, Laxmi Nandkumar Patil, and Shane (Xing) Xu, at the University of Washington Information School—without their support this project could never have been done.

—Bob Larson

ABOUT THE AUTHORS

Bob Larson has been on the faculty at the University of Washington Information School (iSchool) since 2005 assisting graduate students in acquiring the technology skills required in today's information society and information careers. For the previous 20 years Bob headed a company that provided technology trainers and consultants to colleges, universities, private training organizations, and the Boeing Airplane Company. During that time Bob spent ten years teaching Cisco certification courses through the Cisco Networking Academy Program, developing course material and assessment questions for the program; spent three years on the Networking Academy Program Advisory Board; and was part of the visiting faculty teaching CCNP, wireless, and security instructor courses in Europe and Africa. This is Bob's fifth Cisco certification book as the author or coauthor. He has also developed course curriculum and white papers for a variety of organizations. Bob's larger consulting projects include designing and implementing the technology infrastructure for a new medical school, designing and supporting the installation of cellular and Wi-Fi Internet systems on 72 cruise ships, and installing a large VLAN network at an aluminum plant in Ghana, Africa. Bob holds, or has held, numerous industry certifications, including CCNP, CCDP, CCSP, CCNA, CCNP, and MCSE. (http://faculty.washington.edu/blabob/bob/)

Matt Walker is currently an IT security architect working for Hewlett-Packard on NASA's desktop support contract. An IT security and education professional for more than 20 years, he has served as the director of the Network Training Center; as the curriculum lead/senior instructor for Cisco Networking Academy on Ramstein AB, Germany; and as a network engineer for NASA's Secure Network Systems (NSS), designing and maintaining secured data, voice, and video networking for NASA. Matt also worked as an instructor supervisor and senior instructor at Dynetics, Inc., in Huntsville, Alabama, providing onsite certification awarding classes for (ISC)², Cisco, and CompTIA, and after two years came right back to NASA as the IT security manager for UNITeS, SAIC, at Marshall Space Flight Center. He has written and contributed to numerous technical training books for NASA, Air Education and Training Command, and the U.S. Air Force, as well as commercially, and he continues to train and write certification and college-level IT and IA security courses. Matt holds numerous commercial certifications, including CEHv7, CPTS, CNDA, CCNA, and MCSE.

About the Contributing Author and Technical Reviewer

Brad K. Hernandez is an avid technologist, systems integrator, technical trainer, and course developer with 20+ years of experience. Brad is a Cisco-certified systems instructor and senior technical trainer at Skyline-Advanced Technology Services. Utilizing multiple silos of knowledge gained during numerous professional engagements, he now functions as an independent contractor specializing in large-scale data center deployments. He has fulfilled various roles within Fortune 100 organizations, including design, implementation, and knowledge transfer, to ensure an end-to-end successful project. Brad holds more than 20 certifications from industry-leading vendors such as Cisco, Microsoft, VMware, and NetApp. A Florida native transplanted to the heart of Silicon Valley, Brad's journeys have entailed sailing across three seas and one ocean and cycling across a country (www.bradhernandez.com).

CONTENTS AT A GLANCE

CONTENTS

Part 1
Operation of IP Data Networks

Part II
LAN Switching Technologies: Layer 2

4   Switching: Moving Data Inside Your LAN 155

5   Preparing to Configure Cisco Devices 199

Part IV
IP Services, Network Device Security, and IPv6

From Boson Software®

The Cisco CCENT certification requires that you learn and master a number of skills. As you study this book, incorporating Boson NetSim® into your learning process will help you successfully complete the CCENT certification. The Boson NetSim Limited Edition (LE) included with this book will get you started on your way, and additional capability from the full edition is available after purchasing an upgrade.

The Boson NetSim® Network Simulator® is an application that will help you with the practical, hands-on portion of your education. NetSim will ensure that you understand the concepts of routing and switching by challenging you to apply those concepts on Cisco devices. Once you feel that you have mastered both the theory and the practical labs, you can test your knowledge using the exams included with this book and the CD. You may also purchase ExSim-Max™ practice exams from Boson, available at www.boson.com. ExSim-Max practice exams are designed to simulate the complete exam experience, including topics covered, question types, question difficulty, and time allowed. With ExSim-Max, you can be sure you are ready to pass the real exam—guaranteed (www.boson.com/guarantee).

Boson NetSim provides more versatility and support than any other network simulation software on the market. Not only will Boson NetSim help you become CCENT certified, it will actually help you learn and understand how to configure routers, switches, and networks.

The Boson NetSim LE can be upgraded to the full edition for CCENT at any time at www.boson.com/mcgrawhill (with a valid activation code from your qualifying McGraw-Hill Education book). Upgrading enables all other Boson NetSim labs, commands, and advanced features. Don't forget to complete your study with ExSim-Max practice exams.

Best wishes in your future studies!

T he primary focus of our book is to help you achieve the Cisco Certified Entry Networking Technician certification—but there's more to it than that. We've provided all the background and technical knowledge in this book that you'll need to be successful on the exam, as well as a few exercises and hands-on projects to increase your odds. Ideally, though, we'll also succeed in two other, secondary, but just as important, goals.

First, after reading this book and performing the exercises, we'd be happy to see you emboldened with confidence. Yes, we wholeheartedly believe, and would like to make sure you know, *you can do it!* Sure, certifications are hard—they're supposed to be. If they were easy, everyone would do it. But this isn't something you're not capable of. This book was written in the same manner we learned the information—in a simple, easy, and, yes, interesting fashion. Over the last 20 years we've had hundreds of students follow this path to successful exams and successful careers.

Second, after all is said and done, we sure hope you don't stop. CCENT is a great certification, but it's not the end-all and be-all. Instead, it should be a great *beginning* for you. After you pass—and you know you will—follow it up with personal practice, hands-on experience, and study. Put into play what you've been studying for all this time and prove you know it. Then, of course, start on your next certification—the CCNA.

After you've completed the CCENT certification by passing the Interconnecting Cisco Network Devices (ICND1) v2 100-101 exam, you'll be halfway to a CCNA certification. The ICND2 200-101 exam covers the second half of the CCNA body of knowledge.

In This Book

This book covers all the exam objectives posted on Cisco's website concerning the ICND1 100-101 exam. Each chapter explores one or more of the main objectives in this list. You'll also find some repetition from chapter to chapter since some objectives are covered across multiple chapters. The introduction offers a breakdown of Cisco's objectives and which chapter of this book covers each objective.

In Every Chapter

Each chapter has several components designed to effectively communicate the information you'll need for the exam:

- Every chapter begins with the **certification objectives**. These identify the major topics within each section on the exam dealing with the chapter topic. Using these objective headings will help you keep track of where you are with your studies.

- **Practice exercises**, step-by-step exercises providing hands-on experience, are found in chapters with configuration objectives. While some chapters require only knowledge and comprehension levels, other objectives require you to know how a specific configuration option is entered into the switch or router. These practice exercises are designed to reinforce the chapter verbiage and provide insight into the skills that are likely to be an area of focus on the exam. The information covered in these exercises is not simply for reading purposes—you'll be required to perform configuration on a variety of scenario and simulation questions on the exam. Don't fail to prepare for them by simply reading over the practice exercises; practice them and get comfortable with their focus. These exercises will work with the simulator product, produced by Boson and provided with this book, but they can be used anywhere. Practice as much as you can with the simulator and with real equipment, should you have the opportunity. This last part can't be emphasized enough; the two factors that assure success on Cisco certification exams are confidence and the ability to work quickly. Time is your biggest enemy.

- **Exam Watch** notes highlight specific information within the section on which to focus your studies. Do not rely on them totally, but be sure to read over them before the exam.

- An **Inside the Exam** entry is provided at the end of each chapter and basically summarizes the important aspects of the chapter in regard to the exam. Tips and tricks mentioned in this section will definitely help you understand what to expect on the test.

✓   - The **Two-Minute Drill** is a full summary of the chapter, condensed and organized for quick, last-minute review.

 Q&A   - The **Self Test** section at the end of each chapter offers questions similar to those found on the certification exams. Answers and explanations of both correct and incorrect choices are provided to assist in understanding the material.

Some Pointers

This may seem strange to say, since we wrote this book and hope **everyone** in the networking arena gets a copy, but we'll say it anyway: Do not rely on this book alone to pass your CCENT exam. There's not a book on the planet that, by itself, will fully prepare you for the test. Read this book, using the pointers we provide here to guide your study, but never forget to practice, practice, practice. The benefit of hands-on, real-world experience in preparing you for the exam is immeasurable. This book is, we humbly feel, a great guide to follow in preparing for the exam, but you'll definitely need plenty of practice outside its pages to succeed. Once you finish reading this book, be sure to do a thorough review of everything.

- ▇ **Reread all the Two-Minute Drills.** These will serve as an excellent "cram" session just before the exam.

- ▇ **Reread all the Exam Watch notes.** Knowing the information to satisfy each knowledge objective is one thing, but it's only part of the battle. To be truly successful, you'll need to know what to expect on the exam. Reading the Exam Watch notes will give you insights into how the information will be presented on the exam and what to expect. If you know this up front, you won't be surprised on the exam, and your confidence will contribute to your success.

- ▇ **Retake the Self Test sections at the back of each chapter.** Immediately after reading the chapter, give the accompanying Self Test questions a shot. Then, after you're done with the entire book, go back and take each Self Test again. Facing all the questions at one time is similar to the exam itself and will help with your study. Please note that simply memorizing these questions and answers will not help you on the exam. The Self Test questions are similar to what you'll see, but they're not exact replicas. Some of the Self Test questions are intended to make sure that you understand underlying concepts or technologies that you will need to use in the exam.

- ▇ **Use the exam test engine on the CD-ROM.** The test engine, provided by Boson Software on the CD accompanying this book, provides plenty of questions to prepare you for the exam. You can choose to quiz yourself on all questions, much like the exam itself, or target your study by focusing on a single category. Categories roughly match the chapter outline of the book to help mark your progression. Additionally, you can purchase extra tests from Boson Software at its website (www.boson.com).

■ **Do all the practice exercises in each of the chapters.** You will be required to perform configuration and troubleshooting on simulators during the exam. While CCENT doesn't go overboard with these, you'll definitely need to be familiar with *all* the configuration commands and steps included in this text. Use the exercises in the book to reinforce concepts and prepare for the exam. Additionally, feel free to experiment on your own—whether with the simulator or with equipment you have access to. Interject problems to working environments and note various troubleshooting techniques you can use to fix the problem. The configuration of devices is a big part of the exam, but troubleshooting and examining configuration files for errors will play a large role in your success or failure.

■ **Practice your configuration skills.** There will be some simulation questions on the CCENT exam. In simulation questions, you'll be required to perform basic configuration *and* troubleshooting tasks on a Cisco router and/or switch. Therefore, it is important that you have good configuration skills. Use the practice exercises to hone your configuration skills! You may come across a simulation scenario presenting a flawed configuration on the exam. The more you practice with the exercises and Boson's NetSim, the easier it will be to spot these configuration errors right off the bat. Remember that confidence comes only with experience.

Ancillary Media Content

In addition to full coverage of the Cisco CCENT exam objectives, this book comes fully loaded with digital resources to help you study for this challenging exam.

Boson NetSim Networking Simulator, Limited Edition

Hands-on practice and real-world experience are essential in your preparation for the exam. The practice exercises and simulator built for this book are designed with exactly that in mind—giving you hands-on experience and an opportunity to practice to your heart's delight. The network provided in the simulator should allow you ample opportunity to see the command and configuration options in action. The overall network is displayed in Figure 1, with addressing for the exercises spelled out in Figure 2. Each exercise will use a section of this network, with that section's topology included in the NetSim.

This network provides every configuration option covered in the book. As you go through the practice exercises, refer to Figures 1 and 2 to "see" how your configuration should be applied. Additionally, don't just rely on the exercises as written for your study. Feel free to create your own configurations on each device. Use all the **show** and **debug** commands you want to see IOS in action. Finally, after configuring the network to function, purposely change the configuration options to see the results. Using the practice exercises and your own creativity on this network will greatly increase your odds of passing the exam.

Exercises and Bonus Exercises

In addition to the exercises built in Boson's NetSim Networking Simulator, Limited Edition, we've created additional practice exercises you can use to get more hands-on experience. You'll see these called out as exercises throughout the book. For a complete compilation of all the exercises and their solutions, go the PDF lab book in the ancillary digital content. See the appendix for more details.

FIGURE I

A simulator
network for
practice exercises

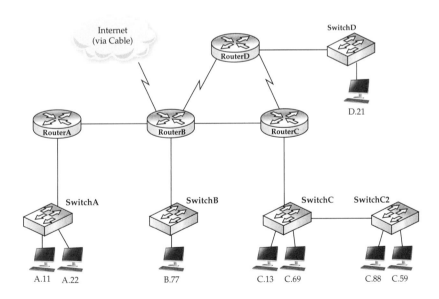

FIGURE 2

Addressing for
the network
topology used
in the practice
exercises

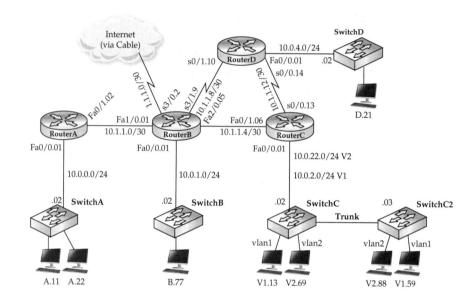

Boson Exam Engine

This book comes with a multiple-choice practice exam in Boson's Exam Engine
(BEE) designed to emulate the actual CCENT exam. Questions are weighted
similarly to the CCENT exam's topics, and you can review your score assessment
report to see your areas of strength and weakness. You can take the test multiple
times, and new questions will draw from the larger pool of questions included in the
Boson Exam Engine. See the appendix for more details.

Video Training from the Authors

Throughout the book, we've looked for opportunities to supplement the book's
content with video training. Check out the video discussion whenever you see one
referenced in the book for discussions of key concepts and onscreen demonstrations.

ACKNOWLEDGMENTS

W e would like to thank the following people:

- This book would not have been possible without the support of the Information School at the University of Washington, specifically, the students, deans, fellow faculty members, staff, and my graduate assistants. Each in their own way supported me and tolerated any periods of distraction on my part.

- My many students each quarter are all master's degree students in either information management (MSIM) or library science (MLIS). They come from diverse career paths, cultures, and home countries, but each represents the best and brightest that a top-tier research university attracts. They inspire and challenge me every day and make me want to go to work and to write a book like this.

- A special thanks to Brad Hernandez, professional trainer extraordinaire, for providing excellent technical insight into the design and flow of this book. Brad's experience and attention to detail proved vital to the success of this project.

- The team from McGraw-Hill Education (Tim Green, Stephanie Evans, Mary Demery, Jody McKenzie, Harleen Chopra, and James Kussow) displayed unbelievable patience and support throughout every stage of this process and was nothing short of amazing. It's been an honor and a privilege to work with such an outstanding, professional, and fun group of people.

- Finally, there is no way this book could have ever even been started, much less completed, without a lot of understanding and patience from my families, friends, and loved ones.

—Bob Larson

How to Take a Cisco Certification Examination

This introduction offers a host of information on your CCENT certification and prepares you for taking the actual examination. In this section, you'll find a brief overview of Cisco's certification program and some guidelines on methods of preparing and studying for the exam, including what to expect on the exam and some simple things you can do on test day to increase your chances of passing.

Cisco's Certification Program

Cisco has a number of certifications, ranging from entry level (CCENT) and advanced routing and switching (CCIE) to network security, wireless, and VoIP. Cisco recommends a variety of classes as training for these individual certifications, but they are not mandatory—all you need to do to hold a certification is pass the appropriate tests. With the right experience, study materials, and a good work ethic, you'll pass any Cisco exam without necessarily attending the recommended course.

Cisco is constantly changing and updating its certification requirements. For more information about Cisco certifications and exams, visit Cisco on the Web at www.cisco.com/web/learning/certifications/index.html.

There is a lot of information about the exam process, requirements, policies, and so on that each candidate should be familiar with before registering for an exam. To protect the integrity of the exams and their certifications, Cisco takes these things seriously and doesn't make exceptions. So, know the rules and processes, and you will do fine. For more information, see www.cisco.com/web/learning/exams/policies.html.

exam
watch
Cisco's website is a veritable gold mine of information regarding your certification. Not only will you be referring to it for certification tracking purposes after your exam, but you can also find plenty of information to help you achieve the certification in the first place. In addition to the objectives being tested for each exam, you will find exam-specific information, sample test questions, information on becoming certified, demonstration tutorial videos, and the latest news on Cisco certification. Take advantage of as many of these resources as you can.

Computer-Based Testing

I know you'd probably prefer to be told that a certification exam actually tests your skills in a real-world, hands-on environment, but unfortunately this just isn't true. Imagine trying to ensure that a stable, secured, unchanging network is available at every test center, worldwide, for candidates attempting a certification. It simply couldn't be; such logistics would preclude anyone from ever offering a certification, especially those as varied and far reaching as Cisco's certifications. To get around this, Cisco (and most vendors, for that matter) relies on a computer-based testing service, operated by Pearson Vue. Pearson Vue provides a secured testing environment in a number of facilities around the world (in fact, there may be a Pearson Vue test center in your own town).

Smile, Sign, and ID

To secure the testing process and protect your investment in your Cisco certifications, the test center admission process requires the facility capture of a digital photo and digital signature from each candidate. In addition, each candidate must provide two types of personal identification, each of which must have the candidate's signature and one of which must be a government-issued photo identification.

Not Like Other Vendors' Exams

No matter how many other certifications you have, don't be surprised. Cisco exams are unlike most others. Tests on a Vue system are relatively straightforward and are similar from vendor to vendor, but there are two big differences that you should be aware of.

- Cisco *does not* use an "adaptive" testing format; you will see all of the questions no matter how well you do. Cisco relies instead on a more traditional format, simply providing test questions in a random order and scoring participants according to their success or failure on each question.

- Cisco tests *do not* allow you to mark a question to return to later. In other words, whether you answer the question or not, once you click the Next button, you are done with that question forever. You can't go back. If you don't know an answer, guess. Don't just skip it—that will always be wrong. Eliminate any obviously wrong answers and then take your best shot. If you are going to run out of time and can't speed up, guess at any remaining ones before the clock runs out. Just keep in mind that once it's gone, you'll never see it again!

Many test-takers will tell you that a good strategy on any exam is to skip the questions you don't know and return to them later. It allows you to better use your time; besides, many times, a question later in the exam will provide insight into those you don't know. Cisco doesn't allow this. Cisco wants you to show that you know the material, not that you can game the system.

General Observations

Each test consists of a random set of questions pulled from a large pool of them. During the "beta testing" of the exam, Cisco will compile and refine a huge amount of questions for this pool. Thus, when you receive your test, it simply retrieves a unique combination of these questions to test your ability. Some are straightforward multiple-choice questions, while others are based on a simulator (forcing you to use your hands-on experience as well as your "book" knowledge). Some questions may not be scored but are included for test validation purposes.

Cisco exams are always timed—lasting usually 75 to 90 minutes, depending on the number of questions and the particular test. The time you have remaining for your specific exam will be displayed in a small box on the corner of the computer screen. Learn to check it to pace yourself, but don't get paralyzed by it. If your time elapses, the exam will be scored based on the questions that you have answered up to that point (of course, all unanswered questions will be counted as incorrect answers). Currently, there are 50 to 60 questions; plan for 60, and you are allowed 90 minutes.

As soon as the exam is over, your score will be calculated and displayed onscreen for you to see. It will also be sent electronically to Cisco for tracking purposes. Whether you pass or not, you'll receive a printed report from the test administrator, showing your overall score and a score for each objective the exam covered. Unfortunately, you will not receive a list of the questions you marked incorrectly.

Question Types

Cisco uses the following question formats in its exams: multiple-choice single answer, multiple-choice multiple answers, drag and drop, fill in the blank, and simulations. While you'll find a brief overview of what to expect here, your best resource on any particular exam is to talk things over with other test-takers. No, it won't do you any good to ask exactly what's on the exam, since each is different, but you can get an idea of what *types* of questions to expect. Check with Cisco's website for forums to get a good idea of what the CCENT exam makeup will be like. Cisco offers an exam tutorial video on the site to demonstrate the various question formats. Google can also lead you to other forums, study groups, and so on. LinkedIn offers a variety of useful forums.

True/False

It won't be that easy, but this is not to say that Cisco doesn't employ true or false logic on its tests; in fact, you'll find quite a few questions where Cisco will test your ability to determine a true or false statement or scenario using a multiple-choice question format. An example would be "Choose the true (or false) statements from the following."

Drag and Drop

This is a basic visual matching question that could be as simple as dragging correct answers from a list to the other side of the screen or dragging labels to the correct location such as on the OSI Reference Model.

Multiple Choice

Multiple choice is the primary format for questions in Cisco exams using multiple-choice single answer or multiple-choice multiple answers. These questions may be posed in a variety of ways; however, no matter which way the question is presented, one tip will always apply on these questions: *Always* read the question carefully. Sometimes you may understand the intent of the question perfectly and know well what the answer is, only to wind up missing it because of a "technicality." For example, if the question asks you to choose two answers, you choose two *only*. And watch for the *negative*—is the question asking which are true or which are *not* true?

Choose the Correct Answer   This is the classic format, requiring you to choose one correct option from the four or five presented. In addition to the wording "Choose the correct answer," indicating a single response, these single-answer questions will display Windows radio buttons—allowing only a single response to be entered. One final tip: If the question states "Select the best answer," it's also a single-answer multiple-choice question.

Choose X Correct Answers   This type of multiple-choice question appears differently than the single-choice version listed earlier. On these, the question will ask you to choose X number of options, where X will be a number from 2 to (sometimes) 4. Instead of the radio buttons used before, you'll find check boxes for marking answers. The testing software prevents too many answers from being selected; if the question asks for two responses, you cannot choose three.

Choose All That Apply   Easily the most difficult, and unfortunately relatively common, type of multiple-choice question you'll see on the exam, the choosing-all-that-apply type lets you choose as many, or as few, answers as you want. Since you don't know how many answers the exam expects, you are at a distinct disadvantage.

Fill in the Blank

You may not see any fill-in-the-blank questions on the CCENT exam. However, Cisco has surprised us from time to time on other issues, so you should at least know what to expect should Cisco slip one in on you. A fill-in-the-blank question provides no choices (or help) at all. You are simply given a scenario with an empty text box and asked which command to enter. You must then type the command, precisely as it should be, into the text box provided.

Obviously, this is challenging and is the reason this type of question usually isn't found on entry-level certifications. If you see one, however, be sure to type the *entire* command—do not use a truncated version that would work just fine on a "real" router.

Exhibits

While not actually a test question type, exhibits are a big part of the exam, and you should know about them up front. You'll find exhibits used constantly throughout your exam, with several questions sometimes referring to a single exhibit. These diagrams and pictures will normally appear in a separate window, which you can enlarge or minimize as you see fit, using a button on the screen.

Scenarios

Scenario questions generally consist of one to two short paragraphs that describe a specific circumstance, network, or event, requiring you to pick the correct choice from a variety of answers. Additionally, you may sometimes find several questions referring to a single scenario. On any scenario question, pay close attention to the wording of the problem (if troubleshooting) and apply simple logic. Oftentimes, reading the question first and then returning to the scenario proves a useful practice in navigating the exam.

Simulations

Simulation questions require you to enter a basic configuration on a Cisco switch or router, given a specific set of instructions and settings required. You'll need to know how to access the device, navigate through the various IOS modes, enter commands, and save configurations. Additionally, sometimes these simulators have existing configurations with built-in errors that require you to troubleshoot and fix the problem. The context-sensitive help and the TAB autocomplete functions within IOS should be available for you within the simulator, but it is always best to prepare as if they won't be.

An important note here with this style of question is your ability to use the simulator itself. In other words, knowing what configuration to enter does you no good if you cannot figure out how to enter the commands into the simulator in the first place. Before the exam begins, you will be presented with a screen asking if you'd like to become familiar with the simulator before the exam starts. *Do not skip this*. It does not affect your time for the exam and ensures you won't be wasting valuable time during it figuring out how the simulator works. Additionally, for a demonstration of what the simulator is like, you can visit www.cisco.com and browse to the certification section to find a simulator demo that is similar to, but not exactly the same as, the simulator you would see on the real exam.

The simulations can either eat up valuable time or make up time if you are comfortable with configuring processes and steps. The other questions take a fairly predictable amount of time, but if you are confident in your configuration skills, you can make all the difference in having time left at the end.

Studying Techniques: Just Do it

When asked "How do I study for a Cisco exam?" the response is something we both agree on. To effectively study for the exam, first schedule the exam. It may sound like lunacy, but trust us, it's the best way. Once your exam is scheduled, you have a deadline and will be forced into studying for it. The world is littered with students who say they are planning to schedule the exam "after I've had time to study for it," who months later have the same excuse. Let us assure you, soon-to-be fellow Cisco networking professional, you'll *never* think you're ready for it without some kind of deadline to push you. Also, the further out you get from a class or reading a book, the softer the details, caveats, and examples become in your mind. Just do it!

Sure, take some time to read this book (and encourage everyone you know to pick up a copy and do the same) and do the practice simulations as you go. Set a schedule for that, but as you see the final chapter approaching, schedule the exam. After reading through this book, schedule your exam no more than a month out; one week out is even better. Spend that time studying, using the tips provided here, and practicing with the NetSim, and then just go knock it out!

There are a million study tips out there and just as many people willing to give them to you. Our suggestions are pretty simple, straightforward, and easy: Make the best use of your time available and practice, practice, practice.

Additionally, you'll be amazed at how easy it is to study during times when you'd least expect it. The principle is known as "stealing time" and works simply: While you're accomplishing one task, make use of the slack time to work on another. For example, create an audio tape (or CD) of yourself asking questions and providing answers. Pop this into your vehicle on the drive to work and, *voilà*, you've just added some free study time. Want another example? How about creating a cheat sheet, or a few flash cards, to keep handy in your jacket, wallet, backpack, or purse? While waiting for your lunch, sitting in the airport, or taking a break from work, bring it out and take a quick peek. There are a thousand ways to do this, but the point is simple: You can find ways to study during your day-to-day activities if you really look for them.

Second, practice, practice, and practice some more. Experiment with both live equipment (if available) and the simulator provided with this book. Just memorizing facts and commands *might* be enough to make it through a single exam, but it's certainly not going to be enough in the real world. Your best bet, on both the exam and your job, is to know not only the "what" but the "how" and "why." The best way to do this is to apply what you've read in this book on a system. Try commands. What are the options? What do they show you? How could you use this output to confirm your work or troubleshoot problems? Set up configurations that work and then break them. Throw in weird configurations to see what happens and, more likely, how to fix them so they work. Of course, there's a little humor here, but you get the point: The more you see the configuration, commands, and traffic in use, the better you'll know how they work and what you need to do.

Temptation of the Dark Side

One last note on studying deals with the "dark side" of the network certification world. A wide variety of study guides and "braindumps" are available on the Internet. Some of these are legitimate vendors wanting to provide helpful insight on making you a better network professional. Others are charlatans pure and simple, hoping to take your money at any cost (pardon the pun). Others are nothing more than the "bait" for the worst of network or computer attacks. Do not rely on a single study guide or any braindump downloaded from the Internet. We can promise you, it's *not* a copy of the Cisco exam and may do more harm than good to your studying. If you do find a practice test or study guide on the Internet, verify the answers through your own research. Simply memorizing test questions, from any resource, will *not* result in a passing score. Far worse, it doesn't provide what you need to keep that IT job that you have been dreaming about and often leaves you with a very short-term job that has to be explained at future interviews or on security background checks.

Thoughts on Simulators

There was a time when simulators were "pretty good" and "better than nothing," but that is not the case today with the Boson NetSim. It is an excellent and accurate replication of the configuration process. If there is anything that is not exactly like the real thing, it would be the time it often takes a real device's CPU to process, which is not a serious issue, but in a few cases the real device might seem a bit sluggish after using any simulator. Even that would vary from model to model, but overall these devices are just a bit slower than the Boson NetSim. The good news is that the exam simulators have the same issue.

The version of the NetSim included is a Limited Edition that you could surely use with the book to pass the exam. But, here's a thought you might want to consider: If you are serious about a career with Cisco devices and you are planning other certifications, consider upgrading the NetSim LE to the NetSim Network Simulator for CCENT or CCNA Full Edition sooner rather than later, if that is within your financial means. It allows you more freedom to experiment and practice more commands and features, and it comes with additional practice labs written by Boson's content experts. Do you need it to pass? No, but unless you are going to gain access to real hardware, you will want the extra features for further study and experience.

Scheduling Your Exam

You can schedule any Cisco exam by calling Pearson Vue or visiting its online registration website at www.vue.com (go to Vue's website to find your local number). Exams can be scheduled up to a year in advance and can be rescheduled with 24 hours' notice. If you miss your test date/time or fail to provide appropriate notice, you will lose your test fee.

Payment for the exam is due upon registration with Vue and is accepted through a variety of means, credit cards being the most convenient. Vue e-mails a receipt and confirmation of your testing date, which typically arrives the same day you schedule the exam. If you need to cancel or reschedule an exam, remember to call at least one day before your exam; otherwise, you'll lose your test fee.

If this is the first time you've ever attempted a Cisco exam, Vue will provide a unique number for testing with Cisco. Be sure to keep this number handy and use it for every Cisco test for which you register. Additionally, address information provided when you first register is used by Cisco to ship certificates and other related material, so make sure you get it right! You will also be required to give a valid e-mail address when registering. If you do not have an e-mail address that works, you will not be able to schedule the exam. Once you are registered, you will receive an e-mail notice containing your registration information for your scheduled exam. Examine it closely to make sure it's correct.

Arriving at the Exam

You should always arrive early for your exam, giving yourself time to relax and review last-minute key facts. While waiting for your exam, take the time to review notes, read over the Exam Watch sections of this book, and look over any cheat sheets and practice cards you have handy. Generally speaking, so long as a computer system is available, you can start your test any time before your scheduled test time. So, after your last-minute cram session, when you're ready, you can begin.

Be sure to bring two sets of identification with you to the testing center. Acceptable forms include government-issued IDs (for example, a passport or driver's license) and credit cards. One form of ID must include a photograph. After the identification, though, you won't need anything else. In fact, testing centers do not allow you to take anything else with you into the exam area: no books, papers, notepads, PDAs, cell phones, nothing.

Consider bringing some hard candy, putting it on the desk when you sit down so that you are not digging through your pockets or purse during the exam. You don't want a coughing attack or throat tickle to distract you or make you leave the room. We've seen people bring fruit and water into the exams, but that may be up to the sites. Call your site in advance and ask.

The test administrator will, however, provide you with a paper and pencil or a small erasable marker board. These are to let you write notes and perform calculations during the exam. A helpful tip, though, is to hurriedly jot down any last-minute tidbits you looked at just before the exam, as soon as the administrator allows you to write. In other words, you could download everything in your brain directly to the paper or marker board before your exam ever starts. Consider putting down your binary conversion table and binary combinations table (number of subnets/number of hosts) so that you don't make silly math errors. Just remember that's the only material you'll have to write on during the test, so leave a little room! You'll have to return the paper (marker board) to the administrator immediately upon completion of the test.

In the exam room, the exam administrator logs you in to your exam, and you have to verify that your name and exam number are correct. If this is the first time you've taken a Cisco test, you can select a brief tutorial for the exam software (which we mentioned before, and you should not skip). If you are nervous, go through the tutorial anyway just to give yourself a minute to relax and become familiar with everything. Additionally, you'll be asked to take a survey before the exam. This does *not* count against your time, so take advantage of it and write down your notes during this survey.

Before the test begins, you will be provided with facts about the exam, including the duration, the number of questions, and the score required for passing. Take a deep breath or two, stretch, make sure that you are as comfortable as you can be, and then start. Once you click Begin Test, the clock starts ticking. The test will appear full screen, with a single question per screen. Navigation buttons allow you to move forward to the next question but, as mentioned earlier, not back. The time countdown will appear in the corner, and a variety of buttons may be available depending on the question asked (a Display Exhibit button, for example). Periodically check to ensure you're budgeting your time wisely. Go to the site knowing that if there are 60 questions and 90 minutes, you should be at approximately question 20 at 60 minutes left, 40 at 30 minutes left, and 57 with 5 minutes left. These are approximations, so don't panic if you are a bit behind; just try to pick up the pace. Remember, once you pass over a question, it is scored immediately (you cannot return to it). Nevertheless, you don't want to waste too much time on any one test question. It is always better to guess than leave a question blank.

Do not try to second-guess the exam or look for a strategy to the questions; there isn't one. They are truly randomized. Know that there will be some simulations and some of each of the different types of questions. Some you will find easy, some more difficult. Don't give up; if you get hit with a series of simulations and/or tough questions up front, keep plugging until you have those out of the way.

While working quickly is important, read every question carefully. Know what the question is asking for sure before you start choosing answers. The simplest question with the most obvious answer becomes something else if you missed or overlooked the word *not*. "Which of the following is not a layer of the OSI model" is a lot different from "Which of the following is a layer of the OSI model?" These are not trick questions; part of your new world is attention to detail.

Generally speaking, you'll receive between 55 and 65 questions and will need to get at least 82 to 85 percent of them correct. Cisco does not provide specifics on either the number of questions or the passing percentile, so you'll never really know until the exam is finished.

The Grand Finale

As soon as your exam is completed, it will be graded automatically. The actual real time that elapses between when you click Score Exam and when the results appear on the screen is just under ten seconds. In your mind, it will most likely seem like an eternity. The result of your exam is displayed showing the minimum passing score, your score, and a PASS/FAIL indicator. With some Cisco tests, the actual score isn't displayed on the screen, only on the printed version of your test results.

If you're curious, you can review the statistics of your score at this time. Normally, though, candidates are either so elated they can't sit still or too dejected to bother looking at the screen. Keep in mind, whether you pass or fail, Cisco does not show you the individual questions answered right or wrong. Instead, you'll get a generic list showing categories and your results within each one. This is also provided on the report that's automatically printed at the exam administrator's desk.

Keep your results in a safe place and check back with Cisco's website over the next 48 hours to make sure your results are posted. After some time (a week or so), you'll receive a folder in the mail from Cisco containing your official certificate and other goodies.

Retesting

If you don't make it the first try and particularly if it is your first Cisco exam, which seems likely, don't panic; you are not alone. Many people, even with other industry certifications, stumble on their first Cisco exam. It is not the end of the world, nor is it an indicator of the future. The good news is that you learn a lot from your first exam, pass or fail. You will know better what to study and how to study. Simply jot down those things you remember and go into the next attempt a little more educated on format, content, and pacing yourself. Additionally, the score report will help guide your study efforts, showing those areas you were weakest in.

Cisco makes you wait five business days before you can sign up for another exam. During this time, continue with the study tips from before, but focus on those areas that need the most attention. When you're ready, contact Vue and schedule another exam. You can track your current certification status by going to www.cisco.com/go/certifications/login. You'll need to use your Cisco testing ID number to log in.

ICND1 100-101

The Exam Readiness Checklist lists the official Cisco CCENT objectives available at the time of publication, but always double-check the objectives at www.cisco.com.

Exam Readiness Checklist					
Official Objective	**Study Guide Coverage**	**Ch#**	**Beginner**	**Intermediate**	**Advanced**
Purpose and Functions of Various Network Devices Such as Routers, Switches, Bridges, and Hubs (6%)					
Recognize the purpose and functions of various network devices such as routers, switches, bridges and hubs	Network Devices: Nodes and Hosts Describing the Network	1 1			
Select the components required to meet a given network specification	Network Devices: Nodes and Hosts Describing the Network	1 1			
Identify common applications and their impact on the network	Common OSI Layer Functions and Protocols	2			
Describe the purpose and basic operation of the protocols in the OSI and TCP/IP models	The OSI Reference Model The TCP/IP Model	2 2			
Predict the data flow between two hosts across a network	Ethernet Fundamentals	4			
Identify the appropriate media, cables, ports, and connectors to connect Cisco network devices to other network devices and hosts in a LAN	Network Media: Transmission or Communications Media	1			
LAN Switching Technologies (21%)					
Determine the technology and media access control method for Ethernet networks	Ethernet Fundamentals	4			
Identify basic switching concepts and the operation of Cisco switches ■ Collision domains ■ Broadcast domains Ways switch forward ■ Store and Forward ■ Cut Through	Switching Fundamentals	4			

Exam Readiness Checklist

Official Objective	Study Guide Coverage	Ch#	Beginner	Intermediate	Advanced
Configure and verify initial switch configuration including remote access management ■ Hostname ■ mgmt ip address ■ Ip default-gateway ■ local user and password ■ enable secret password ■ console and VTY logins ■ exec-timeout ■ service password encryption ■ copy run start	Cisco Internetwork Operating System (IOS) The Command Line Interface (CLI) Basic Initial Configuration Securing the Configuration Interface Configuration	5 5 6 6 6			
Verify network status and switch operation using basic utilities such as ■ ping ■ telnet ■ SSH	Exercises 1-1 and 1-2 Managing Remote Connections	1 6			
Describe how VLANs create logically separate networks and the need for routing between them	Virtual LANs (VLANs)	7			
Explain network segmentation and basic traffic management concepts	Virtual LANs (VLANs)	7			
Configure and verify VLANs	Configure and Verify VLAN Access Ports	7			
Configure and verify trunking on Cisco switches ■ DTP (topic) ■ Auto-negotiation	Configure and Verify VLAN Trunk Ports	7			
IP addressing IPv4/IPv6 (11%)					
Describe the operation and necessity of using private and public IP addresses for IPv4 Addressing	IPv4 Addresses Binary Numbers	3 3			
Identify the appropriate IPv6 addressing scheme to satisfy addressing requirements in a LAN/WAN environment	IPv6 Overview	13			

Exam Readiness Checklist

Official Objective	Study Guide Coverage	Ch#	Beginner	Intermediate	Advanced
Identify the appropriate IPv4 addressing scheme using VLSM and summarization to satisfy addressing requirements in a LAN/WAN environment	Subnet Essentials	3			
Describe the technological requirements for running IPv6 in conjunction with IPv4 ■ Dual stack	IPv6 Transition Strategies	13			
Describe IPv6 addresses ■ Global unicast ■ Multicast ■ Link local ■ Unique local ■ EUI 64 ■ Auto-configuration	IPv6 Overview IPv6 Configuration	13 13			
IP Routing Technologies (26%)					
Describe basic routing concepts. ■ Packet forwarding ■ Router lookup process ■ Process Switching/Fast Switching/CEF	Routing Foundation Routing Table Router Forwarding Process	8 8 8			
Configure and verify utilizing the CLI to set basic Router configuration ■ Hostname ■ Local user & password ■ Enable secret password ■ Console & VTY logins ■ exec-timeout ■ service password encryption ■ Interface IP Address ■ loopback ■ banner ■ motd ■ copy run start	Basic Initial Configuration Securing the Configuration Configuration Fundamentals	6 6 9			
Configure and verify operation status of an Ethernet interface	Configuration Fundamentals	9			

Exam Readiness Checklist

Official Objective	Study Guide Coverage	Ch#	Beginner	Intermediate	Advanced
Verify router configuration and network connectivity using ■ ping ■ Extended ping ■ traceroute ■ telnet ■ SSH ■ how cdp neighbors	Configuration Fundamentals	9			
Configure and verify routing configuration for a static or default route given specific routing requirements	Configuration Fundamentals	9			
Differentiate methods of routing and routing protocols ■ Static vs. dynamic ■ Link state vs. distance vector ■ Next hop ■ Ip routing table ■ Passive interfaces (how they work)	Routing Foundation Routing Protocols	8 8			
Configure and verify OSPF (single area) ■ Benefit of single area ■ Configure OSPv2 in a single area ■ Configure OSPv3 in a single area ■ Router ID ■ Passive interface	OSPF Fundamentals Configuring OSPF	10 10			
Configure and verify interVLAN routing (router on a stick) ■ Sub interfaces ■ Upstream routing ■ Encapsulation	InterVLAN Routing	9			
Configure SVI interfaces	InterVLAN Routing	9			

Exam Readiness Checklist

Official Objective	Study Guide Coverage	Ch#	Beginner	Intermediate	Advanced
IP Services (8%)					
Configure and verify DHCP (IOS router) Configuring router interfaces to use DHCP ■ DHCP options (Basic overview and functionality) ■ Excluded addresses ■ Lease time	Dynamic Host Configuration Protocol (DHCP)	11			
Describe the types, features, and applications of ACLs ■ Standard (editing and sequence numbers) ■ Extended ■ Named ■ Numbered ■ Log option	Access Control Lists (ACLs)	12			
Configure and verify ACLs in a network environment ■ Named ■ Numbered ■ Log option	Configuring ACLs	12			
Identify the basic operation of NAT ■ Purpose ■ Pool ■ Static ■ 1 to 1 ■ Overloading ■ Source addressing ■ One-way NAT	Network Address Translation (NAT & PAT)	11			
Configure and verify NAT for given network requirements	Network Address Translation (NAT & PAT)	11			
Configure and verify NTP as a client	Network Time Protocol (NTP)	11			

Exam Readiness Checklist

Official Objective	Study Guide Coverage	Ch#	Beginner	Intermediate	Advanced
Network Device Security (15%)					
Configure and verify network device security features	Securing the Configuration	6			
	Managing Remote Connections	6			
■ Device password security					
■ Enable secret vs. enable					
■ Transport					
■ Disable telnet					
■ SSH					
■ VTYs					
■ Physical security					
■ Service password					
■ Describe external authentication methods					
Configure and verify switch port security	Configure and Verify Switch Port Security	7			
■ Sticky mac					
■ MAC address limitation					
■ Static/dynamic					
■ Violation modes					
■ Err disable					
■ Shutdown					
■ Protect restrict					
■ Shutdown unused ports					
■ Err disable recovery					
■ Assign unused ports in unused VLANs					
■ Putting Native VLAN to other than VLAN 1					
Configure and verify ACLs to filter network traffic	Configuring ACLs	12			
Configure and verify ACLs to limit telnet and SSH access to the router	Configuring ACLs	12			

Exam Readiness Checklist

Official Objective	Study Guide Coverage	Ch#	Beginner	Intermediate	Advanced
Troubleshooting (13%)					
Troubleshoot and correct common problems associated with IP addressing and host configurations	IPv4 Addressing Virtual LANs (VLANs) InterVLAN Routing	3 7 9			
Troubleshoot and resolve VLAN problems ■ Identify that VLANs are configured ■ Verify port membership is correct ■ Correct IP address is configured	Configure and Verify VLAN Access Ports	7			
Troubleshoot and resolve trunking problems on Cisco switches ■ Verify correct trunk states ■ Verify correct encapsulation is configured ■ Correct VLANs are allowed	Configure and Verify VLAN Trunk Ports	7			
Troubleshoot and resolve ACL issues ■ Verify statistics ■ Verify permitted networks ■ Verify direction ■ Interface	Configuring ACLs	12			
Troubleshoot and resolve Layer 1 problems ■ Framing ■ CRC ■ Runts ■ Giants ■ Dropped Packets ■ Late Collisions ■ Input/Output errors	Interface Configuration Exercise 10-3	6 10			

Part I

Operation of IP Data Networks

1

Network Fundamentals and Terminology

Y ou can't really begin learning any aspect of technology or industry without first mastering the basics. This chapter covers the building blocks you'll need to be successful in the rest of your study and your career. A thorough understanding of this chapter should provide a great bedrock upon which to build the rest of your study! Figure 1-1 shows a basic network drawing.

Any text on networking should begin by defining what, exactly, a network is. In its simplest terms, a *network* is two or more computers connected together to share resources, such as printers, files, music, or an Internet connection. A computer or host provides an interface for us to easily share, store, and access a variety of data. The network devices like switches and routers provide a means to address and send this data between computers, and the media or cable provides a pathway for the data to travel across. It sounds simple (and it really is), but it can get complicated in a hurry. Let's keep it simple and start with the definitions and terminology you'll need to know.

The world of networking has more than its share of terminology and jargon, some of which have common meanings in other parts of our everyday lives. In this section, we'll introduce some terms and concepts you'll need to be familiar with. We'll cover things in a logical order, hitting terms that range from what makes up a network and how data is transmitted on the wire, to how far the network reaches.

FIGURE 1-1   Basic network diagram of where we are going in this book

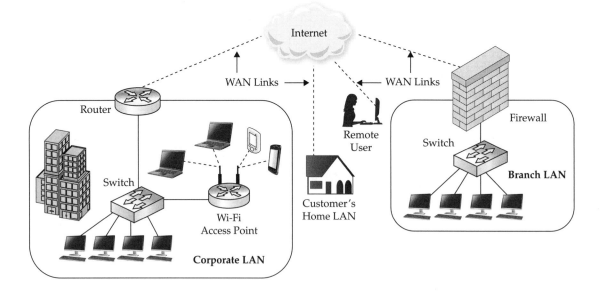

CERTIFICATION OBJECTIVE 1.01

Network Devices: Nodes and Hosts

When thinking about what components make up a network, most observers pick the obvious—the devices they can see or touch. As you'll see, there's more to it than that. A very basic or generic term is node. A *node* is defined as any device that connects to the network that has a recognized address. Most commonly, this address is an Internet Protocol (IP) address, which we'll get to soon enough. Traditionally, nodes can be workstations, servers, printers, switches, wireless access points, or routers. But this term can be used to span other devices on the network, including cameras, cash registers, building access badge readers, videoconferencing systems, and medical or research equipment—just about any device connected to our network that has an IP address can be called a node.

More specific types of nodes are *hosts*: the laptops, desktops, servers, and tablets on our network. For our purposes today, we will use the term *workstation* to include desktop computers, laptops, tablets, iPads, and even smartphones. Our workstations are what we are most used to seeing and working with, but there is a whole other world behind the scenes: our networks! While we have a pretty good idea about what our workstations do, we are here to learn about that other half. The world of networking entails routers, switches, hubs, firewalls, access points, and many other devices. For simplicity, we will just refer to this group of devices as networking equipment.

Network Diagrams

Knowing how all the devices work together helps in the overall design of a network. Two of the most important tasks of a network installer are reviewing network diagrams for technical accuracy and performing troubleshooting. A typical network diagram appears in Figure 1-2.

Most network diagrams follow the same symbology:

- Routers are circles.
- Switches are rectangles with multiple arrows pointing in each direction.
- Hubs (old technology) are rectangles with a single arrow pointing in each direction.

A typical network
diagram

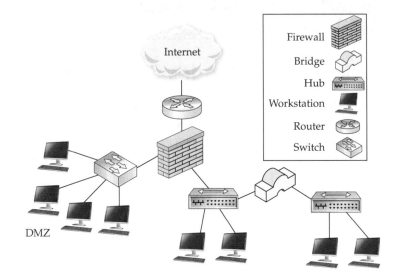

Other oft-used symbols include those for firewalls (comprising a wide variety of symbols, usually including bricks), the cloud (indicating the Internet or another packet switched network that traffic must travel through), lines representing specific connections (such as wireless, serial, Ethernet, and so on), and other networking equipment (PCs, laptops, servers, firewalls, and others).

exam
@atch

Make sure you are very familiar with network diagrams. The exam uses the same symbology discussed in this section but may not label each device on the diagram. In other words, knowing what a switch does will help you in answering the question, but if you are not familiar with the symbol for each, you may misinterpret the network diagram. Be sure to check the

icons used in the diagrams on the exam before the exam starts. The icons should be listed on one of the preparatory pages.

On the CCENT exam, questions will use terms like hosts, nodes, server, workstation, router, and switch. A node is a generic term to include any of the items mentioned. Hosts include workstations or servers. Networking devices are routers, switches, or access points.

Network

Defining where a network starts and stops usually revolves around two things: the geographical area covered and who owns the cables. Networks typically fall into two types: LANs and WANs. Additionally, scale of the implementation and function of these networks can include several other terms, such as SOHO (small office/home office), branch office, and central office.

LANs

A *LAN* (*local area network*) can be defined as a network that serves users within a small geographic area. Usually, LANs are confined to a single room, floor, or building, although they can cover as much as an entire campus. LANs are generally created to fulfill basic networking needs, such as file and printer sharing, file transfers, e-mail, gaming, and connectivity to the Internet or outside world.

In defining a LAN, we usually look at the administrative area of control—if you own all the devices and the connecting cabling within, then it's a LAN. LANs are generally high speed in nature and contain any of the nodes discussed earlier, but typically contain workstations, servers, printers, switches, and wireless access points. Switches and wireless access points are the common connecting technologies for attaching nodes to the network. Hubs are an older, far less efficient connecting technology.

Another traditional characteristic of a LAN is its physical data transmission technology—the cable type. By far, Ethernet is the most common LAN delivery technology. LAN traffic is generally considered *inside* traffic, whereas WAN (wide area network) traffic is considered *outside*. We're using the word *technology* rather than *device* intentionally because today it is not uncommon to have a device that contains switch ports, wireless access point radios, and even a router and firewall capabilities. Rather than have a nice new name for these devices, they are often just called switches, routers, or A/Ps even though they can be much more than that—think about your home all-in-one wireless router with a four-port switch.

Routers connect networks with different address schemes together. In a LAN, they can be used to connect different LAN segments, connecting sales and warehouse departments, or they can be our gateway to the Internet or some other connection to the outside world. Figure 1-2 shows a router on the perimeter of the corporate LAN as a gateway device connecting the LAN to the Internet or an ISP, each of which are different networks. It also shows the branch office LAN using a firewall device, which contains router technology to do the same thing. If you remember that a router technology is always a gateway between networks, LAN or WAN, it is the only technology that performs that function, no matter what device it finds itself in.

A campus network is a large LAN that potentially covers multiple buildings such as a university campus or a large enterprise like Cisco, Microsoft, or Google where many buildings can be connected together via router technologies, but the connections between the buildings are owned by and under the control of the network. The point of distinction is that they all reside within a relatively small geographic region of network connectedness.

A metropolitan area network (MAN) is another network type very much like a campus network, except that the network owner doesn't own the spaces (streets) between the building or sites and therefore requires a WAN service provider to connect the sites. Here we are in a more geographically dispersed environment, perhaps within a city or county. In most instances, you can think of a MAN as LANs connected by WANs even though it might look like a campus.

NICs

A NIC (network interface card) provides the connection from our computers to the media of our network. Typically NICs are built into the motherboard of our workstations or are added as an expansion card.

The NIC installed on the system must match the connection media being used. Many workstations today, particularly laptops, have two NICs, one for copper cabling and one for wireless, which uses radio waves as its media. Other devices like smartphones and tablets support only wireless connections where the built-in two-way radio is the NIC.

NICs listen to the wire or radio signal based on the *media access method* the network uses. When a frame is detected, the NIC reads the physical address (MAC address) and makes a determination on whether to pass it to the operating system (OS) or to ignore the frame. If the address in the frame is unicast (meant for one device) and it matches the NIC's MAC address, it will accept and process the frame. If the address is broadcast (meant for all devices), it will open and process the frame to determine if action needs to be taken. If the address is multicast (meant for two or more specific devices), the frame will be accepted and the devices' protocols will be used to determine if it is processed or discarded.

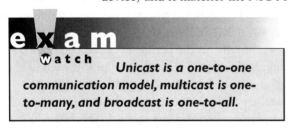

e x a m

ⓦatch *Unicast is a one-to-one communication model, multicast is one-to-many, and broadcast is one-to-all.*

Transceivers and Hubs

Often, multiple types of network media (cabling) will be used in a network design. For instance, a designer may use fiber optic cabling as the media for interconnecting switches, floors, or buildings while using copper cabling for workstation connectivity to the switches. Something has to provide a means to translate the light signals on the fiber to electrical signals for the copper cabling and vice versa. A transceiver is used for just such a purpose.

Transceivers are pass-through devices that do not read or affect the data at all. They simply convert the signal from one media type to another. Because they are "dumb" and work purely on signals (bits), transceivers are known as physical (Layer 1—defined in the next chapter) devices. Transceivers can be a separate device, or more often today this functionality is built directly into routers and switches.

A *hub*, another "dumb" (Layer 1) device, acts as a wiring junction point, allowing systems to plug into a central location. Hubs do not make any decisions on filtering or forwarding data traffic—whatever signal enters the hub on one port is regenerated and flooded out of every other port. To further examine this claim, consider Figure 1-3. Though this is an oversimplified depiction of a hub, the image does show why signals on a hub are sent to all devices. If you take off the top of the hub and examine the wiring within, you'll notice that all ports basically run to a bus in the box. This means all copper cables are touching or spliced together. Therefore, any electrical signal applied to a single port charges all other ports. The hub is nothing more than a junction box that ties all the wires together. A signal sent in to one port is repeated, or flooded, out of all other ports.

Collision Domains

Hubs are rarely used today, but it is still important to understand their function and limitations to better understand how switches work. Recall every cable plugged into

A hub

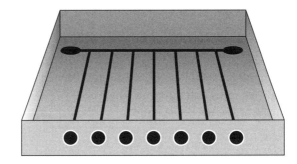

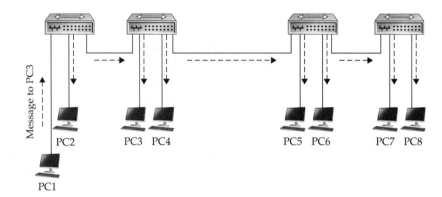

FIGURE 1-4

A collision domain with hubs

a hub terminates with every other cable at a bus so that a signal received on one port is flooded to all ports. Assume, for example, you have four hubs daisy-chained together, as shown in Figure 1-4, and each hub has 10 users on it. After chaining all the hubs together, you have effectively connected all 40 users to the same wire. Since hubs forward all traffic out of all ports, a message from any of the users is repeated to *every other member on the wire* (in Figure 1-4, a message from PC1 to PC3 is flooded to all 40 users).

The chances of a collision (two devices transmitting at the same time) is almost certain as every device is sharing the same media. In this case, 40 systems are all part of the same *collision domain*—a shared segment of media where a message from one system could collide with messages from other systems, garbling both. Collisions greatly slow not only the individual systems that are part of the collision but the network as a whole.

Bridges and Switches

A bridge was a precursor to the switch, typically with only two ports. *Bridges* and *switches* are often used as synonyms; the one big difference is the faster speed at which a switch can make a forwarding or filtering decision. We want you to know what the term *bridge* means, but we will focus on switches as they are what you will find in use today. These devices were designed to have a better understanding of what was being communicated over the wire. Bridges and switches were "smart" … or at least smarter than a hub.

Today, because of their smarter understanding of what is being sent over the media, switches do a better job of segmenting collision domains. When the switch is powered on, it initially acts just like a hub, flooding all messages as they are received. However, it pays attention to whom the data is addressed, both to and from (source and destination MAC address). As the switch watches the communications, it learns who (source MAC) is connected to what port (ingress interface) and records the port it heard each MAC on. After a short amount of time, the switch learns the MAC addresses on each port and can then begin forwarding and filtering traffic intelligently based on these learned addresses. This intelligence or learning of addresses is what allows the switch to move from the behavior of a hub, flooding all communication in a common collision domain, to a high-speed device where traffic is forwarded only to the intended recipients.

Coming back to collision domains, where a hub increases the size of a collision domain by physically attaching many devices to a common delivery path, a switch separates collision paths, providing independent one-to-one communication paths, or separate collision domains.

As with the diagram for a hub, Figure 1-5 displays an oversimplified version of a switch, with the top taken off. Notice that each wire connection from a port ends with a physical switch that does not physically touch the bus. Chips inside the switch monitor both the port wires and the bus itself. As a message hits a port, that wire energizes and the switch at the end closes, touching the bus. These chips, called ASICs (application-specific integrated circuits), inside the device read the source and destination MAC addresses and make a determination as to which port to send the message. The bus then closes the appropriate switch for that one destination port, and the message is delivered. After delivery, the switches are opened, awaiting the next message.

FIGURE 1-5

A switch

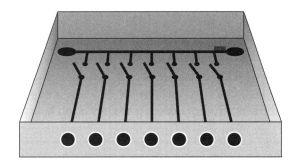

e x a m

Be sure to familiarize yourself with switch operation in regard to separating collision domains and speeding up network performance. Remember, switches initially flood all traffic until the source addresses are learned and entered into an internal table. Exam questions will not only test basic knowledge on this, but will provide scenarios in which you'll have to determine which systems can collide with the source, as well as trace the forwarding of a frame, based on its MAC address. Also, don't forget: switches and bridges both flood broadcast and multicast traffic, no matter where it comes from.

A final advantage switches hold over hubs deals with simultaneous delivery of frames. If a hub receives two frames at the same time, a collision occurs and neither gets delivered; remember, all ports on a hub share the same media, so only one device on the network can transmit at a time. On a switch, ports do not share the media; they see the line as available 100 percent of the time. Because of this design, a switch is capable of simultaneous frame transmission from multiple hosts. The ability to use 100 percent of the bandwidth is known as *full duplex*, the ability to send and receive simultaneously on the same port. In contrast, a hub's behavior is *half duplex*, sending or receiving only when no one else is occupying the wire.

A switch's design and method of operation offers a couple of advantages. First, collisions are effectively eliminated. Second, each device receives 100 percent of the available bandwidth speed. Because bridges and switches read MAC addresses and make filtering decisions on frames, they are considered Layer 2 devices—covered in greater detail in the next chapter.

Routers

While switches, and before them bridges, do a great job of splitting collision domains and improving LAN traffic speeds, they do nothing to limit broadcasts (bridges and switches flood all broadcast and multicast traffic).

Recall that a broadcast is a message meant for all devices. A *broadcast domain* is the area of your network a broadcast can be propagated through. Since hubs and switches flood broadcast traffic, they serve to expand a broadcast domain—any host connected to these devices receives every broadcast sent by any other host connected to the device. Broadcasts are an inherent component of network communications. Administrators should attempt to control broadcast propagation within an area of the network for two main reasons: excessive broadcasts can rapidly consume available bandwidth, and each host must expend CPU time reading or even ignoring the message. Only a router, or Layer 3 device, can split broadcast domains by analyzing the frame to determine the Network layer addresses. (Layer 3, covered in the next chapter).

Providing a gateway out of the network is another job for the router, or Layer 3, device. While switches and bridges can be used to connect multiple nodes to a Layer 2 network segment, they must be in the same IP address subnet. For clarification, consider the post office analogy: A Layer 2 device acts like a single postal clerk for your neighborhood. The clerk can deliver mail inside your neighborhood, where all houses have the same ZIP code, but is not responsible for delivering mail to houses in a different ZIP code. In fact, if the clerk receives a letter destined for another ZIP code, he takes it back to the post office (router) for delivery. So, where switches can deliver data within a ZIP code, we need routers to deliver data to remote networks.

A router is used to connect networks. Acting much like a post office, when a packet is received, the router reads the destination IP (Layer 3) address. It then compares the address to a routing table. This routing table lists the direction (egress interface) of all the remote networks and makes a determination on where to send the packet. If a route exists in the routing table, the router will forward it out of the appropriate port. If there is no entry in the routing table, the router will drop the packet and report the message as undeliverable. (More on IP addresses will be coming.)

Routing tables are built in one of two ways: static or dynamic. Static routing means the administrator defines the routes manually: remember, a route refers to where the destination is and the direction to forward the communication. Dynamic routing allows the routers themselves to share information with each other about the networks they know of and information regarding each link. This information is incorporated into the routing table and keeps it constantly updated. Much more on routing, routing tables, routing protocols, and the like is covered later in this book.

CERTIFICATION OBJECTIVE 1.02

Network Media: Transmission or Communications Media

Now that we have the hosts and networking devices in place, let's talk about what the data is traveling across. Transmission media is the physical pathway over which the data travels.

Just as vehicles need roadways on which to travel, data needs a pathway to use to move from system to system. Network *media* simply refers to the defined pathway data travels within a network. Your choice of media depends on a variety of considerations, such as bandwidth, distance, interference immunity, and cost. Almost every choice when spec'ing out our network comes down to a simple truth. You can have good, cheap, or fast: choose two. In general, installers choose the highest grade of cable available, within cost, for a specific installation. This allows for upgrades in networking devices later on, without removing and installing new cabling. The CCENT exam concentrates on physical media (cabling), while wireless communications are covered in their own CCNA certification.

Media Terminology

Attenuation refers to the weakening or fading of a signal due to imperfections and drag as it travels down our media. A good analogy for attenuation is tossing a pebble into a smooth lake or pool, setting off ripples that fade the farther they get from the impact until they finally disappear. Because of this natural attenuation, each media type has a specific maximum length it is designed to work up to reliably. Some cable types have distance limitations measured in feet/meters, while others are measured in miles/kilometers. Most standards are stated in metric units, meters or kilometers.

Noise immunity is another concern in choosing appropriate media for your network. *Noise* is a catchall term used to refer to the many different forms of interference that can affect a data signal. Electromagnetic interference (EMI)— such as static electricity—and radio frequency interference (RFI) are two common culprits in damaging or corrupting data signals. Depending on your media choice, your network may be susceptible to one, both, or neither. Have you ever heard your computer speakers make a very peculiar noise right before your cellphone receives a call? That is an example of interference or noise and is very bad for our network communication.

Many times, media choice comes down to cost. Generally speaking, the cost of the media increases as its susceptibility to noise and attenuation decreases (good, cheap, or fast). Additionally, media can have several different grades or categories within a specific type. While you may wish to install the best media available, keep in mind that all the devices you purchase for your network must also support that media grade, and some media requires a healthy investment in component/hardware upgrades. In other words, the cost isn't necessarily just about the media, but also includes the upgrades in networking components you may need to utilize the media.

Cabling falls into two major categories: copper-based and fiber-based. Copper cabling uses electrical impulses to send bits, while fiber cabling encodes bits using light impulses. Each category has several defining characteristics and is applied in different situations. In the next section, we'll discuss some basics of cabling at the LAN level. Most, if not all, of the cable discussions following will be applicable to an Ethernet LAN. Ethernet networking is discussed in greater detail in Chapter 4.

Copper Cabling

Copper cables, specifically twisted pair (TP), is the most common media choice for the majority of LAN installations, mainly due to cost and their relative ease of installation.

Twisted pair consists of eight separate wires twisted into four distinct color-coded pairs. The pairs consist of solid color wires and white with a stripe of the same color: orange and white-orange, green and white-green, blue and white-blue, brown and white-brown. Additionally, twisted pair comes in two distinct varieties: shielded (STP) and unshielded (UTP). STP provides a metal shield to help protect against EMI. UTP and, more so, STP offer at least a modicum of protection against EMI, but are ultimately susceptible to noise, interference, and eavesdropping. With any sort of copper cabling, attenuation and EMI are issues to deal with in your network planning.

The Electronic Industries Alliance, the Telecommunications Industry Association (EIA/TIA), and the American National Standards Institute (ANSI) created several categories for twisted pair cabling, setting specific standards of performance and design. The higher the category, the better the cable, and the more options available to you as a network technician. For instance, Category 3 cabling was perfectly acceptable for 10 Mbps Ethernet. However, Category 5 can handle speeds 100 times that of Cat3 running at one gigabit or 1000 Mbps. Today, Category 5e twisted pair is considered the minimum standard in data networking.

Twisted pair categories are listed in Table 1-1.

| TABLE 1-1 | Twisted Pair Categories |

Cable Category	Bandwidth Capability	Application	Maximum Distance
3	10 Mbps	Ethernet	100 meters
4	16 Mbps	Token ring	100 meters
5	100/1000 Mbps	Fast/Gigabit Ethernet	100 meters
5e	1000 Mbps	Gigabit Ethernet	100 meters
6	1000–10,000 Mbps	Gigabit and 10-Gigabit Ethernet	55 meters
6a	10,000 Mbps	10-Gigabit Ethernet	100 meters
7	10,000 Mbps	10-Gigabit Ethernet	100 meters

ⓦatch *Be sure to know the transmission rates, maximum distance, and implementation uses for each of the categories. See Table 1-1.*

Poor connectors are the number one source of physical network connectivity problems. It is generally considered safer and cheaper to purchase machine-made and terminated cables than to attempt to craft your own. A basic understanding of the cables and their connectors is still important for networkers today.

Before learning the appropriate color combination for an RJ45 connector attached to a Cat5 cable, you must first understand the pinouts on the devices you are connecting. A *pinout* is the allocation of a specific function to an individual cable in our bundle of eight. For example, one pin can be set to transmit, while another is set to receive. The pinouts on a device are defined by Ethernet standards, covered more in depth in Chapter 4. The prescribed pinouts are listed in Table 1-2.

Notice from Table 1-2, the transmit pins on an NIC, pins 1 and 2, are different from the transmit pins on a switch or hub port. Switches and hubs have a pinout that is the reverse of the NIC—pins 1 and 2 are set to receive, while 3 and 6 are set to transmit. Considering this, visualize a cable connecting the pins directly to each other, allowing the signal to run straight through, and working perfectly between devices of different pinouts. A cable that has all pins running to their corresponding twin—pin 1 to pin 1, pin 2 to pin 2, and so on—is known as a *straight-through cable*. This cable with a straight-through pinout is what we need to connect an NIC to a switch or a switch to a router.

TABLE 1-2	Devices	Function and Pinout		Function and Pinout		Devices
Device Pinouts	NIC, router, wireless access point, network printers	Transmit	1	1	Receive	Hub, switch
		Transmit	2	2	Receive	
		Receive	3	3	Transmit	
			4	4		
			5	5		
		Receive	6	6	Transmit	
			7	7		
			8	8		

Consider, though, what would happen if you were to plug two devices of the same pinout together. For example, often, network design will call for switches to be plugged together. If a straight-through cable were used in this instance, pin 1 on one switch port would transmit to pin 1 on the other switch port, which is also set to transmit. Therefore, communication could not occur; all we would have is a harmless short and a useless connection. Pins 1 and 2 on both ends would continually transmit to pins not listening, and pins 3 and 6 would always be listening, waiting for a signal that would never arrive. In this instance (plugging two devices of the same pinout together), a *crossover cable* must be used. This cable, configured differently than the previous straight-through, allows the signal to cross over from pin 1(TX) to pin 3(RX) and pin 2(RX) to pin 6(TX). This is accomplished by swapping the copper leads on one end of the cable to a different order than the original. If you examine the connectors at the ends of a crossover cable side by side, you'll find the orange and green pairs are swapped, allowing the signal to cross from pins 1 and 2 to pins 3 and 6.

exam
ⓦatch

Be very aware of which cable to use in a given scenario. Pay particular attention to the devices we are trying to connect before answering a question. For example, a router and a computer have the same pinout; therefore, a crossover cable is the correct choice.

Unlike devices that use a straight-through cable—that is, router to switch ST, NIC to switch ST, printer to switch ST. Like devices use cross-over cables: switch to switch X-over, router to router X-over, NIC to NIC X-over, hub to switch X-over.

The last cable type is more Cisco-specific and is not used to connect networking devices together; it is used to manage our network devices. A *rollover cable* is used to connect our PC's serial port to a router's or switch's console port. All Cisco devices have a console port that provides a direct connect port for performing our configurations. Rollover cables map the pins to their opposite on the end of the wire— pin 1 to pin 8, pin 2 to pin 7, and so on—rolling the signal over to the opposite end. More on rollover cables and console administration will be covered later.

Many new Cisco devices have a capability called auto-sensing MDIx—the port senses the pinout from the far-end device and auto-configures the port's pinouts to match, no matter whether the cable is straight-through or crossover. However, just because this feature is available on some products, you shouldn't throw caution to the wind and simply use any cable lying around. Always choose the right cable for the job.

The Electronic Industries Alliance and the Telecommunications Industry Association (EIA/TIA) created standards for color coding and connectors for twisted pair wiring. The EIA/TIA 568A and 568B standards are used for creating twisted pair cabling for Ethernet networks. 568B pinouts on both ends of the cable create a straight-through, while a crossover can be created by using 568B on one end and 568A on the other.

The color codes for 568B, from left to right, with the tab down and the open end of the RJ45 connector toward you, are white-orange, orange, white-green, blue, white-blue, green, and white-brown, brown. The 568B standard is most commonly used for Ethernet networks. A simple way to remember the color layout is the mnemonic "Only Good Boys Get Brownies." The first letter corresponds to the color, and you always alternate stripe, solid, stripe, solid, and so on. Figure 1-6 shows the cable pinouts.

For more information, there are many how-to videos on YouTube. There are also many cable sources on the Web where you can get general or specific information, but three that we like for images and simple explanations are

http://en.wikipedia.org/wiki/Category_5_cable
http://en.wikipedia.org/wiki/Category_6_cable
www.warehousecables.com/how-to-make-a-cat6-patch-cable.php

FIGURE 1-6

The EIA/TIA
pinouts

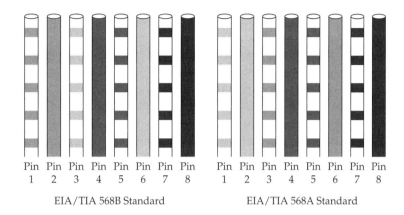

Pin | Pin | Pin | Pin | Pin | Pin | Pin | Pin
1   2   3   4   5   6   7   8

EIA/TIA 568B Standard   EIA/TIA 568A Standard

Fiber Optic or Fiber Cabling

While copper cabling is much more common in data networks, fiber cabling offers many advantages and is used in more and more networks. Fiber cabling encodes bits into light signals, which are totally immune from EMI. Fiber also offers longer segment lengths, much higher bandwidth speeds, and better security than copper cabling. On the other hand, fiber has historically been the most expensive option— not only the cabling itself, but also the devices and NICs used to access the fiber media drive up the installation cost. Until recently, it has also been considered relatively difficult to work with, as connectors are difficult to attach and the cable itself is relatively fragile. While it is possible to connect workstations with fiber, it is far more common in the data closet and LAN backbone connecting routers and switches together. It also works for longer runs like building to building, even over several miles.

Fiber cables contain a glass core that is surrounded by a material known as cladding. Cladding works to contain the light signal in the core. As an analogy, consider a flashlight pointed at a wall. If you turn the flashlight on and begin walking backward, the circle of light on the wall gets larger but dimmer. Light signals inside the wire tend to do the same thing, making the signal weaken the farther down the wire it travels. Cladding controls this *dispersion* and ensures the signal stays clear and focused directly down the core of the wire.

Most fiber cabling in LAN and WAN implementations falls into two major categories: single mode fiber (SMF) and multi-mode fiber (MMF). SMF uses a laser as a light signal source, and has a smaller core (9 microns or less in diameter).

MMF uses an LED as a light source, and has a larger core (50 to 100 microns in diameter). SMF accommodates high bandwidths and very long segment lengths and is the primary fiber choice for lengths measured in multiple kilometers. MMF carries multiple light signals concurrently but at a shorter distance than SMF.

Fiber cables have specific connectors for each cable type. The most common connectors used in fiber cabling are ST, SC, and MTRJ. ST connectors, often referred to as stick and twist connectors, look very much like the BNC connectors used on coax cabling. SC connectors, known as stick and click, are square and have a tab used for securing the connection, much like the tab on RJ45. Lastly, MTRJ connectors are small form factor (meaning they are smaller in physical size than typical connectors) and are normally used for connections to fiber modules in switches or routers.

There are many fiber optic manufacturers and vendors on the Web where you can get general or specific information, but two sources we like for images and simple explanations are

http://en.wikipedia.org/wiki/Fiber_optic
http://en.wikipedia.org/wiki/Optical_fiber_connector

There are many interesting videos on YouTube if you want to see fiber termination or even how fiber optic cable is made, neither of which is required on the exam.

Simplex and Duplex (Half and Full)

A related matter is the method in which devices can send and receive traffic. In *simplex* transmission, devices can only send in one direction, not common except for remote sensors that only report to some type of controller device. An example might be open door sensors reporting to a security system. In *duplex*, devices can send data in both directions. To further hone our definition, duplex has two implementations: half and full duplex. In half duplex, the systems can transmit in either direction but only one at a time. Hubs are examples of half duplex only; another would be a walkie-talkie or CB radio where only one person can talk at a time. In full duplex, both systems can transfer in either direction simultaneously, sending while receiving. A switch's ability to support multiple simultaneous bidirectional or full-duplex conversations is what makes it the preferred choice over the slower one-way hubs.

Whenever possible, network design should include all full duplexing possible. Your duplex setting may be more important than your overall bandwidth/speed available. Incorrect duplex settings could hinder the throughput and perceived performance of the network connection.

CERTIFICATION OBJECTIVE 1.03

Describing the Network

While the device and media make up the network, there are other concepts and terms that you need to be aware of to work in the industry and to pass this exam. We will look at each in the following section and use them in the various chapters of the book.

Data: Bits, Bytes, and Nibbles

The next major term commonly left out in a discussion of networking is *data*, or information. After all, what would a network be without data to transmit? The digital transmissions across a network can include voice, video, or data in many forms (text, presentations, music, pictures, and so on). Each of these requires special attention and functionality to traverse the network correctly. While we cover actual data types and terms later in this chapter, keep in mind that networking isn't just data anymore. Modern networks are often charged with delivering our phone calls, monitoring our premises, and even offering television and entertainment options. Digital data—no matter what its purpose—is composed of a series of *bits*. A bit is the smallest amount of information a computer or network can understand. A single bit is given a numerical value of 1 or 0 (on or off). Bits can be grouped in different quantities to express different information. In data networks we typically work with groups of 8 bits, which create a *byte*. This byte, or grouping of 8 bits, can be used to express up to 256 different combinations. In Chapter 3 when we look at IPv4 addresses we will see that 8 bits can represent any number from 0 to 255, or 256 unique values.

In another common numbering system, bits can be called out as a 4-bit grouping called a *nibble* to signify a hexadecimal or hex digit. Each nibble, or group of 4 bits, represents the 16 numerals represented as 0–9 and A–F that make up the hexadecimal system. Depending on the purpose of a specific combination of bits, bytes, and hex digits received, a device will respond accordingly. Some bit streams, for example, tell the host, "A message is coming and it is intended for you. Please process the information contained within."

Binary data and conversions are covered in Chapter 3, while hexadecimal is covered in Chapter 13.

EXERCISE 1-1

Computer Discovery Techniques

This bonus exercise walks you through some basic computer discovery techniques that will be used throughout the book. The purpose of this lab is to introduce you to the methods for discovering your computer's network connection, hostname, MAC (Layer 2) address, and network (Layer 3) address. Go to the PDF Lab Book on the accompanying media for step-by-step instructions.

Bandwidth and Throughput

Once you understand that your data is made of bits transmitted through media, you should familiarize yourself with a few more terms. There are many analogies for bandwidth, most of which are flawed if you try to apply them directly to data transmission. Common ones are a road with more lanes or a larger diameter of water pipe, each allowing more cars or more water through than their smaller counterparts. The flaw in applying this to networking is that the size of the cable or fiber doesn't similarly increase bandwidth to you. *Bandwidth* is generally considered to be the maximum amount of data (in bits) you can transmit within a given time period (typically one second). Bandwidth can be expressed in bits (b) or bytes (B) per second in digital networking. For example, 10 Mbps would be 10 million bits per second (10 million *bytes* per second would appear as 10 MBps—eight times as much data). Figure 1-7 shows common increments, their value in base-2 (binary) and base-10 approximations, common name, and symbol—the last two are typically combined with bits or bytes.

FIGURE 1-7	Common Units of Measure				
	Base 2	Value	Base 10	Name	Symbol
Bits and bytes units of measure	2^{10}	1,024	10^3	kilo	k, K
	2^{20}	1,048,576	10^6	mega	M
	2^{30}	1,073,741,824	10^9	giga	G
	2^{40}	1,099,511,627,776	10^{12}	tera	T
	2^{50}	1,125,899,906,842,624	10^{15}	peta	P
	2^{60}	1,152,921,504,606,846,976	10^{18}	exa	E
	2^{70}	1,180,591,620,717,411,303,424	10^{21}	zetta	Z
	2^{80}	1,208,925,819,614,629,174,706,176	10^{24}	yotta	Y

Example: 1 Gb = One gigabit, 1 GB = One gigabyte

This notation is important enough to take a moment and emphasize the case of the "B" in 10 Mbps and 10 MBps. They do not mean the same thing. If we remember that 8 bits equal 1 byte, then 8 Mbps equals 1 MBps, or 10Mbps equals 1.25 MBps. It is a common mistake and often not clearly understood, but it has serious implications in communicating bandwidth. Just like when you get an injection from your doctor, you want to know she used the right measurement scale. Make sure you have your bandwidth designated right. If it helps, although it is not a rule, bandwidth or throughput is commonly bps, and volumes of space (RAM, disk space, etc.) are typically Bps.

Another term closely related to bandwidth is *throughput*. While bandwidth is the theoretical *maximum* amount of data a given media can transmit, throughput is the *actual* measurement of the data that is able to pass through the media at any given time. Expressed in the same notation as bandwidth (bps), throughput can be thought of as what you are really getting out of your network. Just as your car may be able to travel at 100+ mph, the actual throughput may well be more like 25 mph because of outside forces such as traffic. In many cases, a gigabit (Gb) network may have far less throughput due to competing network traffic, transmission errors, interference, network devices, slower segments in its path, busy servers, and a host of other variables.

Something to think about on a small scale, increasing the speed of your network at home may let you share files in the house faster, but it will probably have no impact on anything you access over the Internet. In this case, your throughput is limited to whatever your ISP actually delivers to your house, which is typically much less than the speed you can achieve within your home. The old adage applies here: you are only as good as your weakest link. Which is faster, your 100 Mb internal network or your 25 Mb Internet connection? Your 100 Mb LAN is considerably faster.

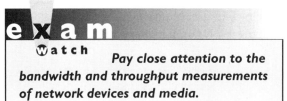

Pay close attention to the bandwidth and throughput measurements of network devices and media.

Network Protocols

Our next definition has to do with the rules of the road. Human beings often make up the rules as they go, while processing information. For example, while you may speak perfect fluent English, your client may not. They may speak slower, or broken, English—occasionally misusing a noun or applying the wrong tense of a verb or two. As a human, you can often figure out the meaning, thereby understanding the communication. Unfortunately, computer systems do not function this way. Standardized, near ritualistic, rules or practices must be in place, or the communication process cannot continue. A *protocol* is simply an agreed upon set of rules for a particular network function. For example, you may agree on a specific method of encoding an electrical signal on a wire to signify a 1 or a 0. Timing sequences, the specific arrangement of bits to signify an address, and how a host can tell that the other end is receiving all the data sent are all examples of protocols in use. Networking protocols are often combined in groups, called a protocol *suite* or *stack*.

Network Topologies

Topology is simply the layout or shape of your network media and the nodes they interconnect. The topology can refer to how the network actually looks (the *physical* topology) or how the data travels on your network (referred to as the *logical* topology).

Physical Topologies

The physical topology of the network refers to how the network actually looks from a bird's-eye view—the physical cabling layout of the network itself. While distinguished by their shape, topologies represent different methods of connecting hosts to the network. Usually, these are very easy to distinguish from one another. The five basic physical topologies are bus, ring, star, mesh, and hybrid. See Figure 1-8 for examples of physical topologies.

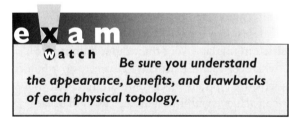

ⓦatch *Be sure you understand the appearance, benefits, and drawbacks of each physical topology.*

Bus Topology   A *bus* topology consists of all devices connecting to a single wire, a coaxial cable (much like your TV cable). A physical bus is often depicted as a straight line—a stick—with connections to hosts coming off in a "T" shape, but the cable can actually snake through the room to connect users. Physical bus topologies are simple to implement and use the least amount of cabling of any topology; however, they are relatively difficult to troubleshoot. A break or gap in the cable in a bus topology can bring all or part of the system down. These breaks can be very difficult to locate. Additionally, terminators that look like a cap must be affixed to both ends of the cable. A *terminator* is a resistor attached to each end of a bus topology network that causes the signal to stop (go to ground) rather than reflect back toward the source like an echo, corrupting the signal. A loose or missing terminator can also bring down the network.

FIGURE 1-8

Physical
topologies

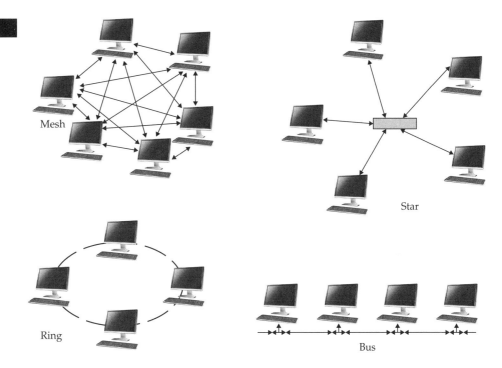

Mesh

Star

Ring

Bus

Ring Topology   In a *ring* topology, all devices are connected to each other in a
continuous loop that is often depicted as a circle, but like coaxial, the cable can snake
around a building or room as long as the cable eventually terminates back into itself
completing the loop (much like a snake biting its own tail). The first device feeds into
the second device, which in turn feeds into the third, and so on and so on until the
loop plugs back into the first device. A break in the cable will bring the entire network
down. However, because of protocols built into many ring technologies, cable faults
can be easier to find and resolve than on a bus topology. Another disadvantage of ring
topology is that it is difficult to expand. Each device must be reconfigured when you
add a new one to the ring. Ring topologies can be either single ring or dual ring. Dual
rings provide redundancy in the case of a line break—if a cable breaks on one ring, the
devices can use the other to communicate until the fault is repaired.

Star Topology   Star physical topology is by far the most common in day-to-day
networking today. In a simple *star* topology, all devices are connected to a single,
central device—usually a switch and historically before that a hub and bridges.

The benefits of a star are fairly easy to see—cable faults only take down the host on that cable (not the entire network), the network is easily expandable, and troubleshooting is very simple. There are two possible drawbacks to a star. First, you have a single point of failure that could disrupt the network. Second, a star uses more cabling than a bus, but the cable is typically much cheaper and easier to work with, plus the number of hosts that can be supported is much larger. Star topologies can also be connected together via links between the switches to create an extended star.

Mesh and Hybrid Topologies   Mesh and hybrid topologies are the last two physical topologies. In a *mesh* topology, every device is directly connected to every other device. Mesh networks have the benefit of complete redundancy—a network break doesn't affect anything. However, they do use the most cable and cable interfaces and have scalability problems. Should you ever have to determine the number of links used in a mesh network, counting them may prove a challenge. The formula for calculating the number of links in a full-mesh network is $N(N-1)/2$, where N is the number of hosts. As an example, 10 nodes would require 45 connections: $10(10-1)/2=45$. *Hybrid* topologies are simply any combination of two or more physical topologies.

Which would you choose? The reality is that almost all business and even home networks use some form of star topology—it is our world today. Support and understanding are plentiful, media and connection devices are relatively inexpensive and readily available, and installation and troubleshooting are easy. Recognize that bus and ring were very early technologies that have faded from networks. That doesn't mean there aren't some rare uses for each, but like mesh and hybrid, they are few and far between in connecting users to networks. Mesh or hybrid topologies are far more likely to be found in the backbone of larger networks, connecting buildings in a campus network or in special-needs environments serving a very specific purpose.

Logical Topologies

The physical layout of the network is only half the picture. The logical topology refers to the path the data actually travels on its way through the network. Regardless of what the network physically appears to be, the pathway of the data itself may be something completely different. The major logical topology is a bus (broadcast) topology.

A bus logical topology broadcasts data to all nodes on the network at the same time. This may seem like a difficult concept to grasp, but consider an analogy. Suppose you are holding a copper wire. Ten other people are holding the same wire with you. You apply voltage to the wire. Who gets shocked? The answer is, of course, everyone. It has nothing to do with the address or even length of wire within limits—you may have been signaling the person at the very end of the cable, but given physics, anyone touching the copper will get shocked.

In a bus topology, a system listens for the wire to get "quiet," then broadcasts its message to the cable. All stations receive it, but only the one it is addressed to will open it. Also known as *contention-based* networking, bus was the original logical topology and is still present today. A star network with hubs was a physical star, but always a logical bus because all links were directly wired to the bus. A star network with switches is physically a star, but technically a logical bus during broadcasts, and a logical star at all other times. With switches, the fewer broadcasts, the more efficient and faster the network.

WANs

A *WAN (wide area network)* is nothing more than a network owned by a third party, a WAN service provider, that connects a LAN to other LANs across an even wider geographic area—perhaps a city, state, nation, or even the whole world! A WAN can connect two branches of a business or they can connect a LAN, like your home or business, to the Internet and millions of other networks.

Aside from the distance, another defining characteristic of WANs is the concept of a leased line or cost for use—the more you use, the more it costs. Most organizations and individuals can't legally install physical cabling across great distances to hook their networks together. Therefore, they lease bandwidth from a provider who already has lines in place or nearby. WAN technologies include dial-up modems, DSL and cable providers, and leased lines across a service provider's network, such as T1 lines from the phone company.

WAN technologies fall into three major categories: circuit switched, packet (or cell) switched, and dedicated connections (point-to-point).

Circuit Switched   *Circuit switched* WAN connections work much like your telephone at home. When you wish to transmit, you make a call and the line is committed exclusively to you until you are finished transmitting. No one else can use the line, and it remains open even when you're not talking. WAN technologies using circuit switching include regular dial-up with a MODEM, using the plain old telephone system (POTS), or Integrated Services Digital Networking (ISDN), using specialized equipment to send digital messages over special phone lines. The advantages of circuit switched technologies include cost (usually cheaper, on-demand service used by others when you are not), scalability (easy to install and expand), and availability. MODEM service can go anywhere there is a phone line. The biggest drawback is that bandwidth is very limited, particularly compared to DSL and cable service providers.

Packet or Cell Switched   *Packet* or *cell switched* technologies work differently than circuit switching. In the case of a leased line, there may be other traffic on the link or parts of the link that originated from other devices on the customer's network. The packets or cells are like trucks driving on a private road. In the case of the Internet, a public network, the packets (not cells) would be traveling with those of the rest of the world, slipping into open spaces in traffic. Cell switching is used in ATM (Asynchronous Transfer Mode, not your bank's automated teller machine) networks and works much like packet switching on leased links, with the main difference being the length of packets. Cell switching uses a standardized cell size like shipping containers you see on the road, whereas with packet switching, sizes of individual packets vary. Packet switching allows multiple connections between multiple locations and it can support quality of service (QoS), providing prioritized treatment for time-sensitive traffic like voice or video.

Point-to-Point (Dedicated)   *Point-to-point*, or *dedicated*, WAN connections are exactly what they sound like—a leased line that directly connects two sites together. The advantage is that the connection is always up and available, and you are guaranteed 100 percent of the bandwidth available 100 percent of the time. The drawbacks are closely related—whether you use the bandwidth or not, you pay for it, and generally speaking, these connections are rather expensive to implement. The cost goes up with both bandwidth and distance. Examples of dedicated connection include the "T" lines, such as T1 (1.544 Mbps), T2 (6.312 Mbps), and T3 (44.736 Mbps).

Due to cost and ease of scalability, most enterprise networks use packet switched technologies, such as frame relay, ATM, or MPLS (Multiprotocol Label Switching). Smaller businesses are finding that cable providers or DSL can offer very high bandwidth at attractive prices.

Location Terminology

Within the LAN/WAN architecture, an organization can have several types of remote connections to their LAN. These include branch offices that can be very large or small, a small office/home office (SOHO) with one or a few users working in a single location, such as a home or office space, and (a growing issue) mobile users.

A mobile user is part of the organization but is not located at one of their facilities. These can be salespeople, technicians, managers, executives, and anyone working from home or traveling on business. Each of these remote connections need to connect back to the central office for any number of tasks. In each case they will need a WAN connection, possibly using the Internet, and may require security in the form of a virtual private network (VPN).

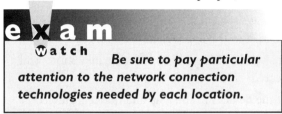

Be sure to pay particular attention to the network connection technologies needed by each location.

EXERCISE 1-2

Media

Network Discovery Techniques

This bonus exercise walks you through some basic network discovery techniques that will be used throughout the book, such as how to ping a router and use tracert. Go to the PDF Lab Book on the accompanying media for step-by-step instructions.

EXERCISE 1-3

MHE Lab

NetSim Introduction

This exercise is a basic introduction to the NetSim simulator. You'll perform this exercise using Boson's NetSim simulator included on the media. The instructions and the topology diagram are included in the simulator.

Task 1: Launch NetSim and View Videos

1. Launch the NetSim program. The Home screen shows a series of windows with mainly text.
2. In the upper-right window, click on the Watch the Video Demo link and watch the videos to learn the basics of using the simulator. They should be displayed in your browser.
3. After viewing the videos, return to the simulator.

Task 2: Explore Lab Host Devices

1. Click on the Labs bar in the lower-left corner of the screen.

2. When the Lab Tree appears above, select Chapter 1 and then 1-3 NetSim Introduction. The lab should load in the upper-right window.

3. Click on the Lab Instructions and NetMap tabs to see what they show. End up with the NetMap tab selected.

4. Put your mouse over each of the devices in the map and notice a Device Statistics box appear next to the device. Click on the one for RouterA and note that it shows the interfaces and connections. Take a moment and look at each device's statistics and note the difference between routers, switches, and hosts.

5. The bottom window is the console display for one of the devices; which device is displayed on the tab below the window. You may have to click on the space below the last line of output and press ENTER to see the current prompt. We'll come back to this in a minute.

6. There are three ways to open the other devices in the console window:
1) Right-click on the device and then click the Configure in Simulator button that appears. 2) Double-click on a device image. 3) Use the Devices drop-down in the top of the console window. Try each of these to open the remaining devices, pressing ENTER to see the prompt for each. You should now have six tabs below the console.

   The red X on the tab can be used to take that device out of the console. Try it and then reopen it so all six tabs show.

7. Select the A.22 tab. A means it is in the A LAN and .22 is the last octet of its IP (the host portion). Make sure the cursor is at the C:> cursor and type **ipconfig** and press ENTER. Make a note of the IP addresses, mask, and default gateway. If you look at the diagram you should see that the gateway is the LAN interface on the router.
Look over the HELP options and the run the ipconfig /all command option. You will notice there is far less output than when you run it on your computer. It is in fact just those items you need for using the simulator to access the Cisco devices.

Task 3: Confirm Connectivity

1. From each host PC, confirm that you can ping the other two computers and then each interface on the routers, and the switches' IP address. Use the diagram for any addresses that you need. Type **ping 10.0.1.77** and press ENTER. You should see that we have connectivity across the entire network.

2. Use the Lab topology at the top of this lab to ping other devices. All pings should work except 10.0.0.2 (SwitchA), which isn't configured yet—you will correct that in the next chapter. Note that it is still passing data properly even so. That is not the case with unconfigured routers.

3. From the prompt, press the UP ARROW key and note that you can recall and rerun or edit earlier commands. That works on all of the devices.

4. Note: The computer tracert command and Cisco device's traceroute command are not featured in the NetSim Limited Edition, so we've shown the output here and in the "Lab Solutions" section in the PDF Lab Book. To run **tracert** from A.22 to 10.0.1.77:

```
C:>tracert 10.0.1.77

"Type escape sequence to abort."
Tracing the route to 10.0.1.77

 1 10.0.0.1 0 msec 16 msec 0 msec
 2 10.1.1.1 20 msec 16 msec 16 msec
 3 10.0.1.77 20 msec 16 msec *
C:>
```

When you are finished you can exit out of NetSim. You can return as often as you like to rerun this part of the lab and to get familiar with navigating through the NetSim. You have a couple of chapters before we return to it, and two of them have no exercises. It would be a good time to familiarize yourself with the tool.

This is the format of all the NetSim labs. Solutions appear in the NetSim simulator and the PDF Lab Book, but are not included in this book.

CERTIFICATION SUMMARY

Much of this chapter is foundational to the rest of the chapters, but there are three exam objectives that pertain to this material. They are as follows:

- Recognize the purpose and functions of various network devices such as routers, switches, bridges, and hubs
- Select the components required to meet a given network specification
- Identify the appropriate media, cables, ports, and connectors to connect Cisco network devices to other network devices and hosts in a LAN

Know the basic data network devices and their purpose. Remember that "hosts" generally refers to servers and workstations, and these aren't addressed in other chapters. The antiquated hubs and bridges could still be used in a question. All of the important devices will be addressed more in the next chapters.

Important media terminology includes attenuation (the degradation of a signal over distance traveled on media), noise (any form of interference affecting the signal), and EMI (interference caused by magnetic interference). Cable falls into two categories: copper and fiber. Copper is generally cheaper and much more prevalent; however, it is susceptible to EMI. Fiber is immune to EMI and can carry data much further, but is often more expensive.

TWO-MINUTE DRILL

Network Devices: Nodes and Hosts

❏ Nodes are any device connected to your network.

❏ Hosts are the computing devices that connect to your network, including servers and workstations. Workstations can include desktop computers and laptops but could also include tablets and smartphones.

❏ Networking devices are routers, switches, wireless access points, and firewalls

❏ Other devices that could be connected to our networks are printers, cameras, telephones, videoconference devices, door access card readers, and more.

Network Media: Transmission or Communications Media

❏ Concerns in selecting media for the network include attenuation, noise immunity, features, and cost.

❏ The two major kinds of twisted pair cabling are unshielded twisted pair (UTP) and shielded twisted pair (STP). Twisted pair cabling consists of four color-coded pairs, with each pair twisted at a specific rate (twist ratio), where segment lengths can reach up to 100 meters.

❏ UTP (and STP) is rated in several categories. Category 5 cabling is the minimum for Fast and Gigabit Ethernet.

❏ The pinout on NIC, router, wireless access point, and printer ports has pins 1 and 2 set to transmit, and pins 3 and 6 set to receive. Hub and switch ports have pins 1 and 2 set to receive, and pins 3 and 6 set to transmit.

❏ Straight-through cables, by far the most common, have all pins on one end of the cable mapped directly to the same pins on the far end and are used between devices with different pinouts.

❏ Crossover cables map pins 1 and 2 on one end to pins 3 and 6 on the far end. They are used between devices with the same pinout.

❏ Rollover cables map pins on one end to their opposites on the far end and are used to connect a PC serial port to a Cisco device console port.

❏ The EIA/TIA 568B standard from left to right, with the tab down, has colors in this order: white-orange, orange, white-green, blue, white-blue, green, white-brown, brown. 568B is the standard used on most straight-through cables.

❏ The EIA/TIA 568A standard from left to right, with the tab down, has the colors in this order: white-green, green, white-orange, blue, white-blue, orange, white-brown, brown. 568A on one side and 568B pinout on the other create a crossover cable.

❏ Single-mode fiber (SMF) has a small core, uses a laser as a transmission light source, and can transmit high bandwidth over very long segment lengths. Multi-mode fiber (MMF) has a larger core and supports shorter segment lengths.

❏ Fiber connectors include ST, SC, and MTRJ connectors.

Describing the Network

❏ All digital data is made up 1s or 0s, called bits, signifying an on or off circuit, as in switch on or switch off.

❏ Binary notation typically looks at grouping these 1s and 0s in 8 bits, called a byte. There are 256 unique combinations of bits (1s and 0s) in a byte. Think of eight light switches side by side; there are 256 combinations of off and on. We will go into this more in Chapter 3 when we cover IPv4 addressing.

❏ Common units of measuring bits or bytes are kilo (1000 bits or 1000 bytes), mega (1000 kilos), giga (1000 mega), and tera (1000 giga) for each. Abbreviations use the first letter, as in 7 Kb or 7 KB, where the lowercase b indicates bits, uppercase B indicates bytes. Therefore, 100 GB is 8 times larger than 100 Gb.

❏ Hexadecimal notation (hex) groups 4 bits into a nibble. There are 16 unique combinations of bits within a nibble that are represented by the numbers 0–9 and letters A–F. We will go into this more in Chapter 13 when we cover IPv6 addressing.

❏ Protocols are the rules within networks; they ensure consistent, reliable behavior. Protocols are often grouped and referred to as protocol stacks or suites.

❏ Topologies are the layout or bird's-eye view of your network.

❏ Topologies can be physical (how they look) or logical (how they behave).

❏ Common topologies are bus, star, ring, mesh, and hybrid, with some variations. By far, the most common LAN topology is the star. Some form of mesh might be used to provide fault tolerance, but is beyond the scope of the exam.

❑ LAN (local area network) is a user network, generally confined to a limited geographic area, under the administration of the network owner. This exam focuses on LANs.

❑ WAN (wide area network) connects LANs or other networks, usually over larger geographical areas. WANs do not have users; they interconnect LANs, where users reside.

❑ Routers connect networks together. A router can connect two LANs together across a larger WAN, and also connect two separate networks together within a LAN.

SELF TEST

The following Self Test questions will help you measure your understanding of the material presented in this chapter. Read all the choices carefully since there may be more than one correct answer. Choose all the correct answers for each question.

Network Devices: Nodes and Hosts

1. Which of the following defines a node?
    A. Any device with a connection to a network
    B. Any device on wireless
    C. Any device processing data
    D. Any device with an address on a network

2. Which of the following is/are true regarding hex digits? (Choose all that apply.)
    A. Hex digits are made of 4 bits.
    B. Hex digits are made of 4 bytes.
    C. Hex can be expressed as 0–9 and A–G.
    D. Hex can be expressed as 0–9 and A–F.

3. Which physical topology has all systems connecting to a central connection device?
    A. Bus
    B. Ring
    C. Star
    D. Mesh

4. Which addresses do Physical layer devices—such as repeaters and hubs—examine in order to make forwarding decisions?
    A. Physical
    B. Logical
    C. Host
    D. None of the above

Network Media: Transmission or Communications Media

5. A network designer is asked to recommend a media type. The customer desires a Fast Ethernet network, but wishes to keep costs at a minimum. Which of the following media types should be recommended?
   A. Cat3 UTP
   B. Cat5 UTP
   C. SMF
   D. MMF

6. A customer maintains a twisted pair network. The customer wishes to attain Fast Ethernet speeds, and wishes to take steps to prevent EMI as much as possible. Which cable type would you recommend?
   A. Cat5 UTP
   B. Cat5e UTP
   C. Cat5 STP
   D. SMF

7. Which of the following is a true statement concerning the UTP cable connection between a PC and a switch?
   A. Pin 1 on the PC end is set to receive and is connected to pin 1 on the switch end.
   B. Pin 3 on the PC end is set to receive and is connected to pin 3 on the switch end.
   C. Pin 1 on the PC end is set to transmit and is connected to pin 3 on the switch end.
   D. Pin 3 on the PC end is set to transmit and is connected to pin 1 on the switch end.
   E. None of the above.

8. Which of the following is a true statement concerning the UTP cable connection between two hubs?
   A. Pin 1 on one end is set to receive and is connected to pin 3 on the other end.
   B. Pin 1 on one end is set to receive and is connected to pin 1 on the other end.
   C. Pin 3 on one end is set to transmit and is connected to pin 3 on the other end.
   D. None of the above.

9. Which cable type would be used to connect a PC to a router?
   A. Straight-through
   B. Crossover
   C. Rollover
   D. None of the above

10. Which cable type would be used to connect a router to a switch?
    A. Straight-through
    B. Crossover
    C. Rollover
    D. None of the above

11. A straight-through cable is created using the 568B standard. Which of the following correctly describes the color-coded cable layout within the connector (from left to right, with the tab down)?
    A. White-green, green, white-orange, blue, white-blue, orange, white-brown, brown
    B. White-green, green, white-blue, blue, white-orange, orange, white-brown, brown
    C. White-orange, orange, white-green, blue, white-blue, green, white-brown, brown
    D. White-orange, orange, white-blue, blue, white-green, green, white-brown, brown

Describing the Network

12. 100 Mb equals which one of the following?
    A. 1.25 MB
    B. 1.25 Gb
    C. 12.5 MB
    D. 12.5 GB

13. Which one of the following is a layout or bird's-eye view of your network?
    A. LAN
    B. WAN
    C. Topology
    D. Protocol suite

14. What does 1 Gb equal?
    A. 10 MB
    B. 100 Mb
    C. 1000 MB
    D. 1000 Mb

15. What does 8 bits equal?
    A. A nibble
    B. A byte
    C. $0.75
    D. 1 Kb

SELF TEST ANSWERS

Network Devices: Nodes and Hosts

1. ☑ **D** is correct. A node is defined as any device with an address on a network (this will normally be an IP address).

   ☒ **A, B,** and **C** are incorrect. **A** is incorrect because not every device touching the network has an address. **B** is incorrect because the media (wireless or wire) has nothing to do with it. **C** is incorrect because a computer (or any device) can process data without being connected to the network.

2. ☑ **A** and **D** are correct. Hex digits are 4 bits in length and can be manipulated to display the alphanumeric characters 0–9 or A–F.

   ☒ **B** and **C** are incorrect. **B** is incorrect because hex digits are made of 4 bits, not 4 bytes. **C** is incorrect because hex digits can only represent characters up to F.

3. ☑ **C** is correct. A star topology connects all devices to a central point.

   ☒ **A, B,** and **D** are incorrect. **A** is incorrect because all devices are connected to a single wire. **B** is incorrect because it connects all devices in a circle, with one device connected directly to the next. **D** is incorrect because it has all devices connected directly to all other devices.

4. ☑ **D** is correct. Physical layer devices do not see addresses at all; they simply forward bits.

   ☒ **A, B,** and **C** are incorrect. **A** is incorrect because physical addresses are used by Layer 2 devices, such as switches and bridges. **B** is incorrect because logical addresses are used by Layer 3 devices, such as routers. **C** is incorrect because "host" is a synonym for logical addresses.

Network Media: Transmission or Communications Media

5. ☑ **B** is correct. Category 5 UTP best fits the scenario. Cat5 UTP is the minimum cable requirement for Fast Ethernet.

   ☒ **A, C,** and **D** are incorrect. **A** is incorrect because Cat3 UTP is only rated for 10 Mbps bandwidth speeds. **C** and **D** are incorrect because both SMF and MMF will comply with the bandwidth requirements; however, fiber is typically more expensive than UTP.

6. ☑ **C** is correct. STP has a metal shield around the twisted pairs to mitigate against EMI.

   ☒ **A, B,** and **D** are incorrect. **A** and **B** are incorrect because UTP has no protection against EMI. **D** is incorrect because SMF is a fiber, not a twisted pair, cable.

7. ☑ **E** is correct. NIC pinouts have pins 1 and 2 set to transmit, and 3 and 6 set to receive. Since both devices have different pinouts, a straight-through (pin 1 to 1, 2 to 2, and so on) cable would be used.

   ☒ **A, B, C,** and **D** are incorrect. **A** and **B** are incorrect because pin 1 on the PC NIC is set to transmit, not receive. **C** and **D** are incorrect because the pinouts listed indicate a crossover cable.

8. ☑ **A** is correct. Hub port pinouts have pins 1 and 2 set to receive, and 3 and 6 set to transmit. Since both devices have different pinouts, a straight-through (pin 1 to 1, 2 to 2, and so on) cable would be used.
☒ **B, C,** and **D** are incorrect. **B** is incorrect because the pinout listed indicates a straight-through cable. **C** is incorrect because pin 3 on hub ports is set to receive. **D** is incorrect.

9. ☑ **B** is correct. PCs and routers have the same pinout; therefore, a crossover cable should be used.
☒ **A, C,** and **D** are incorrect. **A** is incorrect because a straight-through cable will not work between two devices of the same pinout. **C** is incorrect because rollover cables are used between a PC and a router/switch console port. **D** is incorrect.

10. ☑ **A** is correct. Switches and routers have different pinouts; therefore, a straight-through cable should be used.
☒ **B, C,** and **D** are incorrect. **B** is incorrect because a crossover cable will not work between two devices of different pinouts. **C** is incorrect because rollover cables are used between a PC and a router/switch console port. **D** is incorrect.

11. ☑ **C** is correct. This represents the correct pinout for an RJ45 connector using 568B.
☒ **A, B,** and **D** are incorrect because these choices do not represent the correct color-coded pinouts.

Describing the Network

12. ☑ **C** is correct. 8 bits = 1 byte, so 100 Mb = 12.5 MB.
☒ **A, B,** and **D** are incorrect. **A** is incorrect because 1.25 MB = 10 Mb. **B** is incorrect because 1.25 GB = 10 Gb. **D** is incorrect because 12.5 GB = 100 Gb.

13. ☑ **C** is correct. A topology is a layout or bird's-eye view of your network.
☒ **A, B,** and **D** are incorrect. **A** is incorrect because a LAN, or local area network, is a user network, generally confined to a limited geographic area, under the administration of the network owner. **B** is incorrect because a WAN, or wide area network, connects LANs or other networks, usually over larger geographical areas. WANs do not have users. **D** is incorrect because protocols are the rules within networks; they ensure consistent, reliable behavior. Protocols are often grouped and referred to as protocol stacks or suites.

14. ☑ **D** is correct. 1 Gb = 1000 Mb.
☒ **A, B,** and **C** are incorrect. **A** is incorrect because 10 MB is just 10 MB. **B** is incorrect because 100 Mb is just 100 Mb. **C** is incorrect because 1000 GB = 1 TB.

15. ☑ **B** is correct. 8 bits = 1 byte.
☒ **A, C,** and **D** are incorrect. **A** is incorrect because a nibble = 4 bits. **C** is incorrect because, nice try, but that 8 bits = $1. **D** is incorrect because 1Kb = 1000 bits.

2

Networking Models: OSI and TCP/IP

I n just about every aspect of modern industrial life, standards are developed to simplify manufacturing, support, and replacement. Imagine, for example, how difficult it would be to replace a missing bolt on your vehicle if the sizes weren't standardized, or attempt to fix a plumbing problem in your home if every house used different-sized pipes and fittings.

Networking standards have developed over time for the same reasons. Today, fortunately, there are really just two primary standards that we need to concern ourselves with both on the job and for this exam. Figure 2-1 shows the OSI Reference Model and the TCP/IP model, which is the foundation of the Internet. We will look at each in greater detail in this chapter, but for now let's recognize that they are just two different ways of looking at the same thing. The job of these models is to allow us a conceptual model to understand the flow of data in our networks. They provide visibility into the logical steps and components used in networking.

FIGURE 2-1   OSI Reference Model and TCP/IP model

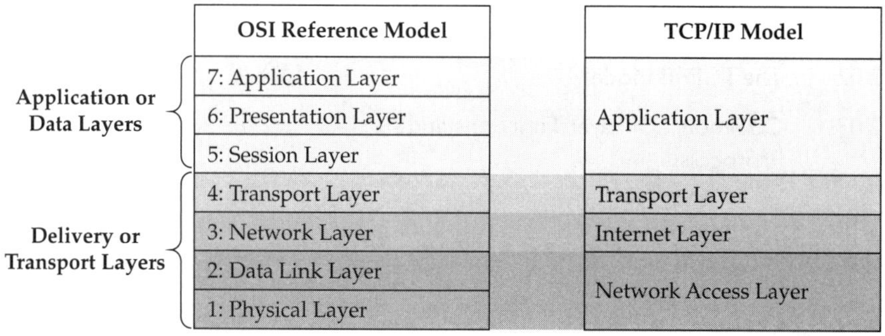

	OSI Reference Model		TCP/IP Model
Application or Data Layers	7: Application Layer		Application Layer
	6: Presentation Layer		
	5: Session Layer		
Delivery or Transport Layers	4: Transport Layer		Transport Layer
	3: Network Layer		Internet Layer
	2: Data Link Layer		Network Access Layer
	1: Physical Layer		

CERTIFICATION OBJECTIVE 2.01

The OSI Reference Model

ISO, the International Organization for Standardization, formed in 1946, develops international standards for almost every industry and everything you can imagine—from simple things like film, pipe, and screw threads to accepted business practices for customer service and ecology-friendly packing materials. Many of these international standards are adopted or incorporated by local standards bodies like the United States' American National Standards Institute (ANSI), either in whole or in part, into national standards. ISO created a set of networking standards or conceptual models called the Open Systems Interconnection (OSI) model (ISO/IEC 7498-1) or OSI Reference Model.

Note that ISO is not an acronym but a short name for the organization to avoid the many acronyms possible in different languages.

Functions and Advantages

A common question asked by new networkers is "What exactly does the OSI Reference Model do?" The answer may be a little surprising. Technically, the OSI Reference Model does ... nothing; it is a conceptual model. You don't buy a box of it, you don't install it, and you don't configure it on devices. The purpose of the OSI Reference Model is to provide a means for us to break down the communications process between two network computers into layers, and easily discuss and describe the steps within each layer, as well as the form in which each layer expects to receive data and is expected to forward data. While not perfect, the model provides a good method of breaking down the communication process in an organized manner for discussion, troubleshooting, and training. It also facilitates interoperability between computers and networking components from different manufacturers, encouraging innovation and competition, which helps keep costs lower.

One word you will hear quite often in regard to the OSI model is encapsulation. *Encapsulation* is the process of adding a header and a trailer to a piece of data.

When ISO developed the OSI Reference Model, every effort was made to distinctly separate logical functions for each of the seven layers. This design concept greatly enhances vendor efficiency in creating new network devices, protocols, and services. For example, a vendor can choose to work in one layer and modify/enhance their product without adversely affecting the functions of the other layers. The OSI Reference Model provides several benefits:

- It simplifies training and learning.
- It reduces complexity in product and services design.
- It provides for vendor interoperability.
- It allows for modular construction.

The Layers

The OSI Reference Model splits the communications process into seven distinct modular layers, with each layer accomplishing specific functions independent of all other layers. Figure 2-2 displays the seven layers. Each layer requires the layers immediately above and below to provide information in an expected form, with certain bits (zeros and ones) attached as a header or trailer providing instructions. Much like a jigsaw puzzle, the layers will only fit to the pieces above and below if the piece is crafted properly—the order can't be mixed up nor can any layer be left out. This process and each layer are discussed in further detail next.

FIGURE 2-2

The OSI
Reference Model
layers

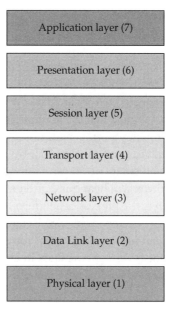

Application layer (7)

Presentation layer (6)

Session layer (5)

Transport layer (4)

Network layer (3)

Data Link layer (2)

Physical layer (1)

Because the OSI model acts as a foundation for the rest of networking, it's very important that you thoroughly understand the stack. It is essential you be able to identify:

- The order of the layers, from top to bottom, and bottom to top
- The number that corresponds to each layer (always starts from the bottom)
- The function(s) of each layer
- The protocols and devices that work at each layer

Memorizing the layers and their numbers is actually fairly easy using a mnemonic. Keeping in mind that the "top" of the stack is Layer 7—Application—simply take the first letter of each layer and create a phrase to help remember their place in the stack. Common examples are "Please Do Not Throw Sausage Pizza Away" and "All People Seem To Need Data Processing." There are many different mnemonics new network technicians use to help remember the layers. Find one that works for you and stick with it! In the remainder of this section, we'll examine each layer in more detail. Refer to Table 2-1 as you read more information about the devices and protocols working at each layer.

e x a m

ⓦatch *Memorize the information in Table 2-1. Questions may or may not be explicit, but you will need to know this information to correctly determine the question's intent.*

TABLE 2-1	Layer	Devices Found in the Layer	Protocols/Standards Working in the Layer
OSI Protocols and Devices	Application	Firewall, Gateway, and IDS (Intrusion Detection System)	SMTP, POP3, IMAP, DNS, DHCP, FTP, HTTP, TFTP, SNMP, VoIP, NNTP, NTP
	Presentation	N/A	JPG, JPEG, TIFF, PNG, GIF, MIME, MP3, MP4
	Session	N/A	NFS, ASP, SQL, RPC
	Transport	Firewall	TCP, UDP, SPX*
	Network	Router	IP, IPX*, AppleTalk*
	Data Link	Bridge, Switch	Ethernet, PPP, HDLC, Frame Relay, ATM
	Physical	Transceiver, Repeater, Hub	RJ45, ST/SC, V series (modem standards)

* IPX/SPX and AppleTalk were early networking protocols vying for market acceptance; both eventually lost out to TCP/IP and the Internet.

The Layers' Role in Handling Network Communications

Before we look at the individual layers, let's look briefly at the process of data communications between two computers, each with its own OSI layers. The sending machine in essence sends the data down through the OSI stack to be processed at each layer (covered later). At each layer, a header is prepended to the beginning of the data package to tell the receiving computer's corresponding OSI layer how to handle or process the package when it arrives. At the receiving computer, the process is reversed. The package travels up the OSI stack, with each layer reading, acting upon, and removing the appropriate header. Figure 2-3 shows the encapsulation process.

This process will be covered in greater detail in this chapter, but it is important enough to understand before discussing the model layers. Make sure that you understand at least conceptually how this encapsulation/de-encapsulation occurs. You might find it useful to go to YouTube and search for *OSI encapsulation* and look for a short animation of the process; the longer explanations will make more sense after you finish the OSI section of this chapter. Note that you want the look and feel of the process, not the exact details—there are many wrong or partially correct explanations.

The Data Layers: Application, Presentation, and Session (7, 6, and 5)

It might help you understand the functions of the seven layers of the OSI model and how they will relate to the TCP/IP model later if you think of them in terms of *data* layers and *delivery* layers. The data layers are the top three layers of the

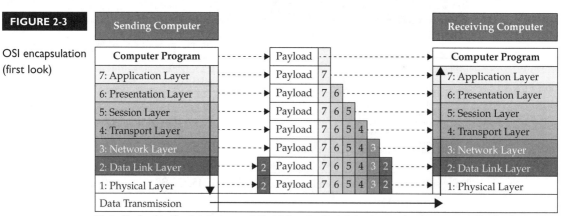

FIGURE 2-3

OSI encapsulation (first look)

Note: Payload is the data being sent. But it is not called data at every layer, so we use Payload.

model. At the top of the stack, we find Layer 7—the Application layer. When we discuss applications in this context, we are talking about network applications, not computer applications like Word, Excel, or Outlook. The *Application* layer holds the protocols that allow computer applications (programs) to access and make use of a network. For example, Microsoft Outlook is an e-mail program, which can work just fine without network connectivity. You can open, edit, create, and delete messages offline. However, if you wish to send and receive e-mail across a network, you need an Application layer protocol to do this—in this example, SMTP. Simple Mail Transport Protocol (SMTP) is the Application layer protocol that any of our e-mail programs rely on to send and receive messages. There are many different Application layer protocols to use depending on what it is you are trying to accomplish.

Continuing the e-mail analogy, imagine you are sending an e-mail from a Microsoft Outlook application to a computer running some other e-mail application. You may have bold, italics, and any number of font settings within your e-mail. Additionally, you may attach a picture file (jpg) for the recipient to enjoy. Enter Layer 6—the Presentation layer. The *Presentation* layer is responsible for formatting and code conversion between systems. This layer accepts the data from the Application layer and ensures it is formatted in a way the receiving station can understand. Once received at the far end, the recipient's Presentation layer will use the same protocols to perform the reverse, handing the processed data back to the Application layer protocol. Some data types, such as JPG, MPEG, or MP3, have protocols that also include encryption (security) and compression (squeezing the spaces out). Both the sending and receiving computers must support all related protocols for a successful exchange.

A small header is prepended to the front of the data to identify any protocols and related instructions or options that will be required at the receiving end.

The Presentation layer encryption and compression are designed to meet the performance requirements of the application and protect the developer's proprietary (ownership) rights. For example, MP3 music files are compressed to a standard that ensures what is received is exactly what is sent by the creator of the MP3 and that it will only play on an MP3-ready device, regardless of what happens to the entire transmission. Modern systems also use encryption and compression at other layers—particularly Layers 2, 3, and 4—to secure or improve the performance of a communication transmission. Network encryption and compression are similar concepts and terminology but applied by different entities for different reasons.

Layer 5—the Session layer—is perhaps the most enigmatic and troublesome of the entire stack. This layer doesn't necessarily do anything to the data at all. Instead, its function is to work in the background, ensuring the communications process between two systems runs smoothly. The standard definition applied to the *Session* layer is that it creates, maintains, and tears down sessions. To correctly understand this, consider an analogy.

A person and their significant other are driving down the road discussing the day's events. While one partner is talking, the other begins to daydream a little. After a few seconds, the one talking says, "Are you listening to me?" BAM!— communications are reestablished and data flow is reestablished and stabilized. Notice the communications process never actually stopped, it just needed a little "massaging" or attention to continue properly. That is exactly what the Session layer does for us. The Session layer provides the attention and continuity that a particular computer application requires, which can be quite different from what the network needs to transmit and receive information. The Session layer takes care of this, providing continuity throughout the communication process. An example of Session layer protocols would be a SQL database session that needs to meet its own continuity, dataflow, and workflow requirements.

Again, another small header is prepended to the front of the data to identify any protocols and related instructions or options that will be required at the receiving end.

Layers 5, 6, and 7 are referred to as the data layers because it is their job to prepare the sender's data and/or remote processing instructions in a completed form that can be understood or used by the receiving device. Problems at these layers are issues for programmers, not network admins. These layers deliver a completed data object to the lower layers, the transport layers, for delivery purposes only. Problems at the transport layers are networking issues, not programmer issues.

The Delivery Layers: Transport, Network, Data Link, and Physical (4, 3, 2, and 1)

Until this point in the process, we still have one giant block or stream of data handed down from the upper layers. Overall network performance can be improved if this data is broken up into smaller, more manageable pieces or segments to be sent across the network. In doing this, segments can be placed on the network and delivered very quickly. As an analogy, think of getting cars and trucks on a freeway compared to putting trains on a track. In the case of trains, you have to wait until an entire train passes your point before a train can access the track, whereas cars and trucks can slip into openings in traffic. Also, like cars or trucks, some segments can take alternative paths to the destination to avoid congestion, but all cars on a train have to follow the same path.

The main job of Layer 4, the Transport layer, is to efficiently transport the data from sender to receiver. It does this via three main functions: segmentation, multiplexing, and flow control.

Transport layer functions are relatively easy to understand.

- Segmentation is simply taking our large data file and breaking it into smaller sequential pieces of the larger data set. At this point, each piece of the original data is referred to as a *segment*.

- Multiplexing is a method of combining multiple digital data streams into one signal over a single cable. Port numbers are specified by the sending device so that the receiving device can direct the segment to the right application.

- Flow control is a method to ensure segments can be released for delivery as quickly as possible without overwhelming the recipient.

A small header is added to the front of each segment telling the receiving device how to process the segment. The segments are then passed down to Layer 3.

Layer 3—the Network layer—answers the question that so far has not been answered: "Just where is the segment going?" The *Network* layer is responsible for logical addressing and routing. Receiving a segment from the Transport layer, the Network layer adds a header that includes a source and destination logical (network) address. This address is read by Layer 3 devices (routers), and best path determinations are made to deliver the segment to its final destination.

At Layer 3, each piece of the original data is referred to as a *packet*.

Now your system has a packet ready to deliver, but it still needs a couple of questions answered. Specifically, how do we get on the media and which device inside our network will deliver this to its destination? Enter the Data Link layer— Layer 2. The *Data Link* layer is responsible for media access, physical addressing, and framing. Media access refers to the method in which your system accesses the media—it transmits when the media is quiet. Layer 2 takes the packet and attaches a header and a trailer. The header contains the source and destination physical addresses needed to move the data inside the next network segment. The trailer contains a frame check sequence (FCS). The FCS is used by Layer 2 devices to ensure that the bits inside the frame have not been changed in transit, to check for errors in transmission. The whole Layer 2 process is called *framing* and completes the encapsulation process so that our original segment is nested between three headers and a trailer. The *Layer 2 header* identifies the next device to handle the frame. The *Layer 3 header* provides logical addressing so that the packet can navigate the larger network. The *Layer 4 header* allows the recipient to reassemble the segments and direct the result to the appropriate application. The *Layer 2 trailer* following the payload allows the receiving device to confirm that the frame is exactly as transmitted.

At this point, each piece of the original data is referred to as a *frame*.

Last, the frame is passed to Layer 1—the Physical layer. The Physical layer forwards bits and nothing more. It neither reads nor understands anything passing through, very much like how a postal carrier does not know the contents of a letter. At this layer, everything is seen simply as bits. There are no addresses, no routing decisions, and no sense of which application is sending or receiving—if you receive an electrical shock, you give one. The *Physical* layer is responsible for actually encoding the bits onto a media. Encoding is the process of manipulating an electrical (or light) signal to represent a 1 or a 0. Standards in the Physical layer vary greatly, and apply to such things as the way connectors are affixed to different cable types, or the impedance allowed on a given copper cable.

As the bits hit the media and arrive at the destination, they are passed up the OSI stack from bottom to top. The process is the exact reverse of what we just covered about the sending device, with each layer processing the information in its own header before removing it. With this information, the recipient can make decisions to continue to process and pass it up the stack or dump it. When you consider that this process occurs for each segment of data traveling back and forth between our systems, it really puts into perspective a few seconds' wait for a web page to load.

Network Components

A thorough understanding of networking components, as well as their functions and placement, is essential to your success, both as a networking technician and as a potential candidate for certification. In this section, we will briefly cover some of the more common network components and discuss several features, functions, and concerns with each. These devices were mentioned in Chapter 1 and will be discussed at greater length throughout the rest of this text, and terminology like collision domain and broadcast domain will also be covered in greater detail. Additionally, the devices are discussed and listed within the layer where they work.

Physical Layer Devices: Layer 1

Physical layer devices do nothing more than physically connect wiring together to complete a path or change the connection from one type to another. Examples of Physical layer devices include transceivers, repeaters, and hubs. Transceivers connect one media type to another, such as a fiber connection to a copper one. Repeaters are used to extend the range of a given media—whatever they take in one port, they regenerate and repeat out the other. Hubs are nothing more than multiport repeaters. Comparatively, where a repeater takes bits in one port to relay to another, hubs have several ports they accept and relay bits on.

Simply speaking, these devices are "dumb" and neither read nor understand data. Physical layer devices will pass on an electric shock, or light signal, exactly as they received it, making no decisions on its path whatsoever. These devices are used to extend the reach of network segments and, in the case of a hub, to share a single media segment between several systems. In other words, if a single network segment is capable of a 10 Mbps transmission, and you connect ten users to it using a hub, each user has an effective bandwidth of 1 Mbps. Physical layer devices extend collision domains, increase network traffic problems, and decrease (effective) available bandwidth.

As mentioned in Chapter 1, these are all early networking technologies that, whenever possible, have been incorporated into or replaced by smarter and more efficient Layer 2 devices, switches.

Data Link Layer Devices: Layer 2

Data Link layer devices actually read your *physical* network addresses—typically Ethernet MAC addresses—and make decisions on forwarding or filtering traffic. The addressing used inside your network segment is akin to the street address on the front of a letter addressed to you—it makes sense to your local postal carrier, but wouldn't mean a thing to someone in a different city or state. These devices have the processing power to read these addresses and make decisions on which port(s) to send the data through.

Layer 2 devices include the older bridges and today's LAN switches. A switch is basically a multiport bridge. Switches and bridges split (or segment) collision domains, decrease network traffic problems, and increase effective available bandwidth to hosts. Keep in mind that a LAN (Layer 2) switch is incapable of acting as a gateway for moving traffic outside your LAN. For that you need a Layer 3 device, a router, or a switch with Layer 3 functionality built in.

Network Layer Devices: Layer 3

Network layer devices play a unique role in your network design. These devices read the *logical* network addresses—typically IP—on your data and make decisions about which route to send the data through. This sounds very much like the switches and bridges discussed earlier, but keep in mind the Layer 3 device not only knows which port to send the data out, but also the best route through outside networks to its final destination. Continuing the analogy from earlier, if the street address on your letter is akin to the physical address of your hosts, the logical address used by Layer 3 devices is equivalent to the ZIP code. When you place a letter in your mailbox, the local carrier doesn't look at the street address; he looks at the ZIP code and makes a determination about which post office should see the letter next. This process continues until the letter reaches a post office that does recognize the street address. Routers and firewalls are Layer 3 devices, and not only split collision domains but also broadcast domains. Routers are placed on the borders of your networks and subnets, for obvious reasons.

Today there are Layer 3 switches, which are actually Layer 2 switches with a router module built in, allowing specified ports to connect to other networks and then pass data between the networks.

Other Devices

Networks can also include a variety of other devices, such as firewalls, gateways, and proxies. A *firewall* is a device that typically works at Layers 3 and 4 and is used to filter network traffic based upon rules the administrator configures on the device. Generally placed between your network and the Internet, firewalls work on an implicit deny principle—if you do not explicitly allow the traffic, it is blocked. *Gateways* work at all layers and are generally used to connect networks and applications of different types together. A *proxy* is a system that provides a specific service to a host. For example, a web proxy will make requests to the Internet for web content on behalf of a host. This increases security and performance since web traffic coming from your network appears from only one system, and hosts can access cached pages on the proxy instead of going out to retrieve them. Generally speaking, these devices are usually placed between your network and the Internet in a special network called a DMZ. Figure 2-4 shows a corporate network with a DMZ safely outside the LAN connected to the perimeter router, but it could as easily be a firewall.

Remember that in today's networks we need to think of each of these devices both as physical devices and as functionality. While the exam may treat each device as a separate item, it is just as likely that a multifunction device, like many home

FIGURE 2-4

Network with
a DMZ

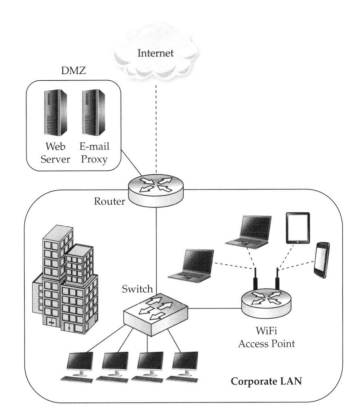

exam

watch *While you may not see
definition-type questions regarding
these devices, it's extremely important
to know the basics of their function and
placement within your network.*

routers, incorporates a four-port LAN switch, a
router, firewall features, and a WiFi access point.

Protocol Data Units

As important as it is for you to know the OSI
model's protocol and devices, it may be even
more important to know the encapsulation
steps as the data moves through systems. As
the process in data exchange moves from one layer to the next, the information is
given a specific name. As you remember from the earlier discussion, each layer adds
a header to the information given to it from the layer above. The combination of
that header and the information passed along from the preceding layer is known as
a protocol data unit (PDU). PDUs can be referenced by a specific name or by their

TABLE 2-2	Layer	PDU	Bits Added
Protocol Data Units	7 – Application	Data	Header
	6 – Presentation	Data	Header
	5 – Session	Data	Depending on the protocol, either none or a header
	4 – Transport	Segment	Header
	3 – Network	Packet	Header
	2 – Data Link	Frame	Header and trailer
	1 – Physical	Bits	N/A

layer. For example, the terms *packet* and *Layer 3 PDU* mean the same thing. The PDUs are listed in Table 2-2.

The process of headers and/or trailers being affixed to data as it moves through the stack is referred to as *encapsulation*. It is vital to your success on the exam and as a network technician to know and understand these PDUs. Much like with the OSI model, a mnemonic can help you. An old mnemonic from the military is "Do Sergeants Pay For Beer?" Again, any mnemonic that helps you remember the terms will suffice. The Sergeants line is only one suggestion.

Lastly, two additional terms need to be discussed here: adjacent layer interaction and same layer interaction. The interaction of a layer with the one layer above and below it on the same device is known as *adjacent layer* interaction. When sending data, the layer accepts a PDU from the layer above and prepares a PDU for the layer below it—the Network layer accepts a segment from the Transport layer and passes a completed packet to the Data Link layer. On the receiving device, the opposite takes place. Each layer is unaware of and never communicates with any other layers than the one immediately above and below.

Same layer interaction refers to a layer on the sending device communicating through the encapsulation and de-encapsulation process with the same layer on the receiving device—the Transport layer on a sending computer communicates with the Transport layer of the receiving computer to take care of retransmission requests, flow control, and acknowledgments. Figure 2-5 demonstrates same layer and adjacent layer interactions. The dashed arrows show the same layer interaction, while the vertical solid arrows show adjacent layer interaction and direction. Just as nonadjacent layers can't communicate on the same device, no other layer on the receiving device can ever interpret or process a PDU from a layer other than its counterpart on the sending machine.

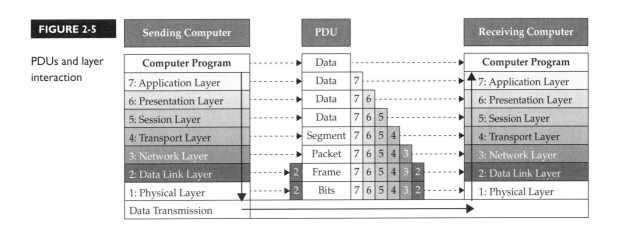

FIGURE 2-5

PDUs and layer interaction

CERTIFICATION OBJECTIVE 2.02

The TCP/IP Model

The OSI Reference Model is an adopted international standard that many protocol stacks complied with in the early days of networking. While the OSI Reference Model provided a defined standard for discussing and studying data communications between two systems, it is not a working protocol stack. TCP/IP is a protocol stack that complied with the OSI model. With the overwhelming success of the Internet based on it, TCP/IP became a de facto standard that almost everyone uses today.

The OSI Reference Model and the TCP/IP suite of protocols are foundational topics covered in almost every text on networking ever written. The OSI model gives us an overall picture of data networking that could support any network protocol suite. The TCP/IP suite, on the other hand, is a specific model of the Internet showing the actual protocols and functions working together to accomplish the task. The rest of this chapter examines the layers, functions, and protocols found within the TCP/IP protocol stack. We start by comparing the TCP/IP suite to the OSI Reference Model. Later we look at each of the individual layers, and the functions and working protocols you would find in each. As with Chapter 1, this information helps complete a solid foundation of networking knowledge.

TCP/IP History

In the late 1970s, and on through the early 1980s, ISO began work on the OSI model in an effort to standardize the burgeoning network protocol field. Work on the OSI model continued and it caught hold in educational and training institutions. Along the same timeline, a small, almost ignored Department of Defense initiative was working on a set of networking rules and functions that would wind up changing the world.

The DOD's Advanced Research Projects Agency Network (ARPANET) was developed and started operations in 1969. The U.S. government had a simple, albeit never before attempted, goal: create a communications method that could connect mainframe computers from different vendors at several universities around the country, allowing operators to actually operate these computers remotely. The government researchers and various educational institutions worked on this open standard. On January 1, 1983, TCP/IP was officially adopted by ARPANET and all systems wishing to communicate with this network, and the Internet as we know it was born.

Like many aspects of computing history, there are countless myths about the government's objectives and methods, but we won't engage in that here. If you are interested in an interesting and factual history of the early days, a good starting point is *Where Wizards Stay Up Late: The Origins of the Internet*, by Katie Hafner and Matthew Lyon, published in 1998 by Simon & Schuster. It is available at Amazon in Kindle and used for as little as $0.01 in hardcover or paperback.

TCP/IP became accepted as the worldwide standard for communication due to its open architecture. Eventually, it moved out of ARPA and U.S. government funding and control to become a truly worldwide public entity. During development, and even today, details on individual protocols and needed functions are released in a *Request for Comment* (RFC). RFCs are open for public discourse; protocols and functions are refined and improved over time as individuals and institutions provide comments and recommendations on them. The eventual adoption of TCP/IP as an accepted standard greatly accelerated the development of the Internet, as well as the systems and devices connecting to it. The OSI model is still referenced in networking, with many of its terms and functionality used interchangeably with TCP/IP. However, the actual working stack of protocols is the TCP/IP model, and it differs slightly from the OSI stack.

TCP/IP and OSI Reference Model Comparison

Earlier, we saw that each layer of the OSI model has a particular function or task to accomplish. The TCP/IP stack works in much the same way, with a few key differences. While the OSI Reference Model provides a platform for discussing and studying data operations between two systems, TCP/IP does conform to the same networking processes and standards defined by the OSI Reference Model.

As with the OSI model, TCP/IP divides networking functions into distinct layers. However, TCP/IP does so with only four layers: Application, Transport, Internet, and Network Access. All the functionality of the OSI model also occurs within the TCP/IP model; however, the layers do not line up exactly. Figure 2-1 displays the OSI and TCP/IP model comparison. While the TCP/IP model has become a de facto standard, the OSI layers and layer numbers are still the ones you need to use for Cisco exams.

CERTIFICATION OBJECTIVE 2.03

Common OSI Layer Functions and Protocols

In this section, we will be looking at common protocols and standards that are used in today's networks and that you can be expected to know for the exam. Figure 2-6 shows both the OSI Reference Model and the TCP/IP model with the related devices and protocols.

Application Layer: Layer 7

Figure 2-6 shows that the Application layer of the TCP/IP model encompasses the top three layers of the OSI Reference Model. Remember that the OSI model

Models, devices, and protocols

OSI Layer	Devices Found	Protocols / Standards Working in the Layer	TCP/IP Layer
7: Application	Firewall, Gateway	SMTP, POP3, IMAP, DNS, DHCP, FTP, HTTP, TFTP, SNMP, VoIP, NNTP, NTP	Application
6: Presentation	N/A	JPG, JPEG, TIFF, PNG, GIF, MIME, MP3, MP4	
5: Session	N/A	NFS, ASP, SQL, RPC	
4: Transport	Firewall	TCP, UDP	Transport
3: Network	Router	IP	Internet
2: Data Link	Bridge, Switch	Ethernet, PPP, HDLC, Frame Relay, ATM	Network Access
1: Physical	Transceiver, Repeater, Hub	RJ45, ST/SC, V series (modem standards)	

and Cisco use the upper three layers, and related protocols are found at each layer according to their purpose:

- Provides applications access to the network through a variety of specialized protocols (Layer 7)
- Provides data formatting, code conversion, and encryption (Layer 6)
- Establishes, maintains, and terminates sessions (Layer 5)

There are literally hundreds of protocols in all of the OSI layers. Some of the more common protocols are covered throughout the rest of this section.

DNS

The Domain Name Service (DNS) may well be the most widely and universally used protocol within the Application layer. Its use is so ubiquitous within Internet communications, it's even used by other protocols! Therefore, it is absolutely essential you understand the purpose of DNS and how it functions.

It probably goes without saying that computers and humans communicate in different ways. For one example, computers cannot communicate with each other unless they are given a specific numerical address. This would work out great if we referred to each other by numbers instead of names: "Hello, 325176652, how are things? Heard from 447987768 lately?" However, people generally speak and communicate with names, and memorizing and using them is much easier for us. Names, though, simply don't mean anything to computer systems. Consequently, we need a mechanism to give us the flexibility of remembering and referring to systems by easy-to-remember names, while simultaneously providing the numerical addresses computers need. This is where DNS enters the picture.

DNS is simultaneously very simple, yet immense in nature and purpose. The main task of DNS is to resolve, or convert, an IP address for a given domain name. This allows a user to type in a name for a resource, and provides a means for the system to find its numerical address equivalent. A domain name—sometimes referred to as a fully qualified domain name (FQDN)—is a name that is associated with one (or more) specific IP addresses. The name itself comes from a portion of something called the DNS namespace. The entire service referred to as DNS is composed of three major components: the namespace, zones, and name servers (resolvers). Figure 2-7 shows a uniform resource locator (URL) for the FQDN *mcgraw-hill.com*, where *http* is the protocol used to access it and *books* is a folder on the *www* server.

The DNS namespace is composed of an inverted tree structure that begins with the root—a single dot (.). The DNS root symbolically provides a starting point for all lookups and names. One step below the root is the *top-level domain*. Many top-level domains (too many to list here) exist, with each established for a specific purpose. Some of the more common top-level domains are com, us, gov, edu, mil, net, and org.

FIGURE 2-7

A URL showing FQDN

Fully Qualified Domain Name (FQDN)

http://www.mcgraw-hill.com/books

Protocol | Specific Domain Host | Domain | Top-Tier Domain | Folder

The level immediately below the top-level domain is known as the *second-level domain*—commonly referred to as the domain name. This portion of the namespace denotes a single organization or entity. For example, cisco.com indicates a portion of the namespace, found inside the .com top-level domain, belonging to the Cisco organization. All computers and systems under Cisco's control that Cisco wants people to locate via a name will be given an FQDN ending in cisco.com. For example, a server may be named srv1.cisco.com. This domain can be further subdivided by additional names. For instance, accounting.cisco.com might contain all the computer names within the accounting department.

Within each defined area of DNS namespace—referred to as a zone—there must be at least one server storing all the records for that particular zone. The zone file contains all the name-to-IP address mappings, and is queried by DNS to find the addresses of domain names. Table 2-3 lists some of the record types found in the zone file.

The last major component of DNS is the servers themselves. Name servers hold the records for a single zone or sometimes for several zones. Name servers *answer* DNS requests from clients to resolve FQDNs. The actual request to a given name server usually comes from a resolver. *Resolvers* are servers on your network that ask name servers for the information. To fully grasp this concept, consider a client trying to resolve the name www.cisco.com.

on the
ⓘ o b   *Caching is a process used to limit the number of queries that have to go all the way to the root. Your computer has a DNS cache, and every name server and resolver along the way caches their results. This means systems can sometimes get the answer to a query very quickly, especially if others on their network have queried for the same record.*

The client operator types www.cisco.com into their web browser. The client system, to resolve to an IP address, sends its resolution DNS request to a local resolver. If the resolver hasn't cached the address from an earlier request, it then queries name servers, all the way up to a root server, to find the one system holding all the records for cisco.com. That server responds to the resolver with the IP address. The resolver caches the request and then responds to the client request, and this all results in the user happily surfing on Cisco's website.

Note: DNS is a wonderful thing, but it can sometimes cause unenviable frustration when working on Cisco products. For example, when working on a Cisco router or switch, if you type in an unrecognized command, the device assumes you want to make a DNS lookup and happily obliges. This lookup doesn't work, obviously, and

TABLE 2-3	Record Type	Definition
DNS Record Types	SOA	Start of authority: Defines the server that owns the zone records, as well as other administrative information (administrator name, current version, and so on).
	NS	Name server: Defines a name server within the zone. Name servers hold all DNS records for the namespace.
	A	Maps an IP address to a domain name.
	MX	Mail exchanger: Denotes the server within a namespace that takes care of e-mail traffic.
	CNAME	Canonical name: An alias used to mask the true identity of a server. This is often used as an alias for specific websites within a domain.

takes a long time to run through iterations before returning to the screen. In order to avoid this problem, use the command **no ip domain-lookup** on your devices (configuration of this command, and others, are covered later in the book—this is solely listed for reference and illustration).

DHCP

Another well-known and often used Application layer protocol is Dynamic Host Configuration Protocol (DHCP). The main function of DHCP is to automatically assign IP addresses from a given pool of addresses to client devices within a specific network segment. The pool of addresses a DHCP server uses is known as a *scope*. In larger networks, servers are configured to provide DHCP services. In smaller networks, a router can be configured as the DHCP server.

Don't be surprised to see DHCP listed as a Network layer utility on the exam. The actual protocol resides in the Application layer; however, the CCENT exam may list it as a Network, or Layer 3, utility.

Every host on a TCP/IP network must have an IP address, which can be defined statically if the administrator has plenty of time, patience, and organizational skills. Once a network grows, however, this becomes much more challenging and can quickly get out of hand. A better choice, and one most administrators choose, is to use DHCP. To correctly apply and use DHCP within a network, you must install or enable the service, configure the scope, the range of IP addresses available to be given out, and other settings, and correctly place the server within the network.

Installing and configuring the service is relatively easy, although there are many situations and configuration options to consider. When configuring the scope, savvy network administrators know to exclude or reserve certain addresses from the pool for servers, switches, printers, and so on. Therefore, administrators can either assign these addresses statically, excluding those addresses from the scope to prevent clients from inadvertently pulling an address already in use, or reserve address space in DHCP so the devices always receive and maintain the same address. Other configuration options include the address of the default gateway, DNS servers, and the amount of time a client is allowed to hold the IP address—known as a lease. Configuring DHCP on Cisco devices is covered later in Chapter 11. See Figure 2-8 for more information on the process a client uses to request and accept an IP address from a DHCP server. There is an abbreviated version of this process to renew the client address lease.

w a t c h **Know the DHCP lease steps, use the mnemonic DORA to help you remember, and know which are** **broadcasts and which are unicasts. DHCP configuration and the** ip helper address **command will be covered in Chapter 11.**

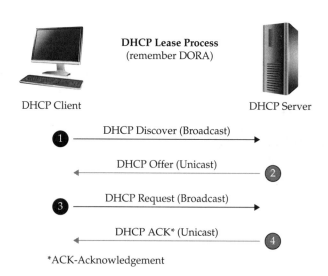

FIGURE 2-8

The DHCP lease process

DHCP Lease Process
(remember DORA)

DHCP Client

DHCP Server

1 — DHCP Discover (Broadcast) →

← DHCP Offer (Unicast) 2

3 — DHCP Request (Broadcast) →

← DHCP ACK* (Unicast) 4

*ACK-Acknowledgement

Finally, placement of your DHCP server is a very important consideration. DHCP works by broadcasting, which makes a lot of sense when you consider the process. When the computer first boots up, it does not know where the DHCP server is. In truth, it doesn't even know its *own* network or address! So the system sends a broadcast message asking for a DHCP server to provide an IP address. Every server running the DHCP service that receives the broadcast will respond, and the client generally takes the first offer it receives. Since routers do not forward broadcasts, it is important to remember to place a DHCP server on each network segment. If it is placed outside the segment, the systems cannot pull IP addresses.

Other Protocols

While there are many more protocols within the OSI Application layer, and an entire book series could be written just about them, this section concentrates on the protocols you'll most likely see on the exam. This is not to say this is all you'll ever need to know about the Application layer; it's just a focused view. Protocols covered in this section perform most of the basic day-to-day functions found in any network, such as file transfers, e-mail, web surfing, and network management. If you are interested in a more complete list, Google "OSI layer protocols" and choose the Wikipedia listing.

File Transfer Protocols File Transfer Protocol (FTP) and Trivial File Transfer Protocol (TFTP) are both found in the Application layer, and they both perform the same function—they transfer files from one system to another. The manner in which they perform these functions differs, as well as where you would traditionally see them in play. FTP is as much a service as it is a protocol and is composed of a server, an authentication method, and the protocol itself. The FTP server is simply a machine that has installed and enabled the FTP service. The server administrator will define an authentication method within FTP, as well as assign permissions through the FTP directory structure. Users log on to the FTP service and, using a variety of commands, pull or put files from or on the server. FTP is considered a connection-oriented protocol, requiring a reliable transport protocol to manage acknowledgments of each packet sent. FTP can be installed on almost any server or workstation, as well as on many Cisco devices.

Note that FTP, while containing an authentication function, is not considered secure. Everything in FTP, including usernames, passwords, and data, is transmitted in clear text over the wire. Additionally, most FTP installations allow for an "anonymous" connection—meaning a user doesn't even have to log on to use the service. There are secure protocols like SFTP, which is an extension of the SSH (secure shell) protocol.

TFTP operates a bit differently. While FTP is a reliable protocol, requiring acknowledgments that each packet was received, TFTP works in a "fire and forget" format: packets are sent as quickly as possible without any acknowledgment required (a process known as connectionless). This results in a much faster file exchange, but it is not suitable for all data types because of its inability to detect loss of packets. Another way this protocol differs from FTP is that TFTP requires no authentication at all—users simply transfer files to and from the server without any login or connection. While there is no authentication method in place, TFTP *does* require the user to know the complete filename and location, as no directory listing is available. It is important to type the filename precisely when transferring to or from a TFTP server.

E-mail Protocols   Another important and very common network function is e-mail. The protocols used to move e-mail through networks are Simple Mail Transfer Protocol (SMTP), Post Office Protocol version 3 (POP3), and Internet Message Access Protocol (IMAP). SMTP is always used to send mail, whether from a user to server or between servers. E-mail works like a post office, where user e-mail goes to its post office, which then forwards it to the recipient's post office where it waits. In other words, we use the SMTP protocol to send our e-mail to a mail server, which in turn uses SMTP to forward the message to the receiver's mail server.

POP3 and IMAP are e-mail retrieval protocols on the recipient's side. When a client connects to an e-mail server, POP3 or IMAP are used to enable viewing of the e-mails. Many implementations of either allow leaving e-mails on the server or copying to the local client. All three protocols are considered connection-oriented protocols, which means a reliable or lossless transport of our data.

Network Management Protocols   Simple Network Management Protocol (SNMP) is another important and often-used Application layer protocol. SNMP provides a much needed, simple-to-use, and powerful method of querying and managing devices on your network. However, it simultaneously opens significant security risks. SNMP consists of three major components: a central monitoring station, an agent on each device, and a database of questions.

In a typical SNMP setting, a central monitoring station, running NMS (network management software), is used to simplify management. The NMS station begins by sending SNMP GET requests to all devices within its network area. This message is received by each SNMP-enabled device, and a small application, known as an agent, processes the request. To answer the request, the agent uses an agreed-upon standard set of questions and answers. These questions can be different per device type and vendor. The database that a particular device answers questions from is known as the management information base (MIB). MIBs are normally unique for each device and vendor and collect the data that the NMS will be retrieving, such as the last time the device was rebooted or the number of bad packets discarded by an interface. The NMS station repeats SNMP requests against the list of MIBs for each device and, eventually, builds a map of the network. This map can be used by a network management specialist to monitor network health, watch for potential problems, and even send configuration updates or changes to devices.

Obviously, SNMP is very powerful in its ability to remotely discover and control our equipment. In an effort to provide at least some security to this process, SNMP was configured with two passwords in which to conduct business—a public and a private community string. The public community string is a password used to read information from SNMP-enabled devices. The private string is used to send configuration updates to devices. By default, the public and private strings on every SNMP-enabled device on the planet are set to (surprise) *public* and *private*, respectively. Should you choose to take advantage of SNMP within your network, these strings should, obviously, be changed to a more difficult password.

Web Surfing Protocols   Lastly, no discussion on popular OSI applications would be complete without at least briefly discussing web surfing. Most Internet browsing and viewing is done using two major protocols: HTTP and HTTPS. The World Wide Web (WWW) application, basically the complex combination of servers and specially formatted documents that make up the Web, is mostly accessed by browsers using Hypertext Transport Protocol (HTTP). The main purpose of HTTP is to transport Hypertext Markup Language (HTML) files; HTML is the language used to create a web page. The HTML instructions tell the browser what to display on the screen.

The entire process is actually pretty simple. A user first enters a uniform resource locator (URL) in the address bar of their web browser. For example, consider what happens when the user types in http://www.cisco.com/ccna.html. The browser makes a request, using HTTP, to get the HTML file named ccna.html, hosted on the server responsible for (or domain) www.cisco.com, listed in the URL. The file is delivered, and the client browser interprets and displays the data encoded in the HTML file—our requested web page.

A URL is made up of three major components: the protocol used, the name of the server (or host) holding the resource, and the name of the page. The protocol comes first, before the //. The domain name listed, such as cisco.com, *comes next and is the host holding the resource. Anything listed after the last "/" is the name of a specific resource (page) or folder on the host. Figure 2-7 showed a URL earlier.*

Hypertext Transport Protocol over SSL (HTTPS) uses much the same process, but adds security, and encryption Secure Sockets Layer (SSL) is an encryption process that secures the communication between the client and the server hosting the site. An exchange of certificates ensures the client can safely exchange data without worrying about third-party interception. HTTPS is very common in online banking, shopping, and secured data-sharing implementations. Both HTTP and HTTPS are reliable, connection-oriented protocols.

Network Time Protocol   Many features benefit from having accurate date and time information. Devices ranging from log entries showing activities to many security features like VPN encryption need to have accurate date and times. In larger networks, one of the servers will often work as a Network Time Protocol (NTP) time server, checking periodically with an Internet-based source, and then keeping any configured hosts and network devices in synch. Many Cisco devices can work as a client for a time server and others can be configured to work as a local time server. In Chapter 11 we look at configuring a device as an NTP client.

Transport Layer: Layer 4

No matter what the application protocol, there must be a protocol in place to transport the request and, eventually, the return data. The Transport layer performs that function—namely, how best to transport the data. The most widely used Transport layer protocols include Transport Control Protocol (TCP) and User Datagram Protocol (UDP). They are used to define how the data will be segmented, what type of flow control to use, and if the data will be sent reliably or not.

TCP

TCP is what is called a connection-oriented and reliable transport protocol used by applications that require packets to be reassembled in the order sent. TCP does this by using sequence numbers. On the plus side, TCP provides the reliability that upper-layer applications may not have built into them. The drawback is that, in order to do so, TCP adds a lot of overhead to the communications process (see Figure 2-9 to view the TCP header). This slows things down, consumes more bandwidth, and requires more processing for hosts during communication. Protocols making use of TCP as a transport protocol include SMTP, POP3, IMAP, HTTP, HTTPS, FTP, and a host of others. The TCP communications process encompasses three major functions: session establishment, error recovery, and flow control.

TCP Three-way Handshake   Every TCP communication process begins with a session establishment process known as the three-way handshake. In the first phase, the requesting system sends a *synchronization* request, known as a SYN. The SYN segment is a simple request to open a communications session, and includes the SYN flag set, a sequence number, and port numbers (covered later in this chapter). When the server receives this request, it creates and sends a *synchronization/acknowledgment* segment, known as a SYN/ACK. This segment includes the SYN and ACK flags set, an acknowledgment of the requestor's sequence number, and a separate sequence

FIGURE 2-9

A TCP header

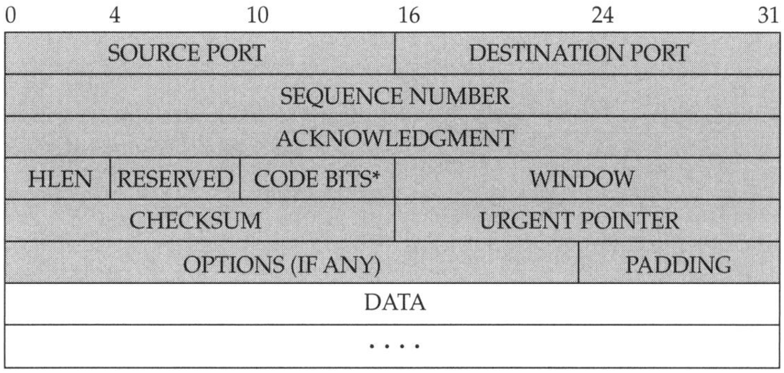

0	4	10	16	24	31
SOURCE PORT			DESTINATION PORT		
SEQUENCE NUMBER					
ACKNOWLEDGMENT					
HLEN	RESERVED	CODE BITS*		WINDOW	
CHECKSUM			URGENT POINTER		
OPTIONS (IF ANY)				PADDING	
DATA					
. . . .					

number. Finally, in the third step, the requesting system sends an *acknowledgment* segment, known as an ACK. This segment includes the ACK flag set, a copy of the acknowledgment of the original sequence number, and an acknowledgment of the server's own sequence number. This process can be seen in Figure 2-10.

A simple analogy for TCP is a phone call where the caller asks to speak to a particular person (SYN), and that person confirms they have reached the right person (SYN/ACK). The caller acknowledges that they are satisfied they have the right person (ACK) and starts sharing their message. The recipient can ask them to slow down or even restate something they may not have heard.

TCP Error Recovery   Once the session is established, data can start flowing between the two systems. During data transmission, sometimes segments get lost due to a variety of reasons. TCP handles error recovery by using the sequence number and acknowledgment fields in the header. The sequence number agreed upon during the three-way handshake is incremented for every agreed-upon number of data bytes sent. For example, if the two systems agree to send 100 bytes at a time, the sequence number would increase by 100 for every segment sent. In other words, each segment that leaves increases the sequence number by a specific amount.

On the receiving end, the recipient system acknowledges the receipt of each segment by incrementing the sequence number to the next expected segment. For example's sake, imagine an established session with an agreed-upon sequence size of 100. If a system sends a segment with a sequence number of 422, the recipient would send an acknowledgment with the sequence number set to 522. An example of this in practice can be seen in Figure 2-11.

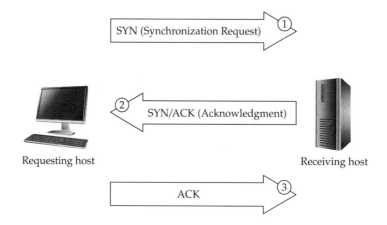

FIGURE 2-10

The TCP three-way handshake

FIGURE 2-11

A TCP
acknowledgment

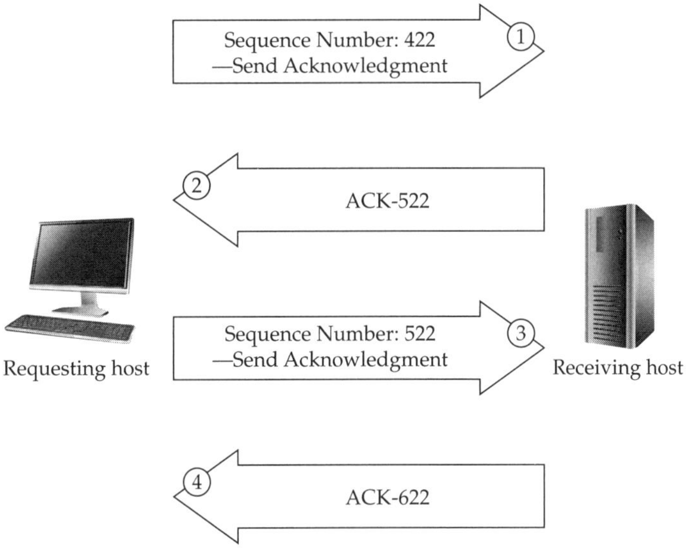

Recovery of lost segments is easy to see within this process. The sending machine will send its allotted 100 bytes and wait until it receives an acknowledgment before it sends the next batch. For example, imagine a sender has transmitted segments with sequence numbers of 122 and 222, and has received an acknowledgment of 322 (the next segment number). The sender knows the recipient has accepted both previous segments and is expecting 100 bytes (322). The sending machine transmits segments 322 and 422, and waits. If all goes well, the acknowledgment will read 522. If the acknowledgment does not come, or is not the expected reply, the sender knows to retransmit the previous segment(s). If the end station loses the last segment, however, the acknowledgment is 422, telling the sender to retransmit the segment with sequence number 422. This process, unexpected sequence number, allows for retransmission of lost segments and ensures all segments are pieced together in the order in which they were sent.

Sequence numbers not only help keep segments in order, but they can also help in reducing the number of retransmissions. For example, consider a conversation occurring between two systems with an agreed-upon sequence increment of 1000 bytes. If the sending device has sent three segments and the sequence number started at 1000, the sending device would expect an acknowledgment of 4000. Suppose, however, the recipient only received the first and third segments. The acknowledgment would be 2000, notifying the sender it needed the second segment to be resent.

The sending device, receiving an acknowledgment of 2000, would assume the second segment never arrived. It would then retransmit sequence number 2000 and wait for an acknowledgment. The recipient now has all three segments, having received the second segment as a resend. It now sends an acknowledgment for what it is expecting next—sequence number 4000. Requesting the retransmission of the third segment would have been a waste since it had already been received.

TCP also makes use of a timer for error recovery. If the sending machine does not receive an acknowledgment within the allotted time, it will retransmit all outstanding segments.

TCP Flow Control The last major function in TCP is flow control. This process ensures data is transmitted as quickly as possible without overwhelming the recipient machine. If TCP required an acknowledgment of each and every segment, flow control wouldn't be needed at all. However, that wouldn't be very efficient, and the communications process would be dramatically slowed. A more efficient solution would be to have the sending machine transmit several segments and wait for an acknowledgment from the recipient of the entire grouping. Both machines could communicate with each other until a maximum size of segment groupings is agreed upon. TCP accomplishes this by using the **window size** field in the TCP header.

The window size field lets each system know the total number of unacknowledged segments that can be outstanding at any time, and can change at any time during the process. Keeping things simple, assume a sending machine sends segments 1, 2, and 3, with a window size of 3. If the path between the two can transmit all segments within the allotted time, and the recipient can handle it, the acknowledgment will read 4. This lets the sender know all three segments were received and it can send the next three. Starting small, the window size will be slowly incremented by the sending machine until a threshold is met. At this point, the sender and recipient are transmitting data as quickly as possible, without congestion problems. Conversely, if the receiving device is overwhelmed or a device along the path starts dropping segments, the act of resending data will cause the slowing down of traffic. This resending of data will, in turn, decrease the number of outstanding segments that are allowed—reducing the window's size and slowing down the conversation. The process of the window size changing during communications is known as **sliding windows**, which finds balance in the rate in which devices communicate.

UDP

The second Transport layer protocol is User Datagram Protocol (UDP), shown in Figure 2-12. Unlike TCP, UDP is a connectionless protocol, meaning it does not require acknowledgments and does not provide for error correction. A much simpler protocol with a smaller header, UDP simply transmits segments as quickly as possible, without regard to the recipient. UDP has the advantage of being much faster than TCP, but it does not provide many of the services that TCP's larger header allows for. If UDP is used as a transport protocol, reliability becomes a function of the applications themselves. An analogy for UDP is sending a simple postcard, where you trust the reliability of the post office to get your message delivered.

UDP is a good choice in a couple of scenarios. If the data transfer is one (or just a few) packets, then the overhead of TCP is unnecessary. Both DNS and DHCP are good examples. In another good UDP scenario, the applications themselves must be capable of tolerating lost packets or have some means by which to ask for retransmissions. For example, streaming video and Voice over IP (VoIP) can both tolerate a packet or two lost along the way, as long as the stream doesn't get too choppy.

Connection-Oriented vs. Connectionless and Reliable vs. Unreliable

These are pretty straightforward concepts. Connection-oriented means the computers go through a handshake process to establish communication before any data is exchanged. TCP is connection-oriented, establishing communication using the three-way handshake. This connection allows the devices to define how flow control, sequence numbers, and acknowledgements will be used.

UDP does not have this handshake process; therefore, it is known as a connectionless protocol. UDP is much more like sending postcards—you drop it in the mail and trust that it arrives—whereas TCP ensures its delivery by sending another postcard if the receiver doesn't acknowledge receiving it.

Reliability refers to a protocol's ability to ensure all pieces of the message are received. TCP does this, so it is called reliable, whereas UDP does not and is therefore

FIGURE 2-12

A UDP header

Source Port Number (16 Bits)	Destination Port Number (16 Bits)
UDP Length (16 Bits)	UDP Checksum (16 Bits)
DATA	

The UDP header is only 8 bytes long.

called unreliable. To recap: TCP is a connection-oriented protocol, and this connection process allows for data to be sent reliably. UDP is connectionless and, therefore, it has no capabilities to detect lost data or request resends.

Port Numbers and Multiplexing

Port numbers work much like office numbers in a building. The address gets you to the building, but the office number (port) gets you to the right department or person. We say that a protocol listens on a particular port number, like setting up office ready for business. Web servers by default listen on port 80, while SMTP (e-mail) listens on port 25. While protocols running as a server or service have "well known" assigned default port numbers, host sessions typically do not. They don't need them; when they initiate a session, they assign a temporary randomly assigned port number greater than 1024 for that session. This allows them to run multiple simultaneous sessions with different protocols or even different servers using the same protocol and yet still keep them separate.

Each segment, TCP or UDP, has two port numbers assigned by the sender. The source port is a temporary, randomly assigned number, like a temporary office location or mailbox, while the destination is typically a known port number assigned to a protocol. A web request might have a source port 50000 and a destination port 80. When the segment gets to the destination device, it is forwarded to port 80 where HTTP is listening. When the server replies, the port numbers are reversed: the source port is now 80 and the destination port is 50000. The host computer knows what session it assigned to port 50000 and sends the segment there.

Consider how confusing things could get if the *same host* asked for two services, HTTP and FTP, from a server. How would we keep the traffic separate? Fortunately, different port number pairs are used to identify each session and which protocol is to answer a request and provide multiplexing for both replies back to the source. Both TCP and UDP use separate port numbers 0 to 65535 (65,536 different ports), which are divided into specific ranges. The first range of port numbers from 0 to 1023 are called *well-known* port numbers and represent applications used by the operating system. Port numbers between 1024 and 49151 are called registered ports, while those between 49152 and 65535 are dynamic ports. Dynamic ports are open for us to use without restriction, and are used by sending machines to identify individual communication sessions. Some well-known ports are listed in Table 2-4.

The Internet Assigned Numbers Authority (IANA) is responsible for the global coordination and registration of commonly used port numbers including, the well-known Internet services. In many cases, both the TCP and UDP port numbers are assigned to the same protocol even though the protocol typically uses only one of them.

TABLE 2-4	Port Number	Application Protocol
	20 (TCP)	FTP (Data)
Well-Known Port Numbers	21 (TCP)	FTP (Control)
	22 (TCP)	SSH
	23 (TCP)	Telnet
	25 (TCP)	SMTP
	53 (TCP/UDP)	DNS
	67, 68 (UDP)	DHCP
	69 (UDP)	TFTP
	80 (TCP)	HTTP
	110 (TCP)	POP3
	161 (UDP)	SNMP
	443 (TCP)	HTTPS (SSL)

e x a m

ⓦ a t c h *Make sure that you know these protocols, at least through 80, and which ones are UDP—the rest will then be TCP.*

Multiplexing To understand the use of port numbers in multiplexing, consider the last example shown in Figure 2-13. First, the client PC requests a web page from the server by choosing a random source port number (5000) in the dynamic range for the source and using the port number for HTTP (80) as the destination. When the server replies, the ports are reversed—80 is now the source, with 5000 as the destination. While surfing the website, the same client decides to transfer a file from the FTP service on the server. A second communications request begins, with the recipient choosing another random port number (5001) as the source port and using the port number for FTP (21) as the destination. Once again, as the data is returned, the port numbers are swapped—21 is now the source, with 5001 as the destination. This process allows both systems to track each session separately, even though the address of the requestor and sender remain the same.

Endpoints and Sockets While we have been focused on the Layer 4 port numbers, the port number is often represented with the IP address or a URL, such as 192.168.1.115:5000 or www.cisco.com:80. This is called a network socket address, which identifies a connection endpoint. In TCP terms, a pair of sockets is a

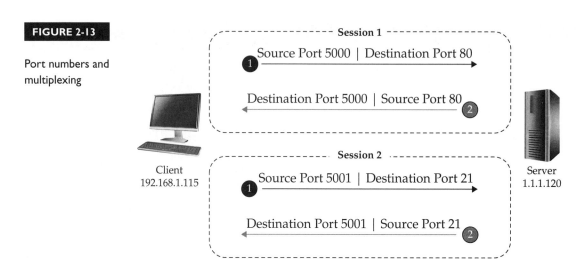

FIGURE 2-13

Port numbers and
multiplexing

connection. In Figure 2-13, Session 1 would be a connection made up of the socket
pair 192.168.1.115:5000 and 1.1.1.120:80. Session 2 would be a connection made up
of the socket pair 192.168.1.115:5001 and 1.1.1.120:21. In each case they represent
a communications session.

Even though ports 1024 through 49151 are considered registered ports, they can
be used as dynamic ports by systems during communications. The combination
of an IP address, a transport protocol, and a port number is known as a socket.
Additionally, just for fun, the ports clients used are also known as ephemeral ports.
They randomly are assigned from a pool of ports the client has available, and are
never reused until a client has exhausted all of its pool of ports.

Network Layer: Layer 3

After the Application and Transport layers have accomplished their functions, the
segment is passed down to the Network (Internet) layer for logical addressing and
forwarding. As shown in Figure 2-1, Layer 3 provides *data forwarding* to devices
on distant (nonlocal) networks via a gateway router that may be connected to the
destination network, or more likely, is just the first step on a journey across a web of
routers that make up the Internet.

In many ways, this is like the duties of the post office in most countries. They
develop an addressing scheme that allows individuals to be located in a city/
neighborhood. They also collect mail from customers, forwarding it into a system
that ultimately uses the destination address to deliver it.

Internet Protocol

The Internet Protocol (IP) is the routed protocol found in this layer. Routed, for now, simply means it will be forwarded through a router toward its destination address. IP provides the hierarchical addressing and routing functions for data delivery across networks. IPv4 addresses are 32 bits in length, like 192.168.7.115, that provide two functions:

1. Identify where the device can be found, the network identifier
2. Identify the particular host device in that network, the host identifier

This dual-function address acts much like house addresses, defining the city, state, and ZIP code (Network) where you can be found, as well as the particular street or house number (host ID) to find your precise location.

While considered a connectionless protocol, IP does make a serious effort to forward all packets. This is commonly referred to as best-effort delivery. However, due to network congestion, cable faults along the way, and a host of other reasons, packets can get lost. While IP by itself has no way to deal with datagram loss, or with issues such as out-of-order delivery, when paired with TCP, it uses TCP's features to deal with these situations. IP paired with UDP is very much like a postcard, a fairly reliable best-effort service, whereas IP teamed with TCP is like certified mail where you get an acknowledgement of receipt. Hopefully you are starting to see how these layers are not disconnected but work together to fulfill the delivery of data.

Layer 3 Header

Within the OSI and TCP/IP layered models, for outbound communications, Layer 3 accepts data *segments* from the Transport layer and constructs a data *packet* adding a packet header as shown in Figure 2-14, which it then forwards to the lower layers for *framing* and transmission. Table 2-5 describes the IP header fields that are used by routers and other Layer 3 devices to perform their functions.

FIGURE 2-14   IP header fields

IPv4 Packet Header																																	
Offsets	Octet	0								1								2								3									
Octet	Bit	0	1	2	3	4	5	6	7	8	9	10	11	12	13	14	15	16	17	18	19	20	21	22	23	24	25	26	27	28	29	30	31		
0	0	Version				IHL				DSCP						ECN		Total Length																		
4	32	Identification																Flags			Fragment Offset														
8	64	TTL (Time to Live)								Protocol								Header Checksum																	
12	96	Source IP Address																																	
16	128	Destination IP Address																																	
20	160	Options (optional)																																	

TABLE 2-5	IP Header Field Descriptions

Field	Description
Version	Identifies the IP version so the device knows what to expect. For IPv4, this value is 4.
IHL	Internet Header Length. The number of 32-bit words in the header (rows in the figure). Due to the IPv4 Options field, the range is 5–15 (20–60 bytes).
DSCP	Differentiated Services Code Point. Identifies packet for special handling, such as real-time data streaming for services like Voice over IP (VoIP).
ECN	Explicit Congestion Notification. A notification feature that would allow end-to-end notification of network congestion to avoid dropping packets.
Total Length	The entire packet (fragment) size, including header and data, in bytes. Range: 20–65535 bytes.
Identification	Uniquely identifies the group of fragments of a single IP datagram.
Flags	Three bits used to control or identify fragments when the network segment requires a smaller frame. (*1)
Fragment Offset	Specifies the offset of a particular fragment relative to the beginning of the original unfragmented IP datagram. The first fragment has an offset of zero. (*2)
TTL	Time To Live. Prevents datagram looping on the network by limiting the datagram's lifetime. When any datagram arrives at a router, the router decreases the TTL field value by 1. When the TTL hits zero, the router discards the packet and typically sends an ICMP Time Exceeded message to the sender. (*3)
Protocol	Identifies the protocol used in the data portion of the IP datagram. (*4)
Header Checksum	16-bit checksum used to error-check the *header*. When a packet arrives at a router, the router recalculates the checksum of the header and compares it to the checksum field. If the values do not match, the router discards the packet. Since the router decrements the TTL field, a new checksum is generated for each network segment. Errors in the *data field* are handled by the encapsulated protocol. Both UDP and TCP have checksum fields.
Source Address	IPv4 address of the sender of the packet. This address may be changed in transit by a network address translation (NAT) device.
Destination Address	IPv4 address of the destination device. This address may be changed in transit by a NAT device.
Options	Not often used. The IHL field must include enough extra 32-bit words to hold all the options.

(*1) The Flags field is 3 bits that indicate whether a packet can be fragmented (broken up into smaller pieces) to accommodate network segments that can't handle the current frame size.

(*2) The Fragment Offset field is a sequence counter used to reassemble the fragments. It indicates that fragment's position in the string of fragments; if it is a zero, it can only be an unfragmented packet or the first fragment.

(*3) TTL, Time To Live, is a handy field. When the initial packet is created, a TTL number is assigned, indicating the number of routers it can pass through before it is considered lost. That number is then decreased by 1 by each Layer 3 device it goes to. When it gets down to zero, the device can't forward it and usually sends an "ICMP Time Exceeded" message to the sender. This keeps any packet from staying in a routing loop forever. Cisco's **traceroute** and the computer's **tracert** commands both use these ICMP messages to display the routers reached by packets as they progress from the source to the destination.

(*4) Protocol number indicates what protocol is carried in the data payload and what kind of data it is.

The IP header, at first glance, seems pretty complicated and can be intimidating. While all of the fields are used by the router, only the destination IP address is used for forwarding decisions about packets through the network. Some fields, such as Version, IHL, and Total Length, tell the device that it is processing IPv4 information and how to know where the header ends and the data begins. Others, such as DSCP, ECN, Flags, and Fragment Free, indicate whether special handling is required of the router. TTL and Header Checksum provide for efficient and reliable forwarding. Like all headers, these fields are populated by the sending device's Layer 3 so that any Layer 3 devices will know how to properly handle the delivery.

These fields, like everything else, are made up of 0s and 1s, but applications and tools can interpret the field values to help us in troubleshooting forwarding problems. The following output from a sniffer shows what many of the field values might look like in HEX form, with friendlier explanations in parentheses:

```
Version: 4
Header length: 5 (20 bytes)
DSCP: 0x00
Total Length: 0x0044 (68 bytes)
Identification: 0xad0b
Flags and Fragments: 0x0000
TTL: 0x40 (64 hops)
Protocol: 0x11 (UDP)
Header Checksum: 0x7272
Source: 0xc0a8024d (192.168.2.77)
Destination: 0x0a801c3 (192.168.1.195)
```

IP addressing is covered in greater detail in Chapter 3.

ICMP

Internet Control Message Protocol (ICMP) is a Network layer protocol that provides error notification and, sometimes, error correction for IP datagram delivery. ICMP can notify sending hosts when packets are lost or congestion occurs. It is used in common troubleshooting commands such as **ping** and **traceroute**, which will be introduced in exercises.

Data Link and Physical Layers: Layers 1 and 2

The OSI Model Data Link and Physical layers are represented in the TCP/IP model as the Network Access layer. Encapsulation, framing, media access, and physical addressing occur at the Data Link layer, while all the physical standards associated with cabling, connectors, and encoding occur at the Physical layer. Each Data Link layer protocol defines a specific frame type in which to encapsulate a packet for delivery within the network segment. In other words, the packet must be delivered somewhere locally first before it can make its way out of the network. If all devices on the media use the same Network Access protocol and standard, the frame type is understood and the frame is delivered to the appropriate device. The Network Access layer encompasses a wide variety of protocols and standards for both LAN and WAN connections, but for CCENT we focus on Ethernet and its MAC addressing for LANs.

Ethernet is, by far, the most common LAN Network Access layer standard. The Ethernet Layer 2 protocol defines a specific frame type, using MAC addresses, and supports a variety of services and functions within the LAN. Multiple devices connected to a common Ethernet segment need methods to determine who the message is intended for, when to transmit data, and how to deal with collisions. These functions, along with more details, are covered in Chapter 4.

Each network segment uses a unique Data Link layer header. As the packet moves from one network segment to the next, the frame's header is stripped off by the router and a new frame header is built for transmission on the next segment. For example, communication may pass across multiple disparate Ethernet segments, or even a wide area network (WAN), on its way to its destination. Each time we transition across a router, we will be stripping and rebuilding Layer 2 headers.

EXERCISE 2-1

Video

Viewing Protocols in Action

The video "Wireshark" with optional exercise in the PDF Lab Book shows TCP/IP applications in action by viewing the packets captured during a live session. Please note the CCENT exam does not test on packet captures at all. This exercise is provided solely to enhance your understanding of TCP/IP by viewing the packets in live action. If you choose to do the follow-along exercise, you will have to install Wireshark on your machine. That process is explained in the exercise.

INSIDE THE EXAM

The OSI Reference Model

The OSI Reference Model does a good job of breaking down the communication process into easily understood, manageable layers. Each layer has specific functions, devices, and protocols. The bits at each layer are known as PDUs, and each PDU has a specific name. Layers 2 through 4 will be tested most heavily on the exam, so pay close attention to the wording of the questions. Look for key words to help with each question: encoding is at the Physical layer, framing and error checking are at

the Data Link layer, routing is at the Network layer, reliability and error correction are at the Transport layer, and encryption and formatting are at the Presentation layer. Lastly, be sure you can identify each layer by name and number, as well as which devices, protocols, and functions occur at each.

Let's summarize the flow of data through the OSI layers for a web browsing session over a corporate network using Figure 2-15. Host A wants to open a browsing session with the web server in the other LAN segment.

FIGURE 2-15   OSI data flow example

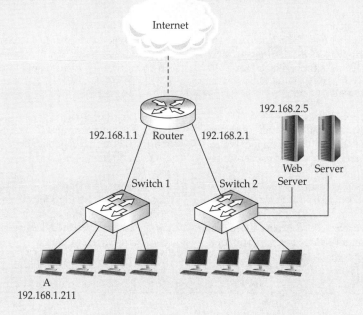

(Continued)

INSIDE THE EXAM

Host-to-Server Communication	Server-to-Host Communication
Host A Layer 7: HTTP protocol used, L7 header added Layer 6: L6 header added Layer 5: L5 header added Layer 4: TCP selected, reliable, handshake to create connection, source port 50000, destination port 80, data segmented and L4 header added, sequence number added Layer 3: Source IP 192.168.1.211, destination IP 192.168.2.5, L3 header added Layer 2: Ethernet selected; L2 header added using source MAC, A's MAC address; destination MAC, router's MAC as default gateway to get to other LAN; frame check sequence (FCS) calculated and L2 trailer added Layer 1: Frames fed on to signal as bits	**Host A** Layer 1: Bits accepted Layer 2: Frame header read, MAC destination confirmed, FCS calculated and compared to L2 trailer; if OK, frame removed and packet sent to Layer 3 Layer 3: Packet header read, destination IP address is ours, so L3 header removed; passed to L4 Layer 4: TCP determined, sequence number confirmed; part of a connection confirmed, acknowledgement sent, header removed and sent to Layer 5 Layer 5: Process the header, remove and send to Layer 6 Layer 6: Process the header, verify any formatting required, remove header and send to Layer 7 Layer 7: Process the header and retrieve data requested for the browser to format and display
Switch 1 Layer 1: Bits accepted Layer 2: Frame header read, FCS calculated and compared to L1 trailer; if OK, destination MAC read and forwarded to outbound interface Layer 1: Frames fed on to signal as bits	**Switch 1** Layer 1: Bits accepted Layer 2: Frame header read, FCS calculated and compared to L1 trailer; if OK, destination MAC read and forwarded to outbound interface Layer 1: Frames fed on to signal as bits
Router Layer 1: Bits accepted Layer 2: Frame header read, MAC destination confirmed, FCS calculated and compared to L2 trailer; if OK, frame removed and packet sent to Layer 3 Layer 3: Packet header read, destination IP address is not ours, so it needs to be forwarded; recognized as local on other interface, sent to L2 for reframing Layer 2: Ethernet selected, L2 header added using source MAC, router's MAC address, destination MAC, web server's MAC; frame check sequence (FCS) calculated and L2 trailer added Layer 1: Frames fed on to signal as bits	**Router** Layer 1: Bits accepted Layer 2: Frame header read, MAC destination confirmed, FCS calculated and compared to L2 trailer; if OK, frame removed and packet sent to Layer 3 Layer 3: Packet header read, destination IP address is not ours so it needs to be forwarded; recognized as local on other interface, sent to L2 for reframing Layer 2: Ethernet selected, L2 header added using source MAC, router's MAC address, destination MAC, host A's MAC; frame check sequence (FCS) calculated and L2 trailer added Layer 1: Frames fed on to signal as bits

(Continued)

INSIDE THE EXAM

Host-to-Server Communication	Server-to-Host Communication
Switch 2 Layer 1: Bits accepted Layer 2: Frame read, FCS calculated and compared to L1 trailer; if OK, destination MAC read and forwarded to outbound interface Layer 1: Frames fed on to signal as bits	**Switch 2** Layer 1: Bits accepted Layer 2: Frame read, FCS calculated and compared to L1 trailer; if OK, destination MAC read and forwarded to outbound interface Layer 1: Frames fed on to signal as bits
Web Server Layer 1: Bits accepted Layer 2: Frame header read, MAC destination confirmed, FCS calculated and compared to L2 trailer; if OK, frame removed and packet sent to Layer 3 Layer 3: Packet header read, destination IP address is ours, so L3 header removed; passed to L4 Layer 4: TCP determined, sequence number confirmed; part of a connection confirmed, header removed and sent to Layer 5 Layer 5: Process the header, remove and send to Layer 6 Layer 6: Process the header, remove and send to Layer 7 Layer 7: Process the header and retrieve data requested	**Web Server** Layer 7: HTTP protocol used, L7 header added Layer 6: Any formatting required, i.e., JPG, etc., L6 header added Layer 5: L5 header added Layer 4: TCP selected, reliable, source port 80, destination port 50000, data segmented and L4 header added; next sequence number added Layer 3: Source IP 192.168.2.5, destination IP 192.168.1.211, L3 header added Layer 2: Ethernet selected, L2 header added using source MAC, web server's MAC address, destination MAC, router's MAC as default gateway to get to other LAN; frame check sequence (FCS) calculated and L2 trailer added Layer 1: Frames fed on to signal as bits

TCP/IP

Much like Chapter 1, questions from this chapter's material on the exam may not be explicit, but instead may be part of scenario-based queries. Direct questions about the material should be fairly straightforward, so a good understanding of the protocols discussed here will help out greatly. On matching questions asking you to identify a particular layer, remember that the TCP/IP layers do not match exactly with the OSI model. The TCP/IP Application layer encompasses the top three layers of the OSI Reference Model, the Internet layer replaces the Network layer, and the Network Access layer encompasses the bottom two OSI layers.

You should commit several key points to memory from this chapter, and be sure to understand the basic functions of each of the application protocols mentioned. At the Transport layer, pay particular attention to the three-way handshake, port numbers, flow control, and multiplexing. Additionally, be very familiar with the differences between TCP and UDP. In the Network Access layer, be sure to remember the frame type changes as the packet travels from network to network.

CERTIFICATION SUMMARY

The OSI Reference Model provides an easily understood, modular description of data as it flows between two systems. The model splits the communications process into seven distinct layers, numbered 7 to 1, from top to bottom. Starting at the top, the layers are Application, Presentation, Session, Transport, Network, Data Link, and Physical. Each layer performs a specific function and relies on the layer above and below it to provide and/or take information. The information at each level has a specific name and is known as the protocol data unit (PDU) for that given layer.

The chapter first compared and contrasted TCP/IP and OSI. All functionality from the OSI Reference Model also occurs within the TCP/IP stack; however, TCP/IP only has four layers. The TCP/IP Application layer comprises layers 7 through 5 and holds several protocols. DNS provides domain-name-to-IP-address resolution, while DHCP dynamically tracks and assigns IP addresses within a network segment. FTP and TFTP are file transfer protocols. FTP is connection oriented, while TFTP is connectionless and faster. SMTP and POP3 combine to move e-mail through networks. SNMP is a very powerful protocol for network management functions. HTTP provides for web surfing and HTML transport, while HTTPS provides secured methods for web access.

Transport layer protocols include TCP and UDP. TCP is connection oriented and uses a three-way handshake to set up a session. Within the session, TCP uses sequence numbers and acknowledgments for reliability and sliding windows for flow control. UDP is connectionless and faster than TCP, but does not have the flow control and reliability features of TCP. Regardless of TCP or UDP, port numbers are used to track multiple communications sessions between systems. Well-known ports are used to identify the Application layer protocol, while dynamic ports are used by requesters to identify the session.

Internet layer protocols include IP and ICMP. IP is a routed protocol, providing hierarchical logical addressing; ICMP provides error notification and other services lacking in IP. Network Access layer standards include SLIP, PPP, and Ethernet.

TWO-MINUTE DRILL

The OSI Reference Model

❑ The OSI simplifies training and education on networking concepts and standards. Its modular design contributes to easier development and maintenance from multiple vendors.

❑ The OSI layers are Application, Presentation, Session, Transport, Network, Data Link, and Physical. The Application layer allows programs to access a network. The Presentation layer formats (and encrypts, if needed) data for transmittal. The Session layer opens, maintains, and closes a session. The Transport layer segments data and provides for reliable end-to-end delivery. The Network layer logically addresses packets and makes routing decisions. The Data Link layer assigns physical addresses, performs media access functions, and conducts framing (aka encapsulation). The Physical layer encodes bits onto the wire.

❑ The bits making up the data payload and the header (and trailer for Layer 2) at each layer are known as a PDU. The PDU at each layer has a specific name. The PDU at the Application, Presentation, and Session layers is known as *data*. At the Transport layer, the PDU is called a *segment*. The Network layer PDU is called a *packet*. At the Data Link layer, the PDU is known as a *frame*, and the PDU at the Physical layer is referred to simply as bits.

❑ In adjacent-layer interaction, layers receive a PDU from a layer above or below them to perform a function on. In same-layer interaction, the same layers on two different machines communicate with each other to accomplish a task.

The TCP/IP Model

❑ The TCP/IP model has four layers: Application, Transport, Internet, and Network Access.

❑ TCP/IP's Application layer maps to the Application, Presentation, and Session layers of the OSI model. The Internet layer maps to OSI's Network layer. The Network Access layer holds the Data Link and Physical layers.

Common OSI Layer Functions and Protocols: Application Layer

❑ DNS provides domain-name-to-IP-address resolution. DNS makes use of resolvers, name servers, and the domain namespace. Top-level domains fall immediately under the DNS root and hold individual zones. Each zone has an SOA record and a name server that holds all the records for the zone.

❑ DHCP provides automatic dynamic IP address allocation within your network segment. A DHCP server is configured with a range of addresses, called a scope, along with other information—such as default gateway and DNS server addresses. DHCP works on broadcasts, so placement of the server must be within the segment. Multiple DHCP servers on the same segment can be problematic, because bogus addresses may be handed out to clients.

❑ Both FTP and TFTP are file transfer protocols. FTP is connection oriented and requires some form of authentication, but is considered insecure because it passes everything in clear text. TFTP is connectionless and much faster, but does not offer directory listing or authentication. TFTP is commonly used to transfer Cisco IOS or configuration files.

❑ SMTP, POP3, and IMAP4 work together to transmit e-mail.

❑ SNMP is used for network management and configuration options and relies on public and private community strings for security.

❑ HTTP transports HTML-formatted pages, and HTTPS adds the SSL protocol for encrypted data transfer.

❑ Transport layer protocols include TCP and UDP. TCP is connection oriented and uses a three-way handshake, with a SYN, SYN/ACK, and ACK transfer to establish a communications channel before data is transmitted. TCP provides reliability by using acknowledgments, and flow control by using a sliding window. UDP is connectionless and does not provide the same services as TCP; however, it is much faster. UDP is typically used to transfer Cisco IOS and configuration files from devices to a server and vice versa.

❑ Port numbers are used to identify the Application layer protocol to be used. A sending machine applies a source port dynamically and a destination port from the well-known range. Upon receiving the response, the port numbers are swapped in the header. The combination of IP address, sequence number, and port number is known as a socket and allows for multiplexing between two systems.

❑ IP is a connectionless routed protocol assigning hierarchical addresses to packets. It allows for both host and network address bits within each address.

❑ ICMP provides error notification services for IP. ICMP responses include request timed out (host did not respond), destination unreachable (no route available in a router), and reply from (success).

❑ Network Access layer standards include SLIP, PPP, and Ethernet, as well as many others. SLIP and PPP are used for point-to-point serial WAN links, while Ethernet is used inside most LANs.

Common OSI Layer Functions and Protocols: Transport Layer

❑ TCP is a connection-oriented, reliable, Layer 4 transport protocol. Application protocols making use of TCP as a transport protocol include SMTP, HTTP, HTTPS, and FTP.

❑ The steps within TCP session establishment (known as the three-way handshake) include synchronization, synchronization acknowledgment, and acknowledgment packets (SYN, SYN/ACK, ACK).

❑ TCP handles error recovery by using the sequence number and acknowledgment fields in the header. The sequence number agreed upon during the three-way handshake is incremented for every byte of data sent.

❑ Flow control in TCP is accomplished using the window size field in the TCP header.

❑ UDP is a connectionless, unreliable, Layer 4 transport protocol. UDP does not require acknowledgments, does not provide for error correction, and does not require a session establishment before data is transmitted. Application protocols making use of UDP as a transport protocol include DNS, DHCP, TFTP, and streaming audio programs.

❑ Port numbers in the TCP or UDP header identify which Application layer protocol is to answer a request, as well as to provide for multiplexing multiple requests from a single source. Port numbers range from 0 to 65535: 0 to 1023 are called well-known port numbers, 1024 to 49151 are called registered ports, and 49152 to 65535 are dynamic ports. Source port numbers are dynamically assigned, and any number over 1023 is an acceptable source port.

Common OSI Layer Functions and Protocols: Internet and Network Access Layers

❑ Routed protocols, like IP, can be routed (forwarded) across networks (or subnets). Routing protocols are used to exchange information between routers to determine the best path availability.

❑ Internet Protocol (IP) is a routed protocol, using a 32-bit hierarchical address. IP is considered a connectionless, best-effort protocol.

❑ ICMP is an Internet layer protocol that provides error notification and, sometimes, error correction for IP datagram delivery.

❑ Encapsulation, framing, media access, and physical addressing, as well as all the physical standards associated with cabling, connectors, and encoding, all occur in the Network Access layer.

❑ Ethernet is the de facto standard Layer 2 technology used within LANs.

SELF TEST

The following Self Test questions will help you measure your understanding of the material presented in this chapter. Read all the choices carefully since there may be more than one correct answer. Choose all the correct answers for each question.

The OSI Reference Model

1. Which OSI layer is concerned with reliable end-to-end delivery of data?
    A. Application
    B. Transport
    C. Network
    D. Data Link

2. At what layer of the OSI model would you find framing?
    A. Transport
    B. Network
    C. Data Link
    D. Physical

3. Logical addressing is found in the _____ layer, while physical addressing is found in the _____ layer.
    A. Physical, Network
    B. Network, Physical
    C. Data Link, Network
    D. Network, Data Link

4. The OSI Reference Model layers, in order from top to bottom, are:
    A. Application, Physical, Session, Transport, Network, Data Link, Presentation
    B. Application, Presentation, Network, Session, Transport, Data Link, Physical
    C. Physical, Data Link, Network, Transport, Session, Presentation, Application
    D. Application, Presentation, Session, Transport, Network, Data Link, Physical

5. What is the PDU at Layer 4 called?
    A. Data
    B. Segment
    C. Packet
    D. Frame
    E. Bit

6. What is the PDU at Layer 3 called?

   A. Data

   B. Segment

   C. Packet

   D. Frame

   E. Bit

7. The Transport layer on the recipient machine requests a retransmission of a segment from the sending machine. This is an example of:

   A. Same-layer interaction

   B. Adjacent-layer interaction

   C. Cross-layer interaction

   D. Split-layer interaction

The TCP/IP Model

8. Which of the following are true when comparing TCP/IP to the OSI Reference Model? (Choose two.)

   A. The TCP/IP model has seven layers, while the OSI model has only four layers.

   B. The TCP/IP model has four layers, while the OSI model has seven layers.

   C. The TCP/IP Application layer maps to the Application, Session, and Presentation layers of the OSI Reference Model.

   D. The TCP/IP Application layer is virtually identical to the OSI Application layer.

9. In which layer of the TCP/IP stack is routing and logical addressing found?

   A. Network

   B. Data Link

   C. Internet

   D. Network Access

10. In which layer of the TCP/IP stack is framing found?

   A. Network

   B. Data Link

   C. Internet

   D. Network Access

11. Formatting and code conversion occurs in the _____ layer of the OSI model and the _____ layer of the TCP/IP stack.
   A. Data Link, Network Access
   B. Network Access, Data Link
   C. Application, Presentation
   D. Presentation, Application

Common OSI Layer Functions and Protocols: Application Layer

12. Which TCP/IP Application layer protocol provides IP address resolution for domain names?
   A. DHCP
   B. DNS
   C. SMTP
   D. SNMP

13. You receive several calls from a group of users about a lack of network connectivity. After investigating, you find all the users are on a brand-new segment off the internal router. Your network uses DHCP and all users on the original segment are functioning fine. What is the most likely cause of the problem?
   A. Every user on the new segment has manually assigned their own TCP/IP address information.
   B. The DHCP server is on the original segment, and DHCP requests are not allowed to cross a router.
   C. Cabling to a single host on the new segment has been severed, taking down the entire network.
   D. This is a temporary problem. Simply waiting longer will fix it.

14. Within SNMP, the _____ community string allows a central device to read MIB information, while a _____ community string provides the authentication to send configuration updates.
   A. Public, Private
   B. Private, Public
   C. Read, Read/Write
   D. Read/Write, Read

15. What signifies the hostname holding the resource in the URL http://www.cisco.com/education .htm?

    A. http

    B. www.cisco.com

    C. education.htm

    D. www.cisco.com/education.htm

    E. www

Common OSI Layer Functions and Protocols: Transport Layer

16. TCP completes a three-way handshake before exchanging data. In order, what are the steps?

    A. ACK, SYN/ACK, SYN

    B. ACK, SYN, SYN/ACK

    C. SYN/ACK, ACK, SYN

    D. SYN, SYN/ACK, ACK

17. What is the well-known port number for SMTP?

    A. 21

    B. 22

    C. 23

    D. 25

    E. 110

18. A client connects to a server and attempts to pull a web page. What port would appear in the destination field of the requesting machine's TCP header?

    A. 23

    B. 25

    C. 80

    D. 88

    E. 110

19. Which of the following port numbers could appear in the source port field of a TCP header leaving a requesting system?

    A. 1022

    B. 1023

    C. 49172

    D. 80

Common OSI Layer Functions and Protocols: Internet and Network Access Layers

20. Which protocol provides error notification services for IP?

    A. ping

    B. SNMP

    C. DNS

    D. ICMP

21. While using ping to test network connectivity, you receive a "Destination Host Unreachable" reply. Which of the following is the most correct interpretation of the result?

    A. The end host is offline.

    B. A Layer 1 problem exists between the two hosts.

    C. A Layer 3 problem exists between the two hosts.

    D. The end host is online.

SELF TEST ANSWERS

The OSI Reference Model

1. ☑ **B** is correct. The Transport layer is responsible for segmentation, flow control, and reliable end-to-end data delivery.
   ☒ **A, C,** and **D** are incorrect. **A** is incorrect because the Application layer allows programs to access a network. **C** is incorrect because the Network layer is responsible for logical addressing and routing. **D** is incorrect because the Data Link layer is responsible for encapsulation, framing, media access, and physical addressing.

2. ☑ **C** is correct. The Data Link layer is responsible for encapsulation, framing, media access, and physical addressing.
   ☒ **A, B,** and **D** are incorrect. **A** is incorrect because the Transport layer is responsible for segmentation, flow control, and reliable end-to-end data delivery. **B** is incorrect because the Network layer is responsible for logical addressing and routing. **D** is incorrect because the Physical layer is responsible for encoding bits onto the media.

3. ☑ **D** is correct. The Network layer is responsible for logical addressing and routing, while the Data Link layer is responsible for physical addressing and media access.
   ☒ **A, B,** and **C** are incorrect. They are out of order.

4. ☑ **D** is correct. From Layer 7 to Layer 1, the order is Application, Presentation, Session, Transport, Network, Data Link, and Physical.
   ☒ **A, B,** and **C** are incorrect. They do not have the order correct.

5. ☑ **B** is correct. The Layer 4 PDU is called a segment.
   ☒ **A, C, D,** and **E** are incorrect. **A** is incorrect because the data is the PDU for the top three layers. **C** is incorrect because the packet is the PDU at the Network layer. **D** is incorrect because the frame is the PDU for the Data Link layer. **E** is incorrect because the bit is the PDU at the Physical layer.

6. ☑ **C** is correct. Packet is the PDU at the Network layer.
   ☒ **A, B, D,** and **E** are incorrect. **A** is incorrect because the data is the PDU for the top three layers. **B** is incorrect because the Layer 4 PDU is called a segment. **D** is incorrect because the frame is the PDU for the Data Link layer. **E** is incorrect because the bit is the PDU for the Physical layer.

7. ☑ **A** is correct. A layer on one machine communicating directly with the same layer on a distant machine is known as same-layer interaction.
   ☒ **B, C,** and **D** are incorrect. **B** is incorrect because this interaction type involves a layer interacting with a layer directly above or below it in the same stack. **C** and **D** are incorrect because they do not exist.

The TCP/IP Model

8. ☑ **B** and **C** are correct. The TCP/IP model has four layers. The Application layer maps to the top three layers of the OSI Reference Model.

☒ **A** and **D** are incorrect. **A** and **D** are incorrect because they are contrary to **B** and **C**.

9. ☑ **C** is correct. Routing and logical addressing occur at the Internet layer of the TCP/IP stack.

☒ **A, B,** and **D** are incorrect. **A** is incorrect because the Network layer is an OSI model layer. **B** is incorrect because Data Link is an OSI model layer. **D** is incorrect because framing, error checking, and media access occur at the Network Access layer of the TCP/IP stack.

10. ☑ **D** is correct. Framing, error checking, and media access occur at the Network Access layer of the TCP/IP stack.

☒ **A, B,** and **C** are incorrect. **A** is incorrect because the Network layer is an OSI model layer. **B** is incorrect because Data Link is an OSI model layer. **C** is incorrect because routing and logical addressing occur at the Internet layer of the TCP/IP stack.

11. ☑ **D** is correct. Formatting and code conversion are Presentation layer functions in the OSI model. The Application layer in TCP/IP maps to the top three layers of the OSI model.

☒ **A, B,** and **C** are incorrect.

Common OSI Layer Functions and Protocols: Application Layer

12. ☑ **B** is correct. DNS resolves an IP address for a domain name.

☒ **A, C,** and **D** are incorrect. **A** is incorrect because DHCP provides automatic dynamic address allocation inside a network segment. **C** is incorrect because SMTP provides e-mail transmission between clients and servers. **D** is incorrect because SNMP provides network and configuration management services.

13. ☑ **B** is correct. DHCP messages are sent broadcast and therefore will not cross the router.

☒ **A, C,** and **D** are incorrect. **A** is incorrect because it is unlikely every client manually changed their TCP/IP configuration at the same time. **C** is incorrect because cabling to a single host would not bring the entire network segment down. **D** is incorrect because waiting will not fix this problem.

14. ☑ **A** is correct. Public and private community strings are used within SNMP to read and write, respectively.

☒ **B, C,** and **D** are incorrect. **B** is incorrect because the choices are backwards. Private allows for writing configuration data, while public allows for reading MIB information. **C** and **D** are incorrect because they do not exist as community strings.

15. ☑ **E** is correct. The host is the www preceding the domain name cisco.com.

    ☒ **A, B, C,** and **D** are incorrect. A, C, and D are incorrect because http is the protocol used, and education.htm is the individual page requested. **B** is incorrect because it includes the domain name cisco.com.

Common OSI Layer Functions and Protocols: Transport Layer

16. ☑ **D** is correct. The three-way handshake begins with a synchronization packet (SYN), which is then acknowledged (SYN/ACK). The last step is an acknowledgment of the sequence numbers (ACK).

    ☒ **A, B,** and **C** are incorrect. The steps are out of order.

17. ☑ **D** is correct. The port number for SMTP is 25.

    ☒ **A, B, C,** and **E** are incorrect. **A** is incorrect because 21 is the port number for FTP. **B** is incorrect because 22 is the port number for SSH. **C** is incorrect because 23 is the port number for Telnet. **E** is incorrect because 110 is the port number for POP3.

18. ☑ **C** is correct. The port number for HTTP, used to pull HTML web pages, is 80.

    ☒ **A, B, D,** and **E** are incorrect. **A** is incorrect because 23 is the port number for Telnet. **B** is incorrect because 25 is the port number for SMTP. **D** is incorrect because 88 is the port number for Kerberos. **E** is incorrect because 110 is the port number for POP3.

19. ☑ **C** is correct. Source port numbers from a requesting machine are dynamic and must not be from the well-known port range 0–1023.

    ☒ **A, B,** and **D** are incorrect. All these answers are from the well-known port range, which cannot be used here.

Common OSI Layer Functions and Protocols:
Internet and Network Access Layers

20. ☑ **D** is correct. ICMP provides error correction and notification services to IP.

    ☒ **A, B,** and **C,** are incorrect. **A** is incorrect because ping is a command-line utility used to test network connectivity. **B** is incorrect because SNMP is an Application layer protocol for network management. **C** is incorrect because DNS provides IP address resolution for a domain name.

21. ☑ **C** is correct. "Destination Unreachable" indicates there is no entry in the route table of your system, or a router on the path, for the end host.

    ☒ **A, B,** and **D** are incorrect. **A** is incorrect because if the packet makes it to the end station's network and the station is offline, you should receive a "Reply Timed Out" message. **B** is incorrect because a "Destination Host Unreachable" message indicates a Layer 3 problem, not Layer 1. **D** is incorrect because if the packet reaches the destination network and the device is online, you should receive a "Reply From" message.

3

IPv4 Addressing and Subnet Masks

T his chapter is dedicated to introducing basic IPv4 address concepts and understanding how they address our networks. We'll cover IP address construction, binary to decimal conversion, the concept of public and private addressing, and subnet masks.

IP addressing is starting a transition from the current version, IP version 4 (IPv4) to IP version 6 (IPv6) for many reasons, but primarily due to a shortage of IPv4 addresses. The focus of this chapter—as well as much of the book and the current CCENT exam—is IPv4, so assume if you see IP that we are referring to IPv4. IPv6 will soon become a part of your networking experience as it is rolled out. We will always designate it as IPv6, and it will be covered in Chapter 13.

CERTIFICATION OBJECTIVE 3.01

IPv4 Addresses

IP addresses are the Layer 3 addresses assigned to every device on our networks as an identity. IPv4 addresses are displayed in *dotted decimal notation*, and appear as four numbers separated by dots, such as 192.168.1.123. Each of the decimal numbers, or octets, is made up of 8 bits (0s and 1s), or a byte. Each octet is numbered by its portion of the address. In our example, the first octet is 192, while 168 is the second octet, 1 is the third, and 123 is the fourth octet. Together they make up what is referred to as a 4-octet address, also called a 32-bit or 4-byte address.

Each IP address actually has two parts. The first part identifies the network that the device belongs to while the second is unique to a particular device. Like your home address where one part is the street you live on, another part is the number that identifies your home on that street. Just as we can assume that 123 Main Street and 212 Main Street are both on the same road, we can assume that 192.168.1.17 and 192.168.1.199 are on the same network.

To separate the network from the device, or host, portion of the address, IP uses a subnet mask that looks like 255.255.255.0 with the IP address. In the subnet mask, 255 indicates this part of the address is part of the network, whereas a 0 indicates the device number section. So in our example, 192.168.1 is the network portion, while 17 and 199 are device identifiers. With this address and mask, any number between 1 and 254 would be a device address on our network. A zero (0) is not allowed as a host address, because it is used to identify the network, as in 192.168.1.0 in our example. Similarly, 255 is not allowed for hosts because that is the broadcast address for that network; 192.16.1.255 would go to all addresses in the network.

While decimal IP addresses and masks are relatively easy for humans to remember, computers and networking devices don't understand decimal numbers. They see IP addresses as 32 bits, 0s and 1s. One thing we will see when we work with binary numbers later in this chapter is that 8 bits can create 256 unique combinations from 00000000 to 11111111 that convert to the decimal numbers 0 to 255. This means that you should never see an IPv4 address or subnet mask with an octet value greater than 255. Figure 3-1 shows a decimal IP address with subnet mask and the binary counterparts, covered later in this chapter.

While the IP address is unique to each device, the subnet mask is shared by every device on that network. Its job is to define the network, not the host. In our networks, or out in the larger Internet, routers use the IP address with the subnet mask to identify the network portion and then forward the data to the router connected to that network. The device portion is only used within the destination network for the edge router and the switch(es) to get it delivered to the right host.

Figure 3-2 demonstrates how each network is unique to the third octet, and then within each subnetwork, the hosts must be unique. While there are two .12 and .15 hosts, when you add the network portion they are unique. An analogy would be that two houses can have the same house number if they are on different streets, as in 123 Main Street and 123 Cisco Avenue, because the postal carrier looks at the street first and then the house number. This design assumes we are using the 255.255.255.0 subnet mask from earlier. Note also that each router interface in a segment has an address from that same address network. The router-to-router links are also in different networks, and, typically, point-to-point networks that have only two addresses, no hosts.

The hosts on each building's LAN all share the same network portion of the IP address as defined by the subnet mask, 255.255.255.0. Each 255 means that

FIGURE 3-1

IP address and subnet mask

	Network		Host
1st Octet	2nd Octet	3rd Octet	4th Octet

192.168.001.123 IP Address
255.255.255.0 Subnet Mask

11000000.10101000.00000001.01111011 IP Address (Binary)
11111111.11111111.11111111.00000000 Subnet Mask (Binary)

Three-building
network with
LANs

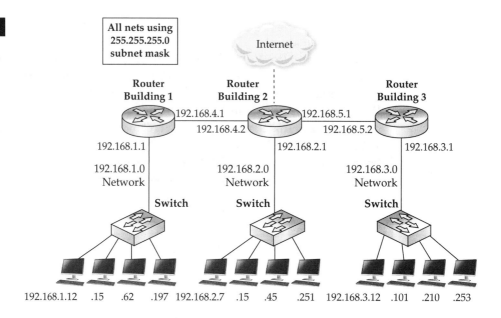

all of this is part of the network, making 192.168.2 the network and anything left identifies the device. This means that in Building 2, hosts 192.168.2.7 and 192.168.2.15 could communicate with each other as well as any other devices on the 192.168.2.0 network without involving the router. They can all talk to their router, which has an interface, 192.168.2.1, in their network. It is in fact their *default gateway* to the outside.

Hosts can't communicate with other LANs without going through their gateway router. We know the diagram makes that seem pretty obvious, but let's walk through an example that demonstrates why the diagram has to look like this. Host 192.168.2.7 can't communicate with any hosts in Building 1 or 3 without going through its gateway router. Even if host 192.168.1.15 could be connected to Building 2's switch, they still could not communicate, because 192.168.2.7, using its own mask, knows that 192.168.1.15 is not part of this network, not local, and therefore would frame the packet to go to the gateway router at 192.168.2.1. The router knows where the 192.168.1.0 network is and would forward the packet to the Building 1 router. In fact, 192.168.1.15 is now an orphan; it can't communicate with any of the local hosts because this computer would frame the packet to go to its own gateway, 192.168.1.1, which would be ignored by Building 2's gateway router because it can't accept frames from any network but 192.168.2.0 on that interface.

Following a Packet

Using our last figure, let's assume host 192.168.3.12 wants to communicate to 192.168.1.197 or any host in Building 1. The host knows the networks don't match, and therefore the destination isn't local, so it builds a frame to its own gateway at 192.168.3.1. It sends the frame.

The Building 3 router accepts the frame because it is addressed to it, but after stripping off the frame it sees the Destination IP address in the packet is to 192.168.1.197. It doesn't have an interface in that network, so it knows the destination isn't local. It checks its routing table and sees that Building 2's router, 192.168.5.1, knows how to get to the destination. It builds a frame to go out its 192.168.5.2 interface to 192.168.5.1. It sends the frame.

The Building 2 router accepts the frame because it is addressed to it, but after stripping off the frame it sees the Destination IP address in the packet is to 192.168.1.197. It doesn't have an interface in that network, so it checks its routing table and sees that Building 1's router, 192.168.4.1, knows how to get to the destination. It builds a frame to go out its 192.168.4.2 interface to 192.168.4.1. It sends the frame.

The Building 1 router accepts the frame because it is addressed to it, but after stripping off the frame it sees the Destination IP address in the packet is to 192.168.1.197. It has an interface in that network, so it knows the destination is local. It builds a frame to go out its 192.168.1.1 interface to 192.168.1.197. It sends the frame.

The 192.168.1.197 host accepts the frame and processes it.

In the next section, we will look at IP addresses, early attempts to group addresses for assignment, what the computer sees as the address, and finally how to confirm the IP address and subnet mask on a computer.

IP Address Classes

As we discussed in Chapter 1, IP addresses to the computer are 32 binary bits acting as little off/on switches to create unique 32-digit numbers (all 0s and 1s). IPv4 can create 4,294,967,296 possible unique addresses between 32 zeroes and 32 ones. Initially, this seemed like plenty of address space, but organizing such a large pool of possible addresses still remained to be figured out. The developers did know that the entire concept of data routing needed to be based on the same principle as the ZIP code system used by the post office, where the destination becomes more specific near the right end. In fact, all routing leads to the network's gateway router or device, and the local network is responsible for delivering the rest of the way.

Therefore, some organization in assigning IP addresses to businesses and ISPs was essential—if there were no organization and addresses were simply handed out at random, routing would break down.

In 1981, more than a decade before the World Wide Web and the public getting interested, it was decided to divide the IP address space into five logical, easy-to-recognize classes and to have a central authority track and assign address allocation. In RFC 791, the IP address space was divided into three host classes plus two special classes for the future, with each one providing address space for a particular need. Over the years, several entities, such as the nonprofit ICANN (Internet Corporation for Assigned Names and Numbers), controlled the allocation of these classes based on need and availability.

Table 3-1 shows the classes and how Class A addresses were to be handed out for large networks, Class B networks for intermediate organizations, and Class C addresses for smaller networks. The organization of addresses into classes followed a very logical—if not practical in the long run—method.

Class A addresses were assigned to allow for very large networks with many host addresses, so the decision was made to allocate only the first octet to the requesting organization. For example, suppose a government entity requested a Class A address. ICANN would assign the first 8 bits, leaving the last 24 up to the network owner to assign as host addresses. If the address assigned was the 9 network, 9.0.0.0, the owner could not change the first 8 bits, but could manipulate the last 24 to assign individual host addresses. Every computer in the network would begin with the number 9 in the first octet (hosts could be addressed 9.0.0.1 to 9.255.255.254).

TABLE 3-1   IP Address Classes

Class	Network Bits	Host Bits	Available Host Addresses per Network	Intended Use
A	First 8 bits	Last 24 bits	$16,777,214$ ($2^{24}-2$)	Large networks (ISPs and so on)
B	First 16 bits	Last 16 bits	$65,534$ ($2^{16}-2$)	Intermediate networks
C	First 24 bits	Last 8 bits	254 ($2^{8}-2$)	Small networks
D	At least 8	Depends on number of network bits	N/A	Reserved for multicast
E	At least 8	Depends on number of network bits	N/A	Reserved for experimental use

The same logic applies for Class B and C networks, only with different numbers of network bits assigned. If an organization received a Class B network, ICANN would assign the first two octets, leaving the last two for hosts. For example, an assignment of the Class B network 188.77.0.0 leaves 188.77.0.1 to 188.77.255.254 as possible host addresses for the administrator to assign. As long as a computer's address begins with 188.77 in the first two octets, it would belong to the network.

If it were a Class C network, the first three octets would be assigned, leaving only the last one for hosts. A Class C example, 195.95.100.0, would leave only the last octet—195.95.100.1 to 195.95.100.254—available for hosts (195.95.100.0 would be the network address, while 195.95.100.255 would be the broadcast).

Remember that routers are only concerned with the network portion of the address, so it was assumed that any connecting network would only have to route packets to the gateway router at the edge of any of these networks and then internal devices would get them to the correct host device.

Allocating Addresses to Class A, B, and C

After much discussion, RFC 791 was accepted as the standard for dividing up the IP address space. This standard stated that the arrangement of the *first* octet determined to which class an address belonged. Since the first octet began with 00000000 and ended with 11111111, it seemed logical that some definable pattern in the arrangement of those bits could be used to satisfy the end goal.

If you follow the arrangements of bits to represent decimals, you discover a repeatable pattern that makes dividing the address space easy. The first arrangement of bits is 00000000, followed by 00000001, 00000010, 00000011, and so on, like eight light switches that can be off (0) or on (1). This pattern repeats until you have 01111111, making an easily definable range of 128 unique combinations. In other words, if the first bit of an IP address is 0, the address is in a Class A network. Class A addresses range from 00000000 (0) to 01111111 (127). We will look at converting to and from binary in another section of this chapter.

The next two classes were just as easy to create. Following the pattern, the next available number looks like this in binary: 10000000 (or 128). Instead of the address starting with a 0, Class B addresses start with 10, and range from 10000000 (128) to 10111111 (191). Class C addresses begin with 110, and range from 11000000 (192) to 11011111 (223). Classes D and E follow similar patterns but are not covered on the CCENT exam. The number ranges for IP address host classes are listed in Table 3-2.

The *default subnet masks* are used by Layer 3 devices like routers and computers to identify the network portion of the IP addresses. The 0s in the mask identify the host portion. Just as the IP address is internally a binary number, so is the subnet

| TABLE 3-2 | IP Address Class Ranges | | | |

Class	Leading Bits	First Octet Range	Hosts per Network	Default Subnet Mask
A	0	1–126	16,777,214	255.0.0.0
B	10	128–191	65,534	255.255.0.0
C	110	192–223	254	255.255.255.0

mask, sometimes called the net mask or just mask, is made up of 1s and 0s in a very special pattern. It begins with 1s and remains all 1s until the end of the network ID, then it flips to 0s to the end. The 255 equals eight 1s or 11111111.00000000.000000 00.00000000 in the case of the Class A net mask. Class B is 11111111.11111111.00 000000.00000000 and Class C would be 11111111.11111111.11111111.00000000.

The number of hosts shown in the table is calculated using the formula 2^n-2, which we will discuss later in this chapter. As you can see, the Class A and B pools are huge and much too large for most organizations. Even the Class C is too large for home networks and most small organizations. Fortunately, today we are not limited to these default masks. We can break these pools up into more efficient and manageable sizes using something called subnetting and subnet masks; these will be covered in later sections of this chapter.

Reserved IP Addresses

You will notice from the table that the 0 and the 127 are not included in the Class A networks. There are several Class As that aren't or won't be assigned—they are reserved addresses. Just remember that while the Class A address pool is 0 to 127, the first and last are reserved and can't be used. The 0 network, where all 8 bits are 0s, identifies all IP addresses; literally, the 0.0.0.0 is the root or beginning of all IP addresses.

Keep in mind the original designers of IP addressing were not fools, but their world was connecting research computers together, initially in the United States, well before personal computers were taken seriously. They were thinking of maybe tens of thousands of connections eventually, not millions and more. As it turned out, their class design and pools of reserved addresses ended up trapping many unusable addresses in Class A and B networks. Let's look at a couple of reserved networks.

Loopback Testing   We saw earlier that the 127 network is reserved. It is set aside for what is called loopback testing, and it is an entire Class A address range

(16,777,214 addresses), just so we could ping ourselves. The IETF (Internet Engineering Task Force) standards reserve the IPv4 127 network address block and the name *localhost* for loopback testing. If you ping any 127.x.x.x address and get a successful response, it confirms that the TCP/IP protocol stack is working properly on that device. Loopback testing runs entirely within the operating system's networking software and sends no packets to any NIC. Any traffic sent to a loopback IP address is simply sent back up the network software stack as if it had been received from another device. The following output shows a loopback test we ran. You can do this on any network computer.

```
C:\Users\bob>ping 127.1.2.3

Pinging 127.1.2.3 with 32 bytes of data:
Reply from 127.1.2.3: bytes=32 time=6ms TTL=128
Reply from 127.1.2.3: bytes=32 time=5ms TTL=128
Reply from 127.1.2.3: bytes=32 time=4ms TTL=128
Reply from 127.1.2.3: bytes=32 time=4ms TTL=128

Ping statistics for 127.1.2.3:
    Packets: Sent = 4, Received = 4, Lost = 0 (0% loss),
Approximate round trip times in milli-seconds:
    Minimum = 4ms, Maximum = 6ms, Average = 4ms

C:\Users\bob>
```

Private Addresses   Another group of reserved address pools that in the end helped prolong the life of IPv4 for more than a decade was a group called private addresses. In the 1990s when it became apparent that the IP address pool was going to be depleted soon, several programs evolved to conserve real public IP addresses. A *public address* is any unique IP address that could be visible in the Internet and routed to from anywhere in the world. The idea was quite simple: many business and home networks don't necessarily need public IP addresses for every device in their network. Private addresses were created to allow administrators to create networks and assign host addresses inside their organizations without using public address space.

While private addresses can be routed within an organization's network, they are not routed by a network's gateway routers to the Internet and wouldn't be forwarded by any Internet service provider's routers if they were. In other words, devices with private IP addresses can't connect directly to the Internet, and computers outside the local network cannot connect directly to a device with a private IP, providing

TABLE 3-3	Network Class	Private Address Range
	A (1 – Class A)	10.0.0.0
Private IP Address Ranges	B (16 – Class B)	172.16.0.0 to 172.31.0.0
	C (256 – Class C)	192.168.0.0 to 192.168.255.0

a bit of security and anonymity. Additionally, many businesses can use the same private IP address range since their networks will never see each other or be routed out to the Internet.

A benefit to private addresses for organizations is that you don't need anyone's permission to use them. More importantly, you don't have to rent them from your ISP on a monthly basis like public addresses—a substantial savings for medium-size and larger organizations.

RFC 1918 created private address ranges within each IP address class for internal networks. The private IP address ranges are listed in Table 3-3.

Another address you might recognize is the *Automatic Private Internet Protocol Addressing* (APIPA) range. Created through a different RFC (RFC 3300), APIPA addresses (169.254.0.0) are used on a variety of different operating systems to automatically assign IP addresses in the event a DHCP server cannot be found. The idea is that, without a DHCP server, all systems booting in the network would randomly choose an address in the *same subnet* (169.254.0.0/24). APIPA addresses can also be used as a troubleshooting indicator, having become a telltale sign that something is wrong between the PC and the DHCP server.

While using private addressing inside the network greatly helped conserve the public IP address space, it's only half the story. Undoubtedly, many of those users will want or need to go out on the Internet. At the same time, a technology called *Network Address Translation* (NAT) became widely available that permits the use of private addressing while also allowing devices in the network to connect to the Internet. NAT is a service that often runs on a perimeter router or firewall that translates private IP addresses into useable public IP addresses, often using the outside interface address of the router or firewall. If you went to a school where hall passes were required to leave a class to go to the library or restroom, NAT-provided addresses work very much like those passes. We will look at NAT in greater detail in Chapter 11.

e x a m

ⓦatch *Make sure that you understand the class addresses and the reserved IP addresses, particularly the loopback and private addresses. Make sure that you understand the differences between public and private addresses.*

Verifying a Host's IPv4 Address

Verifying that a host computer has an IP address is quite simple. Use the Start menu to open the command prompt (DOS-like) window (Start | Programs | Accessories | Command Prompt or Start | Run and type **cmd** and press ENTER).

Type **ipconfig** at the prompt and press ENTER while in the command window; (ipconfig spelling is critical; case is not). Until just a few years ago, you got a very simple IP address, subnet mask, and default gateway—the very things we are looking for. Today, with the transition to IPv6 getting started, there are typically many more things in the output. Figure 3-3 shows the output from a laptop using WiFi.

Figure 3-4 shows just the section of the output that we are interested in today. The longer arrows point at the IP address, subnet mask, and default gateway. The shorter arrows show IPv6 information that we will discuss in Chapter 13.

If you are not familiar with the **ipconfig** command, you can experiment with it on any Windows computer. There are options that you will find useful. The **ipconfig /all** command displays even more detailed information. The **ipconfig /?** command will bring up the help screens showing the other options.

FIGURE 3-3   Example output from ipconfig command

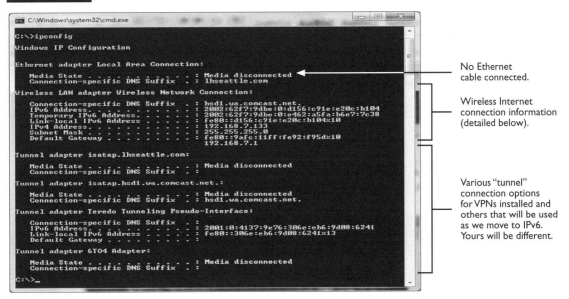

FIGURE 3-4   Detail output of ipconfig command

```
Ethernet adapter Local Area Connection:

   Media State . . . . . . . . . . . : Media disconnected
   Connection-specific DNS Suffix  . : lhseattle.com

Wireless LAN adapter Wireless Network Connection:

   Connection-specific DNS Suffix  . : hsd1.wa.comcast.net.          ◄─── The ISP resolving URLs for you
   IPv6 Address. . . . . . . . . . . : 2002:62f7:9dbe:0:d156:c91e:e20c:b104
   Temporary IPv6 Address. . . . . . : 2002:62f7:9dbe:0:e462:a5fa:b6e7:7c38
   Link-local IPv6 Address . . . . . : fe80::d156:c91e:e20c:b104%10
   IPv4 Address. . . . . . . . . . . : 192.168.7.133                ◄─── Your IPv4 LAN address
   Subnet Mask . . . . . . . . . . . : 255.255.255.0                ◄─── Your IPv4 subnet mask
   Default Gateway . . . . . . . . . : fe80::9afc:11ff:fe92:f95d%10
                                       192.168.7.1                  ◄─── Your IPv4 default gateway
```

You can test your IP address and loopback by using the **ping** command from that same command prompt if you like. The output looks like the following. In addition to both being successful, we see that the network, like most, is using private addresses.

```
C:\Users\bob>ping 192.168.7.132
Pinging 192.168.7.132 with 32 bytes of data:
Reply from 192.168.7.132: bytes=32 time=7ms TTL=128
Reply from 192.168.7.132: bytes=32 time=2ms TTL=128
Reply from 192.168.7.132: bytes=32 time=3ms TTL=128
Reply from 192.168.7.132: bytes=32 time=5ms TTL=128

Ping statistics for 192.168.7.132:
    Packets: Sent = 4, Received = 4, Lost = 0 (0% loss),
Approximate round trip times in milli-seconds:
    Minimum = 2ms, Maximum = 7ms, Average = 4ms

C:\Users\bob>ping 127.0.0.113
Pinging 127.0.0.113 with 32 bytes of data:
Reply from 127.0.0.113: bytes=32 time=7ms TTL=128
Reply from 127.0.0.113: bytes=32 time=6ms TTL=128
Reply from 127.0.0.113: bytes=32 time=6ms TTL=128
Reply from 127.0.0.113: bytes=32 time=5ms TTL=128

Ping statistics for 127.0.0.113:
    Packets: Sent = 4, Received = 4, Lost = 0 (0% loss),
Approximate round trip times in milli-seconds:
    Minimum = 5ms, Maximum = 7ms, Average = 6ms

C:\Users\bob>
```

CERTIFICATION OBJECTIVE 3.02

Binary Numbers

Before we look any deeper into IP addressing, let's look at binary numbers, binary conversions, and just a little bit of binary math, so IP addresses, subnetting, subnet masks, and how routers process addresses will make more sense.

Understanding basic binary is an essential skill not just to pass the CCENT and many other Cisco exams, but to succeed in a networking career of any kind. Considering that network devices, as well as all digital devices, communicate and process only in binary, it is critical to be skilled in three major operations: converting binary to decimal, converting decimal to binary, and determining the number of combinations a specific number of binary digits provides.

So let's look at what all those 0s and 1s mean.

Binary Values

We already discussed that binary numbers are made up of just two digits, 0 and 1, which means it is a base-2 system (two base digits) from which all other numbers must be built. If we look at a single-digit binary there are only two possible values: 0 or 1. Like a light switch, it is either off or on. That's as far as we can go with one digit. So if we put a 1 in the second column and start at 0 in the first column, then 10 = 2. If we add a 1 in the first column, then 11 = 3, which is as far as we can go with two digits. If we put a 1 in the next column and start at 0 again, then 100 = 4, 101 = 5, 110 = 6, and 111 = 7. We could start the process again with 8 (1000) (see Table 3-4).

TABLE 3-4	Binary	Decimal
Binary Numbers and Decimal Equivalents	0	0
	1	1
	10	2
	11	3
	100	4
	101	5
	110	6
	111	7
	1000	8

TABLE 3-5	Binary Position Values								
512	256	128	64	32	16	8	4	2	1

Let's just look at our table a moment. Think of a binary number as a series of columns. The right end column is worth 1, the second column 2, the third column 4, the fourth column 8, and so on, doubling each time. If we have a single-digit binary, it can only contain either a 0 or 1, so 0 ones would be 0, while 1 one would be 1. Look at the top two rows of Table 3-4 to confirm that. When we add a second digit or position, it has a value of 2, allowing us to create 2 (2+0) and 3 (2+1). When we go to a third digit or position, it equals 4, which allows us to create 4, 5, 6, and 7. If we add a fourth digit, it will equal 8 (1000) and then 16 (10000). Look at the pattern: each time we add a digit or position to the left, we double the previous value. The pattern that is forming is shown in Table 3-5. This is the value of each binary bit location. A bit in the third position is worth decimal 4; the seventh position equals 64. This pattern is very important to remember and understand. You will use it a lot. The better you understand it, the easier many things get.

The first column is always 1 and each position (digit) to the left is multiplied by the number of unique digits, 2 in binary. The next section shows how we will use this pattern to create tables that will help us convert binary to decimal and later help us with subnetting and calculating the number of hosts.

Converting Binary to Decimal

Binary numbers are displayed in columns, just like decimal numbers—and, just like decimals, each position to the left in a binary number has more "value" (twice) than the position to the right. We have built our table with eight positions or digits, but it could be extended to the left by doubling the decimal values to infinity. Binary position values are displayed in Table 3-6.

As always, start at the right with 1, then in this case each column to the left is 2 times the one to its right (base-2, remember). Look over the table to see if that doesn't work out. The good news in IPv4 is that we often only need 8 columns for 8 bits. The decimal values will add up to 255, which with 0 is the 256 possible binary values that can be made with 8 bits.

TABLE 3-6	Position value	128	64	32	16	8	4	2	1
Binary Position Values Table	Binary number								
	Decimal equivalent								

	TABLE 3-7 Binary Example converting 11001101								
Position value	128	64	32	16	8	4	2	1	
Binary number	1	1	0	0	1	1	0	1	
Decimal equivalent	128 +	64 +	0 +	0 +	8 +	4 +	0 +	1	= 205

For example, let's translate the binary number 11001101 to its decimal equivalent. As shown in Table 3-7, if you follow the preceding steps and place the values in their appropriate columns, the answer is relatively easy.

The rightmost value was set to 1, as were the third, fourth, seventh, and eighth positions. By adding the decimal values in each of those positions, the decimal equivalent of 11001101 is 205.

We can't emphasize strongly enough the importance of understanding this table, how to build it, and how to use it. Even if you are good at math, the last thing you need when under the stress of the exam is to make math errors. Then practice, practice, and practice some more until you can build the table and do the calculations in your sleep. A good example is shown in Table 3-6. There are many sites on the Internet to check your work—just Google "binary to decimal" or "decimal to binary"—but that won't help you on the test. Let's call this our binary conversion table.

The position row is the value of each binary place/position starting at the right. This first value is always 1 and each column to the left is twice as large. This works regardless of how many digits display in the binary value. The next column value would be 256, then 512, 1024, and so on.

Any time your binary number has fewer digits than the number of columns in your table, make sure to fit the number as far to the right as you can. Any missing digits should be on the left end, otherwise you will get a very large *wrong* number. It is not uncommon but can be confusing to not show zero leading bits. Just as we drop leading zeros in numbers like 00250, some people choose to display 00001100 as 1100, which equals 12 (8 + 4 + 0 + 0).

Spend a little time becoming familiar with your table—how to build it and how it works. A couple of interesting facts that will come in handy: First, there is only one combination of binary bits that equals any decimal value. Looking at Table 3-8,

	TABLE 3-8 Binary Conversion Table to 10 Digits									
Position	512	256	128	64	32	16	8	4	2	1
Binary		1	0	0	0	0	0	0	0	1
Answer		256							1	257

only 100000001 = 257; no other combination can equal 257. Second, pick any value in the decimal value row and the sum of all numbers to the right equals the value that you chose minus one. Look at 16, the sum of all the numbers to the right is 15. For 512, the sum of the numbers to the right is 511. You'll see other uses later for this table and the relationship shown in the value row.

Converting Decimal to Binary

Converting from decimal to binary is an equally important skill. Fortunately, this is also very simple. To convert a decimal to binary:

1. Determine the highest bit position decimal value that is equal to or smaller than your target and set it to 1.

2. Subtract the decimal value from the original number and compare the remainder to the next position to the right.

3. If the next decimal value is equal to or smaller than your remainder, set it to 1 and repeat step 2. If it is bigger, turn the bit to 0 and move one position to the right.

4. Repeat this process until the remainder is 0. As soon as the remainder hits 0, turn all remaining bits to 0.

To see this, let's convert the decimal number 199 into binary. The first binary value equal to or smaller than 199 is 128, so we know it will fit on our 8-bit table. Since the decimal value 128 is smaller than or equal to our target, we will set the binary number to 1.

Another way some people like to test it is that 128 would fit into 199 (division). The result so far is shown in Table 3-9.

In step 2, we subtract 199 − 128 = 71. We now compare that remainder to the next column to the right and see that 64 is smaller than or equal to 71 (would fit into 71), so we put a 1 in the binary number row in that column. At this stage, we get what is shown in Table 3-10.

TABLE 3-9	Position value	128	64	32	16	8	4	2	1
	Binary number	1							
Converting 199 to Binary, Step 1	**Decimal equivalent**								

TABLE 3-10	Position value	128	64	32	16	8	4	2	1
Converting 199 to Binary, Step 2	Binary number	1	1						
	Decimal equivalent								

We repeat the process for each remainder until it zeroes out. Subtract $71 - 64 = 7$. Comparing the 7 to the next three columns (32, 16, and 8), we find them too large, so we set them to 0. At each column, if the decimal value is larger than the remainder, set it to 0 and repeat. If it is smaller or equal, set it to 1, subtract the value, and repeat. Going through each remaining position, we find

1. Subtracting $71 - 64 = 7$. Then 32, 16, and 8 are all larger than 7, so set them to 0.
2. Then 4 is smaller than (would fit in) 7, so set it to 1.
3. Subtract $7 - 4 = 3$. Then 2 is smaller than (would fit in) 3, so set it to 1.
4. Subtract $3 - 2 = 1$. Then 1 is equal to (would fit in) our remainder of 1, so set it to 1.
5. We have zeroed out. Any remaining columns to the right won't be used, so set them to 0.

The bottom row of our table lets us check our answer. The binary equivalent of decimal 199 equals 11000111 (as shown in Table 3-11).

Calculating the Number of Combinations

Another binary math skill is to calculate the number of possible combinations a specific number of binary digits provides. This will become important later in this chapter because this is how we calculate how many total addresses exist and how many subnets we can create. The basic formula is 2^n, where n is the number of bits used. This gives you the total number of possible combinations available. For example,

TABLE 3-11	Position	128	64	32	16	8	4	2	1	
Converting 199 to Binary Result	Binary	1	1	0	0	0	1	1	1	
	Answer	128	64	0	0	0	4	2	1	199

FIGURE 3-5

Bit patterns

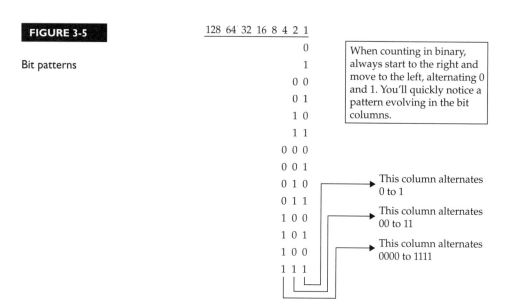

| 128 | 64 | 32 | 16 | 8 | 4 | 2 | 1 |

0

1

0 0

0 1

1 0

1 1

0 0 0

0 0 1

0 1 0

0 1 1

1 0 0

1 0 1

1 0 0

1 1 1

When counting in binary, always start to the right and move to the left, alternating 0 and 1. You'll quickly notice a pattern evolving in the bit columns.

This column alternates 0 to 1

This column alternates 00 to 11

This column alternates 0000 to 1111

suppose you have only one bit. The total number of combinations equals two (2^1): 0 or 1. Two bit positions provide four (2^2) different combinations: 00, 01, 10, and 11. Three positions provide eight (2^3) combinations: 000, 001, 010, 011, 100, 101, 110, and 111 and so on, doubling the number of possible combinations with each additional bit column added. If you list the combinations in columnar format, as shown in Figure 3-5, the pattern becomes fairly clear. Take a moment and study the pattern; with each additional bit the number of possible combinations doubles.

Note also that the first combination at each level is all 0s, the last is all 1s. That too is important, since device host addresses can't be made up of all 0s or all 1s. All 0s identifies the entire network and all 1s is the broadcast address for that network. So while 2^n gives us the number of possible addresses, $2^n - 2$ gives the number of usable addresses.

We are back to using exponents, powers of 2. Fortunately, there is a simple tool you can use that doesn't require doing anything more than multiplying by 2. The number of available combinations per bits available, up to 12, are listed in Table 3-12.

TABLE 3-12

Binary Combinations Table

Number of bits	1	2	3	4	5	6	7	8	9	10	11	12
Possible combinations	2	4	8	16	32	64	128	256	512	1024	2048	4096

FIGURE 3-6

Binary worksheet
tools

Binary Conversion Table								
Decimal	128	64	32	16	8	4	2	1
Binary								
Answer								

Binary Combinations Table	
Bits	Nets
1	2
2	4
3	8
4	16
5	32
6	64
7	128
8	256
9	512
10	1,024
11	2,048
12	4,096
13	8,192
14	16,384
15	32,768
16	65,536

While Table 3-12 conserves space in a book, it is not how to use it when designing networks or taking certification exams. In the upper-right corner of the scratch page, create two columns. In the first, number 1 to 16 (you can always add more if needed). In the second column next to the 1, enter a 2, because we know that one bit gives us two numbers (0 and 1). Then double that in the next row down and continue doing that for at least 8 to 10 rows. It is exactly the same as Table 3-12 but in a handier form to remember and use. It is out of the way, because it is strictly a lookup table. Let's call this our *binary combinations table*. This gives the total possible addresses and all you have to do is subtract 2 to get the number of usable addresses (not all 0s or 1s). Figure 3-6 shows a suggested worksheet to use when designing networks. Write this out on the top of one of the scratch sheets they give you at exam sites (takes about one minute max). It is important to work with both tables enough to be familiar with them. Mixing them up can create bad results.

Boolean AND Operations

Another binary skill is the recognition of Boolean operations in regard to IP addressing. Boolean operations are an integral part of computing in many ways. But in our world today for the CCENT exam, we are only interested in the *Boolean AND operation*.

As discussed at the beginning of the chapter, IP addresses, such as 10.1.2.3, identify a specific device on a network. A subnet mask, such as 255.0.0.0, defines the network that *all* device IP addresses on that network belong to. In our example

FIGURE 3-7

IP addresses: the
network bits

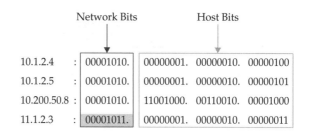

all devices in this network must have an IP address that begins with 10, and their
host portion must be unique on that network. This means the network bits will be
the same, but the host bits can't be the same. For example, 10.1.2.4, 10.1.2.5, and
10.200.50.8 are all on the same network, while a computer addressed 11.1.2.3 would
not be on the same network because the network bits don't match. See Figure 3-7 to
see that network bits are the same.

All Layer 3 devices, such as routers and computers, use the network mask to
determine the network portion of the IP address. The device does this by performing
a Boolean AND operation on the binary values of those two numbers. In a Boolean
AND, the two numbers, IP address and subnet mask in binary form, are the inputs,
and the output is literally a binary map of the network and host parts of the address.

The cool thing is that we are ANDing binary numbers only one digit at a time.
While it is called an AND operation, to us mere mortals, it is multiplication of two
single bits. We saw a minute ago that there are four combinations possible for two
bits: 00, 01, 10, and 11. A Boolean AND multiplies each pair, and all but 11 equal 0
in the result (11 equals 1). Table 3-13 shows the results.

As with anything binary, if you try hard enough, you can overcomplicate the
Boolean AND operation. Keep it as simple as possible in your head. In short, a
Boolean AND simply multiplies the values one bit at a time. Anything multiplied by
0 is 0, and 1 times 1 is always one. Just remember that Boolean AND simply means
multiply.

TABLE 3-13	Inputs		Output
Boolean AND	0	0	0
Operations	0	1	0
	1	0	0
	1	1	1

FIGURE 3-8

172.16.5.19   : 10101100. 00010000. 00000101. 00010011
255.255.255.0   : 11111111. 11111111. 11111111. 00000000
Boolean AND result : 10101100. 00010000. 00000101. 00000000

A Boolean AND
operation

This operation, 0×1,   This operation, 1×1,
came out to 0   came out to 1

To see why we are doing this, look at Figure 3-8. We are ANDing a subnet mask to an IP address. To perform this operation, you simply place the IP address bits above the subnet bits and perform a Boolean AND on each bit column. The result is the network ID.

EXERCISE 3-1

Binary Math Skills Exercises

These bonus exercises walk you through the basic binary to decimal, decimal to binary, and Boolean ANDing covered in this chapter. The step-by-step instructions are included in the PDF Lab Book.

CERTIFICATION OBJECTIVE 3.02

Subnet Essentials

As we saw earlier, the address classes A, B, and C with their default net masks create very large pools of host addresses, particularly in the A and B classes. Table 3-14 shows the three host classes with their default mask and number of hosts.

TABLE 3-14

IP Address Class
Ranges

Class	Leading Bits	First Octet Range	Hosts per Network	Default Subnet Mask
A	0	1–126	16,777,214	255.0.0.0
B	10	128–191	65,534	255.255.0.0
C	110	192–223	254	255.255.255.0

FIGURE 3-9

Classful
subnetting
example

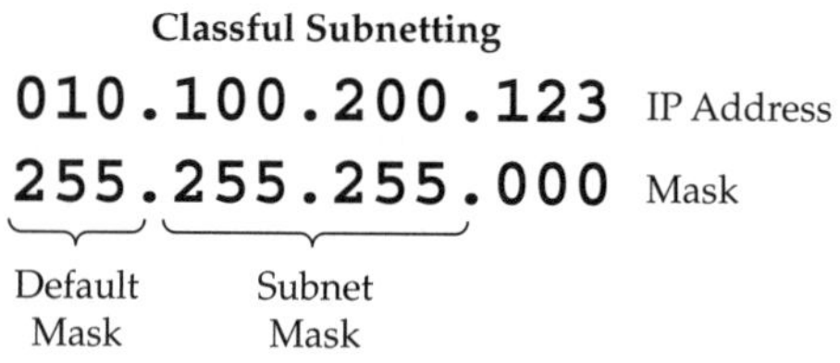

Classful Subnetting

010.100.200.123 IP Address

255.255.255.000 Mask

Default   Subnet
Mask   Mask

As technologies evolved, organizations wanted to segment these large pools into separate networks and then be able to route within those networks. A subnet is nothing more than a smaller portion of a larger address space treated as its own separate network. They came up with a subnetting process that basically amounted to extending the default masks to identify the new subnet. This is called *classful subnetting,* and an example is shown in Figure 3-9 where the Class A 10 network is subnetted to allow network segments with 254 hosts, like a Class C network.

Early routing protocols, the methods used by routers to share routing table information, such as RIPv1 and IGRP, did not share subnet information with IP addresses because they assumed the class default mask. These routing protocols could be manipulated to support these classful subnets with one severe limitation: all subnets had to be the same size in the domain. This was better than before, but still wasteful because subnets had to be based on the largest subnet (most hosts) required.

In 1993, two new standards, Classless Inter-Domain Routing (CIDR) and Variable Length Subnet Masks (VLSM), plus new routing protocols that supported them replaced the old classful system. We now use classless subnetting, which treats all addresses as if they have a single mask, the subnet mask, as shown in Figure 3-10, and a network can have subnets of different sizes as needed.

While the results look the same, the new methods greatly improve efficiency in network design and in routing, which are covered in Part III of this book. For now, let's look at what subnetting is and how we do it.

FIGURE 3-10

Classless
subnetting
example

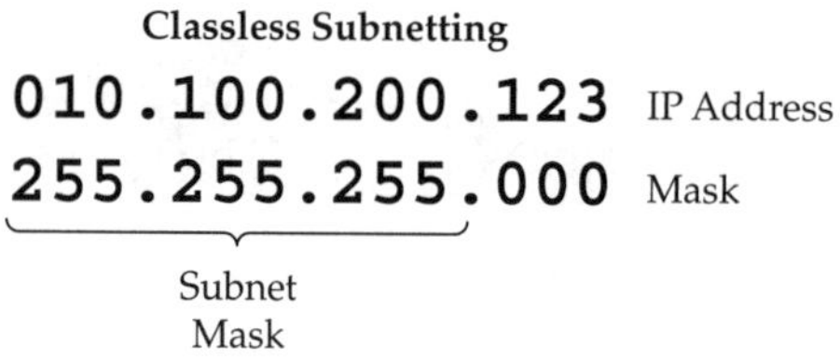

Classless Subnetting

010.100.200.123 IP Address

255.255.255.000 Mask

Subnet
Mask

exam

ⓦatch *The CCENT exam and most networks now use the new protocols and methods, so that is what we will focus on, but the earlier exam and many Internet documents on subnetting still cover classful subnetting, so you should recognize the terms. While the classes are basically irrelevant, they are still referred to, discussed, and even used as units of measurement, as in "I need a couple Class C subnets."*

Defining Subnets

As covered earlier, an IP address is made up of two parts: the network portion and the host portion. Layer 3 devices such as routers use the subnet mask to be able to identify the network portion so they can accept or forward a packet. We also saw that a subnet mask of 255.255.255.0 is made up of 24 1s, 3 octets, and 8 bits of 0s. It is important to remember that the mask starts as 1s, remains all 1s to the end of the network portion, and then changes to 0s clear to the end. There are no exceptions.

Since a router is only interested in the network portion of an address for forwarding, when it examines a subnet mask and an IP address, it stops counting bits as soon as it sees the first 0. It knows the remaining bits are 0s.

Since subnet masks are always a series of 1s from left to right, the decimals corresponding to the bit pattern are unique. The values in Table 3-15 are the *only* values that can possibly be displayed as part of a subnet mask. Any other number would have to have a 0 in amongst the 1s, and that can't happen.

TABLE 3-15	Subnet Decimal Value	Bit Alignment
Subnet Mask Octet Values	0	00000000
	128	10000000
	192	11000000
	224	11100000
	240	11110000
	248	11111000
	252	11111100
	254	11111110
	255	11111111

This means if you have a subnet mask like 255.255.255.192 or 255.255.224.0, you only need to convert the one octet. The rest are either eight 1s or eight 0s. Our two examples would convert to binary as follows:

255.255.255.192 = 11111111.11111111.11111111.11000000
255.255.224.0 = 11111111.11111111.11100000.00000000

e x a m

ⓦ a t c h *Remember that the subnet mask starts as 1s, remains all 1s to the end of the network portion, and then changes to 0s clear to the end—no exceptions. Table 3-15 is very useful, and you will know it by heart as you work more with subnetting. Not only will you see questions on identifying useable subnet masks, but knowing the bit values will allow you to quickly answer questions. Time is your biggest enemy on the exam, and memorizing these values gives you an advantage. Remember that the binary conversion table we used earlier can be used to figure these out, if you have doubts or get confused.*

CIDR Notation (Prefix Notation)

The CIDR standard introduced a method of subnetting, and something called super-netting, classful addresses that were supported by some routing protocols. VLSM has replaced that, and CIDR might be ignored completely except that it introduced an additional way of labeling subnets called CIDR notation, or prefix notation, that is also used in VLSM. It is a syntax that basically replaces the subnet mask by adding a slash character and the number of bits in the network identifier, now called a routing prefix. For example, 192.168.1.1 with a mask of 255.255.255.0 becomes 192.168.1.1/24.

This allows large ISPs to be assigned very large blocks of addresses, such as 3.0.0.0/10, and they can distribute them out in networks as small as 3.0.0.4/30 with two host addresses for serial links. But it doesn't mean subnet masks are going away; many devices still require that they be entered in the traditional form. It means that you have to be able to recognize both forms and be able to quickly and efficiently convert back and forth.

A prefix of /26 is equivalent to 255.255.255.192: the first three octets combined with the first 2 bits of the fourth octet translate to the subnet mask listed. Whether listed as a subnet mask or as a prefix, both indicate the same thing: the number of bits identifies the network portion of the address. Examples of prefix listings and subnet mask comparisons are shown in Table 3-16. Note that only one octet is not all 1s (255) or all 0s (0).

TABLE 3-16	Subnet Mask	Prefix
	255.0.0.0	/8 (old A)
Subnet Mask	255.128.0.0	/9
and Prefix	255.255.0.0	/16 (old B)
Comparison	255.255.192.0	/18
	255.255.240.0	/20
	255.255.255.0	/24 (old C)
	255.255.255.192	/26
	255.255.255.252	/30

Converting Between Prefix Notation and Subnet Masks

Let's take a moment to see how our conversion table can help us move back and forth between these two ways of defining the subnet mask. Because we are working with just one octet, the others are all 1s (255s) or all 0s (0). We can use an 8-bit binary conversion table as shown in Table 3-17.

Prefix to Subnet Mask   If we have a /27 prefix, we know that three octets is 24, so we need 3 bits more. We put them in the first three locations on the left, then we need only to add 128 + 64 + 32 = 224 to know that our mask is 255.255.255.224.

Position	128	64	32	16	8	4	2	1
Binary	1	1	1					
Answer	128	64	32					

If we have a /21 prefix, we know that two octets is 16, so we need 5 bits more. We put them in the first five locations on the left, then we need only to add 128 + 64 + 32 + 16 + 8 = 248 to know then that our mask is 255.255.248.0.

Position	128	64	32	16	8	4	2	1
Binary	1	1	1	1	1			
Answer	128	64	32	16	8			

TABLE 3-17	Position	128	64	32	16	8	4	2	1
	Binary								
8-Bit Binary	Answer								
Conversion Table									

Subnet Mask to Prefix   If we have a subnet mask 255.255.252.0, we can ignore the first, second, and fourth octets, as we know they are all 1s or all 0s. We do our decimal to binary conversion and we will get 11111110. We know the first two octets equal 16, so then 16 + 7 = 23 bits or /23. This conversion is easy because you just keep adding 1s until you hit 252.

Position	128	64	32	16	8	4	2	1
Binary	1	1	1	1	1	1	1	
Answer	128	64	32	16	8	4	2	

If we have a subnet mask 255.224.0.0, we can ignore the first, third, and fourth octets, as we know they are all 1s or all 0s. We do our decimal to binary conversion and we will get 11100000. We know the first octet is equal to 8, so then 8 + 3 = 11 bits or /11.

Position	128	64	32	16	8	4	2	1
Binary	1	1	1					
Answer	128	64	32					

Subnet Address Basics

You may recall when we were discussing classful networks we mentioned that the first address where the host portion is all 0s is the network ID, and the last one where the host portion is all 1s is the broadcast address for that network. That is why we say we lose two addresses from the total available for hosts. The good news is that subnets work exactly the same way. In Figure 3-11 we revisit our earlier example (Figure 3-1) where we looked at the binary and decimal equivalents for private address host 192.168.001.123/24 in the older Class C classful networks. We added a vertical line to show where the network portion ends.

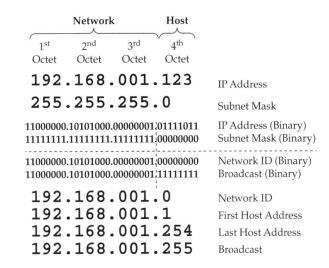

FIGURE 3-11

Network
addresses,
mask, ID, and
broadcast for
192.168.1.123/24

Notice that below the line we added the first address (all 0s in the host network ID), the last (all 1s in the host broadcast), and then we calculated their decimal equivalents (0 and 255). Since everything in between are usable host addresses, we know that they are 1 to 254. While not a rule, many organizations standardize on reserving the first host address for the router interface, which means we can then assign 2 to 254 to hosts. We now know that 192.168.1.123 is a host address in that network since it falls between 1 and 254.

What if we had subnetted using a 26-bit mask instead? Using our binary conversion table (see Table 3-18), we see that 2 bits means our final octet in the subnet mask would be 192.

We also know what our first 26 bits look like since the network bits must be exactly the same for all addresses in a subnet, just like in a network. In Figure 3-12, we can use that information below the line to calculate the first address (all 0s in the host subnet ID), the last (all 1s in the host subnet broadcast). Then we can use the binary conversion table to calculate their decimal equivalents (64 and 127). Since everything in between are usable host addresses, we know that they are 65 to 126.

Position	128	64	32	16	8	4	2	1
Binary	1	1	0	0	0	0	0	0
Answer	128	64						

TABLE 3-18

Binary
Conversion
Table for 2 Bits
(255.255.255.192)

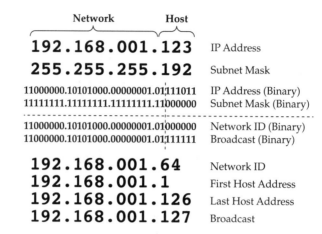

FIGURE 3-12

Network
addresses,
mask, ID, and
broadcast for
192.168.1.123/26

We now know that 192.168.001.123 is a host address in that network since it falls between 65 and 126. We could do this with any prefix mask between 25 and 31 and a variation of it for the other octets, which we will look at in a moment.

Let's try subnetting using a 31-bit mask instead. Using our binary conversion table (see Table 3-19), we see that 31 bits means our final octet in the subnet mask would be 254.

We also know what our first 31 bits look like, so in Figure 3-13, we used that information below the line to calculate the first address (all 0s in the host subnet ID) and the last (all 1s in the host broadcast). Then we can use the binary conversion table to calculate their decimal equivalents (122 and 123). Note that this leaves us with no useable addresses for hosts, so this is not a valid subnet. The smallest subnet you can have is /30 or 252 in the fourth octet, which yields two host addresses. We also now know that 192.168.001.123 isn't a valid host address even if the network had been OK since it is the broadcast address.

TABLE 3-19

Binary
Conversion
Table for 31 Bits
(255.255.255.254)

Position	128	64	32	16	8	4	2	1
Binary	1	1	1	1	1	1	1	0
Answer	128	64	32	16	8	4	2	

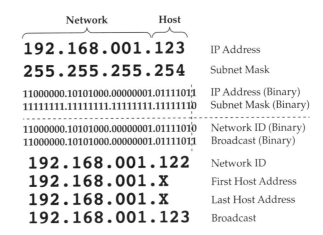

FIGURE 3-13

Network addresses, mask, ID and broadcast for 192.168.1.123/31

Let's do one more subnetting using a 23-bit mask instead. We know that the 23rd bit is in the 3rd octet. Using our binary conversion table (see Table 3-20), we see that 23 bits looks exactly like our last exercise but in the third octet. This means our third octet in the subnet mask would be 254 and the full subnet mask will be 255.255.254.0.

We also know what our first 23 bits, the network portion, looks like, so in Figure 3-14, we used that information below the line to calculate the first address (all 0s in the host subnet ID) and the last (all 1s in the host broadcast). Then we can use the binary conversion table to calculate their decimal equivalents (192.168.0.0 and 192.168.1.255). This gives us 512 total addresses and 510 host addresses. Note it is the equivalent of two Class C networks combined into one. Since everything in between are usable host addresses, we know that they are 192.168.0.1 to 192.168.1.254. We also know that 192.168.001.123 is a host address in that network since it falls in the range.

TABLE 3-20

Binary Conversion Table for 23 Bits (255.255.254.0)

Position	128	64	32	16	8	4	2	1
Binary	1	1	1	1	1	1	1	0
Answer	128	64	32	16	8	4	2	

FIGURE 3-14

Network addresses, mask, ID, and broadcast for 192.168.1.123/23

	Network	Host	

192.168.001.123   IP Address
255.255.254.0   Subnet Mask

11000000.10101000.00000001.01111011   IP Address (Binary)
11111111.11111111.11111110.00000000   Subnet Mask (Binary)

11000000.10101000.00000000.00000000   Network ID (Binary)
11000000.10101000.00000001.11111011   Broadcast (Binary)

192.168.000.0   Network ID
192.168.000.1   First Host Address
192.168.001.254   Last Host Address
192.168.001.255   Broadcast

Subnet Increments

We just used the binary method to figure out where our subnet began and ended, beginning with the subnet ID and ending with the subnet broadcast. That gives us the total number of addresses in our subnet. That number minus 2 is the number of useable host addresses, subtracting out the subnet ID (all 0s host portion) and the broadcast (all 1s host portion). That number of *total addresses* is also the increment, which can be useful in designing our network. In our second example (Figure 3-12), 192.168.1.123/26, our addresses ran from 192.168.1.64 to 127 or 64 total addresses. Don't get confused by 127 − 64 = 63; it is 64 because both 127 and 64 are included.

This means that if we started at the 192.168.1.0 address as our first subnet, we can quickly calculate the subnet IDs since each one is 64 larger than the last one. Since the broadcast is 1 less than the next subnet ID, we can quickly calculate those. The rest of the calculations follow the same pattern and are shown in Table 3-21.

Take a moment and look over the table until you see the relationships. Each row is 64, the increment, larger than the one above. The first host is 1 larger than the

TABLE 3-21	Subnet	Subnet ID	First Useable Host	Last Useable Host	Broadcast
192.168.1.0 Broken into Four Subnets of 64 Addresses	1st	192.168.1.0	192.168.1.1	192.168.1.62	192.168.1.63
	2nd	192.168.1.64	192.168.1.65	192.168.1.126	192.168.1.127
	3rd	192.168.1.128	192.168.1.129	192.168.1.190	192.168.1.191
	4th	192.168.1.192	192.168.1.193	192.168.1.254	192.168.1.255

subnet ID; the last host is the broadcast minus 1. The broadcast is the next subnet ID minus 1. Notice that the first subnet ID and the last broadcast are the network ID and broadcast of our original network 192.168.1.0/24 (see Figure 3-11).

The only things you have to remember are

1. Subnets can't ever overlap. A new one starts right after the last one's broadcast.
2. Subnets can't start just anywhere. They must start on a subnet boundary—host bits all 0s—and must end with host bits all 1s. You can calculate them like we did in Figure 3-11 to Figure 3-14 using the binary, or you can start with the first address in the original network and add the increments as we did in Table 3-21. The next section will show you an easy way to do that.

Magic Number: Using Our Binary Conversion Table

The *magic number*, really the increment number, refers to the position value where your prefix mask or subnet mask ends. Each subnet created with that mask will be a multiple, or increment, of that number, greatly simplifying the time needed to decode information. Using our last example with our binary conversion table (used with Figure 3-12 for 192.168.1.123/26), we see that 2 bits in the fourth octet ends in the 64 column as shown in Table 3-22. That is the magic number or increment value. Therefore, all subnets will be a multiple of 64: 0, 64, 128, 192.

TABLE 3-22	Position	128	64	32	16	8	4	2	1
Binary Conversion Table for 2 Bits (255.255.255.192)	Binary	1	1	0	0	0	0	0	0
	Answer	128	64						

TABLE 3-23	Subnet ID	First Address	Last Address	Broadcast Address
A Magic Number Sample for 192.168.1.0/30	192.168.1.0	192.168.1.1	192.168.1.2	192.168.1.3
	192.168.1.4	192.168.1.5	192.168.1.6	192.168.1.7
	192.168.1.8	192.168.1.9	192.168.1.10	192.168.1.11
	192.168.1.12	192.168.1.13	192.168.1.14	192.168.1.15
	...	...	...	...
	192.168.1.252	192.168.1.253	192.168.1.254	192.168.1.255

This shortcut works no matter where the prefix ends. Suppose, for instance, your prefix is /30 or your subnet mask number is 255.255.255.252. Using our binary conversion table we see that the prefix ends in the 4 column—/30 minus 24 (first three octets) means we need 6 bits in the fourth octet. All subnets created using this mask will be multiples of 4: 0, 4, 8, 12, 16, and so on.

exam
watch *The magic number is only a tip if it helps you on the exam. If this, or any other tip, doesn't help, then stick with the bits—they never lie. Remember, all subnets created using the same prefix mask will be a multiple of the magic number.*

Once we have the magic number, calculating the broadcast address and useable host address range follows the same steps we used for Table 3-21. Assuming we are using the same private address 192.168.1.0/24 subnetted with a prefix /30 or subnet mask of 255.255.255.252, Table 3-23 shows an abbreviated result. Since our increment is 4, we could create 64 subnets (256/4). We've included the first four and the last one.

Prefix Length vs. Number of Hosts

Let's look at the relationship of prefix bits to total available addresses and number of subnets. In Table 3-24 we see our binary conversion table with 10 bits showing. Let's start by looking at the column labeled /24. It is the same as our old Class C or the private address 192.168.0.0/24. As we saw in the last exercise, the position row tells us there are 256 available addresses with a /24 mask. We are assuming we have been given a private Class C to subnet. The next row has been changed to show only the host addresses, having subtracted 2 for the net ID and broadcast. So we have a single network with 256 addresses to serve up to 254 hosts.

TABLE 3-24	Bits	/23	/24	/25	/26	/27	/28	/29	/30	/31	/32
Modified Binary Conversion Table	Position	512	256	128	64	32	16	8	4	2	1
	Hosts (–2)		254	126	62	30	14	6	2	0	0
	Subnets			2	4	8	16	32	64	128	256

If we increase the prefix by 1 bit, we split the addresses in two and now have two subnets, one for 0 and one for 1 in that position. We also know that the increment is 128 so our subnets are 0 to 127 and 128 to 255. *Each bit we add to the right doubles the number of subnets but halves the total addresses per subnet*, from which we subtract 2 to get the number of host addresses. If we used a /27, we could have 8 subnets, each with 32 addresses for 30 hosts. The subnets would be in increments of 32 or 0–31, 32–63, 64–95, 96–127...224–255.

Note our table confirms what we saw earlier, that we can't create subnets with a prefix longer than /30 because it leaves no host addresses.

Before moving on, it is important to realize you just can't make subnets any size or anywhere that you want. They must be in the increments you saw earlier for the fourth octet, and they must start and end on a subnet boundary, where the host bits range from all 0s to all 1s. So if you need 3 subnets with 50 host addresses each, we see that we would have to use prefix /26, with 64 addresses for 62 hosts. Anything longer than /26 wouldn't give us enough addresses; anything shorter would unnecessarily waste addresses. While we could use any of the 4 subnet ranges, it makes sense to be orderly and use 0–63, 64–127, 128–191. That leaves 192–255 for future use in that size or it could be subnetted down further.

Planning Your Network

When breaking up a pool of addresses to subnet a network, your requirements can come in three forms:

- You need a certain number of subnets.
- You need a certain number of hosts per subnet.
- A combination of both—the most common.

In the last section we saw an example of subnetting based on needing 50 addresses per subnet. We were able to use our binary conversion table, but that doesn't really work for figuring a certain number of subnets.

A more useful table is the binary combinations table we introduced back in Figure 3-6, which is shown in Figure 3-15 extended out to 24 bits. If you recall, the first column is the number of bits. Usually 1 to 12 is plenty—you can always extend it. The second column is the total subnets or total hosts following the same pattern we just saw. One bit gives us two subnets, one each for 0 and 1. Each row below is twice the one above; just multiply by 2.

If we need seven subnets, the table tells us that we will need 3 bits. Fifteen subnets would require 4 bits. With hosts we have to remember to subtract the 2; the table gives us total host addresses. So 100 hosts would require 7 bits.

Assuming you are assigned a pool of addresses to work with that is large enough to meet your subnetting need, you need to remember two things:

1. Subnet bits go left to right from the prefix mask you are given. If you are given a /24 pool and you need 7 subnets, it requires 4 bits or /28.

2. Host bits always go right to left starting at the right end (bit 32). If you are given a /24 pool and you need 50 hosts or 6 bits, that means your prefix will be /26 (32-6).

FIGURE 3-15

Binary combinations table to 24 bits

Binary Combinations	
Bits	Nets (Hosts -2)
1	2
2	4
3	8
4	16
5	32
6	64
7	128
8	256
9	512
10	1,024
11	2,048
12	4,096
13	8,192
14	16,384
15	32,768
16	65,536
17	131,072
18	262,144
19	524,288
20	1,048,576
21	2,097,152
22	4,194,304
23	8,388,608
24	16,777,216

Subnet Mask Creation Steps

Creating subnets basically amounts to how many subnets you need, how many host addresses in each subnet, and what pool of addresses you have to get them out of.

Unfortunately, as we've seen, it isn't quite as simple as splitting up a bag of doughnuts, but it needn't be difficult if we follow a plan. Two important things to remember:

exam
watch *You really need to know how these two tables work and how to quickly build them for the exam so that you can quickly create subnets, verify that various subnet/host combinations work, or whether a host is a part of a certain subnet.*

■ There can be no overlap in any of the address pools (subnets).

■ Always start with the largest subnet and work to the smallest. After that you use the skills you have already acquired.

Here are five simple steps to follow to create your subnets:

1. Figure out how many host subnets you need and rank them largest to smallest.
2. Figure out how many host bits will be needed for the largest network.
3. Choose the subnet for the largest network.
4. Note the address range to use so you don't overlap later.
5. Repeat steps 2–4 for the next largest subnet until done.

Subnet Example 1: Simple

Looking at Figure 3-16 as a simple example to start with, we see that we need three host subnets with 50, 60, and 40 host addresses. Let's assume that we have been given the 192.168.0.0/24 private address pool to work with. We rank our subnets, and when we look on our binary combinations table for 60 hosts, we see that all three subnets are going to require 6 bits because they each fall between 31 and 62. Since our /24 prefix gives us 8 bits to work with, that means our prefix mask will be /26 or /24 + (8 − 6). We also know that 2 bits will give us four of these subnets, even though we only need three now. The fourth one will be held for future use. Our result will look like Table 3-25.

	Subnet	Subnet ID	First Host	Last Host	Broadcast
TABLE 3-25					
Simple Subnet Example	B: 60 hosts	192.168.0.0	192.168.0.1	192.168.0.62	192.168.0.63
	A: 50 hosts	192.168.0.64	192.168.0.65	192.168.0.126	192.168.0.127
	C: 40 hosts	192.168.0.128	192.168.0.129	192.168.0.190	192.168.0.191
	Unused	192.168.0.192			192.168.0.255

FIGURE 3-16

Simple subnetting example

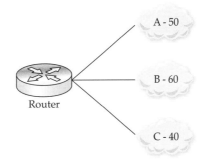

FIGURE 3-17

More complex
subnetting
example

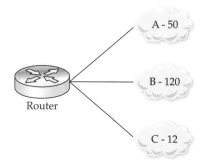

Subnet Example 2: More Complex

Figure 3-17 shows a slightly more common and complex example to work with. We see that we need three host subnets with 50, 120, and 12 host addresses. Let's assume that we have been given the 192.168.1.0/24 private address pool to work with. We rank our subnets, and when we look on our binary combinations table for 120 hosts, we see that we are going to need 7 bits. Since our /24 prefix gives us 8 bits to work with, that means our first prefix mask will be /25 or /24 + (8 − 7). We can add our increment, 128, to get our next subnet ID (0 + 128) = 128, and from that we can complete the calculations for our subnet. The first data row in Table 3-26 shows our result.

We repeat that process for the second subnet, and when we look on our binary combinations table for 50 hosts, we see that we will need 6 bits because it falls between 31 and 62. Our prefix mask will be /26 or /24 + (8 − 6). We start at the next address remaining in our address pool to make sure we don't overlap the first subnet. We can add our increment, 64, to get our next subnet ID (128 + 64) = 192, and from that we can complete the calculations for our subnet. The second data row in Table 3-26 shows our result.

Subnet	Mask	Subnet ID	First Host	Last Host	Broadcast
B: 120 hosts	/25	192.168.1.0	192.168.1.1	192.168.1.126	192.168.1.127
A: 50 hosts	/26	192.168.1.128	192.168.1.129	192.168.1.190	192.168.1.191
C: 12 hosts	/28	192.168.1.192	192.168.1.193	192.168.1.210	192.168.1.211
Unused		192.168.1.212			192.168.1.255

We repeat that process for the third subnet, and when we look on our binary combinations table for 12 hosts, we see that we will need 4 bits because it falls between 9 and 15. Our prefix mask will be /28 or /24 + (8 – 4). We start at the next address remaining in our address pool to make sure we don't overlap the first subnet. We can add our increment, 16, to get our next subnet ID (192 + 16) = 212, and from that we can complete the calculations for our subnet. The third data row in Table 3-26 shows our result. The fourth one will be held for future use.

Decoding Subnet Information

Both on the exam and on the job, one of the most important skills a person needs to master is decoding information from an IP address or network range and a subnet mask pair. The relevant subnet information includes the subnet ID, the broadcast address, and the useable host range, as shown in Table 3-27.

For example, on the exam, several questions will provide an IP address and subnet mask and ask which addresses can be assigned to a system on the same network as the original system. We are going to look at two ways this can be figured. First let's look at the binary method, which involves four very simple steps:

1. Perform a Boolean AND between the address and subnet mask to determine the subnet ID the address belongs to.
2. Determine the broadcast address by turning all host bits to 1s.
3. Determine the first useable address by using the first available combination of host bits (rightmost bit turned on, all other bits turned off).
4. Determine the last useable address by using the last available combination of host bits (rightmost bit turned off, all others turned on).

TABLE 3-27		**Bit Values**	**Decimal Value**
Subnet Information Table	Subnet ID		
	First useable address		
	Last useable address		
	Broadcast address		

As with the subnet mask creation steps, decoding subnet information is best described with a scenario. Suppose you are given the IP address 199.58.7.37 and a subnet mask of 255.255.255.240 or prefix /28. In step 1, you simply perform a Boolean AND to determine the subnet ID the address is on. In this case, the answer is:

```
199.58.7.37          : 11000111. 00111010. 00000111. 0010 | 0101
255.255.255.240      : 11111111. 11111111. 11111111. 1111 | 0000
Boolean AND result : 11000111. 00111010. 00000111. 0010 | 0000
                                                      ↑           ↑
                                                 Network Bits   Host Bits
```

Notice there are 4 host bits left in the subnet. Manipulating these bits allows us to answer the remaining portions of the question:

```
Subnet ID             : 11000111. 00111010. 00000111. 0010 | 0000
First useable address : 11000111. 00111010. 00000111. 0010 | 0001
Last useable address  : 11000111. 00111010. 00000111. 0010 | 1110
Broadcast address     : 11000111. 00111010. 00000111. 0010 | 1111
                                                        ↑            ↑
                                                  Network Bits:   Host Bits:
                                             Must remain the same  Change for
                                                for each entry     each entry
```

Filling the information in, the chart looks like Table 3-28.

TABLE 3-28		Bit Values	Decimal Value
Decoded Subnet Information	Subnet ID	11000111. 00111010. 00000111. 0010 0000	199.58.7.32
	First Useable Address	11000111. 00111010. 00000111. 0010 0001	199.58.7.33
	Last Useable Address	11000111. 00111010. 00000111. 0010 1110	199.58.7.46
	Broadcast Address	11000111. 00111010. 00000111. 0010 1111	199.58.7.47

TABLE 3-29	Position	128	64	32	16	8	4	2	1
Binary Conversion Table for 240 or /18	Binary	1	1	1	1				
	Answer	128	64	32	16				

The second approach for IP address 199.58.7.37 and a subnet mask of 255.255.255.240 or prefix /28 involves using our binary conversion table to convert the last octet of our subnet mask 255.255.255.240, the only one that isn't all 0s or 1s. It is actually easier if we are given a prefix mask /28 because we can see where the network ends as you can see in Table 3-29.

If you recall our magic number discussion, you know that our increment is 16. This means we can calculate the subnet IDs at least up to the address we were given: 0, 16, 32, 48... We know that that 37 falls between 32 and 48. Using our basic math skills from earlier, we know that the first host address is 199.58.7.33, the last host is 199.58.7.46, and the broadcast is 199.58.7.47. You can see that the result is exactly the same either way.

EXERCISE 3-2

Media

Subnetting Exercises

These bonus exercises walk you through the basic subnetting covered in this chapter. The step-by-step instructions are included in the PDF Lab Book.

INSIDE THE EXAM

IPv4 Addressing

You must be very well versed in IP address construction for the exam. Remember that even though they are displayed in dotted decimal format, IP addresses are actually 32 bits, divided into four octets and separated by dots. Each octet can contain from 0 to 255 for 256 values. IP addresses have two subsections—the network portion and the host portion. If all host bits are set to 0s, the address shows the network ID. If all host bits are set to 1s, the address is the broadcast address for the subnet. Any combination of host bits in between is a valid address for the network. Several questions will concentrate on these three options.

Be familiar with classful addressing, including how many octets are available on each class for host addresses, and be prepared to identify and use each class's private address range. Know the difference between public and private addresses, as well as the reserved addresses.

Binary Numbers

Binary math is fairly easy, but it can take time and practice to get comfortable with it. The best way to prepare for the exam is to practice binary conversion as much as possible, and simply memorize common combinations and tips. Be sure you know the position (decimal) values for each position in an octet, remembering that every bit added doubles the total amount of combinations (for example, adding a ninth bit moves the combinations from 256 to a total of 512). Practice manipulating bits up to an octet range. If you convert decimal 1 to 7 to "see" the bits, the pattern will become evident, with 1s moving from right to left in a repeating pattern.

Remember that in converting subnet masks you only need to convert the one that isn't 0 (all 0s) or 255 (all 1s).

Make sure that you understand Boolean ANDing and that if converted to binary, all hosts will have exactly the same binary bits in the network ID.

Know how to quickly build and use both the binary conversion and binary combinations tables. Make sure you really understand the difference between them and when to use each. This can save valuable time on the exam.

Subnet Essentials

Remember what a subnet mask is designed to do: define the network portion of an IP address through the Boolean AND process. The series of 1s from left to right can only create a specific range of numbers: 0, 128, 192, 224, 240, 248, 252, 254, or 255. Also, remember the default subnet masks for Class A, B, and C are 255.0.0.0, 255.255.0.0, and 255.255.255.0, respectively.

INSIDE THE EXAM

Remember that CIDR or prefix notation, such as /24, is the same thing as a subnet mask, but is no longer bound to the old classful system.

Practice creating and applying subnet masks, as well as decoding relevant information from an IP address and subnet pair or prefix. This cannot be stressed enough: if you are not very comfortable with subnetting, you simply will not pass the exam. Review this section and practice as much as possible for the exam. *You cannot practice enough on this topic.*

Remember, if the scenario calls for creating subnets, the formula is simple: 2^n greater than or equal to the number you need, where n is the number of bits. If the scenario calls for supporting hosts, the formula used to determine the number of bits you need is $2^n - 2$ greater than or equal to the number you need, where n is the number of bits. Use your binary combinations table for this if you are not comfortable with powers of 2. Review and know the tables in the subnetting section, and practice subnetting often before challenging the exam.

The exam will have several questions that require applying a subnet mask to a scenario. Practice decoding relevant information— subnet ID, the broadcast address, and the useable host range—from IP address range and subnet mask pairs. You can perform a Boolean AND between the address and subnet mask to determine the subnet ID the address belongs to; determine the broadcast address by turning all host bits to 1s; determine the first useable address by using the first available combination of host bits (rightmost bit turned on; all other bits turned off); determine the last useable address by using the last available combination of host bits (rightmost bit turned off; all others turned on). The magic number and the binary conversion table can also be used for this and are probably quicker.

Make sure that you understand that CIDR replaces the old class system of IP address allocation to assign and use only the IP addresses needed. Understand CIDR notation, or prefix notation, so that you can work with either that or subnet masks, as well as move back and forth between them.

VLSM is subnetting a subnet within your IP network design or plan. Two important things to remember: There can be no overlap in any of the address pools (subnets). Always start with the largest subnet, both calculating it and assigning it addresses. Remember that the magic number is your increment; adding it will give you the start of your next subnet, and minus 1 becomes your broadcast.

CERTIFICATION SUMMARY

IP addressing is probably one of the most tested areas of study on the exam. Familiarity with the concepts in this chapter is essential to success on the exam. Remember and study IP address construction: displayed in dotted decimal format, IP addresses are actually 32 bits, divided into octets and separated by dots. Each octet can be arranged to display numbers from 0 to 255. IP addresses have two subsections—the network portion and the host portion. If all host bits are set to 0s, the address shows the network ID. If all host bits are set to 1s, the address is the broadcast address for the subnet. Any combination of host bits in between is a valid address for the network. Several questions will concentrate on these three options.

The CCENT exam will require you to identify IP address classes, as well as the private ranges within each class. Class A addresses begin with 1 to 126, and each network can host over 16 million addresses. Class A addresses have a default subnet mask of 255.0.0.0, and the private address range is 10.0.0.0. Class B addresses begin with 128 to 191, and each network can host over 65,000 addresses. Class B addresses have a default subnet mask of 255.255.0.0, and the private address range is 172.16–31.0.0. Class C addresses begin with 192 to 223, and each network can host 254 addresses. Class C addresses have a default subnet mask of 255.255.255.0, and the private address range is 192.168.0 to 255.0. This information is in Table 3-1.

Technologies to combat IP address depletion include subnetting, NAT, CIDR, and IPv6. Subnetting allows an administrator to borrow host bits to create smaller networks (called subnets) out of one larger address range. Classful refers to the treatment of every IP address within the class system discussed earlier. In other words, only the default subnet masks and classes are used. Classless refers to the use of subnetting to define network IDs. Routing protocols that are considered to be classful do not recognize subnets, while those that are classless can recognize subnetting.

You should be very familiar with fundamentals regarding private addressing: devices with private IP addresses cannot connect directly to the Internet; computers outside the local network cannot connect directly to a device with a private IP; multiple businesses can use the same private IP address range; and private addressing and NAT provide additional security for hosts on your network.

Basic binary math skills are essential to your success. Make sure you have plenty of practice converting from binary to decimal and from decimal to binary—especially within an octet (8-bit) range. Additionally, be sure you understand the number of combinations you can achieve given a specific number of bits (2^n), as well as how bits are manipulated to achieve these combinations. Start with the rightmost bit turned off, then on for the first two combinations (0 and 1), and repeat with each position to the left (00, 01, 10, 11, for example).

Boolean AND operations use two inputs, the IP address and subnet mask, basically multiplying the bits one pair at a time. A 1 results when both inputs are also 1, otherwise anything multiplied by 0 is a 0. Boolean ANDing is used by routers and hosts to determine the network portion of an IP address. If any of the bits in the network portion don't match, the address is for a different subnet.

The subnet mask is a 32-bit binary number, made up of a series of consecutive 1s from left to right. Once the mask switches to 0s, all remaining digits must be 0s. It is used to determine which portion of an IP address belongs to the network. The only decimal numbers that can possibly be part of a subnet mask are 0, 128, 192, 224, 240, 248, 252, 254, and 255. The default subnet masks for Class A, B, and C are 255.0.0.0, 255.255.0.0, and 255.255.255.0, respectively.

Here are five simple steps to follow to create your subnets:

1. Figure out how many host subnets you need and rank them largest to smallest.
2. Figure out how many host bits will be needed for the largest network.
3. Choose the subnet mask for the largest network.
4. Note the address range to use so you don't overlap later.
5. Repeat steps 2–4 for the next largest subnet until done.

In step 2, if the scenario calls for creating a certain number of subnets, the formula is simple: 2^n greater than or equal to the number you need, where n is the number of bits. If the scenario calls for supporting hosts, the formula used to determine the number of bits you need is $2^n - 2$ greater than or equal to the number you need, where n is the number of bits. Use your binary combinations table for this if you are not comfortable with powers of 2. Practice subnetting often before taking the exam.

Many CCENT questions and scenarios will be based on decoding information from an IP address or network range and a subnet mask pair. The relevant subnet information includes the subnet ID, the broadcast address, and the useable host range. Be prepared to decode information to compare to alternatives—for example, to determine whether a given IP address belongs to the same subnet as another host. The four steps to decode the relevant information are

1. Perform a Boolean AND between the address and subnet mask to determine the subnet ID the address belongs to.
2. Determine the broadcast address by turning all host bits to 1s.

3. Determine the first useable address by using the first available combination of host bits (rightmost bit turned on; all other bits turned off).

4. Determine the last useable address by using the last available combination of host bits (rightmost bit turned off; all others turned on).

Remember that using the binary conversion table and the magic number (increment) process will give you this as well and quicker.

Don't forget to take advantage of the easy subnet numbers (0 and 255) and the magic number when subnetting.

CIDR replaces the old class system of IP address allocation and provides two important advantages. The first is the ability to acquire and use only the amount of IP addresses needed, and the second is to represent multiple subnets with a single route advertisement. CIDR notation, or prefix notation, is a syntax that basically replaces the subnet mask by adding a slash character and the number of bits in the network identifier. This allows large ISPs to be assigned very large blocks of addresses, such as 3.0.0.0/8, and they can distribute them out in networks as small as 3.0.0.4/30 for serial links.

VLSM is a logical way of subnetting a network, making for a more efficient use of all available addresses. It can be thought of as subnetting a subnet within your IP network design or plan. Two important things to remember: There can be no overlap in any of the address pools (subnets). Always start with the largest subnet.

TWO-MINUTE DRILL

IPv4 Addressing

❑ IPv4 addresses are displayed in dotted decimal notation, but are actually made up of 32 bits. Each 8-bit section is referred to as an octet, and numbers can range from 0 to 255. IP addresses have two parts—the network portion and the host portion.

❑ If all host bits are set to 0s, the address is the network ID. If all host bits are set to 1s, the address is the broadcast address for the network. Neither can be assigned to hosts. Any other combination of host bits creates a useable host address on the network.

❑ The subnet mask (255.255.255.128) or prefix mask (/25) defines the network portion of an address; what remains is the host.

❑ Class A addresses are identified in the first octet by numbers ranging from 1 to 126. Class A addresses assign only the first octet, leaving the last three for host bits, and can support 16,777,214 hosts per network. The default subnet mask is 255.0.0.0.

❑ Class B addresses are identified in the first octet by numbers ranging from 128 to 191. Class B addresses assign the first two octets, leaving the last two for host bits, and can support 65,534 hosts per network. The default subnet mask is 255.255.0.0.

❑ Class C addresses are identified in the first octet by numbers ranging from 192 to 223. Class C addresses assign the first three octets, leaving the last octet for host bits, and can support 254 hosts per network. The default subnet mask is 255.255.255.0.

❑ Public addresses can be used on the Internet. Private addresses are used inside a private network (intranet) and require NAT to access outside public resources such as the Internet. The private address ranges are 10.0.0.0, 172.16 to 31.0.0, and 192.168.0 to 255.0.

Binary Numbers

❑ Binary numbering works like decimal numbering, except the base is 2 (not 10) and digits can only be 1 or 0. Place (decimal) value doubles as each position is moved from right to left. Within an 8-bit octet, the position (decimal) values are 128, 64, 32, 16, 8, 4, 2, and 1.

❏ To calculate the decimal equivalent of a binary number, use your binary conversion table.

❏ Binary numbers can have as few as one digit up to an infinite number. For every position added to the left, simply double the value—the ninth position value would be 256, the tenth 512, the eleventh 1024, and so on.

❏ To convert a decimal to binary

1. Determine the highest bit position decimal value that is equal to or smaller than your target and set it to 1.

2. Subtract the decimal value from the original number and compare the remainder to the next position to the right.

3. If the next decimal value is equal to or smaller than your remainder, then set it to 1 and repeat step 2. If it is bigger, turn the bit to 0 and move one position to the right.

4. Repeat this process until the remainder is 0. As soon as the remainder hits 0, turn all remaining bits to 0.

❏ The total number of combinations available for a given number of binary digits is equal to 2^n, where n is the number of bits given. Use your binary combinations table for this.

❏ A Boolean AND takes two inputs, compares (multiplies) them, and comes out with an output based on the comparison: if the two inputs are both 1s, the output is a 1, but if either (or both) is 0, then the output is a 0. Boolean AND is used to match a subnet mask to an IP address—the output is the network ID.

Subnet Essentials

❏ A subnet mask is made up of consecutive 1s from left to right and is used to define where the network bits end and where the host bits begin within an IP address. When a router examines a subnet mask and an IP address, it stops counting bits as soon as it sees the first 0.

❏ The only decimal values allowed within a subnet mask are 0, 128, 192, 224, 240, 248, 252, 254, and 255.

❏ The default subnet masks for Class A, B, and C networks are 255.0.0.0, 255.255.0.0, and 255.255.255.0, respectively. In classful addressing, the line is always drawn on octet boundaries; however, subnet masks are not restricted to the octet boundary. You can borrow as few or as many bits as you need.

❏ CIDR and prefix masking replace classful addressing, so that a network (subnet) can be defined with a prefix /8 to /30; anything longer leaves no hosts.

❏ The five steps to create a subnet mask are as follows:

1. Figure out how many host subnets you need and rank them largest to smallest.

2. Figure out how many host bits will be needed for the largest network.

3. Choose the subnet for the largest network.

4. Note the address range to use so you don't overlap later.

5. Repeat steps 2–4 for the next largest subnet until done.

❏ If the scenario calls for creating subnets, the formula is simple: 2^n greater than or equal to the number you need, where n is the number of bits. If the scenario calls for supporting hosts, the formula used to determine the number of bits you need is $2^n - 2$ greater than or equal to the number you need, where n is the number of bits. Use your binary combinations table for this.

❏ The relevant subnet information that can be decoded from an IP address range and a subnet mask includes the subnet ID, the broadcast address, and the useable host range.

❏ To decode the relevant information use the following steps:

1. Perform a Boolean AND between the address and subnet mask to determine the subnet ID the address belongs to.

2. Determine the broadcast address by turning all host bits to 1s.

3. Determine the first useable address by using the first available combination of host bits (rightmost bit turned on; all other bits turned off).

4. Determine the last useable address by using the last available combination of host bits (rightmost bit turned off; all others turned on).

❏ Subnets created are referred to by their position in a range. The first subnet is created with the first combination of subnet bits (all 0s). The second is created with the next combination available, and so on and so on, all the way to the last (all 1s). To calculate and apply a subnet mask to an enterprise network, first create the subnet mask, then manipulate the subnet bits one at a time.

❏ To save time, take advantage of the "easy" sections of the subnet mask and concentrate your efforts on the portion of the IP address and subnet mask that is more difficult. The subnet mask numbers of 255 and 0 are easy—a 255 means all the bits in the octet above are part of the network ID, while a 0 means all the bits in the octet above can be ignored.

❑ The magic number refers to the position value on the octet where the subnet mask ends. Each subnet created will be a multiple of that number, greatly simplifying the time needed to decode information. Using the magic number can also help find the broadcast address and useable address ranges very quickly. The broadcast address for any subnet is the last combination of host bits available before moving to a new subnet.

❑ CIDR replaces the old class system of IP address allocation and provides two important advantages: the ability to distribute and use an amount of IP addresses closer to the number needed, and router summarization, the ability to represent multiple consecutive subnets with a single route advertisement.

❑ CIDR notation, or prefix notation, basically replaces the subnet mask by adding a slash character and the number of bits in the network identifier (/27).

❑ Two important things to remember with VLSM: There can be no overlap in any of the address pools (subnets). Always start with the largest subnet and work to the smallest.

SELF TEST

The following Self Test questions will help you measure your understanding of the material presented in this chapter. Read all the choices carefully since there may be more than one correct answer. Choose all the correct answers for each question.

IPv4 Addressing

1. PC1 has an IP address of 10.1.1.5, and PC2 has an IP address of 10.1.2.5. Which of the following statements is true regarding these two systems?
   A. If classful addressing is used, both PCs always belong to the same network ID.
   B. If classful addressing is used, both PCs do not belong to the same network ID.
   C. If classless addressing is allowed, both PCs may be on the same network ID.
   D. If classless addressing is allowed, both PCs are never on the same network ID.

2. You are examining a network ID of 172.16.1.0 /24. Which of the following is a useable host address on this network?
   A. 176.16.1.1
   B. 172.16.1.254
   C. 172.16.1.0
   D. 172.16.1.255

3. What is the valid number range for the first octet of a Class B network?
   A. 0–126
   B. 127–191
   C. 128–191
   D. 128–192
   E. 192–223

4. PC1 has an IP address of 172.16.12.5. PC2 is on a separate network subnet. Assuming there is no subnetting (that is, only classful addressing is used), which of the following addresses could PC2 use?
   A. 172.16.250.5
   B. 172.17.12.5
   C. 172.16.0.1
   D. 220.220.200.255
   E. 8.255.255.0

5. How many hosts can be served on a Class B network?
   A. 16,777,214
   B. 65,534
   C. 32,766
   D. 254

Binary Numbers

6. What is the binary equivalent of the decimal number 235?
   A. 11011011
   B. 10101011
   C. 11101010
   D. 11101011

7. How many binary digits are needed to create 1024 combinations?
   A. 8
   B. 9
   C. 10
   D. 11

8. What is the binary equivalent for the decimal number 122?
   A. 01111010
   B. 01111011
   C. 10111010
   D. 10111011

9. What is the decimal equivalent for the binary number 10011011?
   A. 153
   B. 155
   C. 183
   D. 185

10. What is the decimal equivalent for the binary octets 01101111.11100011.11110000.11111110?
   A. 112.227.240.254
   B. 111.226.240.254
   C. 111.227.242.254
   D. 111.227.240.254

11. When performing a Boolean AND between the octets 10010111 and 11111000, what is the outcome?
    A. 00000111
    B. 11111000
    C. 10011000
    D. 10010000

Subnet Essentials

12. Which of the following are valid subnet masks for a Class B address space?
    A. 255.254.0.0
    B. 255.255.0.0
    C. 255.255.245.0
    D. 255.255.254.0
    E. 255.255.192.224

13. Your network design calls for 17 subnets supporting 35 hosts each. Your company provides the 135.72.0.0 address space. Which subnet mask would you create to satisfy the requirement?
    A. 255.255.252.0
    B. 255.255.254.0
    C. 255.255.248.0
    D. 255.255.240.0

14. A customer asks you to create a subnet mask for their network, making sure address space is conserved as much as possible. Each subnet must support 12 hosts, and the address space given is 199.16.7.0. Which of the following answers best fits the customer's needs?
    A. 255.255.255.248, creating 14 subnets and providing 14 hosts per subnet
    B. 255.255.255.240, creating 14 subnets and providing 14 hosts per subnet
    C. 255.255.255.240, creating 16 subnets and providing 14 hosts per subnet
    D. 255.255.255.224, creating eight subnets and providing 30 hosts per subnet

15. Using a Class C address space of 199.88.77.0, you are asked to create a subnet mask for the new network design. Each subnet must be capable of supporting 20 hosts. Which subnet mask best complies with the request, and how many subnets can be created?
    A. 255.255.255.192, creating four subnets
    B. 255.255.255.224, creating eight subnets
    C. 255.255.255.240, creating 16 subnets
    D. 255.255.255.248, creating 32 subnets

16. You have subnetted a Class B address space of 137.99.0.0 using a subnet mask of 255.255.252.0. What is the broadcast address of the third subnet in your design?
- A. 137.99.12.255
- B. 137.99.15.255
- C. 137.99.8.255
- D. 137.99.11.255

17. You have subnetted a Class A address space of 17.0.0.0 using a subnet mask of 255.248.0.0. Which of the following addresses are useable host addresses for the second subnet?
- A. 17.0.8.255
- B. 17.0.14.255
- C. 17.0.11.255
- D. 17.0.15.255
- E. 17.0.19.255

18. You have subnetted a Class C address space of 220.55.66.0 using a subnet mask of 255.255.255.192. What is the useable address range for the first subnet?
- A. 220.55.66.0 to 220.55.66.63
- B. 220.55.66.0 to 220.55.66.62
- C. 220.55.66.1 to 220.55.66.63
- D. 220.55.66.1 to 220.55.66.62

19. A host on a subnet has an IP address of 125.35.88.7 and a subnet mask of 255.255.240.0. What is the broadcast address for the subnet the host belongs to?
- A. 125.35.88.255
- B. 125.35.94.255
- C. 125.35.95.255
- D. 125.35.255.255

20. Which one of the following is the subnet mask equivalent of /27?
- A. 255.255.255.192
- B. 255.255.255.224
- C. 255.255.255.240
- D. 255.255.255.248

21. Which one of the following is the subnet mask equivalent of /17?
   A. 255.255.255.192
   B. 255.255.0.0
   C. 255.255.1.0
   D. 255.255.128.0
   E. 255.255.255.128

22. Looking at Figure 3-18, which three addresses would work for a VLSM solution?
   A. 192.168.1.128/25
   B. 192.168.1.192/26
   C. 192.168.1.0/26
   D. 192.168.1.64/26

23. Looking at Figure 3-18, which one of these pools could be used to efficiently address the three subnets using VLSM?
   A. 10.0.0.0/24
   B. 192.168.0.0/25
   C. 192.168.0.0/23
   D. 192.168.0.0/26

FIGURE 3-18

Questions 22 and
23 exhibit

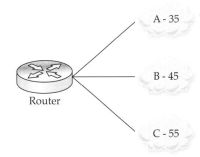

SELF TEST ANSWERS

IPv4 Addressing

1. ☑ **A** and **C** are correct. Classful addressing means the addresses always stay within their class. Since both addresses begin with 10, they are Class A addresses in the same network. If classless addressing is allowed, the class can be subnetted. If the 10.0.0.0 is properly subnetted, both devices could be on the same network.
   ☒ **B** and **D** are incorrect. **B** is not correct because classful addressing places both devices on the same network (10.0.0.0). **D** is not correct because subnetting could allow both to be on the same network.

2. ☑ **A** and **B** are correct. This network has only the last octet available for host bits. As long as they are not all 1s or all 0s, the address is a valid host address.
   ☒ **C** and **D** are incorrect. **C** is not correct because 172.16.1.0 has all host bits turned off (network ID). **D** is not correct because 172.16.1.255 has all host bits turned on (broadcast address).

3. ☑ **C** is correct. The first octet of a Class B address falls in the 128–191 range.
   ☒ **A, B, D,** and **E** are incorrect. These are not valid ranges for Class B addresses.

4. ☑ **B** and **E** are correct. If the network bits are different, then the address is a valid choice.
   ☒ **A, C,** and **D** are incorrect. **A** and **C** are not correct because both of these addresses have the same network bits in common with PC1's address, therefore they cannot be on a separate network. **D** is not correct because 200.220.200.255 is indeed on a separate network, but it is a broadcast address and cannot be assigned to PC2 (all host bits are turned on in the Class C address).

5. ☑ **B** is correct. Class B networks can host 65,534 addresses.
   ☒ **A, C,** and **D** are incorrect. **A** is not correct because this is the number of addresses hosted by a Class A network. **C** is not correct because this choice does not match any IP address class. **D** is not correct because this is the number of addresses hosted by a Class C network.

Binary Numbers

6. ☑ **D** is correct. 11101011 is the correct answer. Following the steps at the beginning of the chapter, the bit positions turned on would be 128 + 64 + 32 + 0 + 8 + 0 + 2 + 1.
   ☒ **A, B,** and **C** are incorrect. **A** is not correct because 11011011 is equivalent to 219. **B** is not correct because 10101011 equates to 171. **C** is not correct because 11101010 equates to 234.

7. ☑ **C** is correct. Ten binary digits provide 1024 combinations ($2^{10} = 1024$).

☒ **A, B,** and **D** are incorrect. **A** is not correct because eight binary digits provide 256 combinations ($2^8 = 256$). **B** is not correct because nine binary digits provide 512 combinations ($2^9 = 512$). **D** is not correct because 11 binary digits provide 2048 combinations ($2^{11} = 2048$).

8. ☑ **A** is correct. 01111010 equates to 122: $0 + 64 + 32 + 16 + 8 + 0 + 2 + 0 = 122$.

☒ **B, C,** and **D** are incorrect. **B, C,** and **D** are not correct because these answers do not match the decimal number 122.

9. ☑ **B** is correct. 10011011 equates to 155: $128 + 0 + 0 + 16 + 8 + 0 + 2 + 1 = 155$.

☒ **A, C,** and **D** are incorrect. The binary equivalent of each of these answers does not match the decimal number 155.

10. ☑ **D** is correct. 01101111.11100011.11110000.11111110 equates to 111.227.240.254: $0 + 64 + 32 + 0 + 8 + 4 + 2 + 1 = 111$, $128 + 64 + 32 + 0 + 0 + 0 + 2 + 1 = 227$, $128 + 64 + 32 + 16 + 0 + 0 + 0 + 0 = 240$, $128 + 64 + 32 + 16 + 8 + 4 + 2 + 0 = 254$.

☒ **A, B,** and **C** are incorrect. These answers do not match.

11. ☑ **D** is correct. When performing a Boolean AND between both octets, put one above the other and simply multiply each pair. The result is 10010000.

☒ **A, B,** and **C** are incorrect. These answers do not match the Boolean AND result.

Subnet Essentials

12. ☑ **B** and **D** are correct. 255.255.0.0 is the default subnet mask for a Class B address space, and 255.255.254.0 is a valid subnet mask.

☒ **A, C,** and **E** are incorrect. **A** is not correct because 255.254.0.0 will not work because it is smaller than the default mask for a Class B address. **C** is not correct because 255.255.245.0 will not work because 245 is not allowed (it is not a consecutive series of 1s) within a subnet mask. **E** is not correct because 255.255.192.224 is incorrect because the subnet mask must always be a series of consecutive 1s from left to right.

13. ☑ **C** is correct. Following the five steps to create a subnet mask, 255.255.248.0 is the correct choice. The Class B address space has a default mask of 255.255.0.0, and we need to borrow 5 bits to accomplish the task (2^n greater than or equal to the number of subnets needed, and 2^5 complies). Counting from left to right, starting with the 17th bit (due to the default mask), the line is drawn after the 21st bit. Setting all bits to 1 on the left of the line, we have 11111111.11 111111.11111000.00000000, which equates to 255.255.248.0.

☒ **A, B,** and **D** are incorrect. These choices do not comply with the scenario needs.

14. ☑ **C** is correct. 255.255.255.240 is the best choice, providing the best "subnets needed to hosts supported" range. The 240 mask creates 16 subnets, leaving 4 bits for up to 14 hosts.

☒ **A, B,** and **D** are incorrect. **A** is not correct because 255.255.255.248 would not work since it only leaves 3 bits for hosts (six hosts on each subnet). **B** is not correct because 255.255.255.240 is the correct mask, but it creates 16 (2^n) subnets, not 14. **D** is not correct because 255.255.255.224 would work in the scenario, creating enough subnets and supporting enough clients; however, it wastes quite a few addresses. The scenario called for only 12 hosts per subnet and conserving address space as much as possible. Therefore, only 4 bits (14 hosts) are needed in the host field, not 5 (30 hosts).

15. ☑ **B** is correct. To support at least 20 hosts per subnet, you must leave at least 5 bits ($2^n - 2$ greater than or equal to the hosts supported), meaning you can only borrow 3 bits to create subnets with. With 3 bits, you can create eight subnets, with each subnet supporting up to 30 hosts. 255.255.255.224 is the correct subnet mask.

☒ **A, C,** and **D** are incorrect. **A** is not correct because 255.255.255.192 will create four subnets, but leaves too many bits in the host field (6). **C** and **D** are not correct because neither choice leaves enough bits in the host field to comply with the scenario.

16. ☑ **D** is correct. The 255.255.252.0 subnet mask for 137.99.0.0 borrows 6 bits from the host field. The third combination of these bits equates to the "8" subnet (000000|xx is the first, 000001|xx is the second, and 000010|xx is the third, where the x's represent the 2 host bits in the third octet). To find the broadcast address, all host bits must be set to 1s: 000010|11.11111111. This equates to 137.99.11.255.

☒ **A, B,** and **C** are incorrect. **A** is not correct because since all host bits are not set to 1s, 137.99.12.255 is simply a host address on the fourth subnet (000011|00.11111111). **B** is not correct because 137.99.15.255 is the broadcast address for the fourth subnet (000011|11.11111111). **C** is not correct because since all host bits are not set to 1s, 137.99.8.255 is a host address on the third octet (000010|00.11111111).

17. ☑ **A, B,** and **C** are correct. The magic number created by the 255.248.0.0 subnet mask is 8 (in the second octet). The second subnet is 17.8.0.0, with a useable range of 17.8.0.1 to 17.15.254.

☒ **D** and **E** are incorrect. 17.0.15.255 and 17.0.19.255 do not fall within the useable range.

18. ☑ **D** is correct. The subnet mask of 255.255.255.192 borrows the first two bits from the last octet. The first subnet is the 0 subnet, and the second is the 220.55.66.64 subnet. The relevant information regarding the first subnet is the subnet ID (220.55.66.0), the useable range (220.55.66.1 to 220.55.66.62), and the broadcast address (220.55.66.63).

☒ **A, B,** and **C** are incorrect. These choices do not fall within the useable range.

19. ☑ **C** is correct. A Boolean AND between the IP address 125.35.88.7 and the subnet mask of 255.255.240.0 shows the subnet ID as 125.35.80.0. Turning on all the remaining host bits, we have 125.35.01011111.11111111, which equates to 125.35.95.255.

☒ **A, B,** and **D** are incorrect. These choices do not reflect the broadcast address of the proper subnet ID.

20. ☑ **B** is correct. The 255.255.255.224 subnet mask is the equivalent of /27.

☒ **A, C,** and **D** are incorrect. **A** is not correct because the 255.255.255.192 subnet mask is the equivalent of /26. **C** is not correct because the 255.255.255.240 subnet mask is the equivalent of /28. **D** is not correct because the 255.255.255.248 subnet mask is the equivalent of /29.

21. ☑ **D** is correct. The 255.255.128.0 subnet mask is the equivalent of /17.

☒ **A, B, C,** and **E** are incorrect. **A** is not correct because the 255.255.255.192 subnet mask is the equivalent of /26. **B** is not correct because the 255.255.0.0 subnet mask is the equivalent of /16. **C** is not correct because the 255.255.1.0 is not a valid subnet mask. **E** is not correct because the 255.255.255.128 subnet mask is the equivalent of /25.

22. ☑ **A, C,** and **D** are correct. The three subnets cover the three networks with no overlap.

☒ **B** is incorrect. That subnet overlaps **A** (192.168.128/25).

23. ☑ **A** is correct. The 10.0.0.0/24 network has enough addresses to cover the three networks. A Boolean AND between the IP address 125.35.88.7 and the subnet mask of 255.255.240.0 shows the subnet ID as 125.35.80.0. Turning on all the remaining host bits, we have 125.35.01011111.11111111, which equates to 125.35.95.255.

☒ **B, C,** and **D** are incorrect. **B** is not correct because 192.168.0.0/25 has only 126 usable addresses. **C** is not correct because 192.168.0.0/23 has only 512 usable addresses and is therefore inefficient. **D** is not correct because 192.168.0.0/26 has only 62 usable addresses.

Part II

LAN Switching Technologies: Layer 2

4

Switching: Moving Data Inside Your LAN

As we prepare to look at LAN switching, we need to look at Ethernet, which is the set of protocols that wired LANs use to communicate and transport data. Ethernet is a common LAN protocol that functions at the OSI Data Link layer (Layer 2) or the TCP/IP Network Access layer. Figure 4-1 shows the model layers as well as the devices and protocols that operate at each layer. Like its WAN counterparts also shown in the figure, the Ethernet protocols define the device addresses, what the data header and footer will look like, and the methods used within that layer.

Ethernet is typically found in a LAN segment with a router at the perimeter that has interfaces in the LAN and one or more interfaces in other LANs or WANs. You will see in Part III of this book that a router works as a gateway between LANs or between a LAN and a WAN, preparing and sending the correct data frame into or out of the LAN. Ethernet, or the other Layer 2 protocols, consists of the local delivery protocols, which function and have relevance only within their network. Figure 4-2 shows the earlier corporate network diagram with one or more LANs within the Corporate and Branch networks. The WAN links could be any of the other Layer 2 protocols shown in Figure 4-1.

FIGURE 4-1   OSI and TCP/IP models showing switches and Ethernet

OSI Layer	Devices Found	Protocols/Standards Working in the Layer	TCP/IP Layer
7: Application	Firewall, Gateway	SMTP, POP3, IMAP, DNS, DHCP, FTP, HTTP, TFTP, SNMP, VoIP, NNTP, NTP	Application
6: Presentation	N/A	JPG, JPEG, TIFF, PNG, GIF, MIME, MP3, MP4	
5: Session	N/A	NFS, ASP, SQL, RPC	
4: Transport	Firewall	TCP, UDP	Transport
3: Network	Router	IP	Internet
2: Data Link	Bridge, Switch	Ethernet, PPP, HDLC, Frame Relay, ATM	Network Access
1: Physical	Transceiver, Repeater, Hub	RJ45, ST/SC, V series (Modem Standards)	

FIGURE 4-2   Network diagram showing LANs and WANs

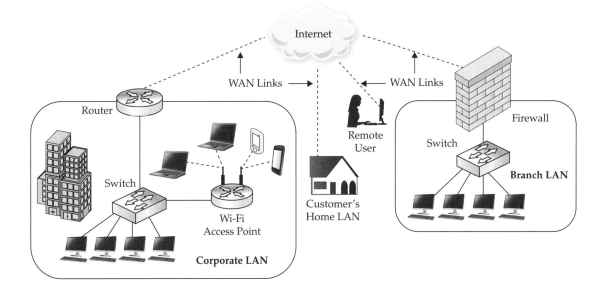

CERTIFICATION OBJECTIVE 4.01

Ethernet Fundamentals

With many iterations, Ethernet evolved to become the most widely implemented networking technology in modern networks. *Ethernet* is a term used to describe a specific group of Layer 2 technologies, media access methods, addressing, and functionality. In this section, we'll cover how an Ethernet network looks and functions, as well as what it takes to put it all together. We'll first start with Ethernet characteristics, such as frame types and addressing, and then briefly look at the media access method CSMA/CD. Finally, we'll wrap up the chapter by covering the various Ethernet standards.

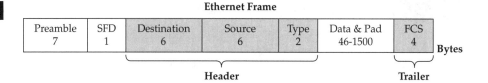

FIGURE 4-3

IEEE 802.3
Ethernet frame

Ethernet Characteristics

Every networking technology has unique characteristics that describe its functionality, and Ethernet is no different. Ethernet networks have distinctive frame types, media access methods, and data flow characteristics. Because Ethernet is the most common LAN technology in modern networks today, it's important to understand how it works. This section will cover Ethernet's defining characteristics.

Ethernet Frame

During our discussion on the OSI Reference Model and the TCP/IP stack, you learned that Layer 2 defines a specific frame type and physical addressing scheme. Each frame consists of bits divided into specific segments known as *fields*. A field contains a certain number of bits and defines specific pieces of information, such as the address, protocol type being carried, and so on. As bits arrive at a network interface card (NIC) one at a time, the NIC looks for them to fall into precise fields. Figure 4-3 is an Ethernet frame layout, and Table 4-1 briefly describes the fields. The highlighted fields are the actual Layer 2 header and trailer that encapsulate the payload (data and padding) from the Network layer. The Preamble and SFD are for synchronization only. They are not actually part of the frame.

TABLE 4-1   IEEE 802.3 Ethernet Frame Field Definitions

Field	Length Bytes	Description
Preamble	7	Synchronization bits.
Start frame delimiter (SFD)	1	Destination address follows this.
Destination MAC address	6	Device to receive frame *in this segment*.
Source MAC address	6	Device that sent frame *in this segment*.
Type	2	Identifies which protocol is contained in the payload, typically a code indicating IPv4 (0800) or IPv6 (86DD).
Data and Pad	46-1500	Layer 3 payload. Padding is added if needed to meet the minimum size.
Frame check sequence (FCS)	4	Check value for CRC test on frame.

SFD is a well-defined and recognizable pattern that the devices use to locate where the important pieces are, namely, that right after the SFD (10101011) comes the destination MAC address.

The preamble and SFD are added at Layer 1 so that the receiving device can tell that a new frame is starting. The Layer 2 frame header and trailer are 18 bytes long and made up of the two MAC addresses, Type and FCS. The size range of acceptable frames is 64–1518 bytes. Anything smaller is a runt, and anything larger is a giant, both of which will be discarded as defective. The data payload field warrants some discussion—it is, after all, the reason the frame is created in the first place. The data payload in an Ethernet frame can be as small as 46 bytes and as large as 1500. If the upper-layer protocol does not place at least 46 bytes in the payload field, the source device will fill the additional space with extra bytes to reach 46. These extra bytes are known as *padding* and do not affect the transmission or the data. The frame is then 46+18=64 to 1500+18=1518 bytes.

The Type (sometimes called EtherType) field is a 2-byte hexadecimal code indicating the payload type. If the entry is larger than 0600, it indicates the Layer 3 protocol being transmitted. If it is an IPv4 or IPv6 packet, the codes are 0800 or 86DD in hex respectively.

The FCS field provides a means for the receiving device to verify that the frame payload has not been modified in transit as the result of a collision or device malfunction. A cyclic redundancy check (CRC) is run before the frame is transmitted, and the value is placed in the FCS field. At the recipient device, the CRC is run again and checked against the FCS. If the values don't match, the frame is discarded.

> **exam**
> **ⓦatch** *You should know the minimum and maximum sizes of an Ethernet frame—from 64 to 1518 bytes. That is, the minimum is a 46-byte payload with an 18-byte header, and the maximum is a 1500-byte payload with an 18-byte header.*

MAC Addresses   Every device on a network segment must have a unique physical address. That address is associated with a NIC on a computer. Ethernet uses the MAC address, also called the *burned-in address* (BIA), which is burned into every NIC/interface by the manufacturer. IPv4 MAC addresses are 48 bits or 6 bytes in length, typically displayed in hex values, and are unique to each NIC. Figure 4-4 shows a description of MAC addresses.

To ensure each MAC address is unique, IEEE assigns an exclusive number, known as the *organizationally unique identifier* (OUI), to a particular manufacturer, and often the OUI identifies the manufacturer and the model of the NIC or the device the NIC is a component of. The OUI makes up the first half (12 bits, or 6 hex digits) of

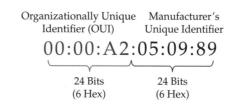

FIGURE 4-4

Ethernet
MAC address
description

Organizationally Unique   Manufacturer's
Identifier (OUI)   Unique Identifier

$00:00:A2:05:09:89$

24 Bits   24 Bits
(6 Hex)   (6 Hex)

the address, with the manufacturer assigning the remaining 24 bits. To avoid conflicts on a LAN and complaints from customers, it is in the manufacturer's best interests to make the last half of the address unique. As stated earlier, the source MAC is the device that created the frame and put it on the network segment. It may not be the original source of the payload. The destination MAC is always the next device to accept and process the frame, which could be the destination device, if local, or the LAN interface of a router, which will process it on its way to its destination. Go back and look at the wording used in Table 4-1. Specifically, look at the description of the destination MAC address: "Device to receive frame *in this segment*." The destination MAC address may be the first stop along the path toward the destination or the tenth. Both MAC addresses are relevant in the current segment only, and they will both be replaced if the frame is forwarded to another network segment. To clarify, segment in this case means Layer 3 devices, computers, and routers. Switches just pass the frame through unchanged.

Address Types   Ethernet and IPv4 both use three types of addresses: unicast, multicast, and broadcast. *Unicast* messages are one-to-one communications addressed to a single device, meaning that the MAC address in the destination field matches only one NIC on the network segment. Other devices might see the frame, but as they examine the MAC address in the destination field, only the NIC matching the destination MAC address will process it—all others discard the frame. An example would be an e-mail being delivered to one host on the network.

Broadcast addresses are one-to-everybody communications; they are meant for every device on the LAN and tell each to open and process the frame. In a broadcast frame, the destination MAC address is always FF:FF:FF:FF:FF:FF, the equivalent of 48 ones. Broadcast messages are often sent when the destination MAC address is unknown, such as when a system powers up and requests an IP address using DHCP. Since it doesn't know the address of the DHCP server, it sends a broadcast to all devices on the segment, and only the DHCP servers will respond.

Broadcast traffic is a necessary evil on Ethernet network segments. However, it should be minimized as much as possible. Not only does broadcast traffic flood your network and take up valuable bandwidth, it also slows each device, requiring processing cycles for each device to open and examine the packet.

Multicast addresses are for one-to-many communications, falling somewhere between unicast and broadcast, where the destination is more than one but less than all hosts. For example, in Chapter 10 you will see that OSPF uses multicast addresses to communicate with other OSPF routers. Another example would be when the user signs up for a live transmission of an event, such as a speech or sporting event.

Collision Domains and CSMA/CD

The problem with Ethernet—particularly with shared media access (hubs)—was how to ensure two devices do not transmit at the same time, causing a *collision* to occur. A *collision domain* is simply any group of devices that, when transmitting, can collide with each other. As a general rule, the smaller the collision domain, the faster and better your network performance.

IEEE defined the carrier sense multiple access with collision detection (CSMA/CD) standard as the media access method on shared media Ethernet networks. Collision detection is reactive in nature, assuming collisions will occur and defining a method to deal with them. A device with a message to send first listens to the wire, waiting for a time when no other device is transmitting to send its signal. If two systems transmit at the same time, they both immediately register an increase in voltage on the line, indicating a collision. Both systems then send a jamming signal to let all devices on the segment know a collision has occurred. The devices involved in the collision then each run a timing algorithm that provides a random wait time of 5 to 50 microseconds before retransmitting. The idea is that the two systems with messages to send will not wind up with the same timer and, thus, will not collide with each other when they attempt to retransmit.

Segmenting Collision Domains With the way CSMA/CD responds to collisions, it should be easy to see why keeping collision domains small is beneficial in any network design. The fewer devices you have contending for the media, the fewer collisions you have and, therefore, the less time your segment spends sending jamming signals and running timing algorithms. Collision domains are segmented and controlled with Layer 2 devices, bridges, and switches. The top diagram in Figure 4-5 shows a small legacy network with 12 hosts connected to two hubs. Even though they may look like two LANs, all 12 devices are contending for the same media (the Layer 1 hubs do nothing but aggregate the wires) and can collide with each other, so the collision domain consists of all 12 hosts.

The lower diagram shows the two hubs separated by a bridge, which splits the collision domains in two. It does this by "learning" which MAC addresses are on which side of the bridge. Then as frames are received on an incoming interface, the

FIGURE 4-5

Collision domains without and with a bridge

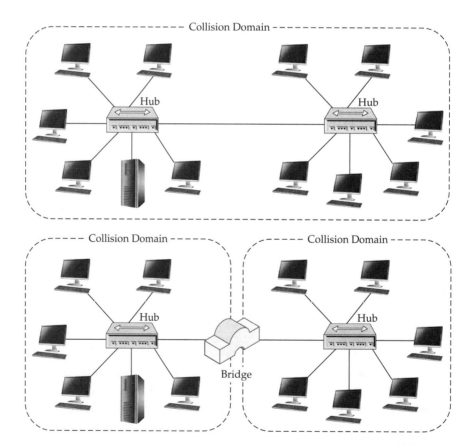

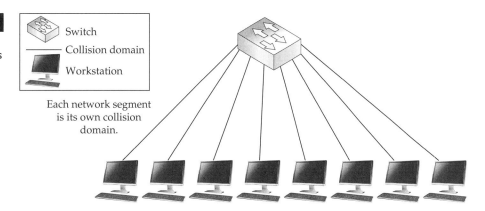

FIGURE 4-6

Collision domains
using a switch

Switch
Collision domain
Workstation

Each network segment
is its own collision
domain.

bridge reads the destination MAC address, forwarding only those frames destined
to the far-side segment. Now computers on the left side only can collide with each
other. The collision domains are now each sized to six.

A switch is functionally a bridge with many ports. Figure 4-6 shows a switch with
eight hosts attached. Now no collisions can occur since each device is separated into
its own collision domain. You will find more information on using switches within
your network to segment collision domains and move traffic efficiently and quickly
in Chapters 5 and 6 of this book.

Data Flow

To start to understand how data flows through a network and particularly how the
Layer 2 frame addresses change, let's look at an example of a larger network, possibly
a campus network where the connections are Ethernet. The process is the same
with WAN connections between the routers except that the frames there would
match the WAN protocol used. In Figure 4-7, host PC1 in the lower-right corner is
sending a message to PC2. Both systems are on Ethernet segments; for the sake of
this discussion, let's assume the routers are in separate buildings and all segments are
using Ethernet.

Address Resolution Protocol   Before we start our first look at data flow
patterns, we need to look briefly at how Ethernet, which is a Layer 2 protocol that
knows nothing about the upper layers, is able to work with Layer 3 IP addresses. In
short, it can't and doesn't. We use Address Resolution Protocol (ARP) to bridge the
two layers together. Technically, ARP is a Layer 2 protocol, but many people define
it as 2.5 because it bridges these layers. The ARP table has the Layer 2 (Ethernet)

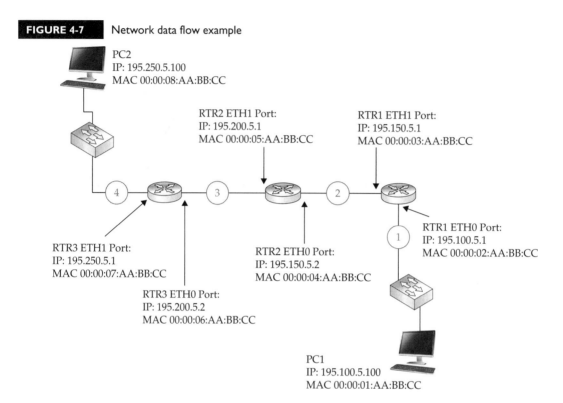

FIGURE 4-7 Network data flow example

address for any IP addresses known on the Ethernet interfaces. If it doesn't have an IP-ARP address entry for the outbound packet, it sends an ARP broadcast into the LAN asking for the IP address. If the device is present, it replies with its MAC address and ARP updates its table. These ARP table entries time out and are dropped if there is no more traffic within the cache timer, assuming that the device has been turned off or removed from the network, as in the case of portable devices.

You can see your local computer's ARP table by opening the command window and typing **arp -a** (or just **arp**) to get a menu of options. The *Physical Address* is the MAC address. The output should look something like the following:

```
C:\>arp

Displays and modifies the IP-to-Physical address translation tables used by
address resolution protocol (ARP).

ARP -s inet_addr eth_addr [if_addr]
```

```
ARP -d inet_addr [if_addr]
ARP -a [inet_addr] [-N if_addr] [-v]

  -a           Displays current ARP entries by interrogating the current
               protocol data.  If inet_addr is specified, the IP and Physical
               addresses for only the specified computer are displayed.  If
               more than one network interface uses ARP, entries for each ARP
               table are displayed.
  -g           Same as -a.
  -v           Displays current ARP entries in verbose mode.  All invalid
               entries and entries on the loop-back interface will be shown.
  inet_addr    Specifies an internet address.
  -N if_addr   Displays the ARP entries for the network interface specified
               by if_addr.
  -d           Deletes the host specified by inet_addr. inet_addr may be
               wildcarded with * to delete all hosts.
  -s           Adds the host and associates the Internet address inet_addr
               with the Physical address eth_addr.  The Physical address is
               given as 6 hexadecimal bytes separated by hyphens. The entry
               is permanent.
  eth_addr     Specifies a physical address.
  if_addr      If present, this specifies the Internet address of the
               interface whose address translation table should be modified.
               If not present, the first applicable interface will be used.
Example:
  > arp -s 157.55.85.212   00-aa-00-62-c6-09  .... Adds a static entry.
  > arp -a                                    .... Displays the arp table.

C:\>arp -a

Interface: 172.30.4.91 --- 0x4
  Internet Address      Physical Address      Type
  172.30.1.1            00-17-c5-10-1b-a0     dynamic
  172.30.3.1            00-1e-0b-c9-b9-7e     dynamic
  172.30.3.5            00-15-5d-03-02-00     dynamic
  172.30.3.105          00-15-5d-03-07-02     dynamic
  172.30.255.255        ff-ff-ff-ff-ff-ff     static
  224.0.0.22            01-00-5e-00-00-16     static
  224.0.0.252           01-00-5e-00-00-fc     static
  239.255.255.250       01-00-5e-7f-ff-fa     static
  255.255.255.255       ff-ff-ff-ff-ff-ff     static

C:\>
```

With that, let's look at the flow of data through our network.

In stage 1, PC1 looks at its routing table to determine whether the destination is on the local network segment. In this case, it isn't, so it uses ARP lookup (and query if necessary) to get the MAC address of its default gateway. The packet is then handed to the Network Access layer for framing.

The frame at stage 1

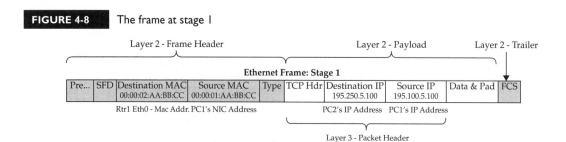

In Ethernet, PC1's MAC address (00:00:01:AA:BB:CC) is used for the source address in the frame, and the router LAN interface (00:00:02:AA:BB:CC) is the destination address for the frame. The frame, shown in Figure 4-8, is then placed on the wire.

The switch reads the destination MAC address as it receives the frame and opens a pathway to the router's port. The router's port receives the frame and begins reading the destination MAC address as well. Since it is intended for the router, the router opens the frame and discards the header and trailer, leaving only the packet. It then reads the destination IP address and compares it to its routing table. Finding a route to the destination by sending the packet through its ETH1 port, the router then goes through the same process as PC1 to find a destination MAC address and build a frame for delivery on ETH1's local network. After ARPing for a MAC address, the router builds a new frame and sends it out ETH1. The new frame appears in Figure 4-9. Notice the packet (containing the IP addresses) doesn't change; however, the frame has new source and destination addresses. In this segment, the sending device is ETH1, and the destination device is RTR2's ETH0 port.

This process of the frame being stripped off, performing another ARP process to determine the new destination MAC address, and frame rebuilding occurs at each link in the delivery chain. Figure 4-10 shows the frame at stages 3 and 4. When the frame is finally delivered to PC2, the frame and packet headers are removed, and the Transport layers between the two systems can begin talking.

Ethernet Frame: Stage 2

Pre...	SFD	Destination MAC 00:00:04:AA:BB:CC	Source MAC 00:00:03:AA:BB:CC	Type	TCP Hdr	Destination IP 195.250.5.100	Source IP 195.100.5.100	Data & Pad	FCS

The frame at stage 2

Rtr1 Eth0 - Mac Addr.   Rtr1 Eth1 - Mac Addr.   PC2's IP Address   PC1's IP Address

FIGURE 4-10

Ethernet Frame: Stage 3

Pre...	SFD	Destination MAC 00:00:06:AA:BB:CC	Source MAC 00:00:05:AA:BB:CC	Type	TCP Hdr	Destination IP 195.250.5.100	Source IP 195.100.5.100	Data & Pad	FCS

Rtr3 Eth0 - Mac Addr.   Rtr2 Eth1 - Mac Addr.   PC2's IP Address   PC1's IP Address

The frame at
stages 3 and 4

Ethernet Frame: Stage 4

Pre...	SFD	Destination MAC 00:00:08:AA:BB:CC	Source MAC 00:00:07:AA:BB:CC	Type	TCP Hdr	Destination IP 195.250.5.100	Source IP 195.100.5.100	Data & Pad	FCS

PC2's NIC Mac Addr.   Rtr3 Eth1 - Mac Addr.   PC2's IP Address   PC1's IP Address

exam

ⓦatch *Make sure you're familiar with the data flow steps shown here. You could be asked to fill in frame fields and to decipher different message types during an information exchange (unicast, multicast, and broadcast). The frame header and trailer are discarded at each router and replaced by a new frame for the next destination port. Don't forget the ARP messages are sent before the frame is ever built. The IP addresses do not change throughout the entire trip with the destination IP address being the basis for all Layer 3 forwarding decisions. Both MAC addresses change at every Layer 3 device. They are point-to-point local delivery only, from host to router, router to router, and finally router to host. Don't assume that the destination MAC for one segment becomes the source for the next; it will always leave from another interface with its own MAC.*

Ethernet Standards

In 1980, the Institute of Electrical and Electronic Engineers (IEEE), a standards-setting body, formed the 802 committee to begin work on defining networking standards. There are 802.x standards for most aspects of networking. The "802" means nothing more than the committee was formed in February 1980. Over time, IEEE developed standards for implementing Ethernet's functionality and, in 1985, released the initial 802.3 standard series. These are the most popular LAN standards used worldwide today. Figure 4-11 shows the current and proposed standards.

Over time, Ethernet has grown to be more than just a small internal Layer 2 LAN technology. In modern networking, Ethernet can run lengthy distances, use a variety of media, and transmit data at high bandwidth speeds. Part of Ethernet's success has to do with the cooperative standards released early on by IEEE, the American

FIGURE 4-11	The Evolution of Ethernet Standards to Meet Higher Speeds			
	Date	IEEE Std.	Name	Data Rate	Type of Cabling
Ethernet standards history (used with permission from Belden, Inc.)	1990	802.3i	10BASE-T	10 Mb/s	Category 3 cabling
	1995	802.3u	100BASE-TX	100 Mb/s*	Category 5 cabling
	1998	802.3z	1000BASE-SX	1 Gb/s	Multimode fiber
		802.3z	1000BASE-LX/EX		Single-mode fiber
	1999	802.3ab	1000BASE-T	1 Gb/s*	Category 5e or higher
	2003	802.3ae	10GBASE-SR	10 Gb/s	Laser-Optimized MMF
		802.3ae	10GBASE-LR/ER		Single-mode fiber
	2006	802.3an	10GBASE-T	10 Gb/s*	Category 6A cabling
	2015	802.3bq	40GBASE-T	40 Gb/s*	Category 8 (Class I & II) Cabling
	2010	802.3ba	40GBASE-SR4/LR4	40 Gb/s	Laser-Optimized MMF or SMF
		802.3ba	100GBASE-SR10/ER4	100 Gb/s	Laser-Optimized MMF or SMF
	2015	802.3bm	100GBASE-SR4	100 Gb/s	Laser-Optimized MMF
	2016	SG	Under development	400 Gb/s	Laser-Optimized MMF or SMF
	Note: *with auto-negotiation				

National Standards Institute (ANSI), the Electronic Industries Alliance (EIA), and the Telecommunications Industry Association (TIA). (The last two develop cabling and connector and termination standards.)

As stated earlier in this chapter, IEEE released—and continues to work on—several standards regarding LAN networking. The IEEE 802.3 series provided a physical blueprint for several network models, including Ethernet. These standards defined the physical and logical topologies, the media used, the equipment needed, and many other characteristics defining a specific network model. The 802.3 series provides OSI Physical and Data Link layer specifications for building a network.

Given the variety of media choices and the advent of full-duplex networks, it's easy to see the need for standards in regard to Ethernet. For the most part, Ethernet framing, addressing, and media access stay the same regardless of the Layer 1 standard in play. The copper categories have standardized on 100-meter maximum distances, but the fiber optic choices can range from approximately 550 meters to thousands of meters. Multimode fiber is the short-haul carrier, whereas single-mode fiber is the long-distance choice.

When designing a LAN or campus network, these Layer 1 IEEE and TIA media standards, including maximum bandwidth and distances, are important to verify if you aren't sure. Table 4-2 shows the details that will be used in the examples and the ones you should know for the exam. We've converted the distances from meters, but it is never too early to start getting used to using them; the standards and much of the literature assumes you will know them.

TABLE 4-2	IEEE and TIA Cabling Details to Know for the Exam		
Ethernet Name	**Maximum Rate**	**Maximum Distance**	**Media**
10Base-T	10 Mb/s	100 m (328 ft.)	TIA Category 3 or higher
100Base-T	100 Mb/s	100 m (328 ft.)	TIA Category 5 or higher
1000Base-T	1 Gb/s	100 m (328 ft.)	TIA Category 5e or higher
1000Base-SX	1 Gb/s	550 m (1,800 ft.)	Multimode fiber (MMF)
1000Base-LX	1 Gb/s	5 km (3.1 miles)	Single-mode fiber (SMF)

For more information on specific cabling standards and termination options and techniques, there are many YouTube videos for both copper and fiber. Both EIA and TIA offer details on their websites. These are a couple of sites I like for basic cabling information and graphics:

http://wiki.networksecuritytoolkit.org/nstwiki/index.php/LAN_Ethernet_ Network_Cable

http://en.wikipedia.org/wiki/Ethernet_physical_layer

ⓦatch   *Here's a quick tip for learning the cable specifications: If the last digit is a T, the cable type is twisted pair;*   *if it's anything else, it's fiber. Make sure you are familiar with the standards.*

CERTIFICATION OBJECTIVE 4.02

Switching Fundamentals

Modern LANs are based on switch technologies that support full-duplex, two-way simultaneous traffic connections to offer high speed, reliability, near 100 percent bandwidth availability, collision avoidance, and other services. While switches were introduced in Chapter 1, this section's main goal is to provide a bedrock of information that can be used to discuss switch configuration in the next chapters. Topics covered include everything from switch basics (modes of operation and startup functions) to advanced features, such as broadcast loop prevention and virtual networking.

Switch Features

An important part of almost every modern Ethernet LAN installation, switches are one of the most important network devices for new network technicians—and CCENT candidates—to know about. Switches provide high-speed data transport inside a network, allow for virtual broadcast domains (VLANs) to control traffic, and help secure network traffic from observers. This section will cover some basic fundamentals of switches, including the switch's physical appearance and basic functions, the modes switches are capable of working in, and what happens when you power on the switch.

Physical Features

Switches come in a wide variety of models and port densities. Cisco provides two major brands of switches: the Nexus and Catalyst series. Generally, Nexus switches are used in high-performance data centers, while Catalyst switches are used in enterprise LAN implementations. Since the CCENT exam concentrates on the Catalyst series, most of the descriptions of switch physical characteristics come from Catalyst switches. As shown in Figure 4-12, a typical switch (Catalyst included) usually has the following common features:

- An LED panel
- A series of ports (aka interfaces) for host connections

The LED panel on a Catalyst switch contains two system indicator lamps and three mode indicator lamps. The system indicator lamps are the system (SYST) and redundant power supply (RPS) LEDs. The SYST LED indicates the overall system status. The RPS LED shows the status of the redundant power supply, if one is present. Table 4-3 lists the LED status and meaning of both system indicator lamps.

FIGURE 4-12

The physical features of a switch

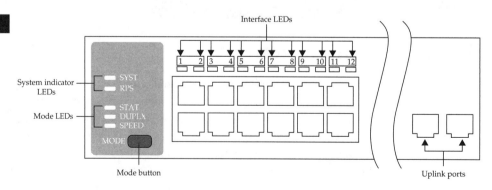

Interface LEDs

System indicator LEDs

Mode LEDs

Mode button

Uplink ports

TABLE 4-3		Switch System Indicator LED Status

LED	Color	Status
SYST	Off	The switch is not powered on.
	Green	Powered on, IOS is loaded, and the switch is functioning normally.
	Amber	POST failed, IOS did not load, and the switch is not functioning.
RPS	Off	RPS is not functioning or connected.
	Green	RPS is connected and ready to provide power. (Blinking green indicates it is providing power to another device.)
	Amber	RPS is in a fault or standby condition.
	Blinking amber	Internal power has failed, and RPS is providing power to the device.

Generally speaking, with LEDs, green equates to good, while amber equates to bad. If you see amber in the system indicator LEDs, don't panic! Usually the fix is fairly simple. If the SYST lamp is amber, turn the device off and on again. If the RPS lamp is solid amber, press the Standby/Active button—it should return to green. If either fix fails, you may have a problem requiring some help, so give Cisco a call.

The mode lamps indicate the LED mode the switch is operating in. The LED mode has nothing to do with switch operation—no matter what mode you choose to display the LEDs in, the switch will continue to forward frames, as it was intended and configured to do. The LED mode is changed by pressing a mode button on the front of the switch. The LED modes simply provide a quick means for administrators to discover information about the switch. Additionally, each host interface port has LEDs, and the LED mode affects how each is displayed. Table 4-4 lists LED modes and their effect on interface LEDs. The LEDs on individual switch interfaces provide a quick means of troubleshooting for administrators and technicians.

Lastly, most modern switches have at least one uplink port. These ports can be RJ45 twisted pair, or fiber, depending on the model of switch. If the uplink port is fiber, a transceiver may be required to transform the bits from electric to light, and vice versa. The uplink ports are often faster, but they don't necessarily have to be used when linking switches.

Catalyst switches not only autonegotiate for speed and duplex, but also have a feature called Auto-Sensing MDIx that detects the cable type connected to the interface. If you connect the wrong cable between switches (for instance, use a straight-through instead of a crossover), no problem—the switch simply changes the pinout to match it, and you're off and running.

TABLE 4-4	Switch Mode LEDs	
LED Mode	**Interface LED Color**	**Status**
STAT	Off	Not in use or administratively down.
	Green	Link present. Blinking green indicates activity.
	Green/amber	Excessive collisions or errors are creating a link fault.
	Amber	Port is blocked by Spanning Tree Protocol (STP). Blinking amber indicates activity on the blocked port.
DUPLX	Off	Half duplex.
	Green	Full duplex.
SPEED	Off	10 Mbps.
	Green	100 Mbps.
	Blinking green	1000 Mbps (gigabit speed).

Switch Initialization Functions

With all the features switches can provide for a network, it is sometimes a daunting task—especially as a junior networker—to install a new switch on the network. Several questions come to mind: What is needed to connect it? What configuration do I need to set up? How do I proceed? Thankfully, installing a switch is a relatively easy task (the configuration is covered in the next chapters). For it to function, the steps are to simply take the switch out of the box, plug it in to the power supply, and connect the hosts. While this is an easy task, it is important that CCENT candidates be familiar with how a Catalyst switch operates at bootup.

For all intents and purposes, a switch (and most networking devices) is basically a specialized computer and performs many of the same tasks your PC does at bootup. The first step in the switch boot process is a simple power-on self-test (POST). Like a PC, the POST checks to ensure memory, processing, and physical components are connected and functioning. LEDs on the front of the switch indicate the boot process, and POST errors will be displayed there. As stated earlier, a POST problem with a switch results in an amber SYST LED.

After the POST runs, a bootstrap program is called from a read-only memory (ROM) location. The bootstrap looks for the device operating system in flash memory and loads it into RAM. The next step calls for the configuration files to be loaded from a special storage location known as NVRAM. After the IOS and configuration files are loaded and active, the switch can begin work.

Cisco's operating system, for both routers and switches, is known as the IOS, which originally stood for *Internetwork Operating System*. There was an early separate switch operating system called the Catalyst Operating System (CatOS). It was dropped in favor of standardizing on IOS for many Cisco devices.

Forwarding Data and the CAM Table

After the operating system and configuration file, if any, are loaded, the switch begins to read and forward frames. The switch can receive three types of frames: unicast, multicast, and broadcast. As discussed earlier, switches filter unicast messages and direct them to the appropriate outbound port while flooding multicast and broadcast messages. But when the switch is first deployed, it floods *all* the frames it receives. The reason for this is simple: Initially, the switch doesn't know where any LAN hosts are located. Before a switch can determine which port to send an incoming frame to, it must first build something called a *content addressable memory* (CAM) table. The CAM table, also known as a MAC address table, contains a list of MAC addresses mapped to specific interfaces on the switch that the MAC address was *learned* on. It is built by reading the *source* MAC addresses as frames are received by the switch. The source MAC address is added to the CAM table for the incoming interface. As the table populates, the switch *learns* to which interface to send the frames.

When powering up, the switch's CAM table is empty. As the first frame enters through an interface, the switch writes the source MAC address and interface mapping in the CAM table. The frame is then flooded to all other ports. This process is repeated until the switch receives a frame with a destination address already in the CAM table. With an entry in the table the switch knows which interface to direct new frames for delivery. This process is true even when a switch is cascaded to other switches—the CAM table simply matches all the connected MAC addresses on the distant end switch to that one interface. See Figure 4-13 for an example of correct CAM table entries.

e x a m

ⓦ a t c h   *The exam focuses on the operation of the switch, but understanding how switches operate at startup and that initially the CAM table is empty will help you understand what happens as a switch becomes operational. All frames are flooded until the interface-to-device MAC address pairings are learned by recording the source address of frames as they enter an interface.*

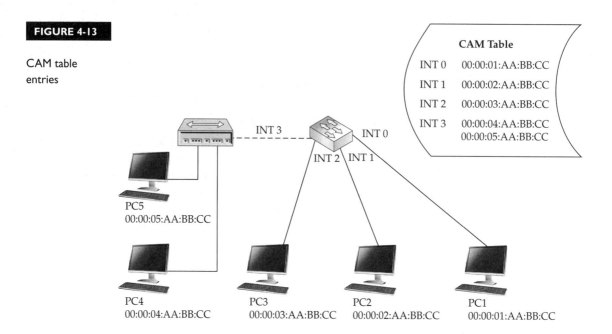

FIGURE 4-13

CAM table
entries

What happens if a host is moved from one port to another? If the CAM table has old information in it, won't frames be delivered to the wrong interface? To answer this, consider how the table updates itself. You already know the switch reads the source MAC address and equates it to the interface on which the frame was received. This process continues for *every* frame received. The switch looks at the incoming frame and compares its source MAC address and incoming port with the CAM table. If there is no entry, it simply adds the pair to the table. If the entry does exist, it verifies that the pair matches. If the new frame entered is on a different interface than the one listed in the table, the switch updates the information. In other words, the CAM table is dynamic, is updated constantly, and allows for systems to be seamlessly added and removed from the switch, as well as to be moved from port to port.

For clarification, consider an example. In the morning, PC1, a laptop, is connected to port 1, and the port address table entry shows 0A:0B:0C:12:34:56 as being located on port 1. So, all messages with the destination address 0A:0B:0C:12:34:56 were sent to interface 1. Later, the user takes the laptop to a meeting and, connecting to a wall jack, places it on switch port 5. When PC1 sends its first frame, the switch compares the source MAC address, 0A:0B:0C:12:34:56, with the port information it has in the table, port 1. Since the message originated from port 5, the port address table is updated, and PC1 will receive all messages on the correct port.

Duplex and Speed

Aside from the collision domain segmentation and bandwidth speed allocation benefits, switches offer two additional advantages in the network design. First, switches can operate using full-duplex, two-way *simultaneous* transmission over separate wires or fibers that virtually eliminates the possibility of collisions while also greatly increasing overall throughput. In theory a 100-Mb segment could have two 100-Mb streams going in opposite directions. The alternative, half-duplex, allows transmissions in both directions, but not at the same time, because they use the same shared media (wire).

Second, switches allow for devices of different speeds to communicate with each other. On most modern switches, systems at 10 Mbps, 100 Mbps, and 1000 Mbps can all communicate freely over the same device. The switch can operate using a store-and-forward process, allowing the frame to be held in a buffer (holding area) until it can be sent to the destination interface.

Both duplex and bandwidth speed settings are assigned per interface and can be manually configured or left to autonegotiation. During the development of the 802.3u standard, IEEE established the principles for autonegotiation on switch interfaces using twisted pair copper media to allow for backward compatibility to 10 Mbps from today's 100 Mbps and faster. By default, every interface on a Catalyst switch is set to autonegotiate, based on the IEEE standard. When a host is connected to an interface, the switch and the host NIC exchange information to discover the speed settings and automatically agree to use the fastest supported on both. Next, both devices determine whether full duplex is enabled on each device.

This works well, as long as both devices are functioning properly and set to autonegotiate. It is the norm for connecting workstations to switches. There is a school of thought when connecting switches together or connecting switches to strategic, higher-volume hosts, such as servers, and that is to manually set both ends to full duplex at the highest speed possible. While this works well and avoids a chance of a suboptimal connection, it is essential that it be properly configured on both ends. If not, the process may not result in the best duplex and speed settings for the connection and may not connect at all.

If autonegotiation fails, the device simply defaults to the settings specified in the set of IEEE rules. For copper links, IEEE specifies using the slowest interface speed and half duplex. This could be a real performance killer for critical links, making servers or entire switch connections look bad.

e**x**a m
ⓦa t c h
Be sure to know the basics on autonegotiation: Cisco switches can match the highest speed that both ends support, but if the speed can't be determined at all, it defaults to the lowest *interface speed (10 Mbps) at half duplex. Keep in mind that gigabit and faster speeds* always **require full duplex; it should make it easier to remember.**

Switch Modes

As covered earlier, all switches read destination MAC addresses to make forwarding decisions on incoming frames. However, the method in which they go about forwarding the frames determines which mode the switch is operating in. Some read just a portion of the frame, while others examine the entire thing, and each switching mode has its benefits and drawbacks. Switches operate in three modes: cut through, store and forward, and fragment free.

Cut-Through Mode   Switches operating in *cut-through* mode forward frames as quickly as possible. As a frame arrives, the switch reads only enough bits to discover the destination address in the correct field of the frame. Once the destination address is determined, the switch makes a quick comparison to its CAM table and opens the pathway to the destination port. The frame is then sent to the destination port *while bits are still being received on the original port.*

Obviously, this mode of switching is fast—frames are forwarded almost as soon as they enter their switch port—but it does have one glaring disadvantage. Because the switch only reads to the destination address, cut-through mode results in the forwarding of frames that may contain errors. Remember earlier in this chapter, the FCS field in an Ethernet frame provides for error checking on the recipient end. Because the switch doesn't read to the FCS field, it could forward frames that are shorter than standard (called *runts*) and longer than standard (called *giants*), both of which are bad frames that will eventually be discarded. This results in retransmission requests and a host of other headaches for your systems—and network—to deal with.

Store-and-Forward Mode   In *store-and-forward* mode, the switch accepts and reads the entire frame before it allows it to be forwarded to the destination port. While this method slows things down a bit, it provides two distinct benefits. First, the switch has the opportunity to verify that frames are error-free by verifying the FCS field before forwarding. Any bad frames are simply discarded.

Second, store and forward allows for systems operating at different bandwidth speeds to communicate on the same switch. For example, assume a switch is rated 10/100/1000 and two hosts are connected, one running at 100 Mbps and the other running at 1000 Mbps. If the faster machine sends a message to the slower machine without store and forward, the slower machine would quickly become overwhelmed and frames would be lost. With store and forward, the entire frame is brought into the switch, held in buffers (think parking lots), and then transmitted at the appropriate speed for the destination port.

Early switches used to default to cut-through mode, but switches today, including Catalyst switches, default to store and forward because of the need to support hosts running at different bandwidth speeds and duplex settings.

Fragment-Free Mode   The third switch mode is somewhat of a compromise between the cut-through and store-and-forward modes. *Fragment-free* switch mode forwards the frame after receiving the first 64 bytes. Much like cut-through mode, this mode opens a pathway to the destination port before all the frame's bits are received; however, it adds the benefit of cutting down on the number of erroneous frames propagated by the switch. Reading the first 64 bytes of the frame allows the switch to determine the most common collision-type error, frame fragments, or runts (smaller than 64 bytes), and can discard them.

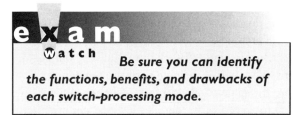

Switched Network Design Considerations

Understanding what the switch looks like and how it operates is only a first step. Applying this knowledge to LAN design and switch placement is just as important. Using a fully switched network and no hubs greatly improves performance and strengthens security, making it the choice for modern networks. However, there are several other considerations to keep in mind while designing and building the network. This section will cover switch installation, broadcast loop mitigation, and VLANs.

Switch Installation and Connections

Network design, with regard to switches, requires consideration of segment lengths, data bandwidth needs, cost, performance, and reliability. Using switches, segment length considerations involve choosing the correct media for each purpose and then staying within standard cable lengths.

Media Considerations   Copper media, UTP or STP, is still the norm for connecting workstations, so cable runs are limited to a total of 100 meters. There are two things to remember: First, be sure to allow for patch cables in the data closet and from the wall to the computer. Second, the actual cable path is often consolidated into cable runs, often in trays, and therefore is often not the shortest path. All of these segments should be straight-through cables. The area that can be serviced from the switches in a data, or wiring, closet is called the *catchment area*.

Connections between switches in the same data closet could be copper or fiber. Connecting data closets, whether building-to-building or even just between floors, often use fiber optic cable, which becomes mandatory when distances might exceed 100 meters. In either case, switch-to-switch connections use a crossover cable. When there is a long backbone run, it is straight through, and a crossover patch cable is used on one end.

Structured cabling for facilities and the standards for it are not part of this exam, but if you are going to work in the field, you should understand how they work, how they impact cable distances, and which cable to use. If you Google *structured cabling*, you will get dozens of hits with varying degrees of detail. Here is a free e-book from BlackBox with a good explanation and graphics: www.blackbox.com/resource/genPDF/Buyers-Guides/Black_Box_Cabling_Guide.pdf

Bandwidth requirements can vary wildly within a single network; segments serving users don't necessarily require the same bandwidth as backbone segments (those connecting switches together) to servers or to routers. Cost and performance are often related. Increasing performance increases the price paid, but replacement costs with infrastructure cabling can be expensive and disruptive. For that reason, new installations offer cable for the future, such as gigabit cabling to all workstations even though some users may still be connecting with 100-Mbps devices.

Switch Roles   Cisco defines three roles for switches within a network: access, distribution, and core. The idea behind Cisco's design is to increase performance, security, and reliability while reducing cost, equipment, and confusion as much as possible. *Access-layer switches* are used to connect end-user workstations to the network. *Distribution-layer switches* provide an aggregation point for the access-layer switches. *Core-layer switches*, if needed, are high-end high-bandwidth devices providing aggregation points for distribution switches in a large enterprise network, such as building-to-building connections in a large campus network.

The concept behind the three layers is relatively simple: End-user workstations must connect to switches, and those switches should not be connected together. Data that travels from one switch to another should go through an aggregation point (a higher-bandwidth switch) rather than daisy-chaining access-level switches.

Today's networks are typically designed with high availability (HA) in mind. In our example design, this means multiple pathways to access-layer switches from different distribution layer switches whenever possible. Figure 4-14 shows this design, which reduces the likelihood that an access-layer switch's users are cut off from the network by a cable failure. HA is provided by using distribution-layer switches. It's more efficient to use the up-layer distribution switch than have data travel from access switch to access switch through daisy-chaining—utilizing only two ports per switch. This concept reduces the amount of cabling required, as well as the likelihood of congested links, thereby increasing performance across the network.

FIGURE 4-14

A Cisco switched network design

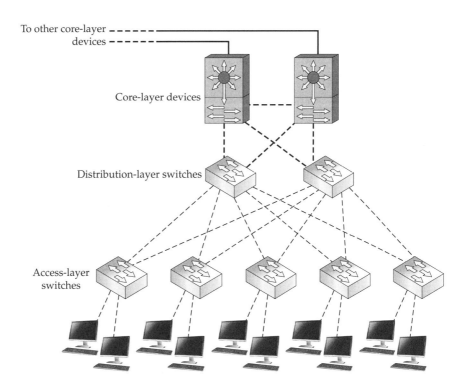

Looping and STP

When designing a switched network for redundancy, it is common to design a network connecting several switches in a redundant fashion, as shown in Figure 4-15. This means a single link failure does not strand any switch or its connected users. But there is a potential problem that must be taken into account. As discussed earlier, switches flood all broadcast traffic. If host A sends a broadcast message to switch A, the switch will, in turn, flood it out every available port. The broadcast message, received by switches B and D, will also flood the broadcast out their ports. Switch C—and A (again)—receive the broadcast and flood it again. This process can repeat for eternity; if a broadcast message enters a switched network that is built with redundant connections, it will loop indefinitely. Since the volume of this looping traffic is growing with each switch, it can often stop the network, at worst, and result in slow performance, at best. In addition, each switch will see traffic arriving from host A coming in on two interfaces and be constantly flipping its CAM table entries. This flipping means that real traffic intended for host A can be sent down the wrong path, which can delay or prevent delivery.

The solution to broadcast looping is built into the Catalyst switches. Spanning Tree Protocol runs on all Catalyst switches by default. STP is the IEEE 802.1d standard that provides a method for switches to negotiate a loop-free solution, allowing you to wire redundancy and rely on STP to iron out the problems. The STP process selects a root bridge (switch) and then calculates and enables only a single path to that root bridge from each other switch. Any remaining redundant links go into a blocking state, which shuts down the port and stops the broadcast from perpetuating through the network. STP is dynamic, so if another segment link fails and it turns out the blocked port is needed, STP will put it back in a forwarding state. For instance, in the network depicted in Figure 4-15, STP would block one of the ports connecting two of the switches together.

FIGURE 4-15

Broadcast loops

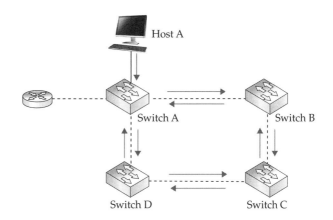

exam
watch

The CCENT exam does not cover STP extensively. You should know what it is and what it does; it prevents loops on Layer 2 switches, but nothing more. The CCNA ICND2 exam covers the details and implementation of STP.

VLANs

As organizations grow and change, people get moved and consolidated into areas that can test your network design. For example, let's imagine a business on three floors, with Administration on floor 1, Engineering on floor 2, and Sales on floor 3. Each floor has its own LAN and switches in a data closet. As the company grows, Sales grows faster than the others and, after running out of space on the second floor, wants to move into unused areas on the other two floors. With separate LANs on each floor, you are separating the traffic nicely, but now you will have users connecting to the wrong LANs and maybe unable to reach needed resources.

Fortunately, Cisco switches support a technology called virtual LANs (VLANs). VLANs allow a single switch to support multiple LANs on a per-port basis. Each virtual LAN or VLAN is a virtual partition of the switch providing a separate broadcast domain and assigned ports that are invisible to any other VLANs or devices. VLANs offer several benefits. Here are some of the more important reasons for using VLANs within a network design:

- VLANs can segment broadcast domains without using a router.
- VLANs can improve performance on hosts, reducing their processing overhead by limiting the broadcast messages and separating traffic types.
- VLANs provide better security by separating devices and their message traffic.

Earlier in this chapter we said that a broadcast domain is basically a network created and bordered by routers. A broadcast from one device in the LAN is transmitted to all devices in the LAN and stops at the router. A virtual LAN works in much the same fashion, except the VLAN is created by joining a group of switch ports together and properly configuring the switch. While normally all ports on a switch would belong to a single broadcast domain, the switch can be configured to treat them as separate networks (broadcast domains).

VLANs are covered in greater detail with configuration options in Chapter 7, but for introduction sake, consider an example. Suppose a network administrator is examining the network in Figure 4-16. The top of the figure shows a switch, using a default configuration, with four hosts connected to it. All four of these hosts belong to the same broadcast domain. If host A sends a broadcast frame, the switch will flood the message, and all hosts will receive it. This worked great in the earlier example when departments were on separate floors, but now say you have Sales personnel on each of the other two floors. The bottom of Figure 4-16 shows the new network. This time the administrator has configured the switch to say, "Hosts A and B are in Virtual LAN 1. Hosts C and D are in Virtual LAN 2." In this instance, if host A sends a broadcast frame, only host B will receive it. The switch still floods the frame but only within the broadcast domain (VLAN) that host A is connected to.

FIGURE 4-16

VLAN switching

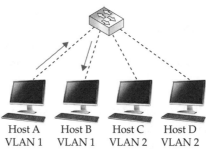

INSIDE THE EXAM

Ethernet Characteristics

Frames are a sequence of bits, received in an expected order and separated into fields. Study Figure 4-3 and Table 4-1 so that you recognize the fields and their purpose. The Ethernet frame consists of a header and trailer that are 18 bytes long. When added to a payload of 46-1500 bytes, you end up with a legitimate frame size of 64-1518 bytes. Anything smaller is a runt; anything longer is a giant; both are bad and discarded by interfaces. If the data in the payload, the Layer 3 packet, is less than 46 bytes, padding or pad (0s) is added to make sure it is at least 46 bytes long.

Ethernet is a contention-based specification, and care should be taken to reduce the size of collision domains. Layer 2 devices—bridges and switches—are used to segment collision domains. Ethernet uses carrier sense multiple access collision detection (CSMA/CD). Devices involved in a collision send jamming signals and then run a timing algorithm before transmitting again.

Ethernet Standards

Ethernet standards define the OSI Physical and Data Link specifications necessary for networking. IEEE 802.3 standards define Ethernet networking. Various physical specifications for cabling exist—such as 10Base-T, 100 Base-T, 1000, Base-T, 1000Base-SX, and 1000Base-LX—and follow the same

format: speed (in Mbps), transmission type (baseband), and cable type/distance rating. The Ethernet standard chosen defines the speed, while the Physical layer specification defines the transmission method involved. Ethernet runs at 10 Mbps, Fast Ethernet runs at 100 Mbps, and Gigabit Ethernet runs at 1000 Mbps. These data rates are achieved using a variety of cable types and duplex options.

Switch Fundamentals

Be familiar with the switch LEDs and the bootup process. The exam will have several questions regarding the treatment of frames by a switch, so it is essential to understand CAM (or MAC) table updates and frame treatment before, during, and after. Switches support simultaneous frame delivery. Duplex operations eliminate collisions and increase bandwidth, and most modern switches can use autonegotiation to determine both speed and duplex. You should be able to identify characteristics of the cut-through, store-and-forward, and fragment-free switching modes.

Switched Network Design Considerations

The exam won't ask you design questions, but you will be faced with a variety of network

(Continued)

INSIDE THE EXAM

diagrams to decipher. Be familiar with Cisco's switched network design terminology, but don't expect any questions dealing directly with it. You should be intently focused on how switches learn MAC address locations, build the CAM table, and handle different message types (unicast, multicast, and broadcast).

Spanning Tree Protocol (STP) details are not on this exam; that's a topic for the ICND2 exam. Just know that it is a loop avoidance technology in a fully switched, redundant network. VLANs are covered in Chapter 7; just know that they allow multiple LANs to run on a switch, controlling broadcast propagation.

CERTIFICATION SUMMARY

In 1980, IEEE created the 802 committee to develop network specifications, including the 802.3 series—defining Ethernet OSI Layer 1 and Layer 2 standards for vendors.

All frames, regardless of type, begin with some sort of "start of frame" notification, followed by destination and source addresses, a Type field, a data payload, and a Frame Check Sequence (FCS) field.

Ethernet uses 48-bit MAC addresses. Each MAC address is unique because of the OUI—the first half of the address assigned by IEEE to a manufacturer, which is then combined with a 24-bit unique ID assigned by the manufacturer. Within Ethernet, MAC addresses are either unicast, broadcast, or multicast addresses. A unicast message is addressed to one host (one-to-one). A broadcast message is addressed to all systems (one-to-all) on the segment (MAC address FF:FF:FF:FF:FF:FF). A multicast address uses a special address (one-to-several) that is recognized only by a specific subset of hosts on the segment.

A collision domain is any group of devices, sharing the same media, whose frames will collide with each other if they transmit at the same time. Collision domains should be kept small and can be segmented with bridges and switches. Within a collision domain, Ethernet uses CSMA/CD as a media access method by listening for a clear line and then attempting to transmit. If a collision occurs, both systems send jamming signals and then run a random timing algorithm to set a delay before retransmitting to avoid colliding again.

Ethernet standards include the 802.3 series, as well as several Physical layer cable specifications. The original Ethernet standard, 802.3, ran at 10 Mbps. Fast Ethernet, 802.3u, runs at 100 Mbps over 100Base-T. Gigabit Ethernet is 802.3z and runs at 1000 Mbps over various copper and fiber cabling. Gigabit always requires full duplex.

Switches provide better network performance, split collision domains into one per port (device), and result in better security on the network. The switch LEDs provide valuable information on system status. While initially flooding frames, switches quickly build a port address (or CAM) table that maps the source MAC address to its arrival interface. This table allows the switch to provide 100 percent bandwidth usage between hosts, delivering the message to only the port that unicast frames are intended for.

Switches also allow for negotiating best duplex and speed options for each device connection. The IEEE autonegotiation standard sets up the highest available bandwidth speed and makes every attempt to run at full duplex between the host and the switch. Switch modes include cut through (fastest but with the most errors), store and forward (the Cisco default behavior; slower but with no bad frames delivered), or fragment free (the compromise version; reads the first 64 bytes of the frame to capture and discards the most common errors, runts or collision fragments, before sending).

Broadcast loops within a fully switched environment are mitigated by STP. VLANs allow multiple LANs on a single switch while containing broadcast traffic and increasing security. Devices within a VLAN (a defined group of switch ports) can transmit data only to members of their own VLAN without the aid of a router.

TWO-MINUTE DRILL

Ethernet History

❏ IEEE began work on the 802.x networking standards, including Ethernet, in 1980. The Ethernet series is the 802.3 specifications.

Ethernet Characteristics

❏ Frames include fields for source and destination MAC addresses, payload types, data payload, and FCS.

❏ CSMA/CD is the media access method used by Ethernet to detect and deal with collisions.

❏ Ethernet nodes, wanting to transmit, first listen to the wire to determine whether it is clear. During transmission, if another device attempts to transmit, a collision occurs. Both devices involved in the transmission send a jam signal and then wait a random amount of time (because of an algorithm) before attempting to transmit again.

Ethernet Standards

❏ IEEE 802.3 standards define OSI Layer 1 and Layer 2 specifications for Ethernet. 802.3 is Ethernet, 802.3u is Fast Ethernet, and 802.3z is Gigabit Ethernet.

❏ The Physical layer, cable, and specifications for networking define the speed, transmission type, and cable type/maximum segment length. 10Base-T, 100Base-T, 1000Base-T, 1000Base-SX, and 1000Base-LX define baseband transmission at different speeds. T is twisted pair copper, and SX and LX are fiber optic cable.

❏ Cable specifications also require a minimum specific cable grade to accomplish their transmission speed. 100Base-T requires Category 5 or higher.

Switch Fundamentals

❏ The LED panel on a Catalyst switch contains two system indicator lamps and three mode indicator lamps that indicate the system status. The LED status and meaning are listed in Table 4-3.

- ❑ Switch ports can be half or full duplex and can run at multiple speeds. IEEE autonegotiation between the switch and the host NIC determines the fastest bandwidth rate and always attempts to use full duplex.

- ❑ Switches run a POST at bootup. If the IOS does not load properly, the SYST LED will glow amber.

- ❑ Switches filter unicast messages and flood multicast and broadcast messages. Unicast messages are flooded only until the CAM table is populated with the destination MAC address/interface pairings.

- ❑ Unicast messages are filtered based on entries in the CAM table, also called the MAC or port address table. The table is built and updated dynamically by comparing the source MAC address and incoming interface pairing with the table. If there is no entry, the pair is added. If there is an entry, the information is updated if necessary and any old entry deleted.

- ❑ Cut-through switching mode begins delivering the message as soon as the destination address is discovered (while bits are still incoming to the switch). This results in faster processing but the delivery of more corrupt or damaged frames (runts and collision fragments).

- ❑ Store and forward buffers the entire frame into memory, recalculates, and compares the FCS before forwarding to the correct interface for delivery. This adds to latency but does not transmit bad frames. It also allows for devices of different bandwidth speeds and duplex settings to communicate on the same switch. This is the current default setting for most switches.

- ❑ Fragment free reads the first 64 bytes and then begins delivering the frame. This catches most (runts) but not all frame errors.

Switched Network Design Considerations

- ❑ Proper design for a fully switched network includes three types of switches. Access-layer switches are used to connect user workstations, distribution-layer switches are used to connect access switches together (for redundancy), and core-layer switches provide high-bandwidth aggregation for distribution-layer switches in large networks.

- ❑ STP is used to automatically protect against data loops in a switched network.

- ❑ Administrators create VLANs by grouping switch ports together. The group of ports is treated as a completely separate physical network, limiting broadcasts and preventing traffic from traveling into or out of it.

SELF TEST

The following Self Test questions will help you measure your understanding of the material presented in this chapter. Read all the choices carefully since there may be more than one correct answer. Choose all the correct answers for each question.

Ethernet Fundamentals

1. Which standards organization defined the Ethernet standard?
   A. IEEE
   B. ISO
   C. ANSI
   D. DIX

2. Which frame field is responsible for error checking?
   A. Preamble
   B. SFD
   C. FCS
   D. Length/Type

3. While examining an 802.3 Ethernet frame from a packet capture, you notice the entry in the Type field is 0800 (in hex). Which of the following are true? (Choose two.)
   A. The entry indicates the length of the frame.
   B. The entry indicates the protocol being transported.
   C. The frame is 0800 bits in length.
   D. The frame is transporting an IPv4 packet.

4. What is the total MTU for Ethernet?
   A. 1500
   B. 1518
   C. 1536
   D. 1537

5. The MAC address of your NIC is 0A:12:3C:4B:67:DE. Which of the following represents the organizationally unique identifier?
   A. 0A:12:3C
   B. 4B:67:DE
   C. 12:3C:4B
   D. 3C:4B:67

6. Twenty hosts are connected to a hub. Host A sends a unicast message to Host B. Which of the following is *not* true?

   A. Only Host B opens and processes the message.

   B. All hosts receive the message.

   C. All hosts open and process the message.

   D. The destination address field holds Host B's MAC address.

7. Your network has 20 computers connected to a hub. You want to increase performance by reducing the size of the collision domain as much as possible. Which of the following devices can be used to do this? (Choose all that apply.)

   A. A hub

   B. A bridge

   C. A switch

   D. None of the above

8. How does CSMA/CD react to collisions?

   A. All systems jam the network, and then all begin transmitting again.

   B. Hosts involved in a collision send an RTS signal indicating a time frame in which to retransmit.

   C. Hosts involved in the collision send a jamming signal and then run an algorithm before retransmitting.

   D. Collisions do not occur on CSMA/CD.

9. On an Ethernet network, PC1 sends a message to PC2. The message must cross two routers along the pathway. Which of the following statements are true concerning the communication between PC1 and PC2? (Choose all that apply.)

   A. The frame header changes twice during the time it is sent from PC1 to finally reaching its destination at PC2.

   B. The frame header changes three times during the time it is sent from PC1 to finally reaching its destination at PC2.

   C. The packet header changes at each router in the delivery path.

   D. The packet header never changes during the delivery path.

   E. PC1 broadcasts a DNS message to determine PC2's MAC address before building the frame.

   F. PC1 broadcasts an ARP request to determine PC2's MAC address before building the frame.

10. Which IEEE standard equates to Fast Ethernet?

   A. 802.3

   B. 802.3u

   C. 802.3z

   D. 802.4

11. What is the maximum segment length on 100Base-T?
    A. 100 meters
    B. 100 feet
    C. 500 feet
    D. 10 meters

Switch Fundamentals

12. You connect a host to a switch. The host is capable only of half duplex. After the connection is negotiated, how should the interface DUPLX LED appear?
    A. Amber
    B. Green
    C. Green/amber
    D. Off

13. A switch is powered on for the first time. Ten devices, Hosts A through J, are connected to the switch. Which of the following are true for the first frame received by the switch? (Choose two.)
    A. The switch records the destination MAC address in the frame and the incoming interface pair in the CAM table.
    B. The switch records the source MAC address in the frame and the incoming interface pair in the CAM table.
    C. The frame is flooded to all other devices connected to the switch.
    D. The frame is sent only to the intended port.

14. Hosts A through J have been connected to a switch for some time, with Host A on port 1, Host B on port 2, and so on. A user moves his system and connects Host A to interface 12. Immediately after the connection, Host A sends a unicast message to Host B. Which of the following are true? (Choose two.)
    A. When the frame enters the switch, it is flooded to all interfaces.
    B. When the frame enters the switch, it is sent directly to interface 2, and no other.
    C. After this unicast message is sent, frames addressed to Host A will continue to be sent to interface 1.
    D. After this unicast message is sent, frames addressed to Host A will be sent to interface 12.

15. A host using a 10/100 NIC is connected to a Catalyst switch. The switch interface is configured for autonegotiate, but the NIC is not. Assuming speed *can* be determined by the switch, which of the following will autonegotiation default to for this scenario?
    A. 10 Mbps, half duplex
    B. 10 Mbps, full duplex
    C. 100 Mbps, half duplex
    D. 100 Mbps, full duplex

16. Host A and Host B are connected to the same switch, and Host A sends a message to Host B. When the switch starts receiving the bits, it reads the destination MAC address, determines the port Host B is on, and immediately opens a channel to that port while bits are still being received. Which switch mode is being used?
    A. Cut through
    B. Store and forward
    C. Fragment free
    D. Full duplex

17. Host A and Host B are connected to the same switch, and Host A sends a message to Host B. When the switch starts receiving the bits, it reads the first 64 bytes, determines the port Host B is on, and opens a channel to that port while bits are still being received. Which switch mode is being used?
    A. Cut through
    B. Store and forward
    C. Fragment free
    D. Full duplex

18. You have 100-Mbps and 1000-Mbps hosts throughout your network. A new trainee asks you which switching method is used on your switches. Which is the correct response?
    A. Cut through
    B. Store and forward
    C. Fragment free
    D. Full duplex

19. A trainee is examining a switch. Port 1 is directly connected to another switch; however, the port's LED is solid amber. The trainee asks whether this is a problem. You determine the LED mode is set to STAT. Which of the following is the correct response?
    A. This is not a problem since all ports are amber in STAT mode.
    B. This is a problem since no port should ever appear amber.
    C. This is a problem. STP has the port in a forwarding state.
    D. This is not a problem. STP has the port in a blocking state.

20. According to Cisco design theory for a fully switched network, hosts do not connect directly to which types of switches? (Choose all that apply.)

    A. Access

    B. Core

    C. Distribution

    D. Cut through

    E. Fragment free

21. Hosts A, B, C, and D are all connected directly to a switch with no additional configuration. Which of the following statements are true? (Choose all that apply.)

    A. There is one collision domain.

    B. There are four collision domains.

    C. There is one broadcast domain.

    D. There are four broadcast domains.

22. Using Figure 4-17, which of the following statements are true? (Choose all that apply.)

    A. Hosts A and B are in the same collision domain.

    B. Hosts A and B are in different collision domains.

    C. Hosts C and D are in the same collision domain.

    D. Hosts C and D are in different collision domains.

    E. Hosts A, B, C, and D are in the same broadcast domain.

    F. Hosts A, B, C, and D are in different broadcast domains.

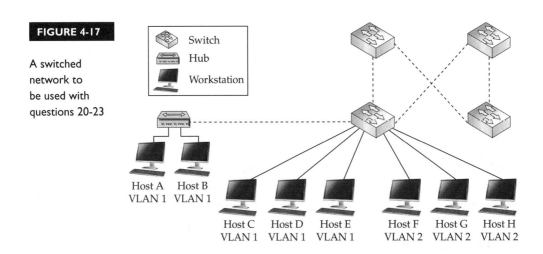

FIGURE 4-17

A switched network to be used with questions 20-23

Switch
Hub
Workstation

Host A   Host B
VLAN 1   VLAN 1

Host C   Host D   Host E   Host F   Host G   Host H
VLAN 1   VLAN 1   VLAN 1   VLAN 2   VLAN 2   VLAN 2

23. Using Figure 4-17, assuming all CAM tables are up to date, if Host A sends a broadcast message, which of the following are true statements? (Choose all that apply.)

    A. Host B will receive the message.

    B. Hosts C, D, and E will receive the message.

    C. Host F will receive the message.

    D. Hosts G and H will receive the message.

    E. The broadcast message is not propagated by the switch.

24. Using Figure 4-17, assuming all CAM tables are up to date, if Host A sends a unicast message to Host E, which of the following is a true statement?

    A. Hosts B and E will process the message.

    B. Hosts C and D will process the message.

    C. Hosts F and G will process the message.

    D. Only Host E will process the message.

    E. The switch cannot forward the message.

25. Using Figure 4-17, assuming all CAM tables are up to date, if Host A sends a unicast message to Host F, which of the following is a true statement?

    A. Hosts B and F will receive the message.

    B. Hosts G and H will receive the message.

    C. Hosts E and F will receive the message.

    D. Only Host F will receive the message.

    E. The switch cannot forward the message.

SELF TEST ANSWERS

Ethernet Fundamentals

1. ☑ **A** is correct. IEEE was the first standards body to create Ethernet standards.

   ☒ **B, C,** and **D** are incorrect. **B** is incorrect because ISO created the OSI Reference Model, not the first Ethernet standard. **C** is incorrect because ANSI is a U.S. standards body that adopts IEEE and other standards. **D** is incorrect because DIX for Digital Equipment Company, Intel, and Xerox teamed to create the first industry standard, but they are not a standards organization.

2. ☑ **C** is correct. The Frame Check Sequence (FCS) field provides a CRC or checksum for error checking.

   ☒ **A, B,** and **D** are incorrect. **A** is incorrect because the preamble indicates a frame is coming. **B** is incorrect because the start frame delimiter indicates the preamble is finishing, and the next bits begin the frame. **D** is incorrect because the length/type indicates the length of frame or type of Layer 3 protocol transmitted.

3. ☑ **B** and **D** are correct. If the entry is larger than 0600, it indicates the Layer 3 protocol being transmitted. IPv4 equates to 0800 in hex.

   ☒ **A** and **C** are incorrect. The entry is larger than 0600, so neither of these can be true.

4. ☑ **B** is correct. 1518 is the largest allowable Ethernet frame size.

   ☒ **A, C,** and **D** are incorrect. **A** is incorrect because 1500 is the maximum payload size. The total MTU includes the frame header and trailer. **C** and **D** are incorrect values.

5. ☑ **A** is correct. The OUI is the first half of a MAC address.

   ☒ **B, C,** and **D** are incorrect. **B** is incorrect because the last six hex digits are the NIC's unique ID assigned by the manufacturer. **C** and **D** are incorrect for the OUI.

6. ☑ **C** is correct. Only the host that the unicast message is addressed to will open and process the message.

   ☒ **A, B,** and **D** are incorrect. All hosts receive the message since they are all connected to a Layer 1 device. Only Host B will open and process the message since the destination address field matches its MAC address.

7. ☑ **C** is correct. While all Layer 2 devices split collision domains, switches create a separate collision domain for each port.

   ☒ **A, B,** and **D** are incorrect. **A** is incorrect because hubs are Layer 1 devices and *extend* collision domains. **B** is incorrect because a bridge is a Layer 2 device, but can split the network only into two collision domains. **D** is incorrect.

8. ☑ **C** is correct. In CSMA/CD, systems involved in a collision send a jam signal to indicate a collision to all devices. They then run a timer algorithm, allowing them to retransmit at a random time interval.

   ☒ **A, B,** and **D** are incorrect. **A** is incorrect because only systems involved in the collision send a jam signal. **B** is incorrect because RTS messages are sent on CSMA/CA, not CSMA/CD. **D** is incorrect because collisions do occur on CSMA/CD.

9. ☑ **A, D,** and **F** are correct. The frame header is removed and replaced by each router along the pathway. Therefore, the frame header will change twice during delivery. The packet information is never stripped off until it reaches its final destination. Finally, PC1 broadcasts an ARP message for PC2's IP address, looking for a MAC. The router will respond.

   ☒ **B, C,** and **E** are incorrect because these are all false statements.

10. ☑ **B** is correct. Fast Ethernet is defined by the 802.3u standard.

    ☒ **A, C,** and **D** are incorrect. **A** is incorrect because 802.3 defines Ethernet at 10 Mbps. **C** is incorrect because 802.3z defines Gigabit-speed Ethernet. **D** is incorrect because 802.4 defines token bus.

11. ☑ **A** is correct. The 100Base-T maximum segment length is 100 meters.

    ☒ **B, C,** and **D** are incorrect because they do not match any standard.

Switch Fundamentals

12. ☑ **D** is correct. If the LED mode is set to duplex, there are only two options: green for full duplex and off for half duplex.

    ☒ **A, B,** and **C** are incorrect. **A** is incorrect because amber LEDs do not appear when the mode is set to duplex. **B** is incorrect because green LEDs indicate a full-duplex connection when the mode is set to duplex. **C** is incorrect because green/amber LEDs do not appear when the mode is set to duplex.

13. ☑ **B** and **C** are correct. As frames enter a newly powered-on switch, the CAM table is empty. The switch records the source address, and its originating interface, in the table and floods the message.

    ☒ **A** and **D** are incorrect. **A** is incorrect because recording the destination address with an incoming interface would not work. Switches record the *source* address. **D** is incorrect because a switch will flood any unicast message it receives that does not match an entry in the CAM table.

14. ☑ **B** and **D** are correct. Moving Host A to a different port would not affect the delivery of frames with a destination MAC for Host B—still on port 2. As the first message from Host A is received, the CAM table will update to the new port (12).

    ☒ **A** and **C** are incorrect. **A** is incorrect because only three types of frames are flooded by switches: broadcast, multicast, and frames without a matching entry in the CAM table. Since Host B is still in the CAM table, the message would be delivered appropriately. **C** is incorrect because the CAM table is updated to Host A's new port number immediately after the frame enters the switch.

15. ☑ **C** is correct. If speed is determined to be less than gigabit, the switch always defaults to half duplex.

    ☒ **A, B,** and **D** are incorrect because none of the remaining options is correct.

16. ☑ **A** is correct. Cut-through switches begin delivering the frame as soon as a destination address is discovered.

    ☒ **B, C,** and **D** are incorrect. **B** is incorrect because store-and-forward switches receive the entire frame before forwarding, injecting additional latency but examining it for errors. **C** is incorrect because fragment free reads the first 64 bytes of the frame before delivering it, thus reducing collision errors and bad frame propagation. **B** is incorrect because full duplex does not apply in this scenario.

17. ☑ **C** is correct. Fragment free reads the first 64 bytes of the frame before delivering it, thus reducing collision errors and bad frame propagation.

    ☒ **A, B,** and **D** are incorrect. **A** is incorrect because cut-through switches begin delivering the frame as soon as a destination address is discovered. **B** is incorrect because store-and-forward switches receive the entire frame before forwarding it, thus injecting additional latency but examining it for errors. **D** is incorrect because full duplex does not apply in this scenario.

18. ☑ **B** is correct. Store-and-forward switches receive the entire frame before forwarding, injecting additional latency but examining it for errors. This allows devices of different speeds/duplex settings to communicate over the same switch.

    ☒ **A, C,** and **D** are incorrect. **A** is incorrect because cut-through switches begin delivering the frame as soon as a destination address is discovered. **C** is incorrect because fragment free reads the first 64 bytes of the frame before delivering it, thus reducing collision errors and bad frame propagation. **D** is incorrect because full duplex does not apply in this scenario.

19. ☑ **D** is correct. Solid amber in STAT mode indicates a port has been placed in a blocking state by the Spanning Tree Protocol, as designed.

    ☒ **A, B,** and **C** are incorrect. **A** is incorrect because all ports should *not* appear amber in STAT mode. **B** is incorrect because ports *can* be amber in STAT mode. When STP is doing its job, a blocking state port prevents routing loops. **C** is incorrect because ports in a forwarding state are green.

20. ☑ **B** and **C** are correct. Hosts do not directly connect to core-or distribution-layer switches.

☒ **A, D,** and **E** are incorrect. **A** is incorrect because access switches provide direct access to users. **D** and **E** are incorrect because cut through and fragment free are switch modes, not design layers.

21. ☑ **B** and **C** are correct. Each switch port represents a separate collision domain. Unconfigured switches do not split broadcast domains.

☒ **A** and **D** are incorrect. These are incorrect choices.

22. ☑ **A, D,** and **E** are correct. Hosts A and B are connected to a hub, putting them both in the same collision domain. Hosts C and D have individual links to the switch, putting them in different collision domains. Hosts A, B, C, and D are all in the same VLAN, putting them all in the same broadcast domain.

☒ **B, C,** and **F** are incorrect. **B** is incorrect because hosts on a hub are in the same collision domain. **C** is incorrect because each host connected to a switch is in its own collision domain. **F** is incorrect because a VLAN creates a broadcast domain.

23. ☑ **A** and **B** are correct. Hosts A, B, C, D, and E are all in VLAN 1, putting them all within the same broadcast domain.

☒ **C, D,** and **E** are incorrect. **C** is incorrect because Host F is in VLAN 2, putting it in a different broadcast domain. **D** is incorrect because Hosts G and H are in VLAN 2, putting them in different broadcast domains. **E** is incorrect because the statement that the broadcast message is not propagated by the switch is not true.

24. ☑ **D** is correct. Only Host E will process the message.

☒ **A, B, C,** and **E** are incorrect. **A** is incorrect because while B will see the message because it is on a hub with A, it will discard it when it sees that the MAC address is not its own. **B** is incorrect because the switch forwards the frame to only Host E's port, based on the CAM table entry. **C** is incorrect because Hosts F and G are in another VLAN and therefore would not receive the frame. **E** is incorrect because the statement that the switch cannot forward the message is not true.

25. ☑ **E** is correct. Host F is in a different VLAN; therefore, the switch can't deliver the frame without a router.

☒ **A, B, C,** and **D** are incorrect.

5

Preparing to Configure Cisco Devices

U p to now, most of this book has explored general networking concepts, which are applicable whether you are taking a Cisco exam or learning basic networking for *any* job in information technology (IT). In this chapter, though, we finally get Cisco-centric. We'll cover some basic methods and practices on Cisco devices, briefly describing device characteristics, and define the differences between the device's operating system and its configuration files. All this leads up to the next chapter where we actually start configuring Cisco devices. Because the configuration terminology and techniques are so similar for all Cisco devices, we will start with switches and then cover the differences as we get to routers in Part III.

CERTIFICATION OBJECTIVE 5.01

Storage (Memory) Locations and Purpose

The switch boot process, or device startup process, was introduced in Chapter 4. Cisco routers follow a similar process, with a few differences that will become important in later certifications. To better understand the boot process and device operation, it's helpful to know the different device storage (memory) locations, their names in the Cisco world, and the role they play. There are four areas of memory: RAM, flash, ROM, and NVRAM.

Random access memory (RAM) on a switch or router is exactly as on any computer—for working storage. It is where the operating system, the configuration (programming), and data are loaded to be available to the CPU for processing. RAM is dynamic, or volatile, clearing the instant the device is rebooted or loses power. This is why it is often referred to as dynamic RAM (DRAM).

Flash memory, or just flash, is a nonvolatile storage location, often on internal chips or cards that function like the hard drive, or better yet, internal solid-state drives, on a computer or tablet. Flash is used to store the Cisco operating system, the IOS (originally Internetwork Operating System).

Read-only memory (ROM) is a permanent memory location, often on a chip, within the device that, like its counterpart in other computers, holds the bootstrap, or startup program. The bootstrap program is run after power-on self-test (POST) when the device is powered up. Its job is to find the IOS image and start it loading into RAM.

TABLE 5-1	Memory Location	RAM	Flash	ROM	NVRAM
Cisco Device Memory Locations	Purpose	Running configuration	IOS image(s)	Bootstrap and ROMMON OS	Startup configuration

Finally, *nonvolatile RAM (NVRAM)* is another nonvolatile storage location within the device that stores the configuration file that will be loaded into RAM once the IOS has been loaded. NVRAM is similar to flash in composition, but unlike most computers, it is actually a separate component on Cisco devices. Both flash and NVRAM are nonvolatile in that they do not disappear if power is lost or a reboot occurs, but unlike ROM, chips are easily changed or erased by administrator commands or by copying a new version into the location. Table 5-1 summarizes this information. Remembering these locations and purposes can make learning device configuration and troubleshooting easier.

CERTIFICATION OBJECTIVE 5.02

Cisco Internetwork Operating System (IOS)

The Cisco operating system, like any computer operating system, is the base level programming that knows how to understand and use the various device interfaces and features. The features supported depend on the type of device and specific IOS image (version), but can include switching, routing, telecommunications, firewall, access control, QoS, and wireless functions. The resulting multitasking operating system can incorporate administrator input and configurations, using English-like instructions or text files, which are then translated into a form the device can understand and efficiently process. Like any other computer operating system, IOS recognizes inputs, provides output, and keeps track of peripheral devices and many configuration settings. The IOS also provides the framework for security and management configuration settings.

PC or tablet operating systems by Microsoft come in versions with different features such as Home, Standard, Professional, Server, etc. Cisco's IOS versions also offer different feature sets for specific implementations. Some versions, for instance, may provide better debug functions, specific command sets, or more compatibility features than others. If a command doesn't seem to be available, or if a service doesn't seem to work, check the IOS version—you may simply need to load a different or newer IOS version.

Not being a consumer product, Cisco images tend to appear cryptic on first examination. The naming convention for each new version of the Cisco IOS provides quite a bit of information for the experienced administrator. Each portion of the name signifies specific information, as shown in Figure 5-1.

After the router is up and running, the command **show version** can be used to check the version number your router is using. A sample output, with key information highlighted, is provided here:

```
classRTR1#show version
Cisco IOS Software, 2801 Software (C2801-IPBASE-M), Version
12.4(1c), RELEASE
SOFTWARE (fc1)
Technical Support: http://www.cisco.com/techsupport
Copyright (c) 1986-2005 by Cisco Systems, Inc.
Compiled Wed 26-Oct-05 08:42 by evmiller
ROM: System Bootstrap, Version 12.4(13r)T, RELEASE SOFTWARE (fc1)
classRTR1 uptime is 1 minute
System returned to ROM by power-on
System image file is "flash:c2801-ipbase-mz.124-1c.bin"
Cisco 2801 (revision 7.0) with 114688K/16384K bytes of memory.
Processor board ID FTX1120Z0T9
2 FastEthernet interfaces
DRAM configuration is 64 bits wide with parity disabled.
191K bytes of NVRAM.
62720K bytes of ATA CompactFlash (Read/Write)

Configuration register is 0x2102
```

FIGURE 5-1

Cisco IOS naming convention

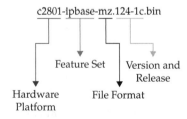

Know what information can be gathered from a show version *command output. Go over the sample output provided and make sure you can pick out the relevant information, especially keying on the configuration register, the IOS version, and the latest reload information.*

The **show version** command holds a lot of information about your device, which we will look at in greater detail when we start configuring and troubleshooting. You should recognize some of the things we have covered, such as the IOS version number, the bootstrap version number, and name of the "System image (IOS) file" used from flash. Information about the system boot procedure is also listed, including system uptime (since last power off) and the reason and time for the last reload of the IOS. Also displayed is information about the system itself: the amount of RAM, the interfaces available, and the amount of NVRAM and flash memory available. Finally, the configuration register setting is also displayed. The 0x2102 indicates the device booted in normal operation mode. This value gets changed when doing password recovery and for some special operations.

CERTIFICATION OBJECTIVE 5.03

Configuration Files

Cisco devices load both an operating system (stored in flash) *and* a configuration file (stored in NVRAM) into working memory called RAM. While the operating system provides the framework for system interaction and the overall functions the device is capable of performing, the configuration file provides the specifics needed to get the job done. For example, the operating system provides a method to recognize the device is a router with Ethernet and serial ports, but the configuration file provides the addresses and security settings for those interfaces. The configuration file provides settings on everything from interface addresses and communications specifics to passwords and protocol specifics. Configuration files are called by the IOS after bootup, and their settings are loaded into memory.

A configuration file is basically a text file of English-like commands that are then interpreted by the operating system into instructions that the CPU will understand. Similar files on other computing devices or implementations might be batch files, script files, or HTML files, if you are familiar with those.

Cisco devices actually have two configuration files—the startup configuration and the running configuration. The startup configuration, known as *startup-config,* is the configuration the router or switch pulls from NVRAM at boot. All configuration information placed into the startup-config remains, even when the router or switch loses power. The purpose of the startup-config should be obvious—a baseline of configurations upon which to operate after a power loss or reboot. Without a startup configuration file, administrators would have to retype all configuration information every time the device powered off. We do not modify the startup-config directly. We make all of our changes in the running-configuration file. Any changes that are made to the running-config file (stored in RAM) take effect immediately. To create the startup-config file we copy the contents of the running-config to the startup-config. In other words, changes are not made directly to the startup-config. Then the running-config is copied into NVRAM to become the new startup-config.

The only time a Cisco device does not start with the startup-config file is when no startup-config exists, or if the *configuration register* is set to ignore the startup configuration. NVRAM can be empty on a new device or if the administrator deletes the startup-config file using the **erase nvram** command (or the older **write erase** or **erase startup-config** command). If no startup-config exists, the device will default into *Setup* mode, asking a variety of questions to lead the administrator through configuring the device.

There are two PDF files you should look over as you go through this chapter. PDF05-01_Sample_switch_(Start) is a Cisco switch that has not been configured; notice that there is quite a bit of information there already because the IOS knows about the interfaces and line connections as well as some basic settings. This is our starting point with any Cisco switch. Some may have more or fewer features, but they all basically start with this type of information. PDF05-02_Sample_switch_(Configured) is basically a sample of where we are going in this chapter and the next two. You are not expected to understand all of this, but note that much of it is recognizable.

e x a m

ⓦatch   *Be sure you understand the differences between the startup configuration file and the running configuration file. Also, remember changes made to the running* *configuration go into effect immediately, and to save the changes you must issue the* **copy** *running-configuration startup-configuration* **command.**

Accessing the Configuration

Knowing that the configuration files hold the settings necessary for the router or switch to function, and that the running configuration is updated by an administrator in real time, an obvious question is raised: How are these changes made to the configuration file? On Cisco devices, the configuration files can be accessed locally or remotely, and using command line or web-based methods. This section introduces the various methods and features of accessing Cisco devices. The information covered in this introduction will provide the bedrock of information needed for success in later chapters and in your day-to-day administration.

Local Connections

The administrator can connect directly to the *console port* on the router or switch using a special console cable. Typically, this method is used for adding at least the initial configuration so that the device could then be accessed using a remote method. While very secure and common in study labs, this method is often inconvenient or impossible for monitoring or making changes in the real world. To access the Cisco router or switch using the console port, the administrator connects a console cable that looks like the one in Figure 5-2. This powder-blue cable ships with most Cisco devices, but is also available very inexpensively from sources like eBay.

The Cisco cable has a DB-9 connector that connects to a PC's serial port and an RJ-45 connector that plugs into the *console port* on the switch or router. The console cable is a rollover cable that maps pin 1 to pin 8, pin 2 to pin 7, and so on, "rolling over" one end of the cable to the other. The connection for local console access is shown in Figure 5-3.

FIGURE 5-2

Cisco console cable

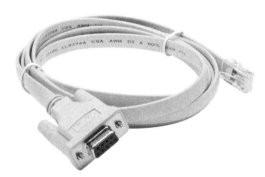

FIGURE 5-3

A console
connection

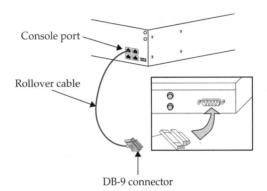

Since many laptops and tablets no longer have a serial port, you may need a USB-to-serial adapter—male to male—to connect to the DB-9 adapter on the console cable. There are several models available today from Amazon, eBay, and many office supply or electronics stores. It should come with a CD or instructions for a site to download the drivers that need to be installed. Once the software is installed, when the adapter is plugged in, the computer creates a virtual serial port (COM3 on mine). A good one is now sold as the Tripp Lite USA-19HS Keyspan High-Speed USB to Serial Adapter, shown in Figure 5-4. A similar unit from Belkin works very well too. Make sure whatever you get supports your computer's operating system.

FIGURE 5-4

USB to DB-9
serial adapter
(photo courtesy
of Tripp Lite)

Once this physical connection is made, the administrator can use a terminal emulation program, such as HyperTerminal or Terra Term, to type in configuration changes. When setting up any terminal emulation program on a console connection, the emulator must be configured properly on the computer's serial port. The default console settings for a Cisco switch or router are

- 9600 bits/second
- No hardware flow control
- 8-bit ASCII
- No stop bits
- 1 parity bit

When using HyperTerminal, Terra Term, or any other emulator, once you attempt to connect over the console port, the system will prompt for the correct communications settings. If you're using HyperTerminal for the connection, you can simply click the Restore Defaults button to set these. The default console settings in HyperTerminal are displayed in Figure 5-5. Once the communications settings are in place, the emulator allows access to the device.

FIGURE 5-5

The default console terminal settings

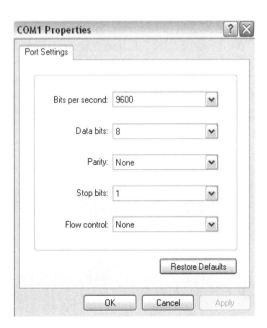

While many terminal emulation programs exist, HyperTerminal is probably the most common—due mainly to the fact it was built in to most Windows operating systems until Vista. HyperTerminal is available as a free trial at www.hilgraeve.com; the latest version supports up through Windows 8.x and offers SSH support. Terra Term can be downloaded for free from www.ayera.com and allows for remote SSH access as well. PuTTY is another free program for Windows. We've worked with MAC users who like iTerm.

Remote Connections

Administrators can, and typically do, access Cisco devices remotely through protocols like Telnet or SSH access. These connections provide the same functionality as a console connection from any location inside or outside the network without requiring a local connection to the device. One obvious concern is security—allowing remote access through any method opens a security concern for your network. When remote access is necessary, the device must be configured to allow this connection. SSH should be used instead of Telnet whenever possible because it encrypts the sessions over port 22. Telnet, on the other hand, runs in clear text over port 23, which would allow others to capture password and configuration information. We will see later that we will disable Telnet as a device security feature.

Remote connections do not require the console cable; they typically start from a computer's LAN connection, our Ethernet connection for this exam. In this case, the Telnet or SSH session is between our PC and the router or switch we are connecting to. In order to allow our Cisco device to accept a remote connection, we typically must first connect through the console to enable this functionality. We will take a look at that in the configuration part of this chapter.

Whereas console connections are limited to the length of the console cable, hence the term *local*, remote sessions can be to devices in the same room or halfway around the world. In one of the author's experience, he routinely connected to routers and switches on cruise ships sailing anywhere in the world via Telnet and SSH. These connections traveled over land circuits and satellite links. As long as there is a known IP address and a path to that address, it is possible to connect and make configuration changes or monitor the device operation.

Configuration Connections

Console and remote (Telnet or SSH) are different connections on the router and can have different features and configurations. The following output is the last few lines of a **show running-config** command with nothing configured. *Line con 0* (number zero) is the console connection, whereas *line vty 0 4* or *line vty 0 15* are virtual connections available for Telnet or SSH sessions (remote sessions). Some devices also have an auxiliary connection *line aux 0*, which can work like a console port via a modem.

```
Switch#show running-config
Building configuration...
---Lines omitted---
line con 0
line vty 0 4
 login
!
end
```

e x a m

ⓦatch   *Know the different methods of accessing Cisco devices. Local access is the most secure, requiring physical access to the device, and using a rollover cable with a DB-9 connector to the serial port of your laptop. Memorize the default settings required for emulator access over the console. The benefit of using SSH over Telnet in configuring routers or switches remotely is that it encrypts the session, preventing sniffers from stealing passwords, and so on.*

Many Cisco devices can be updated using web-based access. A graphical user interface (GUI) can be accessed over a web browser using Cisco Router and Security Device Manager (SDM). Since this technology is not covered on this exam, we will not be covering it here. While web access is relatively easy, often some features or commands can only be implemented from the command line.

CERTIFICATION OBJECTIVE 5.04

The Command Line Interface (CLI)

If you connect via the console or remotely (Telnet or SSH), interaction with Cisco devices is accomplished through the command line interface (CLI). The CLI allows administrators to access the IOS and configuration files using a series of commands to accomplish the configuration goal. Much like any other access functionality, the CLI has rules, syntax, and help functions, and these characteristics should be learned before attempting any device configuration.

The CLI can be a bit intimidating to new users, mainly due to its simplicity bordering on starkness, but with practice the user will become familiar and very proficient in using it. The CLI is divided into three main modes or levels: User, Privileged, and Configuration. Each offers different features and restrictions. We will introduce these modes here and then cover them in greater detail in the next chapter, when we start configuring our first Cisco device, a switch. It is important to know the different modes and how to quickly tell which mode you are currently in, because that controls your options. The screen prompt indicates the mode.

User Exec Mode

User Exec mode, also known commonly as just the *User mode*, is the first mode, or level, that a user reaches immediately after accessing the device in a Telnet (SSH) session. Think of it as the lobby of a building. Only a very basic subset of device commands can be used here, and no device configuration is allowed. Users in this mode can view basic settings (using the **show** command), but cannot change them or reboot or restart the device. The User mode prompt is a >, where the > symbol appears immediately after the device name or hostname, as configured by the administrator. It is a quick way for users to tell which mode they're in.

```
ClassRtr1>
ClassRtr1>?
```

The first prompt shows the User mode for a device named ClassRtr1. The second example shows how to get a list of available command options in any mode. Just type a question mark (**?**) at the prompt. No need to press ENTER. The commands supported will vary depending on the type of device and the version of Cisco IOS software.

Privileged Exec Mode

Privileged Exec mode, also known as just the *Privileged mode* or more commonly *Enable mode*, provides many additional options to the user. Using our building analogy, we are now moving into the operations part of the building, where we can do and see more things but can't really make significant changes yet. To access this mode, the user types in the command **enable**. Again, the **?** command would show the available options. To leave Privileged mode and go back to User mode, use the **disable** command. The # symbol prompt indicates privileged mode.

```
ClassRtr1>enable
ClassRtr1#
ClassRtr1#disable
ClassRtr1>
```

Because of its additional abilities, access to Privileged mode should be restricted and generally protected via a password. We will look at how to do this in the next section.

Global Configuration Mode

Configuration mode allows users to modify the running configuration files on the device, immediately impacting the device operation, as well as issue a command to save the new configuration. Staying with our building analogy, we have moved into the management or control center area. Global Configuration mode is accessed from the Privileged mode by typing the command **configure terminal**. From the Global Configuration mode, the user can enter submodes to configure features such as interfaces. Each submode is accessed by typing in a particular command, and each has its own prompt. We will look at the submodes and prompts in the configuration sections. As always, the **?** will show the commands available in this mode. The **end** or **exit** command returns to the Privileged mode. We will see that CTRL-Z will always exit clear back to Privileged mode from any submode, saving having to backtrack one mode at a time.

```
ClassRtr1#configure terminal
ClassRtr1(config)#
ClassRtr1(config)#end
ClassRtr1#
```

Mode Prompts and Changing Mode Commands

The CLI can be very confusing. However, knowing the purpose and prompt for each mode makes things a little easier to understand. Simply keep in mind that the prompt displays your location within the CLI, and **exit** takes you back one level. Table 5-2 summarizes the CLI configuration modes.

CLI Help Features

The CLI is command-driven, meaning a prompt awaits user input. In other words, much like the old DOS days, pictures and always-on menus simply aren't there to help. In CLI, correct syntax in typing commands is paramount. CLI supports context-sensitive help using the help request (**?**).

The CLI literally contains thousands of command combinations, and each command can have a number of parameter combinations to choose from. New users need to know which commands are even available to them in each mode before they can begin to decide how to proceed, not to mention the parameters for each command. Within the CLI, this is the function of the question mark, the help request. Typing a question mark from anywhere within the CLI displays every command, or command parameter, available in that particular mode. If there are more commands than there is screen space to display them, the commands scroll across the screen, pausing with a - - *More* - - entry. Pressing the SPACEBAR scrolls

TABLE 5-2   CLI Modes

CLI Mode	Prompt	Entry Command	Exit Command
User Exec	*Hostname*>	None—immediately after establishing emulator connection	**exit** or CTRL-C
Privileged Exec	*Hostname*#	**enable** (from User mode)	**disable**
Global Config	*Hostname* (config)#	**configure terminal** (from Privileged mode)	**exit** or CTRL-C
Interface Config	*Hostname* (config-if)#	**interface** *type number* (from anywhere within config mode)	**exit** or CTRL-C
Line Config	*Hostname* (config-line)#	**line** *type number* (from anywhere within config mode)	**exit** or CTRL-C
Router Config	*Hostname* (config-router)#	**router** *routing protocol* (from Global Configuration mode)	**exit** or CTRL-C

through the remainder of the command options one page at a time, while pressing ENTER displays one line at a time. To exit out of the display, press CTRL-C.

A very important note here, though, is that the display shows only the commands from that particular location—if you are in User mode, for instance, you would not see the commands available in Privileged mode, and a user configuring an interface would only see interface commands, not global configuration commands. Additionally, the question mark does not provide the full syntax of the command, only the next word available that is required at that point. At the prompt it would be the command itself. To see parameters of the command, type the command first, a space, and then a question mark. It can build the command, one choice at a time. Remember that as the commands scroll up to fill the page, you can press the SPACEBAR to see the next page of options. Typing anything else, like the next choice, abandons the help request.

The question mark help feature has one uniquely interesting feature. Every other command in the CLI requires that you press ENTER to activate it. When you type the question mark, however, it immediately begins displaying command options—you don't want to press ENTER after typing the ?. This can sometimes get annoying since the display of commands will stop after you press ENTER. Just keep in mind that the ? is instantaneous in its response. Additionally, after all the options display, the CLI presents the command as you previously typed it, awaiting a parameter. The idea is it would save time by not requiring you to retype the command. Unfortunately, many people simply start typing the command in again, entering it twice on the same line. Just remember to pause and view the screen before typing anything!

For example, suppose an administrator wanted to set the time on a router to 9:00 A.M., but is unfamiliar with the command syntax to do so. Using the question mark repeatedly, the commands to continue are displayed:

```
classRTR1#?
Exec commands:
  access-enable     Create a temporary Access-List entry
    ///Output truncated ///
  clear             Reset functions
  clock             Manage the system clock
classRTR1#clock ?
  read-calendar     Read the hardware calendar into the clock
  set               Set the time and date
  update-calendar   Update the hardware calendar from the clock
classRTR1#clock set ?
  hh:mm:ss  Current Time
```

```
classRTR1#clock set 13:58:22 ?
  <1-31>  Day of the month
  MONTH   Month of the year
classRTR1#clock set 13:58:22 4 DEC ?
  <1993-2035>  Year
classRTR1#clock set 13:58:22 4 DEC 2014
```

Notice in the preceding example code that the question mark only displays context-appropriate information for where it was entered. The options for the **clock** command include **read-calendar** and **set** and **update-calendar**, and a short description of each subcommand's purpose follows. Additionally, after typing the **?**, the options will display and the CLI will take you right back to the command so that you can add the next option. In other words, after typing **?** following the command **clock**, the options will display, and the CLI will present the command again, waiting for your input:

CLI Auto-Complete and Command Abbreviations

While the question mark is a helpful feature within the CLI, the auto-complete and abbreviation features are just as valuable. Being a command-driven interactive system, the CLI demands perfection. You can't just get part of the command right; it has to be typed *exactly*. The auto-complete function allows typing just the first characters of a command or word and then using the TAB key to add the rest—up to the next decision point. Note: The TAB key may not work on all keyboards and may not work with some of the USB to DB-9 adapters.

Command abbreviations are supported in the CLI. While we will generally be using the full commands in this book, in practice, most command words can be abbreviated; for example, **enable** can be entered as **en**. It is not always obvious what the abbreviated command is, but simply, it is enough characters to differentiate it from any other command available in that mode. This can be a real time saver both in the exam and on the job. During the exam, you need to make sure you know the full command in case the simulator doesn't support the abbreviation (rare). Help is available in the exam simulations. To see what the abbreviation would be, you can just use the help feature by entering a **?**. We can see that at the User mode, there are only two commands that begin with the letter e, so using **en** would tell the IOS we meant **enable** rather than **exit**.

```
Switch>?
Exec commands:
  access-enable    Create a temporary Access-List entry
  clear            Reset functions
```

```
connect        Open a terminal connection
disable        Turn off privileged commands
disconnect     Disconnect an existing network connection
enable         Turn on privileged commands
exit           Exit from the EXEC
help           Description of the interactive help system
lock           Lock the terminal
```

Other examples include **configure terminal** reduced to **conf t** and **copy running-configuration startup-configuration**, which can be reduced to **copy run start**. Using abbreviations saves a lot of time in switch and router configuration updates.

CLI Command History

The CLI also stores recently entered commands into a history buffer for quick recall and use. By default, the history buffer stores ten commands. Administrators configuring a device can move up and down the command history by using the up and down arrow keys. After scrolling through to find the command, administrators can edit it before reissuing (by pressing ENTER). For example, when configuring an access list, the first portion of the command (**access-list #**) always remains the same. Using the history function, an administrator could simply press the up arrow after entering a command and edit the second half of the command, avoiding having to retype the first portion over and over again. Both on the exam and in day-to-day administration, using the history buffer can greatly speed things up.

CLI Keyboard Shortcuts

The CLI provides several keyboard shortcuts, which work in conjunction with the history buffer. You should know them for the exam, but also to speed up your administration and practice activities. The relevant keyboard shortcuts are displayed in Table 5-2.

Some administrators love keyboard shortcuts, while others despise them. Their use is, of course, a matter of personal preference. One interesting note on them, however, deals with the letters appearing after the CTRL keys. The letter indicates what the keystroke actually does: the "p" is for previous, "n" is for next, "b" is for back, and "f" is for forward. Others include "a" (which is always first and indicates a move to the beginning), "e" (end), "r" (redisplay), and "d" (delete).

| **TABLE 5-3** | CLI Keyboard Shortcuts |

Keyboard Shortcut	Result
Up arrow or CTRL-P	Displays the most recent command entered into the CLI. Pressing repeatedly goes back through history until all commands in the buffer have been displayed.
Down arrow or CTRL-N	Moves forward in the history buffer (from past to most recent). If you have moved past a command using the up arrow, this allows you to return.
Left arrow or CTRL-B	Moves the cursor back through the command without deleting characters.
Right arrow or CTRL-F	Moves the cursor forward through the command without deleting characters.
BACKSPACE	Moves the cursor backwards, deleting characters.
CTRL-A	Moves the cursor immediately to the beginning of the command.
CTRL-E	Moves the cursor immediately to the end of the command.
CTRL-R	Redisplays the command and all parameters.
CTRL-D	Deletes a single character.
ESC-B	Moves back an entire word.
ESC-F	Moves forward an entire word.
ESC-D	Deletes an entire word.

CLI Error Notification

The CLI not only immediately responds with an error message when an erroneous command is entered, but it also provides a caret (^) indicating where in the command the syntax went awry. Granted, this is sometimes as frustrating as it is helpful since the CLI does not provide any indication of what syntax or wording *should* be there; however, it does help narrow down possible causes of problems. In the following example, for instance, an administrator attempted to assign an IP address to an interface but mistyped the command syntax. The caret indicates where the command syntax failed: the last octet of the IP address was not entered.

```
RTR1(config)#int serial 0/3/0
RTR1(config-if)#ip address 172.16.11 255.255.255.0
                                    ^
% Invalid input detected at '^' marker.
RTR1(config-if)#
```

EXERCISE 5-1

Introduction and Explore

In this exercise, we explore some of the skills that you will use in the next chapters as we start configuring switches and then routers. You'll perform this lab using Boson's NetSim simulator. The instructions and the topology diagram are included in the simulator. After starting up the simulator, if you haven't already done so in Exercise 1-3, take a few minutes to view the videos by clicking on the Watch the Video Demo link in the upper-right window. After viewing the videos, return to the simulator.

Task 1: Explore Lab Devices

1. Click on the Labs bar on the lower-left corner of the screen.

2. When the Lab Tree appears above, select Chapter 5 and then 5-1 Intro and Explore. The lab should load in the upper-right window.

3. Click on the Lab Instructions and NetMap tabs to see what they show. End up with the NetMap selected.

4. Put your mouse over each the devices in the map and notice a Device Statistics box appear next to the device. Click on the one for RouterA and note that it shows the interfaces and connections. Take a moment and look at each device's statistics and note the difference between routers, switches, and hosts.

5. The bottom window is the console display for the device displayed on the tab below the window. You may have to click on the space below the last line of output and press ENTER to see the current prompt. We'll come back to this in a minute.

6. There are three ways to open the other devices in the console window:
   1) Right-click on the device and then the Configure in Simulator button that appears. 2) Double-click on a device image. 3) Use the **Devices** drop-down at the top of the console window. Try each of these to open the remaining devices, pressing ENTER to see the prompt for each. You should now have six tabs below the console.

   The red X on the tab can be used to take that device out of the console. Try it and then reopen it so all six tabs show.

7. Select the A.22 tab. A means it is in the A LAN and .22 is the last octet of its IP address—the host portion of the address. Make sure you can see the C:> cursor and type **ping 10.0.1.77** and press ENTER. You should see that we have connectivity across the entire network.

   Use the lab topology at the top of this lab to ping other devices. All should work except 10.0.0.2 (SwitchA), which isn't configured yet—you will correct that in the next chapter.

   Note that it is still passing data properly even so. That is not the case with routers; routers would not pass data if they were unconfigured.

8. Select the RouterA tab. Make sure you can see the RouterA> cursor and type **ping 10.0.1.77** and press ENTER. You should see that we have connectivity across the entire network, but the output is different than when run from a computer; this is Cisco's version of ping. Ping RouterB's interfaces and SwitchB.

9. From the RouterA prompt, press the UP-ARROW key and note that you can recall and rerun or edit earlier commands. This works on all of the devices.

10. Ping other IP addresses from different devices. All should work except pinging SwitchA.

11. Try pinging from SwitchA. That fails too because there is no IP address to return to.

Task 2: Explore Device Configurations

1. From any of the hosts, type **ipconfig** and press ENTER. Then try **ipconfig /all** and compare the results. The **ipconfig** command works only on hosts, not Cisco devices.

2. From RouterA, type **show running-config** and press ENTER. Don't panic—it will fail because that command is not allowed at this level. Look over the error message, then at the prompt type **?** to see the commands available at this level. SPACEBAR displays more; anything else stops the display.

   To see the configuration, we need to be in Privileged mode (enable mode). Type **enable** (or **en**) and press ENTER. When prompted for a password, type **ccent** (*this will be the enable secret password on all Cisco devices in all labs*) and ENTER; it is case sensitive. Note the change in the prompt.

> You should now be able to run the **show running-config** (or **sho run**) command. You can use the scrollbar on the right side to scroll back and look at earlier output.

3. Use these skills to look at the configurations of the other Cisco devices. Don't worry if you don't understand all the output; we are just becoming familiar with the NetSim, the interface, and the CLI.

> Note that if you return to a device, you are still in Privileged mode unless you typed **end** or **exit** to return to User mode.

Task 3: Console vs. Remote Sessions

Up to this point we have been simulating console connections with the Cisco devices—meaning using a PC and a console cable to plug into the console port of each device. We are not connecting over the network. While that is common for initial configurations, we have an established network, so let's look at remote connections using Telnet or SSH.

   We are going to go to each Cisco device from A.22.

1. Close all console sessions (tabs) except A.22 by using the red X in the tabs.

2. At the C:> prompt, type **telnet 10.0.1.1** (LAN interface on RouterB) and press ENTER. When prompted for a password, type **cisco** and press ENTER. *This will be the remote access password you will use on all of your preconfigured devices in all labs unless told otherwise.* You should get the RouterB> prompt.

> Note that you entered in User mode and would have to use the **enable** command and password (**ccent**) to go further.

> After looking around, **exit** out, maybe twice, to return to A.22.

3. Repeat step 2 to Telnet to SwitchB and RouterA, going into Privileged mode on each and running the configuration. You won't be able to Telnet to SwitchA (not configured) or the other hosts (not allowed).

Repeat any or all of these steps until you are comfortable launching a NetSim and starting a console session on all devices. See the configuration of each device and confirm connectivity across all links to all devices (except SwitchA). Make sure that you can successfully Telnet to any Cisco device from any of the hosts. The more comfortable you are with these basic steps, the easier the rest of the labs will be. Return to this lab as often as it takes.

Use File | Exit from the menu or the last icon on the toolbar to exit out of the simulator.

INSIDE THE EXAM

Storage (Memory) Locations and Purpose

Most of the concepts in this chapter apply no matter what Cisco device you are configuring. Test-wise, be sure you know the boot process and the storage locations within a router: RAM, ROM, NVRAM, and flash. Memorize which files are stored in each location, and be able to differentiate between the two different configuration files: running-config and startup-config. Remember, if a startup-config does not exist, the router will boot into Setup mode.

Cisco Internetwork Operating System (IOS)

Be sure you know the naming convention for IOS filenames, and practice the **show version** command. You will definitely be asked to decode information from the **show version** output.

Configuration Files

Access to the configuration files is either local via the console or remote, using Telnet or preferably SSH because of the encryption. Local console connections require a serial port, rollover cable, DB-9 connector, and a terminal emulator, such as HyperTerminal. Be sure to memorize the default settings for a session over the console port. Telnet runs over port 23 and is sent in clear text, while SSH runs on port 22.

The Command Line Interface (CLI)

Be prepared to see numerous questions regarding the basic concepts of the CLI. Know the modes inside and out, and be prepared to identify them based on prompt and type of command entered. Also, definitely know what steps to take to exit out of a mode. These are summarized in Table 5-2.

Be familiar with the context-sensitive help functions within the CLI. Remember the question mark shows all commands *relevant to the mode and command location where it is typed*. Command entries can be abbreviated, so long as enough characters have been entered to allow the CLI to determine the unique command from the list of available options. TAB can be used to complete the command word and the syntax in much the same way. Ten commands are stored by default in the history buffer; using the arrow keys and keyboard shortcuts provides for faster administration and configuration. Remember the caret (^) symbol is used to identify the location of the error within the syntax.

CERTIFICATION SUMMARY

Cisco devices use the configuration register to determine the bootup process, much like the BIOS settings on a PC. There are four storage locations within a router: RAM, ROM, NVRAM, and flash. *Random access memory (RAM)* holds the running-config and is volatile in nature, clearing instantly if the device is rebooted or loses power. *Flash* memory is a nonvolatile storage location, on a chip or removable card, used to store operating system images. *Read-only memory (ROM)* is another permanent memory location within the switch or router that holds the bootstrap program. *Nonvolatile RAM* (NVRAM) is another permanent storage location within the device and holds the startup-config file.

If the startup-config file does not exist, the IOS will load a file called setup, which runs a step-by-step setup program for the administrator. ROMMON is a barebones basic operating system kept in ROM memory that can be used if flash is corrupted.

The Cisco IOS (operating system) recognizes inputs, provides output, keeps track of peripheral devices and bus settings, and provides the framework for security and management configuration settings. The name of the Cisco IOS image signifies specific information: hardware platform, feature set, file format, and version. The command **show version** can be used to check the version number your router is using, and displays information about the IOS version number, bootstrap version number, system uptime, reason and time for the last reload of the IOS, and the source of the current IOS. This command output also displays information about the amount of RAM, the interfaces available, and the amount of NVRAM and flash memory available, as well as the configuration register setting.

Cisco devices have two configuration files: the startup configuration and the running configuration. The startup-config is the configuration loaded from NVRAM into RAM at bootup. By being stored in NVRAM, the startup-config remains, even if the device loses power. The running-config runs in RAM and is the one the CPU uses. Any changes to the running-config go into effect immediately. To save any changes, use **copy running-config startup-config** (or **copy run start**) to update the startup-config.

Configuration files can be modified locally or remotely using the command line interface. A local connection is a direct connection to the device's RJ-45 console port using a rollover cable to a DB-9 connector affixed to a computer's serial port and a terminal emulator program. There are *USB to DB-9 adapters* that create a virtual COM port for newer laptops and table users. The default console settings are 9600 bits/second, no hardware flow control, 8-bit ASCII, no stop bits, and 1 parity bit. A remote connection involves a Telnet or SSH session between the administrator's PC and the Cisco device or between two Cisco devices. A remote session provides the same configuration and monitoring functionality as a console connection. Telnet runs over port 23 and sends all information in clear text, while SSH uses port 22 and encrypts the session, so it is the preferred method.

The CLI is divided into three main modes: User, Privileged, and Configuration. *User mode* allows only very basic viewing commands. Its prompt is a > following the device name. *Privileged mode*—aka Enable mode—offers additional options including viewing system information, restarting the system, or entering Configuration mode. Use the **enable / disable** commands to enter and exit Privileged mode. The prompt for Enable mode changes to a # sign. Configuration mode, or Global Configuration mode, allows users to modify the running configuration files on the device and access the various configuration submodes. Use the **configure terminal** and **exit** or **end** commands to enter or leave. Global Configuration mode commands affect the entire device. The configuration modes, prompts, and how to enter/exit are summarized in Table 5-2. Use CTRL-Z to exit from any Configuration mode to Privileged mode.

The context-sensitive help system is accessed by typing a question mark (?) at any time. The command doesn't require an ENTER. The CLI displays every command, or command parameter, available from that particular mode and cursor location. The CLI supports abbreviated (truncated) commands by typing enough of the command that the CLI can recognize it. If you are unsure of the proper syntax on a particular command, simply type in the first portion of the command and press the TAB key. The CLI also stores recently entered commands into a history buffer for quick recall and use via the up/down arrow keys and a set of keyboard shortcuts. By default, the history buffer stores ten commands but can be increased.

TWO-MINUTE DRILL

Storage (Memory) Locations and Purpose

❑ The configuration register and the boot system command control the boot sequence for Cisco devices much like the BIOS does on computers.

❑ ROM, a nonvolatile memory chip, holds the bootstrap program and the ROMMON basic OS. Bootstrap is used to start the device. ROMMON is only used if flash memory, the IOS files themselves are corrupted, or the administrator purposely changes the configuration register (for password reset).

❑ Flash memory, accessed second in the boot order, is nonvolatile and holds the IOS. NVRAM is nonvolatile and contains the saved startup configuration file. RAM is volatile in nature and holds the running configuration—it is the working area memory that the CPU interacts with.

Cisco Internetwork Operating System (IOS)

❑ The **show version** command displays the IOS version number, system uptime, the reasons for the last reload, the source of the current IOS, the amount of NVRAM and flash memory, and the configuration register setting.

Configuration Files

❑ All changes to the configuration on a Cisco device are made in real time to the running configuration. To make changes permanent, the running configuration must be stored in NVRAM by issuing the command **copy running-config startup-config**.

❑ Device access methods include local, via the console session, and remote, via Telnet or the more secure SSH. Console access requires a rollover cable, DB-9 connector, and a serial port on a system. There are USB to DB-9 adapters that will create virtual serial (COM) ports on newer laptops and tablets. A terminal emulation program can be used to enter configuration commands. The communication parameters for this connection are 9600 bits per second (baud), no hardware flow control, 8-bit ASCII, no stop bits, and 1 parity bit.

❑ Telnet remote access is simple and runs over port 23, but everything is in clear text. A more secure solution is to use SSH (port 22), which encrypts the session.

The Command Line Interface (CLI)

❑ The CLI has three main modes: User, Privileged, and Configuration. User mode is very limited with no ability to change or delete anything. It is identified by a > prompt immediately following the hostname.

❑ The **enable/disable** commands allow access and exit from Privileged mode. The prompt changes from a > to a #. More commands and access to the configuration mode are available here. Access to this mode should be secured with the **enable secret password** command.

❑ Moving from Privileged mode to Configuration mode uses the **configure terminal** command. Configuration starts in Global Configuration mode and can progress to several submodes. Each mode has a distinctive prompt, enter, and exit command. Table 5-2 summarizes this information. CTRL-Z or the **end** command exits out of Configuration mode altogether.

❑ The context-sensitive help feature for the CLI is accessed via the question mark (**?**). Entering a **?** anywhere in the CLI displays all command possibilities for the mode and cursor location. Prefacing the **?** with a letter or series of letters displays all options beginning with the letter(s).

❑ The CLI uses the caret (^) as an error indicator.

❑ CLI commands can be abbreviated (truncated) requiring only as many characters as necessary for the CLI to identify the command or parameter from other options.

❑ The TAB key automatically completes the remainder of the command word when pressed.

❑ Ten commands are kept by default in the history buffer. History is accessed by using the arrow keys (up and down keys scroll through the history). Other shortcut keys let administrators move through and edit commands.

SELF TEST

The following Self Test questions will help you measure your understanding of the material presented in this chapter. Read all the choices carefully since there may be more than one correct answer. Choose all the correct answers for each question.

Storage (Memory) Locations and Purpose

1. Cisco routers and switches use two configuration files. Where is the configuration file used at device bootup stored?
   A. RAM
   B. ROM
   C. Flash
   D. NVRAM

Cisco Internetwork Operating System (IOS)

2. If a device does not have a startup configuration stored in NVRAM, what happens when it is booted?
   A. The system boots into ROMMON.
   B. The system boots directly into Privileged mode.
   C. The system boots into Setup mode, prompting the user for basic configuration information.
   D. Nothing. Without a startup configuration, the boot process cannot occur.

Configuration Files

3. After configuring a switch and saving the configuration to startup-config, the administrator discovers an error has been made in the configuration. Which of the following command entries removes the saved configuration and boots the switch into Setup mode?
   A. **erase nvram**, followed by **reload**
   B. **delete nvram**, followed by **reload**
   C. **erase startup-config**, followed by **restart**
   D. **delete startup-config**, followed by **restart**

4. Which command displays the version number and filename of the IOS image running on the device?
   A. **show running-config**
   B. **show startup-config**
   C. **show ios**
   D. **show version**

5. You have a laptop with a free serial port. Which of the following is/are necessary to establish a connection to the console port on a Cisco device?
   A. A terminal emulator application
   B. A straight-through cable
   C. A crossover cable
   D. A rollover cable
   E. A DB-9 connector

6. Which of the following is true regarding remote configuration access methods to a Cisco device?
   A. Telnet, using port 22, requires a login and is a secure access method.
   B. Telnet, using port 23, requires a login and is a secure access method.
   C. SSH, using port 23, encrypts all communication.
   D. SSH, using port 22, encrypts all communication.

The Command Line Interface (CLI)

7. Which CLI modes let you use the **show running-config** command?
   A. User
   B. Privileged
   C. Global Configuration
   D. Setup
   E. All of the above

8. A network trainee asks for your assistance in configuring a switch. The prompt displayed is *RTR1(config-line)#* and the trainee wishes to return to Privileged mode. Which of the following actions would return the session to Privileged mode?
   A. Using keystroke combination ESC-Z
   B. Using keystroke combination CTRL-Z
   C. Typing **exit** and pressing ENTER
   D. Typing **end** and pressing ENTER

9. How many commands are held in the history buffer on a Cisco device by default?

   A. 10.

   B. 20.

   C. An unlimited number. The history buffer holds all configuration commands entered until a power cycle of the device.

   D. None. History must be enabled before storing commands.

10. An administrator is configuring a Cisco device and has pressed the up arrow three times, moving backward through the command history buffer. Which keystroke entry can be pressed to move forward in the buffer?

   A. Left arrow

   B. Down arrow

   C. CTRL-B

   D. CTRL-N

11. Which of the following commands copies the current configuration to the startup configuration?

   A. **copy running-config startup-config**

   B. **copy running-config nvram**

   C. **copy run start**

   D. **copy system:running-config nvram:startup-config**

   E. All of the above

SELF TEST ANSWERS

Storage (Memory) Locations and Purpose

1. ☑ **D** is correct. The startup configuration is used during the device bootup process and is stored in NVRAM—a nonvolatile storage location retaining all information after power off.
☒ **A, B,** and **C** are incorrect. **A** is incorrect because RAM is volatile and is used to store the running configuration. **B** is incorrect because ROM holds a bootstrap program and the ROMMON basic operating system. **C** is incorrect because flash memory holds a copy of the IOS.

Cisco Internetwork Operating System (IOS)

2. ☑ **C** is correct. Setup mode prompts administrators, step by step, for basic configuration settings when a startup configuration file cannot be found.
☒ **A, B,** and **D** are incorrect. **A** is incorrect because the router will only boot into ROMMON when the IOS is corrupt or the configuration register is set to 2100—the presence of a startup configuration file is irrelevant to this process. **B** is incorrect because a Cisco device never boots directly into Privileged mode. **D** is incorrect because this is a false statement.

Configuration Files

3. ☑ **A** is correct. **erase nvram** removes the startup-config file, while **reload** reboots the system.
☒ **B, C,** and **D** are incorrect. **B** is incorrect because **delete nvram** is not a CLI command. **C** and **D** are incorrect because **restart** is not a CLI command.

4. ☑ **D** is correct. **show version** displays the version number, filename, amount of memory remaining in NVRAM and RAM, the uptime, and the reason for the last reload.
☒ **A, B,** and **C** are incorrect.

5. ☑ **A, D,** and **E** are correct. To use the console port, attach the DB-9 connector to the serial port of the laptop, and then connect a rollover cable between the console port and the DB-9 connector. A terminal emulator application is needed to send configuration commands.
☒ **B** and **C** are incorrect. These are the wrong cable types.

6. ☑ **D** is correct. SSH uses port 22 and encrypts the communication session.
☒ **A, B,** and **C** are incorrect. **A** is incorrect because Telnet does not use port 22. **B** is incorrect because Telnet uses port 23 but is not considered a secure access method since all data is transmitted in clear text. **C** is incorrect because SSH does not use port 23.

The Command Line Interface (CLI)

7. ☑   B is correct. You can run the **show running-config** command in Privileged (Enable) modes.
   ☒   A, C, D, and E are incorrect. A, C, and D are incorrect because the **show running-config** command is not available in these modes. E is incorrect because choices A, C, and D are incorrect.

8. ☑   B and D are correct. Both CTRL-Z and **end** break out of Configuration mode altogether.
   ☒   A and C are incorrect. A is incorrect because ESC-Z is not a correct keystroke combination. C is incorrect because typing **exit** would only bring the user back one level—to Global Configuration mode.

9. ☑   A is correct. History holds ten commands in the buffer by default.
   ☒   B, C, and D are incorrect. B is incorrect because this is an incorrect number. C and D are incorrect because these are false statements.

10. ☑   B and D are correct. Both the down arrow and CTRL-N will move you forward in the command history.
   ☒   A and C are incorrect because neither command choice is correct.

11. ☑   E is correct. All of the commands will result in the running configuration being copied to the startup configuration.
   ☒   A, B, C, and D are all correct choices; therefore, "All of the above" is the correct option.

6

Configuring Cisco Switches

T here are several manufacturers of switches, and many make devices for both the home or consumer market and for the business and enterprise markets. In 2003, Cisco bought the Linksys consumer line and fielded devices with variations of the Linksys and Cisco name. In the spring of 2013, Cisco sold this consumer line to Belkin International, Inc. These consumer units often find their way into the small business market as well. Since the CCENT is a Cisco exam covering the CLI methods for Cisco's Catalyst business class devices, we will not cover the consumer line at all. We only mention it for those looking for a Cisco device to practice on for the exam—these are not what you want. The configuration is typically done with a CD-based wizard and is then modifiable with a fairly friendly web interface.

CERTIFICATION OBJECTIVE 6.01

Cisco Catalyst Switches

Cisco's Catalyst brand was created originally for larger enterprise-type networks and has grown to cover all levels of business class switches. They provide a wide variety of functions available to the administrator, and come in a huge array of sizes and shapes, with each model having a series number assigned to it. The particular Catalyst switch you decide to use in your network depends on both your needs and your pocketbook, and obviously each model may contain specific hardware and configuration options that simply aren't available in other models. While there is no need to be familiar with Cisco's entire switch line for the exam, it can't hurt to look over the different categories and sizes available to start to get a grasp of the field you are playing on. A good online reference would be Cisco's site at www.cisco.com/en/ US/products/hw/switches/.

The configuration examples used throughout this book are created on a Cisco Catalyst 2960 series switch; however, the concepts and techniques apply to any switch in the Catalyst family. For example, the numbering scheme used to configure a specific interface on a 2960 works the same on other Catalyst models. Interfaces on Catalyst switches are numbered x/y, with x being the card number and y being the individual interface on that card. The numbering always starts with 0 and increments from top to bottom for cards and from left to right for interfaces. A 2960 access switch only has one "card" or row of interfaces and, therefore, will always start interface numbering 0/y. From left to right on the switch, the first port would be numbered 0/1, the second 0/2, and so on.

Physical Characteristics

Looking at the switch face, you will see a mode button, two system indicator lamps, and three mode indicator lamps. The system indicator lamps are the SYST (System) and RPS (Redundant Power Supply) LEDs. The SYST LED indicates the overall system status. The RPS LED shows the status of the redundant power supply—if one is present. The LED status and meaning of both system indicator lamps are listed in Table 6-1.

A LAN switch face also contains interface ports to connect to PCs and may contain one or more uplink interfaces to connect to other switches. These uplink interfaces can be the same duplex and speed as the connection interfaces or a completely different physical uplink altogether. For example, on one switch the connection interfaces might be standard RJ45 10/100/1000 Mbps ports, with an RJ45 uplink port capable of up to gigabit speeds. On another switch, the uplink port might be an SC or ST fiber connector. The configuration and layout of the uplink ports and connection interfaces can vary greatly and depend on the model of Catalyst switch purchased.

Each bank of interfaces has a label indicating the speed at which the ports can run. A label of 10/100, for example, signifies that the ports can run at 10baseT or 100baseT Ethernet. A label of 10/100/1000 indicates the port can go up to gigabit speeds.

TABLE 6-1	LED	Color	Status
Switch System Indicator LED Status	SYST	Off	Switch is not powered on.
		Green	Powered on, IOS is loaded, and switch is functioning normally.
		Amber	POST failed, IOS did not load, and switch is not functioning.
	RPS	Off	RPS is not functioning or connected.
		Green	RPS is connected and ready to provide power. (Blinking green indicates it is providing power to another device.)
		Amber	RPS is in a fault or standby condition.
		Blinking amber	Internal power has failed and RPS is providing power to the device.

TABLE 6-2	LED Mode	Interface LED Color	Status
Switch Interface LEDs	STAT	Off	Not in use, or administratively down.
		Green	Link present. Blinking green indicates activity.
		Green/amber	Excessive collisions and jabber errors are creating a link fault.
		Amber	Port is blocked by Spanning Tree Protocol (STP). Blinking amber indicates activity on the blocked port.
	DUPLX	Off	Half duplex.
		Green	Full duplex.
	SPEED	Off	10 Mbps.
		Green	100 Mbps.
		Blinking green	1000 Mbps (gigabit speed).

Each host interface port has LEDs, and the LED mode affects how each is displayed. LED modes and their effect on interface LEDs are listed in Table 6-2. The LEDs on individual switch interfaces provide a quick means of troubleshooting for administrators and technicians.

You will note that there is no power-on button anywhere on the switch. To turn the switch on or off, simply plug in or unplug the electrical power cord. This makes sense when you realize that switches are seldom turned off once turned on, often running years. A power switch introduces another failure point.

Getting Ready

If you take a Catalyst switch out of the box, plug in the electrical cord, and connect systems to interfaces, it will work just fine. Catalyst switches have enough of a default configuration already installed to allow basic switching logic to perform without any intervention on the part of the administrator. Frames will be passed, the CAM table will be built, collision domains will be split, and 100 percent of bandwidth will be made available to each system directly connected.

However, the default configuration settings do not account for other features commonly needed in a business network. VLANs, individual port settings, and security are all examples of configurations an administrator may need for the switch.

ⓦ**a t c h** *Configuration questions may come in the form of multiple choice or as part of a simulation. Pay very close attention to the exact syntax of each command since the help functions may not be available on multiple choice questions. Help using the ? is available in the sims.*

This section covers the configuration of the 2960 access layer switch in a typical business environment—from the initial steps through the more "advanced" settings an administrator may require. VLANs will be covered in the next chapter.

The first step in configuring the switch is, obviously, accessing the CLI. In Chapter 5, we covered the various methods for connecting to a Cisco device for management purposes. Right out of the box, the only way to enter the CLI on a switch is to connect via the console port. Recall this uses a rollover cable, the serial port on a computer, and some form of terminal emulator (such as HyperTerminal). After the physical connection is made, and the steps covered in Chapter 5 have been followed, the switch can be powered on.

EXERCISE 6-1

Connection Methods—HyperTerminal

This exercise demonstrates the proper steps needed to establish an initial connection with a Cisco device using the console port. This exercise obviously requires physical access to a router (or switch), along with a console cable and a properly equipped computer system. If you do not have access to all of the equipment, watch the video and study these steps. They are not tested in the exam, but you will need to know this to work on real devices and better understand the simulations.

Watch "HyperTerminal" for a demonstration of how to configure the HyperTerminal or any terminal client to configure Cisco devices.

1. After connecting the rollover cable to the console port, and ensuring the DB-9 connector is attached to the serial port of the Windows PC, or using a USB to DB-9 adapter, power on the switch by plugging in the power cable.

   On a Windows PC prior to Windows 8, choose Start | All Programs | Accessories | Communications | HyperTerminal, as shown in Figure 6-1. In Windows 8, click on the HyperTerminal Private Edition icon.

FIGURE 6-1   Starting HyperTerminal

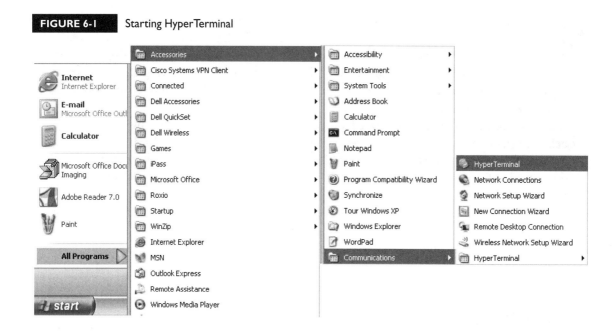

2. Type in **Cisco** as the name of the connection in the Connection Description dialog and then click OK (see Figure 6-2).

3. Choose the COM port you are plugged into or the virtual COM part created by your USB to DB-9 adapter from the drop-down in the Connect To dialog, and then click OK (see Figure 6-3).

FIGURE 6-2

The Connection
Description
dialog

FIGURE 6-3

The Connect To
dialog

4. Click the Restore Defaults button in the COM Properties dialog (see Figure 6-4). Notice the communications parameters default to those required by Cisco console ports. Click OK.

5. HyperTerminal now opens, displaying the connection to the device (see Figure 6-5). You may need to press ENTER a couple times to get the switch's attention. In our example, the switch has no configuration (NVRAM erased).

FIGURE 6-4

The COM
Properties dialog

FIGURE 6-5   HyperTerminal connection to a switch

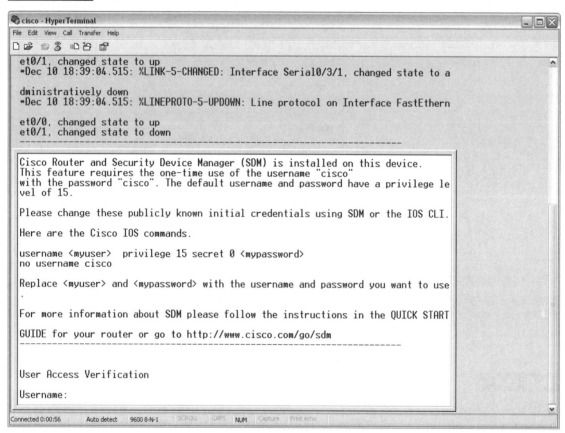

6. Normally we would start work, but this first time we want to save our HyperTerminal setting for the future. Close HyperTerminal by clicking the red X at the top right of the window. When asked about disconnecting, click Yes.

7. HyperTerminal will ask if you would like to save the current settings. To avoid setting up the communications parameters again, choose Yes. HyperTerminal saves the connection as Cisco, and places it in the menu group HyperTerminal.

8. **Windows 7 and earlier:** Access the saved setting by choosing Start | All Programs | Accessories | Communications. Notice that a new group named HyperTerminal appears within the Communications group (see Figure 6-6).

FIGURE 6-6

The
HyperTerminal
group for
Windows 7 and
earlier

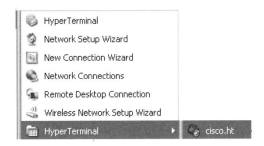

At this point you could use it to start a session with your setting by selecting Cisco, or you could right-click on it and choose Send To…, and then Desktop (Create Shortcut). The shortcut icon appears on the desktop for future use. **Windows 8 users:** Use your HyperTerminal desktop shortcut. When the Connection Description box appears, close it and use File | Open, and you will see your Cisco.ht over on the right side of the screen. At this point you could use it to start a session with your setting by selecting Cisco or you could right-click on it and choose Send To…, and then Desktop (Create Shortcut). The shortcut icon appears on the desktop for future use.

System Configuration Dialog

As discussed previously, when no configuration file exists in NVRAM, the switch defaults to the System Configuration dialog, also known as Setup mode. Setup mode only allows for basic configuration settings and, for the most part, is not used by the majority of administrators. There are easier ways to get a basic configuration. Although it is not a test objective, you should know what it does and how it works. While basically the same concept, all Cisco devices offer a similar wizard-based setup dialog. On some types of Cisco devices it is an easy way to get a basic configuration so that you can then remote in and finish configuring. Note: If you decide to try to use it to see what it does, you always have the option to save or abandon what you have done at the end. CTRL-C will abandon your efforts and return you to the system prompt.

When the switch powers up, a variety of information is displayed. As the operating system loads, a series of #s will display across the screen, followed by the name of the IOS file loaded into memory. Afterward, the IOS version is displayed, as well as information gathered from POST (Base Ethernet MAC address, part numbers, model numbers, and serial numbers). Finally, a prompt appears, asking if you would like to enter setup. Answering "yes" puts you into Setup mode (a "no" provides a User mode prompt):

```
Would you like to enter the initial configuration dialog? [yes/
no]: yes
At any point you may enter a question mark "?" for help.
Use ctrl-c to abort configuration dialog at any prompt.
Default settings are in square brackets "[]".
Basic management setup configures only enough connectivity for
management of
the system, extended setup will ask you to configure each
interface on the system
Would you like to enter basic management setup? [yes/no]:
```

At this point, the system is in setup mode; however, two different methods can be used for setup. In the first, *basic management setup*, the system only prompts for the most basic of settings. In the second, *extended setup mode*, the system will also prompt for the setting on each individual port. The only difference between the two options is that extended setup provides individualized interface configuration, while basic does not. Answering "yes" to the question provides the following output:

```
Configuring global parameters:
Enter host name [Switch]: SW1   /// Notice by default, the name
is "Switch" ///
The enable secret is a password used to protect access to
privileged EXEC and configuration modes. This password, after
entered, becomes encrypted in the configuration.
Enter enable secret: CCENT
The enable password is used when you do not specify an enable
secret password, with some older software versions, and some
boot images.
Enter enable password: Cisco
The virtual terminal password is used to protect access to the
router over a network interface.
Enter virtual terminal password: CCENT
Configure SNMP Network Management? [no]:
Current Interface Summary
```

```
Any interface listed with OK? Value "NO" does not have a valid
configuration

Interface   IP Address    OK? Method Status    Protocol

Vlan1       unassigned    NO    unset up       up
FastEthernet0/1  unassigned    YES   unset up       up
<<<< Output Truncated >>>>
```

exam
watch

Remember, you can enter Setup mode in two ways: first, if there is no configuration in NVRAM (startup configuration), and second, you can enter Setup mode at any time by entering the command setup in Privileged mode. Within Setup, remember that default entries are surrounded by brackets, and extended setup provides configuration options for each interface, while basic does not.

In the preceding example, the hostname of the device was changed from the default (Switch) to SW1. Notice that settings providing a default require only a single press of the ENTER key. Other options set include a few passwords and an opportunity to enable SNMP settings. A summary of the interfaces is then displayed, followed by three options:

```
[0] Go to the IOS command prompt without saving this config.
[1] Return back to the setup without saving this config.
[2] Save this configuration to nvram and exit.
Enter your selection [2]:
```

By default, pressing ENTER will result in the new configuration being saved. Entering a 0 dumps the configuration and provides a command prompt. An entry of 1 simply starts setup all over again. Note: Sometimes, for a fresh start on a switch, administrators will erase the startup configuration (using the **erase startup-config** command) and use the **reload** command to reboot the system. When doing so, the switch IOS will sometimes prompt you with a message stating, "System configuration has changed. Save?(yes/no)" Choosing "yes" copies the running configuration back into NVRAM as startup-config before rebooting. If your intent is to clear the configuration altogether, make sure you choose "no."

Watch "Setup" for a demonstration of how to use the System Configuration dialog.

CERTIFICATION OBJECTIVE 6.02

Basic Initial Configuration

While the System Configuration dialog is a perfectly acceptable way to configure basic settings on a switch, it's typically not the preferred method for configuration. More often than not, switches used in a production environment require more than just the basics. Therefore, since these settings must be made from the command line anyway, most administrators skip setup altogether and go directly to the command line. During a typical configuration, administrators will assign a hostname, apply security settings, configure access methods, configure interfaces, and create any banners. It is a good idea to always follow the same order when configuring to ensure that you don't miss something. It also works as a simple mental checklist after the fact. While the details may vary a bit, the same order will work for all Cisco devices.

Before we start, since this is our first actual configuration exercise, we will be emphasizing things like saving your work, making text file copies, and other basics that will be assumed later when we configure routers. All Cisco IOS devices are very consistent in their commands; for example, **enable** means and is used for the same purpose if supported. So this is both an introduction to configuring a Cisco switch and an introduction to configuring all Cisco IOS devices.

Watch "CLI Help" for a demonstration of how to use the Command Line Interface Help system.

Hostname

Hostname, the device's name, is a basic setting many administrators start out with. The hostname is simply a name that can be used to identify the switch within the prompt and when looking at a configuration on the screen or print output. Unique descriptive names help make sure that when working remotely you are changing the right device.

The syntax is **hostname** *name*, where *name* is the hostname you wish to use for the device. Remember that the **configure terminal** command moves to Global Configuration mode. The hostname is alphanumeric, case sensitive, can contain special characters, and can have a maximum of 32 characters. Note also the prompt changes (after the hostname):

```
Switch>enable
Switch#configure terminal
Switch (config)#hostname CCENTSwitch
CCENTSwitch(config)#copy running-config startup-config
```

```
CCENTSwitch(config)# copy running-config startup-config
                     ^
% Invalid input detected at "^" marker.
CCENTSwitch(config)#exit
CCENTSwitch#
00:38:14: %SYS-5-CONFIG_I: Configured from console by
consolecopy run start
Destination filename [startup-config]?
Building configuration...
[OK]
CCENTSwitch#
```

Notice we used an abbreviated form of the command on our successful attempt. Note also how the prompt changed from Switch to CCENTSwitch instantly. This is an important point for two reasons: first, you'll need to know what the prompt will look like after entering a **hostname** command, and second, it demonstrates that configuration changes go into effect (on the running-config) immediately. They do not change the startup-configuration until we save our changes and would be lost if we rebooted without saving. Lines four to the end are included to demonstrate a couple of configuration issues that we will deal with in the next section.

System Messages and History Buffer

In line four in the last output we attempted to save the change while in configuration mode, which won't work. The next three lines show what an IOS entry error looks like. The ^ under the c of copy indicates "this is where I got lost." The next line shows an **exit** command, which returns us to the Privileged mode, which is where saves must occur.

On the next line, we typed the **copy running-config startup-config** command in abbreviated form, but the IOS sent a system (syslog) message, not an error, while we were typing and therefore our typing appears appended to the end of the message. The command executed properly and asked us to confirm **Destination filename [startup-config]?** At which point we pressed ENTER. It then reported that it was **Building configuration...** and the [OK] indicates it was successful. While nothing more than a confusing irritant, we can tell the IOS not to display these system messages.

The optional **logging synchronous** command suppresses these system messages during a console session. During console sessions, using the console cable, syslog messages are displayed in real time, often right in the middle of typing in a command, as in the last example output.

By default, syslog messages aren't displayed on remote connections (Telnet or SSH). If you wish to see these messages during a remote session, you'll need to enter the **terminal monitor** and **logging on** commands.

While suppressing system messages, it is a good practice to increase the history buffer so that you can recall more commands using the up-arrow key to save typing. By default, the buffer saves ten commands. The contents of the buffer can be viewed using the **show history** command. The buffer size can be changed using the **history size *x*** command, where *x* is the size of the buffer. If an administrator wants a different buffer size during just a specific session, the Privileged mode command **terminal history size *x*** will set the buffer size for that single session only. For example, if the global command **history size 15** was entered on the console, the buffer would save the last 15 commands for recall. If an administrator wanted to move that up to 20, he could enter the **terminal history size 20** command and, during that session, would be able to recall the last 20 commands.

An example of the **history** and **logging synchronous** commands is shown next. Note that the auto-complete help function is used for both the **configure terminal** and **line console 0** commands.

```
!  --unconfigured line connections from show running-config
line con 0
line vty 0 4
 login
line vty 5 15
 login
!
Switch#conf t
Enter configuration commands, one per line.  End with CNTL/Z.
Switch(config)#line con 0 <-- for the only console connection
Switch(config-line)#history size 25
Switch(config-line)#logging synchronous
Switch(config)#line vty 0 15 <-- for all Telnet and SSH
connections
Switch(config-line)#history size 20
!  -- from show running-config after configuring
line con 0
 logging synchronous
 history size 25
line vty 0 4
 login
 history size 20
line vty 5 15
 login
 history size 20
!
```

Notice that the commands become part of the configuration file. If saved, they would be in effect for all future sessions. A Switch# **terminal history size 40** command issued at the Privileged mode wouldn't be saved and would apply only to this session. The **logging synchronous** command doesn't appear on the vty (Telnet or SSH) lines because we didn't enter it for them.

CERTIFICATION OBJECTIVE 6.03

Securing the Configuration

During an initial configuration, one of the most important steps is securing settings. In modern networking, security is not an afterthought to be applied later, but a concern from the get-go, requiring attention and dedication. Common configuration options for security include passwords, setting access method parameters, and interface security settings.

Watch "Basic Security" for a demonstration of how to use the various password and login systems.

Login and Passwords

Usernames and passwords should be created to protect access to the device. It's important to understand that passwords and authentication only work if a login is required in the first place. Look back at the sample output in the last section and you will see that login is on by default on the vty (Telnet and SSH) lines but not on the console line. If you configure the line to require a login, but do not specify a password, as we see on the vty sessions, users attempting to log in will receive an error message stating, "Password required, but none set." They will be effectively locked out. On the other hand, assigning a password but not requiring authentication is a waste of typing.

The console connection is typically open to allow access for configuring. It is assumed that the device is not in production and will be configured with password security before it is put into production. You do find devices without the console port secured "because it is in a secure place," but that means you are trusting everyone with access to that space—including contractors and disgruntled server admins planning a job change. The best strategy is always to secure it and limit access strictly to those needing access.

There are two ways to require a login to occur. In both cases, it is possible to lock yourself out of the device, so consider developing the habit of defining your passwords first and then require the login. Note: There are password recovery processes for all Cisco devices; find them by Googling "Cisco password recovery *device-model*."

The **login** command by itself, as in the vty lines in the last example, means "Use the password assigned specifically to this line, as defined in the configuration." In this instance, the password assigned to the line applies for every connection made on that line, no matter which user attempts to connect. In other words, there is one password, known by all authorized users, allowing access to the devices. The password is created by adding a **password *password*** command just before or after the **login** command—for example, **password Telnet**.

The second method, **login local**, requires a username and password, which are defined in Global Configuration mode. The command syntax is **username *name* password *password***. For example, the command **username CCENT_User1 password Cisco** would create a username of CCENT_User1 with a password of Cisco. There can be a single username/password or separate ones for different admins or groups of admins. While beyond the scope of this exam, various permissions can be assigned to each of these usernames, providing granularity of access for security-minded administrators.

The following code requires that the person attempting to connect to the device over the console know the username is Bob, with a password of Cisco, while those connecting via Telnet would simply need to know the password Telnet. Note that usernames typically are not case sensitive, but passwords always are.

```
Switch#configure terminal
Enter configuration commands, one per line.  End with CNTL/Z.
Switch(config)#username Bob password Cisco
Switch(config)#line console 0
Switch(config-line)#login local
Switch(config-line)#line vty 0 4
Switch(config-line)#password Telnet
Switch(config-line)#login
```

After closing the session in the console and reconnecting, you can see the username and password being enforced:

```
User Access Verification
Username:Bob
Password:
Switch>
```

exam
ⓦatch

Pay close attention to the login *and* login local *settings on questions and simulations on the exam. The* login *command requires that a password be set, and uses the password defined on the line configuration prompt. The* login local *command uses the username/password pairs defined elsewhere in the global configuration. Lastly, the presence—or absence—of login can be the answer you're looking for!*

Privileged Mode Passwords

After protecting access to the device by assigning passwords to individual access lines, two other passwords can be used to protect the CLI itself. Both Enable mode passwords are set using Global Configuration mode and force a user to cite a password to move from User mode to Privileged mode (aka Enable mode). The first, best, and only one you should use is *enable secret* and it is set using the Global Configuration command **enable secret** *password*. The second is an older and less secure *enable password*, which is set using the Global Configuration command **enable password** *password*. The enable secret password never displays on the screen or printouts, so don't forget it. Enable password, on the other hand, displays in clear text when a **show running-config** command is issued. Since **show running-config** can be executed at the User mode, it could then lead an unauthorized person to the next level where they could do some real damage. Additionally, if both the enable password and enable secret are entered into the configuration, the switch will only use the enable secret. For these reasons, most administrators use only enable secret.

To remove or undo commands from the configuration, you simply prepend the word **no** to the basic command: in this case, **no enable password** or **no enable secret**.

While the enable password is stored as a clear-text string, the enable secret is encrypted. But what does that mean? The enable secret is not stored at all in the configuration but goes through an encryption hashing process, mathematical algorithm, and the resulting MD5 hash is what is stored and displayed. When the admin enters a password at the prompt, it is encrypted by the same process and the results are compared. If they are not the same, access is denied.

This does not mean you should forgo passwords; just don't rely on them alone for security. It's much more important to control access to the configuration in the first place. So protect the switch with good physical security, and assign strong console and SSH connection options. In later levels of training, you will learn about even more sophisticated security measures. That is true for the Vigenere/shifting Caesar cipher (level 7), but not MD5 hash—that is, service password-encryption.

Encrypting All Passwords

All passwords—with the notable exception of the enable secret—are stored and displayed in the configuration in clear text. You can, and should, choose to encrypt the passwords using the Global Configuration command **service password-encryption**. This command will deter casual snooping of the passwords, but it is a fairly weak encryption method. Remembering how enable secret passwords are encrypted, be careful that you know the passwords because once the command is run, the password is gone and only the hash remains. Even if you issue a **no service password-encryption** command, the passwords will not revert back—they can't. The hash value becomes the password, at least until you change a password, and then the new one will be in clear text.

The **service password-encryption** command is one of several that is good to have at the end of your configuration checklist to be run only after testing all username/password combinations and any login passwords set on the **line con** and **line vty** access. This way you don't inadvertently lock yourself or remote users out of the device.

ⓦ a t c h *Be very familiar with all aspects of passwords: how they are set and enforced, how they appear within a configuration (both before and after a* service password-encryption *command),* *and how they are encrypted (or hashed). Pay particular attention to the interplay between the enable password and enable secret, as well as the difference between* login *and* login local.

Exec-timeout

Passwords and good physical security work well for securing access methods; however, regardless of whether the session is established locally over the console or remotely using Telnet, an inactive session should not be left open indefinitely. By default, an *inactive* open session disconnects automatically after ten minutes. This can be changed using the **exec-timeout *x* *y*** command, where *x* is the number of minutes and *y* is the number of seconds. Entering the command **exec-timeout 0 0** ensures that the switch will never time out the session, regardless of activity.

Oftentimes, security and usability are at opposite ends of the spectrum, and the **exec-timeout** command is no exception. Administrators don't like their sessions timing out on them while they're troubleshooting or configuring, and will configure the **exec-timeout 0 0** command to prevent just that. However, it's a horrible security practice. If you work in the field very long, particularly as a contractor with multiple clients, you will come across open console sessions. If you see it in a configuration, replace the command with something a little more stringent. Even **exec-timeout 60 0** or something like it would be better than left open.

Banners

Some admins do the hostnames and banners together at the beginning of the initial session. Others tend to do it at the end with the **service password-encryption** as a part of a checklist before wrapping up. A banner is a message displayed to a user of a Cisco device. There are three types of banners, and the type you configure determines when this message is displayed:

- **MOTD** (Message of the Day) banner is shown before login and is typically used for temporary messages of importance.
- **Login** banner is displayed before every login as well, immediately following the MOTD. Its main purpose is to show permanent messages (such as "Unauthorized Access Is Prohibited").
- **Exec** banner displays after login and is intended for messages that would not be shared with unauthorized users.

To configure a banner, use the command syntax **banner *type delimiter* <ENTER>** *message delimiter* <ENTER>. The *type* parameter indicates MOTD, Exec, or Login (MOTD is the default entry). The *delimiter* can be any character to begin and end the message entry that would not appear in the message itself. Many admins use the # symbol unless it is required in the message, such as "School District #7" An example of the **banner** command is shown next:

```
CCENTSwitch#configure terminal
CCENTSwitch (config)# banner #
Enter TEXT message. End with character "#".
```

```
Welcome to CCENT Switch! Please prepare to login.. #
CCENTSwitch (config)# banner login #
Enter TEXT message. End with character "#".
Warning! Unauthorized Access is Prohibited! #
CCENTSwitch (config)# banner exec 7
Enter TEXT message. End with character "7".
Greetings, authorized user! Remember to phone notify (555-1234)
all configuration changes 7
CCENTSwitch (config)# end
```

The first **banner** command did not use a *type* parameter and, therefore, defaulted to the MOTD. The **banner exec 7** example at the end shows that you can use any character as a delimiter (in this case, a 7). A user logging in to this switch would see the MOTD first, followed by the login banner. After entering Exec mode, the last (Exec) banner would be displayed, as shown next:

```
CCENTSwitch con0 is now available
Press RETURN to get started.

Welcome to the CCENTSwitch! Please prepare to login..
Warning! Unauthorized Access is Prohibited!
CCENTSwitch>enable
Password:
Greetings, authorized user! Remember to phone notify (555-1234)
all configuration changes
```

The login banner often has specific wording warning that the device is private property and that unauthorized access will be dealt with severely. It often is specified by network policies and may have been cleared by the legal department. In that case, it can be stored as a text file on your computer and pasted into the configuration. The MOTD then becomes a message to indicate which device is being accessed.

EXERCISE 6-2

MHE Lab

Initial Device Configuration

In this exercise we demonstrate the steps an administrator would take during an initial basic configuration to a router or switch. The steps covered in this lab should become an automatic part of your initial session so that they don't get forgotten. It is possible to change the order if that makes more sense to you.

Task 1: Getting Started

1. Launch the NetSim program, then click on the Labs bar on the lower-left corner of the screen.

2. When the Lab Tree appears, select Chapter 6 and then 6-2 Initial Device Configuration. The lab should load in the upper-right window.

3. Click on the Lab Instructions and NetMap tabs to see what they show. End up with the NetMap tab selected.

4. Right-click on the SwitchA icon in the NetMap and then the Configure in Simulator button that appears. If you press ENTER you should see a Switch> prompt indicating that we are in User mode.

5. Type **enable** and press ENTER to go to Privileged mode. You should note that we weren't prompted for a password as we were in Lab 5-1. That is one of the things we will fix in in this lab.

6. What if we had been working on a real device? When you power on an unconfigured device, the prompt will ask you if you'd like to enter the System Configuration dialog. Reply no, exiting out to User mode, and then go to Privileged mode by typing **enable** and pressing ENTER.

Task 2: Using Help and Command Abbreviations

1. At the prompt, type the **?** but don't press ENTER. You should see a screen full of commands that are available in Privileged mode—every configuration mode has its own commands and none are duplicated in two modes. SPACEBAR displays more; pressing anything else stops the display. Look at the commands that begin with the letter s; it should look like this:

```
rmdir               Remove existing directory
rsh                 Execute a remote command
send                Send a message to other tty lines
setup               Run the SETUP command facility
show                Show running system information
telnet              Open a telnet connection
```

This tells us that **show** is the only command that begins with *sh*, therefore that part of the command could be abbreviated to just **sh. setup**, on the other hand would require *set* to avoid being confused with **send**.

2. At the prompt, type **sh ?** but don't press ENTER (in older IOSs that would stop the display immediately). As you look through the display, these are the **show** options. You'll see that on this device there is only one command beginning with the letter r.

   At the prompt, type **sh r** and press ENTER. You should see a screen full of output. SPACEBAR displays more, anything else stops the display. You can always use longer abbreviations but not shorter than what it takes to be unique from other commands.

   Note that there is a lot of configuration defaults and interface recognition already in an unconfigured device. This initial configuration will be included at the end of the lab if you want to spend some time with it.

3. By now you should see that you need to press ENTER after every command (except **?** for help). To keep from filling the book with "type *xyz-cmd* and press ENTER," let's work with words we often use when talking and when two or more people are troubleshooting. Using *run*, *do*, or *enter* as in *run* **show run**, *do* **show run**, or *enter* **show run** each means the same as "type **show running-config** and press ENTER."

   From here on, some instructions will be in the form *run* **show running-config** or *do* **show running-config**. If you see run or do a command like **show running-config** (sho run) the text in parentheses shows you one abbreviated form of the command, so that you can start getting used to them. You will learn to use them and appreciate them, plus they are supported on the exam. Less typing and less chance of a typo. The IOS hates all typos.

Task 3: Naming the Device

1. Our prompt Switch# is the default for a Cisco switch in Privileged mode. Router# is its counterpart on routers. This prompt is the device name, so we'll change it. But we can't change anything in Privileged mode; we need to go to Global Configuration mode, which requires a **configure terminal** (config t) command.

   Run the command and notice the prompt changes to Switch(config)#. Make sure you recognize the prompt changes so you know what mode you are in. You should be able to recognize commands displayed with the wrong prompt.

   In Global Configuration mode, type **hostname Bubba** and press ENTER. Note the prompt change. Names can be a single word, with no spaces, up to 32 characters long. It can have letters, numbers, and a few special characters like dash and underscore.

Run **hostname Acctg_Switch-27**.

To wrap this up, run **hostname SwitchA** to match our topology map.

Try to run **show running-config** (sho run). It will fail because that is a Privileged mode command and we are in Global Configuration mode.

Do a CTRL-Z to return to Privileged mode and run the command again. You should see at the top of the first screen (you may need to use the scrollbar on the right side of the screen) that the configuration has changed to include your last **hostname** command.

Task 4: Setting Some Passwords

We are going to configure the enable password to *junk* and an enable secret to *ccent* to compare them. Then we'll assign a password (cisco) to the console (CON) port and vty (Telnet) lines. For the console port, we will also suppress the syslog messages, increase the history buffer to 20 commands, and set a timeout on an unattended session to 30 minutes.

1. First do a **show running-config** and look at the very last entries. The two enable passwords don't exist until we create them, but we can see that our 1 console port #0 and our 16 vty (remote access) ports #0–15 have not been configured.

   !

   line con 0

   line aux 0

   line vty 0 15

   !

2. Return to Global Configuration mode with **configure terminal** (config t).

   Type **enable password junk** and press ENTER,

   then type **enable secret ccent** and press ENTER.

3. Make the following entries exactly as you see them for the console port. The order isn't critical but spelling is, as in the case of our password. Password cisco would not accept requests using Cisco or CISCO or anything else.

   line console 0

   password cisco

   history size 20

   login

Two other useful commands that would be added here are **logging synchronous** and **exec-timeout** *minutes seconds*, which are included in the Full Edition of NetSim. The **exec-timeout** *minutes seconds* command could also be added to the vty ports. The **logging synchronous** command is not needed on remote access ports, vty, because system messages are suppressed by default on remote sessions.

4. Make the following entries exactly as you see them to secure all 16 remote access lines at once:

line vty 0 15

password cisco

login

5. Do a CTRL-Z to return to Privileged mode and run **show running-config** (sho run). Look on the first screen for your enable passwords. You may need to scroll back up if it has already gone by. It should look something like this:

!

hostname SwitchA

enable secret 5 sdf6978yhg$jnb76sd

enable password junk

!

Note that the enable secret is encrypted—there is no way to figure it out from here (or if you forget it). But notice that our plain enable password is displayed in clear text. Anyone seeing the configuration, or a printout of it, would know it. What if that password is used on many devices?

Scroll to the bottom of the configuration and look at our console and vty lines.

6. Note the commands are not in the order we entered them, so order in this case doesn't matter.

In the real world, we should have put a password and a login command on the AUX (modem) port as well. The commands would have been:

line aux 0

password cisco

login

Task 5: Creating Some Banners

1. Return to Global Configuration mode with **configure terminal** (config t). In each case, the # is our choice of a "code" to tell the IOS that we are finished with our message. It could be any symbol that doesn't appear in your message, such as @.

   Type **banner MOTD #** and press ENTER, and then type **This is the Message of the Day!** # and press ENTER.

2. Type **banner login** # and press ENTER, and then type **This is the login banner! #**.

   Note that our example is to show where banners appear, but banners are an important part of the configuration, providing the warning to possible unauthorized persons. Here is an example of what an MOTD might look like:

```
banner motd #

---------------Warning!--------------------

Terms of Use
Any or all uses of our server systems, network equipment and all
traffic on this network may be intercepted, monitored, recorded,
copied, audited, inspected, and disclosed to authorized site and
law enforcement personnel. By logging into this network service,
the user consents to such interception, monitoring, recording,
copying, auditing, inspection, and disclosure at the discretion
of authorized site personnel.

Unauthorized or improper use of our servers or network or systems
within the network, may result in administrative disciplinary
action and civil and criminal penalties.

By logging on to this network, you indicate your awareness of
and consent to these terms and conditions of use.

For assistance, contact Network Security at 555-1212.
#
```

Task 6: Securing Unencrypted Passwords

It is possible to force all unencrypted passwords to be encrypted. This is often one of the final steps after testing and making sure that you know all passwords.

1. Return to Global Configuration mode with **configure terminal** (config t).

   Type **service password-encryption** and press ENTER, and then exit back to Privileged mode using CTRL-Z.

Task 7: Seeing Our Work

1. In Privileged mode do a **show running-config** and see that your enable password is now encrypted, as are our passwords for the console and VTY ports. Your banners show up in the configuration near the bottom. Notice the output substituted ^C for the # symbols in the banner messages.
2. Use the **exit** command to get out of Privileged mode and out of the router. Press ENTER and you will see your banners and be prompted for a password because we set one on the console session. Use **cisco** and you should go into User mode.
3. Use **enable** to go into Privileged mode and you get prompted for a password. Try **junk**—it should fail. Try **ccent** and it should work. If you configure both an enable password and enable secret, only the secret is used.

Task 8: Saving Our Work

All of our commands executed and changed the running-config immediately. But remember that the running configuration is lost if the device is rebooted or powered down. Let's save it to the startup-config, which is stored permanently in NVRAM.

1. In Privileged mode, do a **show startup-config** (sho start) and see what is there now. The error message means nothing is stored in NVRAM.
2. Type **copy running-config startup-config** (copy run start) and press ENTER. Very quickly you should get a confirmation that it is done.

   Do a **show startup-config** (sho start) and see that it is there now.

CERTIFICATION OBJECTIVE 6.04

Managing Remote Connections

Using remote connections rather than console connections is very common once a device has a basic configuration. As long as there is a path to the device, we can connect to it from anywhere, such as the comfort of our office or home. This is particularly useful in environments where routers and switches are in cramped, often noisy settings. In worse cases, they can also be humid, such as on cruise ships, and have little lizards in places like Ghana. The easiest and for years the most common protocol was Telnet, which can be accessed via the CMD (command) window on Windows PCs. The steps are as follows:

1. Choose Start | Run. Type **cmd** (for command prompt) and press ENTER.
2. In the command prompt, type **telnet *IP_Address***, using the IP address of the device.
3. Provide the same username and password as before. The prompt changes to the user exec level prompt, letting you know you are in the router. From then on, everything is like the console session.

While Telnet provides a very easy way to access the device remotely, and configuring access is relatively easy using the **login** and **password** commands, Telnet sends all information—including the username and password—in clear text, presenting an obvious security problem. A better option would be to allow remote access only via SSH. We'll look at configuring SSH and disabling Telnet access next.

Configuring SSH

SSH runs over port 22 (Telnet uses port 23) and encrypts the communications path between both systems. Unlike Telnet, which can provide access using just a password, SSH works on a client-server basis and requires a username and a password. This username and password combination can be stored locally on the switch or on a separate server—referred to as an Authentication, Authorization, and Accounting (AAA) server (covered in later exams). The easiest, and most common, application is configuring local usernames and passwords.

Before attempting to set up SSH on your Catalyst router or switch, remember that SSH support is a feature, like anything else. Therefore, you must ensure your switch (or router) IOS supports it. Perhaps the easiest method to check for SSH support is to simply type the question mark (?) at a Global Configuration mode prompt. If the command **crypto** does not appear, your IOS won't support SSH.

Configuring SSH is fairly simple but requires setting several configuration steps on the device. The third and fourth steps are necessary for the generation of the SSH public and private keys. SSH uses these keys to encrypt the communications process. Once they are created, the private key stays on the switch while a copy of the public key must be placed on any client device connecting to the switch.

1. Usernames and passwords must be created, just like we did for the console connection. SSH can use the same ones.

2. The vty lines—those access lines set aside for remote CLI access—must be configured using the **login local** command and the **transport input telnet ssh** command. By default, all vty lines accept Telnet, but this last command is needed to allow SSH access. Optionally, you can, and should, omit the **telnet** parameter, which forces remote sessions to use SSH; Telnet connections are then no longer accepted.

3. To create the keys, a domain name must be created. In the third step, the **ip domain-name** *name.extension* (where *name* is the domain name and *extension* is the three-letter DNS extension) command defines a DNS domain name for the device.

4. The **crypto key generate rsa** command actually creates the public and private keys required for SSH to work (using the hostname and domain name). For example, the following code demonstrates the steps required to set up SSH on a switch, using the domain name of *sample.com*.

```
CCENTSwitch# configure terminal
CCENTSwitch (config)# username Bob password Barker
CCENTSwitch (config)# username Cindy password Cisco
CCENTSwitch (config)# line vty 0 15
CCENTSwitch (config-line)# login local
CCENTSwitch (config-line)# transport input telnet ssh
CCENTSwitch (config-line)# exit
CCENTSwitch (config)# ip domain-name sample.com
CCENTSwitch (config)# crypto key generate rsa
The name for the keys will be: CCENTSwitch.sample.com
Choose the size of the key modulus in the range of 360 to 2048
for your General Purpose Keys. Choosing a key modulus greater
than 512 may take a few minutes.
How many bits in the modulus [512]: 1024
% Generating 1024 bit RSA keys …[OK]
00:05:14: %SSH-5-ENABLED: SSH 1.99 has been enabled
CCENTSwitch (config)# end
```

After SSH is enabled and the keys are created, you can view the public key using the command **show crypto key mypubkey rsa**. The resulting display will show lines of code that make up the key. Each client connecting to the switch will need a copy of this key; the copy can either be added to the client beforehand or handed out by the switch when the client connects. Note: Several SSH client software packages can be installed on client laptops for using SSH. PuTTY is a free, and rather popular, application that provides SSH client services. To connect, open PuTTY (or whatever client you have installed), and connect to the switch, using the IP address or hostname. You'll be prompted for a username and password. Once you are logged in, the public key will be delivered and voilà! The latest version of HyperTerminal also supports SSH connections.

Watch "Configuring SSH" for a demonstration of how to configure SSH support for Cisco devices.

EXERCISE 6-3

SSH Configuration

This exercise demonstrates the steps an administrator would take to configure SSH access for a Cisco device, switch, or router. If you upgrade to the Full Edition of NetSim or get access to real devices with security features set, you can run these lines. The Cisco exam simulator would support the command.

Task 1: Limiting Connections

1. The **transport input telnet ssh** command would be added to the line vty configuration. By default, all vty lines accept Telnet but not SSH. This command is needed to allow SSH access. Ideally you should omit the **telnet** parameter, which forces remote sessions to use SSH only.

   SwitchA(config)#**line vty 0 15**
   SwitchA(config-line)#**transport input ssh**
   SwitchA(config-line)#CTRL-Z

   In Chapter 12, we will learn to create an access control list (ACL) that would secure this even further.

Task 2: Configuring SSH

1. To create the SSH keys, a domain name must be created. The first step here shows the **ip domain-name *name.extension*** command. This would be the organization's domain name, as in e-mail addresses, such as bob@**cisco.com**—the cisco.com is the domain name. It can be faked if one doesn't exist.

   The **crypto key generate rsa** command creates the public and private keys required for SSH to work (using the hostname and domain name supplied). Always use a long key number when prompted, 1024 minimum—the delay mentioned only occurs once.

   ```
   SwitchA(config)#ip domain-name sample.com
   SwitchA(config)#crypto key generate rsa
   The name for the keys will be: CCENTSwitch.sample.com
   Choose the size of the key modulus in the range of 360 to
   2048 for your General Purpose Keys. Choosing a key modulus
   greater than 512 may take a few minutes.
   How many bits in the modulus [512]:1024
   % Generating 1024 bit RSA keys …[OK]
   00:05:14: %SSH-5-ENABLED: SSH 1.99 has been enabled
   SwitchA(config)#end
   ```

2. You can view the public key using the **show crypto key mypubkey rsa** command, but that isn't necessary. As SSH clients connect, they will get what they need from the device.

CERTIFICATION OBJECTIVE 6.05

Interface Configuration

Once the basic configuration, security parameters, and remote access have been set, it's time to turn your attention to other configuration options. The switch may or may not need an IP address; interfaces may need speed, duplex, and VLAN settings enabled; and ports (active or inactive) may require additional security. The settings are all, of course, optional. However, in a production environment, most are used (not to mention heavily tested!).

Assigning the Switch IP Address

You may be wondering, "If switches work at Layer 2, why would I need to install an IP address on a Layer 2 device?" Good question, with an equally good answer: It is needed so that Layer 3 applications and protocols, such as Telnet, SNMP, SSH, and SDM, can remotely access and manage the switch. In other words, if you want to use Telnet or SSH to connect remotely to the switch, there must be a unique IP address to connect to.

Like configuring the TCP/IP properties on a PC, assigning an IP address can be done two ways: statically or dynamically (DHCP). Statically is the more common approach so that the IP address doesn't change over time and to make sure it always has an IP address, even if the DHCP server is unavailable. To assign a static address, the switch will require an IP address, a subnet mask, and a default gateway (you can also optionally configure a DNS server as well). Also, much like configuring a PC, you'll need to tell the switch which interface to use.

We cover virtual LANs (VLANs) in the next chapter, but for now just realize that all switch ports are by default in VLAN 1, which allows devices on any port to communicate with any other connected device. We assign the switch IP address to a virtual interface created specifically for this purpose, known as the *VLAN 1 interface*. This becomes the IP and Ethernet port for the whole switch. By default, the VLAN 1 interface does not have an IP address and is disabled. To use it, you must assign the appropriate TCP/IP options and enable the interface with the command **no shutdown**. The following code demonstrates how to assign an IP address to the VLAN 1 interface:

```
CCENTSwitch#configure terminal
CCENTSwitch(config)#interface vlan 1
CCENTSwitch(config-if)#ip address 192.168.1.5 255.255.255.0
CCENTSwitch(config-if)#no shutdown
```

```
%05:15:12: %LINK-3-UPDOWN: Interface Vlan 1, changed state to up
%05:15:13: %LINEPROTO-5_UPDOWN: Line protocol on Interface
Vlan1, changed state to up
CCENTSwitch(config-if)#exit
CCENTSwitch(config)#ip default-gateway 192.168.1.1
```

e x a m

ⓦ a t c h　　*It's a relatively simple task, but be sure you know how to assign a management IP address to the switch using the VLAN 1 interface. Pay close attention to the syntax of each command, as well* *as the configuration mode on which it is entered. Lastly, don't forget VLAN 1 is disabled by default. For the IP address to do any good at all, you'll need to enable the interface with the* no shutdown *command.*

Notice that the IP address and subnet mask are assigned on the Interface configuration prompt for VLAN 1, while the default gateway address is configured from the Global Configuration prompt. The **no shutdown** command is used to enable the interface and is entered on the interface configuration prompt for VLAN 1. Should you choose to disable the interface, use the **shutdown** command on the Interface configuration prompt for VLAN 1.

On a final note, the **show** command can be used to verify proper IP address and VLAN 1 interface settings. Viewing the IP address is different depending on the method in which it was configured. If you statically assign the address, you can use the **show running-config** command to see the address within the configuration. Lastly, a **show interface vlan 1** command will display the IP address as well as the state of the interface. If all is well, the interface will display the message "VLAN 1 is up, line protocol is up." If the **no shutdown** command has not been entered, it will display the text "Administratively down."

e x a m

ⓦ a t c h　　*Know how to verify IP address assignment within the switch. Also, remember "Administratively down" indicates the interface needs the* no shutdown *command.*

Speed, Duplex, and Descriptions

While interfaces on a Catalyst switch do not need any additional configuration to work (they pass traffic right out of the box), sometimes administrators manually assign speed and duplex settings, as well as define a description on "important" ports.

Interfaces on a Catalyst switch are, by default, configured to autonegotiate speed and duplex with the device connecting through the port. However, it's occasionally a good idea to manually set these options. Additionally, adding a description can help in troubleshooting and during installation. The commands used to configure interfaces are **duplex** {*auto* | *full* | *half*}, **speed** {*10* | *100* | *1000* | *auto*}, and **description** *text*.

Each command is entered individually on each port. For one or two interfaces this isn't a problem, but many times you'll wish to apply certain configuration options to an entire range of ports on the switch. For this, you can use the **interface range** *type port-range* command. Use of these commands is demonstrated in the following code:

```
CCENTSwitch#configure terminal
Enter configuration commands, one per line.  End with CNTL/Z.
CCENTSwitch(config)#interface FastEthernet 0/1
CCENTSwitch(config-if)#duplex full
CCENTSwitch(config-if)#speed 100
CCENTSwitch(config-if)#description File Server port
CCENTSwitch(config)#interface range FastEthernet 0/5 - 10
CCENTSwitch(config-if-range)#description Connection ports to users
CCENTSwitch(config-if-range)#CTRL-Z
```

In this example, we set the speed and duplex on our first port (FastEthernet 0/1) and added a description (File Server port). The **interface range FastEthernet 0/5 - 10** command was used to assign a description to ports 5–10. We could have individually gone to each interface prompt and assigned them, but you can see how the range provides a much quicker and more consistent way of getting it done. After all your interface settings are entered, use the **show interfaces status** command to verify:

```
CCENTSwitch#show interfaces status
Port    Name            Status      Vlan  Duplex  Speed  Type
Fa0/1   File Server port notconnect  1     full    100    10/100BaseTX
Fa0/2                   notconnect  1     auto    auto   10/100BaseTX
Fa0/3                   notconnect  1     auto    auto   10/100BaseTX
Fa0/4                   notconnect  1     auto    auto   10/100BaseTX
Fa0/5   Connection ports notconnect  1     auto    auto   10/100BaseTX
Fa0/6   Connection ports notconnect  1     auto    auto   10/100BaseTX
----Output Truncated----
Fa0/10  Connection ports notconnect  1     auto    auto   10/100BaseTX
Fa0/11                  notconnect  1     auto    auto   10/100BaseTX
Fa0/12                  connected   1     a-full  a-100  10/100BaseTX
----Output Truncated----
```

Take note of several items in this output. First, notice the difference between FastEthernet 0/1, which we manually adjusted settings for, and FastEthernet 0/2, which was left with the defaults. The "not connect" on interface 2 indicates the port is not in use and the "auto auto" indicates it is awaiting an autonegotiation with a connecting system, while interface 1 shows the manually defined settings—even without a device connected to it! Ports 5 through 10 reflect the description assigned by the **interface range FastEthernet 0/5 - 10** command, although the description is truncated due to space. Finally, port 12 displays an active interface. A system has connected to the interface and the switch has autonegotiated full duplex at 100 Mbps (the "a-" indicates autonegotiation).

ⓦ **a t c h** *Familiarize yourself with the interface configuration commands listed here, and make sure you know how*	*to decipher information gleaned from a* show interfaces status *command.*

EXERCISE 6-4

MHE Lab

Interface Configuration

In this exercise we demonstrate the steps an administrator would take to configure switch interfaces and assign an IP address to VLAN 1 for remote connectivity and administration.

Task 1: Getting Started

1. Launch the NetSim program, then click on the Labs bar on the lower-left corner of the screen.

2. When the Lab Tree appears, select Chapter 6 and then 6-4 Interface Configuration. The lab should load in the upper-right window.

3. Click on the Lab Instructions and NetMap tabs to see what they show. End up with the NetMap tab selected.

4. Right-click on the host A.11 icon in the NetMap and then the Configure in Simulator button that appears. If you press ENTER you should see the C:> prompt.

5. We configured various passwords on SwitchA in the last lab. They are included for remote access, thanks to our **copy run start** at the end of the last session.

6. Type **telnet 10.0.0.2** at the prompt to open a remote session. The resulting error message tells us something is wrong.

```
C:>telnet 10.0.0.2
Trying 10.0.0.2 ...
% Destination unreachable; gateway or host down
C:>
```

The message is correct, the destination is unreachable because we have not configured an IP address on the switch yet. This isn't a problem with routers because their interfaces have IP addresses, but switch ports do not. Let's see how we add an IP address to a switch.

7. This must be done with a console (direct) connection and should be a part of your initial task list. To do that, right-click on the host SwitchA icon in the NetMap and then the Configure in Simulator button that appears. If you press ENTER you should get a password prompt and see our banners from Lab 6-2.

Use **cisco**, our standard login password for all of these labs—just so you don't get locked out. You should see the SwitchA> prompt.

8. Type **enable** and ENTER to go to Privileged mode. When prompted for a password, use **ccent**, our enable secret used on all devices for all labs. The prompt should now be SwitchA#.

Task 2: Configuring IP Connectivity on a Switch

We need to assign an IP address to our VLAN 1 as the switch IP address and define the default gateway to RouterA so that the switch can be accessed from outside our LAN. The appropriate information is in the IP Address table at the beginning of the lab.

1. Enter Global Configuration mode by typing **configure terminal** (config t), and press ENTER.

2. Make the following entries:

```
interface vlan 1
ip address 10.0.0.2 255.255.255.0
no shutdown
```

The **no shutdown** enables the interface, disabled by default. Note that the prompt tells you that you are in Interface Configuration mode, a sublevel of Global Configuration mode.

3. Type **exit** and press ENTER to get out of Interface Configuration mode.

4. Type **ip default-gateway 10.0.0.1** and press ENTER and then CTRL-Z to return to Privileged mode.

5. Do a **show running-config** to see that your entries appear down just above the banners, console, and vty port configurations.

6. As a good practice, run a **copy run start** to save our work.

Task 3: Remote Configuring

At this point we can finish configuring our device from the comfort of any workstation with access to our network—in another room, on another floor, even in another country. To simulate that, we are going to finish this lab from host B.77, with our commands traveling through SwitchB and both routers.

1. To get started, start a console session on host B.77. Telnet into our switch, log on, and go to Privileged mode. Try it on your own or follow these steps:

```
C:>telnet 10.0.0.2

This is the Message of the Day!

Trying 10.0.0.2 ... Open

Password:cisco        --Logon password vty 0 15
SwitchA>enable
Password:ccent        --enable secret
SwitchA#
```

We can now do just about anything we could do with a console connection while thousands of miles away.

2. Run **show running-config** (sho run) and look over the switch ports—pretty plain. We will work on that next.

Task 4: Configuring Switch Ports

Switch ports are enabled by default and don't have IP addresses. So what is left to do? We can add descriptions to make troubleshooting easier. While auto-negotiation of speed and duplex is very good, there are times we may want to manually set one or both. In the next chapter we will learn about VLANs and port security. This lab will look at some of the different options and then let you try a few of your own.

1. To add a description to one interface, try these commands:

```
config t
interface fastethernet 0/1     (or int fa 0/1)
description Link to RouterA
interface fastethernet 0/10
description Link to User A.11
```

2. Port 11 is assigned to user A.22; now add a description to the interface.

   Use CTRL-Z to go to Privilegedmode and run **show running-config** (sho run) to see what we have done and check your work. When finished, return to Global Configuration mode.

3. Assume port 2 is dedicated to a legacy device that can't negotiate speed and duplex.

```
interface fastethernet 0/2
description Link to old mainframe
speed 100
duplex full
```

4. We can configure interfaces in groups called ranges.

```
interface range fastethernet 0/3 - 6
description Link to Accounting Dept
interface range fastethernet 0/7 - 9
description Link to IT Dept
interface range fastethernet 0/12 - 15
description Link to Security Cameras
```

   A *range* feature is defined by a hyphen with spaces: **12 - 15**.

   It is possible to add nonadjacent interfaces by separating them with commas. In the Full Edition of the NetSim, that option would work like this: **interface range fastethernet** 0/12 - 15, 24, 22, 20, 18.

5. Add descriptions to ports 16 to 19 for the sales department. Then label ports 20 to 24 as unused.

   Check your work and return.

6. Weren't there a couple of gigabit interfaces on this switch? Yes, and they configure just like FastEthernet. Try this and then add a description to GigabitEthernet0/2 for the accounting server.

interface GigabitEthernet0/1

description **Link to Sales Server system**

Check your work and remain in Privileged mode.

7. Save your work. Hint: Task 2, step 6.

Task 5: Other Ways to Look at Our Work

We used the **show running-config** command to see our results, but there are other commands you should become familiar with, particularly for troubleshooting.

1. Try the **show interfaces status** command and look over the results.
2. Try the **show interfaces** command and look over the results. You should see very detailed info about each interface.
3. Try the **show ip interface** command and look over the results. Notice the output is different from the last command.
4. Try the **show ip interface Fa0/1** command and look over the results.
5. Try the **show ip interface brief** command and look over the results.
6. Experiment with these commands while thinking about how you might use the information, as well as which ones give you the interface status (up or down). Feel free to reconfigure any of the interfaces we did earlier.

Basic Configuration Steps

We've now hit all of the basic configuration steps. It is time to make a list that you can follow in doing the basic configuration of any device and then as a checklist to make sure that you haven't missed anything.

1. Name the device (**hostname** *hostname*).
2. Secure Privileged mode (**enable secret** *password*).
3. Secure console, VTY, and AUX connections, including remote connectivity (SSH).
4. Configure interface(s) and default gateway at least enough to reach remotely.

5. Configure routing and default route—routers and Layer 3 devices only.
6. Verify connectivity (ping to and from).
7. Add Login Banner—Security warnings (**banner login #**).
8. Disable or secure unused ports (switches) and unused services (shutdown).
9. Secure all passwords (**service password-encryption**).
10. Save your work and test everything (**copy run start**).

Once step 6 is done, you can safely complete the configuration remotely if you want or need to. This is not everything you will have to do, but this you do on every device. The other tasks get inserted where appropriate before step 8.

We've provided the ten steps above as a PDF. See "Basic Cisco Configuration Steps" for a handy reference of how to configure any Cisco device.

EXERCISE 6-5

Securing the Connections

In this exercise we demonstrate the steps an administrator would take to configure Cisco devices for more secure connections. You'll perform this exercise using Boson's NetSim. Launch Lab 6-5 and review the topology.

Task 1: Getting Started
1. Right-click on the host A.11 icon in the NetMap and then on the Configure in Simulator button that appears. When you press ENTER, you should see the C:> prompt.
2. We configured various passwords on SwitchA in the last exercise including login passwords for remote access, and they are included thanks to our **copy run start** at the end of the last session.

   Type **telnet 10.0.0.2** at the prompt to open a remote session.

   ```
   C:>telnet 10.0.0.2

   This is the Message of the Day!

   Trying 10.0.0.2 ... Open
   ```

```
Password:cisco
SwitchA>enable
Password:ccent
SwitchA#
```

For years this was considered adequate security, but there are two problems. First, Telnet is a very unsecure protocol. It was developed when all connections were trusted—there was no Internet to be exposed to and no public access. Second, it is what is called single-factor authentication: a bad person only needs one piece of information to gain access to the device. True Privileged mode has a second password, and they never should be the same, but it is better to not allow mischief into the device at all. So we will look at two-factor authentication, such as we use for logging into many accounts requiring both a username and password. Then we will look at securing the transport.

Task 2: Configuring Two-Factor Authentication

1. Assuming you are still Telnetted into SwitchA, go to Global Configuration mode.

2. Make the following entries. The second entry is optional and would only work during the life of this lab, but you can use it for experience. Use any username/password you are comfortable with. Do not omit the first one, though.

```
SwitchA(config)#username student password cisco
SwitchA(config)#username yourname password yourpassword
SwitchA(config)#line vty 0 15
SwitchA(config-line)#login local
SwitchA(config-line)#no password cisco    --gets rid of old
password, not critical but tidy
SwitchA(config-line)#ctrl-z
SwitchA#exit

C:>
```

3. Telnet back into SwitchA and see that you need to supply both a username and password.

   Do a **show run** to see the new entries. Note the passwords are encrypted because of the **service password-encryption** command we added earlier.

4. Open a console session directly to SwitchA. Right-click on the SwitchA icon in the NetMap and then on the Configure in Simulator button that appears. If you press ENTER you should only have to type a password to get in.

   Remember that we only applied two-factor authentication on our vty lines, not *line con 0*. This is somewhat common, because our switches are typically locked in a data facility and then locked again inside a cabinet. Even then, they can only be accessed via a console cable. Others tend to put two-factor authentication on all connections (line AUX too), but we won't do that today.

   For all of these labs we will use this setup: Single-factor on line con 0 with password cisco, two-factor on vty (remote) sessions with username student password cisco (case sensitive).

INSIDE THE EXAM

Cisco Catalyst Switches

Cisco's Catalyst switches are used throughout enterprise networks and service providers. Switch ports are numbered using *x/y* notation, with *x* being the card number and *y* being the individual interface on that card. Numbering always starts with 0 and increments from top to bottom for cards and from left to right for interfaces.

The switch face has five system LEDs (SYST, RPS, STAT, DUPLX, and SPEED), and each bank of interfaces is labeled to indicate capability. Also, remember the basics of switch LEDs: green is good, amber is bad, the SYST lamp indicates the overall health of the switch, and the STAT lamp means the individual port LEDs represent each port's status.

Basic Initial Configuration

Come up with a routine for configuring devices that will become a checklist to make sure you have considered everything. Features to consider are hostname, device access username and passwords, Privileged mode password, message banners (MOTD, Login, and Exec), and enabling encrypted passwords. You may also want to turn off the system (syslog) messages on your console session and increase the history buffer to hold more commands that can then be recalled and edited using the arrow keys and keyboard shortcuts. Be sure to save your configuration changes using **copy run start**.

(Continued)

INSIDE THE EXAM

Securing the Configuration

Pay close attention to the **login** and **login local** settings on questions and simulations on the exam, and be sure you know the difference between the enable password (weak) and enable secret (good). Be sure to review the **service password encryption** command as well. The **exec-timeout** command determines how long an unused session is allowed to remain open.

Managing Remote Connections

SSH should be configured to protect remote access sessions from interception. Be very

familiar with the steps for setting up SSH, and don't forget you can eliminate Telnet altogether with the **transport input ssh** command on the vty lines.

Interface Configuration

Be prepared to see numerous questions on interface configuration, including assigning a device IP address on VLAN 1, as well as setting speed and duplex, and descriptions. Pay close attention to all command syntax, as well as the configuration mode they must be entered on.

CERTIFICATION SUMMARY

Cisco's Catalyst switches were created originally for larger enterprise networks and the Internet backbone. The line now offers a large array of sizes and shapes for different installations; each model has a series number assigned to it. Interfaces on Catalyst switches are numbered x/y, with x being the card or slot number and y being the individual interface on that card. The card numbering always starts with 0 and increments from top to bottom. A 2960 access switch, used in our examples, only has one "card" or row of interfaces and, therefore, will always start interface numbering 0/y, where y=1 to the number of ports.

A Catalyst switch face has a mode button and five system diagnostic LEDs, but no power button (to turn the switch on or off, simply plug in the electrical cord or unplug it). A label on each bank of interfaces indicates the speed at which the ports can be run. A label of 10/100 signifies the ports can run at 10baseT or 100baseT Ethernet. A label of 10/100/1000 indicates the port can go up to gigabit speeds.

Right out of the box, the switch will pass frames and provide service. However, basic configuration is generally needed for VLANs (covered in the next chapter). Individual port settings and device security are all examples of configuration entries an administrator may wish for the switch. Configuration questions may come in the form of multiple choice questions or as part of a simulation. Pay very close attention to the exact syntax of each command since the help functions may not be available on simulation questions.

When no configuration file exists in NVRAM, the switch defaults to the *System Configuration dialog*, also known as Setup mode. Setup mode only allows for basic configuration settings and, for the most part, is not used by most experienced administrators.

During a typical configuration, administrators will assign a hostname, create message banners, apply security settings, configure access methods, and configure interfaces. The hostname is simply a name that can be used to identify the switch within the prompt and configurations. It is assigned using the **hostname** command. There are three types of message banners: Message of the Day (MOTD), Login, and Exec. The *MOTD banner* is shown before login, and is typically used for messages like the device hostname. The *Login banner* is displayed immediately following the MOTD and is often used for set boilerplate-type messages like security and trespass warnings. Finally, the *Exec banner* displays after login, and is intended for messages that should not be shared with unauthorized users, such as contact names and phone numbers. To configure a banner, use the command **banner *type delimiter*** command. Other optional commands include setting **history size** and **logging synchronous**, which suppresses system messages.

Usernames and passwords can be created using the command **username *name* password *password*** to control logins. To secure access to the configuration mode from Privileged mode, use the **enable secret *password*** command, which encrypts the password. The older and less secure **enable password** shouldn't be used and is ignored by the system if both are set. Like many commands, prepending "no" before the command turns it off.

Other device security options include closing inactive open sessions (ten minutes by default). Many admins use the **exec-timeout *x y*** command, where *x* is minutes and *y* is seconds, to extend that time, at least while they are configuring.

Remote access is via the older and unsecure Telnet protocol or, better, the encrypted SSH protocol whenever supported. Configure SSH by creating usernames and passwords; then on the vty line configurations, set **login local** and **transport input telnet ssh** (omit the **telnet** parameter to force SSH only). Then create a domain name using the **ip domain-name *name.extension*** command, and generate the crypto keys with **crypto key generate rsa**. SSH will then share the resulting key with SSH clients that can authenticate.

Interface configuration options include assigning an IP management address and setting speed, duplex, and descriptions. While it is possible to get IP addresses from DHCP, it makes little sense on network devices because we don't want them changing and we want them to always have an IP address, even if the DHCP server is unavailable.

✔ # TWO-MINUTE DRILL

Cisco Catalyst Switches

❑ Catalyst interfaces are numbered x/y, where x is the card number and y is the interface on that card. The 2960 switches used in our examples only have one card in them, so interfaces are numbered 0/1, 0/2, and so on.

❑ Each bank of interfaces includes a label indicating speed and capability. 10/100 indicates 10baseT or 100baseT autonegotiation capability.

Basic Initial Configuration

❑ When no configuration file exists in NVRAM, the switch defaults to the *System Configuration dialog*, also known as Setup mode. This mode is seldom used by skilled admins.

❑ Use the **hostname** *name* command to assign a hostname to the switch.

❑ Use the **banner** *type delimiter* command to create one of the three types of banners: *Message of the Day (MOTD)* is shown before login, the *Login* displays before login immediately following the MOTD, and the *Exec* displays only after login. Login is used for permanent, often longer boilerplate–type messages, such as unauthorized access warnings. Exec messages normally wouldn't be shared with unauthorized users, such as contact info and phone numbers.

❑ Use the **history size** *x* command, where *x* is the size of the new buffer, in a line configuration to change the defined buffer size. Use the global **terminal history size** *x* command to change it for just the single session.

❑ The **logging synchronous** command used on the console line prevents syslog messages from displaying until they are called for.

Securing the Configuration

❑ Use the **login** and the **password** *password* commands to secure the line con or line vty connections. Using **login local** forces the user to know a username and password globally configured on the device, using the **username** *name* **password** *password* command. Either login command can lock users out if the appropriate passwords haven't been configured.

❑ Use the Global Configuration command **enable secret** *password* to secure access to Privileged (Enable) mode. The older **enable password** *password* command is less secure and displays in clear text unless the global **service password-encryption** is used to encrypt the enable password and line passwords; however, its encryption is very weak.

❑ Use the **exec-timeout** *x* *y* command, where *x* is the number of minutes and *y* is the number of seconds, to control how long an inactive session will remain open. The default is ten minutes, but the command allows you to extend it. The **exec-timeout** *0* *0* would stay open until manually closed.

Managing Remote Connections

❑ Telnet is an older clear-text remote access protocol that uses port 23. It should be avoided because any sniffer could view it.

❑ SSH uses port 22 and is encrypted using a client-server agreement with a public and private key. To configure SSH: Create in Global Configuration mode usernames and passwords, and add **login local** and **transport input telnet ssh** on all vty lines—omitting **telnet** would restrict access to SSH. Return to global configuration mode and create a domain name using the **ip domain-name** *name.extension* command, then generate the crypto keys using **crypto key generate rsa**.

❑ To see the public key, use the **show crypto key mypubkey rsa** command.

Interface Configuration

❑ Assign a device management IP address to the VLAN 1 interface using the **ip address** *address subnetmask* interface command and then the **ip default-gateway** *ipaddress* Global Configuration command. Be sure to enter **no shutdown** on the interface (VLAN 1 is disabled by default).

❑ A **show interface vlan1** command will display the IP address, as well as the state of the interface. If the **no shutdown** command has not been entered, it will display "Administratively down."

❑ The commands used to configure interfaces are **duplex** {*auto* | *full* | *half*}, **speed** {*10* | *100* | *1000* | *auto*}, and **description** *text*. Each command is entered individually on each interface. To apply them to several interfaces at once, use the **interface range** *type port-range* command.

❑ On a **show interfaces status** command output, "auto" and "auto" display in the Duplex and Speed columns on unused ports without a manual configuration—manually defined ports will show their duplex and speed settings. When a port is in use, an "a-" indicates autonegotiation with an end system.

SELF TEST

The following Self Test questions will help you measure your understanding of the material presented in this chapter. Read all the choices carefully since there may be more than one correct answer. Choose all the correct answers for each question.

Cisco Catalyst Switches

1. You wish to configure the speed and duplex settings for a port on your Catalyst 2960 switch. The interface is the fifth from the left. Which Global Configuration command will put you in the correct interface configuration mode to enter the new settings?
   A. interface FastEthernet 5
   B. interface FastEthernet 0/5
   C. interface FastEthernet 5/0
   D. interface FastEthernet 1/5

Basic Initial Configuration

2. An administrator wants to use the System Configuration dialog to set up the switch, and intends on assigning manual speed settings on each interface. After clearing NVRAM and restarting the system, a message asking, "Would you like to enter basic management setup [yes | no]?" appears. How should the administrator answer?
   A. Yes, because he wishes to use setup to configure the device.
   B. Yes, because basic management setup allows interface configuration settings.
   C. No, because the message is referring to the management interface and not a setup mode.
   D. No, because basic management mode does not allow for interface configuration.

3. Examining the output of a **show running-config** command, you notice this command:

   banner login welcome to Switch12. Please prepare to login

   What message will display when the switch is accessed from the console?
   A. welcome to Switch12. Please prepare to login
   B. welcome to Switch12
   C. welcome to Sw
   D. None of the above

4. A user wishes to stop syslog messages from interrupting the command prompt display during a console session. Which command accomplishes this?
   A. Switch(config)# logging synchronous
   B. Switch(config-if)# logging synchronous
   C. Switch(config-line)# logging synchronous
   D. None of the above

Securing the Configuration

5. You examine the output of a **show running-config** command and notice two commands: **enable password Cisco** and **enable secret CCENT**. Later on, you establish a console connection to the switch and are prompted for a password to enter Privileged mode. Which password should you use?
   A. Cisco
   B. CCENT
   C. Both. The enable password is first, followed by the enable secret.
   D. Both. The enable secret is first, followed by the enable password.
   E. Neither. Access to a console connection already grants Privileged mode access.

6. After entering the command **service password-encryption**, you notice all passwords appear in encrypted format within the configuration. You then issue a **no service password-encryption** command and save the configuration. The next day, a peer changes the password on the console line, using the command **password Cisco**. After executing a **show running-config**, which of the following would be true?
   A. All passwords, except for the enable secret, will display in clear text.
   B. All passwords, including the enable secret, will display in clear text.
   C. All passwords will continue to display in encrypted format.
   D. The console password will display in clear text; all others will display encrypted.

7. You wish to force users to use two-factor authentication on the console before gaining a command prompt. Which of the following commands are required?
   A. Switch(config)# username Bob password Cisco
   B. Switch(config-line)# username Bob password Cisco
   C. Switch(config)# login
   D. Switch(config-line)# login
   E. Switch(config)# login local
   F. Switch(config-line)# login local

Managing Remote Connections

8. An administrator wishes to force remote access users to connect using SSH. Which command must be entered to disable Telnet access and force SSH use?

A. The **no telnet** Global Configuration command

B. **no telnet** in vty Line Configuration mode

C. The **transport input ssh** Global Configuration command

D. **transport input ssh** in vty Line Configuration mode

Interface Configuration

9. An administrator wishes to add a static management IP address to the switch. Which of the following commands is/are required?

A. The **ip address** *ip_address subnet_mask* Global Configuration command

B. **ip address** *ip_address subnet_mask* on interface Vlan1 configuration mode

C. The **ip default-gateway** *ip_address* Global Configuration command

D. **ip default-gateway** *ip_address* on interface Vlan1 configuration mode

10. A segment of the output from a **show interfaces status** command is displayed next:

```
Fa0/5  File Server port      notconnect   1      full   100    10/100BaseTX
Fa0/6                        notconnect   1      auto   auto   10/100BaseTX
```

Which of the following are true regarding the interfaces?

A. Autonegotiation has been disabled for interface 5.

B. Autonegotiation has been disabled for interface 6.

C. The **speed 100** and **duplex auto** commands have been configured for interface 5.

D. The **speed 100** and **duplex full** commands have been configured for interface 5.

SELF TEST ANSWERS

Cisco Catalyst Switches

1. ☑ **B** is correct. Numbering on Catalyst 2960 interfaces always starts with 0/1, 0/2, and so on.
   ☒ **A, C,** and **D** are incorrect. **A, C,** and **D** are incorrect because the syntax on these commands is not correct.

Basic Initial Configuration

2. ☑ **D** is correct. The administrator can use the System Configuration dialog (setup) to configure interface settings, but only in extended setup mode.
   ☒ **A, B,** and **C** are incorrect. **A** and **B** are incorrect because answering "yes" would start in basic management setup mode, which does not allow interface configuration. The statement in **C** is not correct.

3. ☑ **D** is correct. The first character after the **banner login** command becomes the delimiter. Everything following it becomes part of the banner until the delimiter is seen again. In this instance, "w" becomes the delimiter, which would make the message "elcome to S."
   ☒ **A, B,** and **C** are incorrect because everything between the delimiters (w) would be displayed, but nothing else.

4. ☑ **C** is correct. The command is **logging synchronous**, and it must be entered in Line Configuration mode.
   ☒ **A, B,** and **D** are incorrect. **A** is incorrect because this is the correct command, but it is being entered in Global Configuration mode. **B** is incorrect because again, the correct command is entered, but this time in Interface Configuration mode. **D** is incorrect because this is a false statement.

Securing the Configuration

5. ☑ **B** is correct. In the event the enable password and enable secret are both configured on a device, the enable secret password is always used.
   ☒ **A, C, D,** and **E** are incorrect. **A, C,** and **D** are incorrect because these statements are false; the enable secret will always be used. **E** is incorrect because access to a console connection does not automatically provide access to Privileged mode—that's what the enable password or enable secret is for in the first place!

6. ☑ **D** is correct. After **service password-encryption** has been entered into a configuration, all passwords will remain in encrypted format, even if **no service password-encryption** is entered later. However, if a password is changed after that, it will display in clear text.

   ☒ **A, B,** and **C** are incorrect. A and B are incorrect because the encrypted versions of the passwords will remain after **no service password-encryption** until they are changed. The enable secret always displays in encrypted format, regardless. **C** is incorrect because changing a password after **no service password-encryption** results in a new clear-text entry in the config.

7. ☑ **A** and **F** are correct. Username and password pairs are created in Global Configuration mode. **login local** is required to force users on that line to use their username and password, and is entered in Line Configuration mode.

   ☒ **B, C, D,** and **E** are incorrect. B is incorrect because the command is correct but should be in Global Configuration mode, not Line Configuration mode. C and D are incorrect because **login** does force a password to be used (which would be put on the line with the **password** *password* command), but does not force the use of defined username and password pairs. **E** is incorrect because it is the correct command, but it is not entered in Global Configuration mode.

Managing Remote Connections

8. ☑ **D** is correct. This is the correct command, and must be entered in Line Configuration mode.
   ☒ **A, B,** and **C** are incorrect. A and B are incorrect because **no telnet** is not a valid IOS command. **C** is incorrect because it is the correct command, but it's in the wrong configuration mode.

Interface Configuration

9. ☑ **B** and **C** are correct. The IP address must be assigned to the VLAN 1 interface, while the default gateway address is assigned globally.
   ☒ **A** and **D** are incorrect because these command and configuration mode combinations are not correct.

10. ☑ **A** and **D** are correct. The **speed 100** and **duplex full** commands were issued on interface FastEthernet 0/5. Assigning these commands disables autonegotiation.
    ☒ **B** and **C** are incorrect. B is incorrect because interface FastEthernet 0/6 is still in autonegotiation mode, as shown by the "auto" entries in the display. **C** is incorrect because the duplex command was not set to "auto," as shown by the "full" entry in the display.

7

VLANs and Port Security

S o far we've looked at what switches do in the network and how they forward frames to specific destinations, and we've created a basic configuration for Cisco switches. In this chapter we look at slightly more advanced features: virtual LANs (VLANs) and adding port security to switches.

CERTIFICATION OBJECTIVE 7.01

Virtual LANs (VLANs)

In Chapter 3, we introduced VLANs. Without reiterating too much, we'd like to reinforce some things that should make VLANs easier to understand and then configure.

Why Use VLANs

There are lots of reasons why organizations want to break their LAN into multiple LANs or LAN segments with separate IP address pools. One issue with larger pools of users is that you have more broadcasts, which all hosts have to process at least far enough to ensure that the frames are not for them and then discard them. Another reason for segmenting or breaking up a LAN is that the organization's users may need primary access to quite different resources, such as servers, printers, WAN connections, the Internet, etc. There may also be security or even regulatory reasons why certain departments should be separated from others. Having teachers and students in the same network would make it easier for students to get to resources such as test servers, gradebooks, or student records—all things that should be off-limits to them.

Just as you might put programmers, web developers, engineers, sales, and/or web publishing people in their own departments based on skills, you might also want them in separate networks because of the type and volume of traffic they generate and the impact it has on network performance.

In the old traditional or legacy model, a router would connect each separate network, each with its own switch(es), offices, and workspaces. But as we mentioned in Chapter 3, growth often means people get moved into other areas out of necessity. Putting together project teams often means people from different departments end up working together. The traditional model didn't work so well for this. Also, different sized departments often made it hard to standardize on certain models and sizes of switches. You wouldn't want a 24- or 48-port switch committed to accounting with only six connections, particularly while sales support was out of ports.

Fortunately, VLANs allow us to design networks with individual switch ports assigned to different VLANs, grouped as we need them and where we need them. The number of VLANs in the overall design and on a particular switch is up to the network designer and then easily implemented and changed as needed by the administrators.

To be clear, nothing ever prevented two or more networks from using the same switch, but it led to all the concerns we talked about earlier, plus if there were three networks, then three ports would have to be set aside for router connections so the departments could get to shared resources like e-mail and the Internet. Not a very efficient use of ports if there were many switches like this.

VLAN Interface Types

There are two types of switch interfaces or ports that can be configured on VLAN switches: access ports and trunk ports.

Access ports connect one or more end users to a single VLAN. While the most common form is to connect a single host to their network (hence the name), it is possible to connect to a switch, but all the devices on the switch would have to be in that same network or VLAN.

Trunk ports got their name from telephone networks where a trunk line could carry multiple circuits or phone lines from a central office to a business switchboard. A trunk port connects a cable that carries separate virtual circuits for two or more VLANs between two devices, typically two switches or a switch and a router, but also it is possible between a switch and another VLAN-capable device, such as a firewall or even a server.

The syntax for configuring a port for access or trunk is **switchport mode [access | trunk]** in Interface Configuration mode.

While Cisco Layer 2 switches can segment broadcast domains into two or more separate VLANs, each with their own address pool and broadcast domain, devices in those VLANs still can't communicate with other VLANs without a router. With Layer 2 switches, that means a trunk link to a router. With Layer 3– enabled switches, which are like Layer 2 switches with a router module built into the device, we create what are called switch virtual interfaces (SVIs) to handle the routing. Instead of having to send route forwarding requests to a distant router over a trunk, the local route module would determine if the traffic is allowed to go to the other VLAN and, if so, process the frame accordingly so it could be forwarded.

Figure 7-1 shows a network with two Layer 2 VLAN switches and four VLANs. Looking over the diagram, notice VLAN 4 is not showing. It may no longer be in use or saved for future development or some other reason. VLAN numbers are up to the network designer and need not start with 1 or be contiguous. VLANs 2 and 5 are on both switches, so the trunk between the two switches will have to carry at least VLANs 2 and 5 so that the hosts on Switch B can communicate with their other members on Switch A. Note that would also allow all VLAN 2 hosts to reach the Dev server, but none of the other workstations not in VLAN 2. None of the workstations can reach the File or E-mail servers. What VLANs must the trunk between Switch A and the router be configured for? Would that allow all workstations to get to the three servers?

The trunk between Switch A and the router would have to be configured for VLANs 1, 2, 3, and 5 if all workstations and servers are to have access to the Internet. Would that allow all workstations to get to the three servers? Yes. The router will forward traffic to all three servers, the Internet, and any host on any LAN.

FIGURE 7-1

VLAN switches
with four VLANs
and two trunks

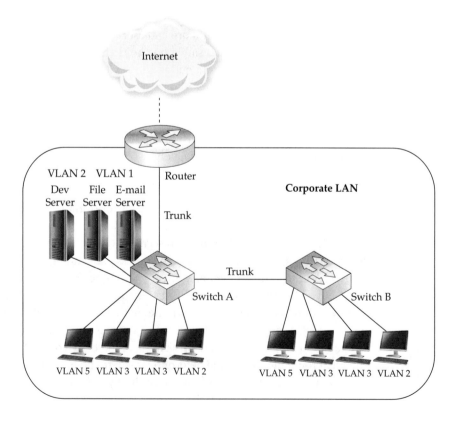

Maybe a more common scenario would be for only the workstations to communicate with the servers. The same is true for access to the Internet. VLANs 2, 3, and 5 would have access to VLAN 1 servers and the Internet, but VLANs 3 and 5 would be denied access to the Dev server. The workstations in VLAN 2 do not need the router to get to the Dev server. Just because all VLANs can reach the router doesn't necessarily mean that we want all of them out on the Internet or going to every server. While the trunk creates a road with lanes for all four VLANs, that doesn't necessarily mean all VLANs should be forwarded by the router to those other lanes. The router could be configured to restrict which frames get re-encapsulated into VLAN 1 or 2 based on something called access control lists (ACLs) configured on the router. We will cover these in Chapter 11.

e x a m

ⓦ a t c h

VLANs offer several benefits. Some of the more important reasons for using VLANs within a network design are

■ *VLANs can segment broadcast domains without using a router.*

■ *VLANs can improve performance on hosts, reducing their processing overhead by limiting the broadcast messages and separating traffic types.*

■ *VLANs provide better security by separating groups of users and their devices and message traffic.*

VLAN access ports connect hosts to a single VLAN. VLAN trunk ports connect to a switch or router and carry two or more VLANs in separate virtual circuits over the connection. While Cisco switches can segment broadcast domains into two or more separate VLANs, each with their own address pool and broadcast domain, devices in those VLANs still need a router to communicate with other VLANs.

IEEE 802.1Q Trunks

As we learned in Chapter 4, the IEEE 802 committee is tasked with developing Ethernet Layer 2 standards. Trunks are no different—to ensure interoperability between vendors, a single standard had to be developed. That standard is called 802.1Q, a VLAN tagging standard that allows Ethernet bridges and switches to keep track of and quickly handle frames from multiple VLANs across a single link, copper or fiber optic.

For our discussion purposes, let's assume that all switches in our network are 802.1Q compliant. For any traffic between switches, a tag is added to each frame when it enters the first switch, indicating exactly which VLAN it is a part of, based on the interface it entered through. Each VLAN has a unique tag, except the native VLAN (VLAN 1 unless changed by the admin). This tag is like a name badge at a really big conference center, which tells all the staff and security which conference you are with so they can efficiently move you along to your destination. Similarly, this VLAN tag allows any intermediate switches to guide the frame to the next trunks. At the final switch, the tag is removed and the frame forwarded normally to its destination interface.

The syntax for configuring a trunk is **switchport mode [access | trunk]** in Interface Configuration mode. The following shows a simple example:

```
Swi_1#configure terminal
Swi_1(config)#interface fa0/2
Swi_1(config-if)#switchport mode trunk
Swi_1 (config-if)end
```

802.1Q Frame Format

802.1Q actually inserts a 4-byte (32-bit) tag inside the Ethernet frame between the source MAC address and the EtherType/Length fields. Figure 7-2 compares an Ethernet frame and an 802.1Q frame. This increases the maximum frame size from 1518 bytes to 1522 bytes. That isn't as big a deal as you might think, because the tag only exists within a group of switches and routers that support 802.1Q and then it is stripped off, returning to normal maximum.

exam

ⓦatch *Know that the IEEE 802.1Q trunk standard is for tagged VLANs that allow multiple VLANs to travel over a single circuit by means of inserting a 4-byte tag on frames from all VLANs except the native VLAN. This tag is only used within and between VLAN-aware switches and is finally removed by the last switch before forwarding out to the final destination.*

FIGURE 7-2									

Preamble 7	SFD 1	Destination 8	Source 8	Type 2	Data & Pad 46-1500	FCS 4	Bytes

Ethernet frame vs. an 802.1Q frame

Preamble 7	SFD 1	Destination 8	Source 8	802.1Q Hdr 4	Type 2	Data & Pad 46-1500	FCS 4	Bytes

Default vs. Native VLANs

Cisco switches have two predefined VLANs, the default and the native VLANs, which many students assume are the same thing or they mix them up. It doesn't help that they both initially default to VLAN 1. VLAN 1 is always the default VLAN on Cisco switches. It can't be changed or deleted because it carries many nondata streams, including many Layer 2 protocols' communication between switches.

The native VLAN is the only VLAN that is not tagged in a VLAN trunk—in other words, native VLAN frames are transmitted without the 802.1Q tag mentioned earlier. So, by default, since the native VLAN is VLAN 1, all VLAN 1 traffic remains untagged. It also means data traffic on VLAN 1 is both untagged and mixed in with all the protocol traffic. If you do not configure this parameter, an 802.1Q trunk port uses the default VLAN as the native VLAN ID. It should be configured the same on all trunk interfaces to avoid getting multiple VLANs in the untagged stream. The following shows how to configure native VLAN for an 802.1Q trunk port:

```
Swi_1#configure terminal
Swi_1(config)#interface fa0/2
Swi_1(config-if)#switchport mode trunk
Swi_1(config-if)#switchport trunk native vlan 3
Swi_1 (config-if)end
```

Dynamic Trunking Protocol (DTP)

DTP is a Cisco proprietary protocol used to negotiate trunking on a link between two VLAN-aware switches. DTP aids with trunk port establishment by negotiating whether a link between two switches should be put into access or trunk mode. It is an attempt to make initial deployment of a switched network easier and minimize configuration errors.

DTP works with the **switchport mode** command by adding a couple of options. The syntax is **switchport mode [access | trunk | dynamic [auto | desirable]]**.

In both access and trunk modes, the interface transmits DTP frames to the other end of the link, trying to get the other end to match up without offering to change.

The two **switchport mode dynamic** options will attempt to negotiate a connection, but will default to access mode if no agreement is reached. With **switchport mode dynamic desirable**, the interface actively attempts to create a trunk link, which it will do if the neighboring interface is set to trunk, desirable, or auto mode. This is the default mode for all Ethernet interfaces. With the **switchport mode auto** command, the interface is willing to convert to a trunk if the neighboring interface is set to trunk or desirable mode. Otherwise, it will become an access interface.

The results of two interfaces sharing a link negotiation are summarized in Table 7-1. Limited connectivity means that only the VLAN the interfaces have in common will be passed. The effect is the same as an access link, except that one end looks like a trunk to anyone troubleshooting the problem.

A related command, **switchport nonegotiate**, added to a trunk or access interface prevents the interface from generating DTP frames. This option requires that the other interface must be manually configured as a trunk interface to establish a trunk link, otherwise the link will be a nontrunking link.

e x a m

ⓦatch　*Know the basics of Dynamic Trunking Protocol (DTP)—its purpose, the options, and the results of ports negotiating as shown in Table 7-1. Note that switchport nonegotiate turns off DTP frames, but then requires that both ends be configured the same.*

Warning: *Do not confuse DTP with VTP (VLAN Trunking Protocol), another Cisco protocol covered in advanced certificates. It is used to share the existence and details of any VLANs on the whole LAN using the client-server relationship between switches.*

TABLE 7-1	Cisco DTP Negotiation Results

	Dynamic Auto	Dynamic Desirable	Trunk	Access
Dynamic Auto	Access	Trunk	Trunk	Access
Dynamic Desirable	Trunk	Trunk	Trunk	Access
Trunk	Trunk	Trunk	Trunk	Limited connectivity
Access	Access	Access	Limited connectivity	Access

Configure and Verify VLAN Access Ports

Creating VLANs is relatively simple. They can be created individually or in ranges when you want to use a consecutive series of numbers. Initially, they are created in Global Configuration mode, but the **vlan** command puts you into VLAN Configuration mode. We can name them in VLAN Configuration mode to make them easier to identify and troubleshoot. Once they are created, we assign interfaces to the VLAN in Interface Configuration mode.

To create a VLAN or modify an existing VLAN from Global Configuration mode:

■ Sw(config)# vlan [*vlan-id* | *vlan-range*] Create a VLAN or edit an existing one. It also puts you into VLAN Configuration mode.

■ Sw(config-vlan)# name *vlan-name* (Optional) Give the VLAN a name, up to 32 characters, while in VLAN Configuration mode.

In the **vlan** [*vlan-id* | *vlan-range*] command syntax, *vlan-id* is a whole number between 2 and 4094 (or 1001 on older IOSs) and *vlan-range* is sequential VLANs, i.e., 2–15. Newer switches also support nonconsecutive numbers separated by commas, i.e., 2-12, 14, 16. Remember that VLAN 1, the default VLAN, already exists and all interfaces are in it by default.

Your vlan-id numbers can follow any pattern useful to the organization. They need not be sequential. They could be 2, 3, 4, 5 or 20, 30, 40, 99. By the same token, if your departments have three- or four-digit budget codes, the department VLANs might be 111, 346, 719, and 999. The following example shows creating VLANs 20, 30, 40, and 50 in one command.

If you use a vlan-id that already exists, the IOS goes to VLAN configuration submode for that VLAN, assuming you want to edit it. To delete the VLAN, just use the **no** form of the same command, **no vlan** [*vlan-id* | *vlan-range*].

Optionally, you can name the VLAN using the command **name** *vlan-name*, where *vlan-name* is a descriptive text string up to 32 characters used by humans to remember what a particular VLAN number is for. The following example shows creating VLANs using the various options:

```
Swi_1# configure terminal
Swi_1(config-vlan)# vlan 13
Swi_1(config-vlan)# name Sales
Swi_1(config-vlan)# vlan 5-10
Swi_1(config-vlan)# vlan 20,30,40,50
```

To add an interface to a VLAN, use the **switchport access vlan** *vlan-id* command on each interface. Recall from earlier that adding the command **switchport mode access** prevents the interface from becoming a trunk.

Suppose you are creating several new VLANs on your switch for the accounting, sales, and engineering departments. Accounting department employees will use interfaces 5 through 10, and interface 12 will be used by sales—the other interfaces will be available for "regular" network users. The following code shows how this might be done. Note you can add the interface **description** option from Chapter 6.

```
Swi_1#configure terminal
Enter configuration commands, one per line.  End with CNTL/Z.
Swi_1(config)# vlan 50
Swi_1(config-vlan)# name Accounting
Swi_1(config)# vlan 77
Swi_1(config-vlan)# name Sales
Swi_1(config)# vlan 123
Swi_1(config-vlan)# name Engineering
Swi_1(config-vlan)# exit
Swi_1(config)# interface range FastEthernet 0/5 - 10
Swi_1(config-if)# switchport access vlan 50
Swi_1(config-if)# switchport mode access
Swi_1(config)# interface range Fa 0/12, Fa 0/14
Swi_1(config-if)# switchport access vlan 77
Swi_1(config-if)# switchport mode access
Swi_1(config-if)# end
```

The first example used the **interface range** option to assign a consecutive group of interfaces at once; the second showed how the newer switches allow you to enter nonconsecutive ports. It also used the abbreviated form for Fast Ethernet. Interfaces can also be assigned one at a time.

Verify VLAN Ports

To verify VLANs exist and which ports are assigned to each VLAN, use the **show running-config**, **show interface status**, or **show vlan brief** command. The running configuration will show interface membership in a VLAN on a per-interface basis, while **vlan brief** shows all VLANs on the switch, as well as the interfaces assigned to each. The **show running-config** (or **show run**) command output looks like this:

```
Swi_1# show running-config
  <<<Output Omitted >>>
!
```

```
interface FastEthernet0/4
!
interface FastEthernet0/5
  switchport access vlan 50
  switchport mode access
interface FastEthernet0/6
  switchport access vlan 50
  switchport mode access
  <<<Output Omitted >>>
interface FastEthernet0/12
  switchport access vlan 77
  switchport mode access
  <<<Output Omitted >>>
!
```

Note that interface FastEthernet0/4 was not assigned to a VLAN, so there is no VLAN notation. The next three interfaces show examples of access ports with the mode set to access to make sure that it does not attempt to form a trunk link.

The **show interface status** command gives us the VLAN confirmation but also shows us connection status (see 0/7 and 0/10). The a-full and a-100 show the interfaces autoconfigured.

```
Switch#sho int status

Port      Name            Status       Vlan    Duplex  Speed Type
Fa0/1                     notconnect   1         auto   auto 10/100BaseTX
Fa0/2                     notconnect   1         auto   auto 10/100BaseTX
Fa0/3                     notconnect   1         auto   auto 10/100BaseTX
Fa0/4                     notconnect   1         auto   auto 10/100BaseTX
Fa0/5                     notconnect   50        auto   auto 10/100BaseTX
Fa0/6                     notconnect   50        auto   auto 10/100BaseTX
Fa0/7                     connected    50       a-full  a-100 10/100BaseTX
Fa0/8                     notconnect   50        auto   auto 10/100BaseTX
Fa0/9                     notconnect   50        auto   auto 10/100BaseTX
Fa0/10                    connected    50       a-full  a-100 10/100BaseTX
Fa0/11                    notconnect   1         auto   auto 10/100BaseTX
Fa0/12                    notconnect   77        auto   auto 10/100BaseTX
Fa0/13                    notconnect   1         auto   auto 10/100BaseTX
Fa0/14                    notconnect   77        auto   auto 10/100BaseTX
Fa0/15                    notconnect   1         auto   auto 10/100BaseTX
   <<<Output Omitted >>>
```

Recall from Chapter 5 that there are two PDF files we looked at earlier. PDF05-01_Sample_switch_(Start) is a Cisco switch that has not been configured, and PDF05-02_Sample_switch_(Configured) is configured with four VLANs and a couple of trunks. It may help you to look those over. You'll see they didn't bother naming their VLANs.

To show all VLANs created on the switch, as well as the interfaces assigned to each, use the **brief** option of the **show vlan** command. The syntax for the command is:

show vlan [all | brief | id *vlan-id* | name *name*]

all	All VLAN details
brief	Each VLAN, name, status, and ports assigned
id *vlan-id*	All data on a single VLAN identified by *vlan-id*, a number: 1 to 4094
name *name*	All data on a single VLAN identified by *name*, a string: 1 to 32 characters

You will notice that most interfaces are still in VLAN 1 because we haven't assigned any to the other two VLANs yet. Also, you will see VLANs 1002 to 1005; these are reserved for old protocols, FFDI and token ring.

```
Swi_1# show vlan brief
VLAN      Name            Status     Ports
1         default         active     Fa0/1, Fa0/2, Fa0/3, Fa0/4, Fa0/11,
                                     Fa0/13, Fa0/14, Fa0/15, Fa0/16, Fa0/17,
               <<<Output Omitted >>>
50        Accounting      active     Fa0/5, Fa0/6, Fa0/7, Fa0/8, Fa0/9,
                                     Fa0/10
77        Sales           active     Fa0/12, Fa0/14
123       Engineering     active
1002      fddi-default        act/unsup
1003      token-ring-default  act/unsup
1004      fddinet-default     act/unsup
1005      trnet-default       act/unsup
Swi_1#
```

exam

ⓦatch   *Make sure you are very comfortable with creating VLANs and assigning access interfaces to them. As always, be sure you pay attention to which configuration mode you are in before* *attempting commands. Be familiar with the output of both the* show running-config *and* show vlan brief *commands and how both allow you to verify a VLAN exists and which ports are assigned to each.*

Configure and Verify VLAN Trunk Ports

Basic trunk configuration is only a little more involved than defining an access port; in fact, you use the **switchport mode [access | trunk]** interface configuration command.

By default, a trunk carries all VLANs on the switch, but it is possible to limit which VLANs are allowed over a trunk with the **switchport trunk allowed vlan** [*vlan-ids* | **all**] command in Interface Configuration mode. In the following example we are configuring interface 2 to be a trunk, and we have changed our native VLAN from VLAN 1 to VLAN 3. We also want it to carry only VLANs 1, 3, 50, and 77 (from our earlier example). We can "prune" the VLANs, leaving out VLAN 123. Remember *prune* and *pruning*, the terms Cisco uses for limiting VLANs allowed on a trunk.

```
Swi_1#configure terminal
Swi_1(config)#interface fa0/2
Swi_1(config-if)#switchport mode trunk
Swi_1(config-if)#switchport nonegotiate
Swi_1(config-if)#switchport trunk native vlan 3
Swi_1(config-if)#switchport trunk allowed vlan 1,3,50,77
Swi_1(config-if)end
```

This configuration assumes the other end of the link will be similarly configured. If we had not used the **switchport nonegotiate** command, the other switch could use the DTP default **dynamic desirable** state to set the trunk. While that would have created the trunk, it wouldn't have pruned the VLANs and wouldn't have known we changed the native VLAN from 1 to 3.

Two commands that can be used to verify the trunk setting are **show interfaces** *type/number* **switchport** and **show interface trunk**. The following output shows the result with key information in bold:

```
Swi_1#show interfaces fa0/2 switchport
Name: Fa0/2
Switchport: Enabled
Administrative Mode: trunk
Operational Mode: trunk
Administrative Trunking Encapsulation: dot1q
Operational Trunking Encapsulation: dot1q
Negotiation of Trunking: Off
Access Mode VLAN: 1 (default)
```

```
Trunking Native Mode VLAN: 3 (Active)
Voice VLAN: none
<<<Output Omitted>>>
```

This output shows the port mode, the native VLAN, and the protocol used on the VLANs—dot1q refers to 802.1Q. Port 0/3 is an example of a trunk formed with DTP; note the word *desirable* under Mode.

```
Swi_1#show interface trunk
Port          Mode          Encapsulation  Status        Native vlan
Fa0/2         on            802.1q         trunking      3
Port          Vlans allowed on trunk
Fa0/2         1,3,50,77
Port          Vlans allowed and active in management domain
Fa0/2         1,3,50,77
Port          Vlans in spanning tree forwarding state and not pruned
Fa0/2         1,3,50,77
Fa0/3         desirable     n-802.1q       trunking      1
Port          Vlans allowed on trunk
Fa0/3         1-4094
Port          Vlans allowed and active in management domain
Fa0/3         1,3,50,77
Port          Vlans in spanning tree forwarding state and not pruned
Fa0/3         1,3,50,77
```

InterVLAN Routing

In this chapter we have focused on switches and switch-to-switch trunks. But for traffic to be able to move from one VLAN to another or out to the Internet, one end of a trunk will be on a switch, just as we have done, and the other on a router. The router would then be configured to allow the forwarding that we need. In Chapter 8 we will demonstrate the router configuration steps and creating SVIs that will work with Layer 3 switches, which have built-in router modules.

EXERCISE 7-1

MHE Lab

Interface and VLAN Configuration

In this exercise we demonstrate the steps an administrator would take to configure VLANs and trunks on a switch. You'll perform this lab using Boson's NetSim simulator. Launch Lab 7-1 and review the topology.

Task 1: Test Lab Connectivity

1. Using the skills from Lab 6-1, open a console session for host V1.13 and verify connectivity to host B.77. Confirm you can ping each router, host V1.59, and SwitchB.

   Confirm that you can't ping SwitchC or SwitchC2. Neither is configured yet. That is what you will do.

   Confirm that you can't ping host V2.69 or host V2.88 even though they are connected to the same switches. They are in another subnet, 10.0.22.0/24.

   Confirm that all of this is true for host V1.59.

2. From hosts V2.69 and V2.88, verify that they can't ping anything but each other. They are currently the only devices in VLAN 2. Note that they can ping each other even though they are on separate switches. An unconfigured switch doesn't care about subnets.

Task 2: Basic Configuration for SwitchC and SwitchC2

1. Using the skills from Lab 6-1 and 6-2, use the Basic Cisco Configuration Steps, Lab Topology, and IP Address sections earlier to configure SwitchC and SwitchC2.

   They should be identical to each other and SwitchB except for their hostname and VLAN 1 IP addresses. Their default gateway will both be the LAN side of RouterC, 10.0.2.1.

   Remember that our login password will always be cisco for these labs and the enable secret will always be ccent.

2. If the first time you do this lab you are not able to do all the steps from the information earlier, SwitchB's configuration information will be listed next as a series of hints. If you get stuck, the configured items will be in the lab solution at the end of the lab.

Note: This is not the entire configuration, just the items to be configured. You might want to log in to SwitchB to see the login banner. Remember this is SwitchB's information. You will need to replace three things to work on SwitchC and SwitchC2:

```
hostname SwitchB
enable secret ccent
interface Vlan 1
 ip address 10.0.1.2 255.255.255.0
ip default-gateway 10.0.1.1
banner login #
---------------Warning!--------------------
Terms of Use
Unauthorized or improper use of our servers or network or systems
within the network, will result in administrative disciplinary
action and civil and criminal penalties.
#
line con 0
password cisco
 history size 20
 login
line aux 0
line vty 0 15
password cisco
 history size 20
 login
```

To confirm that it is probably configured correctly, use step 6 in Basic Cisco Configuration Steps. Make sure that you can ping B.77 (10.0.1.77) from each switch.

Task 3: Create the VLANs

We already assigned an IP address to VLAN 1. We can't name it, delete it, or do anything except change the IP. So we are going to create two new VLANs even though we will only work with one in this lab. You can always come back and apply it if you like later.

1. On the console for SwitchC2, go into Global Configuration mode and make the following entries. Note: It confirms each VLAN and shows the default name that your next command replaces.

```
SwitchC2(config)#vlan 2
VLAN 2 added:
    Name:VLAN0002
SwitchC2(config-vlan)#name Sales
```

```
SwitchC2(config-vlan)#vlan 3
VLAN 3 added:
    Name:VLAN0003
SwitchC2(config-vlan)#name Accounting
SwitchC2(config-vlan)#
```

2. Run the **show vlan** command to see that the VLANs were created and named but no interfaces are assigned yet. Try the **brief** option as in **show vlan brief** and notice it gives us a shorter output with what we want.

3. In Global Configuration mode, run the following commands. Note that we are only adding a description to interfaces 5 through 10 because they are already in VLAN 1, as are all interfaces by default.

```
SwitchC2(config)#interface range FastEthernet 0/5 - 10
SwitchC2(config-if-range)#description IT Department VLAN
SwitchC2(config-if-range)#interface range FastEthernet 0/11 - 15
SwitchC2(config-if-range)#switchport access vlan 2
SwitchC2(config-if-range)#switchport mode access
SwitchC2(config-if-range)#description Sales Department VLAN
SwitchC2(config-if-range)#interface range FastEthernet 0/16 - 20
SwitchC2(config-if-range)#switchport access vlan 3
SwitchC2(config-if-range)#switchport mode access
SwitchC2(config-if-range)#description Accounting Department VLAN
SwitchC2(config-if-range)#
```

4. Run the **show vlan brief** command again to see that our interfaces are now in the VLANs.

   Run a **show running-config (show run)** to see that our interfaces now show the labels and configuration.

   Run **show interface status** to see that you have one host each in ports for VLAN 1 (Fa0/6) and VLAN2 (Fa0/11). Notice also Fa0/1, which connects to SwitchC (Fa0/2), has autoconfigured as a trunk. It doesn't work because SwitchC is not configured with VLANs yet.

5. From hosts V2.69 and V2.88, verify that they can't even ping each other now. They could in Task 2 step 2 because all interfaces were in VLAN 1 and it didn't care what it transported over the link between the switches. But now hosts V2.69 and V2.88 are in ports (Fa0/11) assigned to VLAN 2. Now VLAN 1 can't carry their traffic.

6. As a good practice, run a **copy run start** to save your work.

Task 4: Configuring Trunks

Even though interface Fa0/1 has used Dynamic Trunking Protocol (DTP) to become a trunk, we will configure it ourselves to make sure we get the settings we want. We are going to tell it not to negotiate and to limit the VLANs that can use the trunk to VLANs 1 and 2. Without the **switchport trunk allowed vlan 1,2** command all VLANs could use it by default. We are not using VLAN 3 yet and don't want it included in the trunk.

1. In Global Configuration mode, enter the following commands. The order of the last three is not important.

    ```
    SwitchC2(config)#interface FastEthernet 0/1
    SwitchC2(config-if)#switchport mode trunk
    SwitchC2(config-if)#switchport nonegotiate
    SwitchC2(config-if)#switchport trunk allowed vlan 1,2
    SwitchC2(config-if)#description Trunk to SwitchC
    ```

2. Run the **show interfaces trunk** command and look over the results.

    Run the **show interfaces fa0/1 switchport** command and look over those results.

3. Save your work (**copy run start**).

Task 5: Configuring SwitchC

Now we have to do the same thing on SwitchC—with just a couple of differences. The trunk from SwitchC2 connects to port Fa0/2; Fa0/1 is a trunk to RouterC (already configured—you will do that in Chapter 9), which we will configure the same way. The descriptions on those two need to be changed as needed.

You can try it on your own, or the steps are listed here:

```
SwitchC(config)#vlan 2
VLAN 2 added:
    Name:VLAN0002
SwitchC(config-vlan)#name Sales
SwitchC(config-vlan)#vlan 3
VLAN 3 added:
    Name:VLAN0003
SwitchC(config-vlan)#name Accounting
SwitchC(config-vlan)#interface range FastEthernet 0/5 - 10
SwitchC(config-if-range)#description IT Department VLAN
SwitchC(config-if-range)#interface range FastEthernet 0/11 - 15
SwitchC(config-if-range)#switchport access vlan 2
SwitchC(config-if-range)#switchport mode access
SwitchC(config-if-range)#description Sales Department VLAN
SwitchC(config-if-range)#interface range FastEthernet 0/16 - 20
```

```
SwitchC(config-if-range)#switchport access vlan 3
SwitchC(config-if-range)#description Accounting Department VLAN
SwitchC(config-if-range)#interface FastEthernet 0/2
SwitchC(config-if)#switchport mode trunk
SwitchC(config-if)#switchport nonegotiate
SwitchC(config-if)#switchport trunk allowed vlan 1,2
SwitchC(config-if)#description Trunk to SwitchC
SwitchC(config)#interface FastEthernet 0/1
SwitchC(config-if)#switchport mode trunk
SwitchC(config-if)#switchport nonegotiate
SwitchC(config-if)#switchport trunk allowed vlan 1,2
SwitchC(config-if)#description Trunk to RouterC
```

4. Run the **show vlan brief** command again to see interfaces are now in the VLANs.

   Run a **show running-config (show run)** to see our interfaces now show the labels and configuration.

   Run **show interface status** to see that you have one host each in ports for VLAN 1 (Fa0/6) and VLAN2 (Fa0/11).

5. Run the **show interfaces trunk** command and look over the results.

   Run the **show interfaces fa0/1 switchport** command and the **show interfaces fa0/2 switchport** command and look over those results.

6. The final test is to confirm that not only can hosts V2.69 and V2.88 ping each other now, they also can ping all addresses in the network, including host B.77. All other hosts should be able to ping them. The trunk to RouterC allows both VLANs to get to the router and be routed throughout the network.

   In Chapter 9 you will configure RouterC for yourself, but if you want to preview it, look at its configuration.

7. Save your work.

CERTIFICATION OBJECTIVE 7.04

Configure and Verify Switch Port Security

Designing and installing data cabling for any organization is a combination of meeting current and future needs. That often means there are extra data ports in offices, workrooms, conference rooms, lunchrooms, and even in the lobby or reception area. All of these ports may not be live; they may not be connected to a port in a switch. It may be the plan that an admin will connect it if needed, as is often the case in offices and cubicles. If it is connected to a live switch port, it is a wondrous and helpful thing—not only for employees and other legitimate users, but for those who may not have the organization's best interests in mind. Obviously, this could be a hacker, but it could also be someone wanting to tap into the bandwidth to download pirated movies or music. In this section, we will look at options for protecting those unused ports.

Protecting Unused Switch Ports

One truth about every interface on the switch is that regardless of what configuration has been set, *the port is either in use or it isn't.* On ports that are in use, we've discussed adding descriptions on each port (to help the administrator) and VLAN configurations (for security and broadcast control purposes). However, we haven't discussed anything regarding unused ports or ports connected to unused data jacks. For ports that have a system permanently or regularly connected to them, an additional configuration option—port security—is available and we will look at that in a few moments. For those without a system connected, a couple of additional configuration options are recommended for security purposes.

Unused switch ports and unused live wall data jacks invite use. In some cases, if users—including administrators and contractors—have access to a switch with an open port or a wall jack in an out-of-the-way place, it's only a matter of time before they attempt to use it. Data interfaces on a Catalyst switch begin in an enabled state by default (the **no shutdown** command is not required to enable it). Ports will also attempt to autonegotiate almost everything by default—duplex, speed, even VLAN trunking. A person with a laptop able to emulate a trunk port and a sniffer or network mapping program could learn a lot about the organization and its network in a very few minutes. Even if all they are looking for is free download bandwidth to download things both mentionable and unmentionable, their actions could lead to inquiries and repercussions for the organization, as well as use up organization resources. Obviously, if you have security in mind, leaving these ports open and available is inviting trouble. Some options to secure unused ports:

- Disable each unused interface using the **shutdown** command. An admin would need to issue a **no shutdown** if/when the port or interface is needed.
- Enter the **switchport mode access** command on each interface. (This prevents VLAN trunking at least.)

■ Place each unused port in a VLAN that does not lead anywhere, is inactive, or is connected to limited resources like a printer but with no routing to the rest of the network or the Internet (using the **switchport access vlan** *vlan-id* command).

Looking at the third option earlier, let's revisit something we discussed in the last section. We discussed first that all ports are in VLAN 1 by default and then later that all sorts of Layer 2 device protocols default to using VLAN 1 to communicate. It is this bit of coincidence that makes an open, unconfigured switch port or wall jack connected to it such a gold mine for those wanting to learn about our network with intentions of no good. Layer 2 devices know a lot about our network and they regularly share that information among themselves, often several times per minute, for many very legitimate and necessary reasons.

Note that later in the book we will talk about turning off, for security reasons, unused Layer 2 and Layer 3 features to cut down on the communications traveling in VLAN 1.

Given the previously mentioned risk associated with VLAN 1, maybe part of our VLAN design should be to have one or more special VLANs with very limited access to resources. Maybe one, say VLAN 13, that has no access to organization devices and is always excluded from trunks, then all unused ports are assigned to VLAN 13 until needed. Now plugging in gets you nowhere.

The following shows all three methods applied to interfaces 15–24, which are not assigned for use yet:

```
Swi_1#configure terminal
Swi_1(config)#interface range fa0/15 - 24
Swi_1(config-if)#description Unused
Swi_1(config-if)#shutdown
Swi_1(config-if)#switchport mode access
Swi_1(config-if)#switchport access vlan 13
Swi_1(config-if)#switchport nonegotiate
Swi_1(config-if)end
```

As you gain experience, you may find that it is easier to deal with exceptions by coming up with a default interface configuration, like the one earlier. Then assign it to all interfaces and individually reset the ones that don't follow the standard, such as trunks, assigned ports, etc.

Verifying Our Efforts

To verify our changes, we can use our VLANs from earlier in this chapter. The **show running-config** command will confirm all three methods, while the **show vlan brief** command confirms the last two. The **show running-config** (or **show run**) command output looks like this:

```
Swi_1# show running-config
  <<<Output Omitted >>>
interface FastEthernet0/15
  Description Unused
  switchport access vlan 13
  switchport mode access
  switchport nonegotiate
interface FastEthernet0/16
  <<<Output Omitted >>>
!
```

The **show vlan brief** command confirms our interfaces 15–24 are in VLAN 13. We do still have some in VLAN 1, hopefully waiting for assignment.

```
Swi_1# show vlan brief
VLAN    Name        Status      Ports
1       default     active      Fa0/1, Fa0/2, Fa0/3, Fa0/4, Fa0/11,
                                Fa0/13, Fa0/14,
13      Unused      active      Fa0/15, Fa0/16, Fa0/17, Fa0/18, Fa0/19,
                                Fa0/20, Fa0/21, Fa0/22, Fa0/23, Fa0/24
50      Accounting  active      Fa0/5, Fa0/6, Fa0/7, Fa0/8, Fa0/9, Fa0/10
77      Sales       active      Fa0/12
123     Engineering active
1002    fddi-default act/unsup
            <<<Output Omitted >>>
Swi_1#
```

exam

watch   While these three options to secure unused ports are quite simple and basically extensions of what we have done earlier, understand what each does, why it might be useful, and how it might impact you trying to connect a new host to the network. Understand how the *show running-config* **command will confirm all three methods, while the** *show vlan brief* **command confirms the last two and how that might also help you solve your problem trying to connect.**

Protecting Live Ports for Intermittent Use

In today's cabled networks we have two types of devices that might be plugged in to a data jack, and thereby a switch port, in an office or workspace. One would have a single device plugged into it permanently, at least for the user's life with that device. A workstation or IP telephone might be examples. Another might be a data jack that has one or more devices plugged in at various times, such as a laptop or a label printer. Additional switch configuration can further secure these interfaces.

MAC Address Limitation

Suppose you expect and want only certain systems to access your switch, and you wish to prevent foreign devices (such as an attacker's laptop or PC) from connecting. In this instance, you can assign port security to the switch interface. Port security on an interface allows only a configured maximum number of MAC addresses to connect.

Once the maximum number of secure MAC addresses is reached, if the MAC address of a device attempting to access the port is not one of the stored secure MAC addresses, a security violation occurs.

Secure MAC Address Learning

The switch interface acquires a secure MAC address by a process called learning. By default, an interface can have only one secure MAC address, but you can configure a maximum number up to 128 or 132 depending on the command used. Each interface running port security can learn addresses by the static, dynamic, or sticky method. The maximums apply to secure MAC addresses learned by any of those methods.

Static Method   Static learning means that the admin manually adds or removes MAC addresses as part of the interface configuration and stored in the address table. The static secure MAC address configuration is stored in the running configuration by default and can be made permanent by saving it to the startup configuration. Adding secure addresses by the static method is unaffected by whether dynamic or sticky address learning is enabled.

Dynamic Method   This is the default method enabled when you enable port security on an interface. This method monitors MAC addresses on incoming traffic on the interface. If the address is not yet secured (added to the table) and the device has not reached any configured maximum, it secures (adds the address to the table) and allows the traffic.

Dynamic addresses exist in RAM only and do not survive a device reboot or restarting the interface. Dynamic addresses can be removed individually or the whole lot.

Sticky Method   The sticky method is basically the same as dynamic; they are learned dynamically from the devices connected to the switchport. They are then put into the address table and the running configuration as a static secure MAC address. Like a static secure MAC address, these MAC addresses will be lost unless saved to the startup configuration.

Sticky and dynamic address learning are mutually exclusive. Enabling sticky learning on an interface stops dynamic learning. Disabling sticky learning restarts dynamic learning.

Security Violations   A security violation occurs if any device with a MAC address not in the address table tries to access the interface after the maximum number of secure MAC addresses have been added.

Several things can happen after a security violation occurs depending on how the interface was configured. These are called violation modes:

Protect—Any violation in this mode causes the switchport to drop all traffic from the unknown MAC addresses. The port just won't work for them. It will, however, still permit traffic from known MAC addresses. No notification message is sent when this violation occurs.

Restrict— Any violation in this mode causes the switchport to drop all traffic from the unknown MAC addresses. The port just won't work for them. It will, however, still permit traffic from known MAC addresses. However, unlike the protect violation type, an SNMP (Simple Network Management Protocol) message is prepared indicating that a violation has occurred. The SNMP counter can then be reported by a monitoring system. Basically the system tells any monitoring admin that a violation occurred. It uses a counter so it actually reports how many violations occur.

Depending on the organization and how closely this is monitored, you could get a call or a visit to see what is going on.

Shutdown—Any violation causes the interface to shut down immediately for all devices. This is the more serious approach because the interface is no longer usable until an admin restores it. This may involve the user having to call or issue a trouble ticket to regain access to the port for any use. This is the default setting.

It is possible to modify this option to shut down and then to recover from an error disable after a specified time. The default, if used, is five minutes (300 seconds). The command is **errdisable recovery interval** *interval* in seconds.

Configuring Security Violation Options   To set the action you want to be taken if a security violation is detected, use the **switchport port-security violation** command. The command is used in Interface Configuration mode using either the **interface** or **interface range** command. Use the **no** form of the command to turn it off. The syntax is:

switchport port-security violation [protect | restrict | shutdown]
no switchport port-security violation [protect | restrict | shutdown]

An example would be:

```
Swi_1# configure terminal
Swi_1(config)# interface Fastethernet 0/3
Swi_1(config-if)# switchport port-security violation protect
Swi_1(config-if)#interface range Fa 0/10-20, Fa 0/22, Fa 0/24
Swi_.1(config-if)# switchport port-security violation shutdown
```

Err Disable Recovery   To recover a switch port that is in the error-disabled state, you can manually re-enable it by just shutting down the interface and bringing it back up. Use **shutdown** followed by **no shutdown** in Interface Configuration mode.

Verifying Our Efforts

The **show port-security address interface** *interface_id* and **show port-security address** commands will show that your changes have worked. This first example shows the **show port-security address interface** *interface_id* command:

```
Swi_1#configure terminal
Enter configuration commands, one per line.  End with CNTL/Z.
Swi_1(config)#interface fastethernet 0/19
Swi_1(config-if)#Switchport mode access
Swi_1(config-if)#Switchport port-security
Swi_1(config-if)#Switchport port-security maximum 3
Swi_1(config-if)#Switchport port-security mac-address sticky
Swi_1(config-if)#end
Swi_1#show port-security interface fastethernet 0/19
Port Security              :Enabled
Port Status                :Secure-up
```

```
Violation Mode                :Shutdown  (by default)
Aging Time                    :0
Aging Type                    :Absolute
SecureStatic Address Aging    :Enabled
Maximum MAC Addresses         :3
Total MAC Addresses           :0
Configured MAC Addresses      :0
Sticky MAC Addresses          :1
Last Source Address           :0000.0000.0116
Security Violation Count      :0
```

If all is well, the interface will display "Port Status: Secure-up." If a violation has occurred, resulting in the interface being disabled, the display will read "Port Status: Secure-shutdown." Additionally, the output shows the maximum number of addresses allowed, as well as how many were manually entered or learned by "sticky" methods.

This example shows how to configure a secure MAC address on Fast Ethernet port 0/20 and use the **show port-security address** commands to see the addresses stored in the running configuration. Note that it shows manually adding the sticky addresses, which would not be the norm, but it provides data to see in our example.

```
Switch# configure terminal
Enter configuration commands, one per line.  End with CNTL/Z.
Swi_1(config)# interface fastethernet 0/20
Swi_1(config-if)# switchport mode access
Swi_1(config-if)# switchport port-security
Swi_1(config-if)# switchport port-security maximum 5
Swi_1(config-if)# switchport port-security mac-address 0000.0000.0005
Swi_1(config-if)# switchport port-security mac-address sticky
Swi_1(config-if)# switchport port-security mac-address sticky 0000.0000.0003
Swi_1(config-if)# switchport port-security mac-address sticky 0000.0000.0004
Swi_1(config-if)# end
Switch#show port address
Secure Mac Address Table
------------------------------------------------------------------------
Vlan    Mac Address      Type               Ports    Remaining Age
                                                        (mins)
----    -----------      ----               -----    -------------
   7    0000.0000.0003   SecureSticky       Fa0/20        -
   7    0000.0000.0004   SecureSticky       Fa0/20        -
   7    0000.0000.0005   SecureConfigured   Fa0/20        -

------------------------------------------------------------------------
Total Addresses in System (excluding one mac per port)     : 2
Max Addresses limit in System (excluding one mac per port) : 1024
```

e x a m
ⓦ a t c h *Review the steps for implementing port security and know which commands are used in the process. Make sure you understand the difference* | *between manual configuration and dynamic learning, what the sticky feature means, and how to use the optional commands.*

EXERCISE 7-2

MHE Lab

Switch Port Security

In this exercise we demonstrate the steps an administrator would take to secure the ports on a switch. In the reading, we saw two methods of securing unused ports and one for intermittent-use ports. We will look at the first two in this lab. We will be using the NetSim for this exercise. Launch Lab 7-2 and review the topology.

We will again be working on SwitchC and SwitchC2 so that we can go through one together, and you can try your hand at the second one.

Task 1: Securing Unused Ports: Shutdown

If a port is shut down, it can't be abused.

1. We are going to shut down ports Fa0/3–5 and Gi0/1–2 so that employees or contractors with access to our switch can't tap into it. All we need to do to reenable a port is issue a **no shutdown**. We'll access our devices from host V2.88 and take advantage of the access we created in the last lab.

2. Open a console session on host V2.88 and Telnet to SwitchC, the VLAN 1 IP address from earlier.

   ```
   C:>telnet 10.0.2.2
   ```

   Remember that our login password is always **cisco** in these labs and the enable secret is **ccent**. Log in and go to Global Configuration mode.

3. Run the following commands:

```
SwitchC(config)#interface range Fa0/3 - 5
SwitchC(config-if)#shutdown
SwitchC(config-if)#description Not In Use - shutdown
SwitchC(config-if)#interface Gi0/1
SwitchC(config-if)#shutdown
SwitchC(config-if)#description Not In Use - shutdown
SwitchC(config-if)#interface Gi0/2
SwitchC(config-if)#shutdown
SwitchC(config-if)#description Not In Use - shutdown
SwitchC(config-if)#CTRL-z
```

4. Use the **show interface status (sho int stat)** command to confirm your work.

5. Save your work, exit back to the host, and do the same thing to SwitchC2.

Task 2: Securing Unused Ports: Dead-End VLAN

1. To demonstrate this we are going to reuse the interfaces that we put in VLAN 3. Reopen or return to the console session on host V2.88 and Telnet to SwitchC. Log in and go to Global Configuration mode. Create VLAN 13 and name it Junk. It is not included in our trunk, so it can't leave the switch. It also can't get an IP address from DHCP.

```
SwitchC(config)#vlan 13 name Junk
VLAN 13 added:
    Name:Junk
SwitchC(config-vlan)#interface range Fa0/16 - 20
SwitchC(config-if)#switchport access vlan 13
SwitchC(config-if)#switchport mode access     ← prevents VLAN trunking
SwitchC(config-if)#description Hold
```

2. Use the **show interface status (sho int stat)** command and **show vlan brief** to confirm your work.

INSIDE THE EXAM

Virtual LANs (VLAN)s

VLANs are a common part of modern networks and key features of Cisco switches, so make sure that you understand why organizations would want to use VLANs. What problems do they solve? Know the difference between access and trunk ports and what each does. Look over Figure 7-1 and be able to identify the access ports and how they determine which VLANs need to be included on your trunks. The 802.1Q Trunking Protocol and Dynamic Trunking Protocol are important features to understand. Understanding how DTP negotiation works can help with troubleshooting; Table 7-1 should help with that.

Configure and Verify VLAN Access Ports

Make sure you know how to configure access interfaces to access ports and then how to verify they are there. Practice with the simulations until you can do these as well as all other switch configuration quickly. Make sure you understand at what configuration mode these commands have to be executed.

Configure and Verify VLAN Trunk Ports

Make sure you know how to configure trunk interfaces and the commands you run to verify they are there. Be familiar with both the command and the output. Practice doing access ports and trunk ports together; they are two parts of the same feature. Practice with the simulations. Make sure you understand at what configuration mode these commands have to be executed.

Configure and Verify Switch Port Security

There are two areas of concern here. What to do with unassigned, unused switch ports? There are three possibilities that can be used separately or together. What to do with assigned or live ports? Know how to configure basic port security and what the differences are between the three ways of learning MAC addresses. Understand that dynamic and sticky are mutually exclusive and use the same approach to gather MAC addresses, but where they are stored is different and what that means in case of a reboot.

As always, practice the basic commands for implementing port security and the **show** commands that will confirm it is configured.

CERTIFICATION SUMMARY

There are two types of switch interfaces or ports that can be configured on VLAN switches: access ports and trunk ports.

Know that the IEEE 802.1Q trunks standard is for tagged VLANs that allow multiple VLANs to travel over a single circuit. It accomplishes this by inserting a 4-byte tag on frames from all VLANs except the native VLAN. This tag is only used within and between VLAN-aware switches and is finally removed by the last switch before forwarding out to the final destination.

Know the difference between the default and native VLANs as well as how and why to change the native VLAN.

DTP is a Cisco proprietary protocol used to negotiate trunking on a link between two VLAN-aware switches. DTP works with the **switchport mode [access | trunk | dynamic [auto | desirable]]** command. Table 7-1 summarizes the Cisco DTP negotiation results.

To create a VLAN or modify an existing VLAN from Global Configuration mode, use the **vlan [*vlan-id* | *vlan-range*]** command. Optionally, use the **name *vlan-name*** command to give the VLAN a name, up to 32 characters. To add an interface to the VLAN, use the **switchport access vlan *vlan-id*** command on each interface. Adding the command **switchport mode access** prevents the interface from becoming a trunk. To verify VLANs exist and which ports are assigned to each VLAN, use the **show running-config** or **show vlan brief** command.

Basic trunk configuration is only a little more involved than defining an access port—in fact, you use the **switchport mode [access | trunk]** interface configuration command. By default, a trunk carries all VLANs on the switch, but it is possible to limit which VLANs are allowed over a trunk with the **switchport trunk allowed vlan [*vlan-ids* | all]** in Interface Configuration mode. Two commands that can be used to verify trunk settings are **show interfaces *type/number* switchport** and **show interface trunk**.

To secure these unused ports, disable each unused interface using the **shutdown** command, enter the **switchport mode access** command on each interface (prevents VLAN trunking), and place each unused port in a VLAN that does not exist (using the **switchport access vlan *vlan-id*** command).

Assigning port security additionally secures the device, allowing only known MAC addresses to connect. Commands used include **switchport mode access, switchport port-security, switchport port-security mac-address *option*, switchport port-security maximum *number*,** and **switchport port-security violation *option*.** If a port security violation occurs, the switch can drop traffic, send and log SNMP messages, or disable the interface altogether.

TWO-MINUTE DRILL

Virtual LANs (VLANs)

❑ Some of the more important reasons for using VLANs within a network design are

    ❑ VLANs can segment broadcast domains without using a router.

    ❑ VLANs can improve performance on hosts, reducing their processing overhead by limiting the broadcast messages and separating traffic types.

    ❑ VLANs provide better security by separating groups of users and their devices and message traffic.

❑ IEEE 802.1Q, a VLAN tagging standard, allows Ethernet bridges and switches to keep track of and quickly handle frames from multiple VLANs across a single link.

❑ 802.1Q inserts a 4-byte (32-bit) tag inside the Ethernet frame between the source MAC address and the EtherType/Length fields.

❑ The default VLAN, VLAN 1 on Cisco switches, can't be changed or deleted because it carries many Layer 2 protocols' communication between switches.

❑ The native VLAN is the only VLAN that is not tagged in an 802.1Q VLAN trunk. By default, it is VLAN 1, but can be reassigned.

Configure and Verify VLAN Access Ports

❑ To create a VLAN, use the Global Configuration mode command **vlan vlan-id**, where *vlan-id* is a number between 2 and 1001 (1 is the management interface and 1002–1005 are reserved for old protocols, FFDI and token ring). Optionally, you can also use the command **name vlan-name**, where *vlan-name* is a more descriptive text string for your VLAN.

❑ To add an interface to the newly created VLAN, use the **switchport access vlan vlan-id** command on each interface. Optionally, you can also use the **switchport mode access** command to ensure the interface does not attempt to go into trunking mode.

❑ To verify VLAN creation, use the **show running-config** or **show vlan brief** command. The running configuration will show interface membership in a VLAN on a per-interface basis, while the VLAN brief display shows all VLANs on the switch, as well as their interface ranges.

Configure and Verify VLAN Trunk Ports

❑ Use the **switchport mode [access | trunk]** interface configuration command to create a trunk.

❑ Use the **switchport trunk allowed vlan [*vlan-ids* | all]** in Interface Configuration mode to define the VLANs to be included. The default is All.

❑ Two commands that can be used to verify trunk setting are **show interfaces** *type/number* **switchport** and **show interface trunk**. The first shows the trunk settings for the interface. The second shows the trunk status and the VLANs included.

Configure and Verify Switch Port Security

❑ To secure unused ports, disable each unused interface using the **shutdown** command, enter the **switchport mode access** command on each interface (prevents VLAN trunking), and place each unused port in a VLAN that does not exist (using the **switchport access vlan** *vlan-id* command).

❑ Port security on an interface allows only a configured maximum number of MAC address(es) to connect.

❑ Once the maximum number of secure MAC addresses is reached, if the MAC address of a device attempting to access the port is not one of the stored secure MAC addresses, a security violation occurs.

❑ Secure MAC address learning is the process by which the switch interface acquires secure MAC addresses.

❑ By default, an interface can have only one secure MAC address, but you can configure it to accept more. Each interface running port security can learn addresses by the static, dynamic, or sticky method.

❑ A security violation occurs if any device with a MAC address not in the secure address table tries to access the interface after the maximum number of secure MAC addresses have been added.

❑ Several things can happen after a security violation occurs depending on how the interface was configured. There are three violation modes. Shutdown, the default, requires an admin to re-enable. Restrict causes an SNMP message to be prepared that can then be reported by a monitoring system. It starts a counter so it actually reports how many violations occur. The unauthorized device will not be able to use the port/jack, but authorized devices will still work. Protect is like restrict without the violation reporting.

❑ There are two ways to recover a switch port that is in the error-disabled state. You can bring it out of this state by entering the **errdisable recovery** *cause* global configuration command, or, as many do, you can manually re-enable it by just shutting down the interface and bringing it back up: **shutdown** followed by **no shutdown** in interface configuration mode.

❑ Use the **show port-security address interface** *interface_id* and **show port-security address** commands to show that your changes have worked.

❑ Assigning port security restricts use of the port to the MAC address you specify or the first MAC address the switch learns about on the interface. To assign port security to an interface, place the interface in **switchport mode access** and enable port security using the **switchport port-security** command. Next, allow only the MAC addresses specified, using either the **switchport port-security mac-address** *address* command or the **switchport port-security mac-address sticky** command.

❑ The **sticky** parameter on a port security setting tells the switch to record the source MAC address of the first frame to enter the interface. This address "sticks" as the only allowable secured address on the interface—all other frames with a different source MAC will be discarded.

❑ Optionally, you can specify the number of MAC addresses allowed to use the interface with the **switchport port-security maximum** *number* command, and specify the action taken when a foreign MAC address attempts to use the interface with the **switchport port-security violation [***protect* | *restrict* | *shutdown***]** command.

❑ Port security violation actions can include shutting the port down altogether, discarding traffic, and/or sending SNMP messages.

❑ Verification of port security is done with the **show running-config** and **show port-security interface** *interface#* commands. The running configuration shows the commands assigned to each interface, while the **show port-security interface** output will display the *state* of the interface. If all is well, the interface will display "Port Status: Secure-up." If a violation has occurred, resulting in the interface being disabled, the display will read "Port Status: Secure-shutdown."

SELF TEST

The following Self Test questions will help you measure your understanding of the material presented in this chapter. Read all the choices carefully since there may be more than one correct answer. Choose all the correct answers for each question.

Virtual LANs (VLANs)

1. Which of the following is a reason to create VLANs?
   A. VLANs provide better security by separating groups of users and their devices and message traffic.
   B. VLANs can segment broadcast domains without using a router.
   C. VLANs allow you to forward traffic between networks without a router.
   D. VLANs can improve performance on hosts, reducing their processing overhead by limiting the broadcast messages and separating traffic types.

2. Which protocol is standard for tagged VLANs over trunks?
   A. VLAN Trunking Protocol
   B. 802.1D
   C. Dynamic Trunking Protocol (DTP)
   D. 802.1Q
   E. None of the above

3. Which VLAN must always be VLAN 1?
   A. The static VLAN
   B. The native VLAN
   C. The default VLAN
   D. The Layer 2 VLAN

Configure and Verify VLAN Access Ports

4. Which command is used to add interfaces to VLAN 5?
   A. **switchport access vlan 5** on each interface
   B. **switchport access vlan 5** in Global Configuration mode, followed by **interface range x - y**
   C. **switchport access vlan 5 interface range 0 – 24**
   D. None of the above

5. Which command(s) can be used to view VLAN membership for all VLANs on the switch?

   A. **show vlan brief**

   B. **show membership vlan**

   C. **show running-config**

   D. None of the above

Configure and Verify VLAN Trunk Ports

6. Which command is used to add interfaces to VLAN 5?

   A. **switchport mode trunk vlans All**

   B. **switchport mode trunk** in Global Configuration mode

   C. **switchport mode trunk** on each interface

   D. None of the above

7. Which command(s) can be used to verify your trunk configuration?

   A. **show vlan brief**

   B. **show interfaces type/number switchport**

   C. **show interface trunk**

   D. None of the above

Configure and Verify Switch Port Security

8. Which three are ways to protect unused switch ports?

   A. Enter the **switchport mode trunk** command on each interface.

   B. Enter the **switchport mode access** command on each interface.

   C. Place each unused port in a VLAN that does not exist, is inactive, or is connected to limited resources.

   D. Place each unused port in a VLAN 1.

   E. Disable each unused interface using the **shutdown** command.

9. Which is not a secure MAC address learning for port security?

   A. Sticky method

   B. Restrict method

   C. Dynamic method

   D. Static method

10. If port security is configured, by default what is the result if a security violation occurs?

   A. It goes into Restrict mode until an admin resets it.

   B. It goes into Restrict mode, denying unsecured MAC addresses but allowing secured MAC addresses.

   C. It goes into Shutdown mode for five minutes (300 seconds) and then resets.

   D. It goes into Shutdown mode until an admin resets it.

   E. None of the above.

11. You wish to configure port security on your switch, allowing the switch to learn which MAC address is connected to each port. After setting the interfaces in **switchport mode access** and turning on port security with **switchport port-security**, which command should be entered next?

   A. **switchport port-security mac-address**

   B. **switchport port-security mac-address** *address*

   C. **switchport port-security mac-address learn**

   D. **switchport port-security mac-address sticky**

12. You have configured port security on all interfaces and entered the following command on the interface range: **switchport port-security violation restrict**. Which of the following actions will be taken if a foreign MAC address attempts to use an interface?

   A. The interface will be disabled.

   B. The offending traffic will be discarded.

   C. An SNMP message is sent and logged.

   D. The administrator is notified and decides whether to allow the traffic or not.

13. Which command used to verify port security can be used to determine if the port has been disabled by a port security violation?

   A. **show running-config**

   B. **show port-security violations**

   C. **show port-security interface** *interface#*

   D. **debug mac-address table**

SELF TEST ANSWERS

Virtual LANs (VLANs)

1.   ☑ **A, B,** and **D** are correct. Each is a reason to use VLANs.
     ☒ **C** is incorrect. The statement is untrue because while you can segment a network with VLANs, you still need a Layer 3 device (router) to forward traffic between networks.

2.   ☑ **D** is correct. IEEE 802.1Q defines tagged VLANs for trunking.
     ☒ **A, B,** and **C** are incorrect. **A** is incorrect because VTP is a Cisco protocol for advertising and extending VLANs throughout an entire organization. **B** is incorrect because 802.1 defines untagged VLANs. **C** is incorrect because DTP (Dynamic Trunking Protocol) is a Cisco protocol to help the ends of a link negotiate trunking. **E** is incorrect because this choice is not valid.

3.   ☑ **C** is correct. The default VLAN carries Layer 2 traffic and can't be moved or deleted.
     ☒ **A, B,** and **D** are incorrect. **A** and **D** are incorrect because they do not exist. **B** is incorrect because the native VLAN is VLAN 1 by default, but it can be reassigned to any other VLAN. It is the one untagged VLAN in 802.1Q.

Configure and Verify VLAN Access Ports

4.   ☑ **A** is correct. Each interface must be added to the VLAN individually.
     ☒ **B, C,** and **D** are incorrect. **B** is incorrect because the **switchport mode access** commands are not entered globally. The **interface range** $x - y$ command should have been entered first. **C** is incorrect because this command syntax does not exist. **D** is incorrect because this choice is not valid.

5.   ☑ **A** and **C** are correct. **show vlan brief** displays all VLANs configured on the switch, including their membership. **show run** displays all the commands that create the VLANs, as well as the commands adding the interfaces to them. **show vlan brief** is more concise, but **show run** will work as well.
     ☒ **B** and **D** are incorrect. **B** is incorrect because this command does not exist. **D** is incorrect because this choice is not valid.

Configure and Verify VLAN Trunk Ports

6.   ☑ **C** is correct. **switchport mode trunk** is used on each interface.
     ☒ **A, B,** and **D** are incorrect. **A** is incorrect because this command syntax does not exist. **B** is incorrect because the **switchport mode trunk** commands are not entered globally. **D** is incorrect because this choice is not valid.

7. ☑ **B and C** are correct. **show interfaces type/number switchport** displays the trunk settings for the specified interface. **show interface trunk** displays the trunking status and the VLANs on the trunk.

☒ **A and D** are incorrect. A is incorrect because this command shows the VLANs but not the trunks. D is incorrect because this choice is not valid.

Configure and Verify Switch Port Security

8. ☑ **B, C, and E** are correct. They are all ways to secure unused port interfaces.

☒ **A and D** are incorrect. A is incorrect because creating a trunk with that command would then pass all VLANs, very valuable to an unauthorized user. D is incorrect because VLAN 1 is the default and carries all Layer 2 communications, very valuable to an unauthorized user.

9. ☑ **B** is correct. Restrict is not a secure MAC address learning method.

☒ **A, C, and D** are incorrect. They are all secure MAC address learning methods for port security.

10. ☑ **D** is correct. Going into Shutdown mode until an admin resets it is the default result.

☒ **A, B, C, and E** are incorrect. A is incorrect because it doesn't require a reset and is not the default. B and C are incorrect because they are options, not the default. E is incorrect because this choice is not valid.

I I. ☑ **D** is correct. The **sticky** parameter allows the switch to learn and save the source MAC address from the first received frame as the only MAC allowed to use the port.

☒ **A, B, and C** are incorrect. A is incorrect because this command is missing a parameter after **mac-address**. B is incorrect because this command manually configures an address as the secured MAC. C is incorrect because this command does not exist.

12. ☑ **B and C** are correct. The **restrict** option discards offending traffic and sends an SNMP message to the monitoring station (as well as logging the event).

☒ **A and D** are incorrect. A is incorrect because this action is indicative of the **protect** parameter. D is incorrect because there is no port security violation option to perform this action.

13. ☑ **C** is correct. After entering this command, the interface display will show "Port Status: Secure-up." If a violation has occurred, it will read "Port Status: Secure-shutdown."

☒ **A, B, and D** are incorrect. A is incorrect because **show run** will display the commands used to enforce port security, but does not indicate the state of the interface. B and D are incorrect because these commands do not exist.

Part III

IP Routing Technologies: Layer 3

8

Routing Essentials and Routing Protocols

I n Chapter 2 we saw that any time a computer prepares a message to be delivered to another computer, it passes the message through the TCP/IP stack. At the Internet layer (Layer 3), the destination IP address is placed in the IP header. The packet is then passed to the Network Access layer for frame assembly with a physical address for the destination address. The PC compares the destination IP address to its own and quickly determines that the packet is not intended for any device on the local network (example: 195.100.5.100/24 and 195.250.5.200/24 are not on the same network). The computer then completes the encapsulation frame, placing the default gateway MAC address in the header. The frame is then sent out the NIC, and the switch forwards it on to the router. In this chapter we look at what happens at this point in the process. We will look at the fundamentals of routing in preparation for Chapter 9, where we actually start configuring a Cisco router. We will overview routing protocols in preparation for Chapter 10, where we will configure the OSPF routing protocol. We will also look at some basic commands and then implement them in the next chapters.

CERTIFICATION OBJECTIVE 8.01

Routing Foundation

We start by taking a moment to talk about the word *routing*. Like many words in networking, it was taken from everyday usage because data acted like something we were already familiar with: it followed a route or path to its destination. Mail carriers and delivery truck drivers all have routes and they deliver things to locations on those routes. A delivery gets routed from the supplier to the ultimate customer. Some companies even have a person called a router who plans the routes their trucks will follow.

Data networking grew up within the world of telephony, where routing was the process of selecting best paths in the phone company's circuit switching network. This means that in documents and in conversations with others in the industry, you will hear every form of the word route used and misused. While we have to recognize and work with that, the industry and Cisco are trying to "clarify" the language a bit and hopefully remove some of the confusion. Today, the word *routing*, as in the process of selecting best paths in a network, is now called *forwarding*. Packets are *forwarded* though a network. A router *forwards* traffic based on its destination IP address.

TCP/IP Internet Layer: Layer 3 Revisited

Since routing and forwarding network traffic occurs at Layer 3, the Network layer in the OSI model and TCP/IP's Internet layer, we need to expand a bit on our coverage of Layer 3 that we covered in Chapter 2. As shown in Figure 8-1, Layer 3 provides *data forwarding* to devices on distant (non local) networks via a gateway router that may be connected to the destination network, or more likely, is just the first step on a journey across a web of routers that make up the Internet.

In many ways this is like the duties of the post office in most countries. They develop an addressing scheme that allows individuals to be found in a city/neighborhood. They also collect mail from customers, forwarding it into a system that ultimately uses the destination address to deliver it. Relating it to IP addressing, the Network ID would be the city or community, the subnet mask would be the street or neighborhood, and the Host ID would be the house number.

Within the OSI and TCP/IP layered models, for outbound communications, Layer 3 accepts data *segments* from the Transport layer, constructs a data *packet*, which it then forwards to the lower layers for *framing* and transmission. For inbound communications, it accepts unframed data from the lower layer, processes the packet header, shown in Figure 8-2, and then either forwards it to the Transport layer or processes and returns a new packet to the lower layer for forwarding on toward its final destination. The following briefly describes the IP header fields that are used by routers and other Layer 3 devices to perform their functions.

Version

The version field identifies the IP version so the device knows what to expect. For IPv4, this value is 4; for IPv6, it is 6.

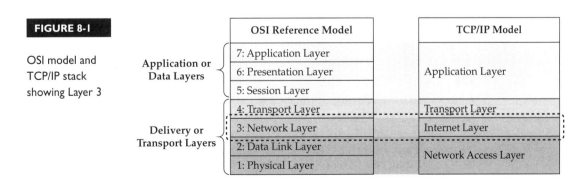

FIGURE 8-1

OSI model and TCP/IP stack showing Layer 3

OSI Reference Model	TCP/IP Model
7: Application Layer	Application Layer
6: Presentation Layer	
5: Session Layer	
4: Transport Layer	Transport Layer
3: Network Layer	Internet Layer
2: Data Link Layer	Network Access Layer
1: Physical Layer	

Application or Data Layers

Delivery or Transport Layers

FIGURE 8-2 IP header information

		IPv4 Packet Header			
Offsets	Octet	0	1	2	3
Octet	Bit	0 1 2 3 4 5 6 7	8 9 10 11 12 13 14 15	16 17 18 19 20 21 22 23	24 25 26 27 28 29 30 31
0	0	Version / IHL	DSCP / ECN	Total Length	
4	32	Identification		Flags / Fragment Offset	
8	64	TTL (Time to Live)	Protocol	Header checksum	
12	96	Source IP Address			
16	128	Destination IP Address			
20	160	Options (optional)			

IHL

Internet header length: The number of 32-bit words in the header (rows in the figure). Due to the variable length of the IPv4 Options field, the range is 5–15 32-bit words (20–60 bytes).

DSCP

Differentiated services code point: Identifies packet for special handling, such as real-time data streaming for services like Voice over IP (VoIP).

ECN

Explicit congestion notification: A notification feature that allows end-to-end notification of network congestion to avoid dropping packets.

Total Length

The entire packet (fragment) size, including header and data, in bytes. Range: 20 to 65535 bytes.

Identification

This field uniquely identifies the group of fragments of a single IP datagram.

Flags

The Flags field is three bits that indicate whether a packet can be fragmented, broken up into smaller pieces, to accommodate network segments that can't handle the current frame size. The following describes what each bit means:

- The first bit, bit 0, is reserved and must always be 0.
- The second bit, bit 1, if set to 1 means don't fragment (DF). If the DF flag is set to 1 and fragmentation is required to route the packet, the packet will be dropped.

■ The final bit, bit 2, the more fragments (MF) bit, when set to 1 tells the receiving device that more fragments are coming—don't reassemble yet. For fragmented packets, all fragments but the last one have the MF flag set to 1. If it is not a 1, then the **Fragment Offset** field is checked. If it is 1, then this is a final fragment. If it is 0, it is an unfragmented packet.

Fragment Offset

Specifies the offset of a particular fragment relative to the beginning of the original unfragmented IP datagram. The first fragment has an offset of 0, the second 1, etc. The Fragment Offset field is a sequence counter used to reassemble the fragments in order. It indicates that fragment's position in the string of fragments. If it is a 0, it can only be an unfragmented packet or the first fragment of a series of fragments.

TTL (Time to Live)

Time to Live: Prevents datagram looping on the network by limiting the datagram's lifetime. When the initial packet is created, a TTL number is assigned, indicating the number of routers it can pass through before it is considered lost. That number is then decreased by 1 by each Layer 3 device it goes to. When it gets down to 0, the device can't forward it and usually sends an "ICMP Time Exceeded" message to the sender. This keeps any packet from staying in a routing loop forever.

Cisco's **traceroute** and the computer's **tracert** commands both use these ICMP messages to display the routers reached by packets as they progressed from the source to the destination.

Protocol

The protocol number indicates what protocol is carried in the data payload and what kind of data it is. Some common ones are listed in Table 8-1 a full list can be found at http://en.wikipedia.org/wiki/List_of_IP_protocol_numbers.

Header Checksum

A 16-bit checksum is used to error-check the **header**. When a packet arrives at a router, the router recalculates the checksum of the header and compares it to the checksum field. If the values do not match, the router discards the packet. Since the router decrements the TTL field, a new checksum is generated for each network segment.

Errors in the **data field** are handled by the encapsulated protocol. Both UDP and TCP have checksum fields.

	Protocol	Protocol Name	Keyword
TABLE 8-1 Sample Protocol Field Values	1	Internet Control Message Protocol	ICMP
	2	Internet Group Management Protocol	IGMP
	6	Transmission Control Protocol	TCP
	17	User Datagram Protocol	UDP
	41	IPv6 encapsulation	ENCAP
	89	Open Shortest Path First	OSPF
	132	Stream Control Transmission Protocol	SCTP

Source Address

The IPv4 address of the sender of the packet. This address may be changed in transit by a network address translation (NAT) device.

Destination Address

The IPv4 address of the destination device. This address may also be changed in transit by a NAT device.

Options

Not often used. The IHL field must include enough extra 32-bit words to hold all the options.

The IP header at first glance seems pretty complicated and can be intimidating. While all of the fields are used by the router, only the destination IP address is used for forwarding decisions about packets through the network. Some fields, like Version, IHL, and Total Length, tell the device that it is processing IPv4 information and how to know where the header ends and the data begins. Others, like DSCP, ECN, Flags, and Fragment Free, indicate whether special handling is required of the router. TTL and Header Checksum provide for efficient and reliable forwarding. Like all headers, these fields are populated by the sending device's Layer 3 so that any Layer 3 devices will know how to properly handle the delivery.

These fields, like everything else, are made up of 0s and 1s, but applications and tools can interpret the field values to help us in troubleshooting forwarding problems. The following output from a sniffer shows what many of the field values might look like in HEX form, with friendlier explanations in parentheses:

```
Version: 4
Header length: 5 (20 bytes)
DSCP: 0x00
```

```
Total Length: 0x0044 (68 bytes)
Identification: 0xad0b
Flags and Fragments: 0x0000
TTL: 0x40 (64 hops)
Protocol: 0x11 (UDP)
Header Checksum: 0x7272
Source: 0xc0a8024d (192.168.2.77)
Destination: 0x0a801c3 (192.168.1.195)
```

Routed vs. Routing Protocols Revisited

We said that a routed protocol is one, like IP, that can be routed, or forwarded, from one network to another to get to its destination. A routing protocol, which will be the focus of this and the next two chapters, refers to how the router learns which routes to put in its routing table. Good enough, but let's take a moment and look at what makes a routed protocol routable.

A nonroutable protocol is one like our Layer 2 delivery protocol, Ethernet. Ethernet uses MAC addressing in its frames to send messages. There is nothing in the MAC address that tells us where a device is located. In fact, if it weren't for the intelligence of switches, we would have to use broadcasts to deliver every packet—literally sending it to every device and relying on the correct device to accept and process it. That is how all earlier networks worked using hubs or coaxial cable. A good analogy is what in the United States is called a Social Security number, which uniquely identifies every citizen, but does absolutely nothing in helping us know where that person is.

These Layer 2 protocols worked well in the early days of networks when networks were small and devices were few, before we started connecting networks together and relying on broadcasts became impossible. Recall that switches had to *learn* every host MAC address that could be accessed on an interface every time the switch was powered on. While that works fine in LANs, it doesn't scale to larger networks or the Internet.

To solve the problem, they needed a hierarchical or logical address model with both a network identifier (where) and a host identifier (who). They had only to look to the telephone industry for a model. Figure 8-3 shows the U.S. telephone coding system that allowed phone switching equipment to connect two phones from clear across the country and eventually anywhere on earth. Using our old classful address model, note that the area code is the network ID (where), the central office code is a subnet (more specific location) within the area code, and the local circuit is the address that connects to a specific phone (the host, the who).

There were several early logical addressing protocols, each following the OSI model requirements, but today, IP is really the only one in common use.

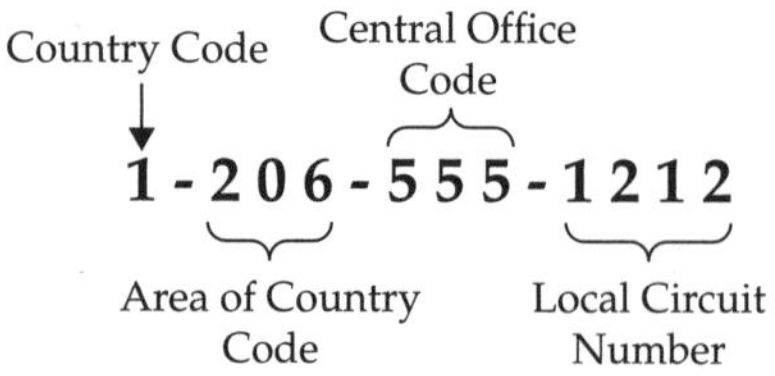

FIGURE 8-3

U.S. telephone number coding scheme

Country Code   Central Office Code

1 - 2 0 6 - 5 5 5 - 1 2 1 2

Area of Country Code   Local Circuit Number

Routed protocols, like IP, provide a method for a packet to be sent outside the local network to anywhere in the world by using logical addresses. In short, they are simply those protocols that are routable or that get forwarded through routers. Layer 2 addresses, such as MAC addresses, are not routable because there is no network identifier telling us *where* the network and host could be located.

exam

ⓦatch

Be sure you know that routed protocols provide a means to address both the host and the network to which the host belongs. In short, routed protocols use logical addresses. Simply stated: routed protocols get forwarded through a router and routing protocols allow routers to dynamically learn about remote destinations/networks.

Router Role and Processes

One of a router's primary roles is to forward data packets between networks. It does this by having at least two interfaces connected to different networks. When a data packet comes in one of the interfaces, the router reads the destination IP address. Then, using information in its routing table, it forwards the packet to the next network on its journey. A data packet is typically forwarded from one router to another through the networks, including the Internet, until it reaches its destination.

A router also provides a broadcast and IP address boundary. While switches forward broadcasts, routers do not forward broadcasts into another network. The router is the gateway or edge of an IP address network or subnet; it should never have the same network directly connected to two interfaces.

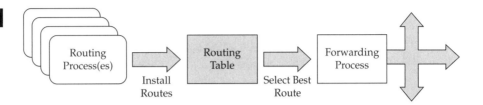

FIGURE 8-4

The three main processes of a router

To perform its role of forwarding packets, the Cisco router uses three processes:

- First, the router engages in one or more *routing protocols* sharing route information with other routers and updating the routing table so that the best route to a destination will be chosen.
- Second, the *routing table* itself accepts information from the routing processes and also replies to requests for route information from the forwarding process.
- Third, the *forwarding process* makes information requests to the routing table to then make packet forwarding decisions.

Figure 8-4 shows a diagram of the three processes and their relationship.

We will look at each of these three processes in this chapter, starting with the routing protocols.

CERTIFICATION OBJECTIVE 8.02

Routing Protocols

A routing protocol defines how routers communicate with each other to exchange network information that enables each to populate a routing table. Initially each router only knows about networks directly attached to it. Through the routing process, all routers gain some knowledge of the network topology so that data can be forwarded efficiently from one host to another anywhere in the network.

There are two ways to categorize routing protocols: interior gateway protocols (IGPs) and exterior gateway protocols (EGPs). IGPs are those protocols used for sharing routing information between routers within an autonomous system (AS), an enterprise or organization's networks. These are the protocols that we will be looking at in our IP networks. There is really just one EGP, Border Gateway Protocol (BGP), the routing protocol of the Internet backbone. It is used to connect large networks and service providers to the Internet, which is beyond the scope of our conversation.

To further break down IGPs, there are two types that you would find in our networks and that would be subjects of the CCENT exam: distance vector routing protocols and link state routing protocols. In this section, we will introduce both.

Distance Vector Routing Protocols

Distance vector protocols are some of the oldest and simplest to implement. They exchange route information only with their directly connected neighbor routers by sharing their entire routing tables. This sharing of route information by passing it from neighbor to neighbor to neighbor is why they are often referred to as "routing by rumor." These exchanges are done using multicasts sent out each router's interface at intervals of 30 seconds. Because of the frequency of these exchanges and the fact they exchange even if nothing has changed, they are considered to be chatty protocols.

When there are two or more routes to the same destination network learned by the same protocol, metrics are methods and units of measurement used to choose the one "best" route to be added to the routing table. Different routing protocols use different metrics. The metric units can be thought of as a *cost*—the lower the metric, the better the route. Distance vector protocols use only hop count as a metric method of measuring distance—hop count being how many routers, or hops, between the two points. The fewer hops, the shorter the distance. This means that when choosing between two alternative routes to a destination, only the one with the shortest hop count is offered to the routing table. Unfortunately, this ignores the possibility that the shorter hop count might be over much slower links. To distance vector protocols, a 3-hop over serial links (1.544 Mbps) looks better than a 4-hop route over Gigabit links.

While easy to implement, the high overhead of frequent broadcasts for communication and the very real chance of choosing a less-than-ideal route mean distance vector protocols are not recommended for large networks.

Examples of distance vector routing protocols include RIPv1, RIPv2, and IGRP. Both RIPv1 and Cisco's IGRP are older protocols and are no longer supported on most devices.

Figure 8-5 demonstrates the downsides of *routing by rumor* protocols. Router A learns about the routes on Router C because Router B told him about it. If changes occur on Router C's end of the network, Router A won't know about it until Router B sends him an update. Since routing tables are exchanged every 30 seconds for RIP, if the change occurs just after an update is sent from Router C to B, it could be

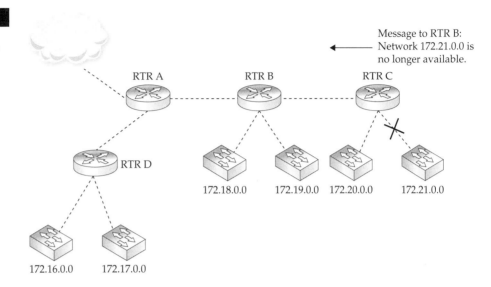

FIGURE 8-5

Distance vector
routing

Message to RTR B:
Network 172.21.0.0 is
no longer available.

60 seconds before Router A learns of the change. Router C will wait for the next
scheduled update to B, which will do the same thing before notifying Router A.
This time it takes for the routers to all have accurate views of the network is called
time to convergence. *Convergence* is when the routing is stable and all routers have
up-to-date and complete routing tables. Only while the network is converged are
packets all being handled properly.

When we say distance vector protocols exchange their routing tables, there is an
exception. A router will not share routes it learned on one of its interfaces back out
that same interface. This is called *split-horizon* and it prevents routing loops. Look
at Figure 8-5 again. If Router B, when exchanging routes with A, tells A about C's
down link, but at the same time also accepts routes about C from A, it would think
it could get to that LAN through A. Split-horizon prevents that by preventing A
from sharing with B anything it learned originally from B. In summary, split-horizon
prevents sending routing updates back to the device that told us the information,
much like trying to tell gossip or a joke to the person who originally told you.

Link State Routing Protocols

Link state protocols are considerably better choices than distance vector for a couple
of reasons. First, they don't waste bandwidth by regularly exchanging the entire
routing table. Instead, they only send updates when a route changes; this is called

a *triggered-update*. These updates are known as *link state advertisements (LSAs)*. As soon as a network drops or is added, the router sends LSAs to all routers within the area. Each router then makes the appropriate update to its table and sends an acknowledgment of receipt—something distance vector routers do not do.

The second major advantage over distance vector protocols is faster convergence time. Link state networks converge often within just a few seconds since the routers hear about any changes as soon as they occur directly from the router that "owns" the network.

Link state protocols use metrics that incorporate different factors in determining which routes to offer to the routing table. For example, consider Figure 8-6. A message received by RTR1 headed to network 192.168.5.0 has two possible pathways—out Serial 0 or Serial 1. The pathway from Serial 0 to the network goes through only two routers (hop count of 2), but each link in the chain is only 56 Kbps. The pathway from Serial 1 to the network goes through three routers (hop count of 3),

FIGURE 8-6

A link state route example

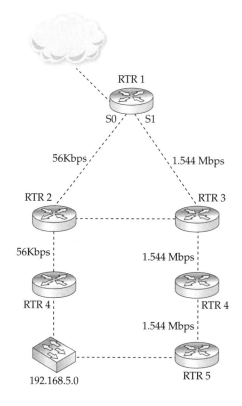

but each link along the chain is T1 (1.544 Mbps) or better. If the network were using distance vector routing, RTR1 would always choose to send messages out interface Serial 0 due to hop count—two hops rather than three. However, the speeds of each link actually make the Serial 1 pathway a much better choice. Link state protocols would take this into account and the message would be sent out Serial 1, reaching the intended recipient faster.

As a rule, the complexity of link state processes and the amount of route information processed means that they require more CPU resources and memory than distance vector protocols. This was more of an issue in the early days of routers. Today's devices—like today's computers—tend to have more than adequate CPU and memory capacity. Since updates are only processed when change occurs, CPU usage can be saved, particularly during periods of network stability.

Examples of link state protocols include OSPF and IS-IS.

exam
ⓦatch
You must be able to compare and contrast the characteristics of distance vector and link state protocols, as well as identify examples of each. Distance vector protocols use hop count as a metric, converge slowly, and exchange their entire routing tables on timed intervals only to their directly connected neighbors. Link state protocols use several different metrics (including bandwidth), converge very quickly, and send LSAs throughout the network as soon as a route changes.

In summary, distance vector routing protocols are easy to configure, do not acknowledge routing updates, can select less-than-optimal routes due to the hop-count metric, and therefore don't work well on larger networks. Link state routing protocols are more memory-and CPU-intensive, but they converge much faster, only send smaller updates, and then only when a network change occurs.

There will be more information on routing protocols and configuration steps covered in Chapter 10 when we look at configuring OSPF.

Cisco has another proprietary routing protocol, called EIGRP. It is a bit of a hybrid distance vector protocol that takes advantage of some link state characteristics as well. EIGRP is covered in the CCENT 2 exam and book.

Routing Logic and Data Flow

When data is received, the router determines the best way of forwarding and proceeds to the next step—encapsulating the packet for delivery in the new network. Examining data flow and routing logic is most easily accomplished by considering an example and watching the data flow between two systems. See Figure 8-7 for an overview of this example.

In our example, PC1 composes a message for PC4. PC1 then passes the message through the TCP/IP stack and, at the Internet layer, the IP destination address 195.250.5.200 is placed in the IP header. The packet is then passed to the Network

FIGURE 8-7

A routing logic example

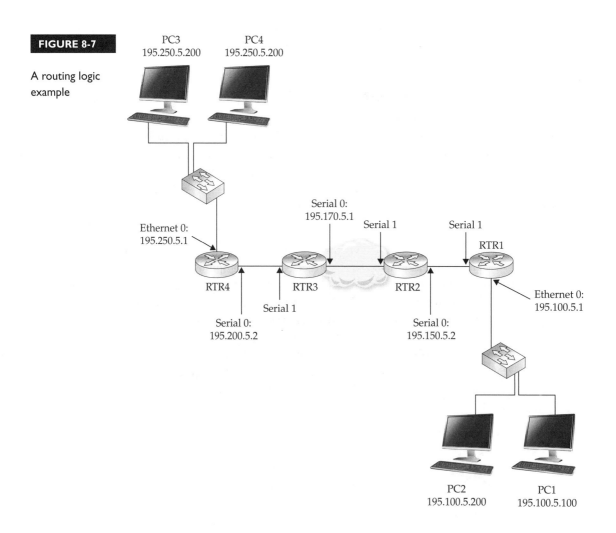

Access layer, at which point a physical address must be determined for the address assigned in the Internet layer. The PC looks at the destination address and quickly determines that the packet is not intended for any device on this network by comparing it to its own (195.100.5.100 and 195.250.5.200 are not on the same network). PC1 then encapsulates the packet and places the default gateway MAC address in the header. The frame, appearing in Figure 8-8, is then sent out the NIC, and the switch forwards it on to the router.

So how does the sending system find the addresses (IP and MAC) to build the packet and frame? The answer is with two protocols: DNS and ARP. *DNS (Domain Name System)* resolves an IP address for a fully qualified domain name or e-mail address. In our example, suppose PC1 is attempting to surf a web page hosted by PC4. As the request is passed through the layers, it pauses at Layer 3 while a separate DNS request is sent out to the nearest DNS server. The DNS requests queries for the IP address of the system hosting the website that PC1 is searching for. When DNS gets its answer, it returns the IP address and it is added to the destination address of the packet. *ARP (Address Resolution Protocol)* then attempts to resolve a MAC address for the IP address it now knows. Since the PC knows the IP address is not local, it gets the MAC address of your network's gateway router, either from its table or by sending out an ARP broadcast.

When the router port (195.100.5.1) receives the frame, it first checks the MAC address to verify the frame was intended for it. Next, the router checks the FCS field and, if the frame is verified as good, the header and FCS are removed. The destination IP address from the remaining packet header is then compared to a routing table within the router. If there is no route in the table, including a default route to your ISP, it is discarded. If there is a route in the table, the router then has to encapsulate the packet for the next network and send it out the appropriate port. The relevant routing tables are listed in Table 8-2.

In our example, Router 1 (RTR1) examines its routing table and finds an entry for the target network. The entry tells the router that to get to network 195.250.5.0 it should send the packet out the interface named Serial 1. Next, the table provides the address of the next router on the pathway: 195.150.5.2. This is an important step because just like devices on any LAN can only communicate directly with devices on that LAN, the next hop address gives RTR1 an address on a shared network to forward the packet to. RTR1 performs an ARP request to find the next hop's physical

FIGURE 8-8

Frame 1

Preamble	Source: PC1 MAC Address	Destination: Router Port MAC Address	Source: 195.100.5.100	Destination: 195.250.5.200	Data	FCS

TABLE 8-2	RTR1 Routing Table		
Routing Table Sample	Destination network	Out (interface)	Next hop (IP address)
	195.250.5.0	Serial 1	195.150.5.2
	RTR2 Routing Table		
	Destination network	Out (interface)	Next hop (IP address)
	195.250.5.0	Serial 1	195.170.5.1
	RTR3 Routing Table		
	Destination network	Out (interface)	Next hop (IP address)
	195.250.5.0	Serial 1	195.200.5.2
	RTR4 Routing Table		
	Destination network	Out (interface)	Next hop (IP address)
	195.250.5.0	Ethernet 0	N/A

address, and then encapsulates the packet using appropriate Layer 2 technology used on the 195.150.5.0 network.

This process is repeated for each router until the packet is finally delivered to the recipient station. In review, the steps a router takes as follows:

1. Verify the frame is addressed for the router port on which it was received and that the FCS field is correct.

2. Remove the frame header and trailer, and compare the destination IP address in the packet header to the routing table.

3. If the address does not match an entry, including a default route, then discard the packet. If it matches an entry, forward the packet to the appropriate interface for delivery.

4. Encapsulate the packet based on the Layer 2 technology on the interface and apply the correct Physical layer address to deliver the new frame to the next hop address.

exam
watch

You must be very familiar with routing logic and the steps routers take when receiving a packet for delivery. Scenario-based exam questions will be much easier to tackle if you know the steps described earlier and understand the basics of routing tables.

CERTIFICATION OBJECTIVE 8.03

Routing Table

Recall that IP addresses and subnet masks or prefix masks allow Layer 3 devices like routers to separate the Network ID portion of the IP address, which is then used for all forwarding decisions. The Host ID, the remaining part of the address, is only used in the destination network.

All Layer 3 devices, including computers, have a routing table stored in RAM that lists the routes to known network destinations and then typically a default route for all unknown networks. These routes indicate the egress interface to use, and in many cases, metrics (distances) for those routes, as well as the next-hop address, the address of the device that we are going to send the frame to for further forwarding. It is inefficient and uncommon that a routing table would include routes to specific host addresses, choosing instead to route to networks and let the destination router and switches deal with the final delivery. The routing table only includes the next-hop router, not the entire path to the destination. The next-hop router will have the next segment.

The routing table contains information about the topology of the network immediately connected to it, routes learned from neighbor routers, and any static routes entered by the admin. Populating and maintaining the routing tables is one of the primary functions of the routing protocols. The following is a simple example of a routing table displayed by using the **show ip route** command:

```
Router1#show ip route
Codes: C - connected, S - static, R - RIP, M - mobile, B - BGP
       D - EIGRP, EX - EIGRP external, O - OSPF, IA - OSPF inter area
       N1 - OSPF NSSA external type 1, N2 - OSPF NSSA external type 2
       E1 - OSPF external type 1, E2 - OSPF external type 2
       i - IS-IS, su - IS-IS summary, L1 - IS-IS level-1, L2 - IS-IS level-2
       ia - IS-IS inter area, * - candidate default, U - per-user static route
       o - ODR, P - periodic downloaded static route
Gateway of last resort is not set
D    192.168.11.0/24 [90/284160] via 192.168.1.1, 00:04:19, FastEthernet0/0
O    192.168.10.0/24 [110/11] via 192.168.2.1, 00:01:01, s0/0
R    192.168.9.0/24 [120/1] via 192.168.4.1, 00:00:07, s0/1
C    192.168.5.0/24 is directly connected, FastEthernet0/1
C    192.168.1.0/24 is directly connected, FastEthernet0/0
S    192.168.3.0/24 [1/0] via 192.168.1.1
```

The seven rows of code are basically a legend that corresponds to the letters at the beginning of each row in the routing table below. Don't be intimidated by all the codes—we will only use a few in this book and on the exam. While we will look at the information below the routes as we work through this chapter, there are some things we can see from the output.

Static Routes

Starting at the bottom of our routing table, the S tells us that the last row is a *static route* that was configured by the admin. It is telling us that to get to all of network 192.168.3.0/24, packets will be sent via a router whose IP address is 192.168.1.1. We can also see that it is the only route to that network.

The syntax for configuring a static route is:

ip route *dest-ip-addr dest-mask* [*next-hop-ip* | *outbound-interface*]

Here are two examples:

ip route 192.168.3.0 255.255.255.0 192.168.1.1

sends all packets destined for the 192.168.3.0 network to 192.168.1.1, the next-hop router.

ip route 192.168.3.0 255.255.255.0 s0/0

sends all packets destined for the 192.168.3.0 network out interface Serial 0/0. This works well with serial, point-to-point, connections because there are only two devices on the segment. Don't use a multi-access interface, such as FastEthernet or Gigabit, as at the egress they would be inefficient and may not work reliably.

Directly Connected Networks

The next two rows up from the bottom of our routing table, the C's tell us that these are directly connected to our router; they are "local networks" for the router. There is no route configuration required. As long as the interface is configured, not shut down, and connected to a live link, the router will discover it and add the information to the table. From the table, we know that they are directly connected networks, we know which interface they are connected to, and since they appear in the table, we know that we can send packets to those networks.

```
C    192.168.5.0/24 is directly connected, FastEthernet0/1
C    192.168.1.0/24 is directly connected, FastEthernet0/0
```

Routing Protocol Entries

The next three rows up of our routing table, the D, O, and R, tell us that these were learned from the routing protocols: D=EIGRP, O=OSPF, and R=RIP. We can also see the IP address of the next-hop address as well as the interface that router is connected to. We will discuss routing protocols in greater length later in the chapter.

```
D    192.168.11.0/24 [90/284160] via 192.168.1.1, 00:04:19, FastEthernet0/0
O    192.168.10.0/24 [110/11] via 192.168.2.1, 00:01:01, s0/0
R    192.168.9.0/24 [120/1] via 192.168.4.1, 00:00:07, s0/1
```

Looking at those three, we can see that there are three other pieces of information for each route. First, near the end is an indication of when the last update occurred in *hours:minutes:seconds*. That can be an indicator of route stability for each protocol, but they can't be compared to each other—what is great for one protocol might be terrible for another.

The other two pieces of information are in the square brackets, [*admin-distance/ metric*]. These were the pieces of information that decided the order in the table (admin-distance) and whether they even got in the table (metric). These will be covered in more detail later, but from the table, we can rightly conclude that smaller admin-distances are preferred.

Default Route

An important static route is a default route, or *gateway of last resort*, for unknown networks. Looking at our routing table example, above the route entries, we can see that the default route has not been configured.

```
     o - ODR, P - periodic downloaded static route
Gateway of last resort is not set
D    192.168.11.0/24 [90/284160] via 192.168.1.1, 00:04:19, FastEthernet0/0
O    192.168.10.0/24 [110/11] via 192.168.2.1, 00:01:01, s0/0
```

Let's look at another example to see what default routes do. In Figure 8-9, let's look at what default routes exist in this network. Hosts 1 through 4 would have a default route to the LAN interface on the gateway router; it is their default gateway. Hosts 6 through 9 would have a default route to the LAN interface on Switch B's side of the warehouse router. The warehouse router would have a default route to the LAN interface on the gateway router. The gateway router would have a default route to the connecting interface on the ISP router. Assuming the ISP is not a top-tier provider, it will have a default route pointing to the next-hop router closer to the Internet backbone. In each case these default routes reduce the size of the local routing table and reduce any routing protocol overhead.

It is entirely likely that the network in Figure 8-9 would not be running a routing protocol at all, instead adding a single static route to the gateway router identifying the warehouse LAN address network and pointing to the second LAN interface on Switch A's side of the warehouse router. The CCENT exam focuses on larger networks with multiple routers running a routing protocol like OSPF. Many

FIGURE 8-9

Network default
routes

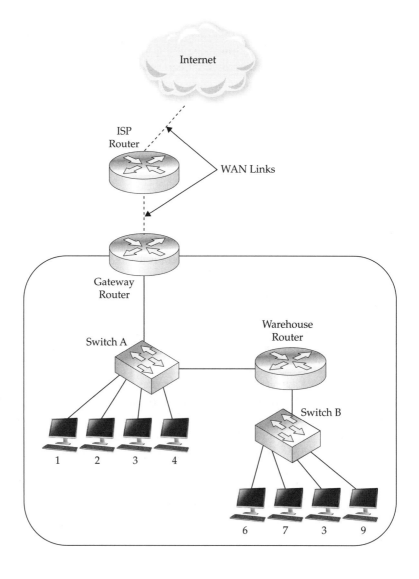

networks, smaller businesses (not necessarily tiny), and homes typically have one or two routers. In these cases, static routes and default routes may be all you need.

Default Route Syntax

The syntax of a Cisco default route can take two forms. The first, 0.0.0.0, quad-zero, means literally any network. The second quad-zero means literally any mask. Taken together it means route all IP networks with any mask. This works with other routes because it is always the last option available in the routing table, hence the name *route of last resort*. Any more specific routes would be seen first and selected. The syntax is:

> **ip route 0.0.0.0 0.0.0.0** [*next-hop-ip* | *outbound-interface*]

Here are two examples:

> **ip route 0.0.0.0 0.0.0.0 10.1.0.2**

sends all packets destined for networks not in our routing table to 10.1.0.2, the next-hop router.

> **ip route 0.0.0.0 0.0.0.0 s0/1**

sends all packets destined for networks not in our routing table out our Serial 0/1 interface.

The second option is used most often with point-to-point connections, where there are only two devices on the segment, such as with T1s. We will configure both static and default routes in the next chapter.

More Specific Routes

Recall when we discussed IP addresses with prefix masks, we saw that the longer the prefix, the more specific the network—the *where* to find a particular host. For example, 192.168.1.192/26 is more specific than 192.168.1.0/24. Any address in 192.168.1.192/26 is also in 192.168.1.0/24, but the first method provides a more direct, smaller target subnet to find the hosts 192.168.1.193–254.

A routing table would include both routes and would choose the more specific route to 192.168.1.192/26 for hosts in that subnet over 192.168.1.0/24 for forwarding packets. The routes could be added to the routing table via any combination of routing methods, as follows:

```
R    192.168.1.192/26 [120/1] via 192.168.4.1, 00:00:07, s0/1
O    192.168.1.0/24 [110/11] via 192.168.2.1, 00:01:01, s0/0
S    192.168.0.0/16 [1/0] via s0/2
S    0.0.0.0/0 via s0/3
```

Traffic to any of the hosts 192.168.1.193–254 would be forwarded out interface s0/1 even though the other routes could deliver the traffic. If interface s0/1 were to go down, the traffic would go out s0/0. If both of those interfaces went down, it would go out s0/2 and, as you have probably guessed, it would use the default route if the others were unavailable.

Static vs. Dynamic Routing

We've seen that the routing table can be built by the device learning the directly connected live interfaces from static routes and default routes manually entered by the admin, and in this section we will look at dynamic routing, which basically means enabling one or more routing protocols and letting the protocols add to and manage routing table entries that are learned about from other routers.

The benefits of static routing include

- **Less overhead on the router's CPU** There is no need to compute routes for the table if they are manually entered and maintained.
- **Less bandwidth usage on the network** No route advertisements need to be sent from router to router. This can be particularly critical on low-bandwidth links like serial T1s or satellite links.
- **Improved granularity** It's possible to have more detailed control over route selection.
- **Security** If routes can only be added or deleted manually by an administrator, there is less chance the routing table can be tampered with by outsiders.

The disadvantages of static routing include

- **Changes are labor intensive** Adding and deleting routes must be done manually and may involve multiple routers.
- **Doesn't scale well** The larger the network, the more difficult it often becomes to maintain. Typically, the more Layer 3 devices you have, the more difficult static routing becomes.
- **Fault tolerance becomes tricky** If the administrator does not have a thorough understanding of the network, disruptive outages can hurt performance and it can be hard to build a work-around.

Dynamic routing, on the other hand, is just about the opposite on each of the points for and against static routing. It is an excellent choice for large networks. It scales well with routers, sharing information about network routes and updating their tables automatically. New network routes are added, outages are dropped or rerouted, and changes can generally be updated on the fly. Dynamic routing is less labor intensive. All of these pluses do come at the cost of increased CPU usage and more bandwidth usage because of the sharing and updating processes.

These two drawbacks are more of an issue on networks running at or near maximum CPU or bandwidth capacity, such as across slow links. Modern routers and LANs using Fast Ethernet or Gigabit links will find these increases minimal.

e x a m

ⓦ a t c h *Be sure you know that routing table entries can be learned by the router in the case of connected networks, configured manually by the admin in the case of static and default routes, and learned by any routing protocols. Know the advantages and disadvantages of static and dynamic routing.*

Building the Routing Table

When trying to understand how entries get added to the routing table, there are three main considerations:

- ■ **Administrative distance** This is a measure of trustworthiness of the source of the route—how trusted is the method that found the route. If a router learns about a destination from more than one routing protocol, it uses administrative distance to compare and rank the routes. Preference goes to the route with lower administrative distance, choosing it as the route to be included in the route listings. For example, a route learned from the RIP routing protocol has an AD of 120, while a route learned from OSPF would have an AD of 110. If both route updates were for the same network ID, the router would put the OSPF-learned route in the table since Cisco trusts OSPF updates more than RIP updates. The RIP route would be available if the OSPF route went down, but the OSPF will always be chosen if available.

TABLE 8-3

Administrative
Distances

Route Type	Administrative Distance
Directly connected network	0
Static route	1
EIGRP	90
OSPF	110
IS-IS	115
RIP (and RIPv2)	120
Unknown	255

- **Metrics** Where administrative distance is used by the router to rank and select routes learned by different methods, a metric unit of measure is used by each routing protocol to rank routes it learned to the same destination. Metrics are how the method, such as OSPF, chooses only its best route to be offered to the routing table. Each routing protocol can use a different metric.

- **Prefix length** Think of CIDR notation: more specific routes—those with the longest prefix or network identifier—will be chosen to offer the forwarding process. 10.1.1.0/24 will be chosen over 10.0.0.0/8 if looking for 10.1.1.25

Administrative distances (listed in Table 8-3) should be committed to memory.

CERTIFICATION OBJECTIVE 8.04

Router Forwarding Process

Router forwarding (or switching) refers to taking a frame from the inbound interface and using one of the router forwarding methods to determine the best path to the destination and then preparing it to be sent through the outbound interface on its way toward the final destination. Don't be confused by the terms *switching* and *forwarding*; they mean the same thing in this case and are used interchangeably even though the industry is trying to move toward forwarding.

Once the frame has been processed and the packet is ready for forwarding, there are three steps to forwarding it through a router:

1. Determine if there is a known route to the packet's destination in the routing table. If not, it is discarded. Remember that a default route is a known route.

2. Determine the next-hop device toward the destination, as well as the outbound interface to use to reach that next-hop device.

3. Rebuild the Layer 2 frame for the packet so that it can reach the next-hop device.

While each of these steps must be done for the packet to reach its destination, you'll find that they are incorporated differently into each of the three forwarding methods covered in the next section.

Router Forwarding (Switching) Methods

There are three different forwarding or switching methods that Cisco routers can use in forwarding packets. The primary differences are the amount of CPU usage and performance (faster throughput).

- **Process switching** requires the CPU to individually handle each packet forwarding decision as if each were a separate message or data stream. This is obviously slow and takes CPU cycles that could be allocated to other activities, such as quality of service.

- **Fast switching** only uses the CPU for the first packet in a data stream to a destination. After that, the forwarding information, such as next-hop address, is stored in a fast-switching cache. As other packets heading to the same destination arrive, the forwarding information can be reused from the cache. This means the processor doesn't have to look up and assemble all the information again. The CPU only gets involved when a new stream to another destination arrives.

- **Cisco Express Forwarding (CEF)** is the latest evolution in router optimization designed to make forwarding packets faster. CEF is able to interact with the routing table and neighboring routers to create a separate little database, called a forwarding information base (FIB), that incorporates information such as the destination, next-hop address, and even Layer 2 information used in building the frame—virtually everything required to forward a packet. This FIB can be accessed very quickly and eliminates CPU involvement. Basically, the CPU has outsourced the forwarding to the much faster switching technologies.

INSIDE THE EXAM

Routing Foundation

Many CCENT questions on routing logic and fundamentals will be simultaneously simple and confusing. To ensure you're prepared, be sure you can recreate the steps a router takes when receiving a packet for delivery, and be prepared for several questions concerning the function of the routing table. Pay particular attention to the concept of the largest prefix match. The exam will also require you to identify and describe routed (IP) protocols, including what makes them routable. Be sure you know what routed protocols provide a means to address both the host (who) and the network (where) to which the host belongs. In short, routed protocols use logical addresses.

Know the three functions of a router and understand the three forwarding methods.

Routing Protocols

Make sure you know the differences between distance vector and link state routing protocols. Be prepared to compare and contrast each.

Routing Table

Be sure you know that routing table entries can be learned by the router in the case of connected networks, configured manually by the admin in the case of static and default routes, and learned by any routing protocols. Know the advantages and disadvantages of static and dynamic routing. Make sure you understand how routing table entries are chosen using administrative distance, metrics, and prefix length.

Router Forwarding Process

Describe the three forwarding methods: process switching, fast switching, and CEF. Be prepared to compare and contrast each.

CERTIFICATION SUMMARY

The steps a router takes when receiving a packet for delivery are: Check the FCS, discard the old frame header, and verify the destination IP address against the routing table. If there is a match, create a new frame header and trailer for the packet, and send it out the appropriate port. If there is no match, discard the packet. You must also be prepared for several questions concerning the function of the routing table. Remember, if there is no entry in the routing table, including route of last resort (default route), the packet is dropped. If there is an entry in the routing table, the router will forward the packet out the interface with the longest prefix, that is, the most matching network bits.

Routed protocols contain logical addresses and can be routed to an end destination. IP is a routed protocol. *Routing* protocols define how routing tables are built and how routers share information with one another. Static routing requires manual updates and has several advantages and disadvantages, while dynamic routing uses routing protocols. Distance vector routing protocols use only hop count as a metric and work well on small networks (example: RIPv2). Link state routing protocols converge much faster, use a variety of metrics in determining route entries, and send LSAs when network outages and changes occur. Examples include OSPF and IS-IS.

TWO-MINUTE DRILL

Routing Foundation

❑ IP is the routed protocol used to transport data to end systems due to the hierarchical, logical addressing found in the header that identifies a network portion that can be located on global networks.

❑ A router's three primary functions are: 1) To use one or more routing protocols to share information with other routers to find the best route to a destination. 2) The routing table itself accepts information from the routing processes and also replies to requests from the forwarding process. 3) The forwarding process makes information requests to the routing table to then make packet forwarding decisions.

Routing Protocols

❑ Routing protocols define how routing tables are built, which metrics are used to determine routes, and how routers communicate with each other.

❑ Dynamic routing is an excellent choice for large networks, as it scales well with routers sharing information about network routes and updating their tables automatically. New network routes are added, outages are dropped or rerouted, and changes can generally be updated on the fly. Dynamic routing is less labor intensive. These pluses come at the cost of increased CPU usage and more bandwidth usage because of the sharing and updating processes.

❑ There are two ways to categorize routing protocols: interior gateway protocols (IGPs) and exterior gateway protocols (EGPs). IGPs share routing information between routers within an autonomous system (AS), an enterprise or organization's networks. There is really just one EGP—Border Gateway Protocol (BGP), the routing protocol of the Internet backbone to connect large networks to the Internet.

❑ IGPs fall into two categories: distance vector routing protocols and link state routing protocols.

❑ Distance vector routing protocols use hop count as their only metric and trade their entire routing table on a timed intervals using broadcasts to their directly connected neighbor. "Routing by rumor" makes for long convergence times. Examples include RIP, RIPv2, and IGRP.

❑ Link state routing protocols use a variety of metrics to compare routes and only send LSAs when a network change occurs using multicast messages. Convergence is much faster with a link state protocol, and they are generally better choices for large networks. Examples include OSPF and IS-IS.

Routing Table

❑ A routing table contains connected networks, static routes, default gateways, and routes learned from routing protocols.

❑ Static routing requires the administrator to add and remove routing table entries manually. Its advantages include less router CPU overhead, less bandwidth usage on the network, and a bit better security. Its disadvantage is slowness and possibly incomplete convergence because network outages and changes have to be manually updated in all routing tables. It doesn't scale well, and fault tolerance and redundancy become tricky.

❑ To determine which interface to send an incoming message out, the router compares the destination IP address to its routing table. If there is no match, the packet is discarded. If there is a match, the routing table entry matching the most number of bits from left to right when compared with the address is used to route the packet.

Router Forwarding Process

❑ When a message is received by a router, it checks the FCS field and discards the header and trailer. The destination IP address in the packet header is then examined and compared against the routing table. The packet is then reframed and sent out the appropriate port.

❑ Router forwarding (switching) methods include: 1) Process switching uses the CPU to handle each packet forwarding decision. It is slow and takes up CPU cycles. 2) Fast switching only uses the CPU for the first packet in a data stream to a destination and puts forwarding information in a fast-switching cache for the rest of the packets. The CPU only gets involved when a new stream to another destination arrives. 3) Cisco Express Forwarding (CEF) router optimization gathers information from the routing table and neighboring routers to create a database, called a forwarding information base (FIB). The FIB incorporates information such as the destination, next-hop address, and even Layer 2 information. With CEF, the CPU has outsourced the forwarding to the much faster switching technologies.

SELF TEST

The following Self Test questions will help you measure your understanding of the material presented in this chapter. Read all the choices carefully since there may be more than one correct answer. Choose all the correct answers for each question.

Routing Foundation

1. Which of the following is/are true regarding router operation?
   A. Routers work at Layer 3 only.
   B. Routers work at Layers 1, 2, and 3 to accomplish their tasks.
   C. Routers only examine Layer 3 addresses.
   D. Routers must examine the Layer 2 address to accept the frame first, and then will look at the Layer 3 address.

2. True/False: The destination device is separated from the sending device by four routers. The largest PDU that makes it intact across all four routers is the original frame.
   A. True
   B. False

3. Which of the following is/are considered routed protocols?
   A. RIP
   B. IP
   C. OSPF
   D. IS-IS

Routing Protocols

4. Which of the following is/are considered to be a distance vector protocol?
   A. RIP
   B. RIPv2
   C. IGRP
   D. EIGRP
   E. OSPF

5. Which of the following is/are considered to be a link state protocol?
   A. RIP
   B. RIPv2
   C. IGRP

    D. EIGRP

    E. OSPF

6. Link state routing protocols have which of the following characteristics?

    A. They use hop count as a metric to determine routes.

    B. They use multiple metrics to determine routes.

    C. They exchange routing information only with their directly connected neighbor routers.

    D. They exchange routing information directly from other routers throughout the network.

Routing Table

7. Which of the following is/are true regarding routing tables?

    A. The next-hop address is irrelevant to router operation.

    B. The next-hop address is used to find an address for the new Layer 2 frame header.

    C. The next-hop address is used to accept routing updates only.

    D. If there is no entry for the packet's destination network address, the packet will be forwarded out the closest matching interface.

    E. If there is no entry for the packet's destination network address, the packet will be discarded.

8. A router receives a message addressed 172.16.15.75. The relevant routing table entries are 172.16.0.0 /20 – Serial 0, 172.16.0.0 /23 – Ethernet 0, and 172.16.15.64 /26 – Ethernet 1. Which interface will the router forward the packet to?

    A. Serial 0.

    B. Serial 1.

    C. Ethernet 0.

    D. Ethernet 1.

    E. None of the above. The packet will be dropped.

9. Which of the following is NOT an advantage of static routing?

    A. Less overhead on router CPU

    B. Less bandwidth usage on the network

    C. More bandwidth usage on the network

    D. Greater security

10. Using the following output, which of the routes is the default gateway?

```
Router1#show ip route
Codes: C - connected, S - static, R - RIP, M - mobile, B - BGP
       D - EIGRP, EX - EIGRP external, O - OSPF, IA - OSPF inter area
       N1 - OSPF NSSA external type 1, N2 - OSPF NSSA external type 2
```

```
         E1 - OSPF external type 1, E2 - OSPF external type 2
         i - IS-IS, su - IS-IS summary, L1 - IS-IS level-1, L2 - IS-IS level-2
         ia - IS-IS inter area, * - candidate default, U - per-user static route
         o - ODR, P - periodic downloaded static route
Gateway of last resort is not set
D     192.168.11.0/24 [90/284160] via 192.168.1.1, 00:04:19, FastEthernet0/0
O     192.168.10.0/24 [110/11] via 192.168.2.1, 00:01:01, s0/0
R     192.168.9.0/24 [120/1] via 192.168.4.1, 00:00:07, s0/1
C     192.168.5.0/24 is directly connected, FastEthernet0/1
C     192.168.1.0/24 is directly connected, FastEthernet0/0
S     192.168.3.0/24 [1/0] via 192.168.1.1
```

A. 192.168.3.0/24 [1/0] via 192.168.1.1

B. 192.168.1.0/24 is directly connected, FastEthernet0/0

C. 192.168.5.0/24 is directly connected, FastEthernet0/1

D. 192.168.10.0/24 [90/284160] via 192.168.1.1, 00:04:19, FastEthernet0/0

E. None of the above

11. Using the output in question 10, which of the routes would be used to get to 192.168.10.45?

A. 192.168.3.0/24 [1/0] via 192.168.1.1

B. 192.168.1.0/24 is directly connected, FastEthernet0/0

C. 192.168.5.0/24 is directly connected, FastEthernet0/1

D. 192.168.10.0/24 [120/1] via 192.168.4.1, 00:00:07, s0/1

E. None of the above

Router Forwarding Process

12. Which are the three primary functions of the router?

A. Routing protocols make information requests and then make packet forwarding decisions.

B. Routing protocols share route information with other routers and update the routing table.

C. Routing table shares route information with other routers and updates its routing table.

D. Forwarding process makes information requests and then makes packet forwarding decisions.

E. Routing table accepts information and also replies to requests.

13. What are the three router forwarding (switching) methods?

A. ASICs

B. Fast switching

C. Process switching

D. CES

E. CEF

SELF TEST ANSWERS

Routing Foundation

1. ☑ **B** and **D** are correct. All devices must work at the Physical layer, and the router must also examine the Layer 2 address to determine if the frame is intended for it or not. After the frame's physical address is verified, the router moves up to Layer 3 and examines the IP address.

   ☒ **A** and **C** are incorrect. When a device is said to work at a given layer, it means the device works at all layers up to that level. Routers work at Layer 3; therefore, they perform functions at Layers 1 through 3.

2. ☑ **B** is correct. Frame headers and trailers are removed and discarded at each router, then rebuilt for the next link in the chain.

   ☒ **A** is incorrect because the statement is false.

3. ☑ **B** is correct. IP is the only routed protocol that contains logical addresses in the headers.

   ☒ **A, C,** and **D** are incorrect. RIP, OSPF, and IS-IS are all routing protocols.

Routing Protocols

4. ☑ **A, B,** and **C** are correct. RIP, RIPv2, and IGRP are all distance vector protocols.

   ☒ **D** and **E** are incorrect. OSPF is a link state protocol and EIGRP is a hybrid.

5. ☑ **E** is correct. OSPF is a link state protocol.

   ☒ **A, B, C,** and **D** are incorrect. RIP, RIPv2, and IGRP are all distance vector protocols and EIGRP is a hybrid.

6. ☑ **B** and **D** are correct. B is correct because link state protocols use multiple metrics in determining and ranking routes. D is correct because LSAs are sent directly to all routers within the network, not just to directly connected neighbor routers.

   ☒ **A** and **C** are incorrect. A is incorrect because link state protocols do not use hop count as a metric to determine routes. C is incorrect because link state protocols exchange routing information only with all routers running the protocol.

Routing Table

7. ☑ **B** and **E** are correct. When the router makes a decision as to which interface to send a message out, it performs an ARP to determine the Physical layer address for the new frame. If there is no matching entry in the routing table, packets are discarded.

   ☒ **A, C,** and **D** are incorrect. A is incorrect because next-hop addresses are used by routers to determine the address for the new frame and are not used solely for routing updates. C is incorrect because there must be an entry for the packet's destination network address. D is incorrect because packets with no matching entry in the routing table are discarded, not forwarded.

8. ☑ **D** is correct. If you translate 172.16.15.75 into binary, it matches 26 bits in the last routing table entry, as opposed to only 20 in the first two.

    ☒ **A, B, C,** and **E** are incorrect. **A** and **C** are incorrect because the address bits match more of the last route entry; it will be chosen over the other two. **B** is incorrect because there is no route for Serial 1. **E** is incorrect because the packet will not be dropped because there is a routing table entry for it.

9. ☑ **C** is correct. Static routing does not use routing updates; therefore, there is less traffic on the network, not more.

    ☒ **A, B,** and **D** are incorrect. **A** is incorrect because static routing uses less overhead on router CPU. **B** is incorrect because static routing uses less bandwidth usage on the network. **D** is incorrect because static routing offers greater security.

10. ☑ **E** is correct. "Gateway of last resort is not set." means there is no default route.

    ☒ **A, B, C,** and **D** are incorrect. Each takes us to one LAN, not all unknown networks.

11. ☑ **E** is correct. The correct route is 192.168.10.0/24 [110/11] via 192.168.2.1, 00:01:01, s0/0. It is the top route to that network worth with the lowest AD to that network.

    ☒ **A, B, C,** and **D** are incorrect because they all lead to the wrong networks.

Router Forwarding Process

12. ☑ **B, D,** and **E** are correct. The three primary functions of the router are routing protocols, routing table, and forwarding process.

    ☒ **A** and **C** are incorrect. **A** is incorrect because the forwarding process makes information requests and then makes packet forwarding decisions. **C** is incorrect because the routing protocols share route information with other routers and update the routing table.

13. ☑ **B, C,** and **E** are correct. The three router forwarding (switching) methods are process switching, fast switching, and CEF (Cisco Express Forwarding).

    ☒ **A** and **D** are incorrect. **A** is incorrect because ASICs (application-specific integrated circuits) is the switching technology in Cisco switches. **D** is incorrect because the acronym should be CEF (Cisco Express Forwarding).

9

Cisco Router Configuration

T he good news is that much of the basics of router configuration is exactly the same as we learned for switches. The concepts of configuration levels, securing the device, banners, login, and so on should look familiar. Routing and interfaces will be the big differences. In this chapter, we'll continue hands-on configuration steps needed for your network's routers. After covering the basics, along with a review of some key concepts, we'll cover initial configuration, static routing, dynamic routing, and we will complete our VLAN coverage from Chapter 7 by showing how to configure our router to support the VLANs. Dynamic routing with OSPF is covered in Chapter 10.

CERTIFICATION OBJECTIVE 9.01

Router Configuration Initial Steps

As we learned earlier, routers provide the means to move data between networks—and for that to work effectively, the correct options and settings must be configured. Before this can happen, however, it's helpful to know a little about the devices themselves. In this section, we'll first cover some basics on Cisco routers, and then follow that with a discussion of installation locations and techniques.

About Cisco Routers

Before getting into the configuration of routers, it's beneficial to know a few things about them—specifically, the physical features of a router, and some basics on the IOS and CLI available on the router. Most LAN switches don't have power (on/off) switches, while routers do. Fortunately, the IOS interface, look and feel, and configuration concepts are very similar. Much like Microsoft Office applications, if you understand one, you generally can at least figure out the basic features of the others. The unique features are what we need to really focus on.

Router Ports and Interfaces

See Figure 9-1 for a look at the back of a typical Cisco router. Routers usually have four different types of ports on their backside: the console port, an auxiliary port, Ethernet ports, and serial ports. The console port was covered in Chapter 6 with

FIGURE 9-1

Router interfaces

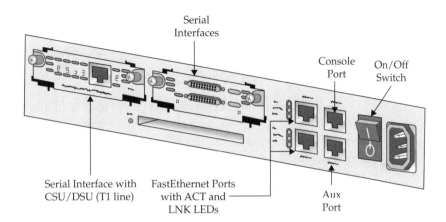

switches, and the same cable and steps for making a console connection apply here as well. The auxiliary port can be used in conjunction with a modem to allow remote dial-in connections over a phone line. It's configured using the **line aux 0** command instead of **line con 0**. The other two types of ports are the ones to focus on for the exam. These are used to connect to switches, other routers, firewalls, and WAN connection devices. As a rule, they are not connected directly to users; that is the function of a switch.

A wide variety of interfaces and options can be added to many Cisco routers. On most newer Cisco routers, the basic "shell" comes with two Fast Ethernet or Gigabit interfaces stacked one on top of another, as shown in Figure 9-1. The interface on the bottom is FastEthernet 0/0, while the one on the top is FastEthernet 0/1. On other models, they could be Gigabit 0/0 and Gigabit 0/1, respectively. The optional modules come in many configurations, including additional Ethernet interfaces, but for our purposes, we will assume a WIC (WAN interface card) to add serial interfaces for WAN connections. The same numbering rule applies: the interface on the bottom will be 0/0, while the top will be 0/1. Each interface is labeled, if you forget.

Ethernet Interfaces   Ethernet interfaces typically provide services for individual Ethernet networks and are numbered using the same scheme covered earlier in this chapter. Each individual port represents an entirely unique LAN or a group of VLANs, and must have an address within each LAN or VLAN host address range. For example, the first Ethernet port might have an address of 192.168.1.1, while the second would have an address in a different subnet (such as 192.168.2.1). While not a rule, many organizations assign the first host address to the router for consistency.

Ethernet interfaces are listed in the CLI according to their speed. While older 10-Mbps Ethernet ports are accessed by the **interface ethernet #** command (where # is the port's number), the more common Fast Ethernet ports are accessed by **interface fastethernet #/#**, and gigabit ports are accessed by the **interface gigabitethernet #/#** command.

The LEDs beside the Ethernet ports can help a lot in quick day-to-day troubleshooting. The ACT light is for "activity" and should blink when the port is sending and receiving traffic. An ACT light that remains solid indicates a problem—either the link is heavily overused or some Physical layer problem is creating a loop or short. The LNK light is for "link" and should remain on, unblinking, if a good connection is present. A flashing LNK light indicates a bad physical connection somewhere along the path (usually at the interface connector itself).

<table>
<tr><td>

exam

watch

This may seem like a simple concept (and common sense, based on what we already know about routers), but be sure you understand that each port must have an address in a unique subnet. The router should not allow you to add any interface (Ethernet or serial) to a subnet that already has an interface assigned within the range, but scenario questions on this can be rather tricky. A scenario question may present a network
</td><td>

diagram, conceived by a coworker, asking you to identify true or false questions about it. The diagram may look fine, but after reviewing the subnetting for each address, you'll find the addresses to be assigned to the interfaces are in the same subnet. For instance, 172.16.16.21 and 172.16.17.21 may appear to be on different subnets; however, if the subnet mask is 255.255.240.0, they are both actually within the same network!
</td></tr>
</table>

Serial Interfaces   Serial interfaces, while also requiring addresses in a unique subnet, are used to provide access to WAN links for your network. Plenty of choices are available when connecting your LANs across long distances—everything from ISDN and T1 lines (point-to-point connections) to frame relay and ATM. (These technologies are covered on other exams.) Serial interfaces are identified like Ethernet interfaces: serial #/#. Serial connections are always point-to-point, meaning there can only be two devices on a segment.

Two other configuration options on serial interfaces are the **bandwidth** and **clock rate** commands. Just as with the frame type, serial interfaces require additional consideration with speed since there are so many different possibilities to choose from. While Ethernet ports run at a predetermined speed (10,100 or 1000 Mbps), serial interfaces can run at a variety of different speeds.

The second command of note on serial interfaces is the *bandwidth speed(kbps)* command. While **clock rate** sets the speed of the connection and is only set on one side of the connection, **bandwidth** does not affect the actual transmitting speed of the interface at all and can be set on both ends. This command is used by certain routing protocols to calculate best routes. The EIGRP and OSPF routing protocols, for example, use the setting configured with the **bandwidth** command as part of their metrics to determine which route is best. By default, all serial interfaces are assumed to be 1544 Kbps (1.544 Mbps)—the rate of a T1 connection—if there is no **bandwidth** command set.

Loopback Interfaces   In Chapter 6, we configured a virtual interface within a switch for VLAN1. We then assigned an IP address to it like any other interface for remote access and administration of the switch. There is a similar virtual interface on routers, called a loopback interface, that is reachable from all interfaces and remains always "up." This address can be used for ping, Telnet, or SSH destination or other troubleshooting, but more importantly, it is used by some routing protocols as a router ID.

To configure a loopback interface, you are actually creating a virtual interface. The commands are the same as other interfaces except you define it with the **interface loopback** *num* command in Global Configuration mode. You then assign an IP address, subnet mask, and optionally a description like any other interface.

The Router IOS

Knowing a little bit about the physical makeup of the router itself and the interfaces you'll be dealing with, you can move forward in preparing to configure your router, but the IOS and CLI are the keys to the configuration kingdom. The IOS, CLI, and memory locations are all virtually identical from a switch to a router. Routers store configuration files and IOS images exactly like switches (in NVRAM and flash, respectively), and use the same commands and techniques to copy and store them. The CLI modes (User, Privileged, Global Configuration, and so on) and the methods in which you move around in them also work the same on routers. Many of the configuration options and commands already covered in Chapter 6 for configuring switches also apply to routers (see Table 9-1). These will be used in the exercises but not covered again. One difference is that switch interfaces are enabled (up) and ready to work by default, while router LAN and serial interfaces are not and require a **no shutdown** command.

TABLE 9-1	Command(s)	Command(s)
IOS Commands Common to Both Routers and Switches	Hostname	Enable secret **password**
	Banner login and banner MOTD	Login and password commands
	Show run and show start	Line con and line vty login options
	Exec-timeout	Service password encryption
	Copy run start	SSH configuration steps
	History	Logging synchronous

In fact, it's probably easier to list the differences in the router CLI when compared to the switch than to go through what is similar. First, of course, the questions asked during setup are different. While, just as with a switch, you can enter setup using the **setup** command, exit using CTRL-C at any time, and have the same ending options (0, 1, or 2), the System Configuration dialog on a router prompts for additional information, such as routing protocol settings and additional interface configuration steps not needed on a switch. Other differences between the two include the configuration of IP addresses, the interface options available (auxiliary and serial ports, for example, are typically router concerns, not switch concerns), and slight differences in the commands available.

The commands common to both switches and routers will be reviewed in the first exercise on the simulator.

exam

watch

Be aware of the differences between a router and a switch IOS. For the most part, this will be common sense— commands dealing with switch functions (show mac address-table dynamic and vlan commands, for example) won't work on a router, and router commands (show ip route and routing protocol commands, such as rip, eigrp, and network) won't work on a switch. Simply pay attention to what the scenario calls for and what device you're working on.

Physical Installation

Once you know a little about the physical makeup of the router and understand the basics of the CLI, and as long as you keep in mind what the router is for, the actual physical installation and connections will seem simple and common sense. Since routers are used to pass traffic between networks, it should make sense that they are actually installed on the "edge" of the network—whether enterprise or small office/home office (SOHO).

As we discussed earlier in this chapter, the serial ports are used for the outside-facing WAN interfaces, while the Ethernet ports connect to switches inside the network, providing access and services to users. For example, consider the simple point-to-point (PTP) network displayed in Figure 9-2. In a fairly common network for a central-to-branch office PTP setup, the central office LAN is connected to the branch office LAN over a *leased line* connection. The individual systems at each location connect to a switch, which has a connection to the router's Ethernet ports. The serial port on each router is connected to the line installed by the WAN service provider or ISP.

Several cable types are used to connect a router to a serial connection, each with its own pinout and (sometimes) strange-looking connectors. Which one you choose depends on the network connection at the CSU/DSU. For all intents and purposes, you simply take a look at the port, order the right cable, and plug it in. Pinouts and data terminals are great, but you don't really need to know what they do and how they work at the WAN end—just pick one that fits the port!

As another example, consider the basic SOHO or branch network displayed in Figure 9-3. With SOHOs, you generally have two options for building your network:

FIGURE 9-2

Router
installation

ISP or WAN Provider Network

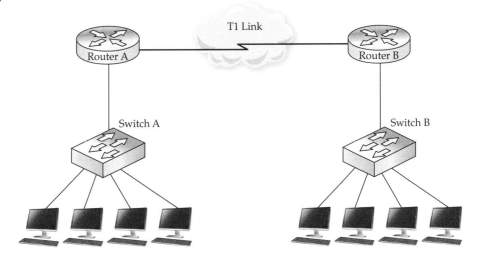

FIGURE 9-3

Two basic SOHO
network options

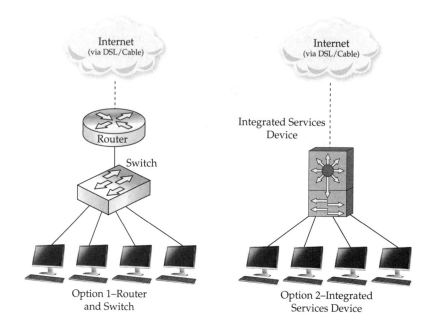

Option 1–Router
and Switch

Option 2–Integrated
Services Device

using a router and switch or an integrated services router. In one option, you can use a cable or DSL modem from the ISP connected to a router and switch.

The second—and more popular—option uses an integrated services device. The integrated services device can perform the functions of the modem, provide for the routing of packets into and out of the network, and even include a switch on the backside for access ports. Many integrated devices can also include firewall features, VoIP functions, act as a wireless access point, and provide for encrypted VPNs.

e x a m

ⓦ a t c h *The information in this section isn't necessarily provided as "verbatim" testing material. In other words, you shouldn't be asked for a blanket definition of an integrated services device or which cable is to be connected first.*

Instead, concentrate on the overall picture and how the devices are connected: UTP cables go to Ethernet ports facing inside a network, serial cables connect the router serial port to the leased line directly.

Configuration Fundamentals

In this section, we'll start with the initial settings required on the router, then follow up with an overview of configuring static or dynamic routing.

Setup Mode

Just as with a switch, the System Configuration dialog, also known as Setup mode, can be used to configure the basic options on a router. Setup won't provide all the options you'll need on your router, nor is it the preferred method, but it is available, easy, and sometimes used by new administrators. There's really no need to rehash setup again—since it was covered in depth in Chapter 6—however, a few things should be noted.

Recall that when an IOS device has no configuration found in its NVRAM, it offers the Setup dialog. Setup mode on a router has many similarities with the Catalyst version but also has a couple of differences. For example, setup on a switch asks for a single IP address (VLAN1), while a router setup calls for an IP address on each interface. Setup on some Cisco routers can also call for something known as Cisco Auto Secure—a feature used to automatically set up common security settings on the router. A sample System Configuration dialog on a router is displayed next. To accept a default in [ ], press ENTER. To exit out of Setup, press CTRL-C.

```
          --- System Configuration dialog ---
Would you like to enter the initial configuration dialog? [yes/
no]: no
At any point you may enter a question mark '?' for help.
Use ctrl-c to abort configuration dialog at any prompt.
Default settings are in square brackets '[]'.
Basic management setup configures only enough connectivity for
management of the system, while extended setup will ask you to
configure each
interface on the system.
Would you like to enter basic management setup? [yes/no]:no
First, would you like to see the current interface summary?
[yes]: no
Configuring global parameters:
  Enter host name [Router]:CCENTRTR1
  The enable secret is a password used to protect access to
```

privileged EXEC and configuration modes. This password, after
it's entered, becomes encrypted in the configuration.
  Enter enable secret: **cisco**
  The enable password is used when you do not specify an enable
secret password. It's also used with some older software
versions and some boot images.
  Enter enable password: **ccent**
  The virtual terminal password is used to protect access to the
router over a network interface.
  Enter virtual terminal password: **password**
  Configure SNMP Network Management? [yes]: **no**
  Configure bridging? [no]
Configure DECnet? [no]
Configure AppleTalk? [no]
Configure IP? [yes]:
Configure RIP routing? [yes]:
Configuring interface parameters:
Do you want to configure FastEthernet0/0 interface? [yes]:
  Use the 100baseTX (RJ45) connector? [yes]:
  Operate in full-duplex mode? [no]:
  Configure IP on this interface? [yes]:
    IP address for this interface: **172.16.1.1**
    Subnet mask for this interface [255.255.0.0]: **255.255.255.0**
    Class B network is 172.16.0.0, 24 subnet bits; mask is /24
Do you want to configure FastEthernet0/1 interface? [yes]:
<<<<Output Truncated >>>>
Would you like to go through Auto Secure configuration? [yes]:
no
Auto Secure dialog can be started later using "auto secure" CLI.
The following configuration command script was created:
hostname CCENTRTR1
enable secret 5 $1$0bri$Y2Iq9S9xs89MrZwu7bRuT/
enable password ccent
line vty 0 4
password password
no snmp-server
!
ip routing
no bridge 1
!
interface FastEthernet0/0
no shutdown
media-type 100BaseX
half-duplex
ip address 172.16.1.1 255.255.255.0

```
no mop enabled
<<<<Output Truncated >>>>
[0] Go to the IOS command prompt without saving this config.
[1] Return to the setup without saving this config.
[2] Save this configuration to nvram and exit.
Enter your selection [2]:
```

Just like Catalyst switches, all configuration options done with setup can be, and usually are, manually configured within the CLI. The basic commands already discussed in Chapter 6 apply here, including how to move around in the CLI, setting passwords, and configuring Telnet, SSH, and console connection parameters, for example. All methods for copying and saving configuration files, as well as how to update the IOS, also apply on routers, just as they did with switches.

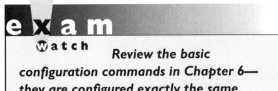

e x a m

ⓦ a t c h   *Review the basic configuration commands in Chapter 6— they are configured exactly the same way on the router. Also, be sure you understand the difference between setup on a switch versus on a router.*

Interface Configuration

One big difference in a router configuration, compared to a switch, is its treatment of interface configuration. While a switch only needs one IP address configured for the VLAN1 interface, *every* active interface on a router requires an IP address. Optionally, you can define a description, duplex, and speed settings just as with a switch.

Remember that the IOS Help system works the same for routers as it does on switches.

Ethernet Interfaces

We enter Interface Configuration mode from Global mode using the following Ethernet interface designations:

For 10 Mb: Router(config)# **interface ethernet** *slot/port*
For 100 Mb: Router(config)# **interface fastethernet** *slot/port*
For Gigabit (1000 mb): Router(config)# **interface gigabitethernet** *slot/port*

If you are not sure what interfaces are on the device or if they are already configured, the **show run** command will tell you. Once in Interface mode you can assign an IP address and subnet mask, add a description, set duplex and speed, and last but not least, issue a **no shutdown** command to bring up the interface.

To configure the IP address on and enable an Ethernet port, use the **ip address** **IP_Address Subnet_Mask** and **no shutdown** commands. You can't use prefix masks here. The simplest configuration is as follows:

```
Rtr1# configure terminal
Rtr1(config)# interface FastEthernet 0/0
Rtr1(config-if)# ip address 199.200.1.1 255.255.255.0
Rtr1(config-if)# no shutdown
```

The following example shows setting some of the options:

```
Rtr1# configure terminal
Rtr1(config)# interface FastEthernet 0/1
Rtr1(config-if)# ip address 199.200.2.1 255.255.255.0
Rtr1(config-if)# description Link to Warehouse
Rtr1(config-if)# full-duplex   ←Options (full/half/Auto)
Rtr1(config-if)# speed 100   ←Options (10/100/Auto)
Rtr1(config-if)# no shutdown
```

Serial Interfaces

As covered earlier, the serial interface requires a little more—a specified encapsulation, if using something other than HDLC, if necessary. The **bandwidth** command is not used by the interface, but communicates to dynamic routing protocols that use bandwidth as part of a metric.

A sample configuration for an interface is shown next:

```
Rtr1# configure terminal
Rtr1(config)# int serial 0/0
Rtr1(config-if)# ip address 135.17.0.1 255.255.255.252

Rtr1(config-if)# no shutdown
```

Note that the IP address is one of only two usable addresses available in subnet 135.17.0.0/30. If you can't see that, go back to Chapter 3 and review with a /30 prefix or 255.255.255.252. This is very common for serial point-to-point connections.

Loopback Interfaces

To configure a loopback interface, you are actually creating a virtual interface. The commands are the same as other interfaces except you define it with the **interface loopback num** command in Global Configuration mode. Then you assign an IP address, subnet mask, and optionally a description from Interface Configuration mode. The interface is enabled by default so you need not issue a **no shutdown**.

```
Rtr1# configure terminal
Rtr1(config)# interface loopback 0
Rtr1(config-if)# ip address 192.168.13.1 255.255.255.0 ← (static IP
address)
Rtr1(config-if)# CTRL-Z
```

Verifying Interface Configuration

While **show run** will give you information about your configuration, the **show ip interface brief** and **show interfaces** commands display the interfaces and more information, including their status. The **show ip interface brief** command provides a quick view of all interfaces and their status.

```
Rtr1#show ip interface brief
 Interface        IP-Address    OK? Method Status                 Protocol
 FastEthernet0/0  199.200.1.1   YES manual up                     up
 FastEthernet0/1  199.200.2.1   YES manual up                     up
 Serial0/0        135.17.0.1    YES manual up                     up
 Serial0/1        unassigned    YES unset  administratively down  down
```

Show Interfaces Command

To see what is going on with your interfaces, you need the **show interfaces** command. Run without options, it displays statistics for all interfaces. If you add the interface identifiers, such as **show interface fa0/0**, it will displays statistics of the specified interface, **fa0/0** in this case. The basic syntax for Fast Ethernet and serial are as follows. Remember that the help (?) feature will display all options.

Router(config)# **show interfaces fastethernet** [*slot/port*]
Router(config)# **show interfaces serial** [*slot/port*]

The following is a sample output for each type of interface:

```
Rtr1#show interfaces FastEthernet 0/0
FastEthernet0/0 is up, line protocol is up
  Hardware is AmdFE, address is 000f.8f4b.a600 (bia 000f.8f4b.a600)
  Description: Internal LAN Interface
  Internet address is 199.200.1.1/24
  MTU 1500 bytes, BW 100000 Kbit, DLY 100 usec,
     reliability 255/255, txload 1/255, rxload 1/255
  Encapsulation ARPA, loopback not set
  Keepalive set (10 sec)
```

```
Full-duplex, 100Mb/s, 100BaseTX/FX
ARP type: ARPA, ARP Timeout 04:00:00
Last input 00:00:07, output 00:00:02, output hang never
Last clearing of "show interface" counters never
Input queue: 0/75/0/0 (size/max/drops/flushes); Total output drops: 0
Queueing strategy: fifo
Output queue: 0/40 (size/max)
5 minute input rate 0 bits/sec, 0 packets/sec
5 minute output rate 0 bits/sec, 0 packets/sec
    417167 packets input, 39317868 bytes
    Received 415431 broadcasts, 0 runts, 0 giants, 0 throttles
    0 input errors, 0 CRC, 0 frame, 0 overrun, 0 ignored
    0 watchdog
    0 input packets with dribble condition detected
    149499 packets output, 17447327 bytes, 0 underruns
    0 output errors, 0 collisions, 3 interface resets
    0 babbles, 0 late collision, 0 deferred
    4 lost carrier, 0 no carrier
    0 output buffer failures, 0 output buffers swapped out
```

On the serial interfaces, the output, while similar, will vary from module type to module type. Note the output is a snapshot in time; you will need to run it again to see changes.

```
Router#show interfaces serial 0/0
Serial 0 is up, line protocol is up
  Hardware is MCI Serial
  Internet address is 150.136.190.203, subnet mask is 255.255.255.0
  MTU 1500 bytes, BW 1544 Kbit, DLY 20000 usec, rely 255/255, load 1/255
  Encapsulation HDLC, loopback not set, keepalive set (10 sec)
  Last input 0:00:07, output 0:00:00, output hang never
  Output queue 0/40, 0 drops; input queue 0/75, 0 drops
  Five minute input rate 0 bits/sec, 0 packets/sec
  Five minute output rate 0 bits/sec, 0 packets/sec
     16263 packets input, 1347238 bytes, 0 no buffer
     Received 13983 broadcasts, 0 runts, 0 giants
     2 input errors, 0 CRC, 0 frame, 0 overrun, 0 ignored, 2 abort
1 carrier transitions
     22146 packets output, 2383680 bytes, 0 underruns
     0 output errors, 0 collisions, 2 interface resets, 0 restarts
```

Loopback output:

```
Router# show interface loopback 0
Loopback0 is up, line protocol is up
  Hardware is Loopback
  Internet address is 192.168.13.1/24
  MTU 1514 bytes, BW 8000000 Kbit, DLY 5000 usec,
     reliability 255/255, txload 1/255, rxload 1/255
  Encapsulation LOOPBACK, loopback not set
```

```
Last input never, output never, output hang never
Last clearing of "show interface" counters never
Queueing strategy: fifo
Output queue 0/0, 0 drops; input queue 0/75, 0 drops
5 minute input rate 0 bits/sec, 0 packets/sec
5 minute output rate 0 bits/sec, 0 packets/sec
   0 packets input, 0 bytes, 0 no buffer
   Received 0 broadcasts, 0 runts, 0 giants, 0 throttles
   0 input errors, 0 CRC, 0 frame, 0 overrun, 0 ignored, 0 abort
   0 packets output, 0 bytes, 0 underruns
   0 output errors, 0 collisions, 0 interface resets
   0 output buffer failures, 0 output buffers swapped out
```

There is a lot of information about an interface using this command, most of which is beyond the scope of this exam. But if you skim over it, you can find out the following information:

- If the interface is up and if the protocol is up (see the next section)
- If the interface has had errors, especially CRC errors
- The speed and duplex of the interface (Ethernet)
- Current utilization and utilization over the last five minutes
- The last time an interface bounced (down then up again)
- The last time the error counters reset
- IP address, subnet mask, and MAC address

We will look at these commands and output in the exercises.

Interface Up and Protocol Up   The first line of output for the **show interfaces** command is probably the most important and useful in troubleshooting or verifying interface connectivity. There are two parts to an interface connection: first there has to be a physical connection (wires connected properly) and second, a recognized signal the device receives. This signal is some form of keep-alive packets, a signal designed specifically to keep a link up. Without periodic signals, the interface would shut down, assuming the connection was lost or communication ended. In many ways, it is like the music that is played over the line when a phone call is on hold. If it was silent, the listener would have no way of knowing that the call hadn't been cut off.

The first part of the message (interface up/down) refers to the physical connection, OSI Layer 1—is there a physical connection? Status down means either no cable connected or no signal detected; there is no electricity on the wire. Status up means a signal is detected; there is electricity on the wire. Ethernet just requires connection to a live switch, but serial interfaces require a properly configured device on the other end of the cable. Interface up means the physical connection works. "Interface is administratively down" means the interface is shut down; issue a **no shutdown**.

The second part of the message (protocol up/down) refers to Layer 2 of the OSI model (Ethernet or serial protocol, like HDLC or PPP). Protocol up means the protocol is configured properly and a communication link is working. The signal is understood or recognized by the interface. If it is improperly configured or configured differently on both ends, there is a signal but it is unrecognized and therefore unusable. Imagine you are near a group speaking a language you are unfamiliar with. You can tell they are speaking, but you can't understand it and won't be successful communicating with them.

If the status is up but the protocol is down on a serial link, it means we can see the electricity on the wire, but we don't understand what is being said. We are not agreeing on protocols: *you are talking PPP, but I only understand HDLC*, like two people trying to communicate in two different languages.

EXERCISE 9-1

Initial Router Configuration

In this exercise, we demonstrate the steps an administrator would take to do basic router configuration. We will review the steps common to both routers and switches, and then begin to address features unique to routers, specifically configuring interfaces. You'll perform this exercise using Boson's NetSim. Launch Lab 9-1 and review the topology.

We will be working on RouterA, then RouterB, and finally RouterC. We can go through the first one together, and you can try your hand at the other two.

Task 1: RouterA: Get Started

1. Using the skills from the other labs, open a console session for Host A.11 and verify connectivity to Host A.22 and SwitchA. But you can't ping any further. That is true for all three LANs; the host and switch can ping each other but no further. This is because the routers are not configured. Unlike switches, they do not work if not configured.

2. Create a console session for RouterA and note there is no security (login or enable passwords).

3. From Privileged mode, do a **show run** and look at the configuration. Most of it should be pretty familiar to you by now. There are a couple of serial interfaces that we won't use until Chapter 10. There are also only five VTY lines.

4. Use the skills you've acquired and, if necessary, the steps in the "Basic Cisco Configuration Steps" from Chapter 6 to create the basic configuration (doing steps 1–3 and then step 10). If you need them, the steps are shown here:

```
hostname RouterA
enable secret ccent
username student password cisco

banner login #

--------------Warning!--------------------

Terms of Use

Unauthorized or improper use of our servers or network or systems
within the network, will result in administrative disciplinary
action and civil and criminal penalties.

#
line con 0
password cisco
 history size 20
 login
line vty 0 4
 history size 20
 login local
```

5. Use the **show run** command to confirm your work.

6. Save your work.

Task 2: Configure Interfaces

1. Looking at the topology diagram or IP address table, we can see that the LAN interface is FastEthernet 0/0 and the IP address should be 10.0.0.1/24. The steps are as follows:

```
SwitchC(config)#interface fastethernet 0/0    (int fa0/0)
SwitchC(config-if)#ip address 10.0.0.1 255.255.255.0
SwitchC(config-if)#description LAN A connection
SwitchC(config-if)#no shutdown    (no shut)
SwitchC(config-if)#CTRL-Z
```

Confirm that you are able to ping the LAN A hosts and switch.

2. Looking at the topology diagram or IP address table, we can see that the interface RouterB is FastEthernet 0/1 and the IP address should be 10.1.1.2/30. The steps are as follows:

```
SwitchC(config)#interface fastethernet 0/1    (int fa0/1)
SwitchC(config-if)#ip address 10.1.1.2 255.255.255.252
SwitchC(config-if)#description Link to RouterB
SwitchC(config-if)#no shutdown    (no shut)
SwitchC(config-if)#CTRL-z
```

You can't ping RouterB until it is configured.

3. Use the **show interfaces (sho int)** or **show interfaces *int-id*** (Fa0/0) command to confirm your work.

4. Save your work.

Task 3: Configure RouterC

RouterC is identical to RouterA except for the hostname and IP addresses. Use the topology diagram and/or IP address table to get the correct information.

1. Try to use Tasks 2 and 3 and the IP address table to configure RouterC.

   If you get stuck, the "Lab Solutions" section in the PDF Lab Book has the correct steps.

Task 4: Configure RouterB

RouterB is a little different from RouterC or RouterA beyond the hostname and IP addresses. First, it has three FastEthernet interfaces, and second, it is a different model of router, so the interface IDs are a bit different, with each being in its own module. Use the topology diagram and/or IP address table to get the correct information.

1. Try to use Tasks 2 and 3 and the IP address table to configure RouterB.

   If you get stuck, the "Lab Solutions" section has the correct steps.

2. You should be able to ping LAN B devices and the adjacent interfaces on RouterC and RouterA, but no further. For that, we will need to implement routing of some kind. That is covered in the next lab.

Configure Routing

Basic configurations aside, let's not forget that the main purpose of a router is routing—the sharing of routing table information with other routers. Therefore, it makes sense that, at some point, you'll need to configure routing settings. In Chapter 8, we covered some of the basics of routing logic and protocols, and how the routing table is used to determine which route for a given packet is best. Basically speaking, routing tables can be updated in three ways: through directly connected routes, through statically added routes, or by routes learned through the use of a dynamic routing protocol. In this chapter, we will look at the first two and then look at dynamic routing in Chapter 10.

We will use this short output from the **show ip route** command for our examples:

```
Router1#show ip route
---Legend omitted---
Gateway of last resort is not set
D    192.168.11.0/24 [90/284160] via 192.168.1.1, 00:04:19,
FastEthernet0/0
O    192.168.10.0/24 [110/11] via 192.168.2.1, 00:01:01, s0/0
R    192.168.9.0/24 [120/1] via 192.168.4.1, 00:00:07, s0/1
C    192.168.1.0/24 is directly connected, FastEthernet0/0
C    192.168.5.0/24 is directly connected, FastEthernet0/1
S    192.168.3.0/24 [1/0] via 192.168.1.1
```

Directly Connected Routes

The first routes added to the routing table are the connected routes, those with a C in the Code column. They are added to the routing table for each enabled interface with a correctly configured IP address. They know about that network because they are a part of the network. The interface makes them a member just like any other device. An analogy would be that you know about your neighborhood because you live there. For example, consider the network in Figure 9-4. Router B will automatically forward packets to the four networks it knows about—1.1.12.0/24, 172.16.4.0/30, 172.16.4.4/30, and 172.16.2.0/24. These routes are added to the routing table as soon as the interface is enabled with the appropriate IP address and subnet mask.

Let's study this diagram a bit to see what we can deduce from it—play a little Sherlock Holmes. Notice that the serial links, represented by lightning bolt lines, are point-to-point connections with a /30 prefix. If you recall from Chapter 3, this is the smallest subnet you can make with just four addresses: subnet ID, two hosts, and the broadcast. This is a common configuration for serial links between routers.

FIGURE 9-4

A sample
network

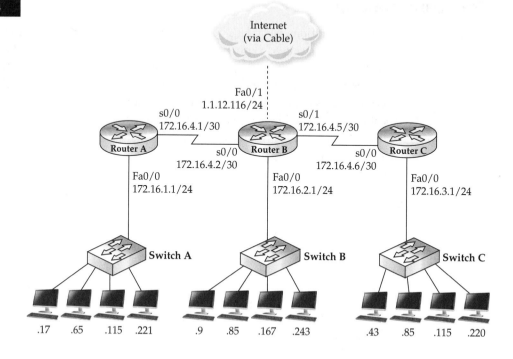

Make sure that you understand it and can figure out the four addresses to use. We can assume these LANs do not represent floors in a building or even buildings in an office park. In both of those cases, we would have connected them with Ethernet, giving us 100 Mbps or even Gigabit connections, instead of maybe 1.54 Mbps from T1 links. Serial links are very slow links.

The LANs have a /24 prefix, so we know there could be up to 253 hosts plus the router in each subnet. We assigned the first available host address to the routers, a common standard practice but not a rule. The numbers below the hosts represent the host portion, fourth octet, of the address pool shared with their router—their default gateway to the outside. In LAN B that would be 172.16.2.9, etc. The gaps in numbers indicate that they are just representative of the hosts on the LAN.

The connection to an Internet cable provider is different. Notice it is Ethernet of some kind, up to 100 Mbps. The actual speed is set by their agreement and controlled by the provider. It is not a point-to-point connection; it has a /24 prefix, meaning the cable company is treating up to 253 of its customers as if they are on a LAN. A point-to-point link eats up four public addresses per customer instead of the one in this configuration. It means the same block of addresses can support 253 customers on the same subnet instead of only 64 customers each on their own subnet. The following output shows what the connected routes would look like in the routing table for Router B.

```
RouterB#show ip route
---Legend omitted---
Gateway of last resort is not set
C    1.1.12.0/24 is directly connected, FastEthernet0/1
C    172.16.2.0/24 is directly connected, FastEthernet0/0
C    172.16.4.0/30 is directly connected, Serial0/0
C    172.16.4.4/30 is directly connected, Serial0/1
```

Static Routes

The next method used to add routes to a table is *static routing*. Exactly what it sounds like, static routing basically has the administrator manually define routes using the CLI. The benefit is lower CPU cycles and processing power on the router. The disadvantage, of course, is that any change on the network (a link going down or something else) must be manually updated on the router, otherwise packets will be misdirected.

In Figure 9-4, a packet received by Router B intended for 172.16.1.65, or any of the hosts on LAN A or C, would be dropped. The router would compare the destination address to the routing table and, finding no match, discard the packet. To ensure this packet reaches the end destination, you could add a static route to Router B's table, telling it to which interface it should forward the packet. Simply allow Router B to route the packet to 172.16.1.5 by providing the destination network ID and subnet mask, and the next-hop address; the next-hop address is the IP address of the destination router point along the pathway to the end destination.

To add a static route, use the **ip route** *network_addr subnet_mask* [*next_hop_ addr* | **egress_int**] command. The following example shows the most common form of entries for Router B so it would know how to forward packets to the other two LANs. It already knows about LAN B. The command basically tells Router B, "If you receive a packet with a destination IP address in the 172.16.1.0/24 range, send it to the next hop, 172.16.4.1. That router knows where the network resides." The second statement does the same for LAN C.

```
Router_B# configure terminal
Router_B(config)# ip route 172.16.1.0 255.255.255.0 172.16.4.1
Router_B(config)# ip route 172.16.3.0 255.255.255.0 172.16.4.6
```

Using the egress interface (outbound interface) would look like the following. In this form, the command tells Router B, "If you receive a packet with a destination IP address in the 172.16.1.0/24 range, send it out interface s0/0. It will get to the destination because there is only one other device on the segment." Using the interface works with Ethernet, but it is not a scalable solution because of the possibility of many other devices on that segment.

```
Router_B# configure terminal
Router_B(config)# ip route 172.16.1.0 255.255.255.0 s0/0
Router_B(config)# ip route 172.16.3.0 255.255.255.0 s0/1
```

The resulting routing table entries would look like the following:

```
RouterB#show ip route
---Legend omitted---
Gateway of last resort is not set
C    1.1.12.0/24 is directly connected, FastEthernet0/1
S    172.16.1.0/24 [1/0] via 172.16.4.1
C    172.16.2.0/24 is directly connected, FastEthernet0/0
S    172.16.3.0/24 [1/0] via 172.16.4.6
C    172.16.4.0/30 is directly connected, Serial0/0
C    172.16.4.4/30 is directly connected, Serial0/1
```

So we're done, right? Well, no. The packet will get to the LAN hosts, but what if they reply? In LAN A, the reply would go to Router A, who knows about Router B's s0/0 interface, but nothing beyond that. The same is true with packets sent to LAN C. The following shows the routing tables for Router A and Router C. Without a route to 172.16.2.0, the routers would drop the packets as undeliverable.

```
RouterA#show ip route
---Legend omitted---
Gateway of last resort is not set
C    172.16.1.0/24 is directly connected, FastEthernet0/0
C    172.16.4.0/30 is directly connected, Serial0/0

RouterC#show ip route
---Legend omitted---
Gateway of last resort is not set
C    172.16.3.0/24 is directly connected, FastEthernet0/0
C    172.16.4.4/30 is directly connected, Serial0/0
```

Look over the routing tables and the diagram and figure out how many static routes need to be added to Router A and Router C. The answer would be two, one for each of the other two LANs. What about destinations on the Internet? Clearly we can't put static routes for every network; there has got to be a better way.

exam

ⓦatch *Be sure you are very, very familiar with the syntax for adding a static route. Keep in mind that you do not need to know every router port along the path— you only need the address of the next hop. Another thing to watch for is to make sure the next-hop address is in the same subnet as the interface on your router (it must* *be in the same subnet for your router to ARP for it). Lastly, don't forget that if you use static routing for your network, you'll have to ensure that the static routes are added appropriately to every router. In other words, in a scenario/troubleshooting situation, verify that the route is added to each router along the pathway!*

Static Route Preference   A last note worth mentioning with static routes concerns administrative distance (AD). In Chapter 8, we learned that administrative distance is used by routers to make a determination as to which route is best and added to the routing table. If the same route is also learned by any dynamic routing protocol, the administrative distance of static routes is 1, which is the lowest AD, except for directly connected routes. Therefore, if a static route is configured, it will always be used in lieu of any route learned, no matter which protocol it learns it from.

Backup Static Routes   There is one exception to this rule about statically defined routes being chosen over any learned route. That is a *backup static route*, which is created by an administrator, is added to the table as a backup if the RIP, OSPF, or other routing protocol–learned route fails. Since by default, a static route is always used first, a workaround is required. The administrators can manually define the administrative distance of the static route by simply adding the *AD* to the end of the command. In the following examples, the static routes with an AD of 150 would only be used if the routing protocol fails. For example, OSPF's AD is 110, so as long as it is running, its routes will be preferred; if it fails, the statics take over.

```
Router_B# configure terminal
Router_B(config)# ip route 172.16.1.0 255.255.255.0 172.16.4.1 150
Router_B(config)# ip route 172.16.3.0 255.255.255.0 172.16.4.6 150
```

e x a m

ⓦ a t c h
You can change the administrative distance on any static route by simply adding it to the end of the command. Sometimes a static route is configured to be used should the learned route fail. This process—a backup static route—is created by changing the AD for the static route to something higher than the routing protocol in use. For instance, to create a backup static route with an AD of 200, the command would look like this: ip route network_id subnet_mask next_hop 200.

Default Routes

There is a special form of static route called a *default route* that is found in most edge routers' routing table. Default routes are created to provide a route for all packets that do not match any other route listed in the table. In other words, a default route basically says to the router, "If you receive a packet with a destination address not listed anywhere else in the routing table, send it here." Perfect for your router sitting on the edge, forwarding packets from one network to the rest of the world and back. A default route would be all you needed to add to the configuration, telling the router, "Send all unknown packet addresses through this interface."

A default route is manually added to the routing table using the **ip route 0.0.0.0 0.0.0.0** *next_hop_addr* command. The four zeroes, called quad-zero, are acting like wildcard characters. The first quad-zero means "any network," while the second quad-zero means "any mask." To see an example, consider the network displayed in Figure 9-4 and look at the following entries:

```
Router_A# configure terminal
Router_A(config)# ip route 0.0.0.0 0.0.0.0 172.16.4.2

Router_C# configure terminal
Router_C(config)# ip route 0.0.0.0 0.0.0.0 s0/0

Router_B# configure terminal
Router_B(config)# ip route 172.16.1.0 255.255.255.0 172.16.4.1
Router_B(config)# ip route 172.16.3.0 255.255.255.0 172.16.4.6
Router_B(config)# ip route 0.0.0.0 0.0.0.0 1.1.12.1
```

Our resulting routing tables would look like the following output:

```
RouterA#show ip route
---Legend omitted---
```

```
Gateway of last resort is 0.0.0.0 to network 0.0.0.0
C    172.16.1.0/24 is directly connected, FastEthernet0/0
C    172.16.4.0/30 is directly connected, Serial0/0
S*   0.0.0.0/0 [1/0] via 172.16.4.2

RouterB#show ip route
---Legend omitted---
Gateway of last resort is 0.0.0.0 to network 0.0.0.0
C    1.1.12.0/24 is directly connected, FastEthernet0/1
S    172.16.1.0/24 [1/0] via 172.16.4.1
C    172.16.2.0/24 is directly connected, FastEthernet0/0
S    172.16.3.0/24 [1/0] via 172.16.4.6
C    172.16.4.0/30 is directly connected, Serial0/0
C    172.16.4.4/30 is directly connected, Serial0/1
S*   0.0.0.0/0 [1/0] via 1.1.12.1

RouterC#show ip route
---Legend omitted---
Gateway of last resort is 0.0.0.0 to network 0.0.0.0
C    172.16.3.0/24 is directly connected, FastEthernet0/0
C    172.16.4.4/30 is directly connected, Serial0/0
S*   0.0.0.0/0 is directly connected, Serial 0/0
```

Notice that for Routers A and C, we no longer need the regular static routes we discussed earlier because the default route sends everything unknown to Router B, which includes the other two LANs. Routers A and C with their LANs are called *stub networks*—they are the end of the line. There are no other networks beyond them, so they can use a single default route much the same as Router B added. Router B still needs our two static routes to find LANs A and C, but now forwards all unknown addresses out to the ISP's gateway address. You will find a route like this on edge routers connected to the Internet.

e x a m
ⓦatch   *Remember that a packet received by a router destined for a network that is not in the router's routing table will be discarded. The default route provides a route for all unknown destination networks* *with one single command. Typically, this is most often seen on border routers or SOHO installations with one interface to the Internet, but you may encounter this in many scenario questions on the exam.*

As we look over another routing table next, let's review the logic of routing:

1. **Is it in the routing table?** If it's not in the table, the packet will be dropped.

2. **Most specific subnet match** Look at 192.168.9.0: there are two entries: first, one with a prefix /30 and then one with /24. The same is true for 192.168.10.0.

3. **Best administrative distance** To get in the routing table, they had to be the best of the best based on administrative distance [AD/Metric]. Directly connected segments with AD of 0 trump all others, followed by static routes with an AD of 1, etc. Here the routing protocol winners compete on AD with other methods with a route to same network.

4. **Best metric** To get to step 3, a route had to have the best metric to that destination that routing protocol had. They compete among themselves and only the best goes on to step 3.

```
Router1#show ip route
---Legend omitted---
Gateway of last resort is 0.0.0.0 to network 0.0.0.0
C    192.168.1.0/24 is directly connected, FastEthernet0/0
S    192.168.3.0/24 [1/0] via 192.168.1.1
C    192.168.5.0/24 is directly connected, FastEthernet0/1
C    192.168.9.0/30 is directly connected, Serial 0/1
R    192.168.9.0/24 [120/1] via 192.168.4.1, 00:00:07, s0/1
C    192.168.10.0/30 is directly connected, Serial 0/0
O    192.168.10.0/24 [110/11] via 192.168.2.1, 00:01:01, s0/0
D    192.168.11.0/24 [90/284160] via 192.168.1.1, 00:04:19,
FastEthernet0/0
S*   0.0.0.0/0 is directly connected, Serial 0/2
```

The *Gateway of last resort* statement means that if there is no entry in the table, the packet will be forwarded via the static default route 0.0.0.0. It means no packets would be discarded at this level; we send everything unknown to the default.

EXERCISE 9-2

MHE Lab

Static Route Configuration

In this exercise, we demonstrate the steps an administrator would take to configure static routes, including default static routes. You'll perform this exercise using Boson's NetSim. Launch Lab 9-2 and review the topology.

Task 1: RouterB: Static Routes

1. Using the skills from the earlier exercises, open a console session for Host B.77 and verify connectivity to SwitchB and any interface on RouterB. But you can't ping any further. That is true for all three LANs. The host, the switch, and the router can ping each other, and the router can ping the near interface on the other two routers because of the shared link but no further. That is because the routers do not have routes in their routing tables yet.

2. Create a console session for RouterB and go to Privileged mode.

3. From Privileged mode, do a **show ip route** and look over the results. You should see that RouterB knows only about its connected routes. That is true of the other two as well.

4. From the topology diagram, we know that LAN A is 10.0.0.0/24 and that we have to get to it through interface 10.1.1.2 on RouterA. LAN C is 10.0.2.0/24. The following commands confirm that RouterB can ping A.11, A.22, and SwitchA (10.0.0.2):

```
config t
ip route 10.0.0.0 255.255.255.0 10.1.1.2
CTRL-Z
```

5. Using the same logic, add a static route to get to LAN C, which is 10.0.2.0/24.

```
config t
ip route 10.0.2.0 255.255.255.0 10.1.1.6
CTRL-Z
```

Confirm that RouterB can ping C.13 and SwitchC (10.0.2.2).

6. From Privileged mode, do a **show ip route** and look at the results. You should see that RouterB now has static routes to the other two LANs in addition to the connected routes. Life is good!

7. Do a **show run** to see where the routes appear in the configuration.

8. Open a console session on Host B.77 and ping A.11. What happened and why? Try A.22 and C.13. Any difference? The ping actually worked, so why didn't you get a successful result? Think about that, and we will fix it in the next task.

9. Save your work.

Task 2: RouterA: Static Routes

Our pings from the last task actually made it to their destinations. Host B.77 sent the echo requests to RouterB, its default gateway, and RouterB knew where each of the LANs were, so it forwarded them. Each host, as requested, sent echo replies back to their default gateway. So far, so good. But RouterA and RouterC do not know where Host B.77 is or anything about the 10.0.1.0/24 network, so it dropped the packets.

1. Looking at the topology diagram, we can see that we can add the following two routes to RouterA to solve this problem. Go ahead and do it.

```
config t
ip route 10.0.1.0 255.255.255.0 10.1.1.1
ip route 10.0.2.0 255.255.255.0 10.1.1.1
CTRL-Z
```

Confirm that Host A.11 or A.22 can now ping B.77 and that B.77 can ping Host A.11 or A.22. We still can't ping C.13 because we don't have routes on RouterC yet. But, don't celebrate yet.

From Host A.11 or A.22, ping 10.1.1.5 and 10.1.1.6, which are the interfaces connecting RouterB and RouterC. How did that work? Try pinging from RouterA. It fails because RouterA doesn't know where that subnet is. Do a **show ip route** to confirm that.

When building static routes, it is important to not overlook any possible destinations. While users would never need to go to connecting links, admins might, so don't overlook them. We do not have full convergence until all destinations can be reached. It looks like we should have done the following. Add the missing route and see whether it solves the problem.

```
config t
ip route 10.0.1.0 255.255.255.0 10.1.1.1
ip route 10.0.2.0 255.255.255.0 10.1.1.1
ip route 10.1.1.4 255.255.255.252 10.1.1.1
CTRL-Z
```

Actually, it solves only half the problem. We can ping 10.1.1.5 but not 10.1.1.6 because RouterC doesn't know where these pings are coming from or how to return them. We'll fix that in the next task.

2. Save your work.

Task 3: Default Routes

It should be obvious by now that static routes can get pretty numerous on larger networks and that it is easy to overlook some subnets. RouterC (and RouterA) are what are called *stub routers*, because there are no more routers beyond them. Notice that all three static routes in the last task pointed to the same destination; the same would be true for RouterC. This means that instead of building all those static routes, we could have put in a single default route.

1. Try the following on RouterC:

   ```
   config t
   ip route 0.0.0.0 0.0.0.0 10.1.1.5
   CTRL-Z
   ```

   Confirm that all hosts can now ping each other and all interfaces on each router.

2. Run **show ip route** to see that you now have a static route (S*) and a *Gateway of last resort is 10.1.1.5 to network 0.0.0.0.*

3. Save your work.

4. Return to RouterA and replace the static routes with a default route. While not necessary for connectivity, it gives you a chance to see how to remove static routes. Adding new ones does not remove old ones.

   ```
   config t
   no ip route 10.0.1.0 255.255.255.0 10.1.1.1
   no ip route 10.0.2.0 255.255.255.0 10.1.1.1
   no ip route 10.1.1.4 255.255.255.252 10.1.1.1
   ip route 0.0.0.0 0.0.0.0 10.1.1.1
   CTRL-Z
   ```

   Confirm that all hosts can now ping each other and all interfaces on each router.

5. Run **show ip route** to confirm your changes.

6. Do a **show run** to see where the routes appear in the configuration.

7. Save your work.

Cisco Discovery Protocol (CDP)

CDP is a Cisco proprietary Layer 2 (Data Link) protocol that is used to discover and share information about any other Cisco devices that are directly connected. Information shared on 60-second intervals consists of the IOS version, type of device, model platform, IP address, and so on. CDP announcements are sent using a multicast out each connected interface every 60 seconds by default. Other Cisco devices that support CDP accept those messages and store them in a table that can be viewed using the **show cdp neighbors** command. The CDP table information is refreshed with every incoming cycle. There is a 180-second holdtime timer that is reinitialized with each update. This holdtime defines how long an entry will stay in the table if no announcements are received.

While a very handy feature in discovering the network, it also presents some security risks so it should always be turned off on interfaces connecting to the outside world. It is on by default in most devices.

There are several commands we should look at, starting with the **show cdp neighbors [detail]** command in Privileged Exec mode. This command displays information about neighboring Cisco devices learned from CDP messages.

```
Router#show cdp neighbors
Capability Codes: R - Router, T - Trans Bridge, B - Source Route Bridge
                  S - Switch, H - Host, I - IGMP, r - Repeater

Device ID       Local Intrfce     Holdtme     Capability  Platform    Port ID
Switch2         Fas 0/0           157         S           2950-12     Fas 0/12
Router2         Fas 0/1           163         R           2621XM      Fas 0/3
--output omitted--
```

Router# identifies which device ran the command (us). **Device ID** is the hostname of the remote device. **Local Interface** is our egress interface. **Port ID** is the remote device's ingress port.

Using the detail option of the **show cdp neighbors [detail]** command in Privileged Exec mode, we can now get quite detailed information about any nearby devices. Since CDP runs in Layer 2, IP connectivity to the other device is not necessary. If you are having trouble reaching a neighbor device by SSH, Telnet, or even ping, you can use this command to see the IP address of the device.

```
Router>enable
Router#show cdp neighbors detail
------------------------
Device ID: Switch2                              ←Device's hostname
Entry address(es):
```

```
  IP address: 192.168.1.243              ←Device's hostname
Platform: cisco WS-C2950-12,  Capabilities: Trans-Bridge Switch
Interface: FastEthernet0/12,  Port ID (outgoing port):
FastEthernet0/0
Holdtime : 137 sec                       ←Time remaining on holdtime
Version :
Cisco Internetwork Operating System Software
IOS (tm) C2950 Software (C2950-C3H2S-M), Version 12.0(5.3)WC(1),
MAINTENANCE INTERIM SOFTWARE             ←Software version and image
Copyright (c) 1986-2001 by cisco Systems, Inc.
Compiled Mon 30-Apr-01 07:56 by devgoyal
advertisement version: 2
Protocol Hello:  OUT=0x00000C, Protocol ID=0x0112; payload
len=27, value=00000000FFFFFFFF010121FF0000000000000006D6AC46C0
FF0001
VTP Management Domain: ''
Management address(es):
-------------------------
Device ID: Router2
Entry address(es):
  IP address: 192.168.1.240
Platform: Cisco 2621XM,  Capabilities: Switch IGMP
Interface: FastEthernet0/3,  Port ID (outgoing port):
FastEthernet0/1
Holdtime : 142 sec
Version :
Cisco IOS Software, C2600 Software (C2600-ADVIPSERVICESK9-M),
Version 12.3(4)T4,  RELEASE SOFTWARE (fc2)
Technical Support: http://www.cisco.com/techsupport
Copyright (c) 1986-2004 by Cisco Systems, Inc.
Compiled Thu 11-Mar-04 19:57 by eaarmas
advertisement version: 2
VTP Management Domain: ''
Duplex: full
Management address(es):
```

Other CDP commands we will look at in the exercises are as follows:

The **cdp enable** / **no cdp enable** command in Interface Configuration mode can be used to disable CDP messages from going out that interface. This is a good idea with any outside router interfaces.

The **cdp run** / **no cdp run** command in Global Configuration mode can be used to enable or disable CDP messages on the entire device.

The **show cdp** command in Privileged Exec mode can be used to display global CDP information, including timer and holdtime information.

```
Router# show cdp

Global CDP information:
Sending CDP packets every 60 seconds
Sending a holdtime value of 180 seconds
Sending CDPv2 advertisements is enabled
```

EXERCISE 9-3

CDP Exploration

In this exercise we demonstrate using the Cisco Discovery Protocol (CDP) features to explore our immediate neighborhood. You'll perform this exercise using Boson's NetSim. Launch Lab 9-3 and review the topology.

Task 1: Run the show cdp neighbors Command

1. Using the skills from the other labs, open a console session for Host B.77.

2. Telnet to RouterB. Remember that the username/password is student and cisco. We could do this from the console of a device, but let's practice remote access.

3. In Privileged mode, run the **show cdp neighbors** command. The result should look like this:

```
RouterB#show cdp neighbors
Capability Codes: R - Router, T - Trans Bridge, B - Source Route
Bridge, S -Switch, H - Host, i - IGMP, r - Repeater
Device ID    Local Intrfce  Holdtme  Capability  Platform    Port ID
SwitchB      Fas0/0         153          T S     2960-24TT-Fas 0/1
RouterC      Fas2/0         153          R       2811        Fas 0/1
RouterA      Fas1/0         153          R       2811        Fas 0/1

RouterB#
```

Device ID is the hostname of the remote device. The Local Interface is our egress interface. Port ID is the remote device's ingress port. Capability is the type of device router/switch. Platform is the model info, and the holdtime is how many seconds before the information is dropped if there is no new update.

4. Notice that you get only adjacent Cisco devices. It also uses the hostname for the device.

5. Run the **show cdp neighbors detail** command. Look at the result, and notice there is a lot of information, including IP address and software version information. CDP runs at Layer 2, so if the other end had a bad IP address (wrong network), you could see that.

6. Run the **show cdp entry RouterC** command and note that you now see the same information except for RouterC.

7. Exit back to Host B.77 and Telnet to at least one other router and a switch. Then run the previous commands again, noting your results and that only Cisco devices appear.

Task 2: Other CDP Commands

CDP does not actually discover anything. Each Cisco device sends out its information every 60 seconds, and other Cisco devices save that information on their neighbors.

1. From RouterB (it could be any Cisco device), remote or console connection, run the **show cdp** command. Note it tells you how often it sends CDP packets and how long the holdtime is set to. It is basically saying it will keep the data until three update cycles have been missed, the device is shut down, or the device is disconnected.

2. Run the **show cdp interfaces** command. It shows us the status of each interface and then whether we have turned CDP off on a particular interface with the **Device(config-if)#no cdp enable** command in Interface Configuration mode. We often do this on interfaces that connect to the outside world. We don't want to share this information.

3. Run the **show cdp traffic** command. It shows us how many packets we've sent and received and a breakdown of any that were received defective.

4. In Global Configuration mode, run the **no cdp run** command and then try any of the **cdp** commands. You should get a message on each: % *CDP is not enabled*. This device is no longer participating in CDP at all.

5. In Global Configuration mode, turn CDP back on with the **cdp run** command and then try any of the **cdp** commands. You should be back in business.

6. Experiment with any of the commands on other devices you want.

7. There's no need to save your work; we haven't made any changes we want to keep.

CERTIFICATION OBJECTIVE 9.03

InterVLAN Routing

In Chapter 7, we looked at VLANs and trunking on Layer 2 switches, during which we configured switch interfaces for our trunks on the two switches shown in Figure 9-5. We were unable to show the routing steps required to finish our work because we hadn't covered routers yet. Now we are going to finish it by introducing you to router on a stick.

Router on a Stick

While VLAN-capable Layer 2 switches allow multiple VLANs to coexist, there is no way for two machines attached to the same switch but in different VLANs to

FIGURE 9-5

Sample network
from Chapter 7

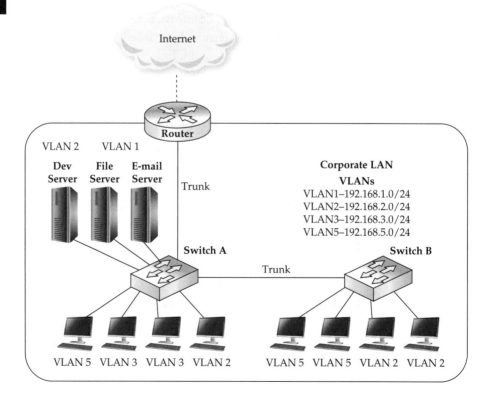

FIGURE 9-6

Historical and
router on stick
implementations

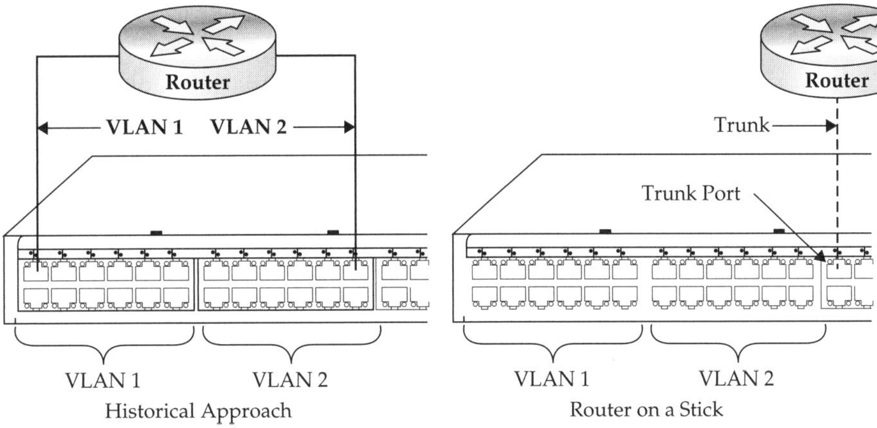

Router

VLAN 1   VLAN 2

VLAN 1   VLAN 2

Historical Approach

Router

Trunk

Trunk Port

VLAN 1   VLAN 2

Router on a Stick

communicate. Even though the Ethernet frames may pass over some of the same
wires, they are blind to each other. To communicate with each other, a router must
be connected to both VLANs, which will then forward the packets between them.
In the early days, to connect two LANs, the router required a separate interface for
each LAN or VLAN. With trunking, the router may have only a single Ethernet
interface with virtual subinterfaces in both VLANs. Hence, names like router on
a stick or one-armed routing. Figure 9-6 shows both methods.

Configuring Router on a Stick

The only things we've added to the figure are the IP subnets that we've assigned
to each VLAN. Notice that we chose to use the VLAN number as the third octet
in our 192.168 address. This is not necessary and doesn't impact the VLANs in
any way, but it is an option and it helps to keep things orderly. It is always useful to
correlate information, so here we chose to correlate VLAN_Number and IP_Subnet.
This will help in understanding and will potentially make troubleshooting easier—in
this way we are encoding metadata.

All four VLANs are included in the trunk between Switch A and the router and
could have been configured with the following commands. Since we didn't include
a **switchport trunk allowed vlan** command, all VLANs are included in the trunk.

```
Switch_A#configure terminal
Switch_A(config)#interface fa0/1
Switch_A(config-if)#switchport mode trunk
Switch_A(config-if)end
```

On the router, we are going to configure the Fast Ethernet 0/0 interface to have what are called subinterfaces. This feature can only be configured on Ethernet interfaces that support 100 Mbps or faster. You can think of these subinterfaces as virtual interfaces that break up our interface opening into four separate openings, like replacing a garage door with four personal size doors. The steps are as follows:

1. Go to the physical interface and issue a **no shutdown** to enable the interface.

2. Create each subinterface by using the **interface** command, adding a unique decimal to the interface ID for each subinterface. (Example: Fa0/0 becomes Fa0/0.1.) While not necessary, we used the VLAN number as the decimal for clarity and ease of understanding and troubleshooting. Note that we underlined the 1s in the first subinterface in the example later. The pattern is repeated on each of the other subinterfaces.

3. Define an IP address and subnet mask.

4. Use the **encapsulation dot1q** *vlan_id* [native] command to enable dot1Q encapsulation on a subinterface for each VLAN. The VLAN ID matches our switch configuration.

5. The **native** option changes our native VLAN to VLAN3 to match our settings on the switch. Recall from Chapter 7 that the native VLAN is the untagged VLAN on an 802.1Q trunked switchport. Whatever we have it set to on the switches must match the router.

6. Optional: On each subinterface, we could add descriptions as shown.

The result might look like this:

```
Router(config)#interface fastEthernet 0/0
Router(config-if)#no shutdown
Router(config)#interface fastEthernet 0/0.1
Router(config-subif)#encapsulation dot1Q 1
Router(config-subif)#ip address 192.168.1.1 255.255.255.0
Router(config-subif)#description Sales Office - VLAN 1
Router(config-subif)#interface fastEthernet 0/0.2
Router(config-subif)#encapsulation dot1Q 2
Router(config-subif)#ip address 192.168.2.1 255.255.255.0
Router(config-subif)#description Manufacturing - VLAN 2
Router(config-subif)#interface fastEthernet 0/0.3
Router(config-subif)#encapsulation dot1Q 3 native
```

```
Router(config-subif)#ip address 192.168.3.1 255.255.255.0
Router(config-subif)#description Research - VLAN 3
Router(config-subif)#interface fastEthernet 0/0.5
Router(config-subif)#encapsulation dot1Q 5
Router(config-subif)#ip address 192.168.5.1 255.255.255.0
Router(config-subif)#description Accounting - VLAN 5
Router(config-subif)#CTRL-Z
```

Confirming the Subinterfaces and Routing Table

It is important to understand that the router now sees these as four interfaces and displays them accordingly on commands like **show run** and **show ip route**. The following is an abbreviated output of the **show run** command:

```
Router #show running-config
Building configuration...
!
!--Output omitted--
interface FastEthernet0/0
 duplex auto
 speed auto
!
interface FastEthernet0/0.1
 encapsulation dot1Q 1
 ip address 192.168.1.1 255.255.255.0
!
interface FastEthernet0/0.2
 encapsulation dot1Q 2
 ip address 192.168.2.1 255.255.255.0
!
interface FastEthernet0/0.3
 encapsulation dot1Q 3 native
 ip address 192.168.3.1 255.255.255.0
!
interface FastEthernet0/0.5
 encapsulation dot1Q 5
 ip address 192.168.5.1 255.255.255.0
!
interface FastEthernet0/1
 no ip address
 shutdown
!--Output omitted--
```

Here is an example of the **show ip route** command with subinterfaces:

```
Router#show ip route
Codes: C - connected, S - static, R - RIP, M - mobile, B - BGP
       D - EIGRP, EX - EIGRP external, O - OSPF, IA - OSPF inter area
       N1 - OSPF NSSA external type 1, N2 - OSPF NSSA external type 2
       E1 - OSPF external type 1, E2 - OSPF external type 2
       i - IS-IS, su - IS-IS summary, L1 - IS-IS level-1, L2 - IS-IS level
       ia - IS-IS inter area, * - candidate default, U - per-user static
       o - ODR, P - periodic downloaded static route

Gateway of last resort is not set

C    192.168.1.0/24 is directly connected, FastEthernet0/0.1
C    192.168.2.0/24 is directly connected, FastEthernet0/0.2
C    192.168.3.0/24 is directly connected, FastEthernet0/0.3
C    192.168.5.0/24 is directly connected, FastEthernet0/0.5
```

Verifying the VLANs

To verify our work and troubleshoot, use the **show vlan** and **show interface** commands. The **show vlan** output shows each VLAN, its interface ID, its IP address, and if there has been two-way traffic. The output looks like this:

```
Router#show vlan

Virtual LAN ID:  1 (IEEE 802.1Q Encapsulation)

   vLAN Trunk Interface:   FastEthernet0/0.1

   Protocols Configured:   Address:            Received:        Transmitted:
          IP               192.168.1.1              0                   2

Virtual LAN ID:  2 (IEEE 802.1Q Encapsulation)

   vLAN Trunk Interface:   FastEthernet0/0.2

   Protocols Configured:   Address:            Received:        Transmitted:
          IP               192.168.2.1              42                 19

Virtual LAN ID:  3 (IEEE 802.1Q Encapsulation)

   vLAN Trunk Interface:   FastEthernet0/0.3

This is configured as native Vlan for the following interface(s): FastEthernet0/0

   Protocols Configured:   Address:            Received:        Transmitted:
          IP               192.168.3.1              36                 34

Virtual LAN ID:  5 (IEEE 802.1Q Encapsulation)

   vLAN Trunk Interface:   FastEthernet0/0.5

   Protocols Configured:   Address:            Received:        Transmitted:
          IP               192.168.5.1              23                 21
```

The **show interface** command by itself displays all interfaces; usually you add the interface identifiers to get just the interface you want. The first line of output confirms that the interface is up and up—enabled and working. We've bolded some of the useful information. Note that the IP addresses are on the subinterface, while duplex and speed are on the physical interface.

```
Router#show interfaces fastEthernet 0/0
FastEthernet0/0 is up, line protocol is up        ←Physical interface is up
  Hardware is AmdFE, address is 0003.e36f.41e0 (bia 0003.e36f.41e0)
  MTU 1500 bytes, BW 100000 Kbit, DLY 100 usec,
     reliability 255/255, txload 1/255, rxload 1/255
  Encapsulation ARPA, loopback not set
  Keepalive set (10 sec)
  Full-duplex, 100Mb/s, 100BaseTX/FX              ←Interface duplex and speed
  ARP type: ARPA, ARP Timeout 04:00:00
  Last input 00:00:00, output 00:00:07, output hang never
  Last clearing of "show interface" counters never
  Queueing strategy: fifo
  Output queue 0/40, 0 drops; input queue 0/75, 0 drops
  5 minute input rate 0 bits/sec, 1 packets/sec
  5 minute output rate 0 bits/sec, 0 packets/sec
     217 packets input, 12884 bytes
     Received 217 broadcasts, 0 runts, 0 giants, 0 throttles
     0 input errors, 0 CRC, 0 frame, 0 overrun, 0 ignored
     0 watchdog
     0 input packets with dribble condition detected
     45 packets output, 6211 bytes, 0 underruns(0/0/0)
     0 output errors, 0 collisions, 4 interface resets
     0 babbles, 0 late collision, 0 deferred
     0 lost carrier, 0 no carrier
     0 output buffer failures, 0 output buffers swapped out

Router#show interfaces fastEthernet 0/0.1
FastEthernet0/0.1 is up, line protocol is up      ←Subinterface is enabled
  Hardware is AmdFE, address is 0003.e36f.41e0 (bia 0003.e36f.41e0)
  Internet address is 192.168.1.1/24              ←Subinterface IP address
  MTU 1500 bytes, BW 100000 Kbit, DLY 100 usec,
     reliability 255/255, txload 1/255, rxload 1/255
  Encapsulation 802.1Q Virtual LAN, Vlan ID  1.  ←Subinterface VLAN ID
  ARP type: ARPA, ARP Timeout 04:00:00
```

To confirm that our VLANs are working and the router is forwarding, we could go to a host in any VLAN and **ping** a post in another VLAN. We could also run the **tracert** command between them. We will do both in the exercises.

EXERCISE 9-4

CDP Exploration

In this exercise we demonstrate the steps an administrator would take to configure the router to connect to a VLAN trunk. You'll perform this exercise using Boson's NetSim. Launch Lab 9-4 and review the topology.

In Exercise 7-1 we created the VLANs and trunk. We were able to test them because the router was preconfigured, but that isn't the case in this lab. We will need to configure the interface to make it work.

Task 1: Test Lab Connectivity

1. From Host V1.13, verify connectivity to Host V1.59 (10.0.2.59). You should also have connectivity to both LAN C switches (10.0.2.2 and 10.0.2.3). Confirm you can't ping Host V2.69 (10.0.22.69) or Host V2.88 (10.0.22.88) even though they are connected to the same switches. They are in another subnet: 10.0.22.0/24.

   Confirm that you can't ping the router or anything beyond it. All of this is because Router C isn't fully configured.

Task 2: Configure RouterC's LAN Interface

1. Either open a console session or Telnet to RouterC from Host B.77.

   Do a **show run** to see that interface Fa0/0, the LAN interface, is not configured. The **show ip interface brief** command would also have told us this.

2. If we put the 10.0.2.1/20 on Fa0/0, VLAN 1 would have connectivity to the network, but VLAN 2 would not, so a regular interface configuration isn't the answer. We need to create subinterfaces, one for each VLAN.

   The first step is to remove any IP address on the *physical* interface Fa 0/0 and then issue a **no shutdown** command to make sure it is enabled. In Global Configuration mode, make the following entries:

```
interface FastEthernet0/0
no ip address
no shutdown
```

   The next thing we need to do is create our subinterfaces, configure them for VLANs, and give them an IP address in one of the VLANs. Since we have only two VLANs, named VLAN 1 and VLAN 2, we will create two subinterfaces using the following commands:

```
interface FastEthernet0/0.1
description LAN C - VLAN 1
encapsulation dot1q 1
ip address 10.0.2.1 255.255.255.0
interface FastEthernet0/0.2
description LAN C2 - VLAN 2
encapsulation dot1q 2
ip address 10.0.22.1 255.255.255.0
CTRL-Z
```

Confirm that you can ping all four of the VLAN hosts.

Run the **show ip route** to see that both networks are now in the routing table.

Run the **show run** command to see what the interfaces look like.

3. Confirm that Host B.77 can ping all four VLAN hosts.

Save your work.

Make sure that you understand what router on a stick is and does—basically providing routing to the VLANs connected to a trunk in a switched network. Know the steps for creating the subinterfaces, assigning IP addresses that *are in the VLAN pool, and placing the subinterface in the VLAN. Know how to use the* show vlan *and* show interfaces *commands to verify the subinterface configuration.*

Switch Virtual Interface (SVI)

Up to this point we've been talking about routers as a separate device to provide Layer 3 services, but what if the switch could handle the interVLAN traffic itself? Layer 3–capable switches can do just that internally. This interVLAN routing on Catalyst switches is achieved by creating Layer 3 interfaces called switch virtual interfaces (SVIs) for each VLAN. The SVIs then provide a connection to the Layer 3 processing for any ports in their VLAN by providing a default gateway for the VLAN.

Being a virtual interface, like the loopback interface, there is no physical interface for the SVI that one could point to or plug a cable into; it exists internally within the architecture and circuitry of the switch. You can think of the SVI as a *portal* that can connect to and communicate with the other SVIs to perform routing functions between the VLANs. Figure 9-7 shows a representation of two VLANs using SVIs within the switch. This is the preferred method today.

In Chapter 7, we saw that by default all Cisco switches already have an SVI created for the VLAN1 (the default VLAN) for IP connectivity to the switch to permit remote administration. On Layer 3–capable switches, we use a similar process to create additional SVIs for each VLAN that allow traffic to be routed between VLANs.

First we enable IP routing using the **ip routing** command. This way, the switch can exchange routes with other network Layer 3 devices. Without this, we would need to configure a static default route to the gateway router.

There are just three commands we use to create the SVI. We create it just like we did the loopbacks using the **interface Vlan#** command and then give it an IP address in the VLAN—the IP we would have given the gateway router interface. The SVI will be the default gateway for the VLAN hosts. We do have to enable the interfaces with the **no shutdown** command. The following output shows the steps for our interVLAN example in the last section using Switch A. Figure 9-5 and related text at the beginning of this section show the steps for the four VLANs. If VLAN1 is already configured, it would not need to be done here as long as the IP address is correct.

```
Switch_A#configure terminal
Switch_A(config)#ip routing
Switch_A(config)#interface Vlan1
Switch_A(config-if)#ip address 192.168.1.1 255.255.255.0
```

FIGURE 9-7

Switch virtual interface (SVI) with two VLANs

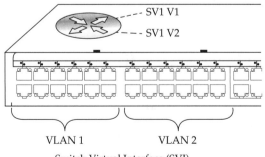

Switch Virtual Interface (SVI)

```
Switch_A(config-if)#no shutdown
Switch_A(config)#interface Vlan2
Switch_A(config-if)#ip address 192.168.2.1 255.255.255.0
Switch_A(config-if)#no shutdown
Switch_A(config)#interface Vlan3
Switch_A(config-if)#ip address 192.168.3.1 255.255.255.0
Switch_A(config-if)#no shutdown
Switch_A(config)#interface Vlan5
Switch_A(config-if)#ip address 192.168.5.1 255.255.255.0
Switch_A(config-if)#no shutdown
Switch_A(config)#CTRL-Z
```

At this point we have our interVLAN routing operational, but let's assume that Switch A will also be connecting to a router as the perimeter router. If the router is not on one of the VLANs, such as VLAN1, then we need to make the following modifications to one of the switch ports that will connect to the router:

```
Switch_A(config)#interface FastEthernet 0/1
Switch_A(config-if)#no switchport
Switch_A(config-if)#ip address 10.0.1.1 255.255.255.0
Switch_A(config-if)#no shutdown
```

The **no switchport** command makes interface FastEthernet 0/1 Layer 3 capable. The IP address is part of the same subnet as the default route.

To verify your configuration, use the **show ip route** command:

```
Switch_A#show ip route
---Codes omitted---
Gateway of last resort is not set
      10.0.0.0/24 is subnetted, 1 subnets
C        10.0.1.0 is directly connected, FastEthernet0/1
C     192.168.1.0/24 is directly connected, Vlan1
C     192.168.2.0/24 is directly connected, Vlan2
C     192.168.3.0/24 is directly connected, Vlan3
C     192.168.5.0/24 is directly connected, Vlan5
```

Watch "VSI InterVLAN Routing" for a video demonstration of how to configure switch virtual interface to perform interVLAN routing on Cisco Layer 3–capable switches.

INSIDE THE EXAM

Router Configuration Initial Steps

Make sure you review the key differences between routers and switches, both physically and configuration-wise, before the exam. When faced with these questions, a healthy dose of common sense will usually see you through. The default encapsulation on a point-to-point serial connection is HDLC, but it can be changed to anything you wish using the **encapsulation** *type* command. Lastly, make sure to review the physical installation information. You may see a question or two that asks you to identify cable types, pinouts, and interface types within a network diagram.

Configuration Fundamentals

It will prove much easier for you to remember CLI differences between a switch and a router. Remember, differences basically come down to the questions asked by setup. If you drop to the command line for configuration, similarities include how to move around in the CLI; setting passwords; configuring Telnet, SSH, and console connection parameters; the methods for copying and saving configuration files; and how to update the IOS.

Knowing the **show ip route** command and understanding administrative distance in regard to the various route types (static, connected, and dynamically learned) is an absolute

necessity for you in taking this exam. Remember connected routes are automatically part of the routing table, while static and dynamic are added or learned, respectively, based on your configuration and the router's placement within the network. Static routing results in lower CPU cycles and processing power on the router, but any change on the network (a link going down, or something else) must be manually updated. The proper syntax for adding a static route is **ip route** *network_address subnet_mask Next_hop_address*. If a static route is configured, it will *always* be used in lieu of any route learned, no matter which protocol it learns it from—the administrative distance of a static route is 1. Default routes provide a route for all packets that do not match any other route listed in the table and are added using the **ip route 0.0.0.0 0.0.0.0** *next_hop_address* command, with the zeroes acting as wildcard characters.

Use the **show cdp neighbors** and **show cdp neighbors detail** commands to discover other Cisco devices close by. Cisco devices by default send out CDP messages every 60 seconds that are used by others to create and maintain a CDP table that is polled using the **show** commands. A 180-second holdtimer keeps information in the table even if two messages have been missed.

INSIDE THE EXAM

InterVLAN Routing

Make sure that you understand what router on a stick is and does—basically providing routing between the VLANs connected to a trunk in a switched network. Know the steps for creating the subinterfaces, assigning IP addresses that are in the VLAN pool, and placing the subinterface in the VLAN. Know how to use the **show vlan** and **show interfaces** commands to verify the subinterface configuration. This is an older technology and seldom used, but you are responsible for knowing it. The modern approach is SVIs on Layer 3 switches. Make sure you know how to create an SVI and that each SVI serves just one VLAN.

CERTIFICATION SUMMARY

Routers typically have four different types of ports on the back: the console port, an auxiliary port, Ethernet ports, and any number of different serial ports. The Ethernet and serial ports are the ones to focus on for the exam, and the only two you can assign IP addresses to. Each individual port represents an entirely unique LAN and must have an address within that subnet's range. While "regular" 10-Mbps Ethernet ports are accessed by the **interface ethernet #** command (where # is the port's number), Fast Ethernet ports are accessed by **interface fastethernet #/#**, and Gigabit ports are accessed by the **interface gigabitethernet #/#** command. Serial interfaces are used to provide access to WAN links for your network. (HDLC is the default frame type on serial point-to-point links, and the frame type must be the same on both ends for communication to work.)

The **bandwidth** *speed(kbps)* command does not affect the actual transmitting speed of the interface at all but is used by certain routing protocols (EIGRP and OSPF) to calculate best routes.

The IOS, CLI, and memory locations are all virtually identical from a switch to a router. Routers store configuration files and IOS images exactly like switches (in NVRAM and flash, respectively), and use the same commands and techniques to copy and store them. The CLI modes (User, Privileged, Global Configuration, and so on) and the methods in which you move around in them also work the same on routers. Rules regarding setting passwords; configuring telnet, SSH, and console connection parameters; all methods for copying and saving configuration files; and methods for updating the IOS apply to routers just as they did with switches. The router CLI differs in the questions asked during setup, the configuration of IP addresses, the interface options available, and some of the commands available.

Typically, UTP cables are used between end systems and the switch, as well as from the switch to the router, with standard RJ45 connectors. Routing tables can be updated in three ways: with directly connected routes, statically added routes, or routes learned through a dynamic routing protocol. *Connected routes* are added to the routing table for every interface with a correctly configured IP address and subnet mask (along with the **no shutdown** command). *Static* has the administrator manually define routes using the **ip route** *network_address subnet_mask Next_hop_address* command. The administrative distance of static routes is 1, which is the lowest AD, except for directly connected routes. Therefore, if a static route is configured, it will *always* be used in lieu of any route learned, no matter which protocol it learns it from. You can change the administrative distance on any static route using the **ip route** *network_id subnet_mask next_hop AdministrativeDistance* command. *Default routes* are created to provide a route for all packets that do not match any other route listed in the table. A default route is manually added to the routing table using the **ip route 0.0.0.0 0.0.0.0** *next_hop_address* command, with the zeroes acting as wildcard characters.

TWO-MINUTE DRILL

Router Configuration Initial Steps

❑ Router Ethernet ports service internal networks. Fast Ethernet ports are accessed by **interface fastethernet #/#**, 10-Mbps Ethernet ports are accessed by the **interface ethernet #** command (where # is the port's number), and Gigabit ports are accessed by the **interface gigabitethernet #/#** command.

❑ The **bandwidth** command does not affect data rate speed at all, but is instead used for metric purposes in certain routing protocols.

❑ The differences in the router CLI when compared to the switch are the questions asked during setup, the configuration of the IP addresses, the interface options offered, and the various commands available. The IOS, CLI, and memory locations are all virtually identical from a switch to a router: routers store configuration files and IOS images exactly like switches, and use the same commands and techniques to copy and store them. The CLI modes (User, Privileged, Global Configuration, and so on) and the methods in which you move around in them also work the same on routers.

Configuration Fundamentals

❑ When no configuration file exists in NVRAM, the router defaults to the System Configuration dialog, also known as Setup mode, just like a switch. The commands to start and end setup are **setup** and CTRL-C, respectively.

❑ You can update routing tables in three ways: through directly connected routes, statically added routes, or routes learned through use of a dynamic routing protocol.

❑ Connected routes are added to the routing table for every interface with a correctly configured IP address and subnet mask—as soon as you add an IP address and subnet mask to an interface, along with the **no shutdown** command (to enable it), the router adds an entry to its routing table for that network.

❑ Static routing has the administrator manually define routes using the **ip route** *network_address subnet_mask Next_hop_address* command. The benefit is lower CPU cycles and processing power on the router. The disadvantage is that any change on the network (a link going down or something else) must be manually updated on the router, otherwise packets will be misdirected.

❑ The administrative distance of static routes is 1, which is the lowest AD, except for directly connected routes. Therefore, if a static route is configured, it will always be used in lieu of any route learned, no matter which protocol it learns it from. You can change the administrative distance on any static route with the **ip route** *network_id subnet_mask next_hop administrative_ distance* command.

❑ Default routes are created to provide a route for all packets that do not match any other route listed in the table. A default route is manually added to the routing table using the **ip route 0.0.0.0 0.0.0.0** *next_hop_address* command.

❑ Use the **show cdp neighbors** and **show cdp neighbors detail** commands to discover other Cisco devices close by.

InterVLAN Routing

To configure a router interface to connect to a trunk link, we need to create subinterfaces on one of our Fast Ethernet or faster physical interfaces. The steps are as follows:

1. Go to the physical interface and issue a **no shutdown** to enable the interface.

2. Create each subinterface by using the **interface** command, adding a unique decimal to the interface ID for each subinterface. (Example: **interface Fa0/0.1**.)

3. Use the **encapsulation dot1q** *vlan_id* [**native**] command to enable dot1Q encapsulation on a subinterface for each VLAN. The VLAN ID matches our switch configuration. The **native** option changes our native VLAN to something other than the default VLAN 1. It needs to match our settings on the switch. The native VLAN packets are not tagged.

4. To verify your work, use the **show run, show ip route**, and **show vlan** commands.

5. To create a switch virtual interface (SVI) on a Layer 3 switch to do the interVLAN routing, use the **interface Vlan#** command for each SVI, give each an IP address in the VLAN, and enable the interface with the **no shutdown** command. The IP address would be the one you would have given the gateway router interface. The SVI will be the default gateway for the VLAN hosts.

6. To verify your work, use the **show ip route** command.

SELF TEST

The following Self Test questions will help you measure your understanding of the material presented in this chapter. Read all the choices carefully since there may be more than one correct answer. Choose all the correct answers for each question.

Router Configuration Initial Steps

1. Based on this chapter, which of the following are true statements about serial interfaces?
   A. They use Ethernet just like the LAN.
   B. They are point-to-point connections.
   C. They can't have more than six hosts attached.
   D. The default encapsulation is HDLC, but it can be changed

2. The router and switch CLI are similar in many ways. Which of the following is/are differences?
   A. Configuring the enable secret
   B. Questions asked during the System Configuration dialog
   C. The commands to move through—and exit—CLI modes
   D. The required amount of configured IP addresses

3. Assume you are installing a business network. Which interface on the router will be linked to the leased line connected to the Internet?
   A. Fast Ethernet 0/0
   B. Serial 0/0
   C. Console
   D. Aux

Configuration Fundamentals

4. Which of the following are commands for configuring Fast Ethernet interfaces?
   A. no shutdown
   B. ip address *IP_Address Subnet_Mask*
   C. bandwidth 100
   D. interface fastethernet *slot/port*

5. Which command generated the following output?

```
Rtr1#
   Interface          IP-Address    OK? Method Status                 Protocol
   FastEthernet0/0    199.200.1.1   YES manual up                     up
   FastEthernet0/1    199.200.2.1   YES manual up                     up
   Serial0/0          135.17.0.1    YES manual up                     up
   Serial0/1          unassigned    YES unset  administratively down  down
```

A. show ip route

B. show interfaces

C. show ip interface brief

D. show ip interfaces serial

6. Which of the following is/are true regarding directly connected networks?

A. The administrator must use the **ip route** command to add them to the routing table.

B. The route is automatically added to the routing table as soon as an interface is properly configured and enabled.

C. The router cannot forward packets to the network until a routing protocol is enabled.

D. The router can forward packets to the network without a routing protocol.

Exhibit 1 will be used in Questions 7–9:

Exhibit I

```
Router1#show ip route
---Legend omitted---
Gateway of last resort is not set
  C    192.168.1.0/24 is directly connected, FastEthernet0/0
  S    192.168.3.0/24 [1/0] via 192.168.1.1
  C    192.168.5.0/24 is directly connected, FastEthernet0/1
  R    192.168.9.0/24 [120/1] via 192.168.4.1, 00:00:07, s0/1
  D    192.168.11.0/24 [90/284160] via 192.168.1.1, 00:04:19, FastEthernet0/0
  O    192.168.10.0/24 [110/11] via 192.168.2.1, 00:01:01, s0/0
```

7. In the last entry in Exhibit 1, what does the number 110 represent ([110/])?

A. It is the routing metric.

B. It is the distance to the network.

C. It is the administrative distance.

D. It is the time since the last update was received.

8. In the last entry in Exhibit 1, what does the number 11 represent ([/11])?
  A. It is the routing metric.
  B. It is the distance to the network.
  C. It is the administrative distance.
  D. It is the time since the last update was received.

9. In the second entry in Exhibit 1, what does the S stand for?
  A. It is the shortest route.
  B. It is directly connected.
  C. It is a manually configured route.
  D. It is the default gateway.

10. You wish to configure a static route to network 192.168.2.0/24. The route must leave interface Serial 0 to the next-hop address of 172.16.5.3. Which of the following commands will configure the route?
  A. ip route 172.16.5.3 192.168.2.0 255.255.255.0 serial 0
  B. ip route 192.168.2.0 255.255.255.0 serial 0 172.16.5.3
  C. ip route 172.16.5.3 serial 0 192.168.2.0 255.255.255.0
  D. ip route 192.168.2.0 255.255.255.0 172.16.5.3

11. You are configuring a router for a small network. Fast Ethernet 0/0 (Fa0/0) is connected to 200.5.4.0/24, Fast Ethernet 1 (Fa0/1) is connected to 200.5.5.0/24, and serial 0/0 (s0/0) is connected to 190.100.100.0/24—an Internet service provider line. The routing table automatically updates for the two directly connected networks. You wish the router to send all other packets through serial0/0, allowing Internet access for your internal clients. Which two of the following configuration commands could create the default route?
  A. ip route 0.0.0.0 0.0.0.0 serial0/0
  B. ip route 0.0.0.0 0.0.0.0 190.100.100.254
  C. ip route 0.0.0.0 0.0.0.0 200.5.4.254
  D. ip route 0.0.0.0 0.0.0.0 200.5.5.254

12. Which of the following commands reports the IP address of nearby Cisco devices?
  A. show cdp
  B. show cdp neighbor ip
  C. show cdp neighbor detail
  D. show cdp neighbor
  E. All of the above

InterVLAN Routing

13. Which of the following commands creates a subinterface on a router?

    A. encapsulation dot1Q 1

    B. ip address 192.168.1.1 255.255.255.0

    C. interface fastEthernet 0/0.1

    D. interface fastEthernet 0/0 subint 1

    E. interface serial0/0.1

14. Which of the following commands would verify the subinterface on a router?

    A. show run

    B. show ip route

    C. show vlan

    D. show interfaces fastEthernet 0/0

15. Which of the following are steps to create InterVLAN routing—router on a stick?

    A. Assign an IP address and subnet mask to each subinterface.

    B. Use the **interface** command adding a unique decimal to the interface ID for each subinterface.

    C. Enable the physical interface with an IP address.

    D. Use the **encapsulation dot1q** *vlan_id* command to enable dot1Q encapsulation on a subinterface for each VLAN.

    E. Enable the physical interface without an IP address.

    F. All of the above.

16. Which of the following are steps to create an SVI for interVLAN routing?

    A. Assign an IP address and subnet mask.

    B. Use the **interface** command, adding a unique decimal to the interface ID for each VLAN.

    C. interface Vlan#

    D. no shutdown

    E. All of the above

SELF TEST ANSWERS

Router Configuration Initial Steps

1. ☑ **B and D** are correct. Serial interfaces by default use HDLC on Cisco routers. They are point-to-point connections.
   ☒ **A and C** are incorrect. A is incorrect because they do not use Ethernet. C is incorrect because point-to-point connections have only two devices attached.

2. ☑ **B and D** are correct. Routers have different questions during setup, and switches only require a single IP address (for VLAN1 interface), while routers need IP addresses configured for each active interface.
   ☒ **A and C** are incorrect. Routers and switches do have these characteristics in common.

3. ☑ **B** is correct. Router serial ports are used to connect to leased-line WAN connections.
   ☒ **A, C, and D** are incorrect. A is incorrect because the Ethernet interfaces service your client networks. C and D are incorrect because the console and auxiliary ports are used for configuration.

Configuration Fundamentals

4. ☑ **A, B, and D** are correct. A is correct because the **no shutdown** command enables the interface. B is correct because the **ip address IP_Address Subnet_Mask** command assigns an IP address. D is correct because the **interface fastethernet slot/port** command takes us to the interface.
   ☒ **C** is incorrect. It is not an Ethernet command; it is a serial command.

5. ☑ **C** is correct because the **show ip interface brief** command displays the output shown.
   ☒ **A, B, and D** are incorrect. A is incorrect because the **show ip route** command displays the routing table. B is incorrect because the **show interfaces** command displays detailed information about the interfaces. D is incorrect because the **show ip interfaces serial** command displays detailed information about the serial interfaces.

6. ☑ **B and D** are correct. Directly connected routes are automatically added to the routing table as soon as the configured interface is enabled with the **no shutdown** command. Because the routes are in the routing table, the router will service these networks.
   ☒ **A and C** are incorrect. A is incorrect because the **ip route** command is used for static routes, not connected routes. C is incorrect because the router *can* forward packets to the network without any routing protocol being enabled.

7. ☑ **C** is correct. It is the administrative distance.

    ☒ **A, B,** and **D** are incorrect. **A** is incorrect because the routing metric is 11. **B** is incorrect because there is no way to know the distance to the network. **D** is incorrect because the time since the last update was received is 00:01:01.

8. ☑ **A** is correct. It is the routing metric 11, as in [110 /11]).

    ☒ **B, C,** and **D** are incorrect. **B** is incorrect because while it may be the shortest route, that is not what the S stands for. It stands for static. **C** is incorrect because the administrative distance is 110, as in [110/11]. **D** is incorrect because the time since the last update was received is 00:01:01.

9. ☑ **C** is correct. It is a manually configured route (or static route).

    ☒ **A, B,** and **D** are incorrect. **A** is incorrect because while it may be the shortest route, that is not what the S stands for. It stands for static. **B** is incorrect because directly connected has a C code. **D** is incorrect because the default gateway is always the last entry in the table and the "Gateway of last resort is not set" indicates no gateway was set.

10. ☑ **D** is correct. The correct syntax for a static route entry is **ip route** *destination_network_id subnet_mask next_hop_address* or in this case **ip route 192.168.2.0 255.255.255.0 172.16.5.3**.

    ☒ **A, B,** and **C** are incorrect. **A** is incorrect because in **ip route 172.16.5.3 192.168.2.0 255.255.255.0 serial 0**, the 172.16.5.3 192 doesn't belong there and breaks an otherwise okay command. **B** is incorrect because in **ip route 192.168.2.0 255.255.255.0 serial 0 172.16.5.3**, the word *serial* doesn't belong there and breaks an otherwise okay command. **C** is incorrect because in **ip route 172.16.5.3 serial 0 192.168.2.0 255.255.255.0**, the word *serial* doesn't belong there. Also, the *destination_network_id subnet_mask* and *next_hop_address* are reversed.

11. ☑ **A** and **B** are correct. The syntax to configure a default route is **ip route 0.0.0.0 0.0.0.0** [*next_hop_address* | *egress_int*].

    ☒ **C** and **D** are incorrect. They are using LAN addresses for the next hop, not the serial0/0 interface.

12. ☑ **C** is correct. The **show cdp neighbor detail** command reports the IP address of nearby Cisco devices.

    ☒ **A, B, D,** and **E** are incorrect. **A** is incorrect because **show cdp** displays global Cisco Discovery Protocol (CDP) information, including timer and holdtime information. **B** is incorrect because in **show cdp neighbor** *ip*, the *ip* is not a valid parameter. **D** is incorrect because in **show cdp neighbor** *interface*, the *interface* is not a valid parameter. **E** is incorrect because some of the options are wrong.

InterVLAN Routing

13. ☑ **C** is correct. The **interface fastEthernet 0/0.1** command creates a subinterface with the decimal .1.
☒ **A, B, D,** and **E** are incorrect. **A** is incorrect because **encapsulation dot1Q 1** sets the encapsulation for the subinterface. **B** is incorrect because **ip address 192.168.1.1 255.255.255.0** assigns an IP address to the subinterface. **D** is incorrect because the **subint** is a command option. **E** is incorrect because serial interfaces can't have subinterfaces.

14. ☑ **A, B,** and **C** are correct. Each would show the subinterfaces.
☒ **D** is incorrect. The **show interfaces fastEthernet 0/0** command would show information about the physical interface only, not the subinterfaces.

15. ☑ **F** is correct. While in the wrong order, all commands would create InterVLAN routing—router on a stick.
☒ **A, B, C, D,** and **E** are each partially correct.

16. ☑ **A, C,** and **D** are correct. While not in the correct order, they will create a SVI.
☒ **B** and **E** are incorrect. **B** is incorrect because that is a subinterface command for a router. **E** is incorrect because of **B**.

10

Open Shortest Path First (OSPF)

I n Chapter 8 we compared static routing and dynamic routing. Then in Chapter 9 we took the network displayed in Figure 10-1 and created the following static routes to make sure that packets from anywhere within the network or from the Internet could find any host in the network.

```
Router_A# configure terminal
Router_A(config)# ip route 0.0.0.0 0.0.0.0 172.16.4.2

Router_C# configure terminal
Router_C(config)# ip route 0.0.0.0 0.0.0.0 172.16.4.5

Router_B# configure terminal
Router_B(config)# ip route 172.16.1.0 255.255.255.0 172.16.4.1
Router_B(config)# ip route 172.16.3.0 255.255.255.0 172.16.4.6
Router_B(config)# ip route 0.0.0.0 0.0.0.0 1.1.12.1
```

FIGURE 10-1

Simple network example from Chapter 9

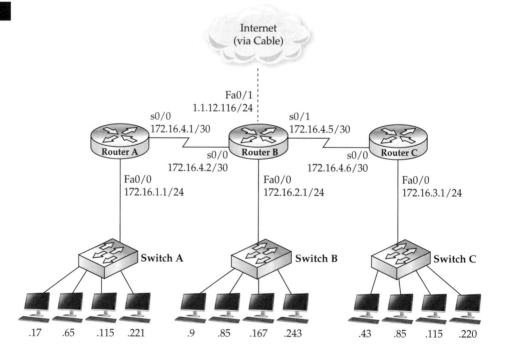

We also discussed the need for the routes so that return traffic could find its way back. Our simple solution accomplishes that, and because they are static entries, there is very little CPU or bandwidth impacts. But are there any downsides?

At least two. The first one applies only if the network is growing. Assuming these three locations, what happens when we add a D network beyond C? Obviously, D would need to be configured. But now Router C's configuration no longer works to find the D network; a route would need to be added for that. Router B also would need a static route for the D hosts. In fact, the only router that wouldn't need to be manually changed is A. When completed, we are back to a point where all hosts can be reached and the network has converged. Convergence is an important concept in routing. A network is converged when all routers have enough information to forward packets to and from any destination within the network. A converged network is the norm and represents stability. But what happens when our next growth adds two LANS, one beyond D and one beyond A? Every device has to be manually updated and the number of changes increases the odds that mistakes could be made. This is why static networks don't scale well. The operational efficiency is more than offset by complexity, labor, and the chance of errors.

The second problem is actually worse even with just the original three LANs. What if Switch A fails? Router B still has a static route to LAN A and will continue to forward traffic from LAN B, LAN C, and the Internet to Router A over a slow serial link, even though Router A can only discard the packets since it no longer has a route to the LAN. It would be better if both Router B and Router C knew that LAN A was gone and handled their own discards.

The bottom line is that static routing doesn't deal well with change, and increased network complexity increases the chances of configuration errors. This is why we use dynamic routing protocols like OSPF (Open Shortest Path First) for our internal routers and networks. We would still use a default route on Router B to forward outside traffic to our ISP. For CCENT and anything but huge networks, outside routers are not included in our router exchanges. In this chapter, we will look at OSPF and how to implement it on our networks.

CERTIFICATION OBJECTIVE 10.01

OSPF Fundamentals

OSPF is an IETF (Internet Engineering Task Force) nonproprietary IP link-state routing protocol. It is becoming the most widely used interior gateway protocol (IGP) and the main link-state protocol used in enterprise networks today. OSPF supports variable-length subnet masking (VLSM), which we covered in Chapter 3. Like all IGPs, it is for routing within a single autonomous system (AS), a single organization.

OSPF uses a variety of link-state advertisements (LSAs) containing the operational state of each link, the cost of the link (metric for ranking), and information about other neighbors. Convergence occurs when all of the OSPF routers have identical link-state databases and a topology view of the network. One of OSPF's greatest strengths is its ability to quickly detect topology changes, such as link failures or additions, react immediately, and then converge to a new loop-free routing structure within literally seconds. This compares very favorably to distance-vector protocols that can take several minutes and the length of time it would take an admin to detect and fix a problem with static routing.

OSPF Version 2 is used in IPv4 networks, while OSPF Version 3 is used in IPv6 networks. In this chapter we will look at version 2; in Chapter 13 when we introduce IPv6, we will introduce version 3.

OSPF Basics

Before getting into the details of OSPF, let's start with an overview of how OSPF works. Each OSPF router develops and maintains two tables. The *neighbor table* contains all neighbor OSPF routers that share a link with this router and have common configurations. These neighbors exchange link-state advertisements (LSAs) to share link or path changes in the network.

The second table is the *topology table*, which is the link-state database (LSDB) made up of the LSAs received. Every router in the segment should share the same topology table after the LSA exchanges. From this information, the router can figure out how all the devices and networks are connected.

From that data, the router can use a process called *shortest path first* (SPF) to calculate the best path from the local device to all remote destinations. At this point the best path to each known destination is offered to the routing table to be considered for inclusion.

In the rest of this chapter we will look at the details about how that all gets done and then what configuration needs to be done to accomplish it.

OSPF Areas

In a larger AS with many networks, each OSPF router would need to keep the LSA information of every other router in its link-state database. But it is possible and advantageous to divide large OSPF enterprise networks into *areas*, as shown in Figure 10-2. Areas are logical groupings of networks, including any routers with

FIGURE 10-2

FIGURE 10-2

Larger OSPF
network with
three areas

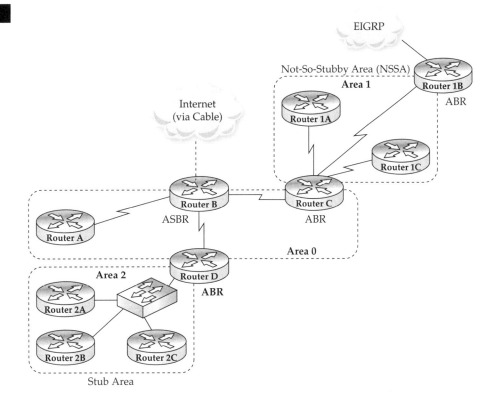

interfaces connected to those networks. Each router within the area maintains a detailed LSDB, which can then be summarized by a connecting router (area border router, or ABR) before forwarding into other areas. This reduces the amount of detail that remote areas must maintain, allowing the internal area to have complete details about the local area and very general or summarized information regarding remote areas, thus reducing the complexity and size of the LSDB and routing table. The smaller or summarized LSDB requires less processing complexity and CPU and memory requirements for the area routers.

This means the exact topology of an area may not be known to other areas, but traffic routed to the border router will be forwarded properly by that router. This is really not very different from what we've discussed earlier with our default gateway router where internal routers need not know anything about the topology of the Internet (represented by a cloud). As long as they direct unknown traffic to the gateway, it will forward the traffic properly.

Areas are assigned a unique 32-bit number by the network designer, which can be displayed as 3 or 0.0.0.3. The OSPF standard defines several special area types.

Backbone Area

The backbone area, also called a transit area (Area 0 or Area 0.0.0.0), is the connecting core of an OSPF network. All other areas must connect to it, and routes can be exchanged via routers with an interface in the backbone area and one in the other area. In our example, Area 2 and Area 0 share routes through Router D. The backbone area also provides connectivity for sharing routing information between nonbackbone areas. In our example, Area 2 can use Area 0 and the ABRs to learn about Area 1's networks.

Figure 10-2 and the following discussion of other areas are not a part of the CCENT exam, but are provided so that you can start to grasp the larger world the OSPF lives in. For the exam, you are focused on single-area OSPF, which means Area 0. Referring to it as the backbone and transit area only makes sense if you see a glimpse of the other areas, each of which must connect to Area 0.

Stub Areas

A stub area is one that has no other networks connected beyond it. Area 2 in our example is a stub area, somewhat like a neighborhood with no other outlets.

NSSA Areas

A not-so-stubby area (NSSA) would be a stub area except that it has one or more connections outside the area, meaning that there is at least one more outlet for the network with an autonomous system boundary router (ASBR).

In our example, Router B is an ASBR that connects to the outside world via the Internet, while Router 1B is an ASBR to connect to a network using EIGRP as its routing protocol. It is outside the OSPF network but still part of the AS or organization's network—remember that IGPs do not extend outside the AS. So why would you do this? You wouldn't by design, but when you acquire or merge with another enterprise, you may need to connect the networks and consider actually integrating them into the OSPF network later.

Router Designations

Looking at Figure 10-2, the routers with no connections outside a single area are called internal routers (IRs). These include Routers A, 2A, 2B, 2C, 3A, and 3C. Routers C and D are area border routers (ABRs) with interfaces in two or more areas but no interfaces outside the AS. If all of the links are physical links, at least one interface will be in Area 0. ABRs link the backbone, Area 0, to other areas. Routers B and 1B are autonomous system boundary routers (ASBRs) with one or more interfaces in an area and one or more to an outside, non-OSPF network. One final designation: all border routers with interfaces in Area 0 can be referred to as backbone routers. A router can be both an internal and a backbone router if all its interfaces are in Area 0.

ⓦatch *Make sure that you can recognize an OSPF diagram. Know the types of areas and the router types. Know that the core or backbone area is Area 0 and that all other areas connect to it via ABRs.*

OSPF Network Types

The CCENT exam focuses on LANs and LAN technologies, but we need to touch briefly on WAN connections a bit because within the AS, OSPF can be running over WAN connections.

Multi-access/broadcast networks are most often thought of as Ethernet LAN connections, but also could include campus and metropolitan area networks (MANs). In our sample diagram, Figure 10-2, Area 2 would be an example. A *loopback* is an interface without a network, which we will see serves some useful purposes when included in routing updates but has no neighbors to share updates with.

WAN connections are beyond the scope of the exam, but include the point-to-point serial WAN connections we configured in Chapter 9 and would be like the links you see in Area 0.

MHE Lab

EXERCISE 10-1

Configuring Serial Interfaces

In this exercise we demonstrate the steps an administrator would take to configure serial interfaces in preparation for configuring single-area OSPF in a network with WAN connections. We will use NetSim for this exercise. Launch Lab 10-1 and review the topology.

To begin with, all hosts and switches are configured. The router FastEthernet links are configured as well, but the serial links are not. Those are the red entries in the IP addresses table in the NetSim instructions IP address table. There is no routing of any kind in place. All devices except the Internet device have our normal usernames and passwords configured.

Task 1: Configure Serial Interfaces

1. Open a console session on RouterB.

   Do a **show run** to see that the serial interfaces are not configured. The **show ip interface brief** command would also tell us this.

2. We are going to configure serial 3/0 first. Use the following steps; it is just like an Ethernet interface in this case. After the **no shutdown** command, you will get a system message that the interface is up (shown in blue here).

```
RouterB#conf t
Enter configuration commands, one per line.  End with CNTL/Z.
RouterB(config)#interface serial 3/0
RouterB(config-if)#ip address 1.1.1.2 255.255.255.252
RouterB(config-if)#description Link to Internet
RouterB(config-if)#no shutdown
%LINK-3-UPDOWN: Interface Serial3/0, changed state to up
%LINEPROTO-5-UPDOWN: Line protocol on Interface Serial3/0,
changed state to up
RouterB(config-if)#ctrl-z
```

   Run a **show ip interface brief** command to confirm that the interface is up/up; notice the status of the other interfaces.

   Ping 1.1.1.1 to confirm that you can reach the Internet.

   Save your work.

3. Repeat step 2 with serial 3/1 using the appropriate IP address from the table or topology diagram. You will get a little different system message and the **show ip interface brief** output. Try it on your own; alternatively, here are the steps:

```
RouterB#conf t
RouterB(config)#interface serial 3/1
RouterB(config-if)#ip address 10.1.1.9 255.255.255.252
RouterB(config-if)#description Link to RouterD
RouterB(config-if)#no shutdown
RouterB(config-if)#ctrl-z
```

   Save your work.

4. Either open a console session on RouterD or Telnet from Host D.21.

   Repeat step 2 with serial 0/1 using the appropriate IP address from the table or topology diagram. You will get a little system message and some **show ip**

interface brief output somewhat like what you got in step 3. Try it on your own; alternatively, here are the steps:

```
RouterB#conf t
RouterB(config)#interface serial 0/1
RouterB(config-if)#ip address 10.1.1.10 255.255.255.252
RouterB(config-if)#description Link to RouterB
RouterB(config-if)#no shutdown
RouterB(config-if)#ctrl-z
```

Notice that you got a single system message telling you that the state is up but no second message telling you that the Line protocol is up. The **show ip interface brief** output confirms that it is up/down. The up indicates that there is now a physical connection (a wire, Layer 1) connecting you; the down means it's not understanding anything on the wire (Layer 2).

Serial connections are different from Ethernet in that they can run at any bandwidth supported by both ends. One end, the Data Communications Equipment (DCE), controls this by setting the clock rate on the interface. The Data Terminal Equipment (DTE), typically the customer's end, will sync to it. The topology diagram tells you which ends are DCEs, but what if that wasn't the case? How would we know? Run the following commands.

This command is featured in the Full Edition of NetSim, so we've included the results here and in the "Lab Solutions" section in the PDF Lab Book. For the Labs, use the DTE/DCE designation on the topology diagram.

You can stop the output at any point. What you need to know is on row 2: DCE cable.

```
RouterD#show controllers s0/1
HD unit 0, idb = 0x1AE828, driver structure at 0x1B4BA0
buffer size 1524  HD unit 0,V.35 DCE cable
cpb = 0x7, eda = 0x58DC, cda = 0x58F0
----output omitted-----
```

To set the clock rate, issue the following commands and then test connectivity to RouterB.

```
RouterD#conf t
Enter configuration commands, one per line.  End with CNTL/Z.
RouterD(config)#interface serial 0/1
RouterD(config-if)#clock rate 64000
%LINEPROTO-5-UPDOWN: Line protocol on Interface Serial0/1,
```

```
changed state to up
RouterD(config-if)#^Z
%SYS-5-CONFIG_I: Configured from console by console

RouterD#
```

Save your work.

5. Use what you've learned and the topology diagram to configure the serial link between RouterD and RouterC. When you have connectivity between them, save your work. If you need help, the steps are included in the "Lab Solutions" section.

OSPF Network Details

OSPF routers create a network of neighbor routers to share link-state advertisements (LSAs). To discover neighbor routers, special messages, called hello packets, are sent out each OSPF-enabled interface at regular intervals using multicast packets. Routers become neighbors when they see themselves included in the other's hello packet. This process requires comparing information in that hello packet to their own to see if they are compatible. Disagreeing on any of the following information in the hello packet would prevent them from forming a neighbor relationship.

Area-Id   Both routers must be connected by interfaces in the same area. Router A could not become neighbors with Router 2A, 2B, or 2C because they are fully (all interfaces) in separate areas. Router D could not become neighbors with Router 2A, 2B, or 2C because it would be connected via an interface in Area 2. Of course, the interfaces should belong to the same subnet and have a similar mask.

Hello Settings   Hello exchanges occur on each segment at fixed intervals. The *hello interval*, in seconds, is the time between the hello packets, while the *dead interval*, in seconds, is how long the router will wait for hello from its neighbors before declaring the router down. The default hello interval is 10 seconds for Ethernet and 30 seconds for nonbroadcast (serial) links. The default dead interval is four times the hello interval, or 40 seconds for Ethernet and 120 seconds for nonbroadcast. *Both settings must match exactly.*

Stub Area Flag   A setting in the hello packets must be the same for the neighbor formation process.

Authentication One of OSPF's features for securing the routing process is the optional configuration of a password for a segment. Routers can only become neighbors if they exchange the same password. If a password is configured on one routers, it must also be configured on the neighbor.

Adjacencies

After a successful neighboring process, the neighbor routers try to establish what is called *adjacency*, which simply means that they synchronize their link-state databases so that they have identical OSPF routing information.

Looking at our example network in Figure 10-2, Areas 0 and 1 are pretty straightforward because each router interface can have only one router neighbor. These are point-to-point connections common in traditional WAN installations. But what about in large Ethernet networks, like campus networks or Area 2 in our diagram? In this case, we have what are called multi-access networks where multiple routers can be connected through switches. These create two efficiency challenges for OSPF:

- **Multiple adjacencies** There is a separate adjacency for every pair of routers. Each router interface in Area 2 could form three adjacencies.

- **Lots of LSA flooding** Each adjacent pair would be exchanging information. The number of adjacencies is $n(n-1)/2$, where n equals the number of routers involved. In our small example that would be $4(3)/2 = 6$ exchanges.

Imagine the number of exchanges as the number of routers increases into dozens. There must be a more efficient way.

DRs, BDRs, and DROthers To make the whole process more efficient, the OSPF standard has a process to elect one router to be a designated router (DR) and a second router to be a backup designated router (BDR). The DR acts as collector and distributor for LSAs for the network, while the BDR collects the same information in case the DR fails. The DR is like the spokesperson for the multi-access network; it sends updates on behalf of the other participants on the multi-access network. All other routers are designated as *DROthers*.

Now instead of all routers flooding LSAs to all other routers in a multi-access network, DROthers send their LSAs specifically to the DR and BDR using a special multicast address, 224.0.0.6. Then the DR uses another special multicast address, 224.0.0.5, to flood the LSAs to all other routers in the network. The idea behind this is simply that the routers have a central point of contact to forward changes to that will then handle notifying the other routers.

DR/BDR Election Process   The process is quite simple and will occur automatically using default settings, but that may not lead to the best solution. You may not want your busiest router to be the DR, for instance. So the process can be configured to get the result that you want.

By default, the DR and BDR are selected by having the highest and second highest interface priority of all involved interfaces. By default, all interfaces have a priority of 1 (one), but they can be configured to set the priority to a number between 0 and 255 using the **ip ospf priority #** command in Interface Configuration mode. A 0 (zero) priority makes the router ineligible to become the DR or BDR.

If the OSPF interface priorities are equal, the highest router ID (RID) is used to break the tie. So the highest RID becomes the DR, and the second highest becomes the BDR. Adding a new router with a higher RID does not trigger a new election. This is known as a nonpreemptive process, because it does not take effect immediately, but in this case is waiting for the next normal DR/BDR election.

The DR remains in that role until it fails, it becomes disconnected from the network (interface down), or the OSPF process fails or is disabled on the DR. If any of these happen, the BDR becomes the DR and an election is held to choose a *new BDR only*.

Router ID (RID)

In addition to being used in the DR/BDR election, OSPF hello packets and LSAs have the router ID (RID), a 32-bit identifier, of the device that originated it. The RID can be specified using the **router-id** *ip-addr* command. If not used, Cisco routers use the highest configured *loopback* address (see Chapter 9). OSPF automatically prefers a loopback interface over any other kind, and it chooses the highest IP address among any loopback interfaces. The advantage to a loopback address is that they never go down. It is common practice on Cisco devices to use a loopback address as the RID.

If there is no loopback configured, the highest active interface when OSPF starts becomes the RID. Figure 10-3 shows Area 2 with RIDs, either from loopbacks or using the **router-id** command, and the results of a DR/BDR election assuming no interface priorities are changed.

If there is no interface with a valid IP address in an up/up state when it starts, OSPF reports can't allocate **router-id** error messages to the log.

OSPF Priority

We can use the **ip ospf priority** *num* command with values from 0–255 to define our preferences for DR and BDR; the higher the number, the more likely it will win the election. The default priority for all interfaces is 1. Since the RID applies to the entire device, not just an interface, it is possible that Router D might have an RID

Area 2 with router IDs and DR/BDR

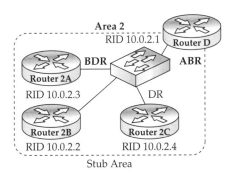

higher than others in Area 2. If we didn't want Router D to ever be the DR/BDR in Area 2, we could use the **ip ospf priority** 0 command in Interface Configuration mode on the Area 2 interface. Then it wouldn't matter what its RID is.

Timing Is Everything with OSPF

OSPF has some timing rules you should be aware of. In choosing the RID, if the **router-id** command isn't used and there is no loopback set, it choose the highest active interface IP address. This means that if only one of your interfaces is active, it becomes the RID and doesn't change when other interfaces are added, including loopbacks. A reboot or disabling and enabling the protocol would correct the problem, but having a loopback set *before* implementing OSPF is also a sure approach.

The DR/BDR election has a similar issue. The process starts when the first OSPF router starts. As soon as it discovers a neighbor and forms an adjacency, if there is no DR, then the election is held right then and those two will become the DR and BDR following the rules stated earlier. They will remain in those roles as other routers are added—adding a new router doesn't trigger an election. If a router comes up and selects the wrong interface as the RID, that could also impact the election, and correcting the RID on the router won't trigger a new DR/BDR election. Imagine how that can mess up your DR/BDR planning.

So how do we get the DR/BDR pair that we designed for initially? First make sure all routers have loopbacks or use the **router-id** command, then bring up the DR first, followed by the BDR and then the DROthers. Another approach is to shut down all connected segment interfaces on all routers, then use **no shutdown** on the DR, then the BDR, and then all DROthers.

Confirming OSPF

OSPF offers many commands with many optional parameters for confirming settings, configuration, and operations. In this section we'll look at a couple of basic commands that confirm the topics just covered; others will be covered in the configuration section.

The show ip ospf neighbor Command   To see the DR and BDR election results and neighbor adjacencies, you can use the **show ip ospf neighbor** command.

```
Router2b# show ip ospf neighbor
Neighbor ID    Pri    State           Dead Time    Address        Interface
10.0.2.1         1    2WAY/DROTHER    00:00:37     192.168.2.1    FastEthernet0/1
10.0.2.4         1    FULL/DR         00:00:34     192.168.2.4    FastEthernet0/1
10.0.2.3         1    FULL/BDR        00:00:39     192.168.2.3    FastEthernet0/1
```

Router 2B sees the neighbor IDs (RIDs). The priorities are all at the default (1). State shows adjacency status and router role. Router 2B only establishes full adjacency with the DR and BDR. All other routers establish two-way adjacency. Only the DR and BDR would show full adjacency to all other routers. Dead time is the seconds left before the entry would be reported as down. The counter gets reset (40 by default) with each hello packet to four times the hello interval (10 for Ethernet default). Address is the interface IP of the neighbor. Interface is the local interface to reach that neighbor.

The show ip ospf interface int_id Command   On a per-interface basis, use the **show ip ospf interface** *int_id* command to see the state, priority, the DR and the BDR with their IPs, and the timer interval settings.

```
Router2b# show ip ospf interface FastEthernet 0/1
FastEthernet 0/1 is up, line protocol is up
  Internet Address 192.168.2.2/24, Area 2
  Process ID 1, Router ID 10.0.2.2, Network Type BROADCAST, Cost: 1
  Transmit Delay is 1 sec, State DROTHER, Priority 1
  Designated Router (ID) 10.0.2.4, Interface address 192.168.2.4
  Backup Designated router (ID) 10.0.2.3, Interface address 192.168.2.3
  Timer intervals configured, Hello 10, Dead 40, Wait 40, Retransmit 5
    Hello due in 00:00:06
  Index 2/1, flood queue length 0
  Next 0x0(0)/0x0(0)
  Last flood scan length is 2, maximum is 2
  Last flood scan time is 0 msec, maximum is 4 msec
  Neighbor Count is 3, Adjacent neighbor count is 2
    Adjacent with neighbor 10.0.2.4  (Designated Router)
    Adjacent with neighbor 10.0.2.3  (Backup Designated Router)
  Suppress hello for 0 neighbor(s)
```

This command shows a lot of information, but for our purposes notice that it shows the local device info, including the RID, state, and priority in the first four rows. Then it shows both the RID and connected interface IP address of the DR and BDR. Next, it shows the hello and dead intervals. Further down, neighbor count is the total number of routers on that interface, while adjacent neighbor count is the DR and BDR for a DROther. It would be all routers if the command was run from the DR or BDR.

The show ip ospf database Command   Another command that can be handy is the **show ip ospf database** command; unfortunately it takes a little working with it to figure out. The following information would apply to a network like the one shown in Figure 10-3. Keep in mind that the link-state database is made up of the LSAs that have been received. This command shows key elements of each LSA's header.

```
Router2b# show ip ospf database
OSPF Router with ID(10.0.2.2) (Process ID 1)
                Router Link States(Area 2)
   Link ID          ADV Router       Age       Seq#           Checksum Link count
   10.0.2.1         10.0.2.1         1292      0x8000010D     0xEF60   2
   10.0.2.2         10.0.2.2         1540      0x800002FE     0xEB3D   2
   10.0.2.3         10.0.2.3         1117      0x80000090     0x875D   3
   10.0.2.4         10.0.2.4         2452      0x800001D6     0x12CC   2
                Net Link States(Area 2)
   Link ID          ADV Router       Age       Seq#           Checksum
   192.168.2.4      10.0.2.4         1278      0x80000237     0x00D860
---output Omitted---
```

The *OSPF Router with ID* line just identifies the requesting device by its RID and shows the OSPF process ID (PID), covered later in this section.

The *Router Link States* (router LSAs) section lists the routers that are showing up in the area. It tells us there are four routers each with two links, except RID 10.0.2.3, which has 3. Note: The link ID is the RID, and the ADV router is the RID of the router that injected (inserted) the LSA. They happen to be the same in this case, but not in the other sections.

The *Net Link States* (network LSAs) section lists the DRs for the area. So it wouldn't be used in areas where there are no DRs. Note: The link ID, 192.168.2.4, is the interface IP address of the DR on that segment, while ADV router is the RID of the router that injected (inserted) the LSA.

OSPF Routing Exchanges

OSPF routers gather link-state information from other routers and develop the same topology (map) of the network, which is then used to determine the routing table entries. When a router initializes or any change occurs in its routing information, it generates a link-state advertisement (LSA) that represents the collection of all link states on that router. All routers exchange link states by means of flooding. Each router receiving a link-state update should store the information in its link-state database (LSDB) and then propagate the update to other routers. Each router maintains a separate LSDB for each area that it has an interface in, so IRs, those routers whole within the area, would have a single LSDB, while ABRs would have one for each area they have interfaces in.

You can think of a link as being an active interface on the router. The link state is a description of the interface and information about its neighboring routers. This interface information would include the IP address and mask, the type of network connected, the other routers on that network, and so on.

If no changes occur in the OSPF network, such as a network being added or deleted, OSPF should remain very quiet except for hello packets.

Route Selection

The second part of the routing process occurs once all routers share the same LSDB and topology. Each router independently runs an algorithm (formula) to build and calculate a *shortest path tree* to all known destinations from itself. OSPF uses a shorted path first algorithm (or just SPF algorithm), an adaptation of Dijkstra's SPF algorithm, to determine the best path to each node. The resulting destinations, the associated cost, and the next-hop address to reach each destination are offered for inclusion in the IP routing table.

OSPF uses the word *cost* for its comparison metric in choosing the best route to a destination. While not referring to money, most people recognize that higher cost is less attractive.

Cost Metric   OSPF uses cost as a metric for route selection; the range is 1 to 65535. Cost in this case is a number reflecting a calculation based on interface bandwidth that results in a lower number as the bandwidth increases. The lower the metric (cost), the better the route. OSPF uses a reference bandwidth of 100 Mbps for the cost calculation. The cost of a link is calculated by dividing the reference bandwidth by the interface bandwidth. Link cost of a 100-Mbps Ethernet link would have a metric of 100/100 = 1. Table 10-1 shows a sample of OSPF default costs for various link types.

Since the result can't be a decimal value, any interface 100 Mbps or faster, such as Gigabit, will have a cost of 1. That could lead the router to make a poor routing decision, so one solution might be to use the **ip ospf cost *cost*** command (range 1–65535) on the 100-Mbps interface to override cost calculation, such as **ip ospf cost 10**. The interface **bandwidth** command can also be used to modify the OSPF cost for an interface by overriding the bandwidth of the interface type. Remember that the **bandwidth** command has no actual impact on available bandwidth, just on how the routing protocol sees the interface.

TABLE 10-1	Interface Type	Interface Bandwidth (bps)	OSPF Cost
	Loopback	8,000,000,000	1
Sample OSPF	Serial	56,000	1785
Cost Defaults	T1	1,544,000	64
	Ethernet	10,000,000	10
	Fast Ethernet	100,000,000	1
	Gigabit Ethernet	1,000,000,000	1

There are other configuration options, such as the **auto-cost reference-bandwidth** *bw* command (range 1–4294967), to solve this problem that are covered in advanced certifications. Care should be used with any command where you modify the metric to make sure that you do not create another problem solving this one.

Total cost to a destination is the sum of the cost of the individual links in the path to the destination.

Shortest Path Tree   Even though all routers share the same link-state database, each router will have its own view of the topology, much like each ballplayer having their own view of the field or court. Therefore the SPF algorithm starts with each router at the root of a tree and calculates the shortest path to each destination based on the cumulative cost of all segments required to reach that destination.

It is important to realize that cost is added on the incoming interface, not added to an outgoing LSA. The receiving router adds its own interface cost to the cost that was advertised in the LSA and then forwards that cost to other routers.

Figure 10-4 shows an example of a simple network and the resulting shortest path tree from Router B's perspective. Notice that Router B would advertise its LAN to A, C, and D with a cost of 1 (100 Mbps), but since it is directly connected, it has no cost to it.

FIGURE 10-4

Shortest path tree example

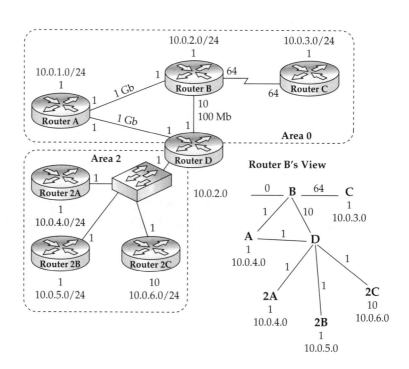

Looking at the 10.0.6.0 LAN, Router 2C would advertise it at a cost of 10 (10 Mbps), Router D would advertise it with a cost of 11, and Router A would advertise it with a cost of 12. Based on that, the route through D looks best (lowest cost), but the admin knows that the Gigabit links between D, C, and B are much faster than the 100-Mb link between D and B. So he used the **ip ospf cost 10** command on the interface to D, giving it a cost of 20 and therefore out of consideration for selection. Does it make sense that we should do the same thing on the D side of that link to make sure that traffic from Area 2 to LANs 10.0.2.0 and 10.0.3.0 take the faster path?

AD Still Trumps All

Remember from Chapter 8 that administrative distance (AD) is a measure of trustworthiness of the source of the route—how trusted is the method offering the route. While a routing protocol, like OSPF, uses metrics like cost to come up with its best path to a known destination, if the router learns about the destination from more than the source, it uses administrative distance to compare and choose the final route. Preference goes to the route with lower administrative distance to be included in the routing table listings. OSPF routes can still be passed over for EIGRP or static routes. Table 10-2 shows administrative distances.

The show ip route Command

In Chapter 9 we saw that the **show ip route** command displays the current status of the routing table, including any default route. The details of the OSPF lines are shown in Table 10-3.

```
192.168.1.0/24 [110/65] via 10.20.20.2, 00:07:38, Serial0/0
```

TABLE 10-2	Route Source	Administrative Distance
Administrative Distances	Connected interface	0
	Static route	1
	Enhanced Interior Gateway Routing Protocol (EIGRP) summary route	5
	Internal EIGRP	90
	OSPF	110
	Intermediate System-to-Intermediate System (IS-IS)	115
	Routing Information Protocol (RIP)	120
	External EIGRP	170
	Unknown Source	255

TABLE 10-3	**[110/65]**	**Administrative distance (AD) / Metric (cost)**
Routing Table OSPF Line Explanation	via 10.20.20.2	Next-hop device
	00:07:38	HH:MM:SS since last update. Indication of stability.
	Serial0/0	Local interface to reach next-hop device

```
Router(config-if)#show ip route
Codes: C - connected, S - static, R - RIP, M - mobile, B - BGP
       D - EIGRP, EX - EIGRP external, O - OSPF, IA - OSPF inter area
       N1 - OSPF NSSA external type 1, N2 - OSPF NSSA external type 2
       E1 - OSPF external type 1, E2 - OSPF external type 2
       i - IS-IS, su - IS-IS summary, L1 - IS-IS level-1, L2 - IS-IS level-2
       ia - IS-IS inter area, * - candidate default, U - per-user static route
       o - ODR, P - periodic downloaded static route
Gateway of last resort is 172.16.4.2 to network 0.0.0.0
     10.0.0.0/30 is subnetted, 3 subnets
C       10.1.1.0 is directly connected, Serial0/1
O       10.10.10.0 [110/128] via 10.20.20.2, 00:05:14, Serial0/0
                   [110/128] via 10.1.1.2, 00:05:14, Serial0/1
C       10.20.20.0 is directly connected, Serial0/0
     172.16.0.0/24 is subnetted, 2 subnets
C       172.16.4.0 is directly connected, FastEthernet0/1
O       172.16.10.0 [110/65] via 10.1.1.2, 00:05:14, Serial0/1
O     192.168.1.0/24 [110/65] via 10.20.20.2, 00:07:38, Serial0/0
O     192.168.2.0/24 [110/65] via 10.20.20.2, 00:09:45, Serial0/0
O     192.168.3.0/24 [110/65] via 10.20.20.2, 00:08:15, Serial0/0
O     192.168.4.0/24 [110/65] via 10.1.1.0, 00:07:12, Serial0/1
O     192.168.5.0/24 [110/65] via 10.1.1.0, 00:06:54, Serial0/1
O     192.168.6.0/24 [110/65] via 10.1.1.0, 00:09:15, Serial0/1
C     192.168.8.0/24 is directly connected, FastEthernet0/0
S*    0.0.0.0/0 [1/0] via 172.16.4.2
Router#
```

Distributing Default Routes

OSPF can share (inject) a default route into a normal area, like Area 0. OSPF routers by default don't propagate a default route throughout the OSPF domain. To share the default route, use one of two forms of the **default-information originate** command. The default routes can be originated by any OSPF router in the normal area. Normal area in this case means one that can accept inter-area routes, routes from other areas. This excludes the various stubby and NSSA areas; they only receive summary or default routes established by their ABR.

Using the command by itself to advertise a default route (0.0.0.0) into the OSPF domain assumes the router running the command already has a default route configured.

The **default-information originate** command will advertise the default route, as long as there is one in the routing table.

Adding the word *always* to the end of the command **default-information originate always** will advertise the default even if there is no default route in the routing table. Assume that a router has a default route received from another router. If it is using **default-information originate** to share the route with its neighbors, and for any reason that default route is removed from the table, the router will stop advertising the default to its neighbors. Adding the **always** option would make sure the route continued to be advertised. In essence it is saying "let's continue to share this route anyway even though it has disappeared from our table."

VLSM and Route Summarization

Earlier in this chapter we mentioned that OSPF supports VLSM, which in Chapter 3 indicated that we can more efficiently segment our networks into usable sizes than we could in the older classful days. Figure 10-5 shows our network from earlier, except that Router C used VLSM to create three subnets, one with 126 (128–2) host addresses and two with 62 (64–2). The three subnets are 192.168.3.0/25, 192.168.3.128/26, and 192.168.3.192/26.

FIGURE 10-5

Our sample
network Area 0
with VLSM

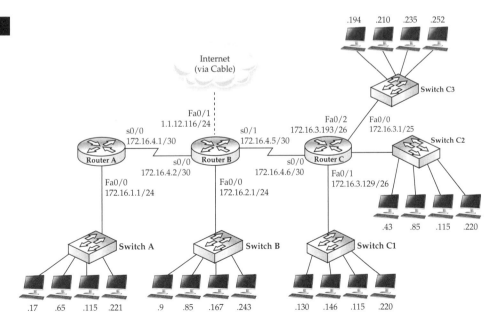

It gets even better—with OSPF, Routers A and B do not need to maintain all three of those routes in their routing tables. OSPF supports something called route summarization, which means that since those three subnets all came from the 192.168.3.0/24 address pool, Router C can share that one address with the others. Any address in LANs C1, C2, and C3 sent to Router C using a route to 192.168.3.0/24 would then be distributed properly by Router C. Okay, it's maybe not all that dramatic in our example, but imagine a network made up of dozens of routers and hundreds of subnets. Route summarization could greatly reduce the number of links shared, the complexity of the topology map on each router, and the size of the routing table on each router.

This same logic applies in designing our IP addressing scheme throughout our AS so that the ABRs can efficiently summarize the routes going into other areas.

So while VLSM allows us to more efficiently use IPv4 addresses, route summarization allows us to simplify our routing process. Just remember that you can design networks to be summarized, but you probably can't summarize a network that wasn't thoughtfully designed.

Load Balancing

While not a CCENT requirement to be able to configure, another advantage to OSPF is that it supports what is called equal-cost load balancing. Normally, if a router has two routes to a destination, it picks one and sends all traffic along that route as long as nothing changes. But if it knows about two to four OSPF routes to the same destination that share the same cost (metric), it will split up the traffic over them, reducing the chances of congestion and lost packets. The default is up to four paths, but can be configured up to sixteen. This means you could run two Gigabit links between two routers for redundancy, in case the link fails, and double your bandwidth as an additional benefit.

It is even possible to manipulate the cost metric to allow or prevent load balancing.

Process ID (PID)

Enabling OSPF uses the syntax **router ospf *process-id*** in Global Configuration mode. An example might be Router1(config)#**router ospf 1**. The process-id (or PID) is any whole number that the router uses internally to keep track of this OSPF routing instance. It can literally be any number unique to this process on the router. Since it is only locally significant on that router, every router could have a different PID if that served some purpose for you. Because that can lead to confusion for admins and increase the chances of configuration errors, many admins just use one PID for all routers in the AS, such as **router ospf 1** on all routers.

It is possible to configure two process IDs on a single router, like Router B with the interfaces to Routers A and D in one (**router ospf 1**) and the interface to router C in the other (**router ospf 2**). This is probably not something you want to do as we now have two separate instances of OSPF, which will not share information between them. There may be a case where this might be useful, but not here or on the CCENT exam.

Wildcard Mask vs. Subnet Mask

In Chapter 3 we learned that a subnet mask like 192.168.0.23 255.255.255.0 is used to identify the network portion of the address, in this case indicating that 192.168.0 is the network identifier. Processes using subnet masks don't care, but the remainder (.23) is the host ID. There is another mask system used by some processes like OSPF that are only interested in the hosts. They use what is called a wildcard mask. It would look like 192.168.0.0 0.0.0.255.

For all practical purposes, a wildcard mask is exactly the opposite of a subnet mask. For example, a subnet mask of 255.255.255.0 (binary: 11111111.11111111.11111111. 00000000) is the opposite of the wildcard mask 0.0.0.255 (binary: 00000000.00000000. 00000000.11111111).

Recalling subnet masks, the consecutive 1s indicated that bit location had to match and the 0s were irrelevant. Wildcards are the opposite: 0s indicate that bit location must match exactly, while the 1s don't matter.

While a process using subnet masks is interested in examining or using the network portion, a wildcard mask indicates which host values are to be examined or included.

Let's look at two extreme examples. 192.168.1.123 0.0.0.0 means all bits must match exactly, so we are talking about exactly the address 192.168.1.123. At the other extreme, 0.0.0.0 255.255.255.255 means any address at all is to be included. A wildcard of 192.168.0.0 0.0.0.255 means the first three octets must be exactly 192.168.0, but any value is acceptable in the fourth octet. While that sounds the same as the subnet 192.168.0.0 255.255.255.0, remember that the processes using the subnet mask only care about the network, while the processes using wildcard masks only care about the hosts to be included.

Using the previous examples, the OSPF command Router1(config-router)#**network 192.168.1.123 0.0.0.0 area 0** would include only the interface with the IP address 192.168.1.123 in Area 0. Router1(config-router)#**network 0.0.0.0 255.255.255.255 area 0** would include all interfaces in Area 0. Finally, Router1(config-router)#**network 192.168.0.0 0.0.0.255 area 0** would include all interfaces with the IP addresses from 192.168.1 to 192.168.1.254 in Area 0.

TABLE 10-4	IP Address	Wildcard Mask	Bits 25 and 26	Hosts Included
	192.168.1.0	0.0.0.63	00	0-63
Wildcard Mask	192.168.1.64	0.0.0.63	01	64-127
0.0.0.63 Examples	192.168.1.128	0.0.0.63	10	128-191
	192.168.1.192	0.0.0.63	11	192-255

So far we have looked at all or nothing, but just as we can subnet like 192.168.1.0/26, we can create its wildcard mask 0.0.0.63 equivalent. In binary that would mean that only the last 6 bits are to be included, as in 00000000.00000000.00000000.00111111—bits 25 and 26 must match. Table 10-4 shows the possible results.

The important thing to understand is that the wildcard mask is the exact inversion (opposite) of the subnet mask. Our binary conversion table from Chapter 3 can help with that. To check your work, Google *wildcard mask calculator*. One we like in particular is SubnetOnline.com because of all the information that it displays. Figure 10-6 shows the output from checking our example. The links on the right show the other calculators included.

Passive Interfaces in OSPF

In Chapter 9 we discussed how we could use a passive interface command to prevent routing protocols from sending routing-related traffic into networks, such as LANs, where there are no routers to use it. Unnecessary routing protocol exchanges increase CPU overhead on the router and pose a security risk in disseminating routing information toward client PCs.

OSPF uses the Router(config-if)#**ip ospf passive-interface** command in Interface Configuration mode to have an interface not participate in OSPF by not sending hello packets and routing updates. The interface is still included in routing updates sent out so that the LAN can be reached as part of the network.

Things to Remember about OSPF

Some things to remember about OSPF over distance-vector or static routing:

- OSPF supports variable-length subnet masks (VLSMs), which allows us to efficiently distribute IP addresses.
- OSPF supports route summarization, which reduces the size of LSA exchanges, the complexity of topology maps on each router, and the number of routes in each router's routing table.

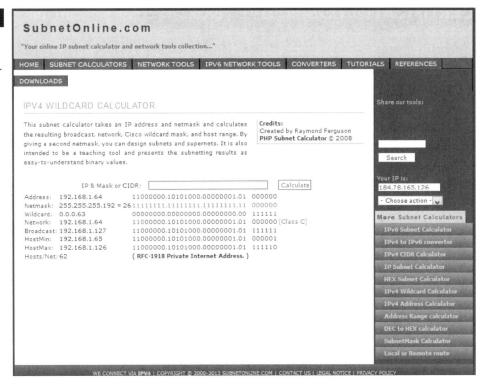

FIGURE 10-6

Wildcard
calculator output.
Used with
permission from
SubnetOnline
.com.

- OSPF uses multicasts (not broadcasts) to send updates, 224.0.0.5 (all SPF routers) and 224.0.0.6 (all designated routers, or DRs).

- OSPF converges much faster because it propagates changes immediately.

- Process ID, or PID, is a whole number identifying internally a router process, OSPF. It is then used like a name badge to keep the process pieces together yet separate from other processes.

- OSPF allows for load balancing with up to six equal-cost paths.

- OSPF uses a wildcard mask, which is basically the opposite of a subnet mask. It identifies the hosts to be included, while the subnet mask identifies the network.

- The **ip ospf passive-interface** command prevents OSPF from sending hello and routing updates out an interface where they are unneeded or unwanted, such as the local LAN segment.

- OSPF does have a few potential disadvantages, including the level of difficulty and understanding required to configure, monitor, and troubleshoot it. It has greater memory and central processing unit (CPU) requirements that can impact router performance.

CERTIFICATION OBJECTIVE 10.02

Configuring OSPF

The actual steps for configuring single-area (Area 0) OSPF is actually quite simple. There are basically two new commands to enable OSPF routing when dealing with a single area. The rest of this chapter looks at configuring and verifying OSPF.

Enabling OSPF: Single Area

To enable a new OSPF routing process on a router, follow these steps:

Router# **configure terminal**
Router(config)# **router ospf** *process-id*
Router(router-config)#**network** *ip-address wildcard-mask* **area** *area-id*
Router(router-config)#**end**

An example, assuming we are going to use a loopback as the router ID, might look like this. Note the mask on the loopback is called a host mask, meaning there is only the one address there, since we are using it only for our RID.

```
Router1# configure terminal
Router1(config)# interface loopback 0
Router1(config-if)# ip address 10.0.0.1 255.255.255.255
Router1(config-if)# exit
Router1(config)# router ospf 1
Router1(router-config)# network 0.0.0.0 255.255.255.255 area 0
Router1(router-config)# CTRL-Z
```

The **router ospf 1** starts the OSPF process. Recall that the *process-id* can be any whole number. It is only used internally by the router to keep track of this routing process. To avoid confusion, we could use the same PID on all of our internal routers.

The **network 0.0.0.0 255.255.255.255 area 0** puts all interfaces, including any loopbacks, into OSPF Area 0, advertising their links if they are active. The *ip-address* and *wildcard-mask* in this case indicate *all networks* with *all masks*, including the loopback address. The *area-id* is the router area these networks belong to. In the case of the core or backbone area, it would normally be 0 and must be 0 if there is only one area.

Confirming OSPF Configuration

While the **show running-config** command will show the configuration, the **show ip protocols** command shows a lot more information.

```
Router1#show ip protocols
Routing Protocol is "ospf 1"
  Outgoing update filter list for all interfaces is not set
  Incoming update filter list for all interfaces is not set
  Router ID 10.0.0.1
  Number of areas in this router is 1. 1 normal 0 stub 0 nssa
  Maximum path: 4
  Routing for Networks:
   0.0.0.0 255.255.255.255 area 0
Passive Interface(s):
    FastEthernet0/0
    FastEthernet0/1
  Routing Information Sources:
    Gateway          Distance       Last Update
  Distance: (default is 110)    ←Administrative Distance
```

Enabling OSPF: More Involved

This example shows using more elaborate wildcard masks, which are definitely required to understand for the exam. Note that the mask on the network statement for the loopback means that only that one address is being advertised.

```
Router2# configure terminal
Router2(config)# interface loopback 0
Router2(config-if)# ip address 10.0.0.2 255.255.255.255
Router2(config-if)# exit
Router2(config)# router ospf 1
Router2(router-config)# network 192.168.1.0 0.0.0.255 area 0
Router2(router-config)# network 192.168.2.0 0.0.0.255 area 0
Router2(router-config)# network 192.168.3.0 0.0.0.63 area 0
Router2(router-config)# network 192.168.3.64 0.0.0.63 area 0
Router2(router-config)# network 10.0.0.2 0.0.0.0  area 0
Router2(router-config)# CTRL-Z
```

Manual Configuration of RID

It is possible to manually define the RID instead of using loopbacks. Any unique IP address can be defined as RID, and (like loopbacks) it is always enabled.

If OSPF is already enabled, a manual configuration change of the RID is performed. It does not take effect until the next router reloads or OSPF routing restarts.

The following commands show how to manually configure the RID. The **clear ip ospf process** command is used to activate the RID on a router that is already running OSPF:

Router(config)#**router ospf** *process-ID*
Router(config-router)#**router-id** *ip-address*
Router(config-router)#**end**
Router#**clear ip ospf process**

An example of using the manual configuration instead of a loopback might look like this:

```
Router3# configure terminal
Router3(config)# router ospf 1
Router3(router-config)# router-id 10.0.0.3
Router3(router-config)# network 192.168.0.0 0.0.0.255 area 0
Router3(router-config)# end
Router3# clear ip ospf process
```

Configuring and Distributing Default Routes

Let's assume that Router 1 is an ASBR with the network's connection to the Internet. We can configure a default route to the ISP using the **ip route 0.0.0.0 0.0.0.0** *next_hop_addr* command as we saw in Chapter 9. Recall that the four zeroes, called quad-zero, are acting like wildcard characters. The first quad-zero means "any network" while the second quad-zero means "any mask."

Then so we don't have to configure it on every other router in the area, we will use the **default-information originate always** command to share the route. The **always** option means the routers will share the default route even if it is not in the routing table.

```
Router1# configure terminal
Router1(config)# interface loopback 0
Router1(config-if)# ip address 10.0.0.1 255.255.255.255
Router1(config-if)# exit
Router1(config)# ip route 0.0.0.0 0.0.0.0 172.16.4.2
Router1(config)# router ospf 1
Router1(router-config)# network 192.168.0.0 0.0.255.255 area 0
Router1(router-config)# default-information originate always
Router1(router-config)#CTRL-Z
```

Verifying Default Route and Distribution

There are three particularly useful commands we can use to confirm the configuration is working properly.

The show ip route Command   Our old friend the **show ip route** command displays the current status of the routing table, including any default route.

```
Router(config-if)#show ip route
Codes: C - connected, S - static, R - RIP, M - mobile, B - BGP
       D - EIGRP, EX - EIGRP external, O - OSPF, IA - OSPF inter area
       N1 - OSPF NSSA external type 1, N2 - OSPF NSSA external type 2
       E1 - OSPF external type 1, E2 - OSPF external type 2
       i - IS-IS, su - IS-IS summary, L1 - IS-IS level-1, L2 - IS-IS level-2
       ia - IS-IS inter area, * - candidate default, U - per-user static route
       o - ODR, P - periodic downloaded static route
Gateway of last resort is 172.16.4.2 to network 0.0.0.0
     10.0.0.0/30 is subnetted, 3 subnets
C       10.1.1.0 is directly connected, Serial0/1
O       10.10.10.0 [110/128] via 10.20.20.2, 00:05:14, Serial0/0
                   [110/128] via 10.1.1.2, 00:05:14, Serial0/1
C       10.20.20.0 is directly connected, Serial0/0
     172.16.0.0/24 is subnetted, 2 subnets
C       172.16.4.0 is directly connected, FastEthernet0/1
O       172.16.10.0 [110/65] via 10.1.1.2, 00:05:14, Serial0/1
O     192.168.1.0/24 [110/65] via 10.20.20.2, 00:07:38, Serial0/0
O     192.168.2.0/24 [110/65] via 10.20.20.2, 00:09:45, Serial0/0
O     192.168.3.0/24 [110/65] via 10.20.20.2, 00:08:15, Serial0/0
O     192.168.4.0/24 [110/65] via 10.1.1.0, 00:07:12, Serial0/1
O     192.168.5.0/24 [110/65] via 10.1.1.0, 00:06:54, Serial0/1
O     192.168.6.0/24 [110/65] via 10.1.1.0, 00:09:15, Serial0/1
C     192.168.8.0/24 is directly connected, FastEthernet0/0
S*    0.0.0.0/0 [1/0] via 172.16.4.2
Router#
```

By adding 0.0.0.0 to the command it displays just the default route info.

```
Router1#show ip route 0.0.0.0
S* 0.0.0.0/0 [1/0] via 172.16.4.2, 00:28:00, Fa0/1
```

The show ip ospf database Command   The **show ip ospf database** command displays a list of the link-state advertisements (LSAs) and adds them to a link-state database. The output shows only the information in the LSA header and in this case includes only the lines relative to what we are working on.

```
Router1#show ip ospf database
        OSPF Router with ID (10.0.0.1) (Process ID 1)

                Router Link States (Area 0)
```

```
Link ID     ADV Router    Age    Seq#           Checksum    Link count
10.0.0.1    10.0.0.1      600    0x80000232     0x9583          1

               Summary Net Link States (Area 0)
Link ID     ADV Router    Age    Seq#           Checksum
10.0.0.1    10.0.0.1      600    0x80000232     0x8E61

               Type-5 AS External Link States
Link ID     ADV Router    Age    Seq#           Checksum    Tag
0.0.0.0     10.0.0.1      601    0x80000232     0xD0D8          0
```

Configuring Passive Interfaces

Let's assume that Router 1 has two serial interfaces connected to two other internal routers in a single-area OSPF. But it also has two LANs that have no routers and therefore do not need OSPF hello and LSAs. We still want the networks advertised to other routers, so we will include them in OSPF and then use the Router(config-if)#**ip ospf passive-interface** command. If at a later time we wanted to remove the passive feature, we use the **no ip ospf passive-interface** command.

```
Router1# configure terminal
Router1(config)# interface loopback 0
Router1(config-if)# ip address 10.0.0.1 255.255.255.255
Router1(config)# interface serial 0/0
Router1(config-if)# ip address 192.168.0.1 255.255.255.252
Router1(config-if)# no shutdown
Router1(config)# interface serial 0/1
Router1(config-if)# ip address 192.168.0.5 255.255.255.252
Router1(config-if)# no shutdown
Router1(config)# interface FastEthernet 0/0
Router1(config-if)# ip address 192.168.2.1 255.255.255.0
Router1(config-if)# ip ospf passive-interface
Router1(config-if)# no shutdown
Router1(config)# interface FastEthernet 0/1
Router1(config-if)# ip address 192.168.3.1 255.255.255.0
Router1(config-if)# ip ospf passive-interface
Router1(config-if)# no shutdown
Router1(config-if)# end
Router1(config)# router ospf 1
Router1(router-config)# network 192.168.0.0 0.0.0.3 area 0
Router1(router-config)# network 192.168.0.4 0.0.0.3 area 0
Router1(router-config)# network 192.168.2.0 0.0.0.255 area 0
```

```
Router1(router-config)# network 192.168.3.0 0.0.0.255 area 0
Router1(router-config)# network 10.0.0.1 0.0.0.0 area 0
Router1(router-config)# CTRL-Z
```

Confirming Passive Interfaces

While the **show running-config** command will show any passive interfaces, so will the **show ip protocols** command.

```
Router1#show ip protocols
Routing Protocol is "ospf 1"
  Outgoing update filter list for all interfaces is not set
  Incoming update filter list for all interfaces is not set
  Router ID 10.0.0.1
  Number of areas in this router is 1. 1 normal 0 stub 0 nssa
  Maximum path: 4
  Routing for Networks:
   192.168.0.0 0.0.255.255 area 0
Passive Interface(s):
   FastEthernet0/0
   FastEthernet0/1
  Routing Information Sources:
   Gateway        Distance       Last Update
  Distance: (default is 110)
```

Configuring OSPF Priority

Let's assume that Router 2 has two Fast Ethernet interfaces connected to two different multi-access networks and we'd like to make sure that Fast Ethernet 0/0 never becomes the DR or BDR for its network segment, but we would like Fast Ethernet 0/1 to win any elections in its segment. To accomplish this we will use the **ip ospf priority** *num* command to change the default priority from 1. The range of values is 0–255, where 0 means never and higher numbers increase the likelihood of winning.

```
Router2# configure terminal
Router2(config)# interface FastEthernet 0/0
Router2(config-if)# ip address 192.168.1.2 255.255.255.0
Router2(config-if)# ip ospf priority 0
Router2(config-if)# no shutdown
Router2(config)# interface FastEthernet 0/1
Router2(config-if)# ip address 192.168.9.2 255.255.255.0
Router2(config-if)# ip ospf priority 50
Router2(config-if)# no shutdown
Router2(router-config)# CTRL-Z
```

Verifying Priority

We can verify the priority on a per-interface basis by using the **show ip ospf interface** ***int_id***. Notice that State reminds us that changing the priority does not trigger a DR/BDR election.

```
Router2# show ip ospf interface FastEthernet 0/1
FastEthernet 0/1 is up, line protocol is up
  Internet Address 192.168.9.2/24, Area 2
  Process ID 1, Router ID 10.0.2.2, Network Type BROADCAST, Cost: 1
  Transmit Delay is 1 sec, State DROTHER, Priority 50
```

We could also see the priority settings of all segment routers using the **show ip ospf neighbor** command. In this case, we see that we have had an election and the priorities are yielding the desired results.

```
Router2# show ip ospf neighbor
Neighbor ID    Pri    State          Dead Time    Address        Interface
10.0.2.1         1    FULL/DROTHER   00:00:37     192.168.9.1    FastEthernet0/1
10.0.2.2        50    FULL/DR        00:00:34     192.168.9.2    FastEthernet0/1
10.0.2.3        10    FULL/BDR       00:00:39     192.168.9.3    FastEthernet0/1
```

Verifying OSPF

After configuring OSPF (or any routing protocol, for that matter), several commands can be used to verify that it's working properly. First, you can verify the route table with the **show ip route** command. Notice that there are two equal-cost routes to network 10.10.10.0, which means we could load-balance over those links.

```
Router(config-if)#show ip route
Codes: C - connected, S - static, R - RIP, M - mobile, B - BGP
       D - EIGRP, EX - EIGRP external, O - OSPF, IA - OSPF inter area
       N1 - OSPF NSSA external type 1, N2 - OSPF NSSA external type 2
       E1 - OSPF external type 1, E2 - OSPF external type 2
       i - IS-IS, su - IS-IS summary, L1 - IS-IS level-1, L2 - IS-IS level-2
       ia - IS-IS inter area, * - candidate default, U - per-user static route
       o - ODR, P - periodic downloaded static route
Gateway of last resort is 172.16.4.2 to network 0.0.0.0
     10.0.0.0/30 is subnetted, 3 subnets
C       10.1.1.0 is directly connected, Serial0/1
O       10.10.10.0 [110/128] via 10.20.20.2, 00:05:14, Serial0/0
                   [110/128] via 10.1.1.2, 00:05:14, Serial0/1
C       10.20.20.0 is directly connected, Serial0/0
     172.16.0.0/24 is subnetted, 2 subnets
C       172.16.4.0 is directly connected, FastEthernet0/1
O       172.16.10.0 [110/65] via 10.1.1.2, 00:05:14, Serial0/1
O    192.168.1.0/24 [110/65] via 10.20.20.2, 00:07:38, Serial0/0
O    192.168.2.0/24 [110/65] via 10.20.20.2, 00:09:45, Serial0/0
O    192.168.3.0/24 [110/65] via 10.20.20.2, 00:08:15, Serial0/0
```

```
O    192.168.4.0/24 [110/65] via 10.1.1.0, 00:07:12, Serial0/1
O    192.168.5.0/24 [110/65] via 10.1.1.0, 00:06:54, Serial0/1
O    192.168.6.0/24 [110/65] via 10.1.1.0, 00:09:15, Serial0/1
C    192.168.8.0/24 is directly connected, FastEthernet0/0
S*   0.0.0.0/0 [1/0] via 172.16.4.2
Router#
```

A variation of the command, **show ip route ospf**, would list only the OSPF routes.

e x a m

ⓦatch   *You will definitely need to know how to configure OSPF on a router. While it's only a couple of commands to remember, it is important that you enable OSPF after configuring your router ID (RID) and your interfaces are up. If you don't, it can have an impact on your RID and DR/BDR elections in multi-access*   *networks. Remember that adding interfaces or changing the configuration doesn't trigger a recalculation of the RID or DR/BDR. You may need to reboot the device—never a good idea in a production network—disable/ enable OSPF, or disable/enable the DR interfaces to trigger the changes.*

EXERCISE 10-2

MHE Lab

Configuring Single-Area OSPF

In this exercise we demonstrate the steps an administrator would take to configure single-area OSPF. You'll perform this exercise using Boson's NetSim. Launch Lab 10-2 and review the topology.

To begin with, all hosts and switches are configured. All links are configured as well. There is no routing of any kind in place, so we will resolve that in these labs. All devices except the Internet device have our normal usernames and passwords configured.

Task 1: Configure OSPF on RouterA

1. Either open a console session on RouterA or Telnet from A.22.

2. We are going to create a loopback interface 0 to become our router ID (RID). Then we enable OSPF using process ID 1, although it could be any number.

Finally, we add a network statement to put all 10.0.0.0 networks into Area 0. Note the wildcard mask, which is not a subnet mask.

```
RouterA#conf t
Enter configuration commands, one per line.  End with CNTL/Z.
RouterA(config)#interface loopback 0
RouterA(config-if)#description OSPF RID
RouterA(config-if)#ip address 10.100.0.1 255.255.255.255
RouterA(config-if)#exit
RouterA(config)#router ospf 1
RouterA(config-router)#network 10.0.0.0 0.255.255.255 area 0
RouterA(config)#CTRL-Z
```

We would usually add the following command in Router Configuration mode so that hellos and LSAs are not unnecessarily sent into our LAN. (You can do this in the Full Edition of NetSim or simply follow along here.)

```
RouterA(config)#interface fastethernet 0/0
RouterA(config-if)#ip ospf passive-interface
```

3. Run **show ip ospf interface**, and you will see information about each interface included in our OSPF session. Notice the interface status, IP address, process ID (PID), router ID (RID), timers, and the neighbor information, which is zero now because this is the only router running OSPF at the moment. For the same reason, we won the election to be the designated router (DR).

4. Run **show ip ospf database**. There should be only one entry now because this is the only router running OSPF at the moment. Note it does show the router ID.

5. Run **show ip ospf neighbor**. There are no entries now because this is the only router running OSPF at the moment.

6. There is another command, **show ip ospf**, that reports the OSPF status and is included in the Full Edition of NetSim. The full output is in the "Lab Solutions" section in the PDF Lab Book, but the key pieces are as follows:

```
RouterA#show ip ospf
 Routing Process "ospf 1" with ID 10.100.0.1
 Supports only single TOS(TOS0) routes
---output omitted (see Lab Solutions)---
 External flood list length 0
    Area BACKBONE(0)
```

```
Number of interfaces in this area is 3
Area has no authentication
SPF algorithm last executed 00:00:00 ago
SPF algorithm executed 3 times
```
---output omitted (see Lab Solutions)---

7. Run a **show ip route** command to confirm that all the router knows about is connected subnets.

8. Save your work.

Task 2: Configure OSPF on RouterB

1. Open a console session on RouterB.

2. You could use the same steps for each of the other routers, but with RouterB you want to make sure you don't include the Internet interface; you don't exchange routes with any outside (non-AS) networks. This time we will list the networks separately for the experience, which is a necessity if you had a mix of IP addresses that didn't mask as easily as our example (a mix like 10.0.0.0, 192.168.0.0, and 172.16.0.0 maybe).

```
RouterB#conf t
Enter configuration commands, one per line.  End with CNTL/Z.
RouterB(config)#interface loopback 0
RouterB(config-if)#description OSPF RID
RouterB(config-if)#ip address 10.100.0.2 255.255.255.255
RouterB(config-if)#exit
RouterB(config)#router ospf 1
RouterB(config-router)#network 10.0.1.0 0.0.0.255 area 0
RouterB(config-router)#network 10.1.1.0 0.0.0.3 area 0
RouterB(config-router)#network 10.1.1.4 0.0.0.3 area 0
RouterB(config-router)#network 10.1.1.8 0.0.0.3 area 0
RouterB(config-router)#network 10.100.0.2 0.0.0.0 area 0
RouterB(config)#CTRL-Z
```

We would usually add the following command in Router Configuration mode so that hellos and LSAs are not unnecessarily sent into our LAN. (You can do this in the Full Edition of NetSim or simply follow along here.)

```
RouterB(config)#interface fastethernet 0/0
RouterB(config-if)#ip ospf passive-interface
```

> **Note:** *Even if you used the passive interface, you still include the LAN in network statements. You want the route advertised to the rest of the routers; you just don't want the updates to be sent into segments that can't use them.*

3. Run the **show** commands from the previous task and notice more information is showing up. The **show ip route** command should now be showing routes learned from RouterA.

   You should be able to ping the RID (10.100.0.1) on RouterA, any interface on RouterA, SwitchA (10.0.0.2), or Host A.22 (10.0.0.22).

4. Before leaving RouterB, you need to deal with the Internet connection since it isn't part of the routing. As you learned earlier, these routes are usually default routes. Since you don't want to have to enter a default route on all routers, you would also use the **default-information originate always** command. Go ahead and enter them; the default route will work, but the second command (**default-information originate always**) isn't featured in the NetSim Limited Edition and you'll get the error message shown next.

```
RouterB#configure terminal
Enter configuration commands, one per line.  End with CNTL/Z.
RouterB(config)#ip route 0.0.0.0 0.0.0.0 1.1.1.1
RouterB(config)#router ospf 1
RouterB(config-router)#default-information originate always

Unsupported Command. Command compatible with NetSim for CCNP.

RouterB(config-router)#CTRL-Z
```

5. Ping 64.0.0.1 to see that the default route sent it to the Internet and the site replied. If the **default-information originate always** command was supported, this would be true from all devices.

6. Run the **show ip route** command to see that your default route appears in two places.

7. Look at the routing table for RouterA. You should see routes learned from RouterB but no default route because of NetSim not supporting the **default-information originate always** command.

8. Save your work.

Task 3: Configure OSPF on RouterC and RouterD

1. Use the skills in Task 2 and Task 3 to configure OSPF on RouterC and RouterD. Use the topology diagram to help with router IDs and anything else you need. Define your networks using either the method in Task 2 or Task 3. When you are done, both hosts should be able to ping each other and everything in between.

   If you need help, the steps are in the "Lab Solutions" section.

2. Save your work.

Troubleshooting OSPF Commands

We've looked at several commands for verifying our configuration and to troubleshoot connection issues. There are many more depending a lot on the technologies you are using for links. Cisco has many fine references, but Google works very well too, bringing up both Cisco and third-party resources. If you haven't already, Google *troubleshooting ospf*. Everyone should Google *cisco password recovery* if you are working in the field or buying used equipment for a lab.

There are two types of commands that are commonly used, show and debug commands. Each has its place and purpose. Show commands are a snapshot in time; they will not change unless you run them again. Debug commands, on the other hand, show activities in real time, occasionally scrolling faster than the user can absorb. In a production environment, debug commands can overwhelm the CPU, particularly if it is already running near capacity. There are two handy commands for stopping runaway debugs: **no debug all** and **undebug all**. The latter can be reduced to **un all**.

OSPF Show Commands:

- show ip protocols
- show ip route ospf
- show ip ospf interfaces
- show ip ospf neighbors
- show ip ospf database
- show ip ospf

Debug Commands:

- ■ debug ip ospf adjacency
- ■ debug ip ospf events
- ■ debug ip spf hello

Debug Example

The following is an example of a debug command, **debug ip ospf events** specifically. Router 1 can't form adjacency with two routers with RIDs 10.0.0.2 and 10.0.0.3. The hello from 10.0.0.2 came in on the Serial0/0 interface from 192.168.2.2, which must be an interface of 10.0.0.2's. It is saying the hello parameters don't match. The third and sixth rows show the problem. The dead interval is 120 on the Received packet but 40 on the Configured machine. The hello intervals match at 30. There are two hello/dead default intervals, 10/40 for faster Ethernet networks and 30/120 for slower serial links. Whoever configured Router 1 got the hello right but flubbed the dead interval.

```
Router1#debug ip ospf events
OSPF events debugging is on
Router1#
06:21:09: OSPF: Rcv hello from 10.0.0.2 area 0 from Serial0/0 192.168.2.2
06:21:09: OSPF: Mismatched hello parameters from 192.168.2.2
06:21:09: OSPF: Dead R 120 C 40, Hello R 30 C 30
06:21:09: OSPF: Rcv hello from 10.0.0.3 area 0 from Serial0/0 192.168.2.6
06:21:09: OSPF: Mismatched hello parameters from 192.168.2.6
06:21:09: OSPF: Dead R 120 C 40, Hello R 30 C 30
Router1#no debug ip ospf events
```

If the output is slow enough, the full no command can be used, but don't forget **un all**—you will need it someday.

EXERCISE 10-3

MHE Lab

Troubleshooting Your Network

In this exercise we demonstrate the steps an administrator would take to troubleshoot general routing issues, OSPF-specific issues, and we will cover some Layer 1 and 2 issues that you might see on the exam and will definitely see in the field. You'll perform this exercise using Boson's NetSim. Launch Lab 10-3 and review the topology.

To begin with, all hosts and switches are configured. All links are configured as well. OSPF is the routing in place. All devices except the Internet device have our normal usernames and passwords configured.

Task 1: Troubleshoot Routing Issues

These are general routing issues. We just happen to be using OSPF for our protocol, but they would apply to any of them.

1. Telnet from A.22 to RouterB using 10.100.0.2, the router ID. You could Telnet to any interface on the device, but it is dependent on that interface being up. This is why loopbacks make more stable device IDs. If we hadn't included them in our routing statements (**network 10.100.0.0.2 255.255.255.255 area 0**), we couldn't do this.

2. From Privileged mode, ping 64.0.0.1, which is a server simulated on the Internet. It should work just fine.

3. Do a **show ip route** to confirm that there is a default route to the Internet.

4. Exit back to A.22 and ping 64.0.0.1. Did it work? We have routing, so why not? We just pinged RouterB, so we know it can find that. We also know that RouterB knows where 64.0.0.1 is; we just proved it. Where do we look?

5. Telnet to RouterA (10.100.0.1) and do a **show ip route**. Where will RouterA forward packets to 64.0.0.1?

   It has nowhere to send them. Remember, if there is no route to the destination, the packet is discarded. That is why we often have a default route to handle cases like this. It's not possible to have any router know every subnet on the Internet. If you recall, NetSim didn't accept our **default-information originate always** command in Exercise 10-2, which would have solved this problem by sharing it with us.

6. Try entering this on RouterA:

   ```
   RouterA#configure terminal
   RouterA(config)#ip route 0.0.0.0 0.0.0.0 10.1.1.1
   RouterA(config)#CTRL-Z
   ```

   Do a **show ip route** and see that you have a shiny new static route.

7. Save your work and return to A.22 to see whether you can ping 64.0.0.1; it should work now.

8. If we had the problem on RouterA, we probably have it on RouterC and RouterD as well.

   Open a console on host D.21 and ping both 10.100.0.2 and 64.0.0.1. Why 10.100.0.2? This is so that when 64.0.0.1 fails, we know we have a routing problem since we can get to the network's edge router.

9. Telnet to RouterD (10.100.0.4) and do a **show ip route** to confirm our diagnosis. Note RouterD knows about all the LANs, all the links, and all other routers, but no default route.

   That's simple to fix, right? Aren't there two paths to B, with one short and one longer? But if the shorter one fails, does it really matter that the other one is longer? Why not put in both?

   Do a **show ip route** and see that you have a shiny new static route.

   In real life, we would add a small AD to the second (least attractive) one so that it would be used only in case the primary went down. NetSim doesn't support it, but this would be the change. We keep the AD small (5 here), so it would still be chosen over a routing protocol.

   ```
   RouterD#configure terminal
   RouterD(config)#ip route 0.0.0.0 0.0.0.0 10.1.1.9
   RouterD(config)#ip route 0.0.0.0 0.0.0.0 10.1.1.13 5
   RouterD(config)#CTRL-z
   ```

10. Save your work and return to D.21 to see whether you can ping 64.0.0.1. It should work now, right? What, it doesn't?

11. Maybe we have a bigger problem, but let's talk briefly about multiple default routes. Ping issues five echo requests, and RouterD treats them as five jobs. Since we didn't add an AD to either one, it is sending three down the first path and two down the second path. If you look at the routing table, it even listed both routes.

    RouterB knows the default route, but RouterC doesn't yet, so we would expect those two to fail (it might take a minute of watching it to think of that). Let's solve C first.

12. Open a console session on RouterC. Try to ping 64.0.0.1, if you like. Then look at the route table; there's no default route. We have the same two paths that it could travel on, so let's add both.

    ```
    RouterC#configure terminal
    RouterC(config)#ip route 0.0.0.0 0.0.0.0 10.1.1.5
    RouterC(config)#ip route 0.0.0.0 0.0.0.0 10.1.1.14
    RouterC(config)#CTRL-z
    ```

    Do a **show ip route** and see that you have a shiny new static route.

13. Save your work and return to D.21 to see whether you can ping 64.0.0.1; it should work now. If all five pings are successful, doesn't that solve all of our problems?

One thing you don't want to do is claim success too early. Three of five should have worked (the ones from D to B) when we added the static routes to RouterD, and yet none did. What's up with that? Now only two of five should work: the ones sent from D to C. But all five work. A little voice in your head should be saying "Yes, but, something doesn't seem quite right…." We'll work on that in the next task because it seems like an OSPF problem.

Just to summarize before we leave this, the real problem is that we couldn't use the **default-information originate always** command on RouterB, which would have then shared the default route. Since that is not available to us, we opted for static routes on each router. It's kind of a pain, and it exposed another possible problem. When one is new, it is common to assume you just made a mistake, but when you know your logic is right and it doesn't work, at least consider that you are looking at a symptom of another problem.

Task 2: Troubleshoot OSPF Basics

Before we start, let's think through our problem. Each router seems to know about all other routers, all LANs, and all links. Run a **show ip route** on each to confirm that, if you like. So, we know that they are talking to each other. The only thing unusual about the network is that we have redundant paths between B, C, and D. Yet our ping from D.21 to 64.0.0.1 failed 100 percent of the time, when we expected it to work either two of five or three of five times. Maybe our redundancy is an illusion.

1. Open a console session on RouterA and do a **show ip route**. It should show all routers, LANs, and links.

2. Leave that session open and open another one on RouterC.

   We are going to shut down the interface Fa0/1 to RouterB and see what that does to RouterA's route table. Common sense says we should lose only that segment. Try it.

   ```
   RouterC#configure terminal
   RouterC(config)#int fa0/1
   RouterC(config-if)#shutdown
   ```

3. Back on RouterA, run your **show ip route** again. You may have to wait a moment for routing to take effect or run the command a couple of times. Did you get what you expected? Wow, we seemed to lose more than one link.

   ```
   RouterA#show ip route

   Gateway of last resort is 10.1.1.1 to network 0.0.0.0
   ```

```
      10.0.0.0/8 is variably subnetted, 5 subnets
C         10.0.0.0/24 is directly connected, FastEthernet0/0
O         10.0.1.0/24 [110/2] via 10.1.1.1, 01:48:22, FastEthernet0/1
C         10.1.1.0/30 is directly connected, FastEthernet0/1
C         10.100.0.1/32 is directly connected, Loopback0
O         10.100.0.2/32 [110/2] via 10.1.1.1, 01:48:22, FastEthernet0/1
S*    0.0.0.0/0 [1/0] via 10.1.1.1
RouterA#
```

Notice we don't see anything beyond RouterB. That tells us there may be a problem with the link between B and D (the one between B and C we shut down).

4. From RouterA, ping 10.1.1.9, the near end of that link. It should work. What does that tell us? The link is not down. Try pinging the other end, 10.1.1.10. It should fail. What does that tell us?

5. It's time to look at RouterB. Open a console session and run a **show ip interface brief** command.

   We should see that both serial interfaces are up/up, meaning both have a physical connection (Layer 1), and it recognizes the signaling (Layer 2). The link to RouterC (Fa2/0) is down/down, which is to be expected since we shut it down at RouterC. Note that it is not administratively down. That is how it would look from RouterC, but RouterB has no idea why there is no connection.

6. Ping 10.1.1.10, the far end of s3/1, to RouterD. It should work. That further confirms the link is good. Now ping RouterD's RID (10.100.0.4). Did it work? What does that tell us?

   The second ping failing, even though it is on the same router, means that RouterB doesn't know about it in the routing table.

   Run a **show ip route** to confirm that.

7. We could start solving this now, but let's look at something first. Return to the console for RouterC and enable Fa0/1 again. Unless you exited, you should be able to just run the command; otherwise, run the following and then return to RouterB:

```
RouterC#configure terminal
RouterC(config)#int fa0/1
RouterC(config-if)#no shutdown
```

8. On RouterB, you may have to wait a moment for the routing to process. You would see a message like the following:

```
*Jun 22 13:22:57.029: %OSPF-5-ADJCHG: Process 1, Nbr 10.100.0.3
on FastEthernet2/0 from LOADING to FULL, Loading Done
```

Run **show ip route** and look over the results.

You should see all routers, switches, and links, but look closely at the entry for RouterD, 10.100.0.4.

```
O       10.100.0.4/32 [110/66] via 10.1.1.6, 00:04:59,
FastEthernet2/0
```

It was learned by OSPF but from RouterC, not RouterD, even though RouterD is directly connected on a functioning link. What does this tell us? It confirms what we suspected at step 6, which is that we have a routing problem, not a connectivity problem.

9. On RouterB, run the **show ip ospf neighbor** command. What is it telling us? RouterB is not neighbored with RouterD.

Run a **show ip ospf interface brief** command. Neither serial interface is listed. s3/0 is expected because that is our link to the Internet, but s3/1 should be there.

Run the **show running-config** command and look for the routing information.

```
RouterB#show run
---output omitted---
!
router ospf 1
 log-adjacency-changes
 network 10.0.1.0 0.0.0.255 area 0
 network 10.1.1.0 0.0.0.3 area 0
 network 10.1.1.4 0.0.0.3 area 0
 network 10.100.0.2 0.0.0.0 area 0
!
---output omitted---
```

Oops! There's no entry for the 10.1.1.8/30 subnet. Fortunately, that is easy to fix. Try it on your own or make these entries:

```
RouterB#configure terminal
RouterB(config)#router ospf 1
RouterB(config-routee)#network 10.1.1.8 0.0.0.3 area 0
RouterB(config-routee)#ctrl-z
```

10. To confirm it worked, run **show ip route** to see that RouterD (10.100.04) is being learned over the 10.1.1.8/30 link.

11. Save your work.

In summary, just because your configuration is working doesn't mean it will always work. Break it and see whether it responds as you expected. If a little voice says "This doesn't seem right," then follow up. You don't want to find out when the network is being used. This process is easier when you have the traceroute tool, Cisco's version of tracert. It would show us the path traffic was taking, and that might have reduced the time to find and confirm the problem.

Task 3: Troubleshoot Layers 1 and 2

We are going to look at some simple troubleshooting steps to make sure our links are working as they should and whether any bad traffic is being received. There will be no failure like the last lab, just some tools to help you troubleshoot Layer 1 and Layer 2, much like we did on in Exercise 10-1 when we configured the serial interfaces. You should know this for the exam, and it is critical in the field.

1. Open a console session on SwitchA and run a **show interfaces fa0/11** command. This is the port that Host A.22 is connected to.

```
SwitchA#show interfaces fa0/11
FastEthernet0/11 is up, line protocol is up
  Hardware is Fast Ethernet, address is 000C.6653.5952 (bia
000C.6653.5952)
  MTU 1500 bytes, BW 100000 Kbit, DLY 100 usec,
     reliability 255/255, txload 1/255, rxload 1/255
  Auto-duplex, Auto-speed              ←Must match other end of cable
  Encapsulation ARPA, loopback not set
  ARP type: ARPA, ARP Timeout 04:00:00
  Last input 02:29:44, output never, output hang never
  Last clearing of "show interface" counters never      ←Counters
  Input queue: 0/75/0/0 (size/max/drops/flushes); Total output drops: 0
  Queuing strategy: fifo
  Output queue :0/40 (size/max)
  5 minute input rate 0 bits/sec, 0 packets/sec
  5 minute output rate 0 bits/sec, 0 packets/sec
     269 packets input, 71059 bytes, 0 no buffer
     Received 6 broadcasts, 0 runts, 0 giants, 0 throttles ←Bad
     0 input errors, 0 CRC, 0 frame, 0 overrun, 0 ignored  ←Bad
     7290 packets output, 429075 bytes, 0 underruns
     0 output errors, 3 interface resets          ←Bad frames out
     0 output buffer failures, 0 output buffers swapped out

SwitchA#
```

So, what are we looking for?

a. If data isn't getting through, do the following:

    i. Make sure the interface is up/up.

    ii. Make sure duplex and speed match the interface on the other end of the cable. This might allow intermittent data through.

b. Look at the packet's input to make sure that number is growing; you may need to ping through the interface to test this (that is, ping from A.22 to D.21). Pinging the interface doesn't count. Pinging from this device doesn't either. Neither passes through the interface.

c. Look for any input errors. Runts are packets that are too small (less than 64KB), and giants are too big (more than 1518KB). Both are usually the result of collisions or a duplex/speed mismatch. CRC errors indicate that the frame has changed since transmission. It could be from a collision or tampering.

d. Output errors are far less common because the device should discard bad frames.

2. Because any **show** command is a snapshot in time, you may need to run it several times to see whether the numbers are growing.

3. Here are some commands you might find useful and are in the Full Edition of NetSim:

a. From a host: **ping** *destination* **-n** *number*; C:>**ping 10.0.4.21 -n 100** would send 100 ping requests.

b. From a host: **ping** *destination* **-t**; C:>**ping 10.0.4.21 -t** would send pings until it gets a CTRL-C.

c. From a host: **tracert** *destination* would show Layer 3 devices between the source and destination.

d. From Cisco devices: **ping** and **traceroute** are supported. Use ? for options.

e. From Cisco devices: **clear counters [*int-id*]**, clear counters Fa0/11 would reset the counter to zero. The **clear counters** command by itself clears all counters. If a device has been running for a long time (years), some of the counters might be high. Clearing them makes changes easier to see between **show** commands.

The third red line in the previous output (*Last clearing of…*) indicates whether the counters have been cleared recently. This might indicate someone else was looking at this problem, if recent.

4. Remember to check both ends of the link; the problem could be on either end. In the case of a switch, it can't hurt to check the link to the router or other switches (Fa0/1 on SwitchA) in case the problem is there.

5. Take a moment and run the **show interfaces fa0/0** and **show interfaces s3/1** commands on RouterB to see that router interfaces will give similar information plus some additional information. The results of step 1 and step 4 are in the "Lab Solutions" section in the PDF Lab Book with the interesting lines in red.

INSIDE THE EXAM

OSPF Fundamentals

Make sure you know the types of areas used by OSPF, including the two proprietary ones Cisco and others added. What are the requirements for linking the areas together? Be sure that you know the router types and where they fit in relation to the areas. Know the difference in the roles of the DR, BDR, and DROther and how they are assigned. Know how loopbacks, RID, and priority are related and how to use them. Make sure you know what a wildcard mask is, how it relates to a subnet mask, and how to use them.

Make sure that you understand how the metric (cost) is used to select the best routes to offer to the routing table. Know that the routing table still uses AD to choose from alternative routes as they are learned from different protocols.

Make sure you understand what the process ID (PID) is and what it is used for. Understand that the benefits of OSPF include the following: distributing default routes, passive interfaces, route summarization, and load balancing. The exam may not ask you to configure all of them, but you should recognize them and what they do.

Configuring OSPF

Make sure that you know what needs to be done before enabling OSPF. Know how to configure OSPF in a single area, including how to define the router ID and use the passive interface feature to prevent updates and hellos from going into the LANs. Know the commands to confirm OSPF and then how to get the router to actually implement the changes you want.

CERTIFICATION SUMMARY

While the exam requirements specify that you be able to configure and verify OSPFv2 (single area), router ID, and passive interface, it also requires understanding the benefit of single-area OSPF.

Understand what OSPF is, an open standard, and that it uses areas to segment large networks.

Having a working knowledge of the areas, their limitations, and the four router roles would be a good foundation. Because of high bandwidth links for connecting large networks or campus networks, understanding the hello process and the DR/BDR election process becomes very important.

OSPF is a huge and complex protocol with many options, making it very versatile and an easy favorite for large IGP. Later you will learn that it integrates well with the Internet's routing protocol, making it a likely candidate to be around for a long time. It's nonproprietary, it scales well, and the standards come from the same organizations and processes as the Internet and its protocols. There is a rich library of help resources through Cisco, but also using Google and the Internet.

While reading this book is important, doing the exercises until you can do the major steps without written instructions and use the various show commands to verify your work will pay dividends on the exam and in your career.

TWO-MINUTE DRILL

OSPF Fundamentals

❑ Every router in an area maintains a duplicate copy of the area link-state database (LSDB) from which it calculates a topology map of the area and generates its routing table entries.

❑ Breaking a larger organization's network domain into areas reduces the size of the LSDB in area routers, the volume of exchanges that need to be done, the complexity of the topology, and the resulting routing table.

❑ The router roles are

    ❑ Area border router (ABR): Connect AS areas and maintain a separate link-state DB for each area

    ❑ Autonomous system boundary router (ASBR): Connect an AS area to the outside

    ❑ Internal router (IR): Routers with all interfaces within one area

    ❑ Backbone router (BR): All the backbone area (area 0) border routers

❑ Each router has an identifier (RID) in the dotted decimal format (e.g., 1.2.3.4) of an IP address. If not explicitly configured with the **router-id** *ip-addr* command, it will be the highest logical IP address at OSPF startup. Cisco devices will choose the highest loopback before looking at physical interfaces. The RID is not an IP address; it does not have to be a part of any routable subnet in the network and often isn't to avoid confusion.

❑ The backbone (normal) area, Area 0, is the only area in a single-area design. When other areas are added, they must all connect to the backbone via a border router or a virtual link. The backbone is the only area that allows links (LSAs) to be injected (or added) from other areas.

❑ Adjacent OSPF area routers form neighbor relationships via hello packet exchanges. If the hello exchanges are successful, they form an adjacency and will exchange LSAs. The hello process can only be successful if

    ❑ They see themselves in the other's hello packets.

    ❑ They are in the same area—area IDs match.

❑ Hello settings match—dead interval and hello interval in seconds. Both configurable, but dead interval is four times the hello interval by default: 40 and 10 for Ethernet or 120 and 30 for most serial WAN links.

❑ Stub area flag must be the same.

❑ Authentication settings must be the same.

❑ In multi-access In multi-access networks (Ethernet), there is a process to elect one router to be a designated router (DR) and a second router to be a backup designated router (BDR). The DR acts as collector and distributor for LSAs for the network. The BDR collects the same information in case the DR fails. All other routers are designated as DROthers.

❑ When a link changes, routers send their LSAs to the DR and BDR using a special multicast address 224.0.0.6. The DR processes and then uses multicast address 224.0.0.5 to flood the LSAs to the routers in the network.

❑ DR/BDR are interface roles, not router roles. A router could have more than one interface with DR or BDR roles.

❑ DR/BDR election is based on highest interface priority (1 by default), highest RID, or highest interface IP address. Priority can be configured between 0 and 255 using the **ip ospf priority #** command in Interface Configuration mode. A 0 (zero) priority makes the router ineligible to become DR or BDR.

❑ Timing is important: both RID and DR processes start when OSPF is enabled (router or network starts). It's important to have RID and interface priority in place. Adding them later changes nothing until the next reboot or DR/BDR election.

❑ The **show ip ospf neighbor** command shows neighbors, priority settings, and adjacency state.

❑ The **show ip ospf interface** *int_id* command shows interface priority, the DR and BDR, hello timers, adjacency state, and the neighbors.

❑ The **show ip ospf database** command shows the neighbors and the DR.

❑ OSPF routers gather link-state information from other routers and develop the same topology (map) of the network, which is then used to determine the routing table entries. All routers maintain an identical link-state database (LSDB) for each area that it has an interface in. IRs, those with all interfaces in one area, have a single LSDB, while ABRs would have one for each area it has interfaces in.

❑ Once all routers share the same LSDB and topology, each router independently uses a shortest path first algorithm to build and calculate a shortest path tree to all known destinations based on cost as metric.

❑ OSPF uses cost for its comparison metric in choosing the best route to a destination. The cost of a link is calculated by dividing the reference bandwidth (100 Mbps) by the interface bandwidth. Link cost of a 100-Mbps Ethernet link would have a metric of 100/100 = 1. Cost can be manipulated on an interface using the **ip ospf cost** *cost* command (range 1–65535) or the interface **bandwidth** command.

❑ OSPF can distribute default routes using the **default-information originate always** command. The **always** option ensures the route is exchanged even if it doesn't exist in the local route table.

❑ OSPF supports route summarization, reducing the size of LSDBs and routing tables.

❑ By default, OSPF supports load balancing over four identical-cost links. That can be increased to 16.

❑ OSPF uses wildcard masks, which for all practical purposes are exactly the opposite of a subnet mask. While the subnet mask identifies the network part of an IP address, the wildcard mask identifies the host portion to be included or processed.

  ❑ With subnet masks, the consecutive 1s indicated that bit location had to match and the 0s were irrelevant. Wildcards are the opposite: 0s indicated that bit location must match exactly, while the 1s don't matter.

  ❑ The subnet mask 192.168.0.0 255.255.255.0 is the opposite of the wildcard mask 192.168.0.0 0.0.0.255. At the extreme, 0.0.0.0 255.255.255.255 means any address at all is to be included.

❑ The **ip ospf passive-interface** command prevents OSPF from sending hello and routing updates out an interface where they are unneeded or unwanted, such as the local LAN segment.

Configuring OSPF

❑ The **router ospf** *process-id* command in Global Configuration mode starts the OSPF process.

❏ The process ID, or PID, can be any whole number. It is only used internally by the router to keep track of this routing process. There are other router features that also use process IDs and they must each be unique to allow the router to keep them separate. To avoid confusion, we could use the same PID on all of our internal routers.

❏ One or more **network *ip-address wildcard-mask* area *area-id*** commands in Routing Configuration mode assign interfaces to areas. The **network 0.0.0.0 255.255.255.255 area 0** command puts all interfaces, including any loopbacks, into OSPF Area 0, advertising their links if they are active.

❏ Other features that can be configured while in Routing Configuration mode include the following:

    ❏ To manually configure a router ID (RID), use the **router-id *ip-address*** command.

    ❏ To distribute (inject) default routes, use the **default-information originate always** command.

❏ The router ID (RID) can be configured using the **interface loopback *n*** command or with the **router-id *ip-address*** command in Router Configuration mode. The RID must be unique but need not be a routable address.

❏ To make an interface passive, use the **ip ospf passive-interface** command in Interface Configuration mode.

❏ To configure OSPF interface priority, use the **ip ospf priority *num*** command in Interface Configuration mode.

❏ Commands to use to verify your configuration and troubleshoot the network include the following:

    ❏ The **show ip route** command shows the routing table and how the route was learned, using a simple code ("C" for connected, "S" for static, and "O" for OSPF). It also displays the next-hop address, outgoing interface, and subnet mask for the route, as well as the administrative distance and metric for the route in brackets.

    ❏ The **show ip route ospf** command would list only the OSPF routes.

    ❏ The **show ip ospf database** command displays a list of the LSAs in the link-state database. The output shows only the information in the LSA header and only the lines relative to the area we are working in.

❑ The **show ip protocols** command shows the details of our OSPF session on this router, including the router ID (RID), number and types of areas with active interfaces, the networks being advertised, any passive interfaces, and the neighbors we are getting information from.

❑ The **show ip ospf interface** *int_id* command shows a lot of info about that interface, including the PID, RID, cost, state, priority, DR, BDR, timer intervals, and neighbor information.

❑ The difference between show and debug commands are as follows: Show commands are a snapshot in time; they will not change unless you run them again. Debug commands show activities in real time, occasionally scrolling faster than the user can absorb.

❑ In a production environment, debug commands can overwhelm the CPU, particularly if it is already running near capacity.

❑ There are two commands for stopping runaway debugs: **no debug all** and **undebug all**. The latter can be reduced to **un all**.

SELF TEST

The following Self Test questions will help you measure your understanding of the material presented in this chapter. Read all the choices carefully since there may be more than one correct answer. Choose all the correct answers for each question.

OSPF Fundamentals

1. In OSPF hello exchanges, which items must match for adjacency to occur?
   A. Hello settings
   B. Stub area flag
   C. Area-Id
   D. Authentication
   E. None of the above

2. In a multi-access network with a DR and BDR, what address is used to send a link change to the DR and BDR?
   A. Their router IDs (RIDs)
   B. 224.0.0.5
   C. Their interface IP addresses
   D. 224.0.0.6
   E. None of the above

3. Which metric increases the chance the route makes it into the routing table?
   A. High hop count
   B. Low hop count
   C. Big PID
   D. High cost
   E. Low cost

4. How many equal-cost links can OSPF load-balance across?
   A. 2 by default up to 4
   B. 3 by default up to 5
   C. 4 by default up to 6
   D. None of the above

5. What would be the IP address and wildcard mask to identify the hosts in 192.168.1.0/24?
   A. 0.0.0.0 255.255.255.0
   B. 0.0.0.0 0.0.0.255
   C. 192.168.1.0 255.255.255.0
   D. 192.168.1.0 0.0.0.255

6. What would be the IP address and wildcard mask to identify the hosts in 192.168.1.0/26?
   A. 192.168.1.0 0.0.0.255
   B. 192.168.1.0 0.0.0.127
   C. 192.168.1.0 255.255.255.192
   D. 192.168.1.0 0.0.0.63

7. What would be the IP address and subnet mask for 192.168.1.64 0.0.0.3?
   A. 192.168.1.0 255.255.255.0
   B. 192.168.1.0 255.255.255.254
   C. 192.168.1.0 255.255.255.252
   D. 192.168.1.0 255.255.255.3

8. We know that we have an OSPF connection to network 192.168.1.0/24, but in the routing table, it is listed as an EIGRP route. How could that happen?
   A. EIGRP has a lower cost than our OSPF route.
   B. The OSPF connection must be down.
   C. EIGRP has a better AD than OSPF.
   D. We have no way of knowing.

Configuring OSPF

9. Which two of the following, if fully configured, would set the router ID?
   A. Router1(config)#interface loopback 10.0.015
   B. Router1(config)#router-id 10.0.0.3
   C. Router1(config)#interface loopback 0
   D. Router1#interface loopback 0
   E. Router1(router-config)#router-id 10.0.0.3

10. Looking at Figure 10-7, what OSPF type of router is this?
    A. ASBR
    B. ABR
    C. IR
    D. There is no way to tell.

FIGURE 10-7

Exhibit for
questions

```
Router1#configure terminal
Router1(config)#interface loopback 0
Router1(config-if)#ip address 10.0.0.1 255.255.255.255
Router1(config-if)#exit
Router1(config)#ip route 0.0.0.0 0.0.0.0 172.16.4.2
Router1(config)#router ospf 1
Router1(router-config)#network 192.168.0.0 0.0.255.255 area 0
Router1(router-config)#default-information originate always
Router1(router-config)#router-id 10.0.0.3
Router1(router-config)#CTRL-Z
```

11. Looking at Figure 10-7, what would be the RID for this router?
  A. 10.0.0.1
  B. 172.16.4.2
  C. 192.168.0.0
  D. 10.0.0.3
  E. There is no way to tell.

12. Looking at Figure 10-7, if there are interfaces with these IP addresses, which would be included in OSPF?
  A. 192.168.0.1 255.255.255.0
  B. 192.168.1.129 255.255.255.128
  C. 10.0.0.1 255.255.255.255
  D. 172.16.5.5 255.255.0.0
  E. 0.0.0.0 0.0.0.0

13. Looking at Figure 10-7, what does **default-information originate always** do?
  A. It ensures all the other routers know the router ID (RID).
  B. It tells other routers that we always want to be the DR.
  C. It makes sure that all of the 192.168.0.0 routes get shared.
  D. It injects the default route into the LSAs.

14. Which command would make an interface passive for OSPF?
  A. Router1# ip ospf passive-interface
  B. Router1(config)# ip ospf passive-interface
  C. Router1(config)# ip ospf passive-interface Fa0/1
  D. Router1(config-if)# ip ospf passive-interface
  E. Router1(router-config)# ip ospf passive-interface
  F. None of the above

SELF TEST ANSWERS

OSPF Fundamentals

1. ☑   **A, B, C,** and **D** are correct. Each must match for adjacency to occur.
    ☒   **E** is incorrect. It is incorrect because this choice is not valid.

2. ☑   **D** is correct. 224.0.0.5 (all SPF routers) and 224.0.0.6 (all designated routers, or DRs) are used to send a link change to the DR and BDR.
    ☒   **A, B, C,** and **E** are incorrect. **A** is incorrect because this router ID is not a destination address. **B** is incorrect because 224.0.0.5 (all SPF routers) is used to send an LSA to all routers. **C** is incorrect because that would require a separate unicast for every other router. **E** is incorrect because this choice is not valid.

3. ☑   **E** is correct. Lowest cost, OSPF's metric, increases the chance that an OSPF route makes it into the routing table.
    ☒   **A, B, C,** and **D** are incorrect. **A** and **B** are incorrect because hop counts are metrics for distance-vector protocols, not link-state. **C** is incorrect because a PID (process ID) has nothing to do with routing; it identifies the OSPF instance. **D** is incorrect because OSPF's metric looks for lowest cost.

4. ☑   **C** is correct. OSPF supports four equal-cost links by default for load balancing but can be configured up to 16.
    ☒   **A, B,** and **D** are incorrect. **A** and **B** are incorrect because they are not the defaults. **D** is incorrect because this choice is not valid.

5. ☑   **D** is correct. 192.168.1.0 0.0.0.255 is the IP address and wildcard mask to identify the hosts in 192.168.1.0/24.
    ☒   **A, B,** and **C** are incorrect. **A** and **C** are incorrect because both have subnet masks, not wildcard masks. **B** is incorrect because 0.0.0.0 255.255.255.0 is a wildcard mask for all /24 subnets.

6. ☑   **D** is correct. The IP address and wildcard mask to identify the hosts in 192.168.1.0/26 would be 192.168.1.0 0.0.0.63
    ☒   **A, B,** and **C** are incorrect. **A** is incorrect because 192.168.1.0 0.0.0.255 would be 192.168.1.0/24. **B** is incorrect because 192.168.1.0 0.0.0.127 would be 192.168.1.0/25. **C** is incorrect because this is not a wildcard mask.

7. ☑ **C** is correct. The IP address and subnet mask for 192.168.1.64 0.0.0.3 would be 192.168.1.0 255.255.255.252.

☒ **A, B,** and **D** are incorrect. **A** is incorrect because the wildcard mask for IP address 192.168.1. 255.255.255.0 would be 192.168.1.0 0.0.0.255. **B** is incorrect because the wildcard mask for IP address 192.168.1.0 255.255.255.254 would be 192.168.1.0 0.0.0.1. **D** is incorrect because it is not a valid subnet mask.

8. ☑ **C** is correct. EIGRP has a better AD than OSPF

☒ **A, B,** and **D** are incorrect. **A** is incorrect because routing protocols are ranked by administrative distance (AD), not metrics, which are incompatible anyway. **B** is incorrect because if the OSPF connection was down, the route would be dropped from the routing table. **D** is incorrect because this choice is not valid.

Configuring OSPF

9. ☑ **C** and **E** are correct. Both a loopback and the **router-id id-*addr*** command, if properly configured, could become the RID. The **router-ip id-*addr*** command would be used for the RID if both were configured.

☒ **A, B,** and **D** are incorrect. **A** is incorrect because the IP address is not part of the **int loopback** command. **B** is incorrect because the correct command is used at the wrong configuration level: it should be Router1(router-config)# router-id 10.0.0.3. **D** is incorrect because the correct command is used at the wrong configuration level: Router1(config)# interface loopback 0.

10. ☑ **A** is correct. The router is an ASBR type because all configured networks are in one area, Area 0, and yet there is a default route to an address not included.

☒ **B, C,** and **D** are incorrect. **B** is incorrect because an ABR would have another area. **C** is incorrect because an IR has all interfaces in the same area. The default route indicates at least one more interface. **D** is incorrect because this choice is not valid.

11. ☑ **D** is correct. The RID was explicitly configured with the Router1(router-config)#**router-id 10.0.0.3** command.

☒ **A, B, C,** and **E** are incorrect. **A** is incorrect because it would have been the RID if the **router-id 10.0.0.3** command hadn't been entered. **B** is incorrect because 172.16.4.2 is the next-hop address for our default route. **C** is incorrect because it is one of the networks to be included in our OSPF network. **E** is incorrect because this choice is not valid.

12. ☑ **A** and **B** are correct. Both addresses fall within the scope defined by the **network 192.168.0.0 0.0.255.255 area 0** command.

☒ **C, D,** and **E** are incorrect. **C** is incorrect because 10.0.0.1 255.255.255.255 is a host address, not a network; even if it was, it is outside the **network 192.168.0.0 0.0.255.255 area 0** command. **D** is incorrect because 172.16.5.5 255.255.0.0. is outside the **network 192.168.0.0 0.0.255.255 area 0** command. **E** is incorrect because 0.0.0.0 0.0.0.0 is a default route, not an interface.

13. ☑ **D** is correct. The **default-information originate always** command injects the default route into the LSAs.

    ☒ **A, B,** and **C** are incorrect. **A** is incorrect because it has nothing to do with the router ID (RID). **B** is incorrect because a high interface priority tells other routers that we always want to be the DR. **C** is incorrect because the **network 192.168.0.0 0.0.255.255 area** 0 command makes sure that all of the 192.168.0.0 routes get shared.

14. ☑ **D** is correct. The Router1(config-if)# **ip ospf passive-interface** command in Interface Configuration mode turns on the passive interface feature.

    ☒ **A, B, C, E,** and **F** are incorrect. **A, B, C,** and **E** are incorrect because they all have attempted to configure the feature at the wrong level. **F** is incorrect because this choice is not valid.

Part IV

IP Services, Network Device Security, and IPv6

11
IP Services

C isco offers a wide variety of IP services as features in its IOS devices and as separate hardware devices. In this chapter, we are going to look at just a few of the services supported by the IOS routers and switches. These services include Dynamic Host Configuration Protocol (DHCP) for assigning and acquiring IP addresses within the network, Network Address Translation (NAT) and Port Address Translation (PAT) for allowing privately addressed network devices to access the Internet, and Network Time Protocol (NTP) for implementing consistent time on all devices within a network or globally.

This just scratches the surface of the many IP services Cisco offers, but these are the ones that are common in many networks and on many devices. It is important to remember that the actual bundle of services on a certain device can depend on the device, the IOS software feature set licensed, and the version.

Customers can select the appropriate Cisco IOS software feature sets to meet their evolving network requirements. Features such as Network Address Translation, Dynamic Host Configuration Protocol, and Hot Standby Router Protocol (HSRP) can be easily deployed individually or in combination with each other across a wide range of Cisco hardware.

CERTIFICATION OBJECTIVE 11.01

Dynamic Host Configuration Protocol (DHCP)

As we discussed in Chapter 2, the main function of DHCP is to automatically assign IP addresses from a pool of addresses, as well as many other useful pieces of information, to client devices within a specific network segment. The pool of addresses a DHCP server uses is known as the *scope*. In larger networks, network servers are configured to provide DHCP services. This can be the server's primary job, or it can be just one of many that it provides.

It is possible to configure a Cisco router to be a DHCP server. This is particularly useful in remote locations such as warehouses or small branch offices that wouldn't normally have network servers. Most home routers provide this service to your small network. While DHCP server configuration is not a CCENT requirement, you should still be aware of the following terms: *scope, excluded addresses* or *excluded range,* and *lease time.* There are a series of commands that allow the router to be configured to provide the many pieces of information a DHCP server can provide, such as the address of the default gateway, any DNS servers, and so on. A pool of IP addresses, such as 192.168.1.0/24, is the scope of IP addresses that can be given out for client requests. The server can maintain more than one scope, so multiple separate segments can get addresses from a single router. There is an **exclude-address** command that holds a range of addresses, such as 192.168.1.1 to 192.168.1.10, out of the pool to be statically assigned by the administrator to network devices such as routers, switches, and so on. Finally, you should know that the lease time is the amount of time the device can use the IP address. This lease time can be renewed if the device is still using the IP address; otherwise, it reverts to the address pool for reuse.

In this chapter we look at configuring DHCP clients on Cisco IOS devices. Before we do, let's review the process a client uses to request and accept an IP address from a DHCP server, as shown in Figure 11-1. Recall that there is also an abbreviated version of this process for renewing the client address lease when it expires.

The best way to remember the steps is the acronym DORA: Discover, Offer, Request, ACK. You can expect to have to know the steps as well as which steps are broadcasts and which are unicasts.

Because of a DHCP server's reliance on broadcasts, the placement of the server can be an important consideration. DHCP using broadcasts makes a lot of sense when you consider the process. When the computer first boots up, it doesn't know where the DHCP server is, and without an IP address of its own yet, it is dependent

FIGURE 11-1

The DHCP lease process

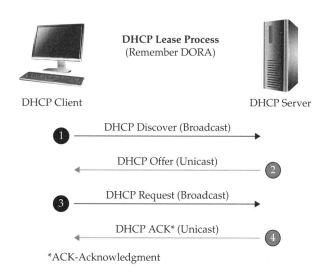

DHCP Client

DHCP Server

DHCP Lease Process
(Remember DORA)

1 DHCP Discover (Broadcast)

DHCP Offer (Unicast) 2

3 DHCP Request (Broadcast)

DHCP ACK* (Unicast) 4

*ACK-Acknowledgment

upon Layer 2 LAN communications. So, the system sends a broadcast message asking for a DHCP server to provide an IP address. Recall that a switch will forward broadcast messages out of every port of this VLAN. If there is a DHCP server on the segment, it will receive this solicitation and respond. Every server running the DHCP service in the segment that receives the broadcast will respond, and the client will generally take the first offer it receives.

Since routers do not forward broadcasts, if there isn't a DHCP server on each network segment, the server would be unreachable to some devices. To get around this, Cisco uses what is called a *relay agent*. This is a device that listens for certain broadcasts on a segment; it then supplies the destination IP address of the DHCP server and forwards the message directly to that DHCP server.

Figure 11-2 shows the example we'll work with in this section. In this example, hosts A, B, C, and D would be able to reach the DHCP server at 10.0.0.5 because they are on the same broadcast segment as the server, but the other nodes would not be able to without help. In this example, the DHCP server will need three pools of addresses, one for each LAN segment, and a relay agent configured on the router's interfaces.

FIGURE 11-2

DHCP example
network

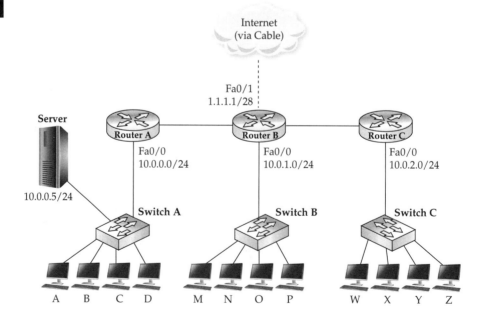

Configuring Relay Agent

To configure a router as a relay agent, you need to first identify the router interface that will receive (hear) the broadcasts for services such as DHCP, DNS, NTP, and others. Then you use the **ip helper-address** *server-addr* command in Interface Configuration mode to define the server address to which the broadcasts should be forwarded. In this example, both Router B's and Router C's LAN interfaces will need the configuration, as shown next.

Relay agents insert the IP address of the interface configured with the **ip helper-address** command into the default gateway IP address field of the DHCP packet. This IP address tells the DHCP server which address scope to pull an IP address from and which subnet gets the return packet. Once the relay agent forwards the packet, it is no longer a broadcast, and therefore no other interfaces need to be configured.

```
RouterB(config)#interface FastEthernet0/0
RouterB(config-if)#ip address 10.0.1.1 255.255.255.0
RouterB(config-if)#ip helper-address 10.0.0.5
RouterB(config-if)#no shutdown
RouterB(config-if)#CTRL-Z

RouterC(config)#interface FastEthernet0/0
RouterC(config-if)#ip address 10.0.2.1 255.255.255.0
RouterC(config-if)#ip helper-address 10.0.0.5
RouterC(config-if)#no shutdown
RouterC(config-if)#CTRL-Z
```

All hosts now should be able to get IP addresses.

Configuring DHCP Client

Business router interfaces connecting to the Internet are typically configured statically, as we have done in earlier chapters, so that the router always has IP addresses and is not dependent on a DHCP server. But, there are exceptions. Smaller networks such as home users and small branch offices often rely on DSL or cable modems that frequently receive IP addresses through DHCP. In that case, we use the **ip address dhcp** command in Interface Configuration mode to enable the feature. The following is an example on Router B from Figure 11-2:

```
RouterB(config)#interface FastEthernet0/1
RouterB(config-if)# ip address dhcp
RouterB(config-if)#no shutdown
RouterB(config-if)#CTRL-Z
```

Watch "DHCP" for a demonstration of how to configure the DHCP client.

CERTIFICATION OBJECTIVE 11.02

Network Address Translation (NAT and PAT)

In Chapter 3 you learned about IP addresses, specifically IPv4 addresses. You also learned that IPv4 address were going to run out and eventually be replaced by IPv6. In the meantime, we needed to preserve the IPv4 address as best we could, and one solution was to create several pools of what are called *private addresses*. These are addresses that can be used by anyone in their local networks but can't be used on public networks like the Internet.

Remember that *private* addresses are free; you don't need permission to use them, and they are not unique and therefore can't be used on the Internet. *Public* addresses (sometimes called *global* or *real* addresses) are unique; they must be assigned by a registering authority or their agents, there is usually a monthly cost involved, and they can be used on the Internet. Note that they can't just be used anywhere; they must be used wherever they were assigned as part of that network. Otherwise, the global router network will not be able to find them. Finally, an organization is not

TABLE 11-1	Network Class	Private Address Range
Private IP Address Ranges	A (1 Class A)	10.0.0.0
	B (16 Class B)	172.16.0.0 through 172.31.0.0
	C (256 Class C)	192.168.0.0 through 192.168.255.0

likely to be able to get a pool of public addresses for all of their devices, and even if it could, the cost would be foolish in most cases.

Recall that RFC 1918 created the private address ranges to be a subset of the three user classes of classful addresses, which were the norm at that time. Table 11-1 lists the private IP address ranges.

While using private addressing inside the network helps conserve the public IP address space, there is a problem. Undoubtedly, many of those users will want or need to go out on the Internet. Fortunately, a technology called Network Address Translation is available that permits the use of private addressing while also allowing devices in the network to connect to the Internet. A translation means exchanging one address for another. NAT is a service that often runs on a perimeter router or firewall that translates inside network IP addresses into usable public IP addresses, or vice versa.

A simple analogy might be that you are known by and referred to by everyone in your organization as Skip, a nickname you picked up in childhood. But when you travel in the business world, you are Mr. Mark Palmer, president and CEO of XYZ Company. This is probably the most common type of NAT translation in most organizations.

Uses of NAT

While the most common use is translating inside private addresses, but there are other situations where they could be public addresses that you want or need to translate for some reason.

The following are four common and yet different reasons to use NAT translation:

- To allow internal users with addresses, typically private IP addresses, that can't be used on the Internet to access the Internet.
- To allow the external devices, typically from the Internet, to access certain internal devices (such as web servers).

■ To redirect TCP traffic to another TCP port or address.

■ To use NAT during a network transition. For example, when merging with or buying another company, it is often necessary to connect the two networks before having the time to readdress the one network into your IP scheme. The newly acquired business could have addresses that overlap with your own. Another common use is to assist you in upgrading network devices or changing IP addresses. Existing users can use NAT translations to access the old address until their configuration is changed.

Inside and Outside Addresses

Before we start configuring NAT, there are a couple of concepts we need to cover.

When we talk about NAT, the interfaces or their IP addresses fall into one of two categories (or locations): inside or outside. *Inside* means within the organization's network. *Outside* means external to the network or not part of the organization's network.

These two categories are used with the terms *local* and *global* to describe whether the addresses are viewed (or seen) from within or from outside the network.

One way to view this is if you think of inside meaning mine or ours and outside meaning someone else's or theirs. Local means private and internal, while global means public or external, open to the world. The four different subcategories are combinations of these, as shown in Table 11-2.

An example of the first two inside addresses might be the private IP address of your workstation that is used by everyone within the organization to reach you; that is your inside local address. But, if you go out on the Internet, NAT will give you a public address, in other words, an inside global address. Now the outside world sees you as that publicly registered IP address and has no way of knowing about your private inside address. A simple analogy might be the one we used for NAT where you are known by and referred to by everyone in your organization as Skip, a nickname you picked up in childhood. But when you travel in the business world,

TABLE 11-2	Inside local address	An inside address as it is seen and used *within the local network*
Inside and Outside Address Categories	Inside global address	An inside address as it is seen and used from *outside the local network*
	Outside local address	An outside address as it is seen and used *within the local network*
	Outside global address	An outside address as it is seen and used *outside the local network*

you are Mr. Mark Palmer, president and CEO of XYZ Company. This is probably the most common type of NAT translation in most organizations.

An example of the two outside addresses is a little less common. An outside local address might be the public IP address of some device outside your network that your organization's NAT is translating so it can be seen and used by everyone within the organization as a local address. Out on the Internet, any remote device with a publicly registered address is known by its outside global address. This is the address that an external organization has leased for its device to be reachable over the Internet.

The analogy of a mail carrier delivering a letter to a company can be used to describe NAT on the router. The postal service has no knowledge of where a letter is going within the company, only that it is delivered to the mailbox in the company (that is, the public IP address). A company person deals with the delivery of mail to individuals (that is, to private IP addresses) and with outgoing mail.

Just remember that inside always refers to located within the network. Outside always means located outside the network, on someone else's network. Local means as seen from within the network. Global means as seen by the outside world.

NAT Types

We will look at three basic types of NAT in this chapter. Table 11-3 shows the three basic NAT types with examples, but combinations of these can be used as well to meet certain needs.

TABLE 11-3	NAT Types
Static NAT	Used when a single inside-local (private) address needs to be translated to a single inside-global (public) address, or vice versa. An example would an internal web server with a private address that needed to be made available to the Internet (public address). That public IP from the outside would always find that internal server.
Dynamic NAT	Used when an inside-local (private) address (or group of addresses) needs to be temporarily translated to an inside-global (public) address (or addresses), or vice versa. This is one method that could be used to allow local users to access the Internet.
Overload (PAT)	Port Address Translation, or as Cisco calls it *overloading*, is a variation on dynamic NAT that allows multiple internal users to be translated to a single public IP address by keeping track of the ports in use. Often, this is the IP address of the router's outside interface. This is the most common method used to allow local users to access the Internet.

Basic NAT Operations

Not only does the NAT device make the inside-to-outside or outside-to-inside translations, it does this by maintaining a table, called the *translation table* or *x-late table*, which keeps track of which internal IP address is using a particular external IP for a particular translation session, thereby maintaining the two-way exchanges while preserving the anonymity of the internal device/user. This way, when an outside device replies to a request from an internal device, the resulting reply traffic can be directed to the right device within the network.

Inside and Outside Interfaces

A NAT router uses two types of interfaces for each translation that work as a team: an inside interface and an outside interface. Traffic entering the inside interface that meets the NAT criteria destined to the outside interface gets a NAT translation. Traffic entering the inside interface destined to any other interface does not get a NAT translation.

A good practice is to always figure out your inside and outside interfaces, but first make sure you understand what NAT is trying to accomplish.

Looking at the sample network in Figure 11-3, if we designate the LAN B interface (Fa0/0) on Router B as inside and Fa0/1 as outside, LAN B users could be translated to public IP addresses to go out on the Internet. Traffic from LAN B going to our server (10.0.0.5), our web server (10.0.3.7), or LAN A or LAN C would not be translated.

As it is now, LAN A and LAN C users would not be able to go to the Internet because their traffic would come into Router B through interfaces not designated as inside. Fortunately, any inside interfaces with traffic that needs to be translated can be configured as inside. Traffic between two inside interfaces is not translated, such as from LAN B to LAN A.

We wouldn't normally want NAT running on Router A or Router C because they have no interfaces to the outside world.

IP NAT [inside | outside] source

Setting up any NAT translation uses a form of the **ip nat [inside | outside] source** command. When you choose **inside**, it means addresses within the network meeting the NAT criteria will be translated to be usable outside the network, including on the Internet.

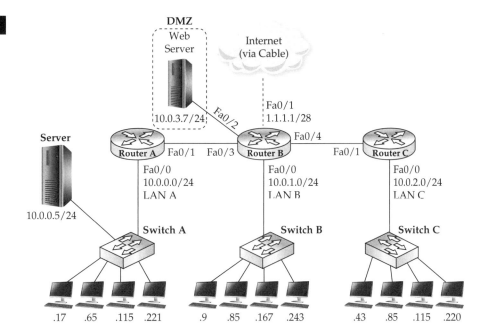

FIGURE 11-3

NAT sample network

NAT Pool

A NAT pool is simply a range of one or more public IP addresses, typically provided by the ISP, which can be dynamically assigned on a first-come, first-serve basis to inside devices so they can access the Internet. This pool could be just a single address or hundreds of addresses. When the last address in the pool has been used in a translation, no other devices can go out until a session ends and its IP address is returned to the pool.

Static NAT

Static NAT is a long-term, one-to-one NAT translation often used to publish services the organization wants the outside world to reach. Since these translations are statically configured, they stay in the NAT table until removed, making them ideal for sharing inside resources such as web and e-mail servers with the outside world. Figure 11-4 shows the static NAT that allows the local web server with a private address (10.0.3.7) to be translated to the public IP address 1.1.1.2 so that it can be accessed from the Internet.

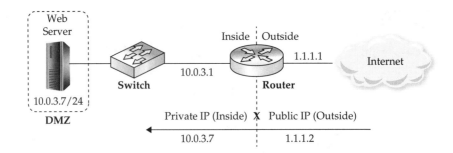

FIGURE 11-4

Static NAT
example

These are the only NAT connections that by default allow outside users to initiate
a session because the NAT server finds an existing translation when the outside
request arrives.

Remember to always figure out your inside and outside interfaces first to make
sure you understand what NAT is trying to accomplish.

There are only three new steps for configuring static NAT, as shown in bold
in the following code. They could be added later if the interfaces were already
configured.

```
Router#configure terminal
Router(config)#ip nat [inside | outside] source static inside-ip outside-ip
Router(config-if)#interface type-number
Router(config-if)#ip address ip-address mask
Router(config-if)#ip nat inside
Router(config-if)#interface type-number
Router(config-if)#ip address ip-address mask
Router(config-if)#ip nat outside
Router(config-if)#end or CTRL-z
```

The **ip nat inside source static** *inside-ip outside-ip* command actually creates
the translation. Using **ip nat inside source static** means we are defining an inside
address to be translated statically. The *inside-ip outside-ip* part is the translation.
The inside local address (server's IP address) is translated to an outside global
(public) address. This static translation means that traffic arriving at the outside
interface looking for the outside global (public) address will get translated to the
inside address and allowed in to reach the server.

The **ip nat [inside | outside]** commands define the inside interfaces and outside
interface between which NAT will take place. These commands are the same in all
NAT types.

The following is an example using Router B and the web server in the DMZ for
the translation. We assume that the ISP has made IP address 1.1.1.0/28 available to

us to use. This gives us 16 addresses, but 1.1.1.1 will be assigned to the router and 1.1.1.15 will be the broadcast. So, we will use 1.1.1.2 for our web server.

```
RouterB#configure terminal
RouterB(config)#ip nat inside source static 10.0.3.7 1.1.1.2
RouterB(config-if)#interface Fa0/2
RouterB(config-if)#ip address 10.0.3.1 255.255.255.0
RouterB(config-if)#ip nat inside
RouterB(config-if)#interface Fa0/0
RouterB(config-if)#ip address 1.1.1.1 255.255.255.240
RouterB(config-if)#ip nat outside
RouterB(config-if)#CTRL-Z
```

Verifying Static NAT

To verify this configuration, use the **show ip nat translations** command in Privileged mode. This command can be run at any time because we manually added the translation that it will always be in the x-late table. It shows that our inside address, 10.0.3.7, can be seen and interacted with on the outside by using the public IP address 1.1.1.2.

```
RouterB#show ip nat translations
Pro   Inside global    Inside local    Outside local    Outside global
---     1.1.1.2         10.0.3.7           ---              ---
```

Dynamic NAT

Dynamic NAT uses a pool of public addresses that are assigned on a dynamic basis to local IP addresses wanting to access the Internet. Figure 11-5 shows that two local hosts with private IP addresses were able to get two public IP addresses from the NAT pool.

There are only two new steps and a different form of the **ip nat inside source** command needed for configuring dynamic NAT; they are in bold in the following code. The **ip nat [inside | outside]** command is the same as before.

```
Router#configure terminal
Router(config)#ip nat pool name start-ip end-ip [netmask mask | prefix-length length]
Router(config)#ip nat inside source list access-list-number pool name
Router(config)#access-list access-list-number permit source-net-it [source-wildcard]
Router(config-if)#interface type-number
Router(config-if)#ip nat inside
Router(config-if)#interface type-number
Router(config-if)#ip nat outside
Router(config-if)#end or CTRL-Z
```

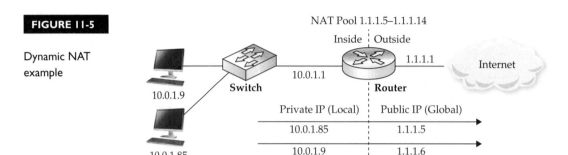

FIGURE 11-5

Dynamic NAT
example

The **ip nat pool** *name start-ip end-ip* [**netmask** *mask* | **prefix-length** *length*]
command is where you define the NAT pool. The name can be anything appropriate,
like net_IPs (no spaces). The *start-ip end-ip* part is just, as the name implies, the
first and last IP addresses to include in the pool. The next option is a choice to use
the subnet mask or prefix length to define the subnet these addresses come from.
They can include any number of the unused available addresses.

The **ip nat inside source list** *access-list-number* **pool** *name* [**overload**] command
defines which hosts can be translated to what addresses. The list means that an
access control list (ACL) will be used to define the eligible hosts. The *access-list-
number* part identifies the specific ACL to be used. Finally, **pool** *name* refers to the
pool name you created in the previous step that contains the global addresses that
will be used for the translations. Basically, it is saying that we will use an ACL to
define our eligible inside addresses to be translated to the global addresses in the
pool we just defined.

We spend the entire next chapter on ACLs, but we need to use one here as part
of dynamic NAT, so we will use a common and yet simple-to-understand ACL.
Simply, an access list is one or more statements that allows us to define something of
interest to us that will be used by another command or process. In this case, we will
define which local source addresses we want to be able to use NAT to go out into the
world. The ACL number or name is nothing more than a label applied to each line
for grouping purposes.

The **access-list** *access-list-number* **permit** *source-net-ip* [*source-wildcard*]
command is the syntax of the statements defining the eligible hosts. The *access-list-
number* part is the same number we used in the **ip nat inside source** command. The
permit part means to include or allow; the alternative is **deny**. The *source-net-ip*
and optional [*source-wildcard*] parts identify the subnet to be permitted. ACLs use
wildcard masks just like we used in OSPF.

In the following example, ACL 10 has three statements that will permit or allow the 10.0.0.0/24, 10.0.1.0/24, and 10.0.2.0/24 subnets:

```
RouterB(config)#access-list 10 permit 10.0.0.0 0.0.0.255
RouterB(config)#access-list 10 permit 10.0.1.0 0.0.0.255
RouterB(config)#access-list 10 permit 10.0.2.0 0.0.0.255
```

To pull this all together in an example, the following assumes we are using Router B from the example in Figure 11-3 to allow all of our LAN users to access the Internet. We assume that our ISP has made IP address subnet 1.1.1.0/28 available to us to use. This gives us 16 addresses, but 1.1.1.1 will be assigned to the router, and 1.1.1.15 will be the broadcast. We used 1.1.1.2 in the previous exercise for our web server NAT address. We want to save two IP addresses for future servers, so that leaves us 1.1.1.5 to 1.1.1.14 (ten addresses) to use for NAT.

We need to designate three interfaces on the router as inside because the hosts will arrive through all three: the LAN B interface (Fa0/0) and the connecting interfaces to Routers A (Fa0/3) and C (Fa0/4). The interface IP configuration is omitted to save space, but it should be routine now.

```
RouterB#configure terminal
RouterB(config)#ip nat pool net_ips 1.1.1.5 1.1.1.14 prefix-length 28
RouterB(config)#ip nat inside source list 10 pool net_ips
RouterB(config)#access-list 10 permit 10.0.0.0 0.0.0.255
RouterB(config)#access-list 10 permit 10.0.1.0 0.0.0.255
RouterB(config)#access-list 10 permit 10.0.2.0 0.0.0.255
RouterB(config-if)#interface Fa0/3
RouterB(config-if)#ip nat inside
RouterB(config-if)#interface Fa0/0
RouterB(config-if)#ip nat inside
RouterB(config-if)#interface Fa0/4
RouterB(config-if)#ip nat inside
RouterB(config-if)#interface Fa0/1
RouterB(config-if)#ip nat outside
RouterB(config-if)#CTRL-Z
```

The addresses in **pool net_ips** are defined by the two following addresses: the beginning and ending IP addresses. The **prefix-length** part *does not* describe the NAT pool net_ips, but instead the subnet that the addresses came from 1.1.1.0/28.

The next statement is saying that we will get the eligible inside hosts from access list 10 and translate them using the pool net_ips we just defined. The next three lines make up ACL 10, with each permitting one of the LAN subnets.

The three **ip nat inside** statements are for the three interfaces the LANs use to enter Router B. The **ip nat outside** command is the interface out of the network.

Verifying Dynamic NAT

After a couple hosts have accessed the Internet, we can verify the configuration uses the **show ip nat translations** command in Privileged mode. If no hosts had gone out, you would get just the row of labels and any static NAT translations.

```
RouterB#show ip nat translations
Pro    Inside global    Inside local    Outside local    Outside global
---    1.1.1.5          10.0.0.65       ---              ---
---    1.1.1.6          10.0.1.9        ---              ---
---    1.1.1.7          10.0.2.43       ---              ---
```

This may not be all translations because they time out shortly after the last activity and get removed from the table. The static NAT entry from the previous example was omitted to focus on this, but it would always be in the output because it never times out.

You can clear the translations by using the **clear ip nat translation *** command, where the asterisk means all. The result would look like the following, if no inside hosts had gone out again:

```
RouterB#clear ip nat translation *
RouterB#
RouterB#show ip nat translations
Pro    Inside global    Inside local    Outside local    Outside global
---    1.1.1.2          10.0.3.7        ---              ---
```

The clear statement can't remove the static translation.

Overload (PAT)

There are two serious problems with the previous dynamic NAT example. First, IP addresses are leased on a monthly basis, so there is a monthly cost associated with maintaining the pool of global addresses. Second, with only ten global IPs in the pool, only ten hosts could go out at one time. Any others would be denied until translations on inactive sessions timed out, returning the public IPs to the pool for reuse. This would be unacceptable in a larger organization, and yet increasing the number of IPs would increase the monthly expense. Fortunately, there is a better solution. Dynamic NAT overload, or more commonly Port Address Translation (PAT), allows many users to use the same global IP but each with a different port number.

Figure 11-6 shows two local hosts with private IP addresses using the same public IP addresses from the NAT pool, but each is being kept track of in the x-late table by the unique port number it is using.

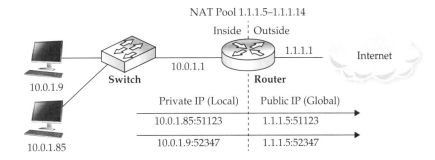

FIGURE 11-6

NAT overload
(PAT) example

With overloading and PAT, there is a one-to-many relationship, with a single public IP address supporting many internal hosts *using different port numbers*. A single IP address can support dozens, hundreds, or even thousands of sessions. *In many instances, routers using overloading use the router's outside address for translation and thereby do not require any additional IP addresses from the ISP.*

The only change required in the previous example is in bold in the following code; it shows using the **overload** parameter to the **ip nat inside source list** *access-list-number* **pool** *name* **[overload]** command:

```
RouterB#configure terminal
RouterB(config)#ip nat pool net_ips 1.1.1.5 1.1.1.14 prefix-length 28
RouterB(config)#ip nat inside source list 10 pool net_ips overload
RouterB(config)#access-list 10 permit 10.0.0.0 0.0.0.255
RouterB(config)#access-list 10 permit 10.0.1.0 0.0.0.255
RouterB(config)#access-list 10 permit 10.0.2.0 0.0.0.255
RouterB(config-if)#interface Fa0/3
RouterB(config-if)#ip nat inside
RouterB(config-if)#interface Fa0/0
RouterB(config-if)#ip nat inside
RouterB(config-if)#interface Fa0/4
RouterB(config-if)#ip nat inside
RouterB(config-if)#interface Fa0/1
RouterB(config-if)#ip nat outside
RouterB(config-if)#CTRL-Z
```

To see what is happening, let's use the **show ip nat translations** command in Privileged mode after a couple hosts have accessed the Internet. That is different.

```
RouterB#show ip nat translations
Pro   Inside global      Inside local       Outside local      Outside global
udp   1.1.1.5:51119      10.0.0.65:51119    1.15.79.4:53       1.15.79.4:53
udp   1.1.1.5:51119      10.0.0.65:51119    1.10.0.11:53       1.10.0.11:53
```

```
tcp   1.1.1.5:52750   10.0.0.65:52750   1.3.159.100:80   1.3.159.100:80
tcp   1.1.1.5:54625   10.0.2.43:54625   1.50.6.4:143     1.50.6.4:143
tcp   1.1.1.5:54626   10.0.2.43:54626   1.50.6.4:143     1.50.6.4:143
tcp   1.1.1.5:54850   10.0.1.85:54850   1.7.19.101:23    1.7.19.101:23
```

First we see that the Pro column is protocol and that PAT identifies the protocol used.

Next let's look at the two inside columns. We see that three of our inside hosts have active translations and that they all got translated to the first IP address in the NAT pool, 1.1.1.5. In fact, NAT will use that address thousands of times before using another, so unless you have a huge network, it doesn't make sense to put more than one or two addresses in the pool. Finally, each inside host picked an unused port number to identify that session, and NAT kept the same port number with the translation.

Looking at the two outside columns, we see they are the same. That will be true in most cases and all of the ones we are looking at. The first two rows show the same LAN A inside host making DNS (port 53) requests to two different servers. The third row shows the same inside host going to a website (port 80), possibly using the IP address supplied by one of the DNSs. The fourth and fifth rows are two e-mail client (IMAP port 143) requests from a LAN C host to the same e-mail server. The last line is a LAN B host sending an outbound e-mail (port 23).

One-Way NAT

In both dynamic and dynamic overload NAT, translation sessions can be instigated and maintained only by an inside host, not by an outside address. Outside devices can respond only to requests started from inside. Also, while inside hosts know the real public address of their destination device, the destination device never knows anything but the public address that NAT supplied. After a particular exchange session is complete, the translation session is removed from the NAT device's x-late table so that if any outside device tries to contact the device again, the NAT router will find no open session in the table and deny the connection.

Troubleshooting NAT

Any time you are trying to determine the cause of an IP connectivity problem, if NAT is involved, it is always a good idea to rule out NAT. It is also important to test your new NAT configurations to make sure they work like you wanted them to work, including not allowing more than you wanted.

These steps can be used to verify that NAT is doing what it is supposed to:

1. Make sure you understand fully what NAT is supposed to do.
2. Does the current configuration accomplish that and no more? Allowing all users to go to the Internet is not the same as allowing LAN B users to go to the Internet even though it is working for LAN B. The problem may be with the configuration. Here are the details to check:
   a. Are the correct inside and outside interfaces defined and configured?
   b. Do any dynamic pools contain the correct range of addresses? Do any of them overlap any used for static mapping?
   c. Do the access lists define the correct addresses to be translated? Check for both addresses left out and any addresses included that shouldn't be.
3. Set up testing to verify that correct translations are in the translation table.
4. The **show** and **debug ip nat** commands (see the following example) can be used to verify that the translation is occurring. Remember that **show** commands are a snapshot in time, while **debug** commands show real-time activity. The **show** commands typically can't impact network performance, but **debug** commands can. The NAT **debug** commands are handy for learning how NAT really works, but probably shouldn't be used on the production equipment because of the volume of NAT activity. In Chapter 12 we look at access control lists, and one of the things we can do is limit the impact of the **debug ip nat** command. Use the **ping** command to generate traffic to test simple NAT configuration.
5. Verify that any routers have the correct routing information to move the packet to where it needs to be. This is a common problem with new NAT configurations; NAT is working fine, but the existing routing table doesn't know about these new addresses. Remember that you are changing a source or destination address in a packet.

The **show ip nat translations** command in Privileged mode that we looked at earlier allows you to see whether the translations exist in the translation table. You might want to run the **clear ip nat translation *** command and retest using **ping**. While the static and dynamic NAT translations are quite simple, the overload option (PAT) is another matter. Don't let the volume of information intimidate you, particularly the inside port numbers. The source host pulls those from the high end of the unassigned port numbers.

```
RouterB#show ip nat translations
Pro   Inside global      Inside local       Outside local       4 Outside global
---   1.1.1.2            10.0.3.7           ---                 ---
udp   1.1.1.5:51119      10.0.0.65:51119    1.15.79.4:53        1.15.79.4:53
udp   1.1.1.5:51119      10.0.0.65:51119    1.10.0.11:53        1.10.0.11:53
tcp   1.1.1.5:52750      10.0.0.65:52750    1.3.159.100:80      1.3.159.100:80
tcp   1.1.1.5:54625      10.0.2.43:54625    1.50.6.4:143        1.50.6.4:143
tcp   1.1.1.5:54626      10.0.2.43:54626    1.50.6.4:143        1.50.6.4:143
tcp   1.1.1.5:54850      10.0.1.85:54850    1.7.19.101:23       1.7.19.101:23
```

Another command that can be useful is the **show ip nat statistics** command to watch the hits counter to verify it is increasing as we send traffic. The hits counter increments every time a translation is used. The output tells us a lot about our NAT configuration, including inside and outside interfaces, ACL name, and pool details. Be sure to look it over.

Clear the statistics first and verify that you have a clean start. Then generate traffic with the **ping** command and check the statistics.

```
RouterB# clear ip nat statistics
RouterB# show ip nat statistics
 Total active translations: 1 (1 static, 0 dynamic; 0 extended)
 Outside interfaces: FastEthernet0/1
 Inside interfaces: FastEthernet0/0, FastEthernet0/2,
FastEthernet0/3, FastEthernet0/4
Hits: 0  Misses: 0
 Expired translations: 0
 Dynamic mappings:
 -- Inside Source
 access-list 10 pool net_ips refcount 0
 pool net_ips: netmask 255.255.255.240
 start 1.1.1.5 end 1.1.1.14
 type generic, total addresses 10, allocated 0 (0%), misses 0
RouterB#
```

After you use the **ping 172.16.11.7** command, the NAT statistics would show as follows:

```
RouterB# show ip nat statistics
 Total active translations: 2 (1 static, 1 dynamic; 0 extended)
 Outside interfaces: FastEthernet0/1
 Inside interfaces: FastEthernet0/0, FastEthernet0/2,
FastEthernet0/3, FastEthernet0/4
Hits: 5  Misses: 0
```

```
Expired translations: 0
Dynamic mappings:
-- Inside Source
access-list 10 pool net_ips refcount 0
pool net_ips: netmask 255.255.255.240
start 1.1.1.5 end 1.1.1.14
type generic, total addresses 10, allocated 1 (10%), misses 0
RouterB#
```

At first glance, it might look all right; you pinged five times, and you got five hits. But five pings should have generated five returned echo reply packets from the destination. For some reason, the echo replies aren't getting translated or are not being sent from the destination. We would need to look the routing tables to see whether routing is working. Then we would need to see whether the destination device refuses pings or any router in between blocks them.

The debug ip nat Command

The **debug ip nat** command can show in real time how and if your NAT translations are occurring. Except for learning environments, because of the heavy output and the impact on performance, the **debug** commands should always be used as a last resort. You should start with the **show** commands.

The following output shows the results of using a **ping** command:

```
RouterB#debug ip nat
IP NAT debugging is on
06:37:40: NAT:  s=10.0.1.85->1.1.1.5, d=3.3.3.3 [63]  (out)
06:37:40: NAT*: s=3.3.3.3, d=1.1.1.5->10.0.1.85 [63]  (in)
06:37:41: NAT*: s=10.0.1.85->1.1.1.5, d=3.3.3.3 [64]
06:37:41: NAT*: s=3.3.3.3, d=1.1.1.5->10.0.1.85 [64]
06:37:42: NAT*: s=10.0.1.85->1.1.1.5, d=3.3.3.3 [65]
06:37:42: NAT*: s=3.3.3.3, d=1.1.1.5->10.0.1.85 [65]
06:37:43: NAT*: s=10.0.1.85->1.1.1.5, d=3.3.3.3 [66]
06:37:43: NAT*: s=3.3.3.3, d=1.1.1.5->10.0.1.85 [66]
RouterB#
06:38:43: NAT: expiring 1.1.1.5 (10.0.1.85) icmp 1536 (1536)
RouterB#undebug all
```

All possible debugging has been turned off. You can see that inside host 10.0.1.85 is being translated to 1.1.1.5 on its way to outside device 3.3.3.3. The **s** indicates the source, and the **d** indicates the destination. The first two are labeled (out, meaning outbound, and in) to see the replies. The pattern follows the rest of the way down. The **[num]** is used to match up requests and replies or to identify an exchange. If you look at the row stamped 06:38:43, it shows an expiring translation.

The debug ip nat detailed Command   The following output shows the results of a ping. Inside host 10.0.1.85 wanted to use port 1536 to ping 3.3.3.3 (outside). See 07:03:50; since that port wasn't already assigned, it wasn't translated (sometimes referred to as *stolen*).

```
RouterB#debug ip nat detailed
IP NAT detailed debugging is on
07:03:50: NAT:  i: icmp (10.0.1.85, 1536) -> (3.3.3.3, 1536) [101]
07:03:50: NAT:  address not stolen for 10.0.1.85, proto 1 port 1536
07:03:50: NAT:  ipnat_allocate_port: wanted 1536 got 1536
07:03:50: NAT*: o: icmp (3.3.3.3, 1536) -> (1.1.1.5, 1536) [101]
07:03:51: NAT*: i: icmp (10.0.1.85, 1536) -> (3.3.3.3, 1536) [102]
07:03:51: NAT*: o: icmp (3.3.3.3, 1536) -> (1.1.1.5, 1536) [102]
07:03:52: NAT*: i: icmp (10.0.1.85, 1536) -> (3.3.3.3, 1536) [103]
07:03:52: NAT*: o: icmp (3.3.3.3, 1536) -> (1.1.1.5, 1536) [103]
07:03:53: NAT*: i: icmp (10.0.1.85, 1536) -> (3.3.3.3, 1536) [104]
07:03:53: NAT*: o: icmp (3.3.3.3, 1536) -> (1.1.1.5, 1536) [104] RouterB#
RouterB#undebug all
All possible debugging has been turned off.
```

The **i:** indicates an inside interface (inbound), while **o:** indicates an outside interface (outbound). The outbound rows go from 10.0.1.85 to 3.3.3.3, while the inbound ones go from 3.3.3.3 to 1.1.1.5. The global address indicates that NAT occurred but wasn't explicitly shown on the outbound transaction.

e x a m

ⓦatch   *Make sure you understand inside versus outside and local versus global. Know the three NAT types, when they would be used, and how to configure them. Remember to always figure out your inside and outside interfaces first to make sure you understand what NAT is trying to accomplish. Many people configure the inside and outside interfaces first so they don't forget them. Use*

the show ip nat translations **command in Privileged mode to see the translations in the translation table. Use the** show ip nat statistics **command to watch the hits counter to verify it is increasing. It also shows you interfaces (inside and outside) and other configuration details. The** clear ip nat translation * **command clears all dynamic translations and resets the statistics counters.**

Watch "NAT" for a demonstration of how to configure a Cisco router for NAT.

Network Time Protocol (NTP)

Network Time Protocol provides clock synchronization for computer and networking devices over packet-switched networks. It is designed to synchronize all participating devices to within milliseconds (1/1,000th of a second) of Coordinated Universal Time (UTC), the time standard for regulating world clocks and time. It replaced the earlier Greenwich Mean Time (GMT). UTC is not just a global Internet or networking standard; it is used by aviation, weather systems, telecommunications, and just about everything else.

NTP puts out a single time worldwide with no adjustment or information about local time zones or daylight saving time. That is why when you set the date and time on your computer, you have to select your time zone, as shown in Figure 11-7. The figure shows that Pacific Standard Time is UTC –8:00, which means your computer will subtract eight hours to get the exact local time. If the device supports daylight saving time, there is usually a check box or a place for entering starting and ending dates.

Why Is NTP Important?

So, why do we care about that level of accuracy in our networks? By having a single source time, devices around the world can share almost the exact time reference, which is critical for managing, securing, planning, and debugging our networks.

FIGURE 11-7

UTC offset

Select time zone:

(UTC-08:00) Pacific Time (US & Canada)

(UTC-08:00) Pacific Time (US & Canada)
(UTC-07:00) Arizona
(UTC-07:00) Chihuahua, La Paz, Mazatlan
(UTC-07:00) Mountain Time (US & Canada)
(UTC-06:00) Central America
(UTC-06:00) Central Time (US & Canada)
(UTC-06:00) Guadalajara, Mexico City, Monterrey
(UTC-06:00) Saskatchewan
(UTC-05:00) Bogota, Lima, Quito
(UTC-05:00) Eastern Time (US & Canada)
(UTC-05:00) Indiana (East)
(UTC-04:30) Caracas
(UTC-04:00) Asuncion
(UTC-04:00) Atlantic Time (Canada)

Time also provides the only frame of reference between all devices on the network. Without synchronized time, accurately correlating log files between these devices is difficult, even impossible. Here are just a few reasons it is important:

- More and more laws and regulations require it. Sarbanes-Oxley and the HIPAA Security Rule both require accurate timestamping.

- Some financial services (banking, stocks, and so on) require highly accurate timekeeping by law.

- Security processes or features will not connect or accept data if timestamps are outside an acceptable range to prevent tampering with the transmission.

- Tracking or logging of network or device events, including security breaches, can be virtually impossible to track or make sense of if timestamps are inaccurate.

- Even shared file systems can have problems if the modification times aren't consistent, regardless of what machine the files are on.

Client-Server Model

NTP uses a client-server model, with a device in the network working as an NTP server. In larger networks, it could be a server, but it could also be the firewall or a router. On most home, small business, or remote systems, the gateway router can perform this function. The server periodically goes out on the Internet to a trusted source and synchronizes; then it sends out NTP packets within the network so that all configured devices share the same time.

While not an exam requirement, these NTP broadcasts are an example of using User Datagram Protocol (in this case, UDP port 123) packets for broadcasting or multicasting, where clients passively listen to time updates. It avoids the overhead of the TCP handshake, and even if one broadcast is missed or lost, another will be out in a few minutes.

The client-server model is important to minimize overhead traffic out over the Internet, plus NTP is typically accurate to within one millisecond over most LANs.

Configuring NTP Client

To configure the NTP client on a Cisco device, you'll simply have to point it to the NTP server with the **ntp server** *server_ip_addr* command in Global Configuration mode. To verify that the Cisco device is learning the time from NTP, use the **show ntp associations** command in Privileged mode. You can use the **show clock [detail]** command in Privileged mode to see the device date and time. The **detail** option shows the source of the time. You can use the **clock timezone** *zone hours-offset* command to display local time, where *zone* is a three-letter designation for your time zone and *hours-offset* is the adjustment from UTC.

```
RTR#configure terminal
Enter configuration commands, one per line.  End with CNTL/Z.
RTR(config)#ntp server 10.0.0.5
RTR(config)#end
RTR#  <- Give it a couple minutes to connect
RTR#show ntp associations

   address     ref clock    st  when  poll reach  delay  offset     disp
*~10.0.0.5   10.1.1.123    3    61   128    4    7.5   11.15     2.4
 *master (synced), #master (unsynced), +selected, -candidate, ~configured
RTR#show clock
15:21:19.467 UTC Fri Apr 18 2014    ←result is UTC time
RTR#configure terminal
RTR(config)# clock timezone PST -8
RTR(config)#exit
RTR#show clock detail
07:22:15.348 UTC Fri Apr 18 2014    ←result is Local time
Time source is NTP
RTR#
```

For CCENT purposes, the only thing you need from the **show ntp associations** command is to confirm that the server address you used is shown in the output, indicating that the two devices are sharing the NTP data. The * before the IP address indicates that the router has synced to the source. The rest of the output can be useful in later Cisco certification exams. The **ref clock** is where the server you defined gets its time; in most cases, this will be a public IP address.

Watch "NTP" for a demonstration of how to configure an NTP client.

INSIDE THE EXAM

Dynamic Host Configuration Protocol (DHCP)

Make sure you know the DHCP lease steps. Use DORA to help you remember, and know which steps are broadcasts and which are unicasts. Know what the scope is, what excluded range and excluded addresses are, and what lease time is. Be sure you know that for those cases when you want a router to get an IP address and other information from a DHCP, use the **ip address dhcp** command in Interface Configuration mode instead of configuring an IP address. Know that the broadcast relay agent is configured with the **ip helper-address** *server-addr* command in Interface Configuration mode on the interface that will receive (hear) the broadcasts for DHCP services.

Network Address Translation (NAT and PAT)

Make sure you can identify the basic operation of NAT, its purpose, and what a pool is. Understand inside versus outside and local versus global in NAT. Know the difference

between three NAT types: static, dynamic, and overload (PAT). Dynamic and overload are one-way NAT; translations can be instigated only by the inside device (**ip nat** *inside* **source**), and outside devices can reply only to inside requests. Be sure you can configure and verify NAT for given network requirements. Remember to always figure out your inside and outside interfaces, but first make sure you understand what NAT is trying to do.

Use the **show ip nat translations** command in Privileged mode to see the translations in the translation table. Use the **show ip nat statistics** command to watch the hits counter to verify it is increasing. The **clear ip nat translation *** command clears all dynamic translations and resets the statistics counters.

Network Time Protocol (NTP)

Understand the basic concept of NTP as a client-server service and its purpose and importance. Be sure you can configure and verify NTP as a client.

CERTIFICATION SUMMARY

This chapter covered three of many IP services that Cisco routers can provide to our networks. DHCP, NAT, and NTP are common in many network implementations. The important thing is to get a basic understanding of what they are, what they do, and why they are important. It is also necessary to be able to do the basic configurations. While DHCP and NTP client configurations are relatively simple, NAT is a little more complex, with three different implementations that require not only configuring and verifying but also choosing which is the most appropriate for a situation.

✔ TWO-MINUTE DRILL

Dynamic Host Configuration Protocol (DHCP)

❏ A pool of IP addresses is the scope of IP addresses that can be given out for client requests. The server can maintain more than one scope.

❏ Use the **exclude-address** command on the DHCP server to hold a range of addresses out of the pool to be permanently assigned to network devices such as routers, switches, and so on.

❏ The lease time is the amount of time the device can use the IP address. This lease time can be renewed if the device is still using the IP address; otherwise, it reverts into the address pool for reuse.

❏ Use DORA (Discover, Offer, Request, ACK) to help you remember the steps, and know which steps are broadcasts (D and R) and which are unicasts (O and A).

❏ A router can be a relay agent, configured with the **ip helper-address** *server-addr* command in Interface Configuration mode on the interface that will receive (hear) the broadcasts for DHCP services.

❏ For a router to get an IP address and other DHCP information, use the **ip address dhcp** command in Interface Configuration mode instead of configuring an IP address.

Network Address Translation (NAT and PAT)

❏ NAT is a service that often runs on a perimeter router or firewall that translates inside network IP addresses into usable public IP addresses, or vice versa.

❏ Four common and yet different reasons to use NAT translation are to allow internal users with private IP addresses to access the Internet, to allow the external devices to access shared internal devices (such as servers), by redirecting inbound traffic to another TCP port or address, and during a network IP address transition.

❏ Inside addresses are within the organization's network. Outside addresses are external to the network. Local and global describe where the addresses are viewed (or seen) from within (local) or outside (global).

❏ There are three NAT types: static, dynamic, and overload (PAT).

❑ A NAT pool is simply a range of public IP addresses to be used for translations.

❑ Static NAT exposes an inside device to the outside world (web or e-mail server).

❑ Determine inside and outside interfaces first. Define them with the **ip nat [inside | outside]** command on the interfaces.

❑ The static NAT **ip nat inside source static** *inside-ip outside-ip* command actually creates the translation.

❑ Dynamic NAT needs three Global Configuration mode commands: **ip nat pool** *name start-ip end-ip* [**netmask** *mask* | **prefix-length** *length*] defines the pool of addresses to use. **ip nat inside source list** *access-list-number* **pool** *name* does the translation linking the list (ACL) of the inside address to the pool of outside addresses. **access-list** *access-list-number* **permit** *source-net-it* [*source-wildcard*] defines by filtering the inside eligible addresses.

❑ NAT overload (PAT) creates a one-to-many relationship, with a single public IP address supporting many internal hosts using different port numbers. A single IP address, even the router's outside interface IP, can support thousands of translations.

❑ Verify NAT configuration with the **show ip nat translations** command in Privileged mode.

❑ To clear the translations, use the **clear ip nat translation *** command, where the asterisk means all.

❑ Troubleshoot using the **show ip nat statistics** command to watch the hits counter to verify it is increasing as you send traffic.

Network Time Protocol (NTP)

❑ NTP provides clock synchronization for computer and networking devices to within milliseconds of Coordinated Universal Time (UTC).

❑ NTP uses a client-server model, with a device in the network working as an NTP server. In larger networks, it could be a server, but could also be a router.

❑ Use the **ntp server** *server_ip_addr* command in Global Configuration mode to configure the NTP client.

❑ To verify NTP, use the **show ntp associations** command in Privileged mode. Use the **show clock [detail]** command in Privileged mode to see the device date and time.

SELF TEST

The following Self Test questions will help you measure your understanding of the material presented in this chapter. Read all the choices carefully since there may be more than one correct answer. Choose all the correct answers for each question.

Dynamic Host Configuration Protocol (DHCP)

1. Which of the following is the correct order for a DHCP IP request?
   A. Request, Discover, Offer, ACK
   B. Discover, Request, Offer, ACK
   C. Discover, Offer, Request, ACK
   D. ACK, Discover, Offer, Request

2. Which of the DHCP steps in the previous question are broadcasts?
   A. ACK
   B. Discover
   C. Offer
   D. Request
   E. All of them

3. Which of the following makes a router a DHCP relay agent?
   A. Router(config)#dhcp relay agent 10.0.0.3
   B. Router(config-if)#dhcp relay agent 10.0.0.3
   C. Router(config)#ip helper-address 10.0.0.3
   D. Router(config-if)#ip helper-address 10.0.0.3

4. Which of the following would allow a router to get an IP address and other DHCP information?
   A. Router(config)#ip address dhcp
   B. Router(config-if)#ip address dhcp
   C. Router(config)#dhcp ip address
   D. Router(config-if)# dhcp ip address

Network Address Translation (NAT and PAT)

5. Which NAT type implements Port Address Translation?
   A. Static
   B. Static overload
   C. Dynamic
   D. Local global
   E. Global local
   F. Overload

6. Using Figure 11-8, which NAT type created the results in this translation table?
   A. Static
   B. Static overload
   C. Dynamic
   D. Local global
   E. Global local
   F. Overload

7. Using Figure 11-8, what is the device IP address of the host that accessed a web server?
   A. 1.1.1.5
   B. 10.0.2.43
   C. 10.0.0.65
   D. 1.3.159.100
   E. 10.0.1.85

	Pro	Inside global	Inside local	Outside local	Outside global
FIGURE 11-8	udp	1.1.1.5:51119	10.0.0.65:51119	1.15.79.4:53	1.15.79.4:53
	udp	1.1.1.5:51119	10.0.0.65:51119	1.10.0.11:53	1.10.0.11:53
NAT	tcp	1.1.1.5:52750	10.0.0.65:52750	1.3.159.100:80	1.3.159.100:80
configuration for	tcp	1.1.1.5:54625	10.0.2.43:54625	1.50.6.4:143	1.50.6.4:143
questions 6 and 7	tcp	1.1.1.5:54626	10.0.2.43:54626	1.50.6.4:143	1.50.6.4:143
	tcp	1.1.1.5:54850	10.0.1.85:54850	1.7.19.101:23	1.7.19.101:23

8. Using Figure 11-9, which NAT type is this configuration for?

    A. Static

    B. Static overload

    C. Dynamic

    D. Local global

    E. Global local

    F. Overload

9. Using Figure 11-9, how many public IP addresses are there in the pool?

    A. 20

    B. 14

    C. 28

    D. 10

    E. 5

10. Which two commands are used to verify NAT configuration?

    A. Router# **show nat translations**

    B. Router# **show ip nat translations**

    C. Router# **show ip nat statistics**

    D. Router# **show nat statistics**

    E. Router# **clear ip nat translation ***

FIGURE 11-9	
NAT configuration for questions 8 and 9	

```
RouterB#configure terminal
RouterB(config)#ip nat pool net_20 1.1.1.5 1.1.1.14 prefix-length 28
RouterB(config)#ip nat inside source list 10 pool net_20
RouterB(config)#access-list 10 permit 10.0.1.0 0.0.0.255
RouterB(config-if)#interface Fa0/0
RouterB(config-if)#ip nat inside
RouterB(config-if)#interface Fa0/1
RouterB(config-if)#ip nat outside
RouterB(config-if)#CTRL-z
```

Network Time Protocol (NTP)

11. Which command is used to configure the NTP client?

    A. Router(config)#**ntp server 10.0.0.5**

    B. Router(config-if)#**ntp client 10.0.0.5**

    C. Router(config-if)#**ntp server 10.0.0.5**

    D. Router(config)#**ntp client 10.0.0.5**

12. Which command is used to verify NTP use?

    A. Router(config)#**show ntp associations**

    B. Router(config-if)#**show ntp associations**

    C. Router#**show ntp associations**

    D. Router>**show ntp associations**

SELF TEST ANSWERS

Dynamic Host Configuration Protocol (DHCP)

1. ☑ **C** is correct. Use the acronym DORA to remember Discover, Offer, Request, ACK as the correct order for a DHCP IP request.
☒ **A, B,** and **D** are incorrect. All have the steps in the wrong order.

2. ☑ **B** and **D** are correct. Discover and Request use broadcasts.
☒ **A** and **C** are incorrect. Both Offer and ACK use unicasts.

3. ☑ **D** is correct. The **ip helper-address** command must be configured on the interface that will hear the DHCP client broadcasts.
☒ **A, B,** and **C** are incorrect. **A** and **B** are incorrect because they are not real commands. **C** is incorrect because while the command is correct, it must be configured on the interface.

4. ☑ **B** is correct. The **ip address dhcp** command must be configured on the interface.
☒ **A, C,** and **D** are incorrect. **A** is not correct because while the command is correct, it must be configured on the interface. **C** and **D** are incorrect because they are not real commands.

Network Address Translation (NAT and PAT)

5. ☑ **F** is correct. Overload NAT implements Port Address Translation (PAT).
☒ **A, B, C, D,** and **E** are incorrect. **A** and **C** are incorrect because static and dynamic NAT do not implement Port Address Translation (PAT). **B, D,** and **E** are incorrect because they are not real commands.

6. ☑ **F** is correct. Overload NAT created the results in this translation table. You can tell by the port numbers.
☒ **A, B, C, D,** and **E** are incorrect. **A** and **C** are incorrect because static and dynamic NAT do not display port numbers and use only two columns. **B, D,** and **E** are incorrect because they are not real commands.

7. ☑ **C** is correct. Host 10.0.0.65 is the device IP address of the host that accessed a web server on port 80.
☒ **A, B, D,** and **E** are incorrect. **A** is incorrect because 1.1.1.5 is the global IP address NAT assigned to the device. **B** is incorrect because while 10.0.2.43 is a device address, it went to an e-mail server (IMAP port 143). **D** and **E** are incorrect because while 10.0.1.85 is a device address, it sent mail to an e-mail server (SMTP port 23).

8.   ☑   C is correct. The configuration is for dynamic NAT.
     ☒   A, B, D, E, and F are incorrect. A is incorrect because Static wouldn't use a NAT pool and would use **ip nat source inside static**. B, D, and E are incorrect because they are not NAT options. F is incorrect because the overload parameter is missing from the **ip nat source inside** statement.

9.   ☑   D is correct. The NAT pool range 1.1.1.5 1.1.1.14 gives you ten addresses.
     ☒   A, B, C, and E are incorrect. A is incorrect because 20 is just part of the NAT address pool named net_20. B is incorrect because 14 is just part of the NAT address pool range. C is incorrect because 28 is the prefix length of the IP pool from which the range was taken. E is incorrect because 5 is just part of the NAT address pool range.

10. ☑   B and C are correct. B is correct because the **show ip nat translations** command shows the translation table. C is correct because the **show ip nat statistics** command shows the translation statistics and many of the NAT elements.
     ☒   A, D, and E are incorrect. A and D are incorrect because they are not real NAT commands. E is incorrect because the **clear ip nat translation *** command erases the translation table, leaving us nothing to work with.

Network Time Protocol (NTP)

11. ☑   A is correct. The **ntp server 10.0.0.5** command is entered in Global Configuration mode.
     ☒   B, C, and D are incorrect. B and D are incorrect because they are not real NAT commands. C is incorrect because the command was entered in Interface Configuration mode, not Global Configuration mode.

12. ☑   C is correct. The **show ntp associations** command is entered in Privileged (enable) mode.
     ☒   A, B, and D are incorrect. All are the right command, just in the wrong configuration mode.

12

Access Control Lists (ACLs)

I n Chapter 11, we used a simple access list with NAT. In this chapter, we will look at how to build and apply access lists to filter traffic. Later in the chapter, we will look at applying them to our remote sessions (line vty).

Access Control Lists (ACLs)

Cisco routers use *access control lists* (also called just *access lists* or ACLs) to provide basic packet filtering. ACLs can be used to filter data of many types, including traffic passing through a router interface, remote access connections, contents of routing updates, and, as in the previous chapter, controlling access to the Internet by defining what traffic will be translated by NAT.

ACLs consist of one or more statements, called *access control entries* (ACEs), that share a common identifier, either a name or a number. The ACL by itself is just a list of statements defining what sort of traffic we are interested in. We will then take that list and apply it to a process to take action on the interesting traffic. It could be as simple as applying the ACL to a router interface to filter incoming or outgoing traffic. Here the router would examine each packet to determine whether to forward or discard the packet, on the basis of the criteria we specified within the access lists. This criteria could be based on the source IP address, the destination IP address, the upper-layer protocol (port number), or other information.

Looking at our example from Chapter 11, shown here, the process using the ACL is the **ip nat inside source** command, which is deciding which inside addresses have access to NAT and therefore the outside world. The **source** *list 10* part indicates that an ACL identified by the number 10 will be used to determine these inside addresses. The ACL has three simple statements that each permit (allow) one subnet based on the source IP address using a wildcard mask like we saw in OSPF. Recall that the wildcard masks define the interesting host bits of the IP address.

```
RouterB(config)#ip nat inside source list 10 pool net_ips overload
RouterB(config)#access-list 10 permit 10.0.0.0 0.0.0.255
RouterB(config)#access-list 10 permit 10.0.1.0 0.0.0.255
RouterB(config)#access-list 10 permit 10.0.2.0 0.0.0.255
```

ACL Processing

There are two important concepts to remember when working with ACLs. First, by default for a router without an ACL, traffic is always allowed to pass through freely. But once an ACL is in place, the default flips to deny, which means that anything not specifically permitted by the ACL will be denied. Looking again at the example, any subnets but the three defined will not be allowed access to NAT. Therefore, to deny subnet 10.0.4.0/24, we don't have to do anything at all. If it helps, you can imagine there is an implicit **deny any** (everything else) statement as the last statement of every ACL.

Second, ACL statements (ACEs) are processed sequentially from the top down so that packets permitted or denied in an early statement never see any other statements. Looking at the previous example, permitting 10.0.0.0/24 with the first line means we can't add a statement afterward to deny a host like 10.0.0.125. Any packets permitted by row 1 never see rows 2, 3, or later. The **deny** statement would need to precede line 1.

ACL Wildcard Mask

ACLs use wildcard masks, like with OSPF routing, not subnet masks. As we saw then, wildcard masks are the inverse (opposite) of a subnet mask. We can subtract the wildcard mask from 255.255.255.255 to get the subnet mask (255.255.255.255 – 0.0.0.255 wildcard mask = 255.255.255.0 subnet mask), or we can subtract the subnet mask from 255.255.255.255 to get the wildcard mask.

At the extremes, 0.0.0.0 255.255.255.255 means any or all hosts on all subnets, while a mask of 0.0.0.0 is a host address for just that one IP (for example, 10.0.0.125 0.0.0.0 from the previous paragraph). It is possible to use the word *any* instead of typing **0.0.0.0 255.255.255.255**. We can also use the word *host* instead of the 0.0.0.0 mask, as in **host 10.0.0.125**. The next two code examples could be added to the example earlier. The first one would block the one host 10.0.3.214 from using NAT, while the second would allow any other hosts.

```
RouterB(config)#access-list 10 deny host 10.0.3.214
RouterB(config)#access-list 10 permit any
```

Note that if we did add these two lines, the last line makes the original three lines redundant. In other words, all five lines could be reduced to just these two: It says to deny host 10.0.3.214 and then allow everyone else. By the same token, just using **access-list 10 deny host 10.0.3.214** by itself would deny all traffic because of the implicit **deny any** that already exists.

e x a m

ⓦ a t c h

Remember that ACLs process the statements (ACEs) in sequential order, testing against each statement from the top down until one matches. Any packet processed by a statement does not see any other statements. Any packet that fails to match any statements is denied by default: implicit deny anything else.

ACLs use wildcard masks like OSPF. The wildcard mask and subnet mask are the inverse (opposite) of each other.

ACL Types

There are two general types of access lists that do basically the same thing: numbered and named. Both are further broken down into two groups: standard and extended. *Standard* ACLs are based solely on source IP addresses. *Extended* can be based on source and/or destination IP addresses as well as upper layer protocols. Named ACLs can do the same as either standard or extended. Not all processes can use numbered and named lists interchangeably, and the trend is toward named ACLs. We will cover each of these options.

Numbered Standard ACLs

Standard ACLs are the original, oldest, and simplest type of ACL based exclusively on source IP addresses. They control traffic by comparing the packet source IP address to the addresses configured in the ACL. If there is a permit statement that includes that address, it is allowed through; otherwise, it is discarded by a **deny** statement or the implicit **deny any** at the end.

Standard ACL numbers are 1 to 99 and 1300 to 1999.

The example earlier (the one originally from Chapter 11) is an example of a numbered standard ACL. It is a filter that, if applied to an interface or a process like NAT, would permit (allow) all hosts in three subnets. The implicit **deny any** at the end would then discard any others. Each packet gets tested against line 1. If not included in that filter, it is tested against line 2, and so on, until there are no more lines, in which case it will be discarded.

```
access-list 10 permit 10.0.0.0 0.0.0.255
access-list 10 permit 10.0.1.0 0.0.0.255
access-list 10 permit 10.0.2.0 0.0.0.255
```

Another possibility might look like the following where we first deny what we want. In this case, we exclude a host and a subnet but then allow everything else. Remember that it is too late to permit 10.0.1.25 and 10.0.4.0/25 because they have already been denied when line 3 was executed.

```
access-list 15 deny host 10.0.1.25
access-list 15 deny 10.0.4.0 0.0.0.255
access-list 15 permit any
```

We can tell these are numbered *standard* ACLs because the number falls within the 1 to 99 range and because there is only one address defined per line.

Numbered Extended ACLs

Extended ACLs can offer more complex traffic filtering by comparing the source and destination addresses as well as the port numbers of the IP packets. Extended ACL numbers include 100 to 199 and 2000 to 2699. They allow for a bit more sophisticated filtering and more flexibility in where we apply the ACL. Let's look at a simple example: Assume we want to deny all hosts in LAN C in Figure 12-1 from being able to reach LAN A. We could create a standard ACL like the following:

```
access-list 15 deny 10.0.2.0 0.0.0.255
access-list 15 permit any
```

FIGURE 12-1

ACL placement example

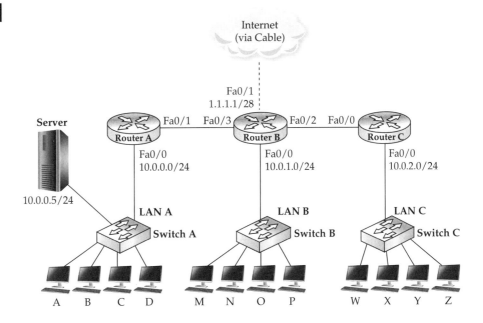

But where would we place it? It would have to go either inbound on Router A's Fa0/1 interface (**ip access-group 15 in**) or outbound on Router A's Fa0/0 LAN interface (**ip access-group 15 out**). It couldn't be applied to Router C because that would also prevent those hosts from reaching LAN B or the Internet, which is more restrictive than we want. By the same reasoning, putting it on Router B's LAN interface or the interface with Router C won't work. What we are seeing is that standard ACLs have to be placed close to the destination, so we don't deny access to other destinations. The downside is that both Router C and Router B as well as the links between have to process and carry packets that are doomed to be dropped when they reach Router A, possibly contributing to congestion.

Let's add another twist. What if all we really want is to prevent those hosts from accessing the server on LAN A? Our standard list doesn't allow that kind of selectivity; it is all of LAN A or nothing. Fortunately, this is where extended ACLs really shine. Look at the following example:

```
access-list 115 deny ip 10.0.2.0 0.0.0.255 host 10.0.0.5
access-list 115 permit ip any
```

Our same source 10.0.2.0/24 is now being denied to just the server (10.0.0.5). So, now the LAN C hosts could access any other hosts on LAN A. Maybe more importantly, since we can now test where the packet is going, we could apply this ACL inbound (**ip access-group115 in**) on the Router C LAN interface, reducing traffic and router processing on the rest of the network.

What we are seeing is that extended ACLs are placed close to the source because we know exactly where the packets are going.

Extended ACL Syntax   To get the more sophisticated filtering, the syntax is also a bit more complex. The basic command syntax is **access-list** *acl-number* [**permit** | **deny**] *protocol* [**host** | *source src-wildcard* | **any**] [**host** | *destination dest-wildcard* | **any**]. The protocol options are [**ip** | **icmp** | **tcp** | **udp**] that can be used to require an optional ICMP type or TCP/UDP port number after each address and mask combination. Table 12-1 shows the main syntax options that we are concerned with. Table 12-2 shows the relational-operators that are available when defining port numbers.

The IP protocol requires only the basic syntax, including designations for the source and destination. Those designations are always one of the following: [**Host** *host-ip-addr* | *ip-addr wildcard-mask* | **any**].

TABLE 12-1 Extended ACL Syntax

(Required)	(Required)	(Choice)	(Choice)	(Required)	(Optional)	(Required)	(Optional)
access-list	*acl-num*	[permit | deny]	protocol	src-id*	[Option]	dest-id*	[Option]
			IP		-		-
			TCP		src-port**		dest-port**
			UDP		src-port**		dest-port**
			ICMP				
			others				

* src-id and dest-id choices: [host ip | ip mask | any]
** src-port and dest-port: relational-operator and port-identifier

TCP and UDP can optionally be asked to match a source port and/or a destination port. When required, they appear immediately after the related IP address designation. The following example shows some samples. The first ACE prevents host 10.0.1.15 from passing through for any reason. The second and third prevent the 10.0.1.0/24 subnet from passing through to access any web or FTP servers; the last statement allows them, with everyone else, to pass through for any other purposes.

```
Router(config)#ip access-list extended 101
Router(config-ext-nacl)#deny ip host 10.0.1.15 any
Router(config-ext-nacl)#deny tcp 10.0.1.0 0.0.0.255 any eq www
Router(config-ext-nacl)#deny tcp 10.0.1.0 0.0.0.255 any eq ftp
Router(config-ext-nacl)#deny tcp 10.0.2.0 0.0.0.255 any ne 80
Router(config-ext-nacl)#permit tcp any host 9.0.1.128 range 8090 to 8095
Router(config-ext-nacl)#deny ip any host 9.0.1.128
Router(config-ext-nacl)#permit ip any any
```

TABLE 12-2

Relational-operators and Their Meanings

Operator	Means	Syntax	Example
eq	equal to	eq port-identifier	eq 80 or eq www
ne	not equal	ne port-identifier	ne 80 or ne www
lt	less than	lt port-identifier	lt 32
gt	greater than	gt port-identifier	gt 1024
range	range x to y	range *port-num* to *port-num*	range 12 to 40

Here's something to think about: Look at the second and third ACEs from the bottom. Notice that we are allowing everyone to access host 9.0.1.128 for something using six TCP ports 8090 to 8095 but blocking anything else. These could be remote monitoring devices or even remote web servers that even 10.0.1.0/24 would be able to access because they are not using port 80.

Table 12-3 lists some port numbers (their ACL keyword that can be used in ACEs) that you should be familiar with for the exam.

Looking at Table 12-1, we see that port number expressions can be part of the source and/or destination in an ACE. Let's take a minute to review IP addresses and port numbers in data exchanges. In Figure 12-2 we have two hosts with sessions to a single server in the Internet somewhere. In the first exchange, host 1.0.1.85 contacted server 3.0.3.3 at port 80 while using port 5000 for any replies. Another way of displaying this is 1.0.1.85:5000 to 3.0.3.3:80. The reply is reversed: 3.0.3.3:80 to 1.0.1.85:5000. So, if we want to filter for port 80, we need to know whether we are filtering outbound requests or inbound replies. The same is true for the second exchange between 1.0.1.9:7100 and 3.0.3.3:21.

TABLE 12-3	Port Number	Protocol	Application	ACL Keyword
Common TCP/ UDP Port Numbers and ACL Keywords	20	TCP	FTP (data port)	`ftp-data`
	21	TCP	FTP (control port)	`ftp`
	22	TCP	SSH	
	23	TCP	Telnet	`telnet`
	25	TCP	SMTP	`smtp`
	53	TCP/UDP	DNS	`dns`
	69	UDP	TFTP	`tftp`
	80	TCP	HTTP/WWW	`www`
	110	TCP	POP3	
	119	TCP	NNTP (News)	
	123	TCP	NTP (Time)	
	161	UDP	SNMP	`snmp`
	443	TCP	SSL/HTTPS	

FIGURE 12-2

IP addresses and
port numbers in
data exchanges

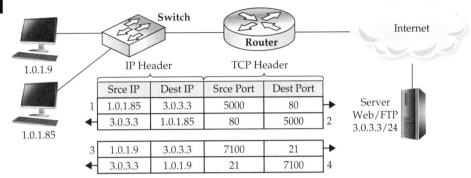

	Srce IP	Dest IP	Srce Port	Dest Port	
1	1.0.1.85	3.0.3.3	5000	80	
	3.0.3.3	1.0.1.85	80	5000	2
3	1.0.1.9	3.0.3.3	7100	21	
	3.0.3.3	1.0.1.9	21	7100	4

The following output would deny the outbound packets if applied to the LAN interface of the router IN (inbound). In this case, ports 80 and 21 are destination ports. We substituted **ftp** for 21 just to show that they are interchangeable.

```
Router(config)#ip access-list extended 105
Router(config-ext-nacl)#deny tcp host 1.0.1.85 host 3.0.3.3 eq 80
Router(config-ext-nacl)#deny tcp host 1.0.1.9 host 3.0.3.3 eq ftp
Router(config-ext-nacl)#permit ip any any
```

The following output would deny the inbound packets if applied to the Internet interface of the router IN (inbound). In this case, ports 80 and 21 are source ports. We substituted **www** for port 80 just to show that they are interchangeable.

```
Router(config)#ip access-list extended 107
Router(config-ext-nacl)#deny tcp host 3.0.3.3 eq www host 1.0.1.85
Router(config-ext-nacl)#deny tcp host 3.0.3.3 eq 21 host 1.0.1.9
Router(config-ext-nacl)#permit ip any any
```

Named ACLs

IP named ACLs allow us to use names for standard and extended ACLs instead of numbers. Named access lists also have a more versatile configuration syntax. Instead of making every line fully able to stand on its own like numbered ACLS, named ACLs break up the process into two parts. First define the type, standard or extended, and assign a name. Then add a series of permit or deny statements. See the following example:

```
ip access-list extended allow-in
deny ip any host 9.0.1.15
deny tcp any 9.0.1.24 0.0.0.0 eq www
deny ip any 9.0.1.128 0.0.0.63
permit ip any any
```

First, the descriptive name *allow-in* helps us remember what the ACL does. It could be any descriptive word without spaces, such as **let-us-in** or **banned-from-net**. In our example, we are allowing our hosts to create IP sessions with anyone except two hosts and a subnet on the 9.0.1.0 network.

Second, each **permit/deny** statement is shorter (less typing) than its numbered ACL counterpart. And while we can add statements to named ACLs like with numbered ones, it is possible to reorder the statements and delete individual statements. Editing has come to ACLs. We will look at that in the configuration section.

While numbered and named can be used interchangeably in many processes, there are some that still require either numbered or named ACLs but not both.

e x a m

watch *There are two types of ACLs: standard and extended. Standard can test on the source IP address only. Extended can test on any combination of source IP, destination IP, and upper-level port information. Both ACL types can use the older number method for identifying or* *can use the newer and much more useful name method. The biggest advantage to named ACLs is the ability to edit them within the CLI.*

Know the common TCP/UDP port numbers and keywords (Table 12-3) that can be used with extended ACLs.

Building and Editing ACLs

As mentioned earlier, ACLs are processed sequentially from the top down. Well, they are built exactly the same way. The first statement created becomes the top item in the ACL, the second entry becomes the second item, and so on.

When designing and building our ACL, try to be aware of all requirements for a particular interface because there can be only one inbound and one outbound per interface. Consider the following when deciding the order of our statements:

- Place statements for frequently encountered packets as close to the top as possible. These packets will then be matched after fewer "tests," saving the router time and processing resources because no more statements will be checked for that packet.

- Place less frequently expected entries closer to the bottom.

■ Place more restrictive statements before more general or less restrictive entries. For example, if we want to block only a host or subnet but then allow the rest of the hosts on the segment, put our **deny** statements first and then the broader **permit** statement.

The following shows how the previous might be implemented. Assume that we have a large network segment 10.0.1.0/24 with more than 200 active users and another segment 10.0.2.0/24 for the warehouse with fewer and infrequent users. In each case, we have a couple addresses for which we want to deny access.

```
access-list 12 deny 10.0.1.0 0.0.0.31
access-list 12 permit 10.0.1.0 0.0.0.255
access-list 12 deny 10.0.2.0 0.0.0.7
access-list 12 permit 10.0.2.0 0.0.0.255
```

We put the 10.0.1.0/24 ACEs first because we expect more of them, but we also put the smaller **deny** subnet first so those hosts have been blocked before the full segment is permitted. Make sure you see why these two statements couldn't be in reverse order.

Here are some other guidelines to consider in building ACLs:

■ There must be at least one **permit** statement. An ACL without at least one **permit** statement denies all traffic. Because of the implicit **deny** statement at the end of an ACL list, any packet that doesn't match any of the ACL statements will be discarded.

■ Be careful with the **permit any** and **permit any any** statements. All traffic meets this test and will pass through the interface. No other statements would be processed. Using this statement at the end of an ACL means the implicit **deny** statement would never be activated. This statement would usually be the only **permit** statement after any **deny** statements, if you want to allow everything but the addresses you denied.

■ Consider using an explicit **deny any** or **deny any any** statement as the last line of your ACLs. The command shows up on the **show running-config** and various **show access-list** commands and **debug** output, which can be helpful with troubleshooting and network monitoring. The implicit **deny** statement do not appear on the **show access-list** command.

ACLs are relevant only on the device on which they are configured. If we want the same ACL on multiple devices, it must be created and applied on each device. By the same token, ACL names or numbers that must be unique on a particular device are relevant only to that device. The same ACL could have a different name, or same name, on another device. Similarly, two different ACLs on different devices might share the same name. While good organizational practice might suggest consistent naming for ACLs doing the same thing on different devices, it is not a requirement.

Remark Statements

The **remark** *text* command can be used to add comments or explanations before or after any ACL command. Anything following the keyword **remark** is ignored by the ACL, but it can save valuable time when we have to figure out what an ACL is doing.

```
access-list 12 remark - Warehouse workstations
access-list 12 deny 10.0.2.0 0.0.0.7
access-list 12 permit 10.0.2.0 0.0.0.255
```

Editing Numbered ACLs

Until the most recent IOS versions, numbered ACLs did not allow editing using the CLI. Any new lines are added to the bottom, and any attempt to delete a row would delete the entire ACL. The following attempt to remove a line from our example would delete the whole thing:

```
RouterB(config)#no access-list 10 permit 10.0.1.0 0.0.0.255
```

To intentionally remove the ACL, the **no access-list 10** command would suffice. The most recent versions of IOS do support editing. An example is shown in the configuration section.

Using a Text Editor to Edit ACLs   Any text editor, like Notepad, can be used to create or edit ACLs. This is particularly useful with numbered ACLs that can't be edited on the router. This at least keeps you from having to retype all of the lines. While this won't be available in the exam, it is a common work practice. Use these steps:

- Run the **show running-config** command.
- Select and copy the ACL statements; then paste them into a text editor.
- Make any changes and deletions using your editor's features.
- If you want to disable the ACL from the interface before the change-over, remove the ACL from the interface using the **no ip access-group** [*acl-name*

| *acl-number*] [**in** | **out**] command. You could make this the first line of your edited list of entries. Be sure to remember to include the commands to get in and out of Interface Configuration mode.

■ Delete the existing ACL so these new lines do not add to it. Use the **no access-list [acl-name | acl-number]** command. You could make this the second line of your edited list of entries.

■ In Global Configuration mode, paste the edited list of statements into the router. The router will verify each statement and report any errors.

■ In Interface Configuration mode, reapply the ACL using the **ip access-group** command. You could make this the last line of your edited list of entries; remember to include the commands to get in and out of Interface Configuration mode.

e x a m

w a t c h *ACLs are relevant only on the device on which they are configured. Make sure you understand the concepts of planning your ACL and how ACLs process packets. Planning, such as putting the most frequent filters near the top, can make your ACLs more efficient, requiring less time and fewer resources. Not understanding*

the sequential processing means that more specific filters may never be seen by the packets because they passed looser tests. Be careful with permit any [any] *and* deny any [any] *statements; all packets meet both. There must be at least one* permit *statement.*

Applying ACLs

ACLs can be built at any time, but they serve no purpose (they do nothing) until they are applied to an interface or used by another process, such as the NAT example. An unapplied ACL is basically a filter waiting for a job. Building ACLs first is a good practice.

Applying a nonexistent ACL is not a good practice. A nonexistent ACL permits all traffic, but the IOS will start filtering as soon as the first statement is entered. Because of the implicit **deny any** statement, everything but that first statement will be denied. The traffic will continue to be filtered by a partial ACL as you add lines, often denying much more than you wanted, causing serious network access issues until the ACL is completed.

In a production environment, you can create a new ACL and the lines to apply it in a text editor like we covered in the previous section, giving you an almost instant cut-over.

Applying ACLs to Interfaces

A common use for ACLs is to filter traffic through a router. In that case, the ACL is applied to an interface using the **ip access-group** [*acl-number* | *acl-name*] [in | out] command. The terms are similar, but we create ACLs with the **access-list** command, and we apply them to an interface with the **ip access-group** command. Use **no** before the same command to remove an ACL from an interface. It does not delete the ACL itself.

The **in** and **out** option refers to whether the traffic is coming in (inbound) to the router or has passed through the router and is on its way out (outbound). Looking at Figure 12-3, traffic from either of our LAN hosts would be coming in the router on interface A and going out interface B on its way to the Internet. But traffic from the Internet to our hosts would be just the opposite. It is coming in on interface B and out on interface A.

In means it is arriving inbound at the router from the source, whereas **out** means the router has already done any processing and forwarding and it is outbound on its way to the destination. There are exceptions, but generally, if we are going to deny traffic, it is best to do it close to the source and on the inbound interface. Why expend router resources on a packet that is going to be discarded anyway? As an analogy, on an airplane, employees check for tickets as the passengers board, denying access to any without tickets or with incorrect tickets. If they wait until the passengers are disembarking (outbound), services have already been provided when passengers are off the plane.

FIGURE 12-3

Router in and out example

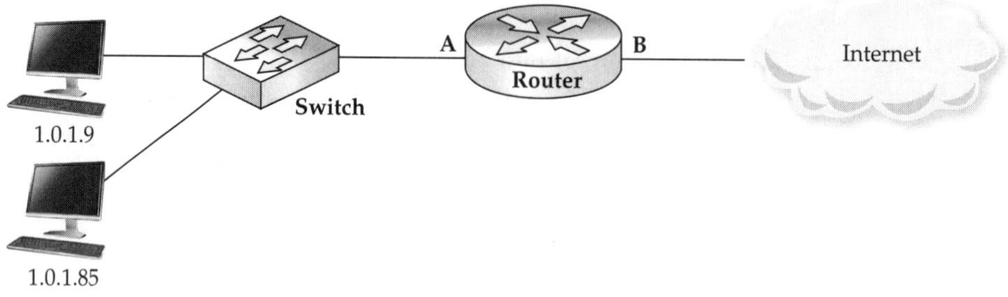

1.0.1.9

1.0.1.85

Switch

A   Router   B

Internet

Organize your interface ACLs because there can be only one per interface inbound and one outbound so that one ACL may have to contain statements for several reasons.

Selecting Interfaces for ACLs

There may be more than one interface that the ACL could be applied to, particularly in larger multirouter networks. Here are a couple guidelines to keep in mind:

- **Apply standard ACLs as close to the destination as possible** Since standard ACLs filter on the source IP address, not the destination, there is no way to apply them closer to the source without possibly restricting access to destinations between those two points, namely, destinations not included in our ACL plan.

- **Apply extended ACLs as close to the source as possible** Since we know exactly where they are going, we can filter them early and save router resources, unnecessary routing of the packet, and reduce traffic over network links.

exam

ⓦatch   *ACLs can be applied to interfaces for traffic filtering. There can be only one in and one out ACL per interface, so a single ACL may be filtering for several objectives. Remember that in/inbound and out/outbound are all relative to the center of the router. Is it heading in toward the center or out from the center?*

When applying ACLs to interfaces, apply standard ACLs as close to the destination as possible. Apply extended ACLs as close to the source as possible.

CERTIFICATION OBJECTIVE 12.02

Configuring ACLs

In this section we will look at the basic ACL configuration for traditional numbered ACLs, named ACLs, and the new configuration method that is like named ACLs using numbers.

Numbered ACLs

We are going to look at both the new method for the latest IOS and the traditional way of building numbered ACLs. While the new method is all you need for the exam, there are thousands, if not millions, of routers in the field that do not yet support it.

Numbered Standard ACL

The command syntax is **access-list** *acl-number* [**permit** | **deny**] [**host** | *source source-wildcard* | **any**]. Standard ACL numbers are 1 to 99 and 1300 to 1999. Remember that the word **any** can be used instead of 0.0.0.0/255.255.255.255. **Host** *ip-addr* can be used instead of 9.0.1.9 0.0.0.0, but then standard ACLs allow you to omit the wildcard on hosts, so the host keyword isn't all that useful here.

The following standard ACL number 5 denies host 9.0.1.15 and all hosts 9.0.1.128 to 9.0.1.191. It then allows all of the 9.0.1.0/24 subnet, which is too late for the ones we denied. Finally, the implicit **deny any** would discard any other hosts.

```
Router(config)#access-list 5 deny host 9.0.1.9
Router(config)#access-list 5 deny 9.0.1.15
Router(config)#access-list 5 deny 9.0.1.128 0.0.0.63
Router(config)#access-list 5 permit 9.0.1.0 0.0.0.255
```

New Method   This method means there is just one way to create numbered or named ACLs, but then if it is going to be the same process, why not just use names? Here are the steps:

```
Router(config)#ip access-list standard 7
Router(config-std-nacl)#deny host 9.0.1.9
Router(config-std-nacl)#deny 9.0.1.15
Router(config-std-nacl)#deny 9.0.1.128 0.0.0.63
Router(config-std-nacl)#permit 9.0.1.0 0.0.0.255
Router(config-std-nacl)#CTRL-Z
```

By far the biggest advantage to this method is the ability to edit the ACLs from the CLI. It is possible using the **insert** statement by going back into the NACL Configuration mode and starting the **new** statement with a new sequence number indicating where you want the line to go. To delete a statement, use the **no** *seq-num* command. The following example shows us adding another denied subnet at line 35 and deleting line 10:

```
Router(config)#ip access-list standard 7
Router(config-std-nacl)#35 deny 9.0.1.192 wildcard bits 0.0.0.7
```

```
Router(config-std-nacl)#no 10
Router(config-std-nacl)#CTRL-Z
Router(config)#show ip access-list 7
Standard IP access list 7

   20 deny 9.0.1.15
   30 deny 9.0.1.128 wildcard bits 0.0.0.63
   35 deny 9.0.1.192 wildcard bits 0.0.0.7
   40 permit 9.0.1.0 wildcard bits 0.0.0.255
```

Applying the ACL   Next we need to apply the ACL to the interface (inbound or outbound) using the **ip access-group** *acl-number* [**in** | **out**] command. Note that while the **access-list** statement doesn't use IP (the number indicates it is for IP), the **ip access-group** statement requires it.

The following code shows the steps for applying either ACL inbound on interface A on our example:

```
Router(config)#interface Fastethernet0/0
Router(config-if)#ip address 9.0.1.1 255.255.255.0
Router(config-if)#ip access-group 5 in
Router(config-if)#CTRL-Z
```

Numbered Extended ACL

The basic command syntax is **access-list** *acl-number* [permit | deny] *protocol* [host | *source src-wildcard* | any] [host | *destination dest-wildcard* | any]. As before, the word **any** can be used instead of 0.0.0.0/255.255.255.255. Host 9.0.1.9 can be used instead of 9.0.1.9 0.0.0.0, but extended ACLs require either the **host** keyword or the wildcard mask; it can't be assumed. In our example, the protocol will be IP, but the options are [**ip** | **icmp** | **tcp** | **udp**] that can be used to require an optional ICMP type or TCP/UDP port number after each address and mask combination.

The following standard ACL number 105 denies IP traffic from anyone to host 9.0.1.15, 9.0.1.24 and all hosts 9.0.1.128 to 9.0.1.191. It then allows all IP traffic to the 9.0.1.0/24 subnet, which is again too late for the ones already denied. Finally, the implicit **deny any** would discard any other IP traffic.

```
Router(config)#access-list 105 deny ip any host 9.0.1.15
Router(config)#access-list 105 deny ip any 9.0.1.24 0.0.0.0
Router(config)#access-list 105 deny ip any 9.0.1.128 0.0.0.63
Router(config)#access-list 105 permit ip any 9.0.1.0 0.0.0.255
```

Next we need to apply the ACL to the interface (inbound or outbound) using the **ip access-group** *acl-number* [**in** | **out**] command. Note that while the **access-list** statement doesn't use the IP (the number indicates it is for IP), the **ip access-group** statement requires it. The following code shows us applying it inbound on interface B of our example:

```
Router(config)#interface Fastethernet0/1
Router(config-if)#ip address 1.1.5.2 255.255.255.252
Router(config-if)#ip access-group 105 in
Router(config-if)#CTRL-Z
```

To use the TCP and UDP protocols, we can add a source port and/or a destination port depending on whether the filter will be applied inbound or outbound for the subnet. The following example shows some statements that might be applied to traffic wanting to leave the subnet. The first and second ACEs prevent the 10.0.1.0/24 subnet from passing through to access any web or FTP servers; the third one prevents 10.0.1.45 from going out for any reason. The fourth would block all outbound UTP; that's pretty severe, but without a port designation, it means everything. The last statement allows everything else to pass for any other purposes.

```
Router(config)#ip access-list extended 101
Router(config-ext-nacl)#deny tcp 10.0.1.0 0.0.0.255 any eq ftp
Router(config-ext-nacl)#deny tcp 10.0.1.0 0.0.0.255 any eq 80
Router(config-ext-nacl)#deny ip host 10.0.1.45 any
Router(config-ext-nacl)#deny utp any any
Router(config-ext-nacl)#permit ip any any
```

Named ACLs

The command syntax has changed for IP named ACLs, requiring the single command **ip access-list** [**extended** | **standard**] *acl-name* followed by a series of **permit/deny** statements. These statements follow the syntax for standard or extended from [**permit** | **deny**] on. Note that numbered access list statements use the number to indicate IP, while the named ones require **ip access-list** in the command. Let's look at our previous example as an extended named ACL:

```
Router(config)#ip access-list extended let-in
Router(config-ext-nacl)#deny ip any host 9.0.1.15
Router(config-ext-nacl)#deny ip any 9.0.1.24 0.0.0.0
Router(config-ext-nacl)#deny ip any 9.0.1.128 0.0.0.63
Router(config-ext-nacl)#permit ip any 9.0.1.0 0.0.0.255
```

Next we need to apply the ACL to the interface (inbound or outbound) using the **ip access-group** *acl-name* [**in** | **out**] command. The following code shows us applying it inbound on interface B of our example:

```
Router(config)#interface Fastethernet0/1
Router(config-if)#ip address 1.1.5.2 255.255.255.252
Router(config-if)#ip access-group let-in in
Router(config-if)#CTRL-Z
```

Editing an ACL

All IOS versions support the ability to edit named ACLs, and the latest versions extend that capability to numbered standard and extended ACLs. When we run the **show access-list** command, we should see autogenerated sequence numbers. We can insert a statement by starting with a new sequence number where we want the line to go. To delete a statement, use the **no** *seq-num* command. The following example shows how we could replace line 30 with a different wildcard mask:

```
router#show access-list
Extended IP access list let-in
    10 deny ip any host 9.0.1.15 (126 matches)
    20 deny ip any 9.0.1.24 0.0.0.0 (248 matches)
    30 deny ip any 9.0.1.128 0.0.0.63
    40 permit ip any 9.0.1.0 0.0.0.255 (1539 matches)
router#configure terminal
Enter configuration commands, one per line. End with CNTL/Z.
router(config)#ip access-list ext let-in
router(config-ext-nacl)#25 deny ip any 9.0.1.128 0.0.0.31
router(config-ext-nacl)#no 30
router(config-ext-nacl)#CTRL-Z
router#
router#show access-list
Extended IP access list let-in
    10 deny ip any host 9.0.1.15 (126 matches)
    20 deny ip any 9.0.1.24 0.0.0.0 (248 matches)
    25 deny ip any 9.0.1.128 0.0.0.31
    40 permit ip any 9.0.1.0 0.0.0.255 (1539 matches)
```

While not necessary for operations, we can resequence the ACL with the **ip access-list resequence** *acl-name start-num incr-num* command.

```
router#configure terminal
Enter configuration commands, one per line. End with CNTL/Z.
```

```
router(config)#ip access-list resequence let-in 20 20
router(config)#exit
router#
router#show access-list
Extended IP access list let-in
    20 deny ip any host 9.0.1.15 (126 matches)
    40 deny ip any 9.0.1.24 0.0.0.0 (248 matches)
    60 deny ip any 9.0.1.128 0.0.0.31
    80 permit ip any 9.0.1.0 0.0.0.255 (1539 matches)
```

EXERCISE 12-1

MHE Lab

Basic Access Control Lists

In this exercise we demonstrate the steps an administrator would take to configure access control lists (ACLs) to control traffic flow. We will use NetSim for this exercise. Launch Lab 12-1 and review the topology.

We will be working on all three routers. Each is configured like it was at the end of Exercise 9-3. All interfaces are configured and we are using static routing so that all devices can reach every other device. We can go through some together, and you can try your hand on others. To see how ACLs work, some of our first efforts will include errors that we will correct.

Task 1: Standard ACL Filtering Traffic

1. Since ACLs work only on the router they are created and applied on, our first step is to make sure we understand what we want to accomplish and select the router we need to configure. We want to block host A.11 from accessing the LAN B subnet. Since we are going to build a standard ACL (a number 1–99), we know it needs to be as close to the destination as possible, so we will apply it on RouterB's LAN interface Fa0/0.

2. Open a console session on RouterB and type these simple commands:

```
RouterB#conf t
RouterB(config)#access-list 10 deny host 10.0.0.11
RouterB(config)#interface fa0/0
RouterB(config-if)#ip access-group 10 out
RouterB(config-if)#CTRL-Z
```

We chose **out** because the traffic will be coming out of the router on that interface. Had we applied it to Fa1/0, it would have been **in** because the traffic would be entering, or going into, the router.

To test our work, open a console session on A.11 and ping host 10.0.1.77, switch 10.0.1.2, and router Fa0/0 10.0.1.1. The first two should be blocked but not the third. Why? Pinging an interface does not pass through the interface, so the filter doesn't apply. So, do we claim success?

Before we do, open a console session on C.13 and ping host 10.0.1.77. Was that supposed to happen?

Open a console session on B.77 and ping hosts 10.0.0.22 and 10.0.2.13. We're pretty sure that wasn't supposed to happen. Both failed.

You might have seen this coming, but we just violated the main rule of ACLs. There must be at least one **permit** statement, or you effectively shut down that interface in the specified direction. Never forget that there is always an implicit **deny everything else** statement at the end. This one is easy to fix; add this line on RouterB:

```
RouterB#conf t
RouterB(config)#access-list 10 permit any
RouterB(config-if)#CTRL-Z
```

Rerun your ping tests to make sure that it works and doesn't restrict any others.

3. Before leaving this, do a **show run** to see the statements you just added. Note that the ACL is near the bottom of the configuration and the line we just added went to the bottom of the list. All new lines are appended to the end.

4. A handy command to remember when an interface is blocking traffic is the **show ip interface fa0/0** command. Run it and look down about seven or eight rows. You will see whether there are any ACLs and in which direction they are filtering. There can be only one ACL per interface per direction. It is much easier than searching the configuration.

```
Outgoing access list is 10
Inbound access list is not set
```

There is a similar command, the **show interfaces fa0/0** command, that is of no use in this case. Try it and make sure you recognize the difference. This is an easy one to get tripped up on when taking the exam or working in the field.

Run the **show access-lists** command to see what ACLs are configured, even if not applied, and the (# matches) will tell you how many times the line has matched a packet. The **show ip access-lists** command does exactly the same thing since there are only IP ACLs. Both have the option of adding the number or name to the end to limit the output to one ACL.

5. Save your work.

Task 2: Extended ACL Filters

1. In this example we want to block host A.22 from accessing the switch in LAN C. In the real world, it might be a printer, server, camera, or some other device, but we'll work with what we have. We know that extended ACLs should go as close to the source as possible. The following does that using both forms of identifying a host address; normally you'd use the one you like. The second line avoids the trap we fell into last time.

   Here is the basic syntax of extended ACL: **access-list** *acl-number* [**permit** | **deny**] *protocol* [**host** | *source src-wildcard* | **any**] [**host** | *destination dest-wildcard* | **any**].

   Make these entries on RouterA:

   ```
   RouterA#config t
   RouterA(config)#access-list 105 deny ip 10.0.0.22 0.0.0.0 host 10.0.2.2
   RouterA(config)#access-list 105 permit ip any any
   RouterA(config)#int fa0/0
   RouterA(config-if)#ip access-group 105 in
   RouterA(config-if)#CTRL-Z
   ```

2. When completed, try to ping and Telnet to SwitchC (10.0.2.2) from host A.22. Both should fail. Try pinging host C.13. Did it work? Why? It's because 10.0.2.2 is the switch management interface, which is what we blocked, not the functioning of the switch. Confirm that A.11 can both ping and Telnet to SwitchC. Use your **show** commands to confirm your work.

3. Time passes, and now we want to restrict host A.11 from accessing 10.0.2.1, RouterC's LAN interface. It sounds like another extended ACL is needed. Closest to the source puts it on RouterA on the LAN interface inbound. But, we already have an ACL inbound on that interface. Moving where it is

applied is not the answer; we need to make our existing ACL 105 serve both purposes, so let's add the following line:

```
RouterA#config t
RouterA(config)#access-list 105 deny ip 10.0.0.11 0.0.0.0 host 10.0.2.1
RouterA(config-if)#CTRL-Z
```

4. When completed, try to ping and Telnet to 10.0.2.1 from host A.11. Both should work. Why? Run a **show access-list** command for a hint. Our new line appears at the bottom after our **permit any any** statement allowed everything through. With named ACLs, we could edit this, but not with numbered ones.

   We are going to have to delete our ACL and redo it in the right order. On any simulator, that is often the case. It is possible to copy the lines to a text editor like we do when working on devices and covered in the text, but generally it takes longer to master the way NetSim works than it is worth.

5. If you want, try it on your own; alternatively, follow these steps. To remove the ACL, you need only the **no access-list 105** command. Since this is a lab environment, we won't remove it from the interface first, but this would make sense in a production environment. Test it when you are through and run your **show** commands from Task 1's step 5 to confirm your work.

```
RouterA#config t
RouterA(config)#no access-list 105
RouterA(config)#access-list 105 deny ip 10.0.0.22 0.0.0.0 host 10.0.2.2
RouterA(config)#access-list 105 deny ip 10.0.0.11 0.0.0.0 host 10.0.2.1
RouterA(config)#access-list 105 permit ip any any
RouterA(config-if)#CTRL-Z
```

6. Save your work.

Task 3: Practice

1. Using the skills covered, assume you have two requirements that you are working on today. You want to block 10.1.1.2 (RouterA) from accessing LAN C hosts. Second, you want to prevent *any* LAN C hosts from accessing 10.0.0.2 while allowing SwitchC to be able to access it.

   Work out your solutions and then make the entries. Test your work and use the **show** commands, particularly **show access lists**, to make sure you are getting the results you expected.

   One solution will be posted in the "Lab Solutions" section in the PDF Lab Book.

2. Save your work.

Limiting Management Access

Our examples so far have been for filtering network data traffic through an interface. We accomplished this by applying our ACL to an interface using the **ip access-group** *acl-id* [in | out] command.

It is possible to filter management traffic using access lists as well. After configuring an appropriate access list, we must apply the access list using the **access-class** command.

The **access-class** command sounds similar to **access-group** that we used to apply ACLs to router interfaces. Many new users confuse the two, but it is an important difference. **Access-class** is used to apply an ACL to a "line" such as **vty**, **aux**, and so on, which are usually management connections that terminate on the router/switch using Telnet, SSH, and HTTP. **Access-group** is used to apply an ACL to a router interface that accepts and forwards data such as through the router.

Use the **access-class** *acl-id* [in | out] command, where *acl-id* can be an ACL name or number, in Line Configuration mode. To remove access restrictions, use the **no** form of this command.

The following example uses a simple standard ACL to permit only IP addresses from a certain subnet (10.0.99.0/24), our admin group, to Telnet/SSH into the router. The implicit **deny any** would discard packets from any other source IP addresses. We want this to protect all of our remote connections, so **0 15** would secure all lines between 0 and 15. If our device supports fewer, **0 4**, it won't create an error.

```
Router(config)#access-list 10 permit ip 10.0.99.0 0.0.0.255
Router(config)#line vty 0 15
Router(config-line)#access-class 10 in
Router(config-line)#exit
```

While this limits access from just certain IP addresses, one of the requirements of the exam is securing the management interfaces so that SSH (port 23), the more secure protocol, would be allowed but Telnet (port 22) would be denied. To do that, we will need an extended ACL like the following example. While not required, we explicitly stated **deny ip any any**.

```
Router(config)#access-list 101 permit ip 10.0.99.0 0.0.0.255 any eq 23
Router(config)#access-list 101 deny ip any any
Router(config)#line vty 0 15
Router(config-line)#access-class 101 in
Router(config-line)#transport input ssh
Router(config-line)#exit
```

Recall in Chapter 6 that we learned to use the **transport input ssh** command to further limit access to SSH traffic. It would be highly suggested here for added security.

Verifying and Troubleshooting ACLs

We can use the **show ip access-list** [*acl-num* | *acl-name*] command to see our ACLs. Without the optional [*acl-num* | *acl-name*], it shows all IP ACLs. While the format is a little different, it is easily recognizable. If there has been any activity, the match count appears in parentheses to the right. The **show running-config** command also shows the ACLs but not the results.

```
Router#show ip access-list
Standard IP access list 10
    permit 10.0.0.0 0.0.0.255
    permit 10.0.1.0 0.0.0.255
    permit 10.0.2.0 0.0.0.255
Standard IP access list 15
    deny host 10.0.1.25 (7 matches)
    deny 10.0.4.0 0.0.0.255 (26 matches)
    permit any (172 matches)
Router#show ip access-list 15
Standard IP access list 15
    deny host 10.0.1.25 (8 matches)
    deny 10.0.4.0 0.0.0.255 (33 matches)
    permit any (252 matches)
```

To confirm which ACLs have been applied to an interface, use the **show ip interface** *int-id* command. Note the **show interfaces** command doesn't include the ACL information.

```
Router# show ip interface Fa0/1
FastEthernet0/1 is up, line protocol is up
Internet address is 1.0.1.2/30
Broadcast address is 255.255.255.255
Address determined by setup command
```

```
MTU is 1500 bytes
Helper address is not set
Directed broadcast forwarding is disabled
Outgoing access list is 10
Inbound access list is 15
Proxy ARP is enabled
Local Proxy ARP is disabled
---output omitted---
```

Debug Feature

The **debug ip packet [*acl*] [detail]** command is a powerful tool for seeing what is happening in the router. Unfortunately, it can cause performance problems for the router because it is generating output on every packet processed. Fortunately, it is possible to use an ACL to get the **debug** command to limit the packets it looks at to just those of interest to us. The optional *acl* is the ACL number or name. Only packets matching the ACL criteria will be processed by **debug ip packet *acl***. The **detail** option displays additional packets, including the packet types/codes and the source and destination port numbers.

This access list need not be applied on an interface because it is applied to the debug operation. In the following example, we are interested in any IP traffic from host 10.0.1.65. To apply the ACL to the debug session, use the **debug ip packet 110 detail** command. Remember to stop the debug process when we are through; see the "Stopping Debug" section.

```
Router(config)#access-list 110 permit ip host 10.0.1.65 any
Router(config)#end
Router#debug ip packet 110 detail
IP packet debugging is on (detailed) for access list 110
```

Similar ACLs could be created to see NAT, NTP, or DHCP traffic after configuring those features as long as we know the protocol and the port number or keyword.

Add Meaningful Timestamps   The **service timestamps datetime** command will show UTC information, without the year, in the following format: MMM DD HH:MM:SS. Adding **msec** to the command will add milliseconds to the output. The commands are entered in Global Configuration mode and assume that the device is using NTP or that the clock has been set.

```
Router(config)#service timestamps debug datetime [msec]
Router(config)#service timestamps log datetime [msec]
```

Stopping Debug   While the debug commands are running, we often can't see the router prompt, especially with intensive debugs. But, in most cases, we can use the **no debug all** or **undebug all (u all)** command. The second option can be abbreviated if we are getting swamped with output. To verify that debugging is off, use the **show debug** command.

ⓦatch   *We use the* show ip access-list [acl-num | acl-name] *command to see our ACLs. If there has been traffic, matches will be displayed after each statement if there are any.*

The show ip interface int-id *command shows the ACLs applied to an interface and the direction (in/out). The* debug ip packet [acl] [detail] *command is a way to reduce the scope of the debug command so that it displays relevant activity. This also saves router performance and resources. A runaway debug can effectively stop a router; know that the* undebug all (u all) *command will stop all debugging.*

Log Option

Adding the **log** keyword to the end of any individual ACL statement causes a system message to be generated showing the ACL number/name and whether the packet was permitted or denied, in addition to port-specific information. These log messages can be stored locally or forwarded to a server for storage. While the feature provides near-real-time insight into traffic being passed or dropped on the network, logging can be CPU intensive and can negatively affect other network performance.

Using the **log** option while testing a new configuration can give us quick results. Then we can edit the line to remove it. In the following code, we are blocking Telnet access to force the use of the more secure SSH, so we have set the log option so we can test it. Since this would ideally be a relatively rare occurrence, the log option shouldn't be a problem. On the other hand, adding it to our **permit ip any any** statement could generate a tsunami of messages on a busy interface and would serve little purpose.

```
Router#show ip access-lists
Extended IP access list No_Telnet
    10 deny tcp any any eq 23 log
    20 permit ip any any
```

If there is an attempt to access the device with Telnet, a system message like the following would appear on our monitor. It tells us that the ACL No_Telnet rejected one packet from host 10.0.1.45 trying to access 1.1.1.7(23), where 23 is the port number.

```
%SEC-6-IPACCESSLOGP: list No_Telnet denied tcp 10.0.1.45(19876)
-> 1.1.1.7(23), 1 packet
```

Remote Sessions

Remember that by default, Cisco IOS does not display log messages to a terminal session over Telnet or SSH connections. Console connections, those where we connect with the console cable, do have logging enabled by default. If we want logging messages to appear on the terminal, then use the **terminal monitor** command (or abbreviated to **term mon**).

```
Router#
Router#terminal monitor
```

EXERCISE 12-2

MHE Lab

Port Filtering with ACLs

In this exercise we demonstrate the steps an administrator would take to configure ACLs using port numbers and the logging feature. We will use NetSim for this exercise. Launch Lab 12-2 and review the topology.

We will be working on all three routers. Each is configured like it was at the end of Exercise 9-3. None of the ACLs from Exercise 12-1 are included. All interfaces are configured and we are using static routing so that all devices can reach every other device. We can go through some together, and you can try your hand on others.

There are several syntaxes for extended ACLs depending on the protocol used. In these labs, we will work with the TCP and UDP protocols. The syntax is as follows: access-list *acl-number* [permit | deny] *protocol* [host | *source src-wildcard* | any] [*operator* [*port*]] [host | *destination dest-wildcard* | any] [*operator* [*port*]] [log].

Optional operators compare source or destination ports. Operands include lt (less than), gt (greater than), eq (equal), neq (not equal), and range (inclusive range, requires two port numbers). The port numbers are in Table 12-1 in the text.

Task 1: Filter Traffic on Port Numbers

1. The most common use of port numbers is on destination addresses for filtering outbound traffic. Recall that on service requests, the destination port is a well-known port number (in other words, 80 for HTTP or 22 for SSH), but the source port is basically a random choice of the computer. But, if you are filtering inbound traffic, the opposite is true. When the web server replies, the source port is well known (80) and the destination is the number your computer assigned. This is when source ports are used; either way, the implementation is the same.

   Here is an example we can build and test. Line 1 prevents host A.11 from Telnetting to SwitchC. Line 3 prevents host A.22 from pinging anything in the C LAN. Line 4 allows anything else. Create it on RouterA.

   ```
   RouterA#conf t
   Enter configuration commands, one per line.  End with CNTL/Z.
   RouterA(config)#access-list 120 deny tcp host 10.0.0.11 host 10.0.2.2 eq 23
   RouterA(config)#access-list 120 deny tcp any any eq ftp
   RouterA(config)#access-list 120 deny icmp host 10.0.0.22 10.0.2.0 0.0.0.255 echo
   RouterA(config)#access-list 120 permit ip any any
   RouterA(config)#int fa0/0
   RouterA(config-if)#ip access-group 120 in
   RouterA(config-if)#CTRL-z
   ```

2. To test it, try to Telnet to SwitchC (10.0.2.2) from host A.11. It should fail, but you can still Telnet to 10.0.2.1 or SwitchB. Note you can still ping 10.0.2.2, the only other thing we can test.

   Try to ping from host A.22 to 10.0.2.2, 10.0.2.13, and 10.0.2.1. Recall that the last one wasn't blocked when we applied a standard ACL on that interface. You can still Telnet to 10.0.2.1 or 10.0.2.2.

   Run **show access-lists** to see your results.

3. Save your work.

Task 2: Logging Option

1. Extended ACLs have a [log] option that causes a system message to display when a match occurs. This is a handy troubleshooting feature but should be removed when you are done. The output displays as a system message on the console and gets saved in the local log file or forwarded to a syslog server, both of which are beyond the scope of this exam. But you should know that logging is an option, how to turn it on/off, and the result on a local console.

For a simple example, make these entries on RouterB:

```
RouterB#config t
RouterB(config)#access-list 120 permit ip any host 10.0.0.2 log
RouterB(config)#access-list 120 permit ip any any
RouterB(config)#int fa0/0
RouterB(config-if)#ip access-group 120 in
RouterB(config-if)#CTRL-z
```

Line 1 just logs any activity out of LAN B to SwitchA (10.0.0.2). Line 2 prevents the implicit deny any from stopping all other traffic. Tip: Don't ever log this line; it can quickly fill your screen with system messages for no real purpose.

2. To test it, from B.77 ping 10.0.0.2 and then return to the RouterB console. You should see a system message like the following. We can see that it is an IP access (list) log for ACL 120 triggered by host 10.0.1.77 and there were five packets.

```
RouterB#
00:22:50:   %SEC-6-IPACCESSLOGDP: list 120 permitted IP
10.0.1.77 -> 10.0.0.2 (8/0), 5 packets
RouterB#
```

Try to Telnet from B.77, and you will see it also triggers a message, but that B.77 pinging the hosts doesn't. They pass through the switch but don't access the management interface. Experiment if you like, such as by Telnetting from SwitchB to SwitchA.

Run a **show access-list** on RouterB and then save your work.

Notice that the ACL is the same number as the one in Task 1; that is possible because they are on different routers. This would be true for named ACLs too.

Task 3: Practice

1. Using the skills covered, assume you have two requirements that you are working on today. You want to block host C.13 from being able to Telnet to RouterA or SwitchA. Second, you want to prevent *any* LAN C devices from being able to ping outside of LAN C.

   Work out your solutions and then make the entries. Test your work and use the **show** commands, particularly **show access lists**, to make sure you are getting the results you expected.

   One solution will be posted in the "Lab Solution" section.

2. Save your work.

exam

ⓦatch

Adding the log keyword to the end of any individual ACL statement causes a system message to be generated. Log messages can be stored locally or forwarded to a server for storage. While the feature provides near-real-time insight into traffic being passed or dropped on the network, logging can be CPU intensive and can negatively affect other network performance.

Remember to use the terminal monitor command (abbreviated to term mon) to allow nonconsole cable sessions to see the messages.

INSIDE THE EXAM

Access Control Lists (ACLs)

Make sure that you know the differences between standard and extended ACLs. Be able to recognize ACLs that have a number incorrect for the type, such as a number less than 100 on an extended ACL. Make sure you understand how to organize an ACL for efficiency and to ensure that all statements can be used. Understand where and how to apply ACLs to interfaces, placing standard ACLs near the destination and extended near the source. Make sure you really know what in | out means when applying an ACL.

Configuring ACLs

Make sure you can configure both types of ACLs using both the older approach and the newer method of named ACLs using a number as a name. Make sure you can recognize the difference and the prompt differences. Make sure you can edit a named ACL to add a line and to delete a line.

Know how to apply your ACLs to an interface in | out for traffic management and to a VTY line in | out for limiting management access.

Know how to use the **show ip access-list** [*acl-num* | *acl-name*] command to see your ACLs and any traffic that matched particular statements. Know that using the **show ip interface** *int-id* command shows the inbound and outbound ACLs, while using **show interfaces** doesn't.

Understand the risks of any **debug** command and how the **debug ip packet** [*acl*] [detail] command can reduce that risk for many types of debugging.

Adding the **log** keyword to the end of any individual ACL statement causes a system message to be generated. Log messages can be stored locally or forwarded to a server for storage. Remember to use the **terminal monitor** command (or abbreviated to **term mon**) to allow nonconsole cable sessions to see the messages.

CERTIFICATION SUMMARY

The exam objectives for this chapter expect you to be able to configure and verify both named and numbered ACLs in a network environment. You need to know what the **log** option does and how to implement it. It is also necessary to know how to apply ACLs appropriately to interfaces, VTY lines, and processes such as the NAT process in Chapter 11 and with various **debug** commands to limit the scope of packets processed and displayed. This is particularly critical in a production environment.

The troubleshooting requirements include identifying and resolving ACL issues, including verifying ACL statistics, verifying permitted networks, and verifying the direction when filtering on an interface.

TWO-MINUTE DRILL

Access Control Lists (ACLs)

❑ Remember that ACLs process the statements (ACEs) in sequential order, testing against each statement from the top down until one matches.

❑ Any packet processed by a statement does not see any other statements.

❑ Any packet that fails to match any statements is denied by default; use an implicit **deny** for anything else.

❑ ACLs use wildcard masks like OSPF. The wildcard mask and subnet mask are the inverse (opposite) of each other.

❑ There are two types of ACLs: standard and extended. Standard can test on source IP address only. Extended can test on any combination of source IP, destination IP, and upper-level port and protocol information.

❑ Both ACL types can use the older number method for identifying or can use the newer and much more useful name method.

❑ The biggest advantage to named ACLs is the ability to edit them from within the CLI.

❑ Know the common TCP/UDP port numbers and keywords (see Table 12-3) that can be used with extended ACLs. Pay particular attention to ports up to 80.

❑ ACLs are relevant only on the device they are configured on.

❑ Make sure you understand the concepts of planning your ACL and how ACLs process packets. Planning, such as putting the most frequent filters near the top, can make your ACLs more efficient, requiring less time and fewer resources.

❑ Not understanding the sequential processing means that more specific filters may never be seen by the packets because they passed looser tests.

❑ Be careful with **permit any [any]** or **deny any [any]** statements; all packets meet both.

❑ There must be at least one **permit** statement.

❑ ACLs can be applied to interfaces for traffic filtering. There can be only one in and one out ACL per interface, so a single ACL may be filtering for several objectives.

❑ Remember when applying ACLs to an interface that in/inbound and out/outbound are all relative to the center of the router. Is it heading in toward the center or out from the center?

❑ When applying ACLs to interfaces, apply standard ACLs as close to the destination as possible. Apply extended ACLs as close to the source as possible to save router and bandwidth resources.

Configuring ACLs

❑ The basic syntax **access-list** *acl-number* [permit | deny] [host | *source source-wildcard* | any] can be used to create a standard numbered ACL.

❑ The basic syntax **access-list** *acl-number* [permit | deny] *protocol* [host | *source src-wildcard* | any] [host | *destination dest-wildcard* | any] can be used to create a standard numbered ACL.

❑ Typically, the protocol will be IP, but the options [ip | icmp | tcp | udp] can be used to require an optional ICMP type or TCP/UDP port number after the appropriate address and mask combination.

❑ Named ACLs require the single command ip access-list [extended | standard] *acl-name* followed by a series of [permit | deny] statements. The **acl-name** can be a number, allowing you to create what amounts to numbered ACLs using the new method.

❑ Numbered access list statements use the number (standard 1–99 and extended 100–199) to indicate IP ACLs, while named ACLs require **ip access-list** in the command.

❑ You can insert a statement by starting with a new sequence number where you want the line to go. To delete a statement, use the **no** *seq-num* command.

❑ Make sure you understand the difference between the **ip access-group** *acl-id* [in | out] and **access-class** *acl-id* [in | out] commands. The latter is used to secure remote management connections.

❑ Use the **show ip access-list** [*acl-num* | *acl-name*] command to see your ACLs. If there has been traffic, matches will be displayed after each statement.

❑ The **show ip interface** *int-id* command shows the ACLs applied to an interface and the direction (**in/out**).

❑ The **debug ip packet [*acl*] [detail]** command is a way to reduce the scope of the **debug** command so that it displays only relevant activity. This also saves router performance and resources. A runaway debug can effectively stop a router; know that the **undebug all (u all)** command will stop all debugging.

❑ Adding the **log** keyword to the end of any individual ACL statement causes a system message to be generated. Log messages can be stored locally or forwarded to a server for storage. While the feature provides near-real-time insight into traffic being passed or dropped on the network, logging can be CPU intensive and can negatively affect other network performance.

❑ Remember to use the **terminal monitor** command (or abbreviated to **term mon**) to allow nonconsole cable (remote) sessions to see the messages.

SELF TEST

The following Self Test questions will help you measure your understanding of the material presented in this chapter. Read all the choices carefully since there may be more than one correct answer. Choose all the correct answers for each question.

Access Control Lists (ACLs)

1. Extended ACLs can filter on which of the following?
   A. Destination IP address
   B. Higher-level protocols
   C. Source IP address
   D. All of the above

2. Standard ACLs can filter on which of the following?
   A. Destination IP address
   B. Higher-level protocols
   C. Source IP address
   D. All of the above

```
access-list 15 deny host 10.0.1.25
access-list 15 deny 10.0.2.0 0.0.0.255
access-list 15 deny 10.0.3.0 0.0.0.255
```

3. Looking at the previous ACL 15, what kind of ACL is it?
   A. Named standard
   B. Named extended
   C. Numbered standard
   D. Numbered extended

4. Looking at the previous ACL 15, what would be the result if it was applied to an interface?
   A. Nothing, no packets would be discarded.
   B. Packets from IP address 10.0.1.25 would be discarded.
   C. Packets from IP address subnet 10.0.3.0/24 would be discarded.
   D. Packets from IP address subnet 10.0.2.0/24 would be discarded.
   E. All traffic would be discarded.

```
Router(config)#ip access-list extended 107
Router(config-ext-nacl)#deny X host 3.0.3.3 host 1.0.1.85 eq www
Router(config-ext-nacl)#deny X host 3.0.3.3 host 1.0.1.9 eq 21
Router(config-ext-nacl)#permit ip any any
```

5. Looking at the previous ACL 107, which of the following could be where **X** is in the statements?

   A. IP

   B. TCP

   C. UDP

   D. ICMP

   E. All of the above

6. Looking at the previous ACL 107, if it were applied to the LAN interface on the perimeter router, what direction would be used in the command?

   A. in

   B. out

   C. Both

   D. None of the above

7. Which command would be used to apply an ACL to a router's VTY lines?

   A. **ip access-group in**

   B. **ip access-group out**

   C. **ip access-class in**

   D. **ip access-class out**

Configuring ACLs

8. What is the implicit command at the bottom of an extended ACL?

   A. **deny ip any**

   B. **deny any any**

   C. **permit ip any**

   D. **permit any any**

   E. **deny ip any any**

   ```
   Extended IP access list test
       10 deny ip host 9.0.1.15 any (126 matches)
       20 deny ip 9.0.1.24 0.0.0.0 any (248 matches)
       30 permit ip 9.0.1.0 0.0.0.255 any (1539 matches)
       40 deny ip 9.0.1.128 0.0.0.31 any
       50 permit ip any any (11691 matches)
   ```

9. Looking at the previous output for ACL test, what command generated it?

   A. **show access list**

   B. **show ip interface Fa0/0**

   C. **show interfaces**

   D. **show access-group**

   E. **show access-list**

10. Looking at the previous output for ACL test, adding the **log** option to which one line could have generated the following message?

    ```
    %SEC-6-IPACCESSLOGP: list test permitted tcp 9.0.1.15(19876) ->
    1.1.1.7(23), 1 packet
    ```

    A. 10
    B. 20
    C. 30
    D. 40
    E. 50

11. Looking at the previous output for ACL test, what can we tell about line 40?
    A. There have been no packets from subnet 9.0.1.128 0.0.0.31.
    B. Line 40 is unnecessary.
    C. Line 40 should be deleted using the **no 40** command.
    D. We should add the line **25 deny ip 9.0.1.128 0.0.0.31 any**.
    E. We don't have enough information.

12. Which of the following commands will let us verify our ACLs?
    A. **show interfaces Fa0/0**
    B. **show ip interface Fa0/0**
    C. **show ip access-class**
    D. **show ip acess-group**
    E. **show access-list**

13. Which statements are true about router interfaces? (Choose two.)
    A. By default they permit all traffic in both directions.
    B. Adding a single ACL changes the default to deny all traffic in both directions.
    C. By default they permit all traffic only in the outbound directions.
    D. Adding a single ACL changes the default to deny all traffic in the applied direction.
    E. By default they permit all traffic only in the inbound directions.

14. Which of the following applies an ACL to a **debug** command?
    A. **debug ip packet**
    B. **show debug ip packet**
    C. **debug ip packet 100**
    D. **debug 100 ip packet**
    E. **debug ip packet detail**

15. Looking at Figure 12-4, to which interface would you apply a standard ACL that would prevent 172.16.3.220 from accessing 172.16.1.17?
    A. LAN C Fa0/0
    B. LAN C s0/0
    C. LAN B s0/0
    D. LAN B s0/1
    E. LAN A Fa0/0
    F. LAN A s0/0

16. Looking at Figure 12-4, to which interface would you apply an extended ACL that would prevent 172.16.3.220 from accessing 172.16.1.17?
    A. LAN C Fa0/0
    B. LAN C s0/0
    C. LAN B s0/0
    D. LAN B s0/1
    E. LAN A Fa0/0
    F. LAN A s0/0

FIGURE 12-4   Exhibit for questions 15 and 16

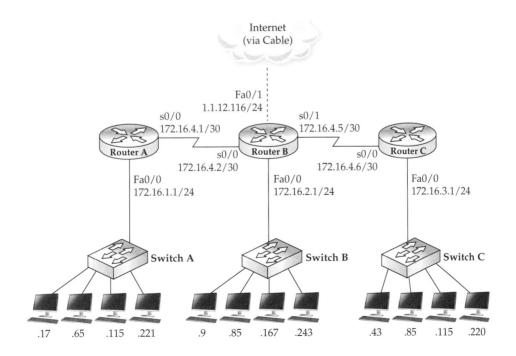

SELF TEST ANSWERS

Access Control Lists (ACLs)

1. ☑ **D** is correct. Extended ACLs can filter on source IP, destination IP, and upper-layer protocols.
   ☒ **A, B,** and **C** are incorrect because while individually correct, the answer includes all three of them.

2. ☑ **C** is correct. Standard ACLs filter on source IP address only.
   ☒ **A, B,** and **D** are incorrect. **A** and **B** are incorrect because only *extended* ACLs can filter on destination IP and upper-layer protocols. **D** is incorrect because the statement is false.

3. ☑ **C** is correct. ACL 15 is a numbered standard ACL.
   ☒ **A, B,** and **D** are incorrect. **A** and **B** are incorrect because it is not a named ACL. **D** is incorrect because 15 can't be an extended ACL; the number would be between 100 and 199. It also has only a source IP, so it must have a destination IP too.

4. ☑ **E** is correct. Because there no **permit** statements, the three statements and the implied **deny any** would discard all packets.
   ☒ **A, B, C,** and **D** are incorrect. **A** is incorrect because packets would be discarded. **B, C, and D,** while individually true statements, together do not describe all that would be discarded.

5. ☑ **B** is correct. Because of the **eq www** and **eq 21**, the protocol must be TCP.
   ☒ **A, C, D,** and **E** are incorrect. **A** is incorrect because IP would not have the **eq www** and **eq 21** qualifiers. **C** is incorrect because UDP uses port numbers but not the **eq www** and **eq 21** qualifiers. **D** is incorrect because ICMP would not use the **eq www** and **eq 21** qualifiers. **E** is incorrect because the statement is false.

6. ☑ **A** is correct. The packets to be filtered would be heading into the router.
   ☒ **B, C,** and **D** are incorrect. **B** is incorrect because it is blocking a specific host from accessing two types of servers. It is common to restrict an inside host while on the Internet. Even if you argued it's blocking an outside host from your servers, then the ACL should be applied "in" on the outside interface. **C** is incorrect. Applying it once impacts only one direction. **D** is incorrect because the statement is false.

7. ☑ **C** is correct. The **ip access-class in** command is correct and in the right direction.
   ☒ **A, B,** and **D** are incorrect. **A** and **B** are incorrect because the **ip access-group** command is used to apply an ACL to an interface, not VTY lines. **D** is incorrect because the **ip access-class out** command has the wrong direction; it should be **in**.

Configuring ACLs

8. ☑ **E** is correct. The implicit command at the bottom of an extended ACL is **deny ip any any**. ☒ **A, B, C,** and **D** are incorrect. **A** is incorrect because **deny ip any** has too few addresses; extended ACLs require both source and destination. **B** is incorrect because **deny any any** is missing the protocol **ip** after the deny. **C** and **D** are incorrect because the implicit statement is a **deny**, not a **permit**.

9. ☑ **E** is correct. The **show access-list** or **show ip access-list** command generated the output. ☒ **A, B, C,** and **D** are incorrect. **A** is incorrect because the **show access list** command is missing a hyphen, as in **access-list**. **B** is incorrect because the **show ip interface Fa0/0** command displays interface information and the names of ACLs are applied, not all ACLs. **C** is incorrect because the **show interface Fa0/0** command displays interface information but no ACL information. **D** is incorrect because **show access-group** is not a real command.

10. ☑ **C** is correct. Adding the **log** option to line 30, **permit ip 9.0.1.0 0.0.0.255**, could have generated the message. Traffic from 9.0.1.15 would have matched the test. ☒ **A, B, D,** and **E** are incorrect because they would not have matched traffic from 9.0.1.15.

11. ☑ **C** and **D** are correct. Line 40 is in the wrong place. Any packets that would match are being permitted by line 30. **C** deletes the old line, and **D** puts it in order at line 25. ☒ **A, B,** and **E** are incorrect. **A** and **B** are incorrect because we haven't actually tested whether there are any packets matching 9.0.1.128 0.0.0.31. **E** is incorrect because the statement is false.

12. ☑ **B** and **E** are correct. The **show ip interface Fa0/0** command shows which ACLs are applied in and outbound. The **show access-list** or **show ip access-list** commands show a list of ACLs plus any traffic matches per statement. ☒ **A, C,** and **D** are incorrect. **A** is incorrect because **show interfaces Fa0/0** doesn't include any ACL information. **C** and **D** are incorrect because neither is a real command.

13. ☑ **A** and **D** are correct. By default interfaces permit all traffic in both directions, and adding a single ACL changes the default to deny all traffic in applied directions. ☒ **B, C,** and **E** are incorrect because each is a false statement.

14. ☑ **C** is correct. The **debug ip packet 100** command applies ACL 100 to the **debug ip packet** command. ☒ **A, B, D,** and **E** are incorrect. **A** and **E** are incorrect because while they are valid uses of the **debug ip packet** command, both omit the ACL option (100 in this case). **B** is incorrect because **show debug ip packet** isn't a real command. **D** is incorrect because **debug 100 ip packet** has the 100 in the wrong place; it should be **debug ip packet 100**.

15. ☑ **E** is correct. Standard ACLs should be applied as near the destination as possible to avoid preventing access beyond the scope that we wanted.

  ☒ **A, B, C, D,** and **F** are incorrect because standard ACLs should be applied as near the destination as possible to avoid preventing access beyond the scope that we wanted. Each blocks the traffic at an earlier point, opening the possibility of denying access to allowed hosts.

16. ☑ **A** is correct. Extended ACLs should be applied as near the source as possible to prevent unnecessary bandwidth and router usage. We know where it is going, so we can drop at the first test point.

  ☒ **B, C, D, E,** and **F** are incorrect because extended ACLs should be applied as near the source as possible to prevent unnecessary bandwidth and router usage. Each of those locations would work but would require router resources and bandwidth to get to them.

13
IPv6 Addressing

T hroughout the first 12 chapters we've been referring to IPv4. IPv4 has served us well for more than 40 years, but as we pointed out in Chapter 3, because of the explosion in interest, due primarily to the Internet and the World Wide Web, the IPv4 address pool is just too small.

Early efforts such as CIDR, VLSM, and NAT have extended the life of IPv4, but they can't solve the problem completely. For that, we need IPv6, the replacement technology for IPv4. That is what we will be looking at in this chapter.

CERTIFICATION OBJECTIVE 13.01

IPv6 Overview

As you've learned, IPv4 is a 32-bit (4-octet) address string that theoretically offered more than 4 billion IP addresses. Even at that, early decisions based on expected address usage and limited knowledge of routing capabilities created an addressing scheme that makes many addresses virtually unusable. Developed with later insight into actual IP usage and the importance of route summarization, IPv6 is a 128-bit address scheme with a huge pool of addresses. If you recall, each time we added a bit to a mask, we doubled the number of addresses. Well, the creators of IPv6 took the 4 billion in 32 bits and doubled that 96 times over. According to Wikipedia, that is about 2^{128}, or 3.4×10^{38}, possible addresses. That's 340 undecillion—in other words, 34 followed by 38 zeroes!

IPv6 also takes care of other limitations of IPv4. When IPv4 evolved, nobody could envision networks spanning the globe and being used by a large percentage of the population. The changes in IPv6 make securing, operating, and managing huge internetworks much easier and more efficient. As a result, some technologies such as broadcasts will no longer be necessary, and others like virtual private networks (VPNs) are built into IPv6. We'll discuss this later when we cover how other protocols have changed to support IPv6.

We'll start with a brief coverage of hexadecimal numbers because IPv6 addresses use them extensively.

Converting Hex to Binary and Decimal

The good news is that each hex digit represents exactly 4 binary bits, or a *nibble*, so each of our conversions is simpler. The not-so-good news is that there are 32 of them in each address. Figure 13-1 shows the hex-to-decimal-to-binary conversions possible. There are only 16 values, and you should know 87.5 percent of them (0–9) by heart by now. The other six (A–F) should also become second nature to you. If it helps, write them a few times with their value as a subscript, such as A_{10} B_{11} C_{12} D_{13} E_{14} F_{15}. The methods you used in converting between binary and decimal are the same here. You build each hex digit 4 bits at a time, and you convert each hex value to 4-bit binary values.

Hex Values Represented

Hex values are used in many ways by many industries and disciplines. They can be displayed in a variety ways, some of which are shown in Figure 13-2. It can get a little confusing when first running into them. Uppercase or lowercase doesn't matter, although consistency makes them easier to read. Single values displayed like 4Fh usually use uppercase for the hex values and lowercase for the *h*, but since there is no *h* hex value, this shouldn't matter. Understanding how to recognize and interpret hex values should make life easier and less stressful during exams. It should also help in converting to and from binary or, when necessary, decimal.

FIGURE 13-1			

Hex-to-decimal-
to-binary
conversion table

Hex		Decimal	Binary
0	=	0	= 0 0 0 0
1	=	1	= 0 0 0 1
2	=	2	= 0 0 1 0
3	=	3	= 0 0 1 1
4	=	4	= 0 1 0 0
5	=	5	= 0 1 0 1
6	=	6	= 0 1 1 0
7	=	7	= 0 1 1 1
8	=	8	= 1 0 0 0
9	=	9	= 1 0 0 1
A	=	10	= 1 0 1 0
B	=	11	= 1 0 1 1
C	=	12	= 1 1 0 0
D	=	13	= 1 1 0 1
E	=	14	= 1 1 1 0
F	=	15	= 1 1 1 1

IPv6 Full Address
2002:3287:82c5:0000:0000:0000:0000:0007

IPv6 Abbreviated/Truncated Address
2002:3287:82c5::7

Ethernet/MAC Address (EUI-48)
00-21-6A-04-B2-46 or 00:21:6A:04:B2:46

EUI-64 MAC Address
02-21-6A-ff-fe-04-B2-46

Individual Values
0xFFFE or 0xfffe | F4h or 99h | F4$_{hex}$ or 99$_{hex}$

For specific purposes, a particular form may be established or evolve as a standard way of displaying the values. IPv6 addresses are typically displayed, as you saw earlier, as eight sets or groups of four digits separated by colons. But, leading 0s in a set can be dropped, and contiguous sets of 0s can be abbreviated with a pair of colons (::).

Traditional MAC addresses (EUI-48), on the other hand, are often displayed as six sets of two digits separated by dashes or colons.

Single values, often showing a field's contents or a value to be entered, are displayed as 0x followed by the hex value, in which case you just ignore the 0x. The other two forms shown in Figure 13-2 also appear in documents and instructions.

Hex-to-Binary Conversion

To convert hex values to binary, make sure you know what you are working with. While not absolutely necessary, many people insert leading 0s where they have been removed. Then take each digit and convert it to a 4-bit binary by first determining its decimal value. While 0–9 are easy, A_{10} B_{11} C_{12} D_{13} E_{14} F_{15} just take a little thinking (or your fingers).

Converting a MAC address like 00-21-6A-04-B2-46 would take 12 conversions, but often you just want to know which string starts with FE80 or FF00 or has FFFE in the middle; in these cases, you need only four conversions. Table 13-1 is a short version of the binary conversion table shown in Figure 13-1 that can help with the conversions and help you avoid silly mistakes during the test.

Position	8	4	2	1
Binary				
Decimal				

For example, FE80 becomes 15, 14, 8, and 0, or 1111 1110 1000 0000 or 11111110.10000000 as bytes. FF00 is 15, 15, 0, 0, or 11111111.00000000. In IPv4, remember that 255 is eight 1s and 0 is eight 0s. In hex, F_{15} is 1111, and 0 is 0000.

Binary-to-Hex Conversion

Binary to hex is just the opposite of the previous. Make sure any dropped leading 0 bits have been replaced. Then start from the right, breaking the bits into nibbles (4 bits), converting the nibbles to decimals (the values 0–15), and converting once again. 10101010.11 becomes 10101010.00000011, and then 1010 1010 0000 0011 or 10, 10, 0, 3, and then $A_{10}A_{10}03$ (AA03).

atch *Understand that hexadecimal values are each 4 bits long (a nibble), and that means they represent values 0–15. The hex digits are 0–9 followed*	*by A_{10} B_{11} C_{12} D_{13} E_{14} F_{15}. Make sure you can move back and forth between hex and binary. Expect to see a binary value and know which hex value it equals.*

EXERCISE 13-1

Media

Hex Conversion Skills

These bonus practice exercises provide extra opportunity to practice the basic binary-to-hex and hex-to-binary conversions covered in this chapter. The instructions are included in the PDF Lab Book on the accompanying media.

IPv6 Address Notation

IPv6 addresses look different from IPv4 addresses. Not only are they four times longer, they are not expressed as decimals, like 192.168.0.27. Instead, they are expressed in hexadecimal (hex) values, which means 16 unique digits. Where binary used just two digits, 0 and 1 (base 2), and decimal numbers use ten digits, 0–9 (base 10), hex uses 0123456789ABCDEF (base 16). Also, instead of using a four-octet, dotted-decimal format like IPv4, IPv46 uses eight sets of four digits separated by colons. A fully displayed

IPv6 address looks like the following example. Notice that there are eight groups, or fields, of four hex digits, separated by colons. Since each hex value is 4 bits in binary, each field is then 16 bits long in binary.
2002:3287:82c5:0000:0000:0000:0000:0007

Abbreviating Addresses

Just as we learned with IP addresses and binary numbers, and as we do every day with our decimal numbers, we can truncate or drop leading 0s, which are the 0s that appear at the beginning of each four-digit set, like the following:
2002:3287:82c5:0:0:0:0:7

Realize that any group that is less than four digits has dropped the leading 0s. The result is a little less typing and, for many, easier to read. As we saw in binary conversions, dropping the leading 0s has no impact on the value, but dropping the trailing 0s does change the value significantly. Think of the difference between $1,000 and $0001 (particularly if it is in our wallet!).

IPv6 supports a second method of truncating that allows us contiguous (consecutive) groups made up of four 0s. In our example, four sets of digits are all 0s. We use a double colon to indicate that we did this. It would look like the following:
2002:3287:82c5::7

To reconstitute the address, count how many fields you have and subtract that from the eight that you need and then fill in the missing field groups of four 0s until there are eight groups again. Our last field has had three leading 0s dropped; they need to be replaced as well.

It is important to remember that *you can do this only once per address*. You can't do it twice even if there are two groups of contiguous 0s. The following example is invalid and would be the wrong answer to any question:
2002::A012::1

We can see that there are three fields displayed, so we know that we are missing five fields. But where do they go, two in the first and three in the second, or vice versa? Or maybe some combination of one and four? That is why we can use this shorthand only once per address.

Masks

IPv6 uses prefix length with slash notation, just like you are familiar with, where the prefix identifies the network part of the address. The prefix length is expressed as an integer between 1 and 128. What is left is the host part. Remember, each digit equals 4 bits, and each group of 4 digits equals 16 bits.

Let's expand on our example of 2002:3287:82c5::/64. The mask is /64, which defines that the first 64 bits of this address is our network, and the remainder will be the host portion. First let's write out the full address. Three fields were given, and :: denotes a undetermined number of successive fields of 0s, in our case, five contiguous fields. So, our address would look like **2002.3287:82c5:0000**:0000:0000:0000: 0000. The bold portion is the network ID, which is the first 64 bits. Recall there are 16 bits per field, so we have four fields. The nonbold part is the host identifier, identifying an individual host on the network, like our **2002:3287:82c5:0000**:000 0:0000:0000:0007 from earlier.

IPv6 Address Types

IPv6 address types are a little different from IPv4. Table 13-2 shows the three basic types of addresses.

Notice that IPv6 does not support broadcasts ever; this is not an oversight. While broadcasts were necessary in the early days of networks, they no longer are. Network segment performance and security will be increased without them. The multicast is the closest thing in IPv6.

TABLE 13-2 IPv6 Address Types		
	Unicast	The same as IPv4; this is a one-to-one transmission from one IPv6 device to one other IPv6 device.
	Multicast	Just like in IPv4; a multicast is a one-to-many transmission from one IPv6 device to one or more IPv6 devices at the same time. IPv6 multicast packets start with the prefix FF00::/8.
	Anycast	A single address assigned to multiple hosts for one-to-many but delivered to only one address. It is similar to a multicast, except that the packet is delivered to only the one closest host according to the routing protocol's calculation of distance. There is no special prefix for anycast addresses.

TABLE 13-3	Global unicast	The equivalent of a public IPv4 address. They are leased from an ISP, registered globally, and routable over the Internet.
Three Types of Unicast Addresses	Unique local	The equivalent of a private IPv4 address. You are free to use them within your network, but they are not routable over the Internet.
	Link local	Every IPv6 interface at startup generates its own link-local address. It is made up of FE80::/10 and usually combines this prefix with the MAC address in EUI-64 format. Routers will not forward it; it is useful only within the local subnet. It is roughly equivalent to the current Automatic Private IPv4 Address (APIPA) range of 169.254.0.0/16.

Unicast addresses are the primary addresses of devices on any network, providing one-to-one transmissions. There are three distinct types of unicasts, and they are described briefly in Table 13-3. Figure 13-3 shows a computer **ipconfig** output, with both the global and link-local types of IPv6 addresses.

In summary, to go on the Internet, you will need a global unicast address. Within your network you could use unique local addresses such as we use with private addresses today. They are routable within your network, making them useful to larger organizations, but they are not routable on the Internet. Link local differs from unique local in that it can be used only within its local subnet. It can't be routed by your internal routers or the Internet. While not the same, it has the same limitations that MAC addresses and the 169.254.0.0/16 (APIPA) addresses do today.

Since NAT no longer exists in IPv6, global unicast addresses are what we want to use to be able to leave the network. Unique local will have some usage within test networks or even the local network, but remember that part of the reason for IPv6 is so that every device will have a globally unique address.

FIGURE 13-3	

Computer ipconfig showing IPv6 addresses

```
C:\Windows\system32\cmd.exe                                    _  □  ×

Wireless LAN adapter Wi-Fi:

   Connection-specific DNS Suffix   . : hsd1.wa.comcast.net.
   IPv6 Address. . . . . . . . . . . : 2002:3287:82c5:0:144e:dc9f:188f:ef43
   Temporary IPv6 Address. . . . . . : 2002:3287:82c5:0:c5aa:9c6d:a2d9:8be0
   Link-local IPv6 Address . . . . . : fe80::144e:dc9f:188f:ef43%3
   IPv4 Address. . . . . . . . . . . : 192.168.7.121
   Subnet Mask . . . . . . . . . . . : 255.255.255.0
   Default Gateway . . . . . . . . . : fe80::9afc:11ff:fe92:f95d%3
                                        192.168.7.1
```

IPv6 Address Allocation

A lot was learned from what turned out to be mistakes made in the original allocations of IPv4 addresses. Plus, the Internet and IP connectivity have both grown exponentially, exposing other issues of scale. For IP routing to work efficiently, addresses assigned to one organization can be subnetted down and assigned to smaller networks, but the original network is ultimately responsible for aggregating those subnets and connecting them upstream toward the Internet. A subset of addresses placed outside that organization's control would be an orphan, unable to communicate beyond its segment.

This is all part of variable length subnet mask (VLSM): As we move closer to the Internet, the prefix masks gets shorter, reflecting each level's routes being summarized as we move from subnet to corporate net to the company's ISP to a higher level ISP, and so on.

This same concept must be applied globally where a huge pool of addresses is assigned to the top-level ISPs for a region, such as South America, which then allocates a smaller subnet pool with many addresses to their client mid-level ISPs. This process continues until an ISP assigns a subnet to an organization or customer.

To manage the process, a not-for-profit partnership called the Internet Corporation for Assigned Names and Numbers (ICANN) coordinates the allocation of IP addresses, including the IPv6 address space. Without that top level of coordination, there wouldn't be a global Internet.

IPv6 Header

IPv6 packets have two parts: a header and a payload. The header consists of a fixed portion, which is the primary header that is 40 bytes (320 bits) in length. It contains the basic functionality that remains consistent for all packets and may be followed by optional header extensions to implement special features. Whereas IPv4 used the term *octet* for 8 bits, IPv6 uses *byte*; however, they both mean 8-bit units. Figure 13-4 shows the fields and their sizes of the fixed header. Note that only the Version field remains unchanged from IPv4; source and destination address labels are the same, but the field is now four times larger.

The Version field, as in IPv4, is 4 bits long and identifies the IP version of the packet. In IPv6, the version is 6.

The Traffic Class field is where Layer 3 quality of service (QoS) can be specified. Simply, QoS is a way of prioritizing traffic so that time-sensitive packets such as voice and video are given preferential treatment by QoS-enabled routers and

FIGURE 13-4

IPv6 header
with a fixed
length at 320 bits,
or 40 bytes

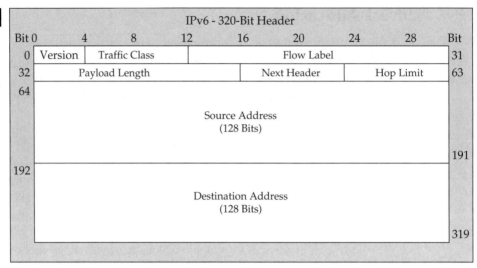

switches. They effectively move to the beginning of the line. The higher the number in this field, the more important or higher priority. QoS is what allows time-sensitive traffic, especially VoIP, to function effectively in our data networks, which are prone to varying volumes and congestion.

The Flow Label field is a number or label that identifies the packet as being part of a single flow, or stream, of packets from a sender to a particular receiver. There are many benefits to recognizing flows, such as ensuring that time sensitive packets like VoIP (voice) from a call get sent along the same routing path so that they arrive at the destination phone in the same order as sent. Recall from Chapter 8 that there are routing efficiencies that allow the CPU to outsource handling packet flows that get treated the same way.

The Payload Length field specifies how big the packet payload is, which can vary. This way, the router can tell where the packet ends. That way, it knows whether anything went missing. This is especially important because there is no header checksum, like there used to be in IPv4.

The Next Header field tells the next Layer 3 device how to interpret the data that follows the header. It basically replaces the IPv4 Options header's role. If the packet contains special options, the Next Header field contains the option type of the next extension header, with any additional required information appended as a header following the IPv6 header. These extension headers that follow the IPv6 *primary* header carry options for special packet treatment, such as routing options or security encryption using IPSec. The Next Header field of the final option always points to the upper-layer protocol that is carried in the packet's payload. Figure 13-5 is a simple example of Next Header with and without extensions.

This method speeds up routing IPv6 packets by maintaining the size and content of its primary header so it can take full advantage of any fast switching features of the router.

The Hop Limit field replaces the TTL (time-to-live) field from IPv4 that prevented routing loops. It did this by decreasing the TTL field, often set initially to 255 hops, each time it was processed by a Layer 3 device. Once it reached 0, the packet was dropped. Hop Limit is an improvement over that by being set to the actual number of hops the packet will pass through on its way to its destination. This hop information comes from the IPv6 routing protocol. The Hop Limit value is still decreased by 1 at each Layer 3 device and is dropped if it reaches 0.

The Source Address and Destination Address fields perform the same basic function as before, except that they are all a full 128-bit address. The specifics of the addresses are covered throughout this chapter.

FIGURE 13-5

Example of Next Header with and without extensions

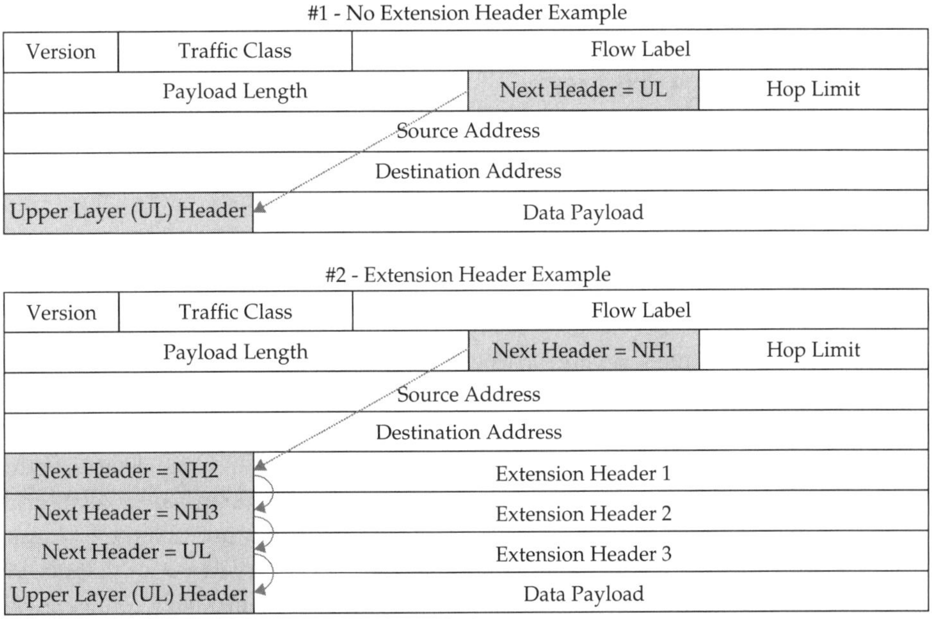

Other Features

When the IPv4 address system had to be upgraded, the creators of IPv6 used four decades of experience to upgrade certain other features and add several more. These include built-in support for encryption (IPSec), support for mobility, a fixed header size to be able to more efficiently take advantage of fast switching options on routers, enhanced ICMP features, and improved router-to-router communications.

CERTIFICATION OBJECTIVE 13.02

IPv6 Configuration

In this section we will look at two configurations: device address configuration and router configuration.

IPv6 Address Options

To use IPv6 addresses, an IPv6 protocol stack must be installed on the device. While this might require an upgrade on older equipment, many devices such as computers, phones, cameras, printers, routers, and most operating systems have been IPv6 ready for some time. They have been just waiting for it to be rolled out.

There are two methods for static addressing on Cisco devices, both of which have all the drawbacks of any manual process: labor-intensive installation and modifications, prone to configuration errors, and typically does not scale well. One method involves the administrator assigning a valid IPv6 128-bit address for that machine on that segment. The other involves the administrator manually configuring the address with the local /64 network prefix followed by the host's MAC in EUI-64 format.

There are also two methods of dynamically addressing hosts. IPv6 can use DHCP to assign IP addresses very much like in IPv4. The administrator configures the DHCP server with a scope of IPv6 addresses to assign. This is called *stateful addressing,* where the DHCP server manages and keeps track of the IPv6 addresses assigned to hosts and the DHCP state of the host address.

There is another option called *stateless auto-configuration with EUI-64.* This feature allows a host to configure an address for itself. The host first learns the /64 network prefix used on the local link and then follows the processes covered in the next section.

EUI-64 and Autoconfiguration

This method allows the device interface to *autoconfigure,* or create its own, IP address by combining the /64 network prefix address with the interface's EUI-64 (64 bit) MAC address. The MAC address provides the unique host identifier while eliminating the need for DHCP or manual configuration.

If there is only a traditional 48-bit MAC, it will be modified to the IEEE's 64-bit extended unique identifier (EUI-64) format. It works by using the unique EUI-48 bit MAC address, which we looked at before in switching, and converts it to a 64-bit value.

It does this in three steps. First, it splits the MAC in half, separating the 24-bit organizationally unique identifier (OUI) and the 24-bit NIC-specific portion. Figure 13-6 shows the steps. Second, a special 16-bit hex value that is always 0xFFFE is inserted between the halves to create a 64-bit address. This hex value is reserved and can't be used by manufacturers.

Finally, in step 3, the universal/local (U/L) flag bit, bit 7 of the OUI portion, is inverted, switching it from 0 to 1.

You don't have to do anything for this to happen; it occurs automatically. But now that you know the process, you should be able to identify any EUI-64 address generated from an EUI-48 (or MAC) by the 0xFFFE in the middle, between the OUI and the NIC-specific portion. If you look at Figure 13-3, you will see an example of the EUI-64 inserted in the IPv6 address for the default gateway.

FIGURE 13-6

MAC to EUI-64
conversion steps

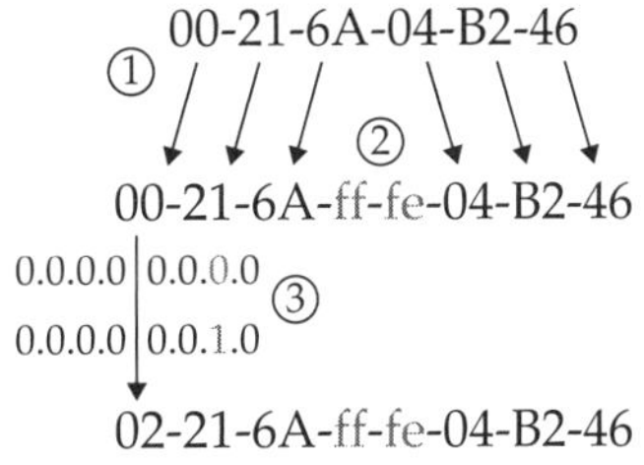

00-21-6A-04-B2-46
① / / /   ② \ \ \
00-21-6A-ff-fe-04-B2-46
0.0.0.0 | 0.0.0.0   ③
0.0.0.0 | 0.0.1.0
02-21-6A-ff-fe-04-B2-46

IPv6 Router Configuration

You need to know the basic IPv6 configuration for the CCENT exam. You may or may not be asked to actually do it on a simulator, but you definitely need to be able to recognize a valid configuration of the following features if you see them. The good news is that there aren't that many features covered on the exam. Let's look at them.

The **ipv6 unicast-routing** command must be run once in Global Configuration mode to enable the forwarding of IPv6 unicast datagrams. Configuring an IPv6 address on an interface is basically the same process as IPv4. The syntax would look like the following:

ipv6 unicast-routing
interface *type int_id*
ipv6 address *prefix/prefix_length* [eui-64]

The **eui-64** part is a keyword that tells the router to use its own EUI-64 (MAC) address appended after the /64 prefix provided. Without that, you would have to enter a full 128-bit address in the command. Here's an example:

```
Router#config t
Router(config)#ipv6 unicast-routing
Router(config)#interface fastethernet 0/0
Router(config-if)#ipv6 address 2002:3287:82c5:0::/64 eui-64
Router(config)#interface fastethernet 0/1
Router(config-if)#ipv6 address 2002:3287:82c5:1::/64 eui-64
Router(config-if)#end
```

Verifying Your Work

Use the **show ipv6 interface** [**interface** *int-id*] [**brief**] command in Privileged mode to verify your configuration. The following is some sample output (with different addresses applied). You can see multiple addresses in use by the interface for global unicast, link-local, and multiple multicast groups.

```
Router# show ipv6 interface fastethernet 0/0

Fastethernet 0/0 is up, line protocol is up
 IPv6 is enabled, link-local address is FE80::215:3EFF:FE47:0861
  Global unicast address(es):
    2002:3287:82c5:0:215:3EFF:FE47:0861, subnet is 2002:3287:82c5:0::/64
  Joined group address(es):
    FF02::1
    FF02::2
    FF02::1:FF47:0861
    FF02::9
  MTU is 1500 bytes
  ICMP error messages limited to one every 500 milliseconds
  ND reachable time is 30000 milliseconds
  ND advertised reachable time is 0 milliseconds
  ND advertised retransmit interval is 0 milliseconds
  ND router advertisements are sent every 200 seconds
  ND router advertisements live for 1800 seconds
  Hosts use stateless autoconfig for addresses.

Device# show ipv6 interface brief
Fastethernet 0/0 is up, line protocol is up
Fastethernet 0/0            [up/up]
    2002:3287:82c5:0::/64
fastethernet 0/1            [up/up]
    2002:3287:82c5:1::/64
Interface        Status            IPv6 Address
Fastethernet 0/0  up                2002:3287:82c5:0:215:3EFF:FE47:0861
Fastethernet 0/1  up                2002:3287:82c5:1:215:3EFF:FE47:0861
Serial0          administratively down unassigned
Serial1          administratively down unassigned
```

Configuring Static Routes

Static routes in IPv6 do the same as IPv4, and the syntax is similar as well. The following command syntax, when executed in Global Configuration mode, sets an IPv6 static route. Basically, this says, "To get to network X, go to this interface on a neighbor router, which will assist you further." If the optional administrative distance [*AD*] argument is not specified, the default administrative distance of 1 will be used.

Router(config)#**ipv6 route** *x:x:x:x::0/[1-128]* [*egress-interface*] [*x:x:x:x:x:x:x:x*] [*AD*]

Remember that the **ipv6 unicast-routing** command needs to be run once from Global Configuration mode to enable forwarding IPv6 unicast datagrams. If you don't know the destination IP address, you can use the **show ipv6 interface** command we just looked at to get it.

When using a link-local address as the next hop, you must specify an interface type and an interface number. The link-local next hop must also be an adjacent device.

The syntax and options for a default static route are similar except the destination network is ::/0 instead of the 0.0.0.0 0.0.0.0 in IPv4. The syntax is shown next. This one is saying "For any unknown networks, go to this interface on a neighbor router, which will assist you further."

Router(config)#**ipv6 route ::/0** [*egress-interface*] [*x:x:x:x:x:x:x:x*] [*AD*]

```
Router#configure terminal
Router(config)#ipv6 unicast-routing
Router(config)#ipv6 route 2001::/64 fa0/1 FE80::C800:10FF:FE1C:8
Router(config)#ipv6 route 2002::/64 s0/1
Router(config)#ipv6 route ::/0 2001:0:1:1221::1
Router(config)#end
Router#
```

Our first example, the third line of output, had to include both the interface type and an interface number and the next hop because it is using a link-local address. It begins with FE80::. The FF:FE in the middle indicates that a EUI-64 conversion occurred. The fourth line shows using an egress interface only, which works fine on serial point-to-point connections. The fifth line uses just the destination address, which works because the router also has an interface in that network segment.

IPv6 ICMP and Ping

ICMP messaging in IPv6 performs very much like ICMP in IPv4. ICMP generates error messages, such as ICMP *destination unreachable* messages, and informational messages, such as *ICMP echo request* and *reply* messages. Ping uses both of the latter.

Ping IPv6   Ping uses both ICMP echo request and reply messages. It also works similar to IPv4 with the **ping ipv6** *address* command. The same /? help feature will help you with options. The following is an example of a simple **ping** command:

```
Router#ping 2002:3287:82c5:0:215:3EFF:FE47:0861

Type escape sequence to abort.
Sending 5, 100-byte ICMP Echos to 2002:3287:82c5:0:215:3EFF:FE47:0861,
timeout is 2 seconds:!!!!!
Success rate is 100 percent (5/5), round-trip min/avg/max = 8/37/68 ms
Router#
```

Configuring OSPFv3

OSPFv3 is the version of OSPF routing that supports IPv6. Configuring it is quite similar to what we did in Chapter 10, if not easier. In OSPFv2, the router ID (RID) is determined by the highest loopback address. If there are no loopbacks, then by the highest IP addresses assigned to a router interface, or, by assigning it manually with the **router-id** command. In version 3, the RID, area ID, and link-state ID can be automatically or manually defined. In each case, they are all still using 32-bit values rather than IPv6-like 128-bit values.

Use the **ipv6 router ospf** command in Global Configuration mode to enable OSPFv3 in the router. The process ID, as in IPv4, is locally assigned and only locally significant. It can be any positive integer from 1 to 65535. The number used here is the number assigned administratively when enabling the OSPF for the IPv6 routing process.

Router(config)#**ipv6 router ospf** *process-id*

OSPFv3 RID is configured under the router configuration process. The networks attached to them are configured directly on the interface in Interface Configuration mode. All we need to do is go to each interface and assign a process ID and area, and we are done. The **area 0.0.0.0** part is the 32-bit form of area 0.

The configuration of OSPFv3 is going to look like this:

Router(config)#**ipv6 router osfp 1**
Router(config-rtr)#**router-id 1.2.3.4**
Router(config)#**interface fastethernet 0/0**
Router1(config-if)#**ipv6 ospf 1 area 0.0.0.0**

The first line enables IPv6 OSPF using process ID 1. The second line creates the RID, and the fourth line configures the interface to be part of area 0.0.0.0 and process ID 1.

EXERCISE 13-2

MHE Lab

Basic IPv6 Configuration

In this exercise we demonstrate the steps an administrator would take to configure simple IPv6 addresses on interfaces. You'll perform this exercise using Boson's NetSim. Launch Lab 13-2 and review the topology.

To begin with, both routers are configured with our normal usernames and passwords.

Task 1: Test Lab Connectivity

1. There is no connectivity at this point.

2. Open a console session on RouterA and do a **show running-config** to see what you have and don't have. You should see no IP addresses, routing, or static routes.

Task 2: Configure IPv6 Interfaces on RouterA

1. Two commands we'll use in this lab are **show ipv6 route** and **show ipv6 interface brief**. Run both in Privileged mode to confirm there is nothing of consequence there.

2. Look at the topology diagram, and you will see that we are basically using the addresses 2002:3287:82C5:X::H/64, where X is our subnet identifier (1 for LAN A, 2 for LAN B, and 0 for the link in between the routers). H is the unique host number, with the router LAN interfaces being 1 like all of our other labs, and the link between the routers being 1 on RouterA and 2 on RouterB.

3. We are going to manually configure our interfaces (what this version of NetSim allows) and enable ipv6 unicast-routing. In your RouterA console session, make the following entries:

```
RouterA#config t
RouterA(config)#ipv6 unicast-routing
RouterA(config)#interface FastEthernet0/0
RouterA(config-if)#ipv6 address 2002:3287:82C5:1::1/64
RouterA(config-if)#interface FastEthernet0/1
RouterA(config-if)#ipv6 address 2002:3287:82C5:0::1/64
RouterA(config-if)#CTRL-Z
```

4. When you are done, run your **show** commands from step 2 and look at the result. You should see both routes and interfaces. The steps and results are also in the "Lab Solutions" section in the PDF Lab Book.

   Notice on the routing table that the C (connected) shows the subnet and which interface it is connected to. The L (local) shows the IP address in that subnet and which interface it is associated with.

   The interface brief is pretty straightforward, showing both the local-link (built-in) and the unicast address we just configured.

   Notice in both outputs that on Fa0/1, the fourth group of our address where we had a 0, the router has just extended the :: to include it. We could have done that as well, but we wanted you to see that was the group we were making unique.

5. Save your work.

Task 3: Configure IPv6 Interfaces on RouterB

1. If you like, use the information in Task 2 to configure the interfaces on RouterB; alternatively, the steps are listed here.

   In your RouterB console session, make the following entries:

   ```
   RouterB#config t
   RouterB(config)#ipv6 unicast-routing
   RouterB(config)#interface FastEthernet0/0
   RouterB(config-if)#ipv6 address 2002:3287:82C5:2::1/64
   RouterB(config-if)#interface FastEthernet1/0
   RouterB(config-if)#ipv6 address 2002:3287:82C5:0::1/64
   RouterB(config-if)#CTRL-z
   ```

2. When you are done, run the **show ipv6 route** and **show ipv6 interface brief** commands and look at the result.

3. Save your work.

Task 4: Default Route

1. Ping each of RouterB's interfaces using **ping ipv6** *ipv6-addr*. Both should work.

   ```
   RouterB#ping ipv6 2002:3287:82C5:2::1

   Type escape sequence to abort.
   Sending 5, 100-byte ICMP Echos to 2002:3287:82C5:2::1, timeout is 2 seconds:
   !!!!!
   Success rate is 100 percent (5/5), round-trip min/avg/max = 1/2/4 ms
   RouterB#ping ipv6 2002:3287:82C5:0::2

   Type escape sequence to abort.
   Sending 5, 100-byte ICMP Echos to 2002:3287:82C5::2, timeout is 2 seconds:
   !!!!!
   Success rate is 100 percent (5/5), round-trip min/avg/max = 1/2/4 ms
   RouterB#
   ```

2. Ping each of RouterA's interfaces. The connected link will work, but the LAN link will fail. Why? Run your route table again to see why.

   ```
   RouterB#ping ipv6 2002:3287:82C5:0::1

   Type escape sequence to abort.
   Sending 5, 100-byte ICMP Echos to 2002:3287:82C5::1, timeout is 2 seconds:
   !!!!!
   Success rate is 100 percent (5/5), round-trip min/avg/max = 1/2/4 ms
   RouterB#ping ipv6 2002:3287:82C5:1::1
   ```

```
Type escape sequence to abort.
Sending 5, 100-byte ICMP Echos to 2002:3287:82C5:1::1, timeout is 2 seconds:
.....
Success rate is 0 percent (0/5), round-trip min/avg/max = 1/2/4 ms
RouterB#
```

To go further, we would need to configure a routing protocol or static routes. The important thing is to get a little hands-on practice with the addresses and to see that the commands are not that different from what we have been doing. Having to type all these addresses should remind you why routing protocols are so handy and why features like interface autoconfigure are so nice.

exam

ⓦatch   *Be sure you know the steps   single area. Know that* show ipv6 interface *will for enabling IPv6 unicasts and configuring   confirm your interface configuration. interfaces, static routes, and OSPFv3 in a*

CERTIFICATION OBJECTIVE 13.03

IPv6 Transition Strategies

IPv6's rollout has been pushed back several times from its originally scheduled global conversion date of January 1, 2000. But it is the future of IP, and it must eventually be rolled out; however, it is going to take time and will be implemented in stages. Cisco and almost all manufacturers and service providers have been supporting both IPv4 and IPv6 for some time and will until some point in the future. If you run an **ipconfig /all** command on your computer today, you will see the IPv6 features are ready for use.

In this section, we will look at the most common strategies for supporting both IPv4 and IPv6 while offering the opportunity for organizations to start moving toward IPv6.

Dual Stacking

The easiest IPv6 transition method is called *dual stack*. It means that the devices maintain side-by-side both the IPv4 and IPv6 protocol stacks and can send and receive both types of packets. This can be done over the same existing interface. This is the preferred IPv6 transition implementation because it avoids the complexities and drawbacks of tunneling, such as security, increased latency, management overhead, and MTU discovery issues. Unfortunately, this can't always be done because older devices on your network may not have an IPv6 stack. Of primary concern are older routers and firewall devices that might not be able to run IPv6. This may require a new OS and maybe memory, if available, or a device replacement.

Tunneling Mode

The terms *tunneling* and *tunnels* are used in different contexts in networking. VPN tunnels are a common usage. The word *tunnel* creates an image of a pipe that our data travels through, but that's not quite right. Virtual tunnels might be closer. Remember that all data is a stream of bits, 0s and 1s. *Tunneling* involves taking the frame created by the OSI layers and encapsulating it, adding another header and trailer, for some purpose.

6-to-4 Tunneling

6-to-4 tunneling means one of the IP protocols is tunneling through the other one, for example, taking an IPv6 packet from one location, encapsulating it inside an IPv4 packet to transition across the service provider network, and then deencapsulating it at the other end to travel on the other location's IPv6 network. This particular tunneling can be either automatically or manually configured. These 6-to-4 tunnels have a special address range of 2002::/16. Other tunneling strategies include the following.

Teredo Tunneling

Teredo tunneling is an IETF technology that encapsulates IPv6 packets in IPv4 UDP datagrams for routing through an IPv4 network such as the Internet. Its primary benefit is that these datagrams can be routed from inside the network through a NAT device. It is considered a temporary or last-resort transition strategy, with full implementation of IPv6 the goal.

ISATAP Tunneling

Intra-Site Automatic Tunnel Addressing Protocol (ISATAP) tunneling uses the IPv4 network as a virtual nonbroadcast multi-access (NBMA) Data Link layer. An IPv6 link-layer address is derived dynamically from the IPv4 address, allowing dynamic neighbor discovery over IPv4 in addition to simple routing. ISATAP is a native capability in most Windows, Linux, and Cisco IOS versions.

NAT-PT

NAT Protocol Translation (NAT-PT) is a standards-based method of taking an IPv6 packet and replacing the IP header with an IPv4 header that approximates the original information as close as possible. It is effectively translating one protocol to the other. One benefit of this method is that no changes are required to existing hosts because all the NAT-PT configurations and translations are done on an NAT-PT router between the networks. The biggest drawback includes increased latency impacting performance and the inevitable loss of header information in the translation process. NAT-PT is not supported in Cisco Express Forwarding (CEF).

Using a protocol translator between IPv6 and IPv4 allows direct communication between hosts speaking a different network protocol. Users can use either static definitions or IPv4-mapped definitions for NAT-PT operation.

If you run an **ipconfig** command, and particularly an **ipconfig /all** command, on your computer, you will probably see that it is ready to support IPv6 and probably a couple tunneling protocols as well. Unless you are using IPv6, not all of the data will be there, but here is enough for you to look at:

```
C:\>ipconfig /all

Windows IP Configuration
    Host Name . . . . . . . . . . . . : LH-Bob-81
    Primary Dns Suffix  . . . . . . . : lhseattle.com
    Node Type . . . . . . . . . . . . : Hybrid
    IP Routing Enabled. . . . . . . . : No
    WINS Proxy Enabled. . . . . . . . : No
    DNS Suffix Search List. . . . . . : lhseattle.com
                                        hsd1.wa.comcast.net.

Ethernet adapter Ethernet:
    Media State . . . . . . . . . . . : Media disconnected
    Connection-specific DNS Suffix  . : lhseattle.com
    Description . . . . . . . . . . . : Intel(R) 82567LM Gigabit Network
Connection                              ←wrapped from row above
    Physical Address. . . . . . . . . : 00-21-70-BE-4F-C8
    DHCP Enabled. . . . . . . . . . . : Yes
    Autoconfiguration Enabled . . . . : Yes

Wireless LAN adapter Wi-Fi:
```

```
     Connection-specific DNS Suffix  . : hsd1.wa.comcast.net.
     Description . . . . . . . . . . . : Intel(R) WiFi Link 5300 AGN
     Physical Address. . . . . . . . . : 00-21-6A-04-B2-46
     DHCP Enabled. . . . . . . . . . . : Yes
     Autoconfiguration Enabled . . . . : Yes
     IPv6 Address. . . . . . . . . . . : 2002:3287:82c5:0:144e:dc9f:188f:ef43
(Preferred)                              ←wrapped from row above
     Temporary IPv6 Address. . . . . . : 2002:3287:82c5:0:244d:5592:d0f7:3bc7
(Preferred)                              ←wrapped from row above
     Link-local IPv6 Address . . . . . : fe80::144e:dc9f:188f:ef43%3(Preferred)
     IPv4 Address. . . . . . . . . . . : 192.168.7.137(Preferred)
     Subnet Mask . . . . . . . . . . . : 255.255.255.0
     Lease Obtained. . . . . . . . . . : Wednesday, May 28, 2014 7:09:25 PM
     Lease Expires . . . . . . . . . . : Thursday, May 29, 2014 7:09:26 PM
     Default Gateway . . . . . . . . . : fe80::9afc:11ff:fe92:f95d%3
                                         192.168.7.1
     DHCP Server . . . . . . . . . . . : 192.168.7.1
     DHCPv6 IAID . . . . . . . . . . . : 50340202
     DHCPv6 Client DUID. . . . . . . . : 00-01-00-01-1A-3B-C4-9D-00-21-70-BE-4F-C8

     DNS Servers . . . . . . . . . . . : 75.75.75.75
                                         75.75.76.76
                                         192.168.7.1
     NetBIOS over Tcpip. . . . . . . . : Enabled

Tunnel adapter isatap.hsd1.wa.comcast.net.:
     Media State . . . . . . . . . . . : Media disconnected
     Connection-specific DNS Suffix  . : hsd1.wa.comcast.net.
     Description . . . . . . . . . . . : Microsoft ISATAP Adapter
     Physical Address. . . . . . . . . : 00-00-00-00-00-00-00-E0
     DHCP Enabled. . . . . . . . . . . : No
     Autoconfiguration Enabled . . . . : Yes

Tunnel adapter Teredo Tunneling Pseudo-Interface:
     Connection-specific DNS Suffix  . :
     Description . . . . . . . . . . . : Teredo Tunneling Pseudo-Interface
     Physical Address. . . . . . . . . : 00-00-00-00-00-00-00-E0
     DHCP Enabled. . . . . . . . . . . : No
     Autoconfiguration Enabled . . . . : Yes
     IPv6 Address. . . . . . . . . . . : 2001:0:9d38:6abd:18e1:39a9:3f57:f876
(Preferred)                              ←wrapped from row above
     Link-local IPv6 Address . . . . . : fe80::18e1:39a9:3f57:f876%6(Preferred)
     Default Gateway . . . . . . . . . :
     DHCPv6 IAID . . . . . . . . . . . : 234881024
     DHCPv6 Client DUID. . . . . . . . : 00-01-00-01-1A-3B-C4-9D-00-21-70-BE-4F-C8
     NetBIOS over Tcpip. . . . . . . . : Disabled
C:\>
```

ⓦatch   *Know the difference between dual stack and tunneling as*   *transition strategies. Pay particular attention to dual stack.*

INSIDE THE EXAM

IPv6 Overview

Understand that hexadecimal values are each 4 bits long (a nibble), and that means they represent the values 0–15. The hex digits are 0–9 followed by the letters A–F as in $A_{(10)}$ $B_{(11)}$ $C_{(12)}$ $D_{(13)}$ $E_{(14)}$ $F_{(15)}$. Make sure you can move back and forth between hex and binary. Expect to see a binary value and know which hex value it equals.

Make sure you know the three basic IPv6 address types and then the three types of unicast addresses and how they could be used. Remember that IPv6 can't broadcast, ever! Any answers with the word *broadcast* in them are deceptions.

Be familiar with the IPv6 header and the fact that the IPv6 creators designed that 40-byte fixed header to be able to take advantage of fast switch features in the routers. The extended headers that are optional follow the primary header and allow for special features to be supported.

IPv6 Configuration

Know that IPv6 supports two forms of static addressing and two forms of dynamic. The one to make sure you really understand is the stateless autoconfiguration with EUI-64.

Be sure you know the steps for enabling IPv6 unicasts and configuring interfaces, static routes, and OSPFv3 in a single area. Know that **show ipv6 interface** will confirm your interface configuration.

IPv6 Transition Strategies

Know the difference between dual stack and tunneling as transition strategies. Pay particular attention to dual stack.

CERTIFICATION SUMMARY

The exam objectives for this chapter expect you to be able to recognize and understand the basics of IPv6 addressing. Know the address types with emphasis on global unicast, multicast, link local, unique local, and autoconfiguration with EUI-64. Be able to identify the appropriate IPv6 addressing scheme to satisfy addressing requirements in a LAN/WAN environment. You should be able to describe the technological requirements for running IPv6 in conjunction with IPv4 with emphasis on dual stack.

Understand and recognize the steps involved in a basic configuration of IPv6 unicast, interfaces, static routes, and OSPv3 in a single area. Remember that all of these are configured in the same mode as their IPv4 counterparts.

TWO-MINUTE DRILL

IPv6 Overview

- ❏ IPv6 is a 128-bit address scheme.
- ❏ Hex digits equal 4 binary bits, or a nibble.
- ❏ Hex digit values are 0–15, using digits 0–9 and A–F (A_{10} B_{11} C_{12} D_{13} E_{14} F_{15}).
- ❏ To convert hex values to binary, convert each digit to 4-bit binary, with the values 0–15.
- ❏ To convert binary values to hex, replace any abbreviated 0s, break into 4 bits, and convert the hex to decimal.
- ❏ There are 32 hex digits in a full IPv6 address in eight groups of four, such as 2002:3287:82c5:0000:0000:0000:0000:0007.
- ❏ You can truncate or drop leading 0s in each group, such as 2002:3287:82c5:0:0:0:0:7.
- ❏ You can replace contiguous groups made up of four 0s and use a double colon, but only once per address, such as 2002:3287:82c5::7.
- ❏ To reconstitute the address, fill in groups of four 0s until there are eight groups again, each with four digits.
- ❏ IPv6 uses prefix length with slash notation, with integers between 1 and 128.
- ❏ Each digit equals 4 bits, and each group of four digits equals 16 bits.
- ❏ There are three types of addresses: unicast (one to one), multicast (one to many), and anycast (one to many, but delivered only to the closest one, based on routing information).
- ❏ Multicast packets start with the prefix FF00::/8.
- ❏ There are three kinds of unicast: global unicast (like IPv4 global), unique local (like IPv4 private), and link local (nonroutable like IPv4 with an APIPA address range of 169.254.0.0/16; made up of FE80::/10 plus MAC address in EUI-64).
- ❏ ICANN coordinates allocation of IPv6 address blocks, with huge subnets going to regional ISPs; they then allocate smaller large subnets to medium-sized ISPs, and so on, to clients. All clients summarize to the ISP that gave them their addresses, and so on.
- ❏ The IPv6 primary header is fixed at 40 bytes (320 bits); optional subheaders can follow.

❑ A fixed header, unchanged in transit, allows fast switching options on routers.

❑ Know the headers from Figures 13-4 and 13-5.

❑ IPv6 has built-in security encryption (IPSec), support for mobility, a fixed header for more efficient use of router fast switching options, enhanced ICMP features, and improved router-to-router communications.

IPv6 Configuration

❑ There are two static (manual) methods to assign IPv6 addresses: a full address and a local /64 network prefix followed by the host's MAC in EUI-64 format.

❑ There are two dynamic methods to assign IPv6 addresses: DHCP like IPv4 (stateful) and stateless autoconfiguration with EUI-64. Make sure you understand the latter, which is a local /64 network prefix followed by the host's MAC in EUI-64 format.

❑ If there is no 64-bit MAC, then split the 48-bit one in half, insert FFFE in between, and flip the universal/local (U/L) flag bit. Bit 7 of the OUI portion is inverted, switching it from a 0 to 1.

❑ Use **ipv6 unicast-routing** once in Global Configuration mode to enable forwarding of IPv6 unicast datagrams.

❑ When configuring the interface, use **ipv6 address** *prefix/prefix_length* [**eui-64**], for example, **ipv6 address 2002:3287:82c5:0::/64 eui-64** in Interface Configuration mode. This is the prefix plus MAC in EUI-64 format.

❑ Use **show ipv6 interface** [**interface** *int-id*] [**brief**] in Privileged mode to confirm.

❑ A static route, in the format **ipv6 route** *x:x:x:x::0*/[*1-128*] [*egress-interface*] [*x:x:x:x:x:x:x:x*] [*AD*], is the network prefix. Here's an example: **ipv6 route 2001::/64 fa0/1 FE80::C800:10FF:FE1C:8. 2001::/64**.

❑ The static default route is the same, but use ::/0 as the network prefix.

❑ With a link-local address as the next hop, you must include the interface ID type, and the next hop must be an adjacent device.

❑ Here's how you configure OSPFv3 (IPv6 version):

```
Router(config)#ipv6 unicast-routing          ← if not already done
Router(config)#ipv6 router osfp 1
Router(config-rtr)#router-id 1.2.3.4
Router(config)#interface fastethernet 0/0
Router1(config-if)#ipv6 ospf 1 area 0.0.0.0
```

The second line enables IPv6 OSPF using process ID 1. The third line creates the RID, and the fifth line configures the interface to be part of area 0.0.0.0 and process ID 1.

IPv6 Transition **Strategies**

❑ There are three methods: dual stack, tunneling, and translation. Focus on dual stack, the preferred method as long as all devices support IPv6.

❑ Dual stack maintains side-by-side both of the IPv4 and IPv6 protocol stacks and can send and receive both types of packets.

❑ Tunneling methods are 6-to-4, Teredo, and ISATAP tunneling.

❑ The translation method is as follows: a NAT Protocol Translation (NAT PT) router between networks, an IPv6 header with an IPv4 header that approximates the original information, and vice versa. Increased latency and some header information are lost.

SELF TEST

The following Self Test questions will help you measure your understanding of the material presented in this chapter. Read all the choices carefully since there may be more than one correct answer. Choose all the correct answers for each question.

IPv6 Overview

1. Which of the following are valid types of an IPv6 address?
   A. Anycast
   B. Multicast
   C. Broadcast
   D. Link local
   E. Unique local
   F. Global unicast
   G. All of the above

2. How many bits in a hex digit?
   A. 1
   B. 32
   C. 16
   D. 8
   E. 4

3. What is the hex value of this binary: 00101110?
   A. 10:1110
   B. A3
   C. 2e
   D. 3d
   E. None of the above

4. What is the binary value of this hex number: FFFE?
   A. 0000000000000001
   B. 0.0.0.0 0.0.0.0
   C. 1111111111111110
   D. 11111110
   E. None of the above

5. Which of the following are valid IPv6 addresses?
   A. 0000:0000:0000:0000:0000:0000:0000:0007
   B. 2002:01b1:0000:0000:0000:ff1a:0016:c217
   C. 2002:1b1:0:0:0:ff1a:16: c217
   D. 2002:1b1::ff1a:16:c217
   E. ::192:168:0:115
   F. ::7

6. Which of the following is a nonroutable type of IPv6 address?
   A. Anycast
   B. Multicast
   C. Broadcast
   D. Link local
   E. Unique local
   F. Global unicast

7. What is the length of an IPv6 primary header?
   A. Variable
   B. 320 bytes
   C. 40 bits
   D. 40 bytes
   E. 320 bits

IPv6 Configuration

8. Which of the following is a stateful method of configuring IPv6 addresses?
   A. Static; manually configure full 128-bit address
   B. Static; manually configure local /64 network prefix plus MAC in EUI-64 format
   C. DHCP
   D. Autoconfiguration with EUI-64

9. Which of the following are not steps in converting EUI-48 MAC to EUI-64 format?
   A. Split the 48 bits in half.
   B. Separate into 24-bit OUI and 24-bit NIC ID.
   C. Insert FEFE between two parts.
   D. Insert FFFE between two parts.
   E. Flip the universal/local (U/L) flag bit, which is bit 17 of the OUI, to 1.
   F. Flip the universal/local (U/L) flag bit, which is bit 17 of the host ID, to 1.
   G. Flip the universal/local (U/L) flag bit, which is bit 7 of the OUI, to 1.

10. Which command enables forwarding of IPv6 unicast datagrams?

   A. Router#**ipv6 unicast-routing**

   B. Router(config)#**ip unicast-routing**

   C. Router(config-rtr)#**ip unicast-routing**

   D. Router(config)#**ipv6 unicast-routing**

   E. Router(config-int)#**ipv6 unicast-routing**

11. Which of the following would configure an address on interface Fa0/1?

   A. Router(config-if)#**ip address 2002:3287:82c5:0::/64 eui-64**

   B. Router(config-if)#**ipv6 address 2002:3287:82c5:0::/64 eui-64**

   C. Router(config)#**ipv6 address 2002:3287:82c5:0::/64 eui-64**

   D. Router(config-if)#**ipv6 address 2002::82c5::/64 eui-64**

   E. Router(config-if)#**ipv6 address 2002:3287:82c5:1::/64 eui-64**

12. Which of the following would verify your configuration in question 11?

   A. Router(config-if)#**show ipv6 interface**

   B. Router(config)#**show ipv6 interface**

   C. Router# **show ipv6 interface**

   D. Router(config)#**show ipv6 interface fa0/1**

   E. Router#**show ipv6 interface fa0/1**

13. Which of the following would not create a valid static route?

   A. Router(config)#**ipv6 route 2001::/64 fa0/1 FE80::C800:10FF:FE1C:8**

   B. Router(config)#**ipv6 route 2001::/64 FE80::C800:10FF:FE1C:8**

   C. Router(config)#**ipv6 route 2002::/64 s0/1**

   D. Router(config)#**ipv6 route ::/0 2001:0:1:1221::1**

   E. All of the above

14. In the following lines of configuration, what command needs to be added to complete the configuration for an OSPF single area?

```
Router(config)#ipv6 router osfp 1
Router(config-rtr)#router-id 1.2.3.4
Router(config)#interface fastethernet 0/0
```

   A. Router1(config)#**ipv6 ospf 1 area 0.0.0.0**

   B. Router1(config-if)#**ipv6 ospf**

   C. Router1(config-if)#**ipv6 ospf 1 area 0.0.0.0**

   D. Router1(config)#**ipv6 ospf area 0.0.0.0**

   E. Router1(config-if)#**ipv6 ospf 1 area 1.2.3.4**

IPv6 Transition Strategies

15. What are the three methods of transitioning from IPv4 to IPv6?
    A. Tunneling
    B. Route aggregation
    C. Translation
    D. Dual stack
    E. Route bridging

16. Which is the preferred method of transitioning from IPv4 to IPv6?
    A. Tunneling
    B. Route aggregation
    C. Translation
    D. Dual stack
    E. Route bridging

17. Which of the following involves side-by-side protocol stacks on the device?
    A. Tunneling
    B. Route aggregation
    C. Translation
    D. Dual stack
    E. Route bridging

18. What is the primary reason that the preferred method of transitioning from IPv4 to IPv6 can't be used?
    A. It costs too much.
    B. It requires a special dedicated router.
    C. The device does not support tunneling.
    D. The device does not have an IPv6 protocol stack.

SELF TEST ANSWERS

IPv6 Overview

1. ☑ **A, B, D, E,** and **F** are all correct. Each is a valid type of IPv6 address.
    ☒ **C** and **G** are incorrect. **C** is incorrect because IPv6 never supports broadcasts. **G** is incorrect because **C** is incorrect, so all of the above doesn't work.

2. ☑ **E** is correct. There are 4 bits, a nibble, in a hex digit.
    ☒ **A, B, C,** and **D** are incorrect.

3. ☑ **C** is correct. 2e is the hex value of this binary: 00101110.
    ☒ **A, B, D,** and **E** are incorrect. **A** is incorrect because the binary value of 10:1110 would be 0001000000001000100010000. **B** is incorrect because the binary value of a3 would be 10100011. **D** is incorrect because the binary value of 3d would be 00111101. **E** is incorrect because there is a correct answer.

4. ☑ **C** is correct. 1111111111111110 is the binary value of this hex number: FFFE.
    ☒ **A, B, D,** and **E** are incorrect. **A** is incorrect because the hex value of the binary 0000000000000001 would be 1. **B** is incorrect because it is an IPv4 wildcard mask. The hex value of the binary 0.0.0.0 0.0.0.0 would be 0. **D** is incorrect because the hex value of the binary 11111110 would be just FE. **E** is incorrect because there is a correct answer.

5. ☑ **A, B, C, D, E,** and **F** are all correct. Each is a valid IPv6 address.
    ☒ None are incorrect. While some are unusual looking, all are valid.

6. ☑ **D** is correct. Link-local addresses are not routable, working only within the local segment and stopping at any router.
    ☒ **A, B, C, E,** and **F** are incorrect. **A, B, E,** and **F** are incorrect because each is routable, even **E**, which is routable within the network but not on the Internet. **C** is incorrect because IPv6 doesn't support broadcasts.

7. ☑ **D** and **E** are correct. The length of an IPv6 primary header is 320 bits, the same as 40 bytes.
    ☒ **A, B,** and **C** are incorrect. **A** is incorrect because the IPv6 primary header is a fixed length at 320 bits, the same as 40 bytes. **B** is incorrect because the IPv6 primary header is 320 bits, not bytes (eight times larger). **C** is incorrect because the IPv6 primary header is 40 bytes, not bits.

IPv6 Configuration

8. ☑ **C** is correct. DHCP is a stateful method of configuring IPv6 addresses. It maintains the address states of each device.
    ☒ **A, B,** and **D** are incorrect. Each is a stateless method with no device maintaining the address states.

9. ☑ **C, E,** and **F** are correct. They are *not* steps in converting EUI-48 MAC to EUI-64 format. C is the wrong insert value; it should be FFFE. **E** is flipping bit 17 of the OUI instead of bit 7. **F** is flipping bit 17 of the host ID instead of bit 7 of the OUI.
☒ **A, B, D,** and **G** are incorrect. They are the steps in converting EUI-48 MAC to EUI-64 format.

10. ☑ **D** is correct. Router(config)#**ipv6 unicast-routing** enables forwarding of IPv6 unicast datagrams.
☒ **A, B, C,** and **E** are incorrect. **A** and **E** are incorrect because they are entered in the wrong configuration mode; it should be Global Configuration mode. **B** is incorrect because while in the right configuration mode, it should be **IPv6**, not just **IP**, in the command. **C** is incorrect because it is entered in the wrong configuration mode and it should be **IPv6**, not just **IP**, in the command.

11. ☑ **B** and **E** are correct. Each would configure an address on interface Fa0/1.
☒ **A, C,** and **D** are incorrect. **A** is incorrect because it should be **IPv6** in the command, not **IP**. **C** is incorrect because it should be in Interface Configuration mode. **D** is incorrect because the IPv6 address is wrong; we have two sets of double colons, which is not allowed.

12. ☑ **C** and **E** are correct. Both forms of the **show ipv6 interface command** would verify your configuration in question 11.
☒ **A, B,** and **D** are incorrect. Each would try to run in the wrong mode; it should be Privileged mode.

13. ☑ **B** and **E** are correct. **B** is correct because the next hop is a local-link address; it starts with FE80::, so it requires an interface ID as well. **E** fails because of **B**.
☒ **A, C,** and **D** are incorrect. Each would create a valid static route. **D** is a default static route.

14. ☑ **C** is correct. Router1(config-if)#**ipv6 ospf 1 area 0.0.0.** would complete the configuration for an OSPF single area.
☒ **A, B, D,** and **E** are incorrect. **A** and **D** are incorrect because they are in the wrong mode; they should be in Interface Configuration mode; **D** also omitted the process ID. **B** is incorrect because it is an incomplete command, with no process ID or area. **E** is incorrect because the RID is entered where the area 0.0.0.0 should be.

IPv6 Transition Strategies

15. ☑ **A, C,** and **D** are correct. Tunneling, translation, and dual stack are the three methods of transitioning from IPv4 to IPv6.
☒ **B** and **E** are incorrect. Neither is a transition method.

16. ☑ **D** is correct. Dual stack is the preferred method of transitioning from IPv4 to IPv6.
    ☒ **A, B, C,** and **E** are incorrect. **A** and **C** are incorrect because they are alternatives for devices that can't support the IPv6 stack. **B** and **E** are incorrect because neither is a transition method.

17. ☑ **D** is correct. Dual stack uses side-by-side protocol stacks on the device.
    ☒ **A, B, C,** and **E** are incorrect. **A** and **C** are incorrect because they do not maintain side-by-side protocol stacks for IPv4 and IPv6. **B** and **E** are incorrect because neither is a transition method.

18. ☑ **D** is correct. The primary reason that the dual stack method of transitioning from IPv4 to IPv6 can't be used is the device does not have an IPv6 protocol stack.
    ☒ **A, B,** and **C** are incorrect. **A** is incorrect because the device will eventually have to support IPv6 or be abandoned. **B** and **C** are incorrect because they aren't applicable to the dual stack method.

A

About the CD-ROM

The CD-ROM included with this book comes complete with unique electronic practice exam questions written by McGraw-Hill Education authors and delivered by the Boson Exam Environment (BEE); the Boson NetSim Limited Edition (LE), with practice labs written by McGraw-Hill Education authors; Boson Software utilities; video training from the authors; a glossary; a PDF Lab Book containing all of the labs and lab solutions from the book along with bonus labs not printed in the book; and a PDF copy of the book for studying on the go.

The software must be installed to access the Boson NetSim LE, BEE, and the Boson Software utilities. Installation is easy.

System Requirements

The system requirements for the Boson NetSim LE and the BEE are as follows:

- **Supported operating systems** Windows 8, Windows 7, Windows Vista, and Windows XP
- **.NET Framework** Microsoft .NET Framework Version 4.0
- **Processor** 1-GHz Pentium processor or equivalent (minimum); 3-GHz Pentium processor or equivalent (recommended)
- **RAM** 512MB (minimum); 2GB (recommended)
- **Hard Disk** Up to 100MB of available space
- **Display** 1024 × 768, 256 colors (minimum); 1024 × 768 high color, 32-bit (recommended)
- **Active Internet connection**

The PDF files require Adobe Acrobat, Adobe Reader, or Adobe Digital Editions to view.

Installing and Running the Boson NetSim LE and BEE

If your computer CD-ROM drive is configured to auto-run, the CD-ROM should automatically start up upon inserting the disc. If the auto-run feature did not launch the CD-ROM, browse to the CD-ROM and click the Setup icon. From the opening screen, you may install the Boson NetSim LE or the BEE by clicking the Install NetSim LE or the Install BEE links and following the steps on the Boson download page.

For information about technical support related to the content of the practice exam, see "McGraw-Hill Education Content Support" at the end of this appendix. Information about customer support for the Boson Software included on the CD-ROM is also shown at the end of the appendix.

Boson NetSim LE

The Boson NetSim LE is a restricted version of the Boson NetSim. Boson NetSim is an interactive network simulator that will allow you to simulate a wide variety of tasks as if you were working on a real network. Once you have installed the NetSim LE, you may access it quickly through Start | Programs | Boson Software.

Register the Boson NetSim LE

The first time the simulator runs, it requires registration. Enter your Boson account information along with the activation code found on the CD-ROM sleeve. If you do not have a valid boson.com account, you will create one when installing the NetSim LE. Once registration is complete, the software will load. To load any of the labs found in this book, select one of them from the Lab Navigator and click the Load Lab button.

BEE and Practice Exams

The BEE is a software-based delivery platform for the electronic practice exams. The electronic practice exams are created to help you review material covered on the CCENT certification exam. You have the option to customize your test-taking environment by selecting the number of questions, the type of questions, and the time allowed in order to assist you in your studies. The BEE also allows you to review questions by topic and offers the option to take an exam in study mode, which includes references and answers. This practice exam has been written by McGraw-Hill Education authors, is delivered by the BEE, and is available by purchasing this McGraw-Hill Education book.

Installing and Running the BEE

To access your practice exam, install the BEE. Then, use the Exam Wizard to activate the practice exam using the activation code from the back of the book. Note that an active Internet connection is required for the initial activation and download of the practice exam content.

Accessing Your Practice Exam

Follow these steps to access the practice exam on the CD-ROM:

1. Install the Exam Engine by clicking the link from the CD-ROM menu and following the instructions on the Boson download page.
2. The first time you run the software, the Exam Wizard should start and will guide you through the process of activating and downloading the exam.

If the wizard does not automatically start, choose the Exam Wizard option or use the Unlock An Exam option, available through Exam Tools.

Using the Exam Wizard

1. Select the Activate A Purchased Exam option.
2. Enter your activation key (located on the CD-ROM sleeve).
3. Select the exam(s) you want to download.

Using the Unlock an Exam Tool

1. Select Unlock An Exam.
2. Enter your e-mail address, password, and activation key (located on the CD-ROM sleeve).
3. Select the My New Exams tab.
4. Select the exam(s) you want to download
5. Click the Download Exam or Download All button.

Video Training from the Author

Video MP4 clips provide detailed examples in audio-video format from the authors of the book. You can access the videos directly from the Video table of contents by clicking the Author Video Index link on the main page.

Glossary

A bonus glossary of key terms from the book has been included for your review.

PDF Lab Book

A lab book containing all of the labs and bonus labs not printed in the book—along with their solutions—is provided in PDF format.

PDF Copy of the Book

The entire contents of the book are provided in a PDF on the CD-ROM. This file is viewable on your computer and many portable devices. Adobe Acrobat, Adobe Reader, or Adobe Digital Editions is required to view the file on your computer. A link to Adobe's website, where you can download and install Adobe Reader, has been included on the CD-ROM.

Note: For more information on Adobe Reader and to check for the most recent version of the software, visit Adobe's website at www.adobe.com and search for the free Adobe Reader or look for Adobe Reader on the product page. Adobe Digital Editions can also be downloaded from the Adobe website.

To view the PDF copy of the book on a portable device, copy the PDF file to your computer from the CD-ROM, and then copy the file to your portable device using a USB or other connection. Adobe offers a mobile version of Adobe Reader, the Adobe Reader mobile app, which currently supports iOS and Android. For customers using Adobe Digital Editions and an iPad, you may have to download and install a separate reader program on your device. The Adobe website has a list of recommended applications. McGraw-Hill Education recommends the Bluefire Reader.

Help

Individual help features are available through Boson's NetSim LE and the BEE. Review the Boson NetSim LE User's Guide for details on registration and how-to directions on completing the practice labs.

Removal Installation(s)

For *best* results for removal of Windows programs, choose Start | Programs | Control Panel | Add/Remove Programs to remove the NetSim LE or the Boson Exam Engine software.

McGraw-Hill Education Content Support

For questions regarding the PDF copy of the book, e-mail techsolutions@mhedu.com or visit http://mhp.softwareassist.com.

For questions regarding book content and content of the practice exam, videos, or additional study materials, e-mail customer.service@mheducation.com. For customers outside the United States, e-mail international_cs@mheducation.com.

Boson Software Technical Support

For technical problems with the Boson NetSim LE (installation, operation, and removal installations) and the Boson Exam Engine, and for questions regarding the Boson activation, visit www.boson.com, e-mail supportissues@boson.com, or follow the help instructions in the help features included with the Boson NetSim LE or BEE.

INDEX

E

I

T

LICENSE AGREEMENT

THIS PRODUCT (THE "PRODUCT") CONTAINS PROPRIETARY SOFTWARE, DATA AND INFORMATION (INCLUDING DOCUMENTATION) OWNED BY McGRAW-HILL EDUCATION AND ITS LICENSORS. YOUR RIGHT TO USE THE PRODUCT IS GOVERNED BY THE TERMS AND CONDITIONS OF THIS AGREEMENT.

LICENSE: Throughout this License Agreement, "you" shall mean either the individual or the entity whose agent opens this package. You are granted a non-exclusive and non-transferable license to use the Product subject to the following terms:

(i) If you have licensed a single user version of the Product, the Product may only be used on a single computer (i.e., a single CPU). If you licensed and paid the fee applicable to a local area network or wide area network version of the Product, you are subject to the terms of the following subparagraph (ii).

(ii) If you have licensed a local area network version, you may use the Product on unlimited workstations located in one single building selected by you that is served by such local area network. If you have licensed a wide area network version, you may use the Product on unlimited workstations located in multiple buildings on the same site selected by you that is served by such wide area network; provided, however, that any building will not be considered located in the same site if it is more than five (5) miles away from any building included in such site. In addition, you may only use a local area or wide area network version of the Product on one single server. If you wish to use the Product on more than one server, you must obtain written authorization from McGraw-Hill Education and pay additional fees.

(iii) You may make one copy of the Product for back-up purposes only and you must maintain an accurate record as to the location of the back-up at all times.

COPYRIGHT; RESTRICTIONS ON USE AND TRANSFER: All rights (including copyright) in and to the Product are owned by McGraw-Hill Education and its licensors. You are the owner of the enclosed disc on which the Product is recorded. You may not use, copy, decompile, disassemble, reverse engineer, modify, reproduce, create derivative works, transmit, distribute, sublicense, store in a database or retrieval system of any kind, rent or transfer the Product, or any portion thereof, in any form or by any means (including electronically or otherwise) except as expressly provided for in this License Agreement. You must reproduce the copyright notices, trademark notices, legends and logos of McGraw-Hill Education and its licensors that appear on the Product on the back-up copy of the Product which you are permitted to make hereunder. All rights in the Product not expressly granted herein are reserved by McGraw-Hill Education and its licensors.

TERM: This License Agreement is effective until terminated. It will terminate if you fail to comply with any term or condition of this License Agreement. Upon termination, you are obligated to return to McGraw-Hill Education the Product together with all copies thereof and to purge all copies of the Product included in any and all servers and computer facilities.

DISCLAIMER OF WARRANTY: THE PRODUCT AND THE BACK-UP COPY ARE LICENSED "AS IS." McGRAW-HILL EDUCATION, ITS LICENSORS AND THE AUTHORS MAKE NO WARRANTIES, EXPRESS OR IMPLIED, AS TO THE RESULTS TO BE OBTAINED BY ANY PERSON OR ENTITY FROM USE OF THE PRODUCT, ANY INFORMATION OR DATA INCLUDED THEREIN AND/OR ANY TECHNICAL SUPPORT SERVICES PROVIDED HEREUNDER, IF ANY ("TECHNICAL SUPPORT SERVICES"). McGRAW-HILL EDUCATION, ITS LICENSORS AND THE AUTHORS MAKE NO EXPRESS OR IMPLIED WARRANTIES OF MERCHANTABILITY OR FITNESS FOR A PARTICULAR PURPOSE OR USE WITH RESPECT TO THE PRODUCT. McGRAW-HILL EDUCATION, ITS LICENSORS, AND THE AUTHORS MAKE NO GUARANTEE THAT YOU WILL PASS ANY CERTIFICATION EXAM WHATSOEVER BY USING THIS PRODUCT. NEITHER McGRAW-HILL EDUCATION, ANY OF ITS LICENSORS NOR THE AUTHORS WARRANT THAT THE FUNCTIONS CONTAINED IN THE PRODUCT WILL MEET YOUR REQUIREMENTS OR THAT THE OPERATION OF THE PRODUCT WILL BE UNINTERRUPTED OR ERROR FREE. YOU ASSUME THE ENTIRE RISK WITH RESPECT TO THE QUALITY AND PERFORMANCE OF THE PRODUCT.

LIMITED WARRANTY FOR DISC: To the original licensee only, McGraw-Hill Education warrants that the enclosed disc on which the Product is recorded is free from defects in materials and workmanship under normal use and service for a period of ninety (90) days from the date of purchase. In the event of a defect in the disc covered by the foregoing warranty, McGraw-Hill Education will replace the disc.

LIMITATION OF LIABILITY: NEITHER McGRAW-HILL EDUCATION, ITS LICENSORS NOR THE AUTHORS SHALL BE LIABLE FOR ANY INDIRECT, SPECIAL OR CONSEQUENTIAL DAMAGES, SUCH AS BUT NOT LIMITED TO, LOSS OF ANTICIPATED PROFITS OR BENEFITS, RESULTING FROM THE USE OR INABILITY TO USE THE PRODUCT EVEN IF ANY OF THEM HAS BEEN ADVISED OF THE POSSIBILITY OF SUCH DAMAGES. THIS LIMITATION OF LIABILITY SHALL APPLY TO ANY CLAIM OR CAUSE WHATSOEVER WHETHER SUCH CLAIM OR CAUSE ARISES IN CONTRACT, TORT, OR OTHERWISE. Some states do not allow the exclusion or limitation of indirect, special or consequential damages, so the above limitation may not apply to you.

U.S. GOVERNMENT RESTRICTED RIGHTS: Any software included in the Product is provided with restricted rights subject to subparagraphs (c), (1) and (2) of the Commercial Computer Software-Restricted Rights clause at 48 C.F.R. 52.227-19. The terms of this Agreement applicable to the use of the data in the Product are those under which the data are generally made available to the general public by McGraw-Hill Education. Except as provided herein, no reproduction, use, or disclosure rights are granted with respect to the data included in the Product and no right to modify or create derivative works from any such data is hereby granted.

GENERAL: This License Agreement constitutes the entire agreement between the parties relating to the Product. The terms of any Purchase Order shall have no effect on the terms of this License Agreement. Failure of McGraw-Hill Education to insist at any time on strict compliance with this License Agreement shall not constitute a waiver of any rights under this License Agreement. This License Agreement shall be construed and governed in accordance with the laws of the State of New York. If any provision of this License Agreement is held to be contrary to law, that provision will be enforced to the maximum extent permissible and the remaining provisions will remain in full force and effect.